The Ardis Anthology of Russian Romanticism

Edited by
Christine Rydel

Ardis, Ann Arbor

Ardis
2901 Heatherway
Ann Arbor, Michigan 48104

Library of Congress Cataloging in Publication Data

The Ardis anthology of Russian romanticism.

    Translated from Russian.
    1. Russian literature—19th century—Translations into
English. 2. English literature—Translations from
Russian. 3. Russian literature—19th century—History
and criticism—Addresses, essays, lectures. I. Rydel,
Christine. II. Title: Russian romanticism.
PG3213.A74 1983   981.7'08'03   83-15494
ISBN 0-88233-741-6 (cloth)
ISBN 0-88233-742-4 (paper)

For my parents,

Chester and Adeline Rydel

СОВРЕМЕННИКЪ,

ЛИТТЕРАТУРНЫЙ ЖУРНАЛЪ,

ИЗДАВАЕМЫЙ

АЛЕКСАНДРОМЪ ПУШКИНЫМЪ.

ПЕРВЫЙ ТОМЪ.

САНКТПЕТЕРБУРГЪ.

ВЪ ГУТТЕНБЕРГОВОЙ ТИПОГРАФІИ.

1836.

CONTENTS

*When no translator's name is given, the translation was done by Christine Rydel.

BALLADS AND VERSE NARRATIVES

PROSE IN RUSSIA: 1790-1841

LITERARY CRITICISM

RUSSIAN ARCHIVE

AFTERWORD

ILLUSTRATIONS

Орестъ К
1835.
Рома

Въ знакъ памяти

17 Марта

PREFACE

The time limits of any literary period, and Romanticism is certainly no exception, are usually as hazy as those mystic lands in which the Romantics liked to spend so much of their time. However, critics generally consider the first forty years of the nineteenth century the romantic era of Russian literature. These are the temporal guidelines of this anthology—except for the inclusion of the "sentimental" Karamzin, who was probably the most influential figure to shape the new Russian literature of the early nineteenth century.

The time frame of Russian Romanticism was easier to determine than the contents of this anthology. Everyone hates anthologies, or at least can think of better things to include in them. I can also think of other things I would like to have included: some Lazhechnikov, Somov, Sollogub and Veltman; a play or two, especially *Boris Godunov* or *Woe from Wit*; more letters, especially Pushkin's and Griboedov's; more memoirs of the period; some of the opposition literature; more criticism written then; poetry by Vyazemsky, Glinka, Dmitriev; fables of Krylov. All of those names and works are important for an understanding of Russian literature in the first half of the nineteenth century. But I had to approach my task with a sense of measure (so out of place in Romanticism) and choose what I considered to be the most representative— not necessarily the best—works of the period.

There is a lot of second-rate literature in this anthology, but a lot of good literature as well; the inclusion of popular literature rather than good literature (although they of course are not necessarily mutually exclusive) gives a truer picture of the age. The Pushkins, Lermontovs and Gogols of an era are the exceptions, not the rule, and usually stand with one foot in their age and the other foot already in the next.

A great deal of poetry is also included in this anthology. Some of the translators have attempted rhymed versions, others have not. Obviously no translation of poetry, however good it may be, is ever as good as the original. And since translations rarely evoke the same response as the originals, the inclusion of so much poetry may seem questionable. However, it is necessary for two reasons: to acquaint readers with the themes of Russian poetry of the first forty years of the last century and to try to demonstrate why this era is called the "Golden Age of Russian Poetry." Poetry really was the most important part of literature in the nineteenth century until prose took over in the 1830s and 1840s.

Another consideration which guided my choice of material is the audience for which this book is compiled. Clearly it is intended for the non-specialist in an attempt to let non-readers of Russian get a taste of the flavor of the period. In trying to make this a useful book, I include an introduction to each section. These introductions serve to provide a general survey of the development of each genre and more specific analyses of the works translated here. On the whole I include more information on the lesser-known authors, since little work in English is available on them.

To help with further research I include a selected bibliography of works available in English. Also provided is a glossary of names which crop up within the text.

In addition, John Mersereau's article, "Yes, Virginia, There Was a Russian Romantic Movement," an attempt to find order in the period, serves as both a general overview of Russian Romanticism and the afterword to this anthology.

Christine A. Rydel
Grand Valley State Colleges
Summer, 1982

A Note on Transliteration

In bibiliographical references and in the glossary, transliterated Russian appears in the Library of Congress system, but without diacritical marks. Within the text Russian names and words appear in their most easily recognized forms, but generally follow the Library of Congress guidelines.

ACKNOWLEDGEMENTS

Although only one name usually appears on the spine of a book, more than one person is in some way responsible for various stages of its development. I wish to thank those contributors here. Of course no one, except me, is responsible for any deficiencies in this anthology.

—The Grand Valley State Colleges Committee on Research and Development for a generous summer grant in 1980. This committee, which is dedicated to scholarly research on our campus, tries—and usually succeeds mainly through the efforts of Professor Howard Stein—to obtain funds to support research and scholarly development, even in these bleak economic times.

—The University of Illinois Russian and East European Center Summer Research Laboratory for the chance to use the marvelous library facilities on the Urbana-Champaign campus. Without the kind support and assistance of the staff, the quiet refuge of my dorm room and the easy access to an excellent Slavic collection, this book would have seen the light of day even later than planned. I especially want to thank several members of the Slavic Library staff who have helped me: Robert Burger and June Pachuta, who are always ready—and even enthusiastically so—to go out of their way to track down elusive clues, sources and allusions; Alla Barabtarlo for help with Russian translation and her quick answers to my many questions; David Aranovsky for his help with some tricky Russian phrases.

—The late Dr. Frank Schwarz for helping me understand, through his encyclopedic knowledge of the city, Turgenev's rapture with Venice.

—Professor Wilhelm Seeger for translations from German and Louise Carpenter for translations from French—and for her general support over the years.

—Lydia C. Thriersen, the guiding force of this book.

—Patti Ward, who typed the manuscript under terrible conditions.

—Lewis Bagby, David Rigsbee and Jamie Fuller—especially Jamie—who took time out from their very busy schedules to do special translations for this anthology.

—Robert Beasecker, research librarian at Grand Valley State Colleges, and researchers at the Bibliothèque Nationale for their efforts in tracking down obscure references.

—Laura Ziemba, Russian Studies student at Grand Valley, who helped with proofreading.

—Mary Ann Szporluk of Ardis and Professor Helena Goscilo of the University of Pittsburgh for editorial assistance.

—Professor Ursula Franklin and Rosalind Mayberry, both of Grand Valley, not only for editorial assistance but also for their support, encouragement and friendship.

—Carl R. Proffer for much more than help and guidance on this anthology, especially for the use of background materials. But there is too much in sixteen years to summarize in an acknowledgement.

—Wayne L. Robart, who puts up with me while I try to work, both at home and away. That is a major task.

C. A. R.

THE GOLDEN AGE OF POETRY: LYRIC POETRY

LYRIC POETRY: INTRODUCTION

By the end of the eighteenth century Russian poetry had a set of rules to follow. After a series of polemics concerning language and meter, poets generally followed Lomonosov's guidelines outlined in *Letters on the Rules of Russian Versification.* In this work Lomonosov set up a hierarchy of genre, with Tragedy and Odes resting in the highest category. Along with a hierarchy of genre he set up a table of language levels ranging from Church Slavonic to the vernacular. Of course, only exalted language could be used in the exalted genres, while vernacular was left to prose. The tone of eighteenth century poetry was usually lofty and impersonal, with odes glorifying heroic exploits and heroic characters, thus engendering patriotic feelings in the hearts and minds of the readers.

The heart began to gain ascendancy over the mind in Russian poetry of the 1790s. The individual and his feelings became a primary theme in poetry. Instead of the well-defined, black and white world of the neo-classicists, the world of contradictions and conflict occupied the first place in the themes of the sentimentalists and pre-romantics.[1] The ideas of individuality and nationality[2] and the relationship between the two were a source of other romantic themes, e. g., the poet's disdain for the masses. Poetry then started to explore man's basic contrariness: his conflict between reason and feeling, his awareness of the chasm separating dream and reality, his boredom with prosaic life coupled with his desire for another reality, his perception of the basic disharmony of life joined at the same time to his quest to find some harmony in the universe. In literature man now looked at reality and tried to define his relationship to it. But above all the mood of the poetry was sentimental, pensive, melancholy, dreamy—feelings played the starring role and reason became a bit-player.

This was the prevailing mood and, by and large, poets looked within man's nature to resolve those conflicts facing him. The most famous representative, and the most influential writer, of sentimental literature was Nikolai Karamzin (1766-1826). A member of the nobility, he received a good education at home and later at Moscow University where he came under the influence of its rector, I. P. Turgenev, who acquainted his students with the moral and patriotic ideals of the Masons. Karamzin himself fell under this influence; for some time he was a Mason, but quit the organization only when it became too mystical for him.[3] But his works reflect this early influence in their themes: problems of ethics, man's spiritual capabilities, the possibility of harmony in all things—especially poetry, man's relationship with God, the role of the poet as creator, a divine correspondence in nature, and man's happiness. The author becomes the main hero of his lyrics.[4]

The tone of Karamzin's poems is sometimes humorous, but almost always intimate and conversational. At times the language comes close to the colloquial diction of the salon. Karamzin's language reforms and his ability to make literature an amusing and pleasurable experience as well as a morally uplifting one were his main literary accomplishments. His reforms became the main topic of the polemics of the groups forming around Karamzin and Shishkov, who wanted to maintain the

Lomonosovian status quo. On the other hand, Karamzin wanted a literature that "the ladies could understand." He did this by simplifying syntax, using short sentences arranged symmetrically by use of parallelism and anaphora, and by purging archaic Russian and Church Slavonic conjunctions. For him and his followers, the diction of the written language would ideally be close to spoken salon Russian with its strong French overtones. He also tried to expand vocabulary by use of calques, neologisms and new meanings for old words. The language became lighter and freer.

This new language fit the kind of sentimental poetry and prose that was becoming popular—shorter, more intimate forms like elegies, epistles and lyrics. The language and themes were to be pleasant, the poems an idyllic refuge from coarseness and harsh reality. These poems followed the example of the English writers whose works were most influential in propagating the idyllic and elegiac moods of the new Russian poetry: Gray's "Elegy in a Country Churchyard," Thomson's *Seasons* and Young's *Night Thoughts.*

The influence of these writers is apparent in the three works by Karamzin included below. In "Spring Song of a Melancholic" we see nature coming back to life after winter's death. All around there is a joyous mood, except in the heart of the lyrical narrator, who longs for a personal spring to chase away his internal, eternally gloomy winter. The poem is written in iambic tetrameter with alternating masculine and feminine lines which do not form any rhyme scheme. Occasionally one or two words do rhyme, but not in the same stanza. Instead Karamzin relies on repetition, alliteration, assonance and near-rhyme to give unity to the poem.

The same lack of rhyme distinguishes the poem "Autumn," in which a wanderer feels the onset of winter, and realizes that man is mortal, but that nature will renew itself in the spring. The poem has a lilting, inconclusive tone, due primarily to its meter and the feminine endings of the lines. In each four-line stanza a dactylic trimeter alternates with a dactylic dimeter. In all cases the final foot is truncated and is therefore trochaic. This is the metric pattern of the poem:

$$/\cup\cup \quad /\cup\cup \quad /\cup$$
$$/\cup\cup \quad /\cup$$

Karamzin creates another interesting metrical pattern in "The Cemetery"; but here he ends each stanza with a masculine line, perhaps underlining the finality of death. The meter of the poem alternates dactyls and trochees in the following manner:

$$/\cup\cup \quad /\cup \quad /\cup\cup \quad /\cup$$
$$/\cup\cup \quad /\cup \quad /\cup\cup \quad /\cup$$
$$/\cup\cup \quad /\cup \quad /$$

Yet again the poem is unrhymed. But this may be a device which gives a natural feeling to a poem in which two voices "debate" the positive and negative aspects of death.

For another poet, Vasily Zhukovsky (1783-1852), death is not an experience to fear, for in death one is reunited in the next world with loved ones who have died.[5] This is but one of the many religiously motivated ideas of this extremely important poet of the "Golden Age" of Russian poetry. Zhukovsky was the illegitimate son of a nobleman, Bunin, and a captured Turkish slave. After Bunin's death his wife brought up young Vasily, who now had two "mothers." The sentimental, mystical tone of his poetry is probably due to his being surrounded by women while he was growing up. Like Karamzin, he studied at the Pensionat for the Nobility connected with Moscow University and also came under the influence of I. P. Turgenev, with whose sons Zhukovsky became close friends. After finishing school he worked in a Ministry office of the salt industry, a job for which he was not suited. His real forte, of course, was literature, and he began his literary life by translating Gray's "Elegy." This was the first of many translations for which he is justly famous.

In 1817 Zhukovsky became Russian language tutor to the Grand Duchess Alexandra Fyodorovna, thus beginning his long association with the Russian court. Later he became tutor to the future tsar, Alexander II, and remained with him until the young tsarevich reached his majority. Even though these years at court occupied much of his time, Zhukovsky continued to write and translate throughout his life.

Zhukovsky is important not only for his own work, but also for the influence he had on the younger generation of poets, including Pushkin. However, his influence on Lermontov, Tyutchev and the Symbolists is more pronounced. And though Zhukovsky did write lyric elegies, he is most renowned for popularizing the ballad in Russia (see below) and for his translations, which are really adaptations of Western literature.

Also original at that time is his experimentation with meter. Since the time of Lomonosov the iambic tetrameter line was the most characteristic meter in Russian poetry. However, Zhukovsky tends to rely more on trochees and ternary meters than on iambics. This gives his poetry a melodious quality, but sometimes leads to a certain cloying monotony not alleviated by his affinity for soft, sweet, musical, liquid sounds. He also wrote in blank verse. Like Karamzin, Zhukovsky uses anaphora (especially "and"), ellipses and dashes for emotional peaks and shifts. Other characteristics of his style are the use of adjectives as nouns, sentences without verbs, interrogative intonation, i.e., three questions followed by an answer, and other parallelisms.

Zhukovsky's style is an apt companion for the typical subject matter of his poetry, set usually in a poetical "other world"—a world of mist, fog, midnight scenes, tears and darkness. He writes of tender feelings, with love and friendship the highest forms of virtue and morality. His idealistic Christianity espouses purity and chastity of feeling in all its manifestations. Zhukovsky also sees the poet as a special being, a symbol of morality. Through the poet we can appreciate beauty as the presence of God; the poet's inspiration is one of God's greatest gifts.

Zhukovsky, with his interest in man and his feelings, was truly a man of his age. Like Karamzin, he fell under the influence of Gray, Thomson and Young, but added to that an interest in Ossian, Goethe, Schiller, Byron, Scott, Uhland, Southey, Stilling, Bürger, Thomas Moore, the Brothers Grimm and Indian literature. In his influences you can see the most important representatives of Sentimentalism, pre-Romanticism and Romanticism itself. Many critics have tried to classify Zhukovsky under one of those three categories. In an excellent analysis of Zhukovsky's life and works, Irina Semenko makes a good distinction among the three, but especially useful is her distinction between Sentimentalism and pre-Romanticism and Zhukovsky's role in both:

> In Russia from the very beginning they were conjoined in the work of Karamzin and his followers. Sentimentalism emphasized a cult of nature, sensitivity, and virtue, coupled

with interest in the intimate "life of the heart," whereas pre-Romanticism utilized the fantastic, the folk element, the exotic, the medieval, the poetry of "mystery and horror," among other things. Zhukovsky did not simply follow in Karamzin's footsteps but was himself strongly influenced by Western pre-Romanticism and developed along the lines it had prescribed. His pre-Romanticism first found expression in his ballads, and subsequently diffused into his lyric poetry.[6]

But Zhukovsky was important for much more; he set Russian poetry on a course which would lead to the great lyric poets—Pushkin, Lermontov and Tyutchev.

A lyric which combines the typical themes, language, intonation and meter of Zhukovsky is "Spring Feeling." In this poem, written in trochaic tetrameter with an aBBa* rhyme scheme, a song-like quality underlines the feeling of lightness and sweetness introduced in the first two lines. The poem uses symbols of transcendence to unite man's feeling with nature, both striving for the "other world."

In "Charm of Bygone Days" (iambic tetrameter, alternating masculine/feminine rhymes), the lyrical narrator is again concerned with another world, but this time it is the "other world" of the past, irretrievable except in memory. Here too Zhukovsky asks questions, but ones which have no answer. He says that only one person can live in the past, a corpse interred with the past itself.

In another poem, "March 19, 1823," the lyrical narrator recalls another dead person, this time one who was very important to him. Her apparition reminds him of the past so dear to him.[7] It is significant that Zhukovsky sets off the last two lines in meter as well as in content. In the last short stanza he draws our attention away from the personal to a scene in nature which encompasses the universe. The first sixteen lines of the poem follow the metric pattern ∪/∪/∪, each ending with a feminine line. Again there are no rhymes in this poem. The last two lines are written in an entirely different meter: /ɯ/, with a definite masculine line.

Another element of nature is the subject of "The Sea, An Elegy." Written in amphibrachic tetrameter, the rhythm of the poem approximates the motion of waves on the sea. The lack of rhyme, a natural closure to lines and stanzas, may also emphasize the limitless formlessness of the ocean. In the poem the lyrical narrator stands near the abyss and asks the ocean to reveal its mysteries and secrets to him. Once more we see in Zhukovsky profoundly anthropomorphic nature.

The sea is a favorite romantic symbol; another is Napoleon. It is interesting that even though Napoleon was Russia's enemy, the greatness of his image is the subject of a significant number of poems and the object of much admiration. In "Night Review," the deceased emperor rises from his grave to review his spectral troops, the pride of France. Once again Zhukovsky does not use rhyme, but depends on repetition, anaphora and syntactic parallels to give structure to his poem. Here too he uses a rare meter, amphibrachic trimeter, with alternating masculine and feminine lines and no skipped beats, so as to emphasize the regular motion, the quick movement of troops on review.

A different view of war and military life emerges in the elegy "The Shade of a Friend" by Konstantin Batyushkov (1787-1855), who with Zhukovsky, was one of the "creators of Romantic psychologism in Russian literature during the second decade of the nineteenth century."[8] But this is only one attribute they have in common.[9] They both developed the intimate lyric into an art form which could portray "general concepts of life,"[10] while concentrating on man's inner life. For both of them man was

---

*lowercase denotes feminine rhymes while capitals denote masculine.

the judge, the arbiter of values in the world. The world they both wanted was an ideal, poetic one in which values would reach perfection. However, it is in this ideal world that the two poets begin to differ. Whereas Zhukovsky is more concerned with moral ideals and sees nothing tragic in life because a heaven does exist, Batyushkov is concerned with aesthetic ideals and is more firmly grounded on earth and this life. In Batyushkov's poetry a melancholy, then tragic, tone emerges because of his awareness that the ideal can never become reality. These differences between the two stem from the literary influences which affected them most: for Batyushkov the epicurean literature of the world of antiquity, with its "world of harmonious humanity";[11] for Zhukovsky the idealistic literature of German and English pre-Romanticism and the Christian Middle Ages, with its religious nature.

In contrast to the Middle Ages with its "other-worldly" orientation, Batyushkov's preferred world of the ancient Greeks and Romans led to his taste for Neo-classical forms, "French hedonistic and erotic verse."[12] This major difference between the two explains Batyushkov's concern with an egocentric hero and a more individualized lyrical narrator as opposed to Zhukovsky's more generalized and self-effacing hero. Batyushkov's classical orientation also explains his method of revealing man's inner feelings. Batyushkov relies on external, physical manifestations to expose inner feelings.[13] Therefore many have called his poems highly visual, plastic, sculptured. On the other hand Zhukovsky concentrates on the emotions themselves, all functioning within man.

Born into a noble family, Batyushkov received a good education and read primarily French literature. He later expanded his horizons with Italian and classical literature. The writers who influenced him were Tasso, Tibullus, Parny, and Petrarch. He knew the latter first through Dmitriev's[14] imitations of the Italian poet. Batyushkov's fascination with Italian literature and language had a lasting effect on his style and language. "Italian" conglomerations of vowels appear frequently in his poetry[15] and make it harmonious and musical. At the same time his verse (even the philosophical poems) remains clear and simple.

Batyushkov especially developed the two genres of epistle and elegy. One of his most famous poems is the verse letter to Zhukovsky and Vyazemsky, *My Penates*. In it he lists the Russian poets he considers his models. Although this work follows earlier examples in French poetry, Batyushkov makes it original by including his contemporaries, Zhukovsky and Vyazemsky, in the list.[16] In *My Penates* Batyushkov also develops his ideas about poetry and the poet; in the epistle he describes the world of the poet and its household gods. He contrasts the poet, with his life of love and poetry, to Philistine existence. Instead of rich mansions, the country of poetry is the poet's abode. Here his companions are: "peace, living beauty, love, other poets, the living and the dead, teachers and friends."[17] This land of poetry, indeed poetry itself, is a triumph over death.[18]

The apparition of a friend killed in battle is the main event of "The Shade of My Friend," an elegy in memory of Batyushkov's comrade, I. A. Petin. It is in the elegy that Batyushkov reached his fullest development. He began writing elegies about war and the burning of Moscow. In "The Shade of My Friend" "the thought of a fallen comrade revives the memory of a sorrowful episode that took place during the war."[19] In this poem we see a device Batyushkov often uses to great effect in his elegies— synchronization of time to reveal man's complex emotions.

Both of Batyushkov's poems included below are written in iambic meters. "Shade" is written primarily in iambic hexameter lines, with nine lines in iambic tetrameter and eight in iambic pentameter. These shorter lines are interspersed in no particular pattern. The rhyme scheme is also varied and the following types of rhymes appear: aBaB, cDDc, EfEf, and GhhG. In addition to these rhyme schemes, *My Penates* contains both masculine and feminine couplets. This poem is written in iambic trimeter, a meter which contributes to the fast pace of the entire poem.[20]

Batyushkov was a major contributor to the modernization and improvement of Russian poetry, but in 1821 insanity ended his career. His influence on future poets, and especially Pushkin, was great. (Some of Pushkin's early verse is difficult to distinguish from Batyushkov's.) It was Batyushkov who brought the "school of harmonious precision"[21] to Russia and did much to instill a new mood in Russian poetry—epicurean eroticism.

Denis Davydov (1784-1839) introduced a heartier eroticism, as well as boisterous liveliness, to Russian poetry with his hussar songs. Known as the "hussar poet," Davydov combined these two careers early in his life. The lyrical hero of his poems is the hussar, a dashing soldier whose conquests in love and war are legendary. Davydov himself entered the Guards Regiment in 1801, but was removed from service and later had to serve in the hussar regiment, all because of a political poem he allegedly wrote. After he retired from service he went to live on his wife's estate, where he farmed and wrote his memoirs as well as a treatise on warfare.

War and military language are an important part of Davydov's poetry; he even uses military terminology in his love lyrics. Epistles, elegies, madrigals, epigrams, and songs make up his small collection of poetry. He basically wrote two types of poems: hussar songs and tender love lyrics inspired by a young girl with whom he fell in love in his later years. The distinguishing characteristics of his poetry are a satiric tone, vulgar language and a penchant for unrhymed trochaic tetrameter.

Although it is written in trochaic tetrameter, "Song of an Old Hussar" does have a rhyme scheme of alternating masculine and feminine lines. Here Davydov conjures up his typical hussar hero; old hussars remember their youth. A more contemplative mood sets the tone of "Evening Bell" (iambic tetrameter with masculine couplets). The bells the lyrical hero hears, though, are not those of a sterile monastery, but those which ring out from a girl's voice—sounds which are full of passion.

Passion for a young girl inspired "Dance," but the poem itself is a conventional love song written in iambic tetrameter, with the rhymes of the first eight lines forming an alternating feminine/masculine pattern, while the rhymes of the last eight lines are: eFFeGhhG. This poem is built on an extended metaphor which compares love to the torrents of spring and culminates in poetic inspiration. The description of the young girl in "To a Pious Charmer," however, is bawdy and playful. It is in the earlier songs and hussar poetry, though, that Davydov is at his most creative. Supposedly "Pushkin had a high opinion of his poetry and used to say that Davydov showed him the way to be original."[22]

Another poet of the era, whose kinship to Pushkin was much greater, is Baron Anton Delvig (1798-1831), one of the most influential men of the Romantic age. A lyceum friend of Pushkin's, Delvig was the son of a Russified Westphalian nobleman and a Russian noblewoman. Life at the lyceum at Tsarskoe Selo was remarkable for encouraging the pursuit of literature. The pupils there not only read literature, but wrote much themselves. Although Delvig was not a good student, he was not without talent and imagination. Even though he himself was a poet, he is more famous for his publishing enterprises, the almanac *Northern Flowers* (1824-32) and *Literary Gazette* (1830-31). Here he published a great deal of important literature of the period.[23]

Delvig may have been part of the "Romantic" camp, but his own inclinations in writing were somewhat more classical. He was clearly aware of genre distinctions and "divides his poems into four groups: Idylls, Songs and Romances, Sonnets, and Miscellaneous, where the second category contains his imitations of folk songs, and the last elegies, epistles, imitations of Horation odes and the like."[24] In his most famous idyll, "The Bathing Women," Delvig describes a highly languorous, erotic scene between two women of the Arcadian past; but he does this with great personal detachment. The form of the idyll is also classical, with its attempt to duplicate Greek poetics in its use of the hexameter—"a basically six-foot dactyllic line, rhymeless, where occasionally a trochaic foot could be substituted for each of the dactyls, except for the penultimate, the sixth foot being truncated to make a trochaic ending."[25]

A less rigidly classical poem is the sonnet "Inspiration," written in iambic tetrameter and the following rhyme scheme: aBBa aBBa Cdd CCd. Here we see some themes later developed by the Romantics: the scorn of the masses for the poet and the poet's favored status with the gods.

Delvig may have looked back to the original Golden Age for inspiration, but it was Pushkin, more than anyone, who justly brought that appellation to his own era. A descendent of the Ethiopian Gannibal (Peter the Great's "Negro") on his mother's side and ancient Russian nobility on his father's, Alexander Sergeevich Pushkin (1799-1837) was educated at home by French tutors until he entered the lyceum at Tsarskoe Selo in 1811. After his 1817 graduation Pushkin entered the civil service and became a part of the social whirl of the capital. Some of his liberal, political epigrams came to the attention of the tsar, who exiled Pushkin to southern Russia, where the poet lived and worked until 1826. After his arrest for alleged complicity in the Decembrist revolt, Pushkin went to Petersburg and an audience with Tsar Nicholas I, who then became his personal censor. In 1831 Pushkin married the beautiful Natalya Goncharova, rumored to be a favorite of the tsar. Pushkin truly seems to have loved his unsuitable wife, a cold, proud beauty who had neither the intellectual ability nor interest to appreciate her husband. Jealous of the attention a Frenchman in Russian service, Baron George d'Anthes, paid his wife, Pushkin challenged him to a duel in which the poet was mortally wounded. After two days of suffering, Pushkin died on January 29, 1837.

According to family tradition, Pushkin already wrote French verse even before the lyceum years, during which he developed his talents. While at the lyceum Pushkin wrote poems in the classical mode and genre, a typical course of literary apprenticeship at that time. His early verses were cold, highly unsentimental, but already technically of a high order. The poets who influenced him at this time were Batyushkov, Zhukovsky, Voltaire, Parny and André Chénier.

Byron was the next influence, in the second stage of Pushkin's poetic development. But unlike the earlier French poets who influenced Pushkin's concise style, Byron's influence was limited to subject matter and genre. Byron's bored, alienated hero found his way into Pushkin's verse narratives set in exotic Eastern lands. Pushkin may have written on romantic subjects, but he never succumbed to Byron's imprecision. In fact, by 1823 Pushkin was already moving away from Byron's influence as he entered the third, more mature period of his artistic career, which culminated in his "Boldino Autumn," the richest, most productive period in his life. It was here that he polished the final version of his novel in verse, *Eugene Onegin*, and wrote some of his greatest lyrics, as well as the *Tales of Belkin*, the comic poem *Little House in Kolomna* and his wonderful plays, *The Little Tragedies*.

The last period of Pushkin's life is marked by a decline in his popularity as well as troubles on the domestic front. Never highly ornamental, Pushkin's poetry became even more devoid of adornment, more restrained and severe. At this time Pushkin continued writing in prose, but never gave up poetry. Besides a number of fairy tales, Pushkin also wrote his poem *The Bronze Horseman*, which stands as a testament to the fact that Pushkin's poetical powers were not on the wane.

Pushkin wrote lyrics in various genres: anacreontics, odes, epistles, elegies, ballads. His highly personal lyrics are about love, usually nostalgic; nature, usually inanimate and aloof from man; friendship; and his own states of mind and soul. Pushkin also wrote a number of poems which outline his views on poetry and the poet.[26] A melancholy pessimism runs through his later poems. And even though we may know the background details of the poems, they are never so subjective that they lose their universal appeal and idealized tone.

Pushkin's poems are difficult to appreciate in translation since their brilliance depends on "untranslatable" qualities: "the choice of words . . .the adequacy of rhythm to intonation, and . . .the complex texture of sound—the wonderful *alliteratio Pushkiniana*, so elusive and so all-conditioning."[27] Pushkin's lyrics depend on these elements rather than on many similes, metaphors and other tropes and figures of speech—although these certainly do appear in his poetry. And even though Pushkin wrote a major portion of his lyrics in iambic tetrameter, he also used other iambic lines, blank verse and some trochaic meters. Often in Pushkin when there is a contrast in meaning, a metrical shift accompanies it. On a syntactical level, Pushkin rarely inverts word order; on a lexical level, his words are simple, color verbs are typical, and Church Slavonicisms do appear. Often Pushkin groups words of the same meaning together. In general Pushkin's language is the salon-style of Karamzin but with more masculine vigor and strength.

One of Pushkin's most famous love lyrics is the beautiful "I remember a wondrous moment" (iambic tetrameter, alternating masculine/feminine rhyme[28]), rich in anaphora, repetition and similes. In this poem the lyrical narrator associates his beloved with everything that gives meaning to his life. He juxtaposes her with divinities, inspiration, tears, life and love itself. The true feelings of love the lyrical narrator feels for the beloved evoke a generous response in "I loved you once" (iambic pentameter). Even though the love affair is over, love has not completely disappeared. In fact, enough remains for him to wish her another love as deep as his.

In "Winter Evening," the narrator drinks to his lost youth, rather than to a former love. Written in trochaic tetrameter, the song-like quality of the poem duplicates the swirling motion of the storm raging outside. A number of pyrrhic feet add to the quick movement of the poem. Another poem in the same meter is "Winter Road." Here the mood is melancholy and anticipatory, a mood at odds with the meter, which again duplicates not only the storm but the movement of the troika as well. Yet another hibernal poem, "Winter Morning," almost sounds like the longed-for destination of the narrator of "Winter Road." In contrast to the storms of the preceding night, the scene is calm and bright. The peaceful mood is echoed in the regular iambic tetrameter lines and the long, lazy sentences, especially the twelve-line sentence with its enjambement from the second to third stanzas. The stanzas themselves have the rhyme scheme aaBccB, one of approximately sixty different stanza forms Pushkin used. In addition, this poem contains Pushkin's typical vocabulary. "Winter Morning" is a good example of a representative Pushkin poem.

An even more contemplative mood surrounds "Autumn," with its long lines (iambic hexameter) and rhyme scheme aBaBaBcc, whose triple repetition adds to the monotony of the season the poem describes. But the poet does not find the season dull, for ironically, during this season of decay and death, the poet becomes most inspired and can write his poetry.

The role of the poet is an important theme in Pushkin's verses. We see that over the years Pushkin views him first as a prophet, then as an ordinary mortal touched by the gods, a mortal who is both inspired and obligated to sing his songs. The obligation goes deeper in "The Prophet." Here Pushkin equates the mission of the poet with the divine mission of a prophet. Like the prophet, the poet must purify himself before he is worthy to impart his message to the masses. To reinforce the comparison Pushkin uses a great many Church Slavonicisms as well as the classical, and liturgical, device of anaphora, which duplicates the form of a litany. In a later poem, "The Poet" (aBaBcDcDEffegHgHiJJi), the intervention of the gods is not as formal. Here we see the poet wrapped in the concerns of the day and of ordinary people. But when he hears the divine voice of inspiration, the poet no longer belongs to the crowd; he rushes off, full of heavenly sounds, to be alone near the sea or in the thick woods.

The romantic theme of the poet's alienation from the masses is the subject of "Poet and Crowd" (various rhyme schemes). But here the poet is not merely alienated; the crowd and poet despise each other equally. They cannot see the use of his poetry, and he condemns them for their mercenary attitude toward everything in life. At the end of the poem Pushkin recalls his early work "Prophet," where the poet tells the crowd that he is born for inspiration, sweet sounds and prayers. In "Echo" (three iambic tetrameters, followed by an iambic dimeter, then another tetrameter and a final iambic dimeter; rhyme scheme AAABAB), the poet learns that he is simply an echo to the sounds of nature. He responds to them, but in keeping with the romantic theme, nothing—and no one—responds to him. Again he is lonely and isolated. In one of his last poems "I erected a monument unto myself" (three iambic hexameters plus a final tetrameter in each stanza), the lyrical poet says that he will achieve immortality through his words as long as a kindred spirit, i.e., a poet, is alive.

In two poems Pushkin describes the writing of verse; in one case the process is annoying, in another it is pleasant. "Verses written at night" has an unusual meter for the subject matter and a complex rhyme scheme: AbbAccDDeeDffGG. In trochaic tetrameter lines he catalogues all of the bothersome distractions which prevent him from sleeping. In a way this sing-song meter is as distracting as the sounds which bother the poet. However, in "Night" the circumstances lead to poetry. Here the poet's voice disturbs the peace of night, but it seems as if his beloved is also his inspiration. Perhaps in imitation of night languor, the meter of the poem is iambic hexameter; the rhyme is alternating masculine/feminine couplets. In an interesting line that calls attention to itself, the poet uses the word "flows" to describe the movement of his poetry. He uses this word twice in one line that he breaks up with three commas, thus breaking up the flow of that very line.

Contradictory sentiments arise in two poems that recall Georgia; however, the sentiments merge into a single feeling of nostalgia for a country from which the lyrical narrator is separated. In "Don't sing, my beauty," the poet asks not to be reminded of Georgia, a land of bittersweet memories. But in "The light of day has gone out" (iambic lines of various lengths, various rhymes), the poet is in the south, exiled far away from home. He describes the coming of evening as he stands on the seashore. His reveries take him back to the shores of his native land, a place he can visit only in his memories.

The sea evokes other feelings in "To the Sea," where the narrator bids farewell to this mighty element of nature. He sings its praises, describing it as a free spirit. He then compares the sea to a pair of Romantic "free spirits": Byron and Napoleon. The many enjambements in the poem duplicate the flow of waters. Although the poem is written in Pushkin's favorite rhyme scheme, two stanzas are five lines long with an AbAbA rhyming pattern. The inclusion of two stanzas different from the norm reinforces the idea of the poem: not everyone, or everything, is subject to the tyranny of rules. Free elements exist in nature, humanity and art.

Tyranny and its awful consequences are the subject of "The Upas Tree," a poem which has an interesting history.[29] The poem tells of a poison tree and the mission of a poor slave for his cruel master. In obtaining the poison from the tree for his master's arrows, the slave himself dies. The main point of the poem is that even though the tree is poisonous, it is not evil. But what man does to man certainly is.

Throughout his career Pushkin wrote many poems with a philosophical, pensive bent; he wrote many introspective, psychological ones as well. When he was still relatively young (twenty-two) he wrote "I've outlived my desires." In this poem Pushkin's narrator presents the pose of a world-weary youth who bemoans the loss of the "summer" of his life and feels "winter" coming all too soon. In a more mature poem, "When I wander along noisy streets" (1829), the poet describes how he can isolate himself in a crowd teeming with life and daily concerns so that he can contemplate death. He sees how transitory are the many trappings of life, but how many other things will remain behind, while we are gone forever.

A later poem describes madness and its ultimate terror—isolation. In "Oh God, Grant I Won't Go Insane" (two iambic tetrameters, then a trimeter, then the pattern again; rhyme AABCCB), the narrator lists what is better than madness: homelessness, poverty, toil and hunger. But then he tells of the ultimate blessing of madness— freedom. However, this does not last for long and, out of fear, men isolate and incarcerate madmen. The madman no longer hears the beautiful sounds of night, only the shrieks and cries of men as mad as himself. Pushkin here debunks the Romantic concept of refuge in madness.

A distinguished contemporary of Pushkin's and close friend of Delvig, Evgeny Abramovich Baratynsky (1800-44) is a member of the so-called "Pushkin Pleiad."[30] Like Pushkin, he combines elements of Classicism and Romanticism in his poetry. After living the first eight years of his life in the Tambov province, Baratynsky moved with his family to Moscow, where they lived until the death of his father in 1810, when the family moved back to their village. Baratynsky enrolled in the Pages' Corps after some preparation in a Petersburg boarding school. While under the influence of Schiller's *Robbers* he collaborated with some schoolmates in the theft of a gold snuffbox filled with rubles.[31] He returned to the country after he was expelled for this incident. Baratynsky later enlisted in the army and after a year he became a non-commissioned officer before his transfer to Finland, where he stayed for five years. After resigning his commission, he married and settled in Moscow. Except for a visit to Petersburg, from 1836 until 1843 he lived with his wife and family at her ancestral estate, Muranovo. In 1843 Baratynsky took his wife and children on a trip to Western Europe, where he died in Italy in 1844.

Baratynsky's first poems appeared in 1819, but his reputation grew only after his elegies began to be published in the twenties. Later he wrote longer narrative poems, but the public did not greet them with enthusiasm. Baratynsky's popularity declined, probably because of his attempts to adapt to Romantic trends, with which he was not really in sympathy. Baratynsky was always closer to French rationalism, due mainly to his early readings in French and to the influence of writers like Voltaire, Delavigne, Parny and Chénier. However, Baratynsky did fall under Schelling's spell, taking themes and motifs from the German's poetry, rather than adopting his philosophical system. While in Moscow, Baratynsky also met members of the *Lyubomudry* group (see below) and grew particularly close to Ivan Kireevsky, with whom he worked on both *The Moscow Herald* and later *The European*. After he broke with Kireevsky and his friends, Baratynsky became very depressed; he also grew gloomy about the decline in the popularity of his poetry.

During his poetic career Baratynsky wrote elegies, epistles, epigrams, light verse and narrative tales. But he is best known for his elegies, meditative in tone. His poems tend to be sad, serious, pessimistic, intellectual, cold, restrained, austere and contradictory. Contradictions exist on several levels: thematic, lexical, and stylistic. Often the content of Baratynsky's poems deals with the irrational, but the form is precise and logical. His style is exact, his syntax complicated by subordinate clauses. Many parallelisms of syntax and rhythms characteristically appear in his poetry, thus adding harmony to the verses.

Lexically Baratynsky's poems can be simple in the shorter works, but heavy in the longer ones. In his poetry he uses many Church Slavonicisms and archaisms along with journalistic prosaisms. Baratynsky also combines various meters and various rhymes, even hyperdactylic ones. His rhymes are "imbued with crisp novelty, and with few exceptions, all of them adhere to high standards of exactness."[32] Almost ninety percent of his poems are written in iambics, with approximately fifty percent iambic tetrameters. But to give a distinct touch to this meter, a fair proportion of the first feet are pyrrhic.[33]

In the "cold metallic brilliance"[34] of his poetic style Baratynsky ponders, among other themes, the role of the poet in society, man's disillusionment with life, the struggle between reason and feeling, inaccessible happiness, nature, and love, which leads to further disillusionment. Baratynsky is clearly a poet of ideas.

Ideas and their transformations are the subject of "A thought when it appears anew" (iambic tetrameter, alternating rhymes). Of course the poet, with his gift for terseness, expresses the thought better than anyone. Unfortunately thought can engulf the poet and make him its victim. In "Poor craftsman of the word" (iambic pentameter, various rhymes), the poet uses his art to expose the truth. But in doing so, he destroys a place of refuge for himself. However, poetry is a comfort to man, a balm for all those who partake of it. In "The lyric poem can heal an aching spirit" (iambic pentameter, alternating rhymes), we see that even the poet, through the act of singing his song, can find release from sorrow.

A poem also transcends time. For Baratynsky, the poet is an exile, an isolated creature. He many find only one friend, but his consolation lies in knowing that sometime in the future someone will find kinship with him through his work. Perhaps in the future he will find the readers he now lacks. Such sentiments appear in "My gift is humble," a poem written in iambic pentameter with an aBBaCddC rhyme scheme. In this poem we see that art is the constant, the element that will survive through time.

A look into the future with its technological world that has no place for the poet is the subject of "The Last Poet." Baratynsky emphasizes the gulf between the poet and mercenary society by switching meters. "In contrast to the ponderous iambic pentameter of the first stanza, the second is written in brisk trochaic tetrameter . . . this makes more distinct the difference between his [the poet's] light-minded spontaneity and their [the masses'] serious existence, devoted to progress and science."[35] The rest of the poem is also built on contrasts of outlooks and descriptive scenes of nature. In "Rhyme" (iambic hexameters and tetrameters with various rhymes), Baratynsky again compares the "fallen status of the modern poet"[36] with the role of the Greek orator in ancient times. Once more Baratynsky uses the devices of "The Last Poet" and builds the poem on sets of contrasts. But in this poem the ending is more optimistic, since poetry still retains its power to comfort man. "Signs" (amphibrachic tetrameters alternating with trimeters, alternating rhymes) is another statement against man's dependence on reason rather than on nature, from which he is now alienated.

In "The mass of men" Baratynsky underlines the difference between the poet and the crowd by contrasting their reactions to night; the crowd fears night, but the poet waits for it so that he can welcome its secrets, terrors and inspiration. Baratynsky uses opposite times of day to emphasize contrasting attitudes. And though he again uses different meters (iambic hexameters and tetrameters), in this poem the pattern does not parallel the contrasts as it does in "The Last Poet." Another interesting poem built on contrasts is "Complaint," an elegiac distich with unrhymed dactylic lines. Here we see how a fly, a detestable creature who lives during beautiful summer, bothers poet and masses alike. But its effects on the poet are devastating.[37]

In "What reason," written in alexandrine couplets, Baratynsky lists a series of phenomena of nature that seem to be free, but are really constrained by natural law. He then shows that man, who also seems to be free, is really ruled and constrained by nature no less than rivers contained by their banks and trees rooted to the ground. Only death unfetters man. In an early (1828) poem, "Death" (written in iambic tetrameters with alternating rhymes), the poet sees death as the bearer of peace rather than the sower of seeds of destruction. Death carries an olive branch rather than a scythe.

In "Hopelessness" the poet finds himself resigned to the fact that he will not have the happiness he seeks. He therefore decides to stop walking along the path that he mistakenly thought leads to it; instead he well greet the passers-by still searching for their elusive goal. Except for the last line, the poem is written in alexandrines, a long regular line. But after the speaker resolves to go no further, the meter changes in the last line to amphibrachic trimeter. A similar sense of hopelessness appears in another of Baratynsky's last poems, "Autumn."

One of his highest achievements, "Autumn" is a poem in the grand manner, its oratorical style replete with archaisms, Church Slavonicisms and neologisms. Written in iambic tetrameter and pentameter lines, the stanzas follow the rhyme scheme, AbAbCdCdEE. In many ways "Autumn" is a compendium of Baratynsky's themes and ideas.[38] Here we see nature vs. reason, the dilemma of the poet, disillusionment, and the pain of being caught between two opposing sides—without any resolution in sight. Autumn itself, clothed in its brilliant colors, is poised between its anticipation of winter and its farewell to summer. Against this background we see a peasant reaping his bountiful harvest. By contrast, the intellectual who relies solely on abstract thought comes up empty-handed. Here Baratynsky uses the vocabulary of the harvest to describe the thinker's plight, thus underscoring even more his own failure.

At this point the theme of the poem itself moves to a higher level and autumn becomes symbolic of the death of the soul and the approaching end to life. Again Baratynsky returns to the disillusioned thinker who finds no resolution to his problems, either in reason or in religion. With winter come the snows that cover him as well as the crops in the fields. But though the crops will grow again, no harvest awaits the intellectual. On this dismal note the poem ends.

After Pushkin and Baratynsky, critics usually consider Nikolai Yazykov (1803-1846) the next major poet of the "pleiad."[39] Son of a rich landowner, Yazykov received an excellent education, both in secondary school and at the university at Dorpat (Tartu), where he learned German and studied philosophy. Like many of his contemporaries, he fell under the influence of Byron and Schiller and, his love of poetry surfaced early in his life. While at the university Yazykov became interested in history, particularly of Old Russia. Eventually Russia, especially in the Middle Ages, became one of his favorite poetic themes; this interest, as well as his friendship with the Kireevskys, finally led to the religious and Slavophile themes of his later poetry. Other themes characteristic of Yazykov are poetry itself, romance, drinking, and in his final poems, illness.

Even though Yazykov had an affinity for the classical system of genres, his poetry in the twenties and thirties basically tended to be genreless. This is especially true of the poems of the "Pushkin cycle," dedicated to that poet and other friends. At the beginning and end of his poetical career, Yazykov wrote mainly elegies. The last ones he wrote at European spas, where he was probably suffering from syphilis. Understandably the tone of his last poems is melancholy, whereas his early poems are happy and energetic.

In his poems Yazykov uses many tropes as well as linguistic and syntactical devices to evoke emotions—especially the use of many verbs and sensuous imagery. Other characteristics of his style are periodic sentences, parallel syntactic constructions, many dependent clauses, and semantic and linguistic pairs. It is not uncommon for Yazykov to repeat sentences and phrases in his poems, or to repeat entire sections of one poem in another. His exuberant style leads him to use rhetorical questions and exclamations, anaphora, alliteration and other tropes whose basis is repetition, such as anadiplosis and epanalepsis. Yazykov's poetic technique is very good. Unfortunately he never developed his talent.

In the drinking song "Pour full the glasses" one can see Yazykov's use of repetition. This poem, as well as "Elegy" and "Prayer," is written in iambic tetrameter with alternating masculine/feminine rhymes. "The Colt" is a lively poem in trochaic tetrameter, a meter more suited to songs and poems on lighter subjects. The longer stanzas have a normal masculine/feminine alternating pattern, but the rhyme scheme of the shorter stanzas is aaBccB.

Like Yazykov, the poet Dmitry Venevitinov (1805-27) did not fulfill the promise of his talent, but his failure was due to an untimely death. The mere forty poems he did write, though, are enough to secure his place among the major poets of the Golden Age.[40] A precocious intellectual, this aristocratic youth had a classical education which included the study of Greek, Latin, French and German. At the time of his death (from a chill) he was studying English and Italian. While at Moscow University he studied philosophy and old Russian literature. Like other intellectuals of the time, Venevitinov became interested in Goethe and Schelling, whose influence on him was strongest of all. He was one of the original members of the *Lyubomudry* (Lovers of Wisdom) group (see below, "Circles and Salons").

The two areas of Schelling's philosophy which found a significant place in Venevitinov's poetry and thought are his ideas about nature and the poet. The main point joining these two areas is the role of the poet, the link between mere mortals and God. The poet is therefore an exalted creature who uses inspiration and his own intuition to penetrate deep enough into nature to perceive its all-pervasive spirit. The poet expresses all of this in his poetry.

This exalted view of the poet is Venevitinov's main poetic theme; others are friendship and love, which is usually unrequited. (This latter view stems from his unfulfilled love for the beautiful and talented Princess Zinaida Volkonskaya, a married woman.) His style is pure, "explicit and discursive, with an emphasis on antithesis...and is coupled with a general sparseness of figurative language and concrete setting."[41] The structure of his poems is logical and abstract. Venevitinov uses typical Romantic imagery and usually writes in the standard iambic tetrameter of the time.[42] What makes Venevitinov stand out among his contemporaries is the "intellectual rigor"[43] of his philosophic poems, which look ahead to the thirties and to poets like Fyodor Tyutchev.

Except for "Sonnet" (iambic hexameter) and "Elegy" (iambic pentameter), the other poems included below are written in iambic tetrameter. The *general* rhyme scheme of most of the poems is alternating masculine/feminine lines; however, Venevitinov's rhymes tend to be more complex than that. It is difficult to assign a "typical" pattern to Venevitinov's rhymes, since the patterns change with each poem. But usually the pattern of the rhymes underscores an idea in the poem, sometimes with antonyms rhyming to emphasize a contrast. Any more detailed description of Venevitinov's rhyme patterns in English would be fruitless, since the translations below do not attempt to duplicate the rhymes of the originals. Suffice it to say that the rhyme schemes are often complex and enhance the ideas of the poems.

In "Sonnet," "Poet," and "Consolation," we see Venevitinov's basic view of the poet: the beloved of the gods, one set apart from the masses. He is calmly privy to the secrets of nature and the gods. In "Sonnet" we see the poet suffer the limits of the world and in "Testament" we see him transcend the world to the hope and promise of a new life for an unfettered spirit.

Part of the pain of this world arises from the faithlessness of friends and lovers. In "To My Signet Ring" the poet asks his ring to be a talisman against the perfidy of life and a faithful companion even in death. The poems "Elegy" and "Dagger" describe the pangs of unrequited and rejected love, while "Life" shows how the excitement of life can soon turn into the boredom of mere existence. Venevitinov treats the transitory nature of love and compares it to friendship and, perhaps, inspiration in a highly symbolic poem, "Three Roses."[44] Again we see a certain disillusionment with life, but faith in the permanence of art and beauty.

Another poet who shares Venevitinov's idealistic view of the poet is Alexei Khomyakov (1804-60). Although Khomyakov made his mark later as a Slavophile, philosopher and theologian, his early poems reflect the age as well as the ideals of the *Lyubomudry* group of which he was a member. The descendent of an ancient noble family, Khomyakov received his education at Moscow University. After serving in the Guards during the war with the Turks, he settled down in 1829 to a life of study and writing. Khomyakov's philosophical bent is apparent in his poetry, whose main characteristic is his rigorous thought.[45] Of course, the early poems reflect the influence of the writers popular in his circle—Schiller, Schelling and Goethe; the verse is full of pantheistic ideas, stressing the unity of man's soul and nature. The role of the poet is his most important and lasting theme. The five poems included below are a compendium of his ideas about the poet, a tragic and immortal figure. The poet's "immortality lies in his ability to create life, his tragedy in his constant inability to give flesh and material reality to the world which lives in his imagination."[46]

In "Dream," Khomyakov describes the value he places on the poet and the immortality he receives when his song outlives him. Almost like the crown God places on the poet, "Dream" itself has a circular pattern in the repetition of the first stanza as the poem's last one. The movement of God's gift is from the crown, to the fingers, to the heart, to the greedy ears of his listeners, who hear not only his voice, but the voice of nature itself. In the first half of the poem Khomyakov leads up to this identification through his use of similes, connecting the poet to nature: the sounds of his strings are like thunder, his song is like living water. When the poet lies in the grave, his lips are sealed, but the song still thunders and his voice still sounds out. Unlike "Two Hours," "Inspiration " and "Lark, Eagle and Poet," all written in iambic tetrameter with alternating masculine/feminine rhymes, this poem is written in iambic pentameter, except for lines four and twenty-four (iambic tetrameter) and line eight (iambic hexameter); the rhyme scheme is AbbA, an additional circular pattern.

Another poem written in iambic pentameter is "A Vision" (alternating masculine/feminine rhyme), in which Khomyakov's lyrical narrator describes the advent of inspiration and its life-giving qualities. In "Two Hours" he describes the unhappy time when inspiration does not visit the poet and denies life to the world born in his soul. But in this poem the lyrical narrator also describes the happy hour when inspiration does indeed fill the poet's heart. "Inspiration" is another work which calls the poet to seize the moment when inspiration arrives; failure to make the best use of this time leads not only to his own poetic death, but to the deadening of the world. Khomyakov's vision is more joyous in "The Lark, Eagle and Poet," where he unites the three as symbols of transcendence in their quest for inspiration and freedom in their native land.

A true Russian patriot peripherally connected with the *Lyubomudry* group through publication (with V. F. Odoevsky) of the almanac *Mnemosyne* (1824-25) is the poet, critic and Decembrist, Wilhelm Küchelbecker (1797-1846). As Mirsky point out, Küchelbecker is a contradictory figure: "Though of German blood, he was the most ardent of Russian patriots, and though in reality the most advanced of the Romantics, he insisted on calling himself an extreme literary conservative and a supporter of Admiral Shishkov."[47] After the Decembrist revolt he fled to Poland but was apprehended before he reached the border. He spent the last twenty years of his life in Siberian exile. Very little of his work appeared in print during his lifetime; what is left is a collection of lyrics, epics, diaries, essays and stories.

As a student at the Tsarskoe Selo lyceum, he was a classmate of Pushkin, Delvig and Baratynsky. Küchelbecker was always a liberal in his political views, so it is not surprising that he became a Decembrist after he met Ryleev (see below). In exile he led a hard life, living in poverty and trying to eke out an existence by tutoring and farming. He became blind and died of tuberculosis.

Küchelbecker's hardships are reflected in the poems of his last years, personal lyrics about lack of poetic inspiration and the deaths of his friends. These poems contrast with his early verses—elegies, epistles, odes—which are full of enthusiasm, passion, and poetic idealism. Always a practitioner of the "high style," with its proclivity for the odic tradition, Küchelbecker nevertheless was an innovator who gave greater scope to that tradition through experiments in metrics (especially with dactyls) and drama. Early in the twenties his poems became more public in theme, emphasizing republican ideas. Of course, this trend ended with his exile.

In "Tsarskoe Selo," which in retrospect sounds like a prophecy of his exile, Küchelbecker takes us on a stroll through his youthful haunts. Already here we see the themes of freedom and friendship which characterize a significant portion of his work. The poem is written in iambic hexameters, with a number of shorter lines (tetrameters, pentameters and even a trimeter) at irregular intervals. The ryhme scheme is very complex in the first part of the poem: aBBaCddCeeB/aCCaCCeeFggFhhI/IeeJeJJk-kLmLm. In the last section of the poem, where he focuses attention on himself and his sorrows, the rhyme scheme becomes more conventional: NoNoPqPqRssRttUvvU.

In his farewell to Pushkin, "October 19, 1837," Küchelbecker devises stanzas in which the rhyme scheme is AbbAcDcD and the meter is iambic pentameter. Although twenty years separate this poem from "Tsarskoe Selo," their structure has common elements. Again he praises his friend and grieves at the loss of a great poet. But then Küchelbecker directs attention toward himself and describes his exile, in this case a fate that really does seem worse than death. Significantly only about a third of the early poem concerns his own unhappiness, while four-fifths of the later poem discusses his plight—a horrendous one indeed.

Another poet-Decembrist who also wrote about his terrible life in prison and exile is Alexander Ivanovich Odoevsky (1802-39). A fiery character, this man published only about four poems before his arrest. After a year's imprisonment he was sent to hard labor, first to Irkutsk and then to the Caucasus, where he was allowed to serve as a private soldier. He died of malaria in 1839.

As a poet Odoevsky provides a link between the early Romantics and Lermontov, who knew and liked his works. His poems are often about specific subjects, events and people rather than about generalized concepts—although he wrote some philosophical poems similar to Venevitinov's. His interests center on Russian history, especially on the struggles for freedom of various cities against Moscow. His poems about Novgorod made that city's bell a symbol of freedom and a probable source for the name of Herzen's journal *The Bell*. Pan-Slavic and Georgian elements also appear in his work. Odoevsky's views of the poet are not as lofty as those of his contemporaries; he thought the poet should be a comforter of the people, someone who would also fight for them.

On a technical level, the poet Odoevsky was not a real innovator, although he wrote many poems without rhymes. In long works he uses various rhythms, but contributes nothing new to his lexicon, which is often archaic and full of romantic clichés. Odoevsky made no genre changes of importance.

Even though none of his poetry written after 1826 was published in his lifetime, friends back in the capital did not forget him. In answer to Pushkin's poem "Deep in Siberian Mines," which he sent to Siberia with the wife of Nikita Muravyov, Odoevsky wrote "The Ardent Sounds of the Seer's Strings" (iambic tetrameter, alternating feminine/masculine rhymes, except stanza two: aBBa). Pushkin writes to assure the exiled Decembrists that they are not forgotten and that someday they will be free. Odoevsky answers that they, the exiled Decembrists, will forge swords from their chains. "Sparks will grow into flames," a line from the poem, later became the epigraph to Lenin's newspaper, *Iskra* (*The Spark*).

On a more resigned note Odoevsky wrote "The Dying Artist" (iambic tetrameter, various rhyme schemes) on the death of D. Venevitinov. At first the lyrical narrator seems to be speaking about another poet, but then the voice changes and the dying poet tells about his own life cut short. This poem contains the famous metaphor likening the poet's life to "unripe fruit." The poet does not get to sing his song; he will do it in heaven.

Another poet whose song was cut short is the leading Decembrist Kondraty Fyodorovich Ryleev (1795-1825), executed for the major organizational role he played in the 1825 revolution. Brought up by a cold, miserly father, Ryleev spent almost his entire life in a military atmosphere. However, he did get a chance to go to Europe with the troops; this trip, especially his stay in France, led him to see a need for constitutional reforms in Russia. After the war Ryleev could not stand the conditions in the army and so, after marrying in 1819, he resigned his commission and moved to Petersburg, where he got a job in the civil service as a judge. By all accounts he was a just judge whose eyes were opened to the deplorable social conditions in Russia.

During this period he met the "literary men" of the capital and began his own career as a writer, and later, as a publisher of *The Polar Star*. His early works, like those of most of his contemporaries, were mainly odes. Ryleev was closer to the eighteenth century than to the nineteenth, with his propensity for a rhetorical, solemn style, full of apostrophe, patriotism, and a somewhat imperative tone. However, there are traces of Romanticism in his works of a patriotic, Byronic tint.

After his apprenticeship with odes, Ryleev went on to write elegies, idylls, and romances. He is most famous for his *dumy*, a genre akin to Ukrainian folk songs. While living on his wife's estate in Voronezh, near the Ukraine, Ryleev became interested in the history of that country and in the Cossack tradition. His *dumy* (1821-23), with their didactic intent, fit into Ryleev's idea of the role of literature and the poet. Literature is meant for agitation, propaganda, general education, and moral teaching. The poet, above all, is a citizen, one ready to sacrifice himself and all of his personal concerns—even family—for his fatherland. Even though he may be aware that he is fated to destruction, the poet must nevertheless wish to battle for his country's freedom.

Admirably suited to these themes, the *dumy* (based on the historical songs [1816] of the Polish poet Julian Niemcewicz) are historical ballads which go back to Russian history to depict ancient heroes in their struggles with the villainous enemy. Typically they describe a hero, his situation, and his psychology through flashbacks, soliloquies, or speeches to the troops. One of the better *dumy*, "Ivan Susanin," breaks out of the standard pattern and evokes the past with a fair measure of authenticity. The ballad, written in amphibrachic tetrameter with rhymed couplets, tells of Ivan Susanin's successful attempt to divert the Polish enemy from finding Mikhail Fyodorovich Romanov, the future tsar. He achieves his goal, but not without sacrificing his life.

"The Citizen" castigates those who waste their lives in idle pleasures without fighting for freedom. This selfish generation which ignores its duty will scarcely produce heroes. The poem is written in iambic lines of various length, with hexameters predominant. The rhyme is alternating masculine/feminine lines, except for lines five to eight, which form the pattern cDDc. "The Citizen" is important not only as an example of Decembrist rhetoric, but as the model for the whole school of "Civic Poetry" which flourished in later years.

A real "people's poet" is Alexey Vasilievich Koltsov (1809-42), known primarily for his "Russian Songs," a literary example of native folk music. The son of a coarse cattle dealer from Voronezh, Koltsov was allowed to go to school for only a year. After that his father brought him home to help with the cattle trade. However, while he was at school, Koltsov became interested in literature and he completed his schooling alone upon returning home. He grew up friendless, envied by the crude rustics. Koltsov fell in love with a family maid, but his father sent her away to someone in the Kuban, where she got sick and died. Koltsov took a long time to recover from this incident and eventually fell in love again. Once more the father forbade the marriage and the girl gradually turned into a prostitute. Koltsov led a lonely existence until his death in 1842.

Despite his dreary life, Koltsov managed to achieve some literary success. His poems were very popular, even though they were written in the thirties, when prose was already in style and poetry out of favor. For a while Koltsov was a protégé of Stankevich and Belinksy, who valued his work. He tried to educate himself and asked Belinsky for books; he wanted to learn everything. Zhukovsky helped him materially, but this aid angered Koltsov, who thought that Zhukovsky did not consider him to be on the same level. Koltsov did not want to be dependent on anyone.

Koltsov began to write at twenty-five, after finding a book on poetics describing Neo-classicism; so his early poetic efforts followed that mode. In his songs Koltsov tried to give the peasants' views on life, their feelings, their circumstances. Though Koltsov was sympathetic to the peasants, his poems are not political attacks against serfdom. Koltsov's best poems follow the spirit of the folk song. They are usually unrhymed and lack a defined metrical pattern—although a trochaic rhythm predominates.[48] The poems contain many repetitions, parallels, epithets, exclamations and diminutives. The poems "Song," "Song of a Ploughman," "Peasant's Meditation," and "Bitter Fate" follow these general outlines; the even-numbered lines in "Bitter Fate" end in feminine rhymes. Only "Nightingale," an imitation of Pushkin, follows an iambic tetrameter pattern with alternating masculine/feminine couplets.

The nightingale, a traditionally romantic bird, figures in several of Koltsov's poems. In three of the poems the nightingale elicits a sad mood and betrays the melancholy feelings of the poet/singer. "Nightingale" is really a conceit, an extended simile, comparing a nightingale and a poet, both captivated by beauty: the bird with a rose, the singer with a young maid. But the real link between the two is the sad song they both sing. In "Song" the young lover sends a nightingale to sing of his love to his beloved, from whom he is parted. "Bitter Fate" describes the lyrical narrator's life and compares his youth to the flight of a nightingale. Again in an extended metaphor Koltsov compares the peasant's life to seasons, cycles and phenomena of nature.

Koltsov uses more nature imagery to describe the face of a young maiden at the moment of parting from her beloved in "Separation." Loss of one's beloved is not as tragic, though, as the wasted lonely life described in "A Peasant's Meditation." It is only in "Song of a Ploughman" that we see the joyous side of the peasant's life. When all else fails in life, damp mother earth will nurture the crops and provide a livelihood for the ploughman.

Koltsov's songs renewed an interest in folk motifs so popular at the beginning of the century. The work of Alexander Ivanovich Polezhaev (1805-38) also recalls an earlier mood of Romanticism—stormy rebellion.[49] Polezhaev, the illegitimate son of a landowner and peasant girl, was a tortured man whose life of debauchery and degradation serves as a model for the demonic, destructive lyrical heroes of his poems. After leading a wild life at Moscow University, Polezhaev wrote a burlesque poem, *Sashka*, a parody of Pushkin's *Eugene Onegin*; but Polezhaev's poem is coarse and vulgar. Because of his liberal political views, Polezhaev came under close police scrutiny and was summoned to an audience with Nicholas I, who allowed him to serve as a private soldier. His various escapades, including an attempt to desert, got him into even more trouble up until his death.[50]

Polezhaev's poetry is largely personal, pessimistic, and often bitter. Hugo and Byron influenced him early, and he never outgrew their effect on him. Polezhaev's poems are about personal liberty and the boundless freedom of art and life.[51] According to Mirsky: "Looseness, turgidness, and garrulity are his besetting sins . . . in about a dozen of his poems are passionate force, a rhythmic rush, and a romantic rush that are his alone."[52] "Song of the Captive Iroquois," perhaps his most famous poem, may be an allegorical statement of the individual's struggle against despotism. Each section begins with two lines in anapestic trimeter, followed by anapestic dimeter lines. The longer lines have couplets for rhymes, followed by an ABBC pattern and another couplet. Only the last section, with its lack of a final couplet, deviates from this scheme. The poem describes the bravery of a captive waiting to die.

The attitudes of four different countries is the topic of "Four Nations," in which Polezhaev describes the English as brave freedom fighters, the French as impetuously childish jokesters, the Germans as uncomprehending bookworms, and the Russians as abject slaves. The poem is set in a strange meter—iambic dimeter; its masculine couplets add to the "staccato"[53] quality of the rhythm. The only deviation from the rhyme occurs in the third stanza, whose final lines form an ABBA pattern.

Polezhaev experiments with meter in "The Bitter One," where iambic pentameter lines alternate with iambic tetrameters; the alternating feminine/masculine rhymes parallel the intersecting meters. This poem, as well as "Indignation," explores with great self-pity the agony of the lyrical narrator's life and his fear of death. Of course he blames fate for his piteous existence. "Indignation" also has an interesting metrical pattern. Basically written in trochaic tetrameter, the odd-numbered lines end in dactyls. Trochaic meter, usually associated with songs, adds another dissonant note to this tale of woe and bitterness.

The only relief from this dreariness comes in "Waterfall," a description of nature which turns into a metaphor for the poet's lost youth, with its brief flash of freedom. Written in iambic tetrameter with alternating feminine/masculine rhymes, this poem—like most of Polezhaev's—is inner-directed. Polezhaev shares this tendency to be highly autobiographical in his lyrics with another Romantic poet, Mikhail Yurievich Lermontov (1814-41).

The son of an army officer/petty landowner and an aristocratic mother who died when he was three, Lermontov was raised by his maternal grandmother, who quite early turned him into a spoiled child. She took him to the Caucasus when he was nine, where his life-long love affair with the area began. Probably because he was surrounded and brought up by women, Lermontov turned into a vain, pampered man. When he was sixteen Lermontov entered Moscow University; two years later he went to Petersburg, where he entered the Cadet school rather than the university. So began his stormy military career.

Although Lermontov was a brave, courageous hussar who distinguished himself in battle, he was twice reduced to the ranks and fought in the lines in the Caucasus. He was first reduced to the ranks for his poem "Death of a Poet" (see below) and the second time for his participation in a duel. Another duel ended his life in 1841.

Lermontov began his literary career when he was thirteen; at that time he began to develop a cult of Byron in his verses.[54] His early poems (1828-32) are largely imitative, full of clichés, flamboyant similes and Byronic sentiments. The next stage in his career (1832-35) is largely pornographic. Lermontov began to write his mature verses (about eighty in all) in 1836 and continued to write poetry until he died, although in the last years he turned mostly to prose. The main genres of his last period consist of oratorical *dumy*, pseudo-ballads and melancholy meditations.

The themes of Lermontov's poetry are typical for the Romantic Age. Byron's influence accounts for Lermontov's poems about individual liberty, dissatisfaction with life, loneliness, and the egotism which played a large role in shaping the character of Lermontov's heroes—both in the lyrics and in prose. The lyrical heroes are lonely, try to lead an intensely intellectual life, yearn for earlier and better times, seek higher realms as a result of their evaluation of the world of reality, and ultimately are children of fate (though rebellious rather than passive children). The fate which tries to rule them is ineffable. Indeed everything in Lermontov's world is ineffable.

Nature in Lermontov's poems is usually pure and fresh, unlike that of stifling civilization. Many of his works are set in the Caucasus, which he describes in the rich visual images of a painter (which Lermontov was). His landscapes are rarely neutral, and the phenomena of nature are full of emotional shading and symbolic value.

Lermontov also writes often of love. He usually describes the negative aspects of love, tragic because it is unrequited. His lyrical hero suffers because of love and expresses his bitterness and jealousy toward the woman who caused his pain; he wishes her to suffer and feel pain as deep as, or deeper than, his own. Love exists only in the past and memories are sad and bitter. The poet as well as the lover must suffer, for that is his fate. The poet also suffers loneliness because he is misunderstood by the crowd whom he views with disdain.

Many of Lermontov's poems are based on contrast, the tension between polar opposites, especially reason and feeling. Early in his career Lermontov's poems are filled with borrowed, hackneyed similes. He has a tendency to combine metaphors that do not fit and to express himself in imprecise syntax. But those defects are dimmed by his emotional intensity and oratorical style. Sounds are important to Lermontov and as a result his poems have a musical quality.

Lermontov's preference for ternary meters over iambs also contributes to the musicality of his verses. He ordinarily uses iambic tetrameters for satirical poems or indignant indictments of those people and things that he hates. Lermontov uses irregular iambs for his civic poetry, but experiments with other meters in his verse.

In an early poem, "My House" (alternating iambic tetrameters/pentameters with corresponding masculine/feminine rhymes), Lermontov describes the poet's domain—the entire world. In this poem we see that though he has no limits in life, the poet must nevertheless suffer. Contradictions also form the basis of another early poem, "The Sail." Written in iambic tetrameter with alternating masculine/feminine rhyme, this poem is a symbolic representation of someone searching for an indefinable object or an unknown land. The sail, like Lermontov's heroes, is rebellious: it seeks peace in storms.

The disillusionment with life that is the subject of two poems—one early, one late— motivates Lermontov's lyrical hero's quest for some sort of comfort. In "Cup of Life" (alternating masculine/feminine rhymes in iambic tetrameter/trimeter lines), we are told that we go through life with our eyes closed. When we open them before death, we find we have not missed anything. Life is merely a dream, and not even ours. In a later poem, "It's Both Boring and Sad," Lermontov again paints a bleak picture. Once more he recalls the empty cup of life when he says that life is but an empty joke. It is ironic that a poem which describes poverty of life is so rich in metric experimentation. The lines are composed of three-, four- and five-footed amphibrachs with alternating masculine/feminine rhymes. Within this meter Lermontov varies the rhythm with ellipses, dashes and enjambement—all resulting in a poem that sounds like natural speech which disguises a very regular meter.

Occasionally Lermontov's narrator finds relief from life, sometimes in prayer, sometimes in nature. In one of his poems, called "Prayer," he tells us he gets relief from the difficult times of life through a special prayer. This poem is also interesting from a metrical angle; in it iambic trimeters alternate with lines that are iambic tetrameters, with the last foot always a pyrrhic: $\cup/\ \cup/\ \cup/\ \cup\cup,\ \cup/\ \cup/\ \cup/$. The rhymes correspond to the alternating lines. In another "Prayer," the poet beseeches the Mother of God to grant a happy life and peaceful death to a young girl. This poem, which consists of dactylic tetrameter lines with alternating rhymes, is a touching, tender statement of affection.

The lyrical narrator finds hope not only in prayer, but in nature as well. In "I walk out alone upon the road" (trochaic pentameter, alternating masculine/feminine rhymes), he looks for peace in the heavens and searches the night sky. He cannot understand why nature can sleep while life is hard and painful for him. He tells us he is already resigned to expect nothing from life. He would like to find freedom, peace and oblivion—those very attributes the sleeping world has at night. The narrator knows he will find those things in death, but does not want death, only peace. And he finds it in the nature described in "When the yellowing cornfield sways" (iambic hexameter, alternating masculine/feminine rhymes). But he does not find peace within nature itself. He can merely understand happiness on earth and see God in the heavens, where he finds some comfort.

Tears, not comfort, are the result of a natural encounter in "The Cliff" (trochaic tetrameter, abba rhyme scheme). A gentle cloud rests on a cliff and leaves the next morning. A trace of it is left behind—or is the cliff really shedding tears? Could it be lonely after the fleeting companionship of a gentle cloud?

No ambiguity of feeling shows through in "Wherefore" (iambic hexameter, couplets) and "Thanksgiving" (iambic tetrameter, alternating masculine/feminine rhyme). Both reveal bitterness at the end of a love affair. But bitterness runs even deeper in Lermontov's political poems—"Farewell, Unwashed Russia" (iambic tetrameter, alternating feminine/masculine rhyme), and *Duma* (iambs of various lengths, alternating masculine/feminine rhyme). The first is a derisive leavetaking, while the second is a contemptuous look at Russia and the age.

The poem which made Lermontov famous was also a political one, "Death of a Poet," in which he blames the government (tsar) for the death of Pushkin. In the first half, written in the iambic tetrameter he saves for his "indignant" poetry, Lermontov recreates the circumstances of the duel and castigates Pushkin's false friends. Then in iambic lines of various length, he puts the blame on the court. The poem is rhetorical and follows an odic pattern with its irregular rhymes.

The mood of yet another of his poems is quite different from the public high-style ode on Pushkin's death. "Dream" (iambic pentameter with alternating rhyme scheme) is a complex poem which has three frames of narration, a device Lermontov uses in his novel *A Hero of Our Time*. Lermontov's lyrical narrator dreams that he is dying in Dagestan; within this dream, the dying man dreams of a young woman in the city who dreams of the dying man. Written just a few months before Lermontov himself died in a duel in the Caucasus, this poem is a mini-narrative which tells a story in the romantic fashion, i.e., with intensity, fragmentariness, and mystery.

A poem by Fyodor Ivanovich Tyutchev (1803-73), "Dream At Sea," also tells a story, but one with deeper philosophical ramifications—a hallmark of his verse. A descendent of an old noble family, Tyutchev received an education at home and at Moscow University.[55] His tutor was the poet Raich (see below). In 1822 Tyutchev entered the diplomatic service and went to Germany, where he met Schelling and Heine. During his twenty-two years abroad he served mainly in Munich, but then was sent to Turin. While in Europe he married a Bavarian woman. After her death Tyutchev married again, another German. After he returned to Russia in 1844 he became a fixture in the salons flourishing in the capital at that time. Tyutchev was a brilliant conversationalist and his wit enlivened many a social gathering. In his private life he spoke only French, and all his political articles and correspondence were written in that language. But he wrote his poems in Russian.

After his return to Russia Tyutchev received a job on the Censorship Board where he worked for many years. About 1850 he met Elena Alexandrovna Denisieva, who became his daughters' governess. She and Tyutchev fell deeply in love, and she bore him three children. This love is the subject of the poems known as the "Denisieva cycle," an exceptional collection of love poetry. She died in 1864.

During the last years of his life Tyutchev became even more involved with politics and his poems reflect this. The poems, not very good as poetry, reflect his conservative pan-Slavic views. To this period also belong a number of religious poems, artistically on a level with the political ones. This period of his life also marks Tyutchev's physical decline. After three strokes, Tyutchev died in 1873.

Some of Tyutchev's early poems appeared in various almanacs, but his first "major" publication of sixteen poems appeared only in the mid-thirties in Pushkin's journal, *The Contemporary*. Tyutchev's first volume came out in 1854. Unfortunately this was not an auspicious time for poetry in Russia, with the literary trends veering toward prose. The Symbolists "discovered" Tyutchev in the 1890s and rekindled interest in this unjustly forgotten poet.

Besides poems on political and religious themes, Tyutchev's lyrics fall into three major categories: poems about love, nature and temporal affinities, i.e., times of the day and of the year. Poems from each of these categories also constitute, with other poems, a larger, more inclusive collection—the metaphysical lyrics. In Tyutchev's works we can see similarities with Baratynsky, another philosophical poet who combines traits of romanticism and classicism. But unlike the restrained Baratynsky's, Tyutchev's poems are highly personal and often full of emotion.

Most critics tend to categorize Tyutchev as a poet who wrote on Romantic themes but was a classicist in style. Close examination of his poems shows that this judgment is not particularly true. Although Tyutchev does use archaisms, Church Slavonicisms, and compound adjectives—all signs of a classical bent—the archaisms and Church Slavonicisms form a small portion of his vocabulary, which mainly consists of highly Romantic semantic fields.[56] Another characteristic of Tyutchev's lexicon is a high index of synonyms in a given poem, a device which contributes to his "intensive method." And while he does use composite adjectives with some frequency, his *composita* are more neologistic than those of another writer who used them often— Derzhavin.

If Tyutchev bears any resemblance to Derzhavin at all, it is in his syntax. The majority of his sentences are written in standard word order; but he often separates nouns and adjectives, reverses adjectives and nouns, and displaces natural word order. However, he usually does this so that his lines can fit a metrical pattern. Tyutchev's poems are full of parallel syntactical patterns which he often uses to underline comparisons and contrasts in his subject matter. Also not uncommon is his use of triplets, i.e., series of three nouns, adjectives and verbs. Even though these devices seem rhetorical and oratorical on the surface, they appear in poems with conversational intonation. These poems are often intimate love lyrics.

The meter of Tyutchev's poems is normally binary. Approximately 87 percent of his lyrics were written in iambic lines; 57 percent of these are iambic tetrameters. In spite of this, Tyutchev experiments within the form and creates rich rhythmic modulation through use of spondees, pyrrhics, and full lines, i.e., lines with the fewest possible number of words. He also uses trochaic lines, usually reserved for songs and light verse, in very serious poems.

Tyutchev's rhymes at first glance also seem to be mundane, with few innovations. Alternating rhymes comprise 65 percent of his verse and circular rhymes (AbbA) make up 12 percent. But the rhymes are significant in that they underscore the meaning of the poem. Tyutchev often puts the most important words of the poem in rhyming position. Tyutchev also effectively uses all types of tropes and figures of speech. Perhaps the most characteristic use of a rhetorical device is Tyutchev's use of the simile as the basic structural device of a poem, much in the manner of the Metaphysical Poets and their use of the conceit.

"Fountain" (iambic tetrameter, AbbA rhyme) is an excellent example of a poem which is really an extended simile. In the first stanza the poet describes a fountain with water spouting up into the air. But a strong natural force, gravity, causes it to come back to earth. In the second stanza he describes how man's thought also works like a fountain, also straining toward heaven. But nature, the stronger force, wins over man, the weaker force of the two.[57]

Another poem which contains a Romantic theme is *Silentium!* (basically iambic tetrameter, with variations for emphasis). Here Tyutchev emphasizes the poet's isolation from the masses who cannot understand his message by exhorting the poet to remain silent. Why bother to express something which no one will understand? Is it not better to keep it to yourself? For in expressing a truth, you invariably change it into a lie. Tyutchev emphasizes his point in the rhyme scheme of masculine couplets. Each stanza ends with a command that echoes the one in the first line; each of these lines rhymes with the other. And as a frame, the first and last words of the poem are identical: "Be silent."

Another of Tyutchev's poems which fits within a frame, but here a more elaborate one, is "Dream at Sea." In order to duplicate the rocking, lulling motion of the sea which puts the poet to sleep, Tyutchev uses amphibrachic tetrameter lines. Masculine couplets form the rhyme scheme. The first seven lines are a preface which "opens the way for the dream."[58] The two infinities which the poet possesses are the chaos of the sea and the heights of his dream, a vision of a magic, unknown land. The same sea which lulled the poet to sleep now breaks in to wake him and bring him back to reality. In ending the vision with the poet's claim to resemble God, Tyutchev is writing a parable of the "romantic apotheosis of man and its dangerous consequences."[59]

The sea again appears as chaos, but political chaos, in "Sea and Cliff." The entire poem is a metaphor where the cliff is Russia and the sea her enemies. In this poem Tyutchev takes two insentient forces of nature and elevates them to abstract concepts. The result is more than mere personification, for it approaches the higher plane of allegory. Once more Tyutchev uses meter to enhance the poem. He deviates from iambic lines to write a poem in trochaic tetrameter with alternating feminine and masculine rhymes. By beginning the poem with a trochee he imitates the action of the wave on the cliff, first the impact of a wave and then its lapping away.

Tyutchev uses the same rhyme and meter in yet another political poem, "Huddled Hamlets." The dissonance between the light meter and the sad tone is striking. In this lyric Tyutchev no longer glories in Russia's power, but despairs over the poverty of the land. The tone is depressing and the landscape is bleak. But we see another view of nature in "Autumn Evening," where Tyutchev returns to iambic lines (pentameters) and an alternating rhyme scheme. Here he creates a tender, gentle mood, even though the land is orphaned and sad during this time of decline. But if one experiences pain at this time, the suffering is modest. Perhaps this view of nature, even of nature in its decline, is not pessimistic because it can be autumn anywhere, not necessarily in Russia. And even though we get a glimpse of night, it is not as terrifying as it usually is in Tyutchev's poems.

Tyutchev's lyrics about the Night present a number of attitudes. Sometimes night is negative, with its terror or its periods of insomnia. At other times night is a positive force, a time of transcendence and inspiration. Three of Tyutchev's poems are often grouped together as representative of his reactions to the night. These poems are also bound together by common words and motifs—especially the grouping of night, the abyss and chaos. Two of them share a common meter, iambic tetrameter, and all three have alternating rhyme schemes.

In "About What, O Night Wind, Do You Cry?" the irrational elements of night, insomnia and madness, which lead to spiritual chaos, become a frightening consequence of night's activities. However, this terror may be due to the lyrical narrator's desire not to have his "precarious inner balance"[60] upset, as Gregg suggests. The possibility exists because the poet is drawn to the night, the time when this process of self-revelation would take place.

Night is no less frightening in "Holy Night" (iambic pentameter). But it is important that here night is holy, and therefore a positive force. Contrasted to day with its protective cover over the abyss, night becomes the time when man, now orphaned, faces that very abyss which is his own soul. However, as Pigarev points out, the day and its golden pall are merely a cover for man's reality and the infinity of chaos, which can only be discovered at night.[61] Night is man's time of truth.

"Day and Night" is probably Tyutchev's most famous poem about these antithetical hours. Like the others, this poem describes night as a time when man must face the truth about himself—however frightening it may be. And also like the others, this poem contains the "vocabulary of the night." The words of the "Night-Cycle" poems form semantic fields which describe the themes of solitude, mystery, irrationality, chaos, and the abyss; these words and themes are certainly Romantic in character. Significantly these words are not only Romantic, but also Schellingian in nature. It is probably in these three poems that Tyutchev is closest to Schelling.

The contradictory nature of love also appears in a number of poems. In "Yesterday in Charmed Dreams" (iambic tetrameter, alternating rhyme), we get a highly erotic picture of a sexual encounter and the deep pleasure it brings. In a later poem, "Malaria" (alexandrines with an aBBa rhyme), a new strain appears, one akin to those described by Mario Praz in his *Romantic Agony*. "Malaria" comes from Tyutchev's second German period when, according to Richard Gregg, love equalled both sex and pain. During this period, Tyutchev saw love as being sinful, and sin as being lovely. The poem advances the view that evil exists even in the most beautiful objects and the most sensual experiences.[62]

In "Oh, How Murderously We Love," written in Tyutchev's most characteristic rhyme pattern and meter, love is no longer sensual. An example of a poem from the "Denisieva" cycle, this lyric expresses the destructive quality of mindless passion. The beloved has faded and dried up. After the description of the horrible consequences of passion, the narrator begins to put the blame on the lover, whose love now inflicts so much pain on the beloved.

It is appropriate to conclude our brief survey of the poetry of the Golden Age with Tyutchev, for he is its last major representative. He is also a link to the end of the century, when poetry again became the dominant form in Russian literature. During the Romantic Age all the poets began writing poems grounded in the classical tradition, and all somehow were enchanted by Romanticism—some more than others. Various groups of poets emerged: the Decembrists, the Wisdom Lovers, the Pushkin Pleiad. But within these groups each poet developed his own style. Some poets, like Pushkin, Baratynsky, Koltsov and Tyutchev, fit in no group at all. In fact, the one characteristic they share is that they exemplify a theme they all investigated: the inspired poet's individuality in opposition to the crowd.

Notes

1. N. D. Kochetkova, "Poeziia russkogo sentimentalizma. N. M. Karamzin. I. I. Dmitriev," in *Istoriia russkoi poezii*, ed. B. P. Gorodetskii, Vol. I (Leningrad: Nauka, 1968), pp. 163-90.

2. For definitions of nationalism see Lauren G. Leighton, *Russian Romanticism: Two Essays* (The Hague: Mouton and Co., 1975).

3. It also became too dangerous to be a Mason because of government oppression.

4. Henry M. Nebel, Jr., *N. M. Karamzin* (The Hague: Mouton and Co., 1967), p. 85.

5. Irina M. Semenko, *Vasily Zhukovsky* (Boston: Twayne Publishers, 1976), p. 26.

6. Semenko, p. 55.

7. Masha Protasova Moyer, his half-niece, whom he loved and wanted to marry. This poem recalls the date of her death.

8. Ilya Z. Serman, *Konstantin Batyushkov* (New York: Twayne Publishers, 1974), p. 169.

9. Semenko, pp. 67-69.

10. Semenko, p. 67.

11. Semenko, p. 67.

12. Semenko, p. 67.

13. Semenko, p. 68 and Serman, p. 167.

14. I. I. Dmitriev is an important sentimentalist poet whose influence is second only to Karamzin's.

15. Serman, p. 166.

16. Serman, p. 73. For a detailed discussion of *My Penates*, see this source, pp. 72-92.

17. Serman, p. 85.

18. Serman, p. 89.

19. Serman, p. 100.

20. Serman, p. 85. He also discusses the swift succession of episodes.

21. Serman, p. 169.

22. D. S. Mirsky, *A History of Russian Literature*, ed. Francis J. Whitfield (New York: Alfred A. Knopf, 1966), p. 79.

23. See John M. Mersereau, Jr., *Baron Delvig's* Northern Flowers (Carbondale: Southern Illinois University Press, 1967) for a detailed study of Delvig's journalistic work.

24. Ludmilla Koehler, *Anton Antonovič Delvig* (The Hague: Mouton and Co., 1970), pp. 11-12.

25. Koehler, p. 47.

26. See Victor Erlich, *The Double Image* (Baltimore: Johns Hopkins Press, 1964) for an analysis of Pushkin's metapoetry.

27. Mirsky, p. 92.

28. Since most of Pushkin's poems discussed here follow both this rhythm and this rhyme pattern, I shall mention meter and rhyme scheme in the text only when it deviates from this pattern.

29. Richard F. Gustafson, "The Upas Tree: Pushkin and Erasmus Darwin," *Publications of the Modern Language Association*, 75 (1960), 101-9.

30. This was not a real group, but is a term which applies to a number of Pushkin's contemporaries, e.g., Baratynsky, Yazykov, etc.

31. Benjamin Dees, *E. A. Baratynsky* (New York: Twayne Publishers, Inc., 1972), p. 17.

32. Dees, p. 136.

33. Dees, p. 136.

34. Mirsky, p. 102.

35. Dees, p. 100. For a detailed analysis see this source, pp. 100-105.

36. Dees, p. 122.

37. Dees, p. 108.

38. Dees, pp. 115-22.

39. Information for this discussion of Yazykov comes from Benjamin Dees, "Yazykov's Lyrical Poetry," *Russian Literature Triquarterly*, 10 (Fall 1974), 316-30, and K. K. Bukhmeyer, "N. M. Yazykov," in *Polnoe sobranie sochinenii* by N. M. Yazykov (Moscow-Leningrad: Sovetskii pisatel, 1964), pp. 5-52.

40. Larry Andrews, "D. V. Venevitinov: A Sketch of His Life and Work," *Russian Literature Triquarterly*, 8 (Winter 1974), 373-84.

41. Andrews, p. 379.

42. Andrews, pp. 380-81.

43. Andrews, p. 380.

44. Andrews, p. 381.

45. E. A. Maimin, "Filosofskaia lirika poetov-liubomudrov," in *Istoriia russkoi poezii*, ed. B. P. Gorodetskii, Vol I (Leningrad: Nauka, 1968), pp. 438-41.

46. Maimin, p. 439.

47. Mirsky, p. 106.

48. Renato Poggioli, *The Poets of Russia* (Cambridge, Mass.: Harvard University Press, 1960), p. 27.

49. V. S. Kiselev-Sergenin, "A. I. Polezhaev," in *Istoriia russkoi poezii*, ed. B. P. Gorodetskii, Vol I (Leningrad: Nauka, 1968), p. 468.

50. Mirsky, pp. 123-24.

51. Kiselev-Sergenin, pp. 468-69.

52. Mirsky, p. 124.

53. Mirsky, p. 124.

54. For a detailed study of Lermontov's style, see B. M. Eikhenbaum, *Lermontov*, trans. Ray Parrot and Harry Weber (Ann Arbor: Ardis, 1981).

55. Richard A. Gregg, *Fedor Tiutchev. The Evolution of a Poet* (New York: Columbia University Press, 1965) is the source of my biographical information.

56. See Christine A. Rydel, "A Formal Analysis of the Poems of Fedor Ivanovič Tjutčev," Diss. (Indiana University, 1976) for a detailed analysis of his lexicon, syntax, rhyme, meter and tropes and figures of speech.

57. Gregg, p. 82.

58. Gregg, p. 98.

59. Gregg, pp. 99-100.

60. Gregg, p. 101.

61. K. V. Pigarev, *Zhizn' i tvorchestvo Tiutcheva* (Moscow: Akademiia Nauk, 1962), pp. 199-200.

62. Gregg, pp. 74-75.

LYRIC POETRY

N. M. KARAMZIN

Spring Song of a Melancholic

Raging winter has vanished,
Frosts, rime and snow have vanished too;
And the gloom which enshrouded everything on earth
Has faded away like smoke, and vanished.

We no longer hear the roar of stormy winds
Which frightened the wanderer on his way;
We don't see heavy, black clouds
Drifting from north to south.

Spring arrives smiling;
And peace drifts in, hard on its heels.
And a Zephyr gambols and plays
On Nature's tender breast.

Quiet rain pours down from the sky
And all of creation comes to life;
All of the grass grows green in the fields,
And the meadow is completely covered with flowers.

The violet has already blossomed
And blooms peacefully under a bush,
And feeds ambrosia to the air;
Without waiting for praise, it does good.

On the branches little birds sing
Songs of praise to an all-bountiful Creator;
And love gives harmony to their songs,
And love gladdens their hearts.

Meek little lambs wander about
And nibble the grass in the meadows;
They nourish a love for the Creator in their hearts—
And thank Him without words.

Lying carelessly on the grass,
A shepherd plays his pipes;
Nourished by a fragrant scent,
He praises the beauty of spring.

Joy is beaming all around, all around,
Only gaiety is all around;
But I, burdened with sadness,
Wander despondently in the woods.

Sadness wanders along the meadows with me.
Looking into a brook, I shed tears;
I disturb the water with my tears,
I alarm it with my sighs.

Most wise and merciful Creator!
When will my Spring come,
And my winter of sadness depart,
And the gloom in my soul fade away?

1788

Autumn

Autumn winds blow
  In a gloomy oak grove;
Yellow leaves noisily
  Roll about the earth.

Field and garden have become deserted;
  The hills lament;
Songs have turned to silence in the groves—
  Little birds are now in hiding.

A flock of late geese
  Rush to the south,
Rising in smooth flight
  Into the celestial heights.

Grey mists whirl
  In the quiet valley;
Mixing with the smoke in the village,
  They ascend to the sky.

Standing on a hill, a wanderer
  Sighs languidly,
While with despondent eyes
  He looks at pale autumn.

Be comforted, mournful wanderer!
  Nature withers
But for a short time;
  Everything comes back to life.

Everything renews itself in spring;
  Smiling proudly,
Nature will arise again,
  Dressed up in her wedding clothes.

Ah! a mortal withers forever!
  In the springtime, an old man
Still feels the cold winter
  Of his feeble life.

1789
Geneva

The Cemetery

A voice
It's terrifying in the grave, so cold and dark!
The winds wail here, the coffins shiver,
  White bones rattle.

A second voice
It's quiet in the grave, so soft, peaceful.
The winds blow here, it's cool for those who sleep;
  Grasses, little flowers grow.

The first
A worm with a bloody head gnaws away at the dead.
Toads make their nests in yellow skulls,
  Snakes hiss in the nettles.

The second
The sleep of the dead is deep, sweet, gentle;
There are no storms in the coffin; tender little birds
  Sing their song on the grave.

The first
Black ravens, the greedy birds,
Live there; howling beasts of prey
  Rummage in the earth.

The second
A small rabbit rests in the grass
With its dear little friend there;
  A dove sleeps on a branch.

The first
Densely commingling, dampness and shadow
Drift along in the stuffy air;
  A leafless tree stands nearby.

The second
Aromatic vapors of blue violets,
White jasmine and lilies
  Stream into the bright air.

The first
A wanderer fears the valley of death;
Feeling terror and trepidation in his heart,
  He hurries past the grave.

The second
A tired wanderer sees a place
Of eternal peace—and casting off his staff,
  He remains there forever.

1792

V. A. ZHUKOVSKY

The Sea. An Elegy

Silent sea, azure sea,
I stand enchanted over your abyss.
You are alive; you breathe; you are filled
With a confused love and a disturbing thought.
Silent sea, azure sea,
Reveal your deep secret to me:
What moves your immense bosom?
How does your strained breast breathe?
Or does the distant, bright sky draw you
Out of your earthly captivity to itself?..
Full of sweet, secret life,
You are pure in its sweet presence:
Its bright azure flows over you,
You sparkle in its evening and morning light,
You caress its golden clouds
And joyfully glitter in its stars.
And when dark clouds gather
To take the clear sky away from you—
You churn, you howl, you stir up the waves,
You rage and tear the inimicable haze to pieces...
And the haze disappears and the clouds go away,
But, full of your former alarm,
You raise up the frightened waves for a long time,
And the sweet glitter of the skies which appeared
Does not return you to complete stillness;
Your appearance of immobility is deceptive:
You hide your confusion in the peaceful abyss,
Admiring the sky, you tremble for it.

1822

March 19, 1813

You stood
Silently before me.
Your doleful eyes
Were full of feeling.
They reminded me
Of the sweet past...
They were the last things
On this earth.

You moved away
Like a quiet angel;
Your grave is
As peaceful as paradise!
All earthly memories
Are there,
All holy thoughts of
Heaven are there.

Stars of the heavens,
Quiet night!..

19 March 1823

Song

Enchantment of days long forsaken,
Why have you come so suddenly
To life? Who seeks to reawaken
Long-silent dreams and memory?
This worldly soul your whispers greeted;
Familiar looks at it you cast;
And that which had been long secreted
Was briefly visible at last.

O holy Past, why are you swelling
Within my breast and crowding me?
Dear guest, will hope live at my telling?
And shall I say to what was: *Be*?
New brilliance can I see, revealing
A lovely, withered dream? Once more
Can I cast down a pall, concealing
The naked life I knew before?

Why does my spirit rush forever
Toward a land of days long gone?
Land bare of people, it will never
Be filled, or past years linger on.
A *lone* inhabitant stands mute—he
Beholds antiquity so dear;
There he and all the days of beauty
Are laid into a lonely bier.

Second half of 1818

Spring Feeling

Little breeze, so soft and light,
Why are you so sweetly blowing?
Magic stream, why are you growing
Clear and playing in your flight?
What has filled your soul anew?

What has sent excitement through it?
What has once more come back to it,
Passing spring, along with you?
I stand gazing at the sky...
There the clouds are brightly glowing;
As they shine, they fly off, going
To where distant forests lie.

Or from off the heights once more
Does familiar news come pouring?
Is antiquity's dear voice now soaring,
Ringing loudly as before?
Or that place where small birds sail,
Wandering and then returning,
Land that holds our deepest yearning,
Is it still beneath a veil?
Will someone direct us where
Leads the path to shores we've never
Seen? Ah, tell me, can we ever
Locate that enchanted *There*?

1816

Night Review

At night when the hour strikes twelve
The drummer gets up from his coffin;
He walks back and forth as he beats
And rapidly sounds out the warning.
The infantry in their dark tombs
Are roused by the drum's steady rhythm:
Arise now the old grenadiers,
Arise brave chasseurs, young and able,
Arise from beneath Russian snows,
From Italy's fields, rich and fertile,
Arise from the African steppes,
From Palestine's hot, sandy desert.

At night when the hour strikes twelve
The trumpeter leaves his grave, gallops
Now forward, now back, as he blows,
And loudly he blares out a warning.
The infantry in their dark graves
Are roused by the sound of the trumpet:
Gray-headed hussars now arise,
Arise cuirassiers in mustaches;
From north and from south, cavalries
One after the other are flying;
They rush from the east and the west
Upon light, ethereal horses.

At night when the hour strikes twelve
A captain gets up from his coffin;
He wears a small cap and a sword,

His uniform coat thrown upon him;
The captain, astride his old horse,
Along the front lines slowly travels;
And marshals are riding behind,
And after him adjutants follow;
And as he approaches and stops,
He sees the whole army salute him;
Before him the regiments pass
To music, one after the other.

He gathers his generals and
Arranges them all in a circle,
And then to the one standing near
He whispers the password and slogan;
Throughout the whole army are spread
That same password, that very slogan:
And that very password is *France*,
And their slogan is *Saint Helena*.
Thus, just so that he might preside
At this review of his old soldiers,
At night when the hour strikes twelve
The dead emperor leaves his coffin.

January 1836

K. N. BATYUSHKOV

To My Penates

Fatherland Penates! come,
Kind protectors of my home!
Not in gold or jewels rich—
Can ye love your simple shrine?
Smile, then, sweetly from your niche
On this lowly hut of mine.
Thus removed from worldly care,
I, a wearied wanderer,
In this silent corner here,
Offer no ambitious prayer.
Here, if ye consent to dwell,
Happiness shall court my cell.
Kind and courteous ever prove,
Beaming on me light and love!
Not with streams of fragrant wine,
Not with incense smoking high,
Does the poet seek your shrine—
His is mild devotion's sigh,
Grateful tears, the still soft fire
Of feeling heart: and sweetest strains,
Inspired by the Aonian choir.
O Lares! in my dwelling rest,
Smile on the poet where he reigns,

And sure the poet shall be blest.
Come, survey my dwelling over;
I'll describe it if I'm able:
In the window stands a table,
Three-legged, tott'ring, with a cover,
Gay some centuries ago,
Ragged, bare and faded now.
In a corner, lost to fame,
To honor lost, the blunted sword
(That relic of my fathers' name)
Harmless hangs, by rust devoured.
Here are pillaged authors laid—
There, a hard and creaking bed:
Broken, crumbling, argile-ware,
Furniture strewn here and there.
And these in higher love I hold
Than sofas rich with silk and gold,
Or china vases gay and fair.
    Kind Penates! thus I pray—
O may wealth and vanity
Never hither find their way,
Never here admitted be!
Let the vile, the slavish soul,
Let the sons of pomp and pride,
Fortune's spoilt ones, turn aside;
Not on them nor theirs I call!
Tottering beggar! hither come,
Thou art bidden to my home:
Throw thy useless crutch away;
Come—be welcome and be gay!
Warmth and rest thy limbs require,
Stretch thee by my cheerful fire:
Reverend teacher! old and hoary,
Thou whom years and toils have taught,
Who with many a storm hast fought,
Storms of time and storms of glory!
Take thy merry balalaika,[1]
Sing thy struggles o'er again;
In the battle's bloody plain,
Where thou swungst the rude nagaika,[2]
Midst the cannon's thunder roar,
Midst the sabres clashing o'er;
Trumpets sounding, banners flying
O'er the dead and o'er the dying,
While thy never-wearied blade
Foes on foes in darkness laid.
And thou, Lisette! at evening steal
Through the shadow-cover'd vale
To this soft and sweet retreat;
Steal, my nymph, on silent feet.
Let a brother's hat disguise
Thy golden locks, thy azure eyes;
O'er thee be my mantle thrown,
Bind my warlike sabre on:
When the treacherous day is o'er,
Knock, fair maiden, at my door;

Enter then, thou soldier sweet!
Throw thy mantle at my feet;
Let thy curls, so brightly glowing,
On thy ivory shoulders flowing,
Be unbound: thy lily breast
Heave, no more with robes opprest!
"Thou enchantress! Is it so?
Sweetest, softest shepherdess!
Art thou really come to bless
With thy smiles my cottage now?"
O her snowy hands are pressing
Warmly, wildly pressing mine!
Mine her rosy lips are blessing,
Sweet as incense from the shrine,
Sweet as zephyr's breath divine
Gently murmuring through the bough;
Even so she whispers now:
"O my heart's friend, I am thine;
Mine, beloved one! art thou."
What a privileged being he,
Who in life's obscurity,
Underneath a roof of thatch,
Till the morning dawns above,
Sweetly sleeps, while angels watch,
In the arms of holy love!
But the stars are now retreating
From the brightening eye of day,
And the little birds are greeting,
Round their nests, the dewy ray.
Hark! the very heaven is ringing
With the matin song of peace:
Hark! a thousand warblers singing
Waft their music on the breeze:
All to life, to love are waking,
From their wings their slumbers shaking;
But my Lila still is sleeping
In her fair and flowery nest;
And the zephyr, round her creeping,
Fondly fans her breathing breast;
O'er her cheeks of roses straying,
With her golden ringlets playing:
From her lips I steal a kiss;
Drink her breath: but roses fairest,
Richest nectar, rapture dearest,
Sweetest, brightest rays of bliss,
Never were as sweet as this.
Sleep, thou loved one! sweetly sleep!
Angels here their vigils keep!
Blest, in innocence arrayed,
I from fortune's favors flee;
Shrouded in the forest-shade,
More than blest by love and thee.
Calm and peaceful time rolls by:
O! has gold a ray so bright
As thy seraph-smile of light
Throws o'er happy poverty?

Thou good genius! in thy view
Wealth is vile and worthless too:
Riches never brought thee down
From thy splendour-girded throne;
But beneath the shadowy tree
Thou hast deigned to smile on *me*.
Fancy, daughter of the skies,
Thoughts, on wings of light that rise,
Waft my spirit gay and free,
When the storm of passion slumbers,
Far above humanity,
To the Aonian land of numbers,
Where the choirs of music stray;
Rapture, like a feather'd arrow
Bursting life's dark prison narrow,
Bears me to the heavens away.
Sovereigns of Parnassus! stay
Till the morning's rosy ray
Throws its brightness o'er your hill,
Stay with nature's poet still.
O, reveal the shadowy band,
Minstrels of my fatherland!
Let them pass the Stygian shore,
From the ethereal courts descending:
Yonder airy spirits o'er,
O! I hear their voices blending:
List! the heavenly echoes come
Wafted to my privileged home;
Music hovers round my head,
From the living and the dead.
Our Parnassian giant,[3] proud,
Tow'ring o'er the rest I see;
And, like storm or thunder loud,
Hear his voice of majesty.
Sons and deeds of glory singing
A majestic swan of light;
Now the harp of angels stringing,
Now he sounds the trump of fight;
Midst the muses', graces' throng,
Sailing through the heaven along;
Horace's strength, and Pindar's fire,
Blended in his mighty lyre.
Now he thunders, swift and strong,
Even like Suna o'er the waste;[4]
Now, like Philomela's song,
Soft and spring-like, sweet and chaste,
Gently breathing o'er the wild,
Heavenly fancy's best-loved child!
Gladdening and enchanting one![5]
History's gayest, fairest son!
He who oft with Agathon
Visits evening's fane of bliss:
Or in Plato's master tone,
Near the illustrious Parthenon
Calls the rays of wisdom down
With a voice sublime as his.

Now amidst the darkness walking,
Where old Russia had her birth,
With the ancient princes talking,
As they ruled o'er half the earth:
Or Sclavonian heroes hoary,
Cradled in a night of glory!
    Sweetest of the sylphs above,[6]
And the graces' darling, see!
O how musically he
Tunes his Citra's melody,
To Dushenka[7] and to love.
Now Meletzy does appear,
Mutual thoughts their souls employ;
Hand in hand the two stand near
And sing a song of joy;
Next engaged with love in play,
Poets and philosophers,
Close to Phaedrus and Pilpay,[8]
Lo! Dmitriev appears
Sporting like a happy child,
Midst the forest's tenants wild,
Garlanded with smiling wreaths;
Truth unveiled beside him breathes.
See two brothers toying there,
Nature's children—Phoebus' priests:
Krylov leading Khemnitser!
Teaching poets! ye whose song
Charms the idle moments long,
When the wearied spirit rests.
    Heavenly choir! the graces twine
O'er you garlands all divine;
And with you the joys I drink,
Sparkling round Pierian brink,
While I sing in raptured glory,
"*Ed io anche son pittore.*"
    Friendly Lares! O, conceal
From man's envious, jealous eye
Those sweet transports which I feel,
Those blest rays of heart-born joy!
Fortune! hence thy treasures bear,
And thy sparkling vanities:
I can look with careless eyes
On thy flight—my little bark,
Safely led through tempests dark,
Finds a peaceful haven here—
Ye who basked in Fortune's ray
From my thoughts have passed away.
    But ye gayer, wiser ones,
Glory's, pleasure's cheerful sons!
Ye who with the graces walk,
Ye who with the muses talk,
Passing life's short hours away
In intellectual children's play;
Careless, joyous sages!—you,
Philosophers and idlers too!
Ye who hate the chains of slavery!

Ye who love the songs of bravery!
In your happiest moments come,
Come, and crowd the muses' home.
Let the laugh and let the bowl
Banish sorrow from the soul:
Come, Zhukovsky, hither hieing,
Time is like an arrow flying—
Pleasure, like an arrow fleet:
Here let friendship's smile of gladness
Brighten every cloud of sadness—
Wreathe with cypress, roses sweet.
    Love is life;—thy garlands bring,
Bobrov, while they're blossoming:
Bind them blooming round our brow—
Bacchus, friends! is with us now.
Favorite of the muses, fill:
Pledge and drink, and pledge us still!
Aristippus' grandson—thou!
O thou lov'st the Aonian lasses,
And the harmonious clang of glasses;
But when evening's silence fills
All the vales and all the hills,
Thou, remote from worldly folly,
Tak'st thy walk with melancholy;
And with that unearthly dame
(Contemplation is her name)
Who conveys the illumined sense
In sublime abstraction hence—
Up to those high and bright abodes
Where men are angels—angels, gods.
    Give me now thy friendly hand;
Leave for me thy spirit land!
Come, companion of my joy,
We will all time's power destroy
On our *chasha zolotoi*.[9]
See behind, with locks so gray,
How he sweeps life's gems away;
His remorseless scythe is mowing
All the flowers around us blowing.
Be it ours to drive before us
Bliss—though fate is frowning o'er us!
Time may hurry, if he will;
We will hurry swifter still;
Drink the cup of ecstasy,
Pluck the flow'rets as we fly,
Spite of time and destiny:
Many a star and many a flower
Shine and bloom in life's short hour,
And their rays and their perfume
For *us* shall shine—for *us* shall bloom.
    Soon shall we end our pilgrimage;
And at the close of life's short stage
Sink smiling on our dusty bed:
The careless wind shall o'er us sweep;
Where sleep our sires, their sons shall sleep
With evening's darkness round our head.

There let no hired mourners weep;
No costly incense fan the sod;
No bell pretend to mourn; no hymn
Be heard midst midnight's shadows dim—
Can they delight a clay-cold clod?
No! if love's tribute ye will pay,
Assemble in the moonlight ray,
And throw fresh flow'rets o'er my clay:
Let my Penates sleep with me—
Here bring the cup I loved—the flute
I played—and twine its form, though mute,
With branches from the ivy-tree!
No grave stone need the wanderer tell
That he who lived and loved so well
Is sleeping in serenity.

1811-1812

Translator's Notes

1. The balalaika is a two-sided musical instrument
of which the Russian peasants are extremely fond.
2. The nagaika is a hard throng used by the Cossacks
to flog their horses, but sometimes employed as a
weapon of warlike attack.
3. Derzhavin.
4. In the original *steppe*; a long, mighty barren
desert, such as the Siberian river (Suna) flows over.
5. Karamzin.
6. Bogdanovich.
7. Dushenka (the diminutive of Dusha—the Soul), or
the Little Psyche, is the title of the most celebrated
poem of Bogdanovich.
8. The wise man who, according to the oriental
story (current also in Russia), received *Truth* after she
had been inhospitably driven from place to place....
Pilpay's Fables were translated into French by Galland
in 1714. There are also several English translations.
9. The golden cup.

The Shade of My Friend

Sunt aliquid manes: letum non omnia finit;
Luridaque evictos effugit umbra rogos.
Propertius*

I left the misty shores of Albion:
It seemed as if they were drowning in the leaden waves.
    A halcyon hovered behind the ship,
And its quiet voice amused the sailors.
    The evening breeze, the lapping of the waves,
The monotonous noise and flutter of the sails,
    And on the deck the helmsman calls to
The guard, dozing to the murmur of the waves—
    All of this nourished my sweet pensiveness.
Like one bewitched, I stood near the mast
    And through the mist and cover of night
I searched for my beloved northern star.
    All of my thoughts were clothed in reminiscence
Under the delightful sky of my fatherland,
    But the noise of the breezes and the rocking of the sea
Brought a languorous oblivion to my eyelids.
    Reveries turned into other reveries
And suddenly . . .was it a dream? . . .before me stood a
                                                   a comrade, one
    Fallen in a fatal battle, who met
An enviable death near the waters of Pleisse.
    But his appearance was not frightening; his brow
    No longer retained his deep wounds;
It bloomed with gaiety, like a May morning,
And reminded my soul of all that is heavenly.
"Is it you?"—I cried—"O warrior forever dear!
By the frightful glow of Bellona's fire,
Did I not, along with your faithful friends,
    Inscribe with my sword your heroic deed upon
                                                   the tree,
Over your untimely grave . . .
And did I not, with supplication, sobbing and tears,
    Bid farewell to your shade on its way to its
                                                   heavenly home.
Shade of my unforgettable friend! Answer me,
                                my dear brother!
Or was all that happened just a dream, a daydream;
Everything, everything—the pale corpse, the grave,
                                                   the rite
Performed in friendship in your memory.
O! Utter just one word to me! Let that familiar sound
    Caress my greedy ears again,

*The souls of the dead are no apparition:
  everything does not end in death;
A pale shade slips away,
  having vanquished the pyre.
        (Propertius, "Cynthia's Shade")

Let my hand, o unforgettable friend!
    Clasp yours in love..."
And I flew to him...But the heavenly spirit disappeared
Into the bottomless blue of the cloudless sky,
Like smoke, like a meteor, like a midnight apparition,
He disappeared—and sleep left my eyes.

Everything around me slept under the shelter of silence.
The threatening elements seemed mute.
By the light of the moon, covered by a cloud,
A tiny breeze was scarcely blowing, the waves were barely
                              gleaming,
But sweet peace fled from my eyes,
    And my soul still flew after the apparition,
And still wanted to stop the heavenly guest—
You, dear brother! O best of friends!

1814

D. V. DAVYDOV

To a Pious Charmer

He who knows our pious charmer
Likewise knows delicious evil;
One sly glance from this disarmer
Sings profanely of the devil.

Sweetness is exchanging glances,
While she kneels before the altar,
Adding curses to her phrases
Murmured sweetly from her psalter.

Pleasing is her intonation,
Sounds which hint at lewd transactions,
Her rebuff means affirmation:
No in words and *yes* in actions.

Ever fearful, all reluctant,
First refusal, then entreaties:
"O barbaric sin! I'm ruined!"
Later: "O my darling, more please...."

1820s

Song of an Old Hussar

Whither friends of bygone days,
Whither hussars brave and earthy,
Tale-tellers of battle-frays,
Drinking comrades aged and worthy?
    Grandads, I remember you
    Drinking vodka by the bucket,
    Sitting by the campfire's hue,
    Which your noses red reflected!
Caps on heads are tilted tip-sides,
Cloaks on knees, you lightly sway,
Swords and pistols at your hip-sides,
For divans a pile of hay.
    Blackened pipes between your lips,
    All so quiet, smoke curls wander
    Over curly mustache tips
    And dark temples as you ponder.
Not a murmur! Smoke in columns...
Not a murmur! As if dead
They all drink and, bowing head,
Fall asleep like tired young ones.
    But when scarce the dawn appears,
    Each onto the field goes flying;
    And with caps cocked over ears,
    Skirted cloaks like whirlwinds playing,
Horses seethe beneath their men,
Sabres whistle, foes go falling...
And the battle ends—Again
In the night the bucket's swinging.
    But my God! Now what do I see?
    My hussars in fashion dressing:
    Uniforms with boots to knee,
    Even on a parquet waltzing!
People say: "How fine are they!"
And you hear their watchers' fervor:
"*Jomini*, yes *Jomini!*"
But of vodka not a murmur.

1817

Those Evening Bells*

Those evening bells, those evening bells—
How many a tale their music tells!
Not those which at the end of day
From chapel tower wend their way,
But that which at the gloomy hour
Is sung so true by maiden pure . . .
Those evening bells, those evening bells—
How many a tale their music tells!

How sweet, how pure, how sad it sounds!
My heart, my past, my soul resounds,
When first its vibrant notes appear,
And softly, sweetly brush my ear! . . .
'Tis not mere sound, but passion's sighs,
A sound with which my spirit cries!
Those evening bells, those evening bells—
How many a tale their music tells!

For all in life makes swift reply:
The moon responds from clouded sky,
The desert wastes in murmured moan,
A virgin's soul in faithful tone,
And love beset with passing years,
And eyes caressed by poignant tears . . .
Those evening bells, those evening bells—
How many a tale their music tells!

1836

Dance*

A spring appears in oaken dell,
And seethes with ceaseless undulation,
And scatters sand and stones pell-mell
In senseless, raging flagellation.

But tranquilized by charming grace,
The spring subsides to soft caressal,
And bears from shore in light embrace
The spring's first fragile flower petal.

And thus, in quickly fleeting dance,
And thus, distinguished from the proudest,
Careens, majestic in her stance,
My youthful love, my charming goddess,

Inciter of my aspirations,
My hopes, my dreams, my inspiration,
And my poetic agitations,
And my poetic consecration!

1834

*A response to Thomas Moore's well-known St. Petersburg air, "Those Evening Bells." Davydov probably knew Ivan Kozlov's translation.

*One of Davydov's "autumn love" poems to Evgenia Zolotarova, the sixteen-year-old girl with whom he fell in love in his early fifties. [Translator's note]

A. A. DELVIG

Inspiration.
A Sonnet

It's not often that inspiration flies down to us
And burns in our soul for a brief moment.
But the pet of the muses values this moment
As much as a martyr values his separation from
                                        the world.

He has forgotten the deceit in friends, the
Dissuasion in love, and the poison in everything
Which the heart holds dear: the ecstatic poet
Has already read through his destiny.

And despised, persecuted by people,
Wandering alone under the skies,
He speaks to future ages;

He places honor above all things,
He swears to avenge himself in glory
And share immortality with the gods.

1822

The Bathing Women
An Idyll

"What! You've burst into tears! You don't even want to
                        listen to an old friend!
A frightful affair: Daphne won't say a word to you,
Won't sing songs with you, won't dance, and just as she's
                                about to cry,
She'll immediately meet Licorice's mocking eyes, and
                                both of them
Blush in a flash, redder than the sky on an evening
                        before a storm!
You big baby, you ought to be ashamed! or don't you
                know this gray-haired satyr?
Who spoiled you as a baby? All day long, poor you would
Sit on the hill, all alone, and look after your flock:
In my heart I would take pity on you, and I, an old man,
                would come to have a laugh with you,
To argue a bit while rolling the dice, to play the pipes.
                        And what came of it?
Who can play dice and who has mastered the pipes
                        as you have?
You yourself know: no one. From whose basket did you
                        eat fruit?
Everything from mine: I myself chose the fine honeysuckle
And braided it with light-colored straw to form their
                                designs.

You also drank milk from my cups and goblets:
                                I dried and
Hollowed out round pumpkins, which looked like the
                                cheeks of a young
Satyr, and skillfully carved clusters of grapes,
                                flowers, and
Figures of powerful gods and heroes on their skin.
(I can brag) that no one else had such
Cups and goblets and light baskets. Often, after
Bacchanalian orgies, other satyrs used to hurry off
To their caves to rest on fragrant beds,
Or to the groves to frighten and chase the
                                young shepherds;
But I came to you, forgetting both peace and love;
Drunk, I would dance to your song with a trained kid;
Frisky, I got up on my hind legs and jumped
                                about clumsily,
Shaking my head, I grew irritated with my horns
                                and beard.
You choked with merry laughter, tears shone
In the hollows of your puffed-out cheeks—and sorrow
                        was completely forgotten.
What kind of sorrow did you have then, when you were
                                a child?
You would smash my pumpkin, break my pipe—and
                                that's all.
Won't I comfort you now? Will I leave you now? trust me.
And dry away your tears! calm down and listen to an
                                old friend."

Thus did the ancient satyr talk to young Micon,
Lying silently melancholy in a dark chestnut grove.
The young shepherd's childlike heart was inflamed
                        with love for Daphne,
With ardent, pure, first love: he loved, and loved not
                                in vain.
Until last evening everything heralded happiness for him:
Daphne readily danced and sang with him, once she even
Clasped his hand and quietly and sweetly whispered
Something to him when he said to her: "Love me,
                                Daphne!"
For the last two evenings why hasn't Daphne been the
                        same as before, that former Daphne?
He goes to her—but she goes away from him.
                                Knowing glances,
Tenderly childish speeches, a smile from those purple lips,
Glowing in sweet bliss—all of this has flowed away,
                                like waters in spring!
What has happened to the beautiful shepherdess?
                                But doesn't our
Old satyr know all about this? Not without reason does he
                        repeat: "Listen to me!"
The night is beautiful; it's quiet and there's not a cloud
                                in the sky.
If the goddess Diana sends a kiss with every ray
                                of moonlight

To the fortunate Endymion, then there has not been
                                            another mortal on earth
Kissed so often and so passionately in the entire
                                            history of love!
There isn't and there won't be. The rays of light do
                                            shine that way, the earth is
Drowning in their charming light; the river Ilissos
                                            flows like
Silver from a cool urn; nightingales trill out their
                                            sweet songs;
The shore breathes in the languid fragrance of
                                            aromatic grass;
The heart lives more fully and the soul revels in
                                            sweet bliss."
Poor Micon listened to the satyr, slowly lifted his head,
Sat down, leaned against the tall chestnut tree, quietly
Folded his arms, and directed his gaze at the satyr; and the
Old satyr reclined on his elbow on a long branch and,
                                            rocking, began this way:
"I woke up yesterday at early dawn: it was really cold!
Didn't I cover up the evening before? Where is my
                                            warm hide blanket?
Didn't I spread aromatic, fresh grass beneath me?
I looked out and screwed up my eyes! the blinding light
                                            of morning had not yet blended
With the lazy gloom of the cave! What's this?
                                            My legs throbbed:
My legs were tied to a tree! My hand went for
                                            my mug: o gods!
My mug was smashed, my priceless mug was smashed!
Ah, I wanted to cry out: old man, you're still as zealous at
Bacchic battles as you were before, but not as strong
                                            as before, my friend!

You didn't get to your cave, you probably fell
                                            on the way;
And overcome by wine, you fell into the hands of scoffers!
But the lapping of the water, the merry cries of women
Put ideas in my mind, but the words stopped on my
                                            open lips.
Not daring to breathe, I just barely lifted myself; thick
Bushes were in front of me; I pulled the leaves apart
                                            gently; I
Moved my head a little into the bushes and looked: there
                                            the waves sparkle and turn blue;
I moved a little farther and I saw: Licorice and Daphne in
                                            the waves,
Both are as beautiful as maiden-Graces and as naked
                                            as nymphs;
They had two swans with them. You know, their
                                            favorite swans:
You saved the poor things last spring; their mother was
                                            pecking at them cruelly—
You chased the mother away, took them and gave them as
                                            a gift to Licorice:

You already loved Daphne then, but were afraid to give
                                            them to her.
I remember that the first feelings of love are bashful
                                            and timid:
You love but fear that you will bore your dear one with a
                                            superfluous caress.
Licorice grasped the white necks of the swans and
Suddenly began to swim, but Daphne dove into the
                                            crystalline waters.
Daphne reappeared and laughter met her: "Daphne,
                                            I am Leda,
A new Leda." "But I am Venus! You see, like her,
Wasn't I just born from gleaming sea foam?"
"True, but the former Leda is nothing before the new one!
                                            Two
Zeuses serve me. What can you boast of before
                                            Aphrodite?"
"Crippled, old Hephaestus won't be my husband!"
"That is also true, my dear Daphne; I'll say it again:
                                            that's true!
Your Micon is beautiful; you won't find a shepherd better
                                            than he!
He has three rows of curls; his eyes are a heavenly color;
Their glances pierce your heart; he's young, and like a
                                            peach picked
At its peak, he's fresh and rosy and adorned with
                                            shining down;
And what kind of lips has he? Fragrant, crimson roses,
Full of sounds and words sweeter than all the
                                            heavenly songs.
Daphne, my friend, kiss me then! soon you won't be
Readily kissing your Licorice too often; you will say:
'The lips of the shepherd, young Micon, kiss much
                                            more sweetly!' "
"My crafty friend, you are always laughing! You make me
Blush all in vain! And what is your Micon to me?
                                            he is fine—
Better for him! I am indifferent to him." "Why are you
                                            blushing, then?"
"I'm blushing against my will: why are you badgering
                                            me so?
You only talk about Micon! Micon, yes, Micon; but what
                                            is he to me?"
"Why are you trembling and nestling me with your
                                            breast? Why
Are you breathing so ardently, so unevenly? Listen:
If (I call on the immortal gods as witness that I do not
                                            wish this),—
If, chasing after a stray sheep, Micon were to appear
Right here, on the shore—what would you do?" "What
                                            would I do? I'd drown myself!"
"Exactly, and I'd drown myself too! But why? What kind
                                            of strange behavior is this?
Are we really worse like this? watch, I'll swim:
                                            Aren't these

Tender breasts, these waves of hair in a golden stream,
                                             beautiful?
And here you've swum up; look, your little foot in the
                                    water has grown as
White as the snow which adorns the mountains! But all of
                                         you is so white!
Your neck, arms—look at yourself and you'll say—a
                                           great Master
Has trimmed them in ivory, but Zeus has filled them with
                                          a surplus
Of sweetly-captivating life. Daphne, what are we
                                           ashamed of!"
"Friend Licorice, I don't know; but I do know that it's
                                 wonderful to feel ashamed!"
"True; but a lot of incomprehensible things are still
                                      hidden! Just think:
Really, what are men? Aren't they people exactly like us?
The very same beautiful creation of the wondrous Zeus-
                                            Chronidus.
Why are we ashamed in front of men, when we joke freely
                                   with another, alien
Creature, the swan: first when caressing its long neck,
We bring his beak to our lips and kiss it; then when we
                                      tenderly ruffle
Its white wings and press our bosoms to its downy breast.
Do their eyes have a horrible power, the power of a
                                            Medusa,
Which turns us into stone? So what will you tell me?"—
                                        "I don't know!
Only that I would willingly be Leda! And in the same way
I would not tire of caressing and kissing my beloved in this
                                    modest form,
In the beauty of blinding whiteness! I pray, o gods,
Turn this impudent one (whoever he may be) into a stag,
Just like the hunter Actaeon, a sacrifice to Diana's wrath!
Ah, Licorice, horns!" "What do you mean, horns?"
"There are horns behind the bushes!"
"Daphne, it's Micon's satyr!" "Let's swim away!" "He's
                                      heard everything
And will tell everything to Micon! poor us!" "We are
                                             lost!"

"And though I was as careful as a passionate youth, I thus
                                  unexpectedly ended
Their conversation! and I was totally pleased: you see,
                                            Daphne
Loves you, and this innocent girl deserves a wonderful
                                               fate:
To possess Micon's heart on earth and in Pluto's realms!
But you're not crying as you did before, you big baby!
                                           obviously
It's useful to listen to an old satyr, isn't it? Then, go into
                                        your hut!
Give yourself over to the sweet powers of Morpheus! Eros
                                     will not abandon
A beautiful affair! trust me and calm down: it will end as
                                         it began."

1824

A. S. PUSHKIN

The light of day has gone out;
The evening mist has fallen on the dark blue sea.
     Sound out, sound out, obedient sail,
Gloomy ocean, be rough beneath me.
     I see the distant shore,
The magic regions of a southern land;
I hurry there in sorrowful agitation,
     Intoxicated with memories . . .
And I feel the tears that rose again in my eyes;
     My soul seethes and then grows calm;
A familiar dream flies around me;
I remembered a reckless love of years gone by,
And everything that made me suffer, and everything
                                    dear to my heart,
The tedious deceit of hopes and desires . . .
     Sound out, sound out, obedient sail,
Gloomy ocean, be rough beneath me.
Fly, my boat, and carry me to the distant borders
Along the menacing whims of the deceitful seas.
     But only not to the sad shores
     Of my misty motherland,
     The land where the flame of passion
     Ignited my first emotions.
Where the muses secretly smiled at me,
     Where my lost youth
     Faded early in the storms,
Where lightwinged joy deceived me
And gave my cold heart over to suffering.
     A seeker of new impressions,
     I fled you, native lands;
     I fled you, stepchildren of pleasure,
Fleeting friends of fleeting youth;
And you, confidantes of prophetic delusions,
To whom I lovelessly sacrificed myself,
My peace, my glory, my freedom and my soul.
But you, whom I forgot, young traitresses,
Secret friends of my golden spring,
And you whom I forgot . . . But nothing has healed
The former wounds of my heart, the deep wounds
                                        of love . . .
     Sound out, sound out, obedient sail,
Gloomy ocean, be rough beneath me.

1820

I've Outlived My Desires

I've outlived my desires, despising
My former dreams; now all that's left
Is suffering and pain, comprising
The sad fruits of a heart bereft.

I wove my crown of flowers under
The tempests of a cruel fate;
Alone and sad I live, and wonder:
Is my end drawing near? I wait.

Just so, when struck by late-arriving
Cold, as the winter's blizzards shrill,
Alone on a bare branch surviving,
A last leaf shivers in the chill.

1821

Night

The silence of the night at this late hour is broken
By my voice calling you, words faintly, fondly spoken.
Beside my bed a candle casts a mournful glow;
My verses run together, murmuring, they flow,
Flow, filled with thoughts of you, love's little rivers
                                        streaming
Before me in the dark your eyes are softly gleaming,
I see them smile, and then I hear you say to me:
My friend, my dearest friend . . . I love you tenderly.

1823

To the Sea

Farewell to you, unharnessed Ocean!
No longer will you roll at me
Your azure swells in endless motion
Or gleam in tranquil majesty.

A comrade's broken words on leaving,
His hail of parting at the door:
Your chant of luring, chant of grieving
Will murmur in my ears no more.

Oh, homeland of my spirit's choosing!
How often on your banks at large
I wandered mute and dimly musing,
Fraught with a sacred, troubling charge!

How I would love your deep resounding,
The primal chasm's muffled voice,
How in your vesper calm rejoice,
And in your sudden, reckless bounding!

The fisher's lowly canvas slips,
By your capricious favor sheltered
Undaunted down your breakers' lips:
Yet by your titan romps have weltered
And foundered droves of masted ships.

Alas, Fate thwarted me from weighing
My anchor off the cloddish shore,
Exultantly your realm surveying,
And by your drifting ridges laying
My poet's course forevermore.

You waited, called . . . I was in irons,
And vainly did my soul rebel,
Becalmed in those uncouth environs
By passion's overpowering spell.

Yet why this sorrow? Toward what fastness
Would now my carefree sails be spread?
To one lone goal in all your vastness
My spirit might have gladly sped.

One lonely cliff, the tomb of glory . . .
There chilling slumber fell upon
The ghost of mankind's proudest story:
There breathed his last Napoleon.

There rest for suffering he bartered;
And gale-borne in his wake, there streams
Another kingly spirit martyred,
Another regent of our dreams.*

He passed, and left to Freedom mourning,
His laurels to Eternity.
Arise, roar out in stormy warning:
He was your own true bard, o, Sea!

His soul was by your spirit haunted,
In your own image was he framed:
Like you immense, profound, undaunted,
Like you nocturnal and untamed.

Bereft the world . . . where by your power,
O, Sea, would you now carry me?
Life offers everywhere one dower:
On any glint of bliss there glower
Enlightenment or tyranny.

Farewell, then, Sea! Henceforth in wonder
Your regal grace will I revere;
Long will your muffled twilit thunder
Reverberate within my ear.

To woods and silent wildernesses
Will I translate your potent spells,
Your cliffs, your coves, your shining tresses,
Your shadows and your murmurous swells.

1824

*Lord Byron, who had perished at Missolonghi that year.
[Translator's note]

To ...

I recollect that wondrous meeting,
That instant I encountered you,
When like an apparition fleeting,
Like beauty's spirit, past you flew.

Long since, when hopeless grief distressed me,
When noise and turmoil vexed, it seemed
Your voice still tenderly caressed me,
Your dear face sought me as I dreamed.

Years passed; their stormy gusts confounded
And swept away old dreams apace.
I had forgotten how you sounded,
Forgot the heaven of your face.

In exiled gloom and isolation
My quiet days meandered on,
The thrill of awe and inspiration,
And life, and tears, and love, were gone.

My soul awoke from inanition,
And I encountered you anew,
And like a fleeting apparation,
Like beauty's spirit, past you flew.

My pulses bound in exultation,
And in my heart once more unfold
The sense of awe and inspiration,
The life, the tears, the love of old.

1825

Winter Evening

Storm has set the heavens scowling,
Whirling gusty blizzards wild,
Now they are like beasts a-growling,
Now a-wailing like a child;
Now along the brittle thatches
They will scud with rustling sound,
Now against the window latches
Like belated wanderers pound.

Our frail hut is glum and sullen,
Dim with twilight and with care.
Why, dear granny, have you fallen
Silent by the window there?
Has the gale's insistent prodding
Made your drowsing senses numb,
Are you lulled to gentle nodding
By the whirling spindle's hum?

Let us drink for grief, let's drown it,
Comrade of my wretched youth,
Where's the jar? Pour out and down it,
Wine will make us less uncouth.
Sing me of the tomtit hatching
Safe beyond the ocean blue,
Sing about the maiden fetching
Water at the morning dew.

Storm has set the heavens scowling,
Whirling gusty blizzards wild,
Now they sound like beasts a-growling,
Now a-wailing like a child.
Let us drink for grief, let's drown it,
Comrade of my wretched youth,
Where's the jar? Pour out and down it,
Wine will make us less uncouth.

1825

Winter Road

Through the waves of fog a clouded
Moon serenely makes its way,
And on fields in sadness shrouded
Pours its melancholy ray.

While along the wintry, dreary
Road a troika runs pell-mell
To a monotone, the weary
Jingling of its tedious bell.

In the long songs of the trusty
Driver something speaks to me
Of my home: now bold and lusty,
Now a heartfelt misery ...

Neither fires nor black huts greet me
As my lonely way I go ...
Only mileposts rise to meet me
Through the thickets and the snow.

I am bored, sad, but tomorrow
When I'm seated by your fire,
Nina, I'll forget my sorrow,
Gaze at you and never tire.

In a resonant progression
The clock will complete its sphere;
Midnight, banishing depression,
Will not separate us here.

Nina, I am sad: my plodding
Path grows dull, the bell persists,
Quiet now, my driver's nodding,
And the moon is wrapped in mists.

1826

The Prophet

Suffering from a spiritual thirst,
I crawled through the desert's gloom,
When a six-winged seraph burst
Through clouds and above a crossroad loomed;
His fingers as light as a dream
Touched the very pupils of my eyes
And opened them to prophecy,
These eyes so like a frightened eagle's.
He touched my ears,
And filled them with noise and sound:
And I heard the shudder of heaven,
And the ethereal flight of angels,
And the underwater movement of vile sea creatures,
And the growth of vines in the valley.
And he pressed close to my lips
And tore out my tongue so sinful
And cunning and given to idle chatter;
And into my senseless mouth
With his bloody right hand he placed
The sting of a wise serpent
And he clove my breast with a sword,
And pulled out my quivering heart,
And a coal, blazing with fire,
He thrust into my open breast.
I lay like a corpse in the desert,
And the voice of God called out to me:
"Rise up, prophet, and see, and hear,
And be filled with My will,
And, travelling over land and sea,
Set the hearts of the people on fire with the word."

1826

The Poet

When on the poet Lord Appollo
Does not for mystic homage call,
To worldly bustle, pastimes hollow,
He lives in petty-minded thrall:
Then the celestial lyre is muted,
Chill torpor does his heart befall,
Amid life's idle and unsuited,
He seems the idlest wretch of all.

Yet once the god-engendered word
But touches on the vivid senses,
The poet's soul awakens, tenses
Its pinions like an eagle stirred.
He chafes in worldly dissipation,
From human colloquy he flees,
Before the idol of the nation
He is too proud to bend his knees.
Then will he rush, uncouth and somber,
Astir with sounds and wild unease,
Toward the shores of desolate seas,
To murmuring wildwoods' vast penumbra.

1827

The Poet and the Crowd

The poet strummed his inspired lyre
With a distracted hand.
He sang—but the cold and haughty
Unenlightened people all around
Listened to him without comprehension.

And the slow-witted rabble said;
"Why does he sing so loudly?
Striking our ear in vain,
To what goal does he lead us?
About what does he strum? what does he teach us?
Why does he disturb and torture our hearts
Like a willful sorcerer?
His song is as free as the wind,
And in return, like the wind, also barren.

Poet

Be silent, uncomprehending people,
Day laborer, slave of need and worries!
Your impudent grumbling is unbearable to me,
You are the worm of earth, not the son of the heavens;
You would like everything to be of use—
You value the idol Apollo Belvedere for its weight,
You do not see any use in it at all.
But you see the marble itself as the god...And why not so?
A cooking pot is more dear to you:
You can cook some food in it for yourself.

Rabble

No, if you are the chosen one of the heavens,
Then, divine envoy, use your gift
For our benefit:
Improve the hearts of your brothers.
We are faint-hearted, we are insidious,
Shameless, malicious, ungrateful;
In our hearts we are cold eunuchs,

Slanderers, slaves, fools;
Vices make their nests around our hearts.
Loving your fellowman, you can
Give us bold lessons,
And we will obey you.

   Poet

     Get away from me—what business
Does a peaceful poet have with you!
Boldly petrify in your lewdness:
The voice of the lyre will not revive you!
You are as offensive to the soul as coffins.
For your stupidity and malice
Until now you've had
Scourges, dungeons, axes;
Enough from you senseless slaves!
In your cities they sweep up the litter
From noisy streets—that's useful toil!
But, having forgotten their service,
Altar and sacrifice,
Do the priests take your brooms from you?
[We're not born] for everyday emotion,
Or for profit, or for battles;
We are born for inspiration.
     For sweet sounds and prayers.

1828

          * * *

Don't sing songs of sad Georgia
To me, my beauty, for
They remind me of
Another life and a distant shore.

Alas! your cruel harmonies
Recall the steppes and a night long ago,
And the features of a poor
Distant maid in moonlight all aglow.

Even though looking at you, I
Forget that dear, fateful woman,
Then I hear you sing, and I
Imagine her phantom before me again.

Don't sing songs of sad Georgia
To me, my beauty, for
They remind me of
Another life and a distant shore.

1828

Anchar (The Upas Tree)

Upon the desert's blazing sands,
In harsh and arid desolation,
Like some dread sentry Anchar stands,
Austere, alone in all creation.

Once on those thirsting plains to him
By angered Nature life was granted,
And in each mortal leaf and limb
And root the poison was implanted.

The venom trickles through the bark,
Beneath the noon sun liquefying,
And cools when day's heat yields to dark,
In thick transparent resin lying.

To Anchar's boughs no bird dare fly
Nor tiger come; the wind's black eddy
Enwraps the death tree, then whirls by,
With evil vapors charged already.

And if some storm cloud, as it goes,
The tree's dense leaves should chance to moisten,
Into the burning sands there flows
A rain that bears in it the poison.

But once with regal glance a man
To Anchar did a man send faring,
Who thus obediently ran
And hastened back, the poison bearing.

He brought as well a withered bough
As homeward with the gum he wended,
And meanwhile from his pallid brow
The sweat in icy streams descended.

He brought the gum—but in his cave
Upon his bed of bark did sicken,
Until by death the wretched slave
Before his mighty lord was stricken.

His prince the poison used to coat
The arrows faithful to his orders,
With which he ruinously smote
The tribes that dwelt across his borders.

1828

          * * *

As down the noisy streets I wander
Or walk into a crowded shrine,
Or sit with madcap youth, I ponder
Bemusing reveries of mine.

I say: the years speed by unhalting,
And we, as many as are here,
Will pass beneath the eternal vaulting,
And someone's hour is drawing near.

Or gazing at an oak tree lonely,
I muse: this patriarchal sage
Did not outlast my forebears only,
It will outlive my own dim age.

Or fondling some dear child is reason
For me to think: I make thee room,
Farewell to thee! It is the season
For me to fade, for thee to bloom.

Each day, each passing year of aging,
In deep abstraction now I spend,
At pains among them to be gauging
The year-day of the coming end.

And where, fate, is my death preparing?
At sea, a-roving, in the fray?
Or will this nearby vale be bearing
Within its earth my feelless clay?*

Although my flesh will be past caring
About the site of its decay,
Yet would I gladly still be sharing
The dear haunts of my earthly day.

And close to my sepulchral portals
I want young life to be at play,
And Nature, unconcerned with mortals,
To shed its beauty's timeless ray.

1829

Winter Morning

Frost and sun; miraculous day!
My charming friend, still dozing away—
It's time, my beauty, get up, rise forth:
Wake up your eyes, so blissfully closed,
To meet Aurora's northern pose,
Appear like the star of the north!

Recall, last night, the storm did rage and fly,
While shadows rushed o'er the lacklustre sky;
The moon, like a colorless stain,
Grew yellow 'mid the gloomy clouds,
And you sat there so sadly bowed—
But now...look through the windowpane:

Beneath the skies so blue and light
Like rugs magnificently white,
Agleam in the sun, the snow does lie:
'Tis forest transparent that darkens the scene,
'Tis fir trees, through frost, all turning to green,
And under the ice the river is bright.

The room for us is all aglow
With amber light. The kindled stove
Does crackle in a merry way.
It's nice to think on a bench near the fire.
You know—though—I do so desire
The brown mare all hitched to the sleigh.

Gliding along the morning snow
Dear friend, we'll let ourselves go.
To flee with our impatient horse
And go to see the fields so empty,
The woods not long ago so leafy,
And shores, so dear to me, those shores.

1829

* * *

I loved you: love, it very well may be,
Within my soul has not quite died away;
But let it give you no anxiety;
I do not wish to grieve you, come what may.
I loved you silently and hopelessly,
By jealousy and shyness overcome;
I loved you so sincerely, tenderly...
May you be loved thus by some other one.

1829

*This query is echoed by, among many others, Heinrich Heine when he asks ca. 1825 in "Wo?":

Wo wird einst des Wandermüden/ Letzte Ruhestätte sein?/ Unter Palmen in dem Süden?/ Unter Linden an dem Rhein?// Werd' ich wo in einer Wüste?/ Einge- scharrt von fremder Hand?/ Oder ruh' ich an der Küste/ Eines Meeres in dem Sand?// Immerhin! Mich wird umgeben/ Gotteshimmel, dort wie hier,/ Und als Toten- lampen schweben/ Nachts die Sterne über mir. [Trans- lator's note.]

Lines Written at Night during a Time of Insomnia

I cannot sleep, there is no fire near;
All about is darkness and annoying sleep.
Only monotonous voices of the hours keep
Resounding round me here,
The womanish babbling of the Parcae,
The trembling of the sleeping night,
The mouse-like scurry of daily life . . .
Why do you cause me all this strife?
What can this tedious whispering mean?
Is it the reproachful grumble
Of a day I wasted away?
What do you want of me?
Do you call out or do you prophesy?
I want to understand you,
I search for meaning in you.

1830

Echo*

Where beasts in trackless forests wail,
Where horns intone, where thunders flail,
Or maiden chants in yonder vale—
        To every cry
Through empty air you never fail
        To speed reply.

You listen to the thunder knells,
The voice of gales and ocean swells,
The shepherd's hail in hills and dells
        And you requite:
But unrequited stay . . . This spells
        The poet's plight.

1831

*The motif of this lyric appears to have been drawn from Barry
Cornwall. [Translator's note.]

Autumn (A Fragment)

> *What will not enter then into my pensive mind?*
> *DERZHAVIN*

I

October—and the groves already shaking,
From naked boughs what foliage clings there still;
The road congeals beneath the fall-wind's raking;
The stream still courses babbling past the mill,
But icebound lies the pond; my neighbor's taking
His hunt in haste to fields far overhill,
The fall crop suffers from their reckless playing,
And drowsing woods wake to the hounds' sharp baying.

II

This is my season: spring is not for me;
The thaw nags; slush and smells—spring makes me vapid;
The blood's in sap, both head and heart unfree.
Remorseless winter finds me more intrepid,
I love her snows; in moonlit nights, what glee
In sleighrides with a friend, so light and rapid,
When fresh and cozy under sable fur
She grips your hand, all glowing and astir!

III

What fun on sharpened irons to be curving
The level gloss of an encrystalled lake!
And winter balls' resplendent stir and swerving? . . .
But draw the line: six months of flake on flake
Our very troglodyte must find unnerving,
The northern bear. One can't forever take
Young charmers gliding through the snows, or cower
'Twixt stove and double windows, turning sour.

IV

Fair summer—ah! But can I call you friend,
By heat and dust and flies and midges harried,
When, draining all fine faculties, you rend
Our vitals like parched fields, and leave us arid?
Keep cool is all we think of, and we end
By wishing drab old wintertime had tarried;
Ashamed of wine and pancakes at her wake,
We now clink frosted glasses for her sake.

V

The fading autumn almost none admires,
Yet, reader, I am fond of her, I own,
Fond of her muted glow of half-banked fires.
Like a poor child unloved among her own
She calls to me. If anyone enquires,
Her of all seasons I hold dear alone.
There is much good in her. A frugal wooer,
My whim finds some appeal quite special to her.

VI

What is her hold? It may be—let me try—
Like a consumptive girl's who, meek and ailing,
Endears herself to you. Condemned to die,
She droops, poor thing, without revolt or wailing;
Upon her bloodless lips a smile will lie,
The very grave-pit's yawning hollow failing
To blanch the cheek that flushes play upon.
Today she is alive, tomorrow gone.

VII

I find you eye-beguiling, mournful season,
Your valedictory splendors make me glad—
For sumptuous in her death is nature, pleasing
The forest all in gold and purple clad;
The wind-sough's whisper in the treetops breezing,
The brooding sky with swirling vapor sad,
The virgin frost, the sun's infrequent glinting,
And hoary winter's distant ominous hinting.

VIII

With each new autumn I come fresh in bud;
The Russian winter makes my nature stronger;
With newfound zest I chew old habits' cud,
Sleep wafts below on time, on time comes hunger;
Serene and brisk beats in my heart the blood,
Desires well up, I'm gay again and younger,
I'm full of life—my organism's such
(If you will pardon this prosaic touch).

IX

They bring a steed to me; through open spaces
It bears the rider on with tossing mane,
Beneath the gleaming hooves' impatient paces
The sheet-ice crackles, rings the frozen plane.
The brief day spent, the orphaned fireplace's
Dead embers come to life—now flare again,
Now smolder low; before it I sit reading
Or in my pensive mind long fancies feeding.

X

And in sweet silence I forget the world,
Imagination drugs me with its sweet slow current,
And poetry is in my soul unfurled:
It grows embattled with its lyric warrant,
It stirs and throbs and, yet in slumber curled,
It gropes to clear its way, an uncurbed current—
And then guests call on me, invisible swarms,
My fancy's fruit, in long familiar forms.

XI

And in my mind conceits grow bold and caper,
Light rhymes fly out to meet them on the wing,
And fingers itch for pen, and pen for paper,
And in a moment verse will freely ring.
Thus dreams a ship becalmed in stagnant vapor,
Till, look! she crawls with sailors, scampering
Up, down, the sails swell out and swing to quarters,
The great hulk gathers way and cleaves the waters.

1833

Don't let me lose my mind, oh, God;
I'd sooner beg with sack and rod
    Or starve in sweat and dust.
Not that I treasure my poor mind,
Or would bemoan it should I find
    That part from it I must:

If they but left me free to roam,
How I would fly to make my home
    In deepest forest gloom!
In blazing frenzy would I sing,
Be drugged by fancies smoldering
    In rank and wondrous fume.

And I would hear the breakers roar,
And my exultant gaze would soar
    In empty skies to drown:
Unbridled would I be and grand
Like the great gale that rakes the land
    And mows the forest down.

But woe befalls whose mind is vague:
They dread and shun you like the plague,
    And once the jail-gate jars,
They bolt the fool to chain and log
And come as to a poor mad dog
    To tease him through the bars.

And then upon the evenfall
I'd hear no nightingale's bright call,
    No oak tree's murmurous dreams—
I'd hear my prison-mates call out,
And night attendants rail and shout,
    And clashing chains, and screams.

1833

* * *

Exegi monumentum

I have erected unto myself a monument, not made
                                                by hands;
The path to it that people take will not be overgrown.
It has raised its unruly head higher
Than Alexander's column.

No, I shall not die completely—my soul in its sacred lyre
Will outlive my dust and will escape decay—
And I shall be renowned, as long as even one poet
Is alive in this sublunary world.

Rumors about me will pass through all of mighty Rus,
And each of her people will call my name in their native
                     tongues,
Both the proud grandson of the Slavs and the Finn,
                     and today's
Tungus, and the Kalmyk—the friend of the steppes.

And for a long time I shall be beloved by the people
                     because
I awakened kind feelings with my lyre,
And because in my cruel century I celebrated freedom
    And urged mercy for the fallen.

O muse, be obedient to God's command while
Neither fearing insult nor demanding a crown;
Accept praise and calumny with indifference,
    And don't dispute a fool.

1836

E. A. BARATYNSKY

Hopelessness

My wish for happiness was of divine creation;
And I demanded it from earth and heav'n above,
Then I crossed halfway into life, the victim of
Illusion's faraway temptation.
But now I'll serve no longer fate's capricious ways:
Akin to happiness, repose will satisfy me;
Henceforth onto the main track I'll direct my gaze—
And humbly greet those passing by me.

1823

* * *

My gift is humble and my voice is quiet,
But I am living, and upon the earth
To someone my existence is of worth:
My faraway descendent will descry it
Within my lines of verse; how can this be?
It seems my soul to his bears a relation;
I found a friend in this my generation,
And will find readers in posterity.

1828

Death

O death! what awesome trepidation
Your name inspires in us: In all

Our thoughts you are the dark's creation,
A sentence called for by our fall.

To those who do not understand you
You often are portrayed as one
Who bears an ugly scythe in hand, you
Are thought a loathsome skeleton.

But you are beauty, shining brightly,
The daughter lofty Ether made:
An olive branch you cling to tightly,
And not a sharp, destructive blade.

And when the world arose in flower
Out of wild forces' symmetry,
Almighty God gave you the power
To guard his structured harmony.

Above creation you are flying—
You spread forgetfulness of strife
While with a cool breath pacifying
The dreadful violence of life.

And you calmed Phoebus' brothers, sowing
The seeds of peace; you quenched the fire
That through mad Phaedra's blood was flowing,
A painful, unrestrained desire.

You, holy maid, appearing to us,
Assuage our anger instantly;
The heat of passion coursing through us
Beneath your cooling hands will flee.

Uneasy life's bright variation
Of hues, excess diversity,
Has undergone a transformation
To decent, white monotony.

A fate unfriendly and distressing
Makes people friends with gentle you:
The very same hand is caressing
The servant and the ruler too.

Confusion, pressure, and misgiving
Are what each anxious day contains:
You solve all mysteries of living,
You are the loos'ning of all chains.

1828

* * *

What reason has the captive to indulge in dreaming
Of freedom? For observe: the river's calmly streaming
Within appointed banks it is accustomed to;

Now still the mighty fir tree stands where first it grew,
Incapable of moving. And an unknown force is
Empowered to draw stars along in heav'nly courses.
Nor does the roving wind know freedom, and a law
Determines the direction of its gusty breathing.
And even we for final burial are fated,
When our rebellious dreams, forgotten, have abated;
Slaves who possess intelligence, we're only free
To reconcile desires and fate obediently—
And with our happy, peaceful fate will be contented.
Fool! Is there not a higher will that has presented
Us with our passions? And is the voice that sounds
In their voice? Oh, it is a heavy life that pounds
Within the heart of man, a mighty wave's pulsation
Confined in narrow borders of fate's designation.

1833

* * *

The lyric poem can heal an aching spirit.
And the mysterious pow'r of harmony
Makes error's heavy burden disappear; it
Restrains a seething passion's ecstasy.
The poet's soul, harmoniously outflowing,
From all its many sorrows finds release;
And poetry seems hallowed then, bestowing
On all communicants the purest peace.

1834

The Last Poet

The era marches in its iron progression;
Self-interest fills their hearts, and how to earn
A daily living is their main obsession,
Their common dream, a shameless, clear concern.
The childish dreams of poetry have perished
In an enlightened world devoted to
Industrial pursuits, no longer cherished
By generations caught up in the new.
    Hellas now is born anew, her
    Freedom triumphs as before,
    And she draws her people to her,
    Lifts her capitals once more:
    Learning is again in flower,
    Taste shines, luxury abounds;
    But in the primeval bower
    Of the Muses, no lyre sounds!
The winter sets the waning world to glowing;
It shines!...Man wears a stern and pallid mien;
But forests, hills, and shores of rivers flowing
In Homer's fatherland are lush and green.
Parnassus blooms! A living stream is springing

Before it, and as in the former years
It gently beats. Now going forth and singing,
A poet—the last Attic son—appears.
    Artlessly both love and beauty
    Has the poet glorified,
    To which silence owes no duty
    In its emptiness and pride.
    Curing momentary grief in
    Each light-hearted turn of phrase,
    Mortal! Earth thus finds relief in
    Those uncultivated days.
To cold Urania's followers he praises,
Alas! the blessings passion can bestow:
The people's hearts inspire his lyric phrases,
As stormy Aeolus makes pastures grow.
Unfolded by the breath of inspiration,
Like Aphrodite rising silently
From out the foamy deep at her creation,
Arises now poetic fantasy.
    Why do we appear unwilling
    To submit to smiling dreams?
    We surrender to more chilling
    Thoughts but not to them, it seems!
    Trust in the sweet declarations
    Offered by caressing eyes
    And the soothing revelations
    Of the sympathetic skies!
Stern laughter was the sole response they offered...
His fingers stilled the strings, and to the crowd
He did not speak the words he could have proffered;
Before them all his head remained unbowed.
He takes a new course, lost in contemplation,
To some place uninhabited by men,
A silent spot...on earth no isolation
Remains; the world's no more an idle den.
    Only the rebellious sea has
    Never given in to man:
    Spacious, affable, and free as
    It roams through its azure span.
    And its face has never varied
    Since the day th'ethereal light
    By Apollo first was carried
    Upward to the heav'nly height!
And now against a cliff it loudly crashes.
The Singer stands there, his thoughts disarrayed...
But suddenly delight in his eyes flashes:
Those rocks...the ocean's murmur...Sappho's shade!
Where Thyona, her lover, buried the sad passion
Of a rejected love that she once knew,
Apollo's foster child in the same fashion
His dreams and useless gift will bury too!
    As before the world is glowing
    With cold luxury: its old
    Lifeless skeleton is growing
    Silver and is edged with gold.
    But the ocean's voice is clear—it

Leads man to confusion; he
Walks away with grieving spirit
From the pounding of the sea.

1835

* * *

A thought, when it appears anew
Within the poet's verse succinctly,
Is like a young girl, obscure to
A world that sees but indistinctly;
Then it grows bolder, speaking through
Words that are eloquent and clever,
On all sides coming into view,
Like a seductive woman who
In novel prose is present ever;
Becoming, in the final stage,
A chatterbox, old, rudely shrieking,
Drags on in journalistic speaking,
Polemic now grown stale with age.

1837

Autumn

I

And now September! each day the sun delays
Its rising, and its glow grows colder;
In mirrors of unsteady water, rays
Of untrue gold are now seen trembling.
A gray mist curls itself around the hills;
The morning dew leaves flatlands sodden;
The curly crowns of oak turn yellower still
And red are the rounded leaves of aspen;
The birds no longer raise their vivid cries,
Silent are the forests, tuneless the skies.

II

And now September! the evening of the year
Approaches. Frosted fields and mountains
Display at dawn a freshly dabbed veneer
Of silver, intricately patterned.
Soon foul Aeolus will rouse himself from sleep;
Before him flying dust will scatter,
The swaying groves will howl and leaves will heap
Until the dales fill with their falling,
And heavy clouds will mount toward heaven's dome;
The darkened river will begin to foam.

III

Farewell, farewell to heaven's radiance!
Farewell, farewell to nature's splendors!
To the magic rustle and fair luxuriance
Of forests, and to gold-scaled waters!
To the pleasant dream of summer's short-lived charm!
In groves stripped bare the echo lingers
As woodsmen with their axes sound alarm.
Soon now a whitened, dim reflection
Of groves and hills in winter garb will show
Upon the surface of the stiffened flow.

IV

Meanwhile the idle peasant gathers in
The good fruit of his year-long labor;
The hillside grain stacked ready for the bin,
He strides with sickle toward the meadow.
The sickle moves among the falling rows
And bright sheaves stretch beside the stubble
Or line the furrows, and the wagon slows
And creaks beneath the heavy harvest.
Then glorious as a city of golden domes
Bright grain-ricks rise above the peasant homes.

V

The villages, their sacred festive days!
How cheerfully the barnsmoke rises!
How quick the rhythm that the flail now plays
And the mill's great wheel turns ever more lively.
Come, winter! many a good thing is stored away
As, warm and cheerful in his cottage,
The herdsman, ready for a sterner day,
Relaxes with his sons and daughters.
The bread and salt, the foaming homebrewed beer:
His harvest in, he has no cause for fear.

VI

But you, herdsman of the broader field,
Life's watcher, when your days are autumn
And when your portion of the wide earth's yield
Is shown to you in all its grandeur;
And when, as fit reward for your long toil,
Life's overseers start the harvest
Of grain you sowed once in your own life's soil
And see the harvest is accomplished
And you at last are free to contemplate
Your gathered thoughts, the full bins of man's fate—

VII

Are you as rich as one who tills the earth?
Did you, as he did, sow, believing

And trusting time would prove your labor's worth?
Did you count gold as you lay dreaming?...
Take out your wealth—admire it and be proud!
Count everything, each acquisition!
Alas! Your only asset is avowed
Contempt for passions, dreams, and labors!
Vile wrongs, deceits—what further can you claim?
Your harvest brings you unremitting shame.

VIII

Your day has dawned, how clear to you now seems
The impudence of youth's presumptions,
For you have felt the depths and the extremes
Of man's hypocrisy and madness.
Once you were light amusement's closest friend,
An ardent seeker of responses,
A tsar of bright obscurities—and then
A contemplator of fruitless thickets,
Alone and longing, and only endless pride
Could stifle the death moan that rose inside.

IX

But if that terrible, indignant cry,
If that great howl of bitter longing
Were from the heart's depths to be lifted high
In all its savagery and grandeur—
Then in the midst of gaiety and play
The very bones of youth would tremble
The playing child would throw his toys away,
And nevermore would joy light his eye;
And inside him the living man would die.

X

So now call in the world to celebrate!
Good host, be generous, but hurry!
Invite each honest guest to load his plate
And taste each intricate concoction!
The table shines! Each dish deserves acclaim
For its uniqueness. Such abundance!
But, strangely, every morsel tastes the same,
And, like the grave, that taste is frightening;
So sit alone, complete the funeral feast—
For your soul's earthly joy is now deceased.

XI

No matter what dawn rises in you then,
No matter what illuminations,
No matter how the last twist of the wind
Of thoughts and feelings in you surges—
Let the mocking grandeur of the mind
Becalm the heart's now futile beating
And let it stifle the lingering, plaintive whine,

The earnest, vain, belated babble.
And then accept as life's own gift and goal,
As its best treasure, the death chill to the soul.

XII

Or, shake off visions of the earth, break free
With bursts of life-renewing sorrow,
And peer beyond the final boundary
To glimpse a shoreline bright with flowers,
The judgment land beyond the lightless mists,
And then believe those long-dreamt tidings
That contradict the world as it exists,
And then hear peace, as if on harpstrings,
As upward the grand hymns of concord soar
To heights that you could not have known before—

XIII

Bow low before the grand, ordained design
And find new hope, be grateful, humble,
And mark no limits, let your troubled mind
Find respite from vain cerebration—
Know now your soul will nevermore echo
The noise of earth, nor will it ever
Permit the vapors of life's passing show
To recontaminate your learning.
Know now the mountain's and the valley's worth
Were never measured on or for the earth.

XIV

Hear now the fury of the whirlwind's roar;
The forest howls, and with a mindless
Intensity the sea foams at the shore;
So, on occasion, roused from slumber,
The lazy-minded crowd sends out its word,
Its oracle of empty knowledge,
And then a voice, a banal voice is heard
And everywhere it finds responses;
But no response awaits the blessed word
That speaks beyond all passions earth has heard.

XV

Its chosen course a wrong one from the start,
Its line impossible to alter,
Let now the star rush toward the vacant heart
Of heaven and forever vanish;
The loss to earth is nothing you should fear;
The distant wait of her long falling
Will never reach as far as this world's ear;
Nothing disturbs the peace of heaven:
Neither the newborn star's first ray of light
Nor her sister's disappearance in the night.

XVI

Winter is coming; emaciated earth
Each day looks older, balder, weaker;
Abundance in the fields has turned to dearth;
The golden ears are gone forever—
Life dies with death, prosperity with woe,
The past year's sharp configurations
Are now all levelled by a shroud of snow
Whose hue has everywhere a sameness—
The world before you offers nothing new,
No future harvest lies ahead of you!

1836-37

Signs

As long as a man has left nature untried,
    By furnace and by scales untested,
But childishly on nature's teachings relied,
    Her signs to him on faith have rested.

And while he loved nature, she loved him in turn;
    It also was typical of her
To show toward him always a friendly concern;
    His language she helped him discover.

The raven, who sensed that ill luck lay in wait,
    Cawed out to him its premonition,
And musing, he humbled himself before fate,
    Restraining his bold disposition.

A bristly wolf ran from the forest onto
    His pathway with turning and twisting,
Then foretelling conquest, his forces he threw
    Against the foe, boldly resisting,

Above him a couple of pigeons had flown,
    Love's ecstasy gaily foretelling.
In peopleless wilds yet he was not alone,
    A life not unknown in him swelling.

But, trusting his reason, he yielded to vain
    Inquiry and cast aside feeling . . .
Then nature to him closed her heart with disdain,
    No prophecies on earth revealing.

1839

The mass of men accept a troubling day but fear
The silent, awesome night. For in it there appear
The self-willed visions of unchained imagination.
'Tis not the lightwinged child of magic dark that we
        Would fear, but daydreams, vanity
        Of man, and worldly tribulation.

        The stirred-up gloom won't linger on—
        And with it in that dark confusion,
        The fright'ning phantom will be gone,
Your terror then will smile at senses' false illusion.

O son of fantasy! The fairies' favorite, blessed
By fortune, you are present at the merrymaking
Of formless powers, in the absent world are taking
        Part in it as a frequent guest!
        Take heart, let not despair come o'er you
        At earthly griefs that lie in store: you
Know that your dream will give your soul a giant's mien;
Touch with unshaking hand a cloud—'twill be no more;
                                            you
Will once again perceive that opened up before you
Are gates behind which cloistered spirits can be seen.

1839

Rhyme

        Once at the Olympic games
On squares of Grecian cities of the recent past
He sang, the stepchild of the Muse, amid the vast
Waves of people, greedy for musical delights.
In him there dwelled a total faith in sympathy;
        And like a surging harvest blowing,
        His free and spacious meter flowing
        Poured forth in lovely harmony.
A crowd in rapt attention gathered all around,
        When all at once a great vibration
Came over them—applause, a full and endless sound;
        It made the singer's strings resound
        And filled them with new inspiration.
        When there arose an orator
        Upon a platform standing near him,
By turns he'd glorify and then he would deplore
The people's fate. They all moved close enough to hear
                                            him,
And every eye was turned upon him—no one stirred;
        The power of his every word
Enabled him to rule by popular discretion:
He knew himself and understood
How mighty was the god that could
Control his solemn, grave expression.
But now who asks our lyres to say
What friendly secrets they've protected?
And who to heav'n's been borne away

By voices for so long neglected?
With us the poet does not know
Whether his flight is high or low!
Let both judge and defendant question:
What ails the bard—some foolish ill?
Or could it be a lofty skill?
And let them offer a suggestion!
Amidst a lifeless sleep at night,
In daylight's cold, sepulchral places,
You only, rhyme, with your embraces
Can fill the poet with delight.
And like the Ark's dove, gently winging,
So from your native shore you're bringing
A living branch; and you, it seems,
Can reconcile the poet to you,
Divine impulses rushing through you,
And recognize all of his dreams!

1840

* * *

Poor craftsman of the word! One thought progresses
Behind another! And from memory
He can't escape. The priest of thought is he.
All things—death, life, and truth—a thought expresses.
Brush, chisel, organ! He is lucky who
Can see their boundary and not step o'er it;
The world's feasts make him drunk! In front of you,
As if before a sword, thought pierces through
A light! And earthly life grows pale before it.

1840

Complaint

Bane of a beautiful summer, troublesome fly, why
                                        annoy me
      Hovering, circling about, sticking to fingers
                                        and face?
Who is it that has endowed you, through your sharp sting,
                                        with the power
      To interrupt love's hot kiss, or a strong-winged idea?
You've made a wild-tempered Scythian out of a peace-
                                        loving dreamer,
      Child of the luxuries of Europe, now death's
                                        eager foe.

1841

N. M. YAZYKOV

Songs

I

Pour full the glasses, sing by ear!
To wine—respectful veneration:
To it a solemn, festive cheer!
To it—obeisance and prostration!

The hero, set by wine ablaze,
Sweeps off to death, more daring, gallant;
The poet sings, to Bacchus prays,
A new Apollo in his talent.

The lover, his sweetheart's affair,
Forgets, when with the glass elated,
And while he drinks, does not despair,
But suffers, unintoxicated.

On earth below, it's true, I think,
Deprived of Bacchus life is galling:
Anacreon tells us to drink—
And we affirm: until we're falling!

Pour full the glasses, sing by ear!
To wine—respectful veneration:
To it a solemn, festive cheer!
To it—obeisance and prostration!

1823

Elegy

She drew me on in fascination,
In her I all the charms divined,
All the ideals and consummation
Of my transcendent dream sublime.

From gods above did I solicit
A simple destiny in vain,
Unfettered heart and peace of spirit
As precious jewels I retained.

The captivating power of yearning,
Just as a spark of Zeus' fire,
Has all of me inflamed and burning,
Has all of me filled with desire.

But let not me receive her favors;
She is my star, my paradise

In moments of repose and labors,
In moments of intemperate vice.

To youthful urges of emotion
I acquiesce without design,
And I admire in wild devotion
The beauty which cannot be mine.

1825

A Prayer

I turn to Providence, appealing:
Allot to me tormented days,
But grant endurance firm, unyielding,
But steel my heart to hardened ways.
Oh, let me reach, with change arrested,
Another life's mysterious doors,
Just as a Volga wave whitecrested,
Unbroken, whole, draws near the shore.

1825

The Colt

Gaily, eagerly he's breathing
Meadow breezes fresh and light;
Dove-gray steam is puffing, seething
From his nostrils fiery, white.
Full of strength and free, courageous,
Loudly he began to neigh,
Stirred the colt—with hooves audacious
To the field he dashed away!
Dashes he, with eyes dilating,
Savagely his head inclined;
In the wind in waves cascading
Jet-black mane unfurled behind.

Just as wind: if slope advances
On the path? The brave one prances—
On it now! Be there descent
And a swirling current? —Sweeping
All at once with mighty leaping
Over them—and off he went!

Take your pleasure, colt so clever!
Show your strength so rugged, fine!
Mane cascading not forever
You've in wind unfurled behind!
Life with freedom not forever
On a wild one is bestowed,
And the cold air of the meadow,
Daring steepness of the road,

Current fatal and rampageous,—
Soon, so soon locked up for keeps!
Gratify your hooves courageous,
Powerful run and mighty leaps!

Colt so clever, work is calling!
In a harness light, enthralling,
With a saddle lustrous, smart,
And with tinkling reins enlacing,
In precise and splendid pacing
With a rider you'll depart.

1831

D. V. VENEVITINOV

Sonnet

Within the value of life my days would flower calmly;
There revelry would nurture me with dreams. A world
Of fantasy, to me the fatherland's clear limit,
With its familiar beauty, it attracted me.

But early flame of feelings, outbursts of emotion
Destroyed me with their magical, enchanted strength:
Alas, I love the happy beam of life delightful,
Preserving but remembrances of former days.

And I have come to know, o Muse, your fascination!
The lash of stormy waves and lightning's flash I've seen;
I've heard the howl of storms and heard the crash
                                        of thunder.

What is there to match the poet filled with passion?
Forgive me! But through you your nursling can
                                        but perish,
And yet, in perishing, he only blesses you.

1824

The Poet

Oh do you know the son of gods,
The muses', inspiration's darling?
Could you among the sons of earth
Discern his certain speech, his movements?
Not fiery, his ascetic mind
Won't shine in boastful conversations,
But a clear ray of lofty thoughts
Shines in his gaze, involuntary.

Let near him in a haze of joy,
Let thoughtless youth create an uproar,
A reckless cry, immodest laugh,
And unrestrained, unbridled gladness:
All this is foreign, strange to him,
He looks around at all things calmly,
And only seldom from his lips
Will something drive his fleeting smile.
His goddess is simplicity,
And meditation's quiet genius
From very day of birth had settled
The seal of silence on his lips.
What are his dreams, and what his longings,
His hopes, his fears; they are all secret,
All silent kept within himself:
He thoughtfully within his soul
Preserves his unsuspected feelings . . .
When something unexpectedly
Disturbs his fiery breast—his soul
Is ready to pour forth in language
Without alarm or artifice
And shines in his impassioned eyes . . .
And he anew grows quiet, bashful
And lowers to the earth his gaze,
It is as if he hears reproach
For his irrevocable outburst.
Oh, if you meet him with his brow
Austere set deep in meditation—
Then pass him by without a sound,
Do not disturb with your cold phrases
His ever sacred, quiet dreams;
Look with a tear of adoration;
Be still: this is the son of gods,
The muses', inspiration's darling.

1826

My Consolation

How blessed he on whose lips fortune
Has placed the lofty gift of speech,
To whom she has with magic strength
Delivered over hearts of people:
The spring of life, the wondrous flame
He, like Prometheus, has stolen
And animates the icy stone
Around himself as did Pygmalion.

A lucky few the heavens' gift
Are given as a happy fortune,
And seldom to the lips express
The fire of hearts obediently.
But if into a soul is placed
The smallest spark of noble passion,—

Believe me, 'tis not there in vain,
It will not glimmer fruitlessly . . .
Fate would not fire a soul with this
So that the cooling ash of death
Forever should put out the ember:
No! What is in the depths of souls,
Because the grave cannot remove it,
Survives and will live after me.

The prophecies of souls are truthful.
I knew the heartfelt fits of passion,
I was their victim, felt their pain,
And of my suff'ring, ne'er complained;
I found in life my consolation:
A secret voice has promised me
That it was not just useless torment
That rent my breast before its time.
It said to me, "Some time the fruit
Will ripen of this secret torment.
A potent word will accidentally,
In unexpected fire of speech,
Be torn from deep within your breast:
You will not let this word fall vainly;
'Twill set afire another breast,
Will fall into it as a spark
And as a fire will there awaken."

1826

Testament

Now is the hour of final suffering!
Listen: a dead man's will
Is fearful, like the voice of prophecy.
Listen: remove not
This ring from my cold hand;
Let my sorrows die with it
And be buried with it.
To my friends—regards and comfort:
My best moments of enthusiasm
Were dedicated to them.
And listen, my goddess:
Now the sanctuary of your soul
Is more open and clear to me;
Passion's voice in me has fallen silent,
Love's enchantment is forgotten,
The iridescent haze has disappeared,
And that which you called paradise
Before me now is open.
Draw near! Here is the door of the tomb!
All is now permitted to me:
I do not fear society's judgments.
Now I can embrace you,
Now I can kiss you,

As in the first joy of greeting
In paradise we would kiss
Our angels with pure lips,
If we in ecstasy should meet them
Beyond the gloomy grave.
But forget this speech:
In it there is frenzy's mysterious voice;
Why do I pour out
Cold doubts into a burning breast?
To you one, only one supplication!
Do not forget!. .away with protestations—
Swear!. . You believe, dear friend,
That beyond this limit of the grave
My soul will bid the body farewell
And will live, as a free spirit,
Without form, without darkness and light,
Clothed in imperishability.
This spirit, like an eternally vigilant gaze,
Will be your relentless companion,
And if by criminal memory
You are unfaithful, thenceforth woe!
I shall secretly take the shape of reproach;
I shall stick to your treacherous soul,
In it I shall find food for vengeance,
And your heart will be sad and languorous,—
And I, like the worm, shall not fall away.

1827

Elegy

Enchantress! How delightfully you sang
About the wondrous land of fascination,
The ardent fatherland of loveliness!
Oh, how I used to love your reminiscing,
How avidly I harkened to your words,
And how I saw this unknown land in dreaming!
You in this wondrous air have grown enraptured
And fervently your speech now breathes its fragrance!
You long looked on the color of the heavens,
And heaven's colors brought us in your eyes.
Your ardent soul flared up, it flamed so clearly
And lit within my breast a second fire.
But this fire is tormenting and rebellious,
It does not burn with love that's quiet, tender—
No! It consumes, and torments, and grows cold,
It's agitated by a fickle longing;
Now stormily it seethes, and now subsides;
The heart anew with suffering awakens.
Oh, why, oh, why did you so sweetly sing?
Oh, beauty's singer, why then did I harken
So avidly to you, and from your lips
Drink poison of a dream, of cheerless passion?

1827

To My Signet Ring

You were unearthed in a dusty grave,
Herald of age-long love,
And again to the dust of the grave
Will you be consigned, my signet ring.
But now it was not love that blessed
With you the eternal flame
And over you, in tender melancholy,
Pronounced a sacred vow . . .
No! Friendship in the bitter hour of parting
Gave you to a sobbing love
As a token of compassion.
O be my faithful talisman!
Save me from grave wounds,
And society, and the worthless crowd,
From biting thirst for deceitful fame,
From seductive dreams,
And from emptiness of spirit.
In times of cold doubt
Revive my heart with hope,
And if in the sorrows of seclusion,
Far from the angel of love,
A crime is contemplated,—
You subdue with wondrous strength
My fits of hopeless passion,
And from my rebellious breast
Avert the lead of madness.
And when in death's hour I shall bid
Farewell to that which I love here,
I will not forget you in parting:
Then I will entreat my friend
Not to remove you, signet ring,
From my cold hand,
So that even the grave would not divide us.
And this request will not be fruitless:
He will affirm his vow to me
With the words of a fatal oath.
Ages will pass, and perhaps
Someone will disturb my dust
And unearth you again;
And shy love anew
Will whisper superstitiously to you
The words of agonizing passion,
And you again will be its friend
As you were mine, my faithful signet ring.

c. 1827

The Dagger

Abandon me, don't think of me!
I loved but you in this existence,
But I have loved you as a friend,

As one would love a star in heaven,
As one would love a bright ideal,
Or as a vivid dream of fancy.
I have discovered much in life,
In love alone I knew no torment,
And my descent into the grave
Should be as of a fool enchanted.

Abandon me, don't think of me!
But look—here is my hope, my purpose;
You see—but why then did you start?
No, do not tremble, death's not dreadful;
Don't whisper now to me of hell:
Believe me, hell's on earth, my darling!
Where there's no life, there is no pain.
Now kiss me as a farewell token . . .
Why is it that your kisses tremble?
Why does your gaze now burn with tears?

Abandon me, and love another!
Forget me, I will soon myself
Forget the grief of our existence.

c. 1827

Life

Life captivates us all at first;
All's warm in it, all warms the heart,
And it, like an enchanting tale,
Caresses our capricious minds.
Then something frightens from afar,—
Yet in this fright we find enjoyment;
Amusing our imagination,
Like tales of magical adventure
The old men often tell at night.
But then illusion playful ceases!
For we grow used to wondrous things.
And soon we look on all things, torpid;
How hateful life becomes for us.
All its entanglements, its riddles
Are now too boring, long and old,
As is a tale retold too often
To wearied ones ere hour of rest.

1826

Three Roses

As paradisal beauty's emblem,
In lonely steppe of earthly path,
The gods have tossed to us three roses,
Most beautiful of Eden's blooms.

The first beneath the skies of Kashmir
Now flowers near a sparkling stream;
It is the mistress of the zephyr,
Inspirer of the nightingale.
And neither day nor night it withers,
And if by someone it is plucked,
No sooner gleams a ray of morning,
Than this first rose still fresher blooms.

But still more beautiful the second:
For this one with the crimson dawn,
In early morning heavens blooming,
With vivid beauty dazzles us.
The fragrance of this rose is fresher,
More cheering, too, this rose to meet:
It only for an instant reddens,
But with each day it blooms again.

The third has still a fresher fragrance,
Although it is not in the skies.
But for impassioned lips love fosters
This rose upon a maiden's cheeks.
This third rose, though, is timid, tender,
And after blooming quickly fades,
Then morning's ray will gleam through vainly—
This rose will never bloom again.

c. 1826

A. S. KHOMYAKOV

Dream

I had a dream I was a poet,
And a poet was a wondrous occurrence,
And in the poet the Most High placed
    A crown on all of His creation.

I had a dream I was a poet,
And strings beneath my finger breathed,
Their sounds rang out like thunder-gods,
And pierced with an arrow the depth of the heart.

And just like living waters in the wild steppe,
My song caressed the greedy ear;
In it was heard the mysterious voice of nature,
And the mortal's upward-soaring spirit.

But the hour came. They closed me in the grave,
The cold of the tomb froze up my lips;
Yet out of its darkness, out of cold dust,
The song rang out and the sweet voice sounded.

Ages passed by, and other generations
Covered the land where lay the poet's dust;
Yet the golden strings did not grow still,
And the sweet voice sounded as before.

I had a dream I was a poet,
And a poet was a wondrous occurrence,
And in the poet the Most High placed
 A crown on all of His creation.

1828

The Lark, the Eagle, and the Poet

When the East, awakened,
Brightens with dewy dawn,
The invisible lark hovers
In the plain of the azure sky;
And, inspired, he creates
His artless song, and haughtily
Scatters the silver notes
On the path of the airy breeze.
The eagle, forgetting his prey,
Takes flight, and higher than blue-gray storm-cloud,
Wings spread out like a sail,
He rises, exultant and mighty.
Why do they sing? Why do they fly?
Why do ardent dreams
Allure the poet to the sky
From the valley's gloom and vanity?
Because inspiration is in the sky,
And in songs a surplus of powers,
And rapture of proud freedom
In the spreading of wings over clouds;
Because from the height of the sky
The other song! that song of my native land,
Is drawn-out, sad, and plain,
Full of melancholy, tears, and sorrows.
How many thoughts it suddenly evokes
About our steppe, our ringing snowstorms,
About the joys and griefs of youthful days,
About the cradle's quiet melodies,
About the house of father, kin, and friends.

1831

Inspiration

Seize the moment of inspiration,
Drink down the cup of ecstasy
And do not slay your soul
With a dream of lazy oblivion!

Seize the moment! It slips by
Like a bright streak of lightning;
But it holds many years
Of earthly existence.
But if once with cold soul
You reject the heavenly gift
And extinguish inspiration's fire
In the vanity of the barren earth;
And if once in carefree indolence,
Grown fond of the world's paltriness,
You bind with the chain of pleasure
The soul's rebellious transport,—
Then the pure dew of sacred poetry
Will not descend on you,
And before your blinded sight
The heavens will not swing open.
And your poor heart will shrivel,
And the rich field of your former thoughts,
Like the arid steppe, will go to seed
Under the thorns of earthly notions.

1831

Two Hours

There is for the poet an hour of bliss,
When by a momentary dream
His soul is suddenly warmed within
As if by a burst of fire.
Tears of inspiration gleam,
His breast is filled with wondrous strength,
And songs pour out harmoniously,
Like a sweet-sounding wave.
But there is for the poet an hour of suffering,
When the whole splendor of glorious creation
Will arise in the darkness of night
Before his pensive soul;
When in his breast will be stored up
A whole world of images and dreams,
And this new world will burst into life,
Strive for sounds, beg for words.
But there are no sounds on the poet's lips,
His fettered tongue is silent,
And the ray of light divine
Fails to penetrate his vision.
In vain he suffers, frenzied;
Miserly Phoebus heeds him not,
And the newborn world perishes
In his mute and impotent breast.

1831

W. K. KÜCHELBECKER

Vision

How vastly the darkness has fallen!
How still the noise of daily existence!
How sweetly my beautiful beloved
Has drifted into drowsiness!
The whole world lies in solemn peace,
Enwreathed by dream and deep silence;
And choruses of stars, a festival of night,
Perform their journey above the earth.

What rushed by like a breath of spring?
What flew over me so quickly?
And what sound, like the shudder of a harp,
Like the whirring wing of a swan?
Suddenly a light flashed, half the sky swung open;
I started to tremble, speechless, scarcely breathing . . .
Before whom, O heart, have you begun to throb?
Whom do you await? —speak, my soul!

You are here, lord of song, you are here,
Beautiful master of my young dream!
Celestial friend, my beneficent genius,
Again, again you have appeared to me!
Still the same spring on your lively cheek,
The same luster on your ethereal wings,
And the same lips with inspired smile;
You are still the same—yet you are not what you were.

You lived a long time in that azure space,
And the heavens' ray remained on your brow;
A whole world lies in your deep gaze,
A world of clear thoughts and creative wonders.
More beautiful, deep and sonorous
Is the melodious wave of your words;
Your sturdy frame more boldly rises,
And the span of your ringing wings is more terrible.

Before you the tremor of love blends
With a mysterious tremor of fear.
Incline toward me; lift me from the dust,
Bless my dreams as before!
Touch my head, celestial brother,
With your ethereal breath, as before;
Fill my whole heart with inspiration;
Take earthly shadows away from my eyes!

Then filled with strength, solemn and calm,
I shall rise above the abyss of life . . .
Awake, timbrel! Awake, voice of the lyre!
Awake in my soul, O my song!
Heed me, ye suffering people;
Ye strong ones, bend a shy ear;
Ye dead and stony hearts, when you hear
This song, take in a breath of life!

1840

Tsarskoe Selo

Over me the canopies of native trees bowed,
The quiet coolness of spreading birches!
Here is our familiar meadow; here is the cliff we love:
On its heights, we—sons of young freedom,
Disciples and favorites of Phoebus and Nature—
Would break through the thick of the trees
And leave the smooth path to the weak with scorn!
O sweet and sorrowless time!
Has the peace of my soul really vanished forever,
Have enchanting dreams abandoned me?
Happiness I find only in memories:
      My eyes are filled with unwanted tears!
Indeed, you have flown by, my golden years;
But—praise be to fate: again, again I am here.
In this peaceful refuge I completely revive!
I stand—and the watery expanse like a mirror
Shows me the bridge, the knolls, the shores and
                              shore wood,
And the brilliant azure of the cloudless skies!
How often, sitting here in the glimmer of midnight,
Have I looked at the moon in enraptured silence!
The lovely places, where exalted muses,
Their glorious flame, their sacred joys,
A passion for the great, a love of the good—first
We knew, and where our alliance of three,
A pure and sacred alliance of young poets,
Contracted by friendship and omnipotent skill,
      Was strengthened by the fraternal Camenae!
May it not be forgotten by us to the grave:
Neither serene happiness, nor gloomy suffering,
Nor comfort, nor profit, nor the striving for honors—
Nought will banish my soul from you!
And the rivalry of sweet songs and glory
Will unite the rivals and friends more closely!
Why are you not here, chosen ones of the Charites,
You, O my Delvig, my lazy sage,
Unconcerned, and happy in your unconcern!
You, my fiery, sensitive bard
      Of love and the good Ruslan,—
You, on whose brow I foresee the crown
Of Ariosto and Parny, of Petrarch and Bayan!
O friends! Why am I not roaming with you?
Why am I not conversing, contending here with you?
Why am I not looking from this tower onto the luxuriant
                              garden with you?
      Or, linking our arms,
Why are we not listening together to the sound
                              of the water
Striking the rocks in sparks and foam?
Why are we not looking at the sunrise together,
And at the flame dying out at the edge of the sky?

Everything would seem a fantasy to us,
   An incoherent, dim dream,
Everything, everything that I encountered, when I took
                              leave of solitude
That—alas!—has taken away happiness and peace,
And serenity of youthful soul,
And has rent my poor heart so painfully apart!
With you, my companions, my blood will be soothed,
And in my native land I will forget for a moment
The cares and the melancholy, the boredom and emotion,
And perhaps I will forget even love itself!

July 14, 1818
Tsarskoe Selo

October 19, 1837

Blissful is he who has fallen like the youth Achilles,
Beautiful, mighty, bold, and majestic,
In the midst of a career of victories and glory,
Full of invincible strength!
Blissful is he! His ever youthful countenance
Shines like the eternally golden sun,
Like the first dawn of Eden,
With the splendor of immortality.

But I, alone among a people alien to me,
Stand in the night, weak and forlorn,
Over the terrible grave of all my hopes,
Over the dark tomb of all my friends.
Into that bottomless tomb, smitten by lightning,
Has fallen the last poet close to my heart . . .
And here again is the sacred day of the Lyceum;
But Pushkin is no longer among you!

He will bring no new songs to you,
And by them your hearts will not be stirred;
He will not drink of the toasting cup with you:
He has ascended to his friends beyond the clouds.
He is feasting now with our Delvig;
Now he is with my Griboedov:
After them, after them my soul yearns;
Avidly I reach out my hands to them!

It is time, as well, for me! Long has fate been
                              threatening me
With the tortures of an insufferable blow:
It is depriving me of the gift
With which my spirit is inseparably fused!
It is so! I have endured the years of prison,
Exile, and shame, and orphanhood;
But under the shield of holy inspiration
Here in me a deity has blazed.

The time has come! Neither flame nor lightning stroke
Has slain me; no, I sink in the midst of a bog,
Crushed by a mountain of needs and anxieties,
And I have grown unaccustomed to the forgotten strings.
In a stifling dungeon an angel once created for me
A paradise of songs from golden dreams;
But am I not a soulless corpse without him
Among corpses just as cold and dumb?

October 19, 1838
Siberia

A. I. ODOEVSKY

(Answer to Pushkin's Epistle)

The ardent sounds of the seer's strings
Reached our ears.
Our hands rushed to our swords,
But they found only fetters.

But be calm, bard: we are proud
Of our chains, of our fate,
And behind the locks of our prison
We laugh in our soul at the tsars.

Our sorrowful work will not be lost:
The spark will kindle a flame—
And our enlightened people
Will gather under a holy banner.

We will forge swords from our chains
And will again light the flame of freedom,
It will appear unexpectedly to the tsars—
And nations will breathe joyfully again.

(1826)

The Dying Artist
(On the Death of D. V. Venevitinov)

All of my impressions crowded into a sound
And a color and a well-formed word;
And the muses were proud of the youth
And said: "He is a poet! . . ."
But no; the rays of a dawn had scarcely
Touched my eyes,
When the light darkened in my sight:
The fruit of my youthful life has blown away!
No! my daring brush did not succeed

In bringing heavenly dreams to life;
The sound of my song, which I never finished singing,
Will not be played out on any earthly strings.
But I, clothed in imperishability,
Will hear it all in the heavens.
But on earth, where I did not pour forth
The fire of my soul into a pure flame,
I died completely...And a coarse stone,
The usual cover of silent graves,
Will lie on my cold skull,
Not telling my tribesmen
That a newly built lyre
Fell too early from my hands
And that I did not succeed in pouring forth
The beauty and order of the world into a harmonious
sound.

1827

K. F. RYLEEV

Ivan Susanin

As a result of 1612, the young Mikhail Fyodorovich Romanov, last representative of the Riurik dynasty, was hiding in the Kostroma region. At that time the Poles occupied Moscow: these strangers wanted to seize the Russian throne for the tsarevich Vladislav, son of King Sigismund III. One detachment penetrated the Kostroma borders and tried to capture Mikhail. Near his hide-out the enemy captured Ivan Susanin, an inhabitant of the village of Domnino, and demanded that he secretly lead them to the home of the future wearer of the crown of Russia. Like a true son of the fatherland, Susanin wanted to die rather than save his life by being a traitor. He led the Poles to the opposite side and informed Mikhail of the danger. Those staying with him managed to get him away. The exasperated Poles killed Susanin. At the ascension to the throne by Mikhail Fyodorovich (in 1613), a charter was given to the heirs of Susanin for a piece of land near the village of Domnino; the subsequent tsars confirmed it.

"Where are you taking us?.. It's pitch dark here!"
The enemies testily cried to Susanin.
"We will get stuck and sink into the snow drifts;
We won't reach any place to spend the night.
Truly, brother, you have lost the way on purpose;
But you won't get to save Mikhail that way.

Let us then get lost, let the blizzard rage:
But your tsar will not escape death at the hands of the
the Poles!..

Lead us, then—and you'll get something for your
troubles;
Or resist: and you'll soon come to grief at our hands!
We've been forced to spend the whole night fighting
through the storm...
But what shows dark there in the valley, beyond the
fir tree?"...

"A village!" the peasant answered the Sarmatians.[1]
"There, see the threshing floors, a fence and even a
little bridge.
After me! to the gates!—this little hut
Is always kept warm for guests.
Go in—don't be afraid!"—"Well, aha, a Russian!..
Well, brothers, what a hell of a distance!

I have never seen such an infernal night,
My falcon's eyes were blinded by the snow...
My *zhupan*[2] is wringing wet, not a thread is dry!"
After we entered, thus grumbled the young Sarmatian.
"Landlord, bring us wine! we're soaked, frozen to
the marrow!
Quickly! don't make us resort to using our sabres!"

A simple tablecloth was spread on the table;
Beer and a mug of wine,
Both Russian kasha and shchi[3] were put before
the guests,
As well as big slices of bread for each of them.
The raging wind knocks at the window;
The sadly crackling wood burns away.

It's already long past midnight!.. Wrapped in deep sleep
The Sarmatians lie serenely along the benches.
Everything in the smoky hut partakes of the peace.
Only grey-haired Susanin is on guard and
In the corner, near the icon, prays under his breath
For the sacred defense of the young tsar!

Suddenly someone on horseback rode up to the gates.
Susanin got up and stealthily went to the doors...
"It is you then, my own?.. But I have come for you!
Where are you going in such nasty weather?
It's after midnight...and the wind has still not
died down;
You will only bring anguish to the hearts of those near
and dear!"

"God himself led you to this house;
My son, hurry to the young tsar;

1. Sarmatian is a term prevalent in eighteenth-century Poland which signifies backwardness and a rural mentality opposed to Enlightenment.
2. An article of men's clothing worn by Ukrainians and Poles in ancient times, a *zhupan* resembles a half-caftan.
3. Barley groats and cabbage soup.

Tell Mikhail to hide quickly;
Tell him that these proud Poles, out of malice,
Are secretly planning to kill him
And threaten Moscow with new misfortune!

Tell him that Susanin will save the tsar,
Burning with love for his country and his faith.
Tell him that escape lies only in flight
And that the murderers are spending the night here
                                    with me."
"But what have you undertaken? think, my father!
The Poles will kill you . . . What will become of me?

And also of my young sister and sickly mother?"
"The Creator will save you through his holy power.
He won't let you perish, my dear ones:
He is protector and helper of all orphans.
Farewell then, o my son, time is precious to us;
And remember: I will perish for the Russian people!"

Sobbing, young Susanin jumped on his horse
And hurried off like a whistling arrow.
In the meantime the moon made a half-circle
And the whistle of the wind died down, the blizzard
                                    quieted.
The dawn was growing red in the eastern sky:
The Sarmatians awoke—those villains, harmful to
                                    the tsar.

"Susanin!" they shouted, "why are you praying to God?
There's no time for that now—it's time we were on
                                    the road!"
After they left the village in a noisy crowd,
They entered the dark forest by a roundabout path.
Susanin leads them . . . Morning has arrived.
And in the forest the sun began to shine through
                                    the branches.

First it quickly hides, then flashes brightly,
Then dimly lights up, and then disappears again. Not even
Not even stirring, both the oak and birches stood;
Only under their feet does the snow squeak from the frost,
Only occasionally does a raven make noise after
                                    taking wing,
And a woodpecker pecks away at a hollow willow.

All of the Sarmatians silently follow
Their grey-headed guide farther and farther.
The sun is already shining high in the sky;
The forest becomes more and more remote and
                                    more wild!
And suddenly the little path disappears before them:
And the pines and firs, gloomily bending

Their thick branches to the ground itself,
Weave a wooden wall out of twigs;

In vain is an anxious ear on the alert.
Everything in this godforsaken place is deaf and quiet . . .
"Where did you bring us?" screamed an old Pole.
"There where I needed to!" Susanin answered.

"Kill me! torture me!—my grave is here!
But know this and writhe in grief: I have saved Mikhail.
You thought that in me you found a traitor:
There are none nor will there ever be any on Russian soil;
Here everyone loves his fatherland from his infancy
And would not soil his soul in treason."

"Villain!" cried the raging enemies,
"You will die under the sword!" "Your anger doesn't
                                    frighten me.
Whoever is a Russian at heart will cheerfully, bravely,
And joyfully die for a just cause!
I fear neither punishment nor death;
Without hesitating I will die for the tsar and for Rus'!"

"Die then!"—the Sarmatians cried to the hero—
And the whistling sabres extended over the old man
                                    began to sparkle!
"Perish, traitor! Your end has come!"
And covered with wounds, the steadfast Susanin fell!
And the purest blood turned the pure snow crimson!
It saved Mikhail for Russia!

1823

The Citizen

At the fatal hour shall I
Disgrace a citizen's dignity
By imitating you, pampered race
Of degenerate Slavs?
No, I am incapable of dragging out my young century
In passion's embraces and shameful idleness,
    And with my soul seething, I am incapable of
                                    pining away
Under the heavy yoke of autocracy.
    Let the youths, who have not yet guessed their fate,
Not desire to perceive the destiny of the century,
Nor prepare for future battle
For the oppressed freedom of man.
With their cold souls, let them cast cold glances
    On the disasters of their fatherland
And not read in them their own future disgrace
And the just reproaches of their descendants.
They will repent when the people, in revolt,
    Will find them in the embraces of idle bliss
And, seeking rights of autonomy in stormy revolt,
They will not find either a Brutus or a Riego* in them.

(1824-25)

*A leader of the Spanish revolution of 1820.

A. V. KOLTSOV

The Nightingale

Captivated by a rose, the nightingale
Sings over it both night and day;
But the rose listens silently to the songs
And innocent sleep engulfs it . . .
Thus does another singer with his lyre
Sing for a young maid;
He is consumed by ardent passion,
But the sweet maid does not know—
For whom is he singing? Why
Are his songs so sad?

1831

Song

Don't you sing, nightingale,
Under my window;
Fly away into the forests
Of my native land!

Take a fancy to the window
Of my soul-maiden . . .
Tenderly chirp out to her
About my yearning;

You tell her how I
Wither and dry up without her,
Like grass in the steppe
Before autumn.

Without her, at night
The moon seems gloomy to me;
In the middle of the day, the
Little sun has no fire.

Without her, who will
Caress me?
On whose breast will I
Bow my head to rest?

Without her, at whose speech
Will I smile?
Whose song, whose greeting
Will touch my heart?

Why are you singing then, nightingale,
Under my window?
Fly away, fly away
To my soul-maiden.

1832

Song of a Ploughman

Hey! drag on, gray horse,
Along the field, along the acres.
Let's whiten the iron
Against the damp earth.

Little dawn, a beautiful girl,
Has already caught fire in the sky,
The little sun emerges
From the large forest.

It's merry in the field.
Hey, drag on, gray horse,
You and I, both together,
Are master and servant.

Merrily I clamber up on
The harrow and wooden plow,
I get the cart ready
And scatter the seeds.

Merrily I gaze
At the threshing floor, at the ricks,
I thresh and winnow . . .
Hey! drag on, gray horse!

My gray horse and I
Plow up the field early,
We make a cradle
For the holy seedlet.

Damp mother-earth
Will nurture it, feed it;
A little blade of grass will appear in the field—
Hey, drag on, gray horse.

A little blade of grass will appear in the field—
And then an ear of corn will spring up;
It will begin to ripen, to dress
Itself up in golden material.

Our sickle will begin to shine here,
Our scythe will begin to ring out here;
Our rest on the heavy
Sheaves will be sweet!

Hey, drag on, gray horse!
I'll feed you to your heart's content,
I'll give you water to drink,
Spring water.

I will plow and sow
With a silent prayer:
Oh God, let me grow
Grain—my wealth!

November 21, 1831

A Peasant's Meditation

I'll sit down at the table—
And think a bit:
How can one live on earth
All alone?

The young man has
No young wife,
The young man has
No faithful friend,

No golden coffer,
No warm corner,
No harrow or wooden plow,
No ploughman's horse;

Along with my poverty
God the father gave me
Only one gift—
Great strength;

But bitter need
Has even used up
This very thing—
All for other people.

I'll sit down at the table—
And think a bit:
How can one live on earth
All alone?

April 9, 1837

Bitter Fate

Like a stray nightingale,
My youth flew by,
My happiness has roared past
Like a wave in foul weather.

There was a golden time,
But it hid itself;
My youthful strength
Is worn out along with my body.

Blood has congealed in my heart
From sorrowful brooding.
Even that which I loved as my own soul
Has betrayed me.

The winds sway the
Young man, like a blade of grass;
Winter chills his face,
The sun burns it.

For the time being
I've become completely worn out by everything,
And my blue caftan
Has fallen down from my shoulder!

Without love, without happiness
I roam over the world:
When I part with misfortune
I meet up with sorrow.

On a steep hill
A green oak once grew,
But now it lies and rots
Beneath the hill...

August 4, 1837

Separation

At the dawn of my misty youth
I loved my darling with all my soul;
She had a heavenly light in her eyes;
The flame of love burned on her face.

May morning, what are you compared to her,
You, green mother-oak;
Steppe grass is silken brocade,
Evening sunset, night the sorceress!

You are good when she is not here,
When a person shares his grief with you,
But when she is present—it's as if you didn't exist;
With her, winter is spring, night is a clear day!

I can't forget, how for the last time
I said to her: "Farewell, my darling!
You know, this is how God willed it—we will part,
But we'll see each other again..."

In an instant her face turned as red as a flame,
Then covered over with white snow—
And, sobbing like a mad woman,
She hung on my breast.

"Don't go, stay! Give me some time
To hold back my grief, to cry out my sadness,
For you, for my bright falcon..."
It took her breath away—words died out...

May 21, 1840

A. I. POLEZHAEV

Four Nations

I

The British lord is
Proud of his freedom—
He is a citizen,
He is a true son
Of his native land.
Neither kings
Nor papal intrigues
Will stealthily
Raise their
Bloody paws
Against the daredevil.
Like a new Brutus,
He carries a sword
To trim his talons.

II

The Frenchman is a child,
Joking, he'll overthrow
Your throne
And give the law;
He is tsar and slave,
Mighty and weak,
Proud,
Impatient.
He is as quick as a glance,
And as empty as nonsense.
But he will both astonish
And make you laugh.

III

The German is brave,
But overripened
In the cauldron of his mind;
He, like the plague
Of neighboring countries,
Is dead drunk;
Himself wearing a cap,
With his nose full of tobacco,
He sits,
At least for five centuries now,
Over a pile of books
Ready to bite his tongue
And to curse
His mother and father
Over a couple of lines
Of Chaldeon dates,
Whose meaning
He couldn't understand.

IV

In [Russia] they revere
The [tsar] and the [knout];
There the [tsar] with his [knout]
Is like a [priest] with his [cross];
He lives by it,
And eats and drinks [by it];
But the Russians,
Like fools,
With gawking mouths
Cry out as an entire
Nation: "hurrah!
It's time to beat us!
We love the knout!"
And so, without
Further ado, they beat
Them, like asses,
Without letting up
Both night and day:
The more they beat
The more they reap,
Just put pitchforks in his side
Then [you get] a wisp of hay!
But without beatings
All of Rus' would be just a howl—
And would fall,
And would disappear!

1827

Song of the Captive Iroquois

I'm to die! In disgrace to the swarm
I'll defenselessly give up life's form!

Nonchalantly will they
For amusing the young
All my sinews taut-strung
From my rib-bones unsplay!
They will beat me, revile,
Then my corpse they'll defile!

But I'll persevere! Not a word will I say,
Not a wrinkle my brow will display!

Like the aged oak tree
That one's arrows can't move,
Calm and brave will I prove
Death has no fear for me.
As a warrior and man
Will I cross to soul's land.

To assemblies of ghosts I will sing
Of my perishing's last fearless fling,

And my tale will convey
To all those within sound,
That war spirit's still found
In old warriors grey.
Then will rise great acclaim
From the mouths of the same.

They will say in a voice as if one:
"You are truly our ancestor's son!"

Then as aggregate massed
We'll return as before;
Into our kin we will pour
All the fire of our past.
And they'll win in the end
The revenge that we send!

I'm to die! In disgrace to the swarm
I'll defenselessly give up life's form!

Like the aged oak tree
That one's arrows can't move,
Calm and brave will I prove
Death has no fear for me!

1828

The Bitter One

Oh, why did fate ruin me?
Why did nature exclude me forever
From the bonds of existence,
And why did I die, still terribly alive?
A flame of inextinguishable passion
Still struggles within my breast,
And conscience, a sworn enemy, like a stone
Oppresses an outcast of the people!
But my gaze, roving but swift, still
Occasionally is directed toward heaven,
Though I am deprived of the holy, comforting
Spark of a deity, of hope, and of faith!
And everything in creation breathes love,
Even the worm, the earth and a leaf are all alive,
But I, a villain, am like one marked
With the blood of Abel! I am an atheist!
And I see, like a pitiful witness,
The radiance of the morning star;
And each day virtue repeats to me:
"Be afraid, be afraid of the recompense prepared
                                         for you!..
And it is formidable, the voice of impending doom;
And my blood grows as cold as ice,
And my hair automatically stands on end,
And sweat streams down!

If only I could flee to a distant wilderness,
If only I could despise the horror of the grave!
My soul seethes, but the hand of this slave
Cannot break its fateful vessel!
And my life is more agonizing than hell,
And the thought of death is ponderous . . .
But eternity . . . oh! it's no reward for me—
I am the son of ruination and evil!
O Providence, for what reason did I rise up from
The darkness of the ages to appear before you?
Oh, again turn over to destruction
This atom punished by fate!
Earth, open up your gluttonous belly,
Flow over me like a burning Etna,
And you, stormy whirlwind, divert my
Sorrow and spite and memory with ash!

1832

The Waterfall

Amid the rapids, clear streams
Babble down from the high mountain,
And suddenly, flowing together in a wide current,
Turn into a menacing waterfall.
Masses of waves, like hillocks, gush
In their swift and steep descent,
And after flying away, brightly gleam
All around like silver rain;
Protracted roaring howls and moans
Along the raucous river
And, disappearing with damp foam,
Grows deadly silent in the distance.
That's our life! that's a true
Picture of my lost youth!
In sincere beauty, at first
It rolled on like a stream;
Then, in a fit of mindless passions,
As quick as mountain waterfalls,
It suddenly disappeared in noisy splashes
Like the peal of a distant echo.
Sound out, sound out, O son of nature!
At a dismal time you
Reminded a singer of a flash of freedom
With your free play!

1832

Indignation

Where are you, irretrievable time
Of never-to-be-forgotten antiquity?
Where are you, beneficent sun
Of my golden spring?
Like a beautiful vision,
In the brilliance of rainbow rays of light,
You flash despotically
And hide from our eyes!
You don't shine as you once did,
Nor do you burn within my breast—
Given over to my inevitable fate,
I am on the path of life,
While gloomy, thunderous clouds
Sound out over my head;
Grim portents
Weigh upon my melancholy spirit.
Ah, how much of value
Have I lost in this life!
How I did worship a
Contemptible idol—the pitiful world!
With the wondrous conceit and strength
Of a volunteer warrior
And with the jealous love
Of a frenzied priest,
I served it solemnly;
I suffered without repentance
And exchanged reason—
That divine light—for madness!
Like a criminal, only fettered
By a just hand—
My mind was formidable, disenchanted
With the light of naked truth!
What then? . . . I concealed
Insatiable passions within fire,
And friends—secret villains—
Maliciously betrayed me!
Under the aegis of affection,
Under the guise of love,
The fateful dagger of betrayal
Drowned in my blood!
It's sad to see a black abyss
After you've seen the sky and flowers;
But it's sadder still to waste
A shameful life among slaves.
And to one trampled by insult,
It's sadder to see forever behind you
Irresponsible plunder
Along with persistent Nemesis!
Where are you then, rumbling destroyers,
Why are you hiding in the gloom
While oppressors
Celebrate on earth!
People, depraved people—
Whether you are slaves or hangmen—
Throw down your spears and

Swords, honed by spite!
Don't disturb the cold steel—
Idol of cruel rage!
The whole world will not fill up
Your hungry innards!
Your bloodthirsty teeth
Gleam like the blades of a scythe—
Carnivores—thus fight to the
Finish, like dogs! . .

1835

M. YU. LERMONTOV

My House

My house is everywhere where there's a firmament,
Where one only hears the sounds of songs;
Everything in which there is a spark of life lives in it,
But it's not crowded for a poet.

Its roof reaches to the very stars
And from one wall to another—
A distant path which its inhabitant
Measures out not with a glance, but with his soul.

There is a feeling of truth in the heart of man,
The holy seed of eternity:
It embraces limitless space and
The flow of a century all in a short moment.

And my omnipotent beautiful house
Is built for that feeling,
And I am doomed to suffer in it a long time,
But only in it will I be at peace.

c. 1830

The Cup of Life

1.
We drink from the cup of what is,
    Our eyes blindfolded so we cannot see.
The cup's rim is teary and moist,
    Evidence of our misery.

2.
Then just before death the blindfold
    Gives way to light,
And all that once propped up our vanity
    Disappears from sight.

3.

Then we see that the golden cup
    Was always dry,
That we dreamed a wine that was
    Not ours: it too a lie.

1831

The Sail

A lone sail whitens
In the light blue mist of the sea! ..
For what is it searching in a distant land?
What has it left in its homeland?

The waves play—wind whistles,
And the mast bends and creaks ...
Alas! It does not search for happiness
Nor from unhappiness does it run!

Under it is the stream of bright azure,
Above it a golden ray of sun ...
But it rebelliously asks for a storm,
As if in storms there is peace!

1832

The Death of a Poet

Honor's hostage, the poet, is dead,
The victim of careless and deceitful talk.
D'Anthès drilled out his heart with lead
And felled him like a clover stalk.
His soul had never any room to spare
For dishonor, shame, embarrassment, or spleen.
But when the world had an opinion to air
He revolted (as usual!). Now death intervenes,
For he was murdered. So what use
Are these crocodile tears? These fatuous eulogies?
This gross retching up of lame excuses?
Death was Fate's unalterable decree.
When you first knew him, didn't you
Run after, a pack of sycophantic liars,
And just for fun pucker up and blow
The kindling of his barely lighted fires?
So what now? You should rejoice—
The last tortures were ghastly! Death
Consumed him as fire to a stick: his voice
(His garland!) died out with his breath.

As his blasé murderer took aim,
Mercy figured as the least of his vices.
Though empty, his heart beat the same

As always, and his trigger-hand was ice.
Why should it tremble? Like them,
Like all the kiss-ass flunkies who bank
On perquisites, money, favor, and rank,
He was tossed our way by Fate's whim.
A foreigner, he loathed our country too
(Our barbarous country!), its language and traits;
He was bored stiff by our national debates
And by the poet he raised his hand to.

He's dead now, the grave's done its part.
Just like the unknown singer whose curse
Was that cat-like jealousy chose him for its mouse,
His Lensky, sung in immortal verse,
Proves how subtly life follows art.

Why did he exchange his true friends' trust
For the envy, hypocrisy, anxiety, and lust
Of the suffocating *haut monde*?
Why did he offer slanderers his hand
And make hollow men his confidants
    Who could, from youth, show wisdom on demand?
Once they snatched the old wreath from his head
They put on thorns disguised with laurel leaf.
    The hidden needles made their poison spread
    As they cut his forehead underneath.
So the dissembling and shabbiness persisted
Until the final days were frantic with alarms
Of his decline. His death consisted
Of hope and revenge dying in each other's arms.
    The music that moved us—it gave
    Us such delight—is gone, the air is still.
    The singer's only refuge is his grave,
    His lips clamped tight with the Reaper's seal.

And you, so hypersensitive to your worth
(Your only pedigree's the blood of brutes),
Would wreck the few whose misfortune (besides birth)
Was to cross the wide path of your dirty boots.
You who crawl and fester around the throne
Are the antithesis of Freedom, Fame, and Genius.
    You hide behind the law's skirts and groan
    In ecstasy when Justice shrivels from disuse.
But God judges, you masters of irrelevance!
    His justice is sure, though he bides his time.
    He reads your reptilian thoughts in advance
And counts your *baksheesh* a spiritual crime.
Your denunciations will be totally passé
    At the Judgment; your wits will desert you
And even your black blood will not wash away
    The good poet's blood, which comes from virtue!

1837

Prayer

Mother of God, I stand in prayer before
Your image with its bright halo,
Not for salvation, not before battle,
Not with gratitude or in repentance;

It's not for my desolate soul that I pray,
Not for the soul of an orphaned wanderer on this earth;
But I want to entrust an innocent maiden
To the warm patroness of a cold world.

Surround this worthy soul with happiness;
Give her companions, full of attention,
A bright youth, a peaceful old age, and
A world of hope to her gentle heart.

And when her span of days approaches its final hour,
Whether it is in the noisy morning or in the silent night—
Send the best of angels to her sad bed
To receive her beautiful soul.

February 1837

* * *

When the yellowing cornfield ripples,
And the cool forest rings out with the sound of the wind,
And a crimson plum hides in the garden
Under the delightful shade of a green leaf;

When at rosy evening or at morning's golden hour,
A lily-of-the-valley, sprinkled with fragrant dew,
Nods its head out from under a bush
In a friendly greeting;

When an icy spring plays along a ravine
And, merging thought into vague dreams,
It murmurs to me a mysterious saga
Of a peaceful land whence it rushes—

Then my soul's anxiety grows calm,
Then the wrinkles in my brow disperse—
And I can perceive happiness on earth,
And I can see God in the heavens.

February 1837

* * *

I'm bored and sad and have no one to whom I can
    Give my hand in a moment of spiritual adversity . . .
Desires! . . what's the use of forever desiring in vain? . . .
    And years go by—all of the best years!

To love . . . but whom? . . for a little while—it's not worth
                                    the trouble,
    Yet it's impossible to love forever.
What if you look within yourself?—not even a trace of the
                                    past is there:
    And joys and sorrows, and everything is worthless
                                    there . . .

What of passions?—you know that sooner or later their
                                    sweet disease
    Will disappear at the sound of a rational word;
And when you look around with cold attention, life
    Is such an empty and stupid joke . . .

January 1840

Meditation

Sadly do I look at our generation!
Its future is either empty or dark,
While under the burden of knowing and doubt,
    It grows old in idleness.
    From the time when we are scarcely out of the cradle,
                                    we are
Rich with our fathers' errors and their hindsight,
And life already oppresses us, like a straight path without
                                    a goal,
    Like a feast at an alien holiday.

    We are shamefully indifferent to good and evil alike;
At the beginning of our careers we wither without a fight;
We are shamefully faint-hearted in the face of danger,
And in the face of power—we are despicable slaves.
    Thus does some puny fruit, when come to ripeness
                                    too soon,
Gladdening neither our tongue nor our eye,
Hang among the flowers, an orphaned newcomer,
And the time of their beauty is the time of their downfall!

We have dried out our minds with fruitless learning;
Enviously hiding our best hopes and noble voice
From our family and friends
    With scepticism of derided passions.
We have barely touched the cup of pleasure,
    But that has not preserved our youthful strength;
Fearing a surfeit, we extract forever the very
    Best out of every joy.

Dreams of poetry, creations of art do not
Stir our minds in sweet ecstasy;
We greedily preserve some remnant of feeling in our
                                    our breasts—
A useless treasure covered in miserliness.
We both hate and love by chance

Without sacrificing anything to hate or to love,
And a certain secret coldness reigns in our souls
    While fire seethes in our blood.
And our fathers' luxurious amusements and
Their honest, childish debauchery bore us;
And looking back derisively we hurry to our graves
    Without happiness and without glory.

And like a sullen crowd which is soon forgotten,
We pass over the world without a noise, without a trace,
Without casting a fruitful thought to the centuries,
    Without the genius of a work begun.
And our heirs will insult our dust with contemptuous
                           verse,
With the austerity of a citizen and a judge,
With the bitter mockery of a deceived son
    Over his bankrupt father.

1838

The Prayer

In a difficult moment of life
If in my heart sadness grips,
One wondrous prayer
I repeat over and over by heart.

There is a benevolent force
In the harmony of living words,
And an incomprehensible beauty
Breathes in them.

From the soul when the burden rolls away,
Doubt distantly
Swirls and cries,
And it becomes so light, so light . . .

1839

Goodbye to Russia

My unwashed Russia, goodbye to you,
Land of slave-and-master race,
And you, phalanxes of official blue,
And you, their obedient populace.

Maybe beyond the Caucasian wall
I can manage for once to steer clear
Of your ubiquitous bigwigs' all-
Seeing eyes, and their all-hearing ears!

1837

Thanksgiving

I render thanks to you for all, for all,
For passion's torment that in secret rends,
For poisoned kisses, tears of bitter gall,
For vengeful enemies and slandering friends;
For springs of feeling in the desert drained,
For all life lavished on me to delude . . .
All I could wish to beg is that you deigned
To shorten now my term of gratitude.

1840

Wherefore

I grieve, because I love you, and I know
This flowering youth of yours that moves me so
Will not be spared vile slander's cunning torment.
For every shining day, each joyous moment
In tears and anguish fate will make you pay.
And so I grieve . . . because you are so gay.

1840

The Dream

In a Caucasian gorge, in noon-blaze dreaming,
Inert, a bullet in my breast, I lay;
And from the deeply gaping wound, still steaming,
Drop after drop, my lifeblood drained away.

Alone I lay upon the sandy clearing,
And craggy ledges clustered close and steep,
The sun stood high, the tawny summits searing,
And searing me—but I was dead asleep.

And in a dream I saw an evening rally,
Lights blazing, in the land from where I came,
And heard young girls in garlands gaily dally
In conversation, mentioning my name.

But 'mid the carefree chatter one, refusing
To join in it, sat pensive and apart,
In some forlorn and melancholy musing,
The Lord knows how, engrossed her girlish heart.

Of a Caucasian valley she was dreaming,
In that far vale a man she knew lay dead,
And from a black and gaping heart-wound, steaming,
The lifeblood trickled in a chilling thread.

The Cliff

Once a cloud-wisp spent the night
On an old cliff-giant's breast.
When morning came she left the nest
And whirled, coquette-like, out of sight.

And yet a trace of her still sleeps,
As dampness on his wrinkled height.
Now self-absorbed, an anchorite,
He persists in being, he weeps.

1841

I Walk Out Alone

I walk out alone along the road;
The stony passage glows through the cover
Of fog. Dead of night; the desert listens for God,
And one star talks with another.

In the sky everything is solemn and wonderful!
The earth is sleeping in a soft blue light . . .
Why am I so troubled then, and ill? Do I still
Have expectations, or merely feel contrite?

No, from life I expect nothing more;
Of my past there's nothing to regret.
It's freedom and peace I'm looking for!
I'd like to fall asleep and forget

But not with the cold zero of oblivion . . .
Still, I'd like a kind of eternal rest
So that a pulse in me would be living on,
And when I breathed, it would stir my chest.

So that, caressing my ears night and day,
A peaceful voice would sing of love
As I lay beneath, and green-leaved always,
A dark oak would bend and sway above.

1841

F. I. TYUTCHEV

Autumn Evening

There lingers in an autumn evening's light
A tender charm, mysteriously occurring;
A strange, foreboding glitter fills the night,
And gently now the purple leaves are stirring.
While overhead a quiet, cloudy sky
The sad and orphaned earth is calmly viewing.
From time to time cold gusts of wind rush by
As if to warn us that a storm is brewing.
Exhausting, damage, loss hang over all;
A gentle smile of fading marks the season—
It is a modest suffering which we call
Divine pain, in one capable of reason.

1830

Malaria

I love this wrath of God! I love the overflowing
And secret evil force that moves invisibly
In flowers, in the spring's glass-like transparency,
And in Rome's very sky, in rainbow colors glowing.
That same unclouded vault, and always your sweet breath
That pours so gently from your bosom, lightly lifting,
That same rose scent, the same warm breezes gently
                                          drifting,
That rock each leafy branch, and all of this is Death!
Thus do we recognize how nature can present us
With colors, voices, sounds, aromas that portend,
As harbingers for us, the last hour we will spend,
And ease the final pangs of anguish that torment us.
Someone has sent to us this envoy from the Fates,
Who calls the sons of Earth away from life, concealing
His face behind a veil, and thereby not revealing
To us his dread approach, and what beyond awaits!

1830

Silentium

Be still, efface ourself, and sink
The dreams you dream, the thoughts you think
Deep in the soul's most inward root;
Let them swim up and wane as mute
As stars of night in silence mill—
Rejoice in them—and be still.

How can the heart communion find?
How can another plumb your mind,
Or share what you are nourished by?
A thought outspoken is a lie;
By stirring it, you cloud the rill—
Partake of it—and be still.

Be compassed to your inner pole—
The soul within, believe, is fraught

With worlds of secret, magic thought
That noise without can but dispel,
And rays of day would surely kill—
Attune to them—and be still.

1830

Dream on the Sea

The sea and the storm rocked our boat violently;
I, sleeping, was left to the whim of the sea.
In me two infinities, merging, arose,
And I was their plaything, to move as they chose.
Around me, like cymbals, the rocks raised a clang;
The winds called each other; the waves crashed and sang.
Deaf in the chaos of sound, there I lay,
But over this chaos my dream made its way.
Magically muted and painfully bright,
It soared lightly over the thund'ring dark night.
In feverish rays its own world was revealed—
The ether shone bright; earth displayed its green yield;
Labyrinth-gardens and castles were seen,
And silently multitudes swarmed in between.
There, faces once unknown I now found I knew,
And magical beasts and strange birds met my view.
I walked like a god over creation's height;
Beneath me the still world poured out its soft light.
But through all these dreams, like a sorcerer's cry,
I heard the loud thunder of waves crashing by,
And into the still realm of these fantasies
Burst roaring waves pouring out foam on the seas.

1836

About What, Night Wind, Do You Cry?

About what, night wind, do you cry?
What are you mindlessly bemoaning?
What does your strange voice signify
With dull complaints, then louder groaning?
You tell in words known to the heart
Of pain beyond all comprehension—
You dig into the soul and start
The raging sounds of mad dissension.

O do not sing these frightful songs
Of chaos long ago created!
The night soul's world avidly longs
To hear its favorite tales related,
To burst from out the mortal breast
And with the Boundless be united!
O do not wake the storms from rest—
Beneath them chaos stirs, excited!

1836

The Fountain

Look how the shining fountain seems
So like a cloud, alive and whirling;
See how it flames, its damp smoke swirling,
To shatter in the sun's bright beams.
In rays of light the fount reached for
The sky, those sacred heights attaining—
Condemned to fall, its droplets raining
In fiery dust, on earth once more.

O fountain that reminds us all
Of death, your flow is never-ending!
What law beyond our comprehending
Directs and shapes your rise and fall?
How greedily you make your way
To heaven! But your stubborn beaming
Some unseen hand refracts, and gleaming,
It sparkles in the towering spray.

1836

In Yesterday's Enchanted Dreaming

In yesterday's enchanted dreaming,
You slumbered through the quiet night
While on your eyelids, softly gleaming,
The moon poured out its ebbing light.

A peaceful quietude surrounded
You, and the shadows deepened where
You lay; your even breathing sounded
More clearly in the evening air.

But through the curtains, gently swaying,
For a short while night's darkness crept
Upon your floating ringlets playing
With some unseen dream as you slept.

Now something suddenly came blowing
Into the room with quiet ease,
Light as a mist-draped lily, flowing
As if transported by a breeze.

And now some unseen being darted
Across the carpets, dimly lit,
And clutching at the blanket, started
To climb along the rim of it—

Now like a snake it wriggled, curling,
And then upon the bed it crawled,
Now like a ribbon, lightly swirling,
Among the coverings it sprawled . . .

With sudden bright illumination,
It touched your youthful breast, and then
It opened, with loud exclamation,
Your silken lashes once again!

(1836)

Day and Night

A veil with gold threads woven by
The high will of the gods is stealing
Across a nameless gulf, revealing
A secret world where spirits lie.
That brilliant veil which clothes the sky
Is day, which wakens all things living
And, friend of men and gods, is giving
Relief from pain to souls that cry.

But day grows dark as eventide
Begins: night comes again, and tearing
The blessed veil that day was wearing
Off of the world, throws it aside.
And now the chasm greets our sight
With its dark terrors; once we've seen it,
There is no obstacle between it
And us—that's why we fear the night!

1839

The Sea and the Cliff

Bubbling up, the ocean gushes,
Whistles, rises with a roar,
Toward immobile heights it rushes,
To the stars it longs to soar . . .
Was a devil's fire set burning
By some hellish force—did this
Underneath the ocean's churning
Kettle, cause the overturning
Of its cavernous abyss?

With its raging breakers crashing
On the shore, the surging sea,
Roaring, whistling, shrieking, smashing,
Pounds the cliff incessantly,
But not under subjugation
To the waves' whim, calm and proud,
Unmoved, without alteration,
Present at the world's creation,
You, our giant, stand unbowed!

Mounting one last onslaught, wailing,
Galled at being thus defied,
Once again the waves are scaling

Your enormous granite side.
But their fierce attack is shattered
On that changeless rock, and they,
Penitent and weak, have splattered
Lightly and at last are scattered,
Flowing in a muddy spray . . .

Stand then, mighty and exalted
Cliff! Wait but an hour or two—
Till the rumbling wave has halted
Its exhausting war with you . . .
Tired out, its spirit waning,
It will stop its evil game—
And from howling fights refraining,
Your gigantic heel restraining
It, will once again grow tame . . .

1848

* * *

Holy night rose in the firmament
And rolled up the day so comforting,
The day so kind, like a golden pall—
A pall flung over the abyss.
And like a vision, the external world was gone . . .
And man, like a homeless orphan,
Now stands, both weak and naked,
Face to face with the dark abyss.
He is hurled back upon himself—
His mind abolished, and his thought orphaned—
He is plunged into his own soul, as if it were the abyss,
And from outside there is no support, no limit . . .
And now everything bright and alive
Seems like a dream from long ago . . .
And in that which is strange, unsolvable, nocturnal,
He finds his native legacy.

(1848-50)

We Love in Such a Deadly Fashion

We love in such a deadly fashion,
Destroying, while we are in thrall
To violent and blinding passion,
That which we hold most dear of all!

How long since you, victorious lover,
Declared, "Now she belongs to me . . ."
Not yet a year—now you discover
What's left of all she used to be.

What happened to her smile, the glitter
In her bright eyes, the touch of rose

That graced her cheek? Tears, hot and bitter,
Have singed and burned away all those.

Do you recall the circumstances
When you first met that fateful day,
Her childlike laugh and magic glances,
The charming things she used to say?

And what of all this now? Where is it?
Was this a long-lived dream? Alas!
It's over, like a guest's brief visit,
As northern summers quickly pass!

Like some dread sentence placed upon her
By fate, your love for her became
A kind of undeserved dishonor
That only filled her life with shame!

O life of anguish and rejections!
Within her soul's depths she held fast
To what remained, her recollections...
But they betrayed her at the last.

Her charms then disappeared; she cowered
Just like a creature in the wild...
And that which in her soul had flowered
The surging crowd crushed and defiled.

What then did she succeed in keeping,
Like ashes, from this misery?
Pain without comfort, without weeping,
Pain that persists unyieldingly!

We love in such a deadly fashion,
Destroying, while we are in thrall
To violent and blinding passion,
That which we hold most dear of all!

1851

                         * * *

Huddled hamlets, scanty granges,
Frugal nature's desolation,
You, long-suffering's native ranges,
Homeland of the Russian nation!

Past the alien mind's divining,
Past the haughty viewer's guess,
Is the secret radiance shining
Through your humbled nakedness.

Bent beneath the cross' load,
Heaven's king has walked in tattered
Slave's attire your every road,
Homeland mine, and blessings scattered.

1855

BALLADS AND VERSE NARRATIVES

BALLADS AND VERSE NARRATIVES: INTRODUCTION

Two genres which represent the Age of Romanticism particularly well are the ballad and the verse narrative. In Russia these literary forms also encompass two tendencies which dominated the culture of the period: reliance on Western models and a search for "nationality," especially in folk literature and Russia's historical past. In early nineteenth century Russia both of these tendencies merged in the ballad form.

Ballads are traditionally short folk songs (thirty to eighty lines) which tell a story without narrative comment or digressions. Their action is concentrated, compressed and highlighted in a form full of repetitions, refrains, parallelisms and stylized speech. Love in its infinite variety forms the main theme of most ballads which concentrate on ordinary characters who do not quarrel with their fate.[1] Critics of the ballad talk of a "code" which describes the world of the ballad as concrete reality which is "at best apathetic, at worst hostile."[2] The supernatural world is real, accepted as a normal part of life and "frequently appears in dreams, superstitions, premonitions and omens."[3] These elements of the folk ballad also appear in the "literary" ballad which differs from its traditional cousin mainly in its artificiality. Instead of evolving from a folk tradition, the literary ballad is the product of an author's conscious decision to use the specific ballad form.

Perhaps the revival of the "natural" ballad form in eighteenth-century Europe was a reaction against the artificial rules and regulations of neo-classical literature. But whatever the cause, the revival of the ballad was a widespread phenomenon. The influence of writers such as James Thomson, Edward Young, Thomas Gray, James Macpherson, Robert Southey, William Shakespeare and Gottfried Bürger spread into Russia along with the popularity of ballads.[4] Instead of relying on its own tradition, Russia relied on western literature to provide a model for the ballad.

The authors of the first original ballads in Russia are M. N. Muravyov, N. M. Karamzin and I. I. Dmitriev.[5] However, the most important balladeer to appear in Russia is Vasily Zhukovsky, with his poetic renderings/translations of forty ballads. But as all critics point out, Zhukovsky did not merely translate; he created his own works patterned on the European originals. His *Lyudmila*, a translation of Bürger's *Lenore*, appeared in 1808. Written in trochaic tetrameter with rhyming couplets, each of the twenty-one twelve-line stanzas advances the story of a young girl who awaits the return of her beloved from the wars. She falls into despair when he does not return. But during the night, he does return and Lyudmila rides off with him. When they arrive at their destination in the morning, Lyudmila discovers that her lover is really a corpse and his home, a grave. Lyudmila dies in punishment for her rejection of God.

Zhukovsky's ballad follows the storyline of *Lenore*, but differs from it significantly on a stylistic level. Zhukovsky's setting is abstract[6] and the language is sweet rather than colloquial. Where Bürger uses conversational German, vivid physical descriptions and dynamic verbs, Zhukovsky writes his ballad in a far more literary language, relying on emotional epithets.[7]

In 1813 another reworking of *Lenore* and *Lyudmila* appeared in Zhukovsky's ballad *Svetlana*. Its twenty stanzas are each fourteen lines long, with the rhyme scheme AbAbCdCdEEfGGf. Each of the masculine lines is written in trochaic tetrameter with a truncated final foot ($/\cup/\cup/\cup/$) while the feminine lines are trochaic trimeters. *Svetlana* begins with young girls telling their fortunes, here a stylized folk motif. Svetlana participates in the activities and then settles down to sleep. Her beloved appears and she, like Lyudmila, rides off with him only to discover that he is a corpse. But Svetlana does not die; she awakens in the morning to find out that the horrors of the night were all merely a dream. Zhukovsky ends the poem with an epilogue where he calls Svetlana's attention to the fact that her adventure was only a dream and asks her to smile upon his ballad. This epilogue is a mild example of Romantic irony; it may also be an indication that *Svetlana* is really a parody of both *Lenore* and *Lyudmila*.[8]

Zhukovsky's renditions of *Lenore* certainly soften the language and actions of the original. His hero and heroine in *Svetlana* follow the patterns of sentimental rather than folk models.[9] But folk elements, however stylized they may be, certainly do appear in *Svetlana*—more than in the rest of his works. The very beginning of the poem is a catalogue of fortune telling traditions as well as an introductory frame to the narrative portion of the ballad. Also Zhukovsky uses the folk device of the epithet to describe Svetlana and her dream lover; however, his epithets are derived from typical sentimental vocabulary: Svetlana is quiet, sad and sweet, while her beloved is pale and despondent.[10] And even though Zhukovksy does occasionally resort to colloquialisms and "folk" forms such as diminutives and folk-style epithets, his vocabulary in *Svetlana* is consonant with that of his poems, i.e., sweet, gentle and refined—the language of the salon so favored by the Karamzinians and the members of Arzamas.

The language reform of the Karamzinians, with its aestheticism and elegance, did not appeal to another important "balladeer" of the period, Pavel Alexandrovich Katenin (1792-1853). Educated at home, this product of a noble family of the Kostroma region entered the military at an early age. By 1819 he had already served his country with enough distinction to be promoted to the rank of colonel. He retired to his estates in 1820 under police surveillance which resulted from his membership in an underground group which eventually became a part of the Decembrists. However Katenin was saved from the repercussions of the Decembrist uprising because of his exile to his estates. In 1832 the government lifted its ban restricting Katenin from visiting Moscow or Petersburg. Because of financial difficulties Katenin was forced to join the military again. He served in the Caucasus and describes his experiences there with bitterness. However, he became commandant of the Kizlyarsky fortress in 1836 and retired from the military in 1838. After this Katenin returned to his estate, where he lived until his death in 1853.[11]

Vague rumors describe Katenin as a friendless eccentric (especially after Pushkin's death) living out his last years on his estate, voluntarily isolated from the capital and the literary activity which marked his earlier years. Katenin was proficient in various genres and, like many of his contemporaries, translated much from western literature, including works of Racine, Corneille, parts of the El Cid legends, Tasso, Ariosto and Dante, whom he especially admired. The last he translated into the Italian octave and terza rima forms.

In addition to translations Katenin wrote four original plays (one in collaboration with Griboedov), the best of which is *Andromache* (1809-27). This play was too old-fashioned for the period, although Pushkin admired it. Katenin's tendency to prefer old forms is also clear in his heroic poem *Mstislav Mstislavich* (1819). Another indication that he was a literary "old-believer" is his opposition to the Arzamas trend in poetry. A partisan of the Shishkov faction, Katenin attacked the sweetness of the language of the "Zhukovsky school." In spite of his "classical" preferences, Katenin was considered by many—including Pushkin—to be a romantic, mainly because of his works, which contain many "national" and folklore elements. He violently maintained that he was *not* a romantic and that no Russian could be one, since romanticism is a Western phenomenon which has no relation to Russian history and culture. However, he did not attack any kind of subject matter, but maintained that a writer should choose national topics since he knows his own nation better than foreign ones. To Katenin *nationality* was an important theme, along with patriotism and hatred of tyranny. It is not surprising that his poems have a didactic tone.

An example of a ballad which demonstrates the lesson that God's punishment corrects man's imperfect justice is *The Murderer* (1815). An orphan who murders the kind peasant who gave him a home finds no peace until he confesses to his crime. The moon haunts the orphan and almost acts like his conscience. Written in alternating iambic tetrameter/iambic trimeter lines with corresponding feminine and masculine rhymes, this ballad contains the literary devices of the genre: a prosaic style, folk epithets, "rhetorical questions and the repetition of the epithet *strashnyi* [frightful]."[12] In addition to this, the dialogue of the ballad is colloquial and sometimes prosaic. The language is sometimes coarse or "low" (according to contemporary critics[13]), a characteristic the ballad shares with *Olga*, Katenin's version of *Lenore*.

Olga appeared in 1816 as an answer to Zhukovsky's melancholy, sentimental version, *Lyudmila*. Tired of Zhukovsky's periphrastic style and softened versions of the original, Katenin restores elements of Bürger's original: his heroine's blasphemies, her despair, the lover's transformation into a corpse, the heroine's death, and the setting placed in a definite time and locale. The tone and moral of *Olga* are also closer to Bürger's *Lenore*.[14] Olga's emotional reaction to her lover's failure to return is more elemental and violent than that of Zhukovsky's heroines. Written in trochaic tetrameter with the rhyme scheme aBaBccDD, *Olga* is a more striking and forceful evocation of the terror, evil and ugliness of a desperate woman's midnight ride with her dead bridegroom than Zhukovsky's could ever be.

A bride, her groom, her rejected suitors, a strange wedding night, supernatural events, folk motifs—and even Zhukovsky—all figure prominently in a lighthearted verse narrative by Pushkin. *Ruslan and Lyudmila* (1820) is his first major narrative poem, a hybrid of lyric, ballad, mock heroic, fairy tale and parodic forms. Its appearance confounded the readers, who were in a quandary over its genre and style. *Ruslan and Lyudmila* combines Lomonosov's three levels of language (high, middle and low) into a delightful blend of Church Slavonicisms and contemporary Russian. In actuality the language of the poem most nearly resembles the spoken speech of the gentry. A similar melange of genres imparts a playful mood to the poem. In the dedication the narrator even asks the Muses (or some young ladies) to accept his "playful work." He then says he will be happy if some young maid will look lovingly upon his "sinful songs." Pushkin sustains this lightly ironic tone throughout the work.

In the preface to the poem Pushkin's narrator recites a catalogue of fairy tale characters and motifs, thus tempering a ponderous classic device with frivolous subject matter. Perhaps this is Pushkin's sly way of warning his audience that they are not about to read a simple fairy tale. Later, in Canto Four, the narrator pokes gentle fun at Zhukovsky in his parody of the older poet's "Twelve Sleeping Maidens." Throughout *Ruslan and Lyudmila* we can find more parodic devices, such as a comic Homeric simile in Canto Five. All of this carefree experimentation contributes to the poem's overall mood of playfulness. Here we have a poem in which the prevalent sentimental mood of terror turns into laughter, and fantastic elements lack logic. Add to everything else a dollop of mild eroticism and the result is an entertaining breath of fresh air in the "gloom-doom" literary atmosphere of contemporary ballads.

Another aspect of *Ruslan and Lyudmila* which reinforces its mood of lightness is its iambic tetrameter lines in a varied rhyme scheme. In Russian the iamb is a versatile foot, the use of which can give rise to various tones. Here Pushkin uses it in a meter which, after him, became the standard in Russian poetry. But meter is only the rhythmic organizing factor of the poem. The total structure of this work depends on a series of contrasts. Tender scenes alternate with frightening ones (cf. wedding scenes vs. disappearance of Lyudmila), happy scenes with sad ones.[15] Moreover, Pushkin patterns the entire poem on contrasts of setting, action and characters. In addition, a frame surrounds the entire poem of six cantos, each of which has its own frame story which encloses another narrative.

The story of *Ruslan and Lyudmila* is straightforward but the plot does not have unity or logical development, though the narrator never disorders the chronology of the tale—even when he interrupts. Essentially the poem is a series of lyrical scenes. Perhaps the poem does not need a complex plot with valid motives since the characters are not very real. But they do have enough personality to be distinguished from each other. The characters do not resemble the heroes and heroines of fairy tales but instead act like those in contemporary literature. Ruslan is not a *bogatyr*[16]; he is a romantic hero on a quest to find his lady-love. Lyudmila also does not act like a folk heroine; she resembles "those nice and absent-minded girls from Pushkin's lyrics."[17] The narrator does not hesitate to smile tenderly at his heroine, even in her most frightful moments.

> She cries—however she "does not glance away" from the mirror; she decided to drown herself—but she didn't drown; she says that she won't eat, but then "she thought it over—and began to eat." This does not bother us: it is completely within the style of the whole tale, and we know ahead of time that this misfortune is not genuine misfortune here, and that all will end well, as in a fairy tale.[18]

We know that everything will turn out happily, because the narrator sets up the proper expectations.

The narrator's comments throughout *Ruslan and Lyudmila* assure us that he can make things come out all right simply because he is the narrator. Using Romantic irony, he makes fun of his readers by assuring them that, after all, they are reading poetry. The narrator's attitude to poetry in general parallels his attitude to the story he is telling. His digressions reveal his opinions about the offhand role of the poet (cf. Canto Four) and poetry and comment on literature in general. His remarks about literature also include answers to his critics. The narrator's comments, more than anything else, truly make *Ruslan and Lyudmila* a playful work, a realization of the theme of the poem: this work has no edifying theme, no ideological significance; it is merely a playful exercise.

After completing this poem, Pushkin was sent off to the Caucasus where he fell under the influence of Byron's Eastern Tales and began writing *poemy*[19] in Byron's manner. During the twenties he also wrote *Eugene Onegin*. It was not until 1830 that Pushkin returned to folk motifs, when he wrote his verse fairy tales. Although the fairy tales are full of national feeling, most of them have foreign sources. *The Tale of the Golden Cockerel* is most probably based on "The Tale of the Arabian Astronomer," one of the stories in Washington Irving's *The Alhambra,* which Pushkin knew in its French translation.[20]

Like *Ruslan and Lyudmila*, the fairy tales are neither reworkings nor imitations of folk stories, but original poems.[21] Of course, genuine folk elements do appear in *The Tale of the Golden Cockerel*. In it we find the traditional legendary motif "of the ruler sending out a succession of armies and finally going out to battle in person."[22] Added to this are the golden cockerel itself, an animal who shows up in Russian children's songs, as well as the "miraculous sentry" and "unwitting promise" of Russian fairy tales.[23] Pushkin also commences the narration with a traditional fairy-tale beginning and ends with a folklore formula. The people who inhabit the world of the tale are themselves folkloric types rather than developed characters. Pushkin even uses folk epithets to describe Dadon's sons.

Pushkin's treatment of Dadon, however, makes him a bit more complex than a simple folk hero (or villain). In the course of his adventures Dadon reveals several different aspects of his nature. He demonstrates good will when he promises to grant the astronomer who gave him the cockerel his first wish. But when the astronomer asks for the Princess of Shemakha as his reward, Dadon shows he is quick to anger, cunning (when he asks what use the maiden would be to a eunuch), and ruthless in his brutal murder of the magician. The tsar betrays a certain shallowness of character when he first sets eyes upon the young princess. Her presence alone prompts Dadon to forget immediately his two sons killed in battle, the sons whom he had so recently mourned.

The princess herself turns out to be a heartless match for Dadon. All of the people are shocked when the tsar murders the astronomer. But the princess merely looks on and laughs. This incident not only reveals something about the princess, but about Dadon as well. While the princess laughs the tsar flashes her an ironic grin.

Light irony is the basic tone of the tale, a tone which the lively narrator sustains throughout. He accomplishes this through his skillful use of rhyme and meter. Written in trochaic tetrameter with alternating masculine and feminine couplets, Pushkin's fairy tale conveys a playful tone while it retains the aphoristic quality of the couplets. The couplets reveal the moral of the story, while the meter makes it easier to accept. The narrator's virtuosity also shines through in the use of various levels of language in the tale. He employs the low comic style of chapbooks for some parts of the tale and a bookish literary style for others.[24] In his description of Dadon he uses the comic style, probably to emphasize his comic grotesque nature. But he resorts to a literary style when he describes the princess.[25] Pushkin's method of letting his narrator depict Dadon in a "comic-grotesque"[26] light is a subtle protest against Nicholas I. Pushkin wrote *The Golden Cockerel* soon after his conflict with the Tsar in 1834. Several lines in an early fragment of the tale make clear that the work may be a mild satire on the real Tsar.[27]

However, Pushkin's work is not simply a narrow topical piece; its implications are more far-reaching. The *Tale of the Golden Cockerel* does contain a lesson, even though it may be light and airy. Pushkin here looks at the implications and responsibilities of power. Tsar Dadon may know how to exercise the rights of power but sorely fails to understand its responsibilities. He learns too late that even a tsar is not above the law. Dadon breaks his promise to the astronomer and is therefore punished. But Dadon's punishment is another example of the subtle irony of the fairy tale. The task of the golden cockerel is to warn the tsar of the enemy's approach. Perhaps what the cockerel does at the end is identify and punish the tsar's own worst enemy—himself.

In the *Tale of the Golden Cockerel* Pushkin does not write of a real historical figure, but Lermontov certainly returns to Russia's past in *The Lay of Tsar Ivan Vasilievich, A Young Oprichnik and the Daring Merchant Kalashnikov* (1837). Set in Muscovy during the era of Ivan IV (The Terrible), this romantic narrative poem uses the language of the times to evoke the spirit of the age. *The Lay of Kalashnikov* may imitate a traditional folk genre; however, like Pushkin's tales, it still remains an original literary creation. Without duplicating the exact rhythm and meter of the oral model, Lermontov still manages to reproduce the "feel" of a traditional historical folk song in his successful stylization of that form.

The *bylina*, or historical song, falls into two categories: Kievan and Novgorodian. The former tell of heroic warriors (*bogatyr*) while the latter usually have historical or topical subjects.[28] *The Lay of Kalashnikov* clearly follows the second tradition. Lermontov's song begins with a *zapev* (a striking up) and finishes with an *iskhod* (ending), two characteristics of the *bylina*.[29]

Perhaps the most distinctive feature of the historical song is its adherence to a non-rhymed, accentual verse scheme, usually with three predominant stresses in no fixed position. However, the end of the line is always dactylic, with the foot normally spread over two words. Lermontov's song follows the *bylina* pattern closely; the lines most often begin with anapests and end in dactyls. "One of the peculiarities of this poem distinguishing it from the bylina is a pause, amounting almost to a caesura, after the word which bears the second stress. The force of the metre is thereby emphasized."[30]

Consonant with Lermontov's meter is his use of formulas and syntactic patterns which appear in folk poetry. Throughout we can find lines like "*Da pro lyubimogo kuptsa, pro Kalashnikova*" (about a beloved merchant, about Kalashnikov) rather than "about a beloved merchant Kalashnikov." Here Lermontov retains the repetition which the folk poets used as a mnemonic device. Related to this trope is the parallel syntactic formula, such as "*I prichityvali da priskazyvali*" (And we read it loud and we chanted it); "*V udovol'stvie svoe i veselie*" (in his pleasure and merriment) with the possessive adjective following the first noun only; "*Lish' odin iz nikh, iz oprichnikov*" (only one of them, of the oprichniki); "*klich klikat'*" (to cry out the cry); and "*Ne shutku shutit', ne lyudei smeshit'*" (not to joke a joke, not to make the people laugh). Another folk device is the fixed epithet, a figure of speech we see in *Kalashnikov:* "beautiful little sun," "orthodox tsar," "bold warrior," and "daring merchant."

All of the devices Lermontov uses in *Kalashnikov* not only conjure up the past, but also are intended to strike a responsive chord in the reader's heart. It is difficult not to be angry with the *oprichnik* or not to cheer brave Kalashnikov on as he seeks revenge for the dishonor brought on his family, or not to mourn his death. Lermontov journeys back to Russia's exotic past to arouse emotions and responses which belong to every age.

The "exotic" also took shape in the verse tales of Pushkin where its source was not Russia's history, but Byron's Eastern Tales, such as *Lara, The Giaour* and *The Corsair.*

Lands of the East, such as Turkey and Persia, fascinated the Romantics; they held a sway over Pushkin as well. His first poem in the Byronic mode is *The Prisoner of the Caucasus* (1820-22) and the second is *The Fountain of Bakhchisaray* (1822-24); both poems resemble the English poet's *Corsair*. But the most sophisticated of Pushkin's Byronic poems (and therefore the least Byronic) is *The Gypsies*, whose hero is the most developed of all.

Pushkin's early heroes are Byronic in that they are naive youths who have met treachery, sometimes at the hands of a woman. They lack belief in the moral worth of humanity and delight in voluptuousness. The heroes of Byron's Eastern Tales are normally outcasts, criminals or exiles, while their beloved women are either Eastern beauties or pure Christian blondes. The hero's antagonist is the pasha. In Byron's tales the hero meets obstacles to his love, tries to overcome them, and ends up dooming his beloved or himself. Common motifs of the tales include abduction of the beauty, disguise, secret murder, revenge, punishment of the criminal, pictures of battle, robber scenes, the harem, and a phantom. [31]

Pushkin's tales do not contain all of the Byronic motifs, but retain enough to banish doubts about the Englishman's influence. The main difference between the tales of the two poets is that Pushkin's tales are less "hero-centered." Other characters have lives and worlds of their own. Sometimes Pushkin even criticizes his hero (*The Gypsies*) or puts him off to the side (*The Fountain of Bakhchisaray*). In addition to this, Pushkin's heroine is more active, as in *The Prisoner of the Caucasus* which, in spite of its being closest in plot to any of Byron's tales, has no real antagonist.

The heroine of *The Gypsies*, Zemfira, wanders off into the steppe one night and brings home an exiled outsider, Aleko, and thus starts a chain of events that leads to her death. Aleko soon becomes the center of attraction in the poem, for we come to know him better than any of Pushkin's Byronic characters. In the early stanzas the narrator himself furnishes clues to the character of a faceless Aleko. As the tale progresses we learn more about Aleko through his actions and dreams—which sometimes merge. The situation of the hero, i.e., expecting faithful love from a woman as free as the wind, provides enough of a motive for the murder of Zemfira. However, Aleko decides to kill Zemfira at the scene, but only after he overhears her scornful remarks about him.

Zemfira, a dark-eyed beauty, has grown tired of Aleko's confining love. She must be totally free. Not only is she compared to the wind in the poem, her name itself means "wind." These devices are not as subtle as the oblique clues to her personality: her song and her mother's actions. The conflict between Zemfira and Aleko is a microcosmic version of a theme dear to the hearts of the Romantics, the clash between two civilizations—the noble savage and civilized man. To underline the theme, Zemfira's father tells Aleko the story of another isolated exile who cannot adjust to the way of life in his new country; he tells the story of Ovid.

Within the entire narrative there is little action; but more happens in the dreams which sometimes overlap with the story. The ill-defined limits between waking and dreaming contrast to the precision of the poem's language and structure. Symmetries and parallels form the basic pattern of *The Gypsies*. Notice how burial mounds appear at the beginning and end of the poem. The poem also has a cyclical pattern, almost like the moon to which Zemfira is compared; in the beginning Aleko arrives and approaches a crowd, while at the end, the crowd moves away from him.

Pushkin also conveys the idea of movement through the enjambement he uses in the tale. All of this emphasis on movement certainly is appropriate in a poem about a group of people who lead an itinerant life. The meter of *The Gypsies* is the versatile iambic tetrameter and the rhyme scheme varies. Pushkin even retains the meter in the conversations, which sound natural and unstrained. He deviates from iambic tetrameter in Zemfira's song, with its unusual configuration of stressed and unstressed syllables: /∪/ /∪/, a pattern which resembles most the amphimacer of classical poetry. The strong and repeated emphasis on the key words in Zemfira's song leaves no doubt about her feelings.

Perhaps Zemfira's song is overly melodramatic, as are the story and plot of *The Gypsies*. But is spite of the melodrama, Pushkin's style, technique and subtlety more than make up for this. Other characteristically dazzling devices which we see in *The Gypsies* are dreams and catalogues. They also occur in *Ruslan and Lyudmila*, but here they work on a more advanced level. Pushkin will hone these devices to perfection in *Eugene Onegin*, the work towards which *The Gypsies* is advancing.

Evgeny Baratynsky was not as successful in adopting Byronic models to Russian themes as was his contemporary, Pushkin. More a classicist by taste and temperament, Baratynsky could not feel at ease with a genre so alien to his pen. However, he did try to write narrative poems; the result was not entirely felicitous. Baratynsky wrote *Eda,* the most famous of his *poemy*, in 1824. Not well-received by the public or by critics, this extremely romantic poem centers on the trite story of the love of a simple Finnish girl for a "civilized" Russian officer who leaves her in a most predictable manner: his division must go to war. Eda and her lover are typical romantic characters; she is an idealized heroine and he is a cad. However, Baratynsky does portray Eda's father more realistically; the old man is coarse, his speech is elliptical and his actions well-motivated and believable. [32] Also good is the description of Eda's indecisiveness about admitting the young soldier into her bedchamber. The movements of her hand betray the state of her mind. [33]

Baratynsky also uses nature skillfully to parallel Eda's moods. Throughout the poem we see a variation of the pathetic fallacy: when she is sad, nature is dark and bleak. In fact after her lover leaves, Eda's beauty turns lifeless and winter sets in. [34] Another sentimental touch is the description of Eda's grave at the end of the poem.

In spite of the banality of much of the poem, *Eda* is not without merit. The descriptions of the Finnish landscapes are very beautiful and evocative. They offer a contrast to the more predominant eastern scenes we find in the popular Byronic tales. On a more formal level, Baratynsky skillfully manipulates a recurring vocabulary to underline the action and themes of the poetry: destruction, duty and trust. [35] He tells the tale in iambic tetrameter in stanzas of various lengths with no consistent rhyme schemes. Although *Eda* is in no way the best example of Baratynsky's extensive talent and genuine poetic skill, it is a good example of the pervasiveness of Romanticism in Russian culture. Even Baratynsky, a philosophical and predominantly classical poet, felt compelled to write a Romantic verse tale.

The twenties and thirties of the nineteenth century were the heyday of verse tales in Russia. Another poet who wrote them and who is worthy of consideration is Ivan Kozlov (1779-1840). A member of the Moscow gentry, Kozlov was well-acquainted with French, Italian and Polish; he later learned English and German. [36] In 1795 he joined his regiment but disliked military life and transferred to the Civil Service two years later. After serving in Moscow and distinguishing himself in his career, in 1807 he moved to Petersburg, where he began to lead the life of a "cultural dandy." [37] A year later Kozlov met Zhukovsky and began his activity in literary circles. By 1809 he felt financially secure enough to marry. But soon he began to suffer from a disease which gradually led to paralysis and, in 1821, to blindness. In spite of this handicap Kozlov wrote poetry and kept on working in literary spheres. He worked on Delvig's *Northern Flowers*. The poetry of Kozlov's later years was reflective and grew more and more religious. He died on January 30, 1840.

A product of the sentimental age, Kozlov found his inspiration in Zhukovsky, Karamzin, Ossian, Young, Moore and Lamartine. He also looked to Byron for themes and heroes. His most famous verse narrative, *The Monk* (1825), is a reworking of Part Two of Byron's *Giaour,* with Karamzinian touches. [38] In a sentimental setting of mountains, valleys, night, clouds and a solitary monastery perched high on a crag, a Byronic hero "submits to God's will." [39] The introductory setting is effective and sets the proper mood. We are ready to find out the mystery which led the dying monk to the monastery. We hear the conventional tale of a young man who loses the woman and child he loves when she apparently dies in childbirth because she hears of her father's curse. Mad with grief, the youth wanders about until he is "born again" in Christianity. In spite of his new life, the young man kills the old rival who was the initial cause of his flight with his beloved. A vision of his wife fills him with grief and remorse, which drive him to the monastery.

The monk, the young girl and the rival are all stock characters from the Byronic-Romantic tradition. She is an ideal beauty and the rival is a low, villainous antagonist. The monk is a true Byronic hero who suffers pain beyond endurance. A creature of nature, he is happiest in the wilds.

The form of the poem is as conventional as the story. The meter of *The Monk* is iambic tetrameter and the stanzas are of various length with no fixed rhyme scheme. However, Kozlov does make good use of enjambement in sections where he wants to stress movement. [40] *The Monk* may be an unremarkable poem, but its importance lies in its place in the history of Russian poetry. Kozlov's verse tales were an early influence on Mikhail Lermontov. [41]

Lermontov experimented with the verse narrative in poems such as *The Boyar Orsha* (1836), *Mtsyri* (1839) and *Fairy Tale for Children* (1840); and he reached Romantic heights in *The Demon* (1841), his best-known—though not necessarily best—*poema*. Lermontov worked on this poem for many years and reworked it five times. It is written in iambic tetrameter with stanzas of various lengths and no consistent rhyme scheme. [42] Set in Georgia, the poem tells the story of a demon who loves a mortal whose soul belongs to God. Lermontov's protagonist is the Byronic hero in his most extreme form—a suffering outcast who is not merely demonic, but is the demon himself.

Lermontov elicits a sympathetic response from the reader for his hero with the very first word of the poem: melancholy. From that point on Lermontov's narrator describes the Demon as an outcast, an exile from heaven and hell, a creature caught in the endless torment of eternal life without hope or love. Memories of the time when he was an angel plague his isolation, and lack of challenge from men removes the pleasures from temptation. Only vacillation between contempt for creation and desire for love relieve his perpetual boredom.

Once while flying over the mountains of Georgia, the Demon spots Tamara, a beautiful young girl, on the eve of her wedding. The Demon falls in love with her and plots to win her for himself. Tamara's bridegroom is traveling through the mountains and stops to spend the night in a chapel, safe from brigands. But the Demon fills his mind with dreams of Tamara and tempts him to travel through the night. The bridegroom meets his death and Tamara becomes prey for the Demon.

The evil spirit promises to assuage the young girl's grief by filling her eyes with golden dreams, bright dreams. The dreams of light and darkness which the Demon brings to Tamara and the groom are one example of the many instances of conflicts and contrasts in the poem. Throughout the narrative we see the opposing forces of light and dark, day and night, and good and evil struggle for Tamara; we also see them within the Demon himself.

Good and evil also struggle within Tamara, who wants God, yet desires the devil. Lermontov's narrator describes her on the eve of her wedding as a future exile in an alien land. Perhaps here he is establishing a mild connection between her and the Demon—the ultimate exile. But Tamara's exile springs from a joyous cause—her impending marriage. The demon frees her from this exile, but causes one more severe: in order to escape the devil's temptations and because she does not wish to marry, Tamara leaves her family and joins a convent. However, even there the young girl is not safe from the blandishments of the Demon, who claims he wants love and regeneration.

The Demon's speeches to Tamara contain the anguish of his love and desire; they move Tamara to succumb to his temptation. The suffering which causes him to cry and scorch the mountains with a tear flows out sincerely in his words to his beloved. But we see his true nature when the angels carry Tamara's soul to God while the Demon curses his dreams and vents his spite and arrogance in his curses. The internal struggle between good and evil which was carried on in the hearts of Tamara and the Demon now culminates in an archetypal battle between the angels and the spirit of darkness. The angels win and the demon is left as we first found him—again alone, without consolation or love.

In the Demon we see the culmination of the Byronic hero, convinced that only *he* has the power to love Tamara as she deserves and that only *he* suffers with infinite pain. Lermontov conveys the emotional force of the hero not only through characterization, but also through his language. His style, full of formulae and clichés, is emotionally rhetorical. [43] Lermontov's use of such devices as "emotional antitheses, repetition, parallelisms and formulae which exert an influence through their rhythmic-intonational vigor" [44] tends to become artificial, however. This is certainly a flaw in the poem. According to a famous critic of Lermontov, in *The Demon* and *Mtsyri* the poet found "sufficiently vivid and complete expression." [45] But the result was not fortuitous.

> The traditional Russian narrative poem appeared in a new guise—aiming at declamation and decorativeness, emphasizing emotional expressiveness, rhetoric, the "memorability" of lyrical formulae. As a result, the form disintegrated, the genre turned into a schema and the Russian lyrico-epic narrative poem had run its course. [46]

The very elements of stylized rhetoric which make *The Demon* artificial, in the hands of Pushkin, the greatest poet of the era, make *The Bronze Horseman* (1833) a sincere, natural, literary masterpiece. Since Lermontov specifically calls *The Demon* an "Eastern Tale" in the Byronic mode, he must set the poem in some exotic place; and so he sets it in Georgia. He describes only the general features of a landscape which does not become an integral part of the narrative, as does Petersburg in Pushkin's *Bronze Horseman*. [47] In this poem Pushkin also uses stylized rhetorical devices, but they indeed do parallel and enhance the content of the poem.

The *Bronze Horseman*, a Petersburg novella, [48] concerns the fate of a young clerk who blames Peter the Great for the loss of his beloved Parasha in a great flood which washes over the city "built on swamps." The entire poem is based on a pattern of contrasts in stanza and rhyme scheme, diction and vocabulary. As one critic has ably demonstrated, the sections of the poem which deal with Peter use the eighteenth-century ode tradition with formal syntax within quatrains that have an abba rhyme scheme. The other sections which deal with the poor clerk Evgeny and trivial Petersburg activities have irregular rhyme schemes without stanzaic patterns. The tone of these sections is closer to that of Pushkin's *Eugene Onegin*. [49] The contrasting sections of *The Bronze Horseman* are a testament to the skill of Pushkin, who can use iambic tetrameter throughout the poem, but with various effects.

Though Pushkin contrasts Peter and Evgeny, he introduces them in the same way. [50] We first see Peter contemplating the Neva and are privy to his plans of grandeur. Here he plans to build a city, a testament to his and Russia's greatness. When Evgeny first appears on the scene, he goes home to dream of his future simple life with his beloved Parasha. He has no pretensions to greatness. But the consequence of Peter's dream—Petersburg itself—puts an abrupt end to Evgeny's. Because of its location, Petersburg periodically has floods, one of which kills Parasha and hundreds of others.

In Pushkin's hands the flood almost becomes human and cruel. It sweeps over the city like an invading horde and destroys everything in its wake. The flood turns into Evgeny's enemy. When the young clerk sees the ruins of Parasha's home, he goes insane and wanders over the city. Once he shakes his fist in anger at the statue of Peter the Great (the Bronze Horseman) which is located on the banks of the Neva. In a famous passage the statue comes to life and pursues Evgeny around the city; the sounds and quick rhythm of these lines imitate the galloping of the horse as it chases the clerk.

The entire poem is a symphony of sounds which echo the moods of each section. Evgeny's increasing insanity is reflected in the instrumentation which suggests howling. Many "oo" sounds accompany times of sadness while loud, cacophonous sounds herald the storm.

The storm, in some ways, is like Peter—magnificent in power but cruel in its disregard of the people. The narrator of the *Bronze Horseman* has an ambivalent attitude toward the founder of the city. He loves "Peter's creation," but also accuses the tsars of not really caring for their people. Notice the ironic overtones of the sections which describe the way officials hurry to save the tsar during the flood but ignore the common folk. Poor Evgeny wanders many days before he dies at Parasha's gates.

Pushkin wrote *The Bronze Horseman* in 1833, years before Lermontov began to write *The Demon,* in which the genre ran its course. Nevertheless, Pushkin's Petersburg tale is the true masterpiece of the period.[51] *The Bronze Horseman* is the source of several themes in Russian literature: Petersburg as a city where mysterious things happen, the plight of the poor clerk, and ambivalent views of Peter's role in Russian history. Yet in another way this poem looks to the end of the era of Romanticism by debunking one of its most popular myths—that madness is a refuge.

The verse narrative or *poema* is an important genre in the history of Russian literature. It was most popular during the Romantic age but still appears in our time. The *poema* is also important as a transitional form that aided the development of prose genres in Russia. Significantly it was Pushkin and Lermontov who really set the early standards of *excellence* in Russia's prose through serving their apprenticeship writing and perfecting the verse narrative.

Notes

1. Michael Katz, *The Literary Ballad in Early Nineteenth Century Russian Literature* (London: Oxford University Press, 1976), pp. 3-4. I base most of my discussion of the ballad in Russia on this text.

2. Katz, p. 5.

3. Katz, p. 5.

4. Katz, pp. 8-11.

5. Katz, pp. 22-33.

6. Katz, p. 52.

7. Katz, p. 55.

8. Katz, p. 59.

9. Katz, p. 58.

10. Katz, p. 59.

11. G. V. Ermakova-Bitner, "P. A. Katenin," in P. A. Katenin, *Collected Works*, Poet's Library Series (Moscow-Leningrad: Soviet Writer, 1965), pp. 5-57. My discussion of Katenin is based on this introduction to his works.

12. Katz, p. 124.

13. Katz, p. 125.

14. Katz, pp. 126-29.

15. A. Slonimsky, *Masterstvo Pushkina* (Moscow: Khudozhestvennaia literatura, 1959), pp. 194-95.

16. Epic hero of Russian folk tales.

17. Slonimsky, p. 191.

18. Slonimsky, pp. 192-93.

19. Russians differentiate between lyric poems (*stikhotvoreniia*) and narrative tales (*poemy*).

20. John Bayley, *Pushkin. A Comparative Commentary* (Cambridge: Cambridge University Press, 1971), pp. 52-53.

21. Slonimsky, p. 413.

22. Bayley, p. 53.

23. Slonimsky, pp. 425-26.

24. Slonimsky, p. 425.

25. Slonimsky, pp. 427-28.

26. Slonimsky, p. 427.

27. Slonimsky, p. 424; Bayley, pp. 52-53.

28. M. A. Poltoratskaya, *Russian Folklore* (New York: Rausen Language Division, 1964), p. 21.

29. Poltoratskaya, pp. 21-22.

30. B. O. Unbegaun, *Russian Versification* (Oxford: The Clarendon Press, 1963), p. 106.

31. V. M. Zhirmunsky, *Bairon i Pushkin* (Leningrad: Academia, 1924), p. 100. Most of my discussion is based on this source.

32. Benjamin Dees, *Evgeny Baratynsky* (New York: Twayne, 1972), p. 61.

33. Dees, p. 62.

34. Dees, p. 63.

35. Dees, p. 62.

36. G. R. V. Barratt, *Ivan Kozlov: A Study and a Setting* (Toronto: Hakkert, 1972), pp. 19-47 is the source of my information on Kozlov's life. I rely on this text for my brief biography of the poet.

37. Barratt, p. 23.

38. Barratt, p. 140.

39. Barratt, p. 140.

40. Barratt, p. 145.

41. Kozlov wrote two other verse tales, *Princess Natalya Dolgorukaya* and *The Mad Girl*. The form of *The Monk*, with the dying man confessing his adventures before death, resembles Lermontov's *Mtsyri*, in which a young boy makes his confession to the monks who brought him up.

42. The Demon's song in stanza fifteen is written in trochaic tetrameter.

43. B. M. Eikhenbaum, *Lermontov*, tr. Ray Parrott and Harry Weber (Ann Arbor: Ardis, 1981), p. 113.

44. Eikhenbaum, p. 114.

45. Eikhenbaum, p. 117.

46. Eikhenbaum, p. 117.

47. Eikhenbaum, p. 109.

48. Pushkin's subtitle calls the poem a "*Peterburgskaya povest*," thus linking it to the Romantic tradition of mixing genres and to the growing popularity and development of prose in Russia in the early nineteenth century.

49. Walter Vickery, "*Mednij vsadnik* and the 18th Century Heroic Ode," *Indiana Slavic Studies*, No. 3 (1963), pp. 140-42.

50. Notice also how only poor fishermen are on the river at the beginning and end of the poem.

51. Only after Pushkin's death did the entire poem appear in print in *The Contemporary* in 1837.

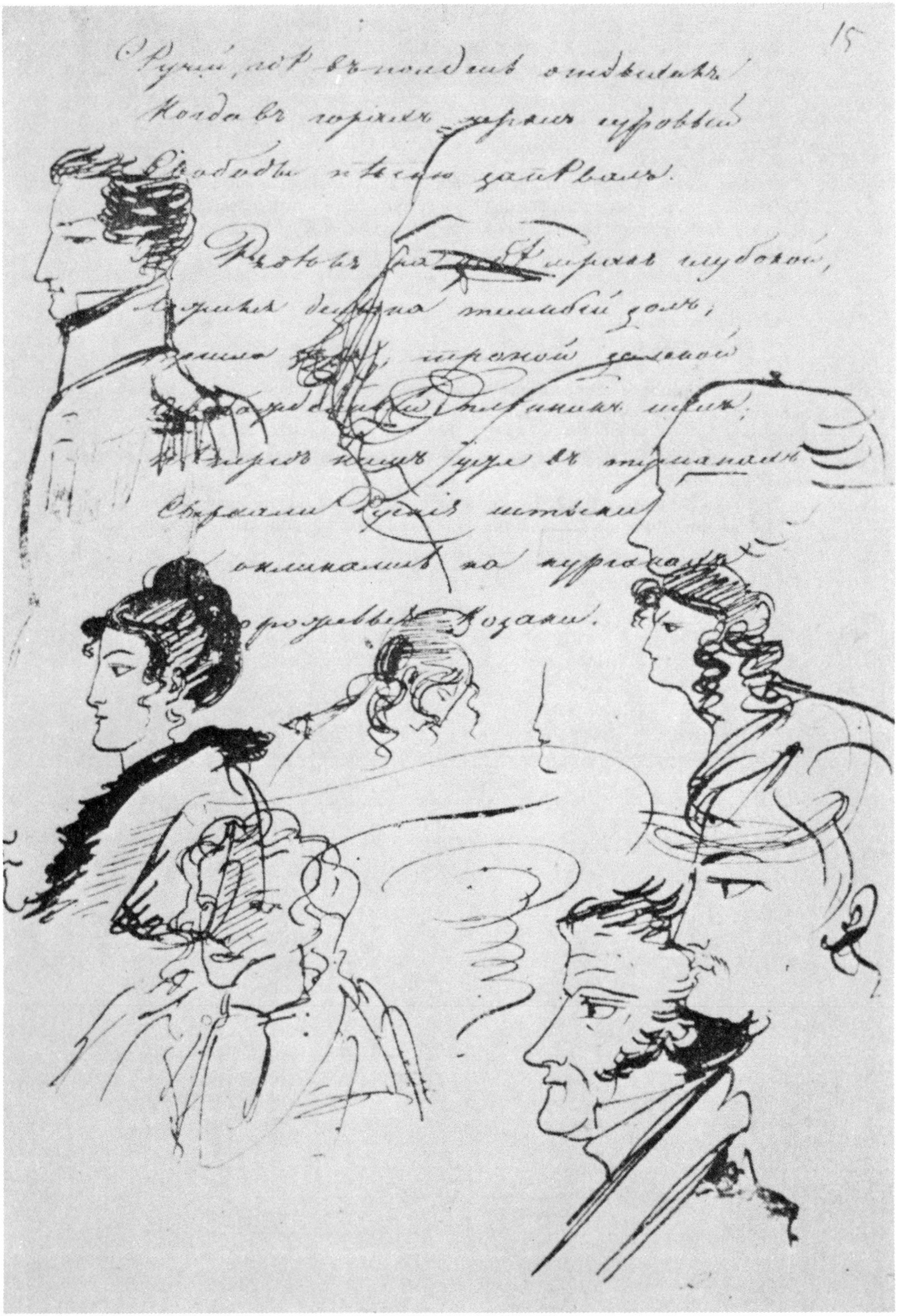
15

BALLADS AND VERSE NARRATIVES

V. A. ZHUKOVSKY

Svetlana

To A. A. Voeykova

Once on Twelfth Night
   Girls were telling fortunes:
They removed their shoes from their feet
   And threw them over the gates;
They raked the snow;[1] they listened
   Under the window; they fed
A chicken a certain number of pieces of grain;
   They put hot wax in water;
They put a gold ring
And emerald earrings
   Into a glass of pure water;
They laid out a white kerchief
And over a cup they sang
   Ritual songs in harmony.

The moon shines dimly
   In the hazy mist—
Dear Svetlana
   Is quiet and sad.
"Little friend, what's wrong with you?
   Say something;
Listen to the round-song;
   Pull out a little ring for yourself.
Sing, my beauty: 'Smithy,
Forge me a new golden crown,
   Forge me a golden ring;
I'll be married with this crown,
I'll become engaged with this ring
   In front of the holy lectern.' "

"How can I sing, my dear little friends?
   My darling sweetheart is far away;
It's my lot to die
   In solitary grief.
A year has gone by—there's no news;
   He doesn't write to me;
Ah! but the world is beautiful only because of him,
   My heart beats only because of him . . .
Or don't you ever think about me?
Where are you, in what country?
   Where is your home?
I pray and shed tears!
Alleviate my sorrow,
   Comforting angel."

Here in the *svetlitsa*[2] a table is covered
   With a white shroud;
And a mirror and candle
   Are on this table;
Two place settings are on the table.
   "Tell your fortune, Svetlana;
At midnight, without any lies,
   You'll find out what your lot will be.
When you look into the pure glass of the mirror,
Your sweetheart will knock at the door
   With a light hand;
The bolt will fall from the door;
He will sit at his place
   To sup with you."

There's the beauty all alone;
   She sits down at the mirror;
With hidden shyness she
   Looks into the mirror:
It's dark in the mirror; deathly
   Silence is all around;
In a quivering flame the candle
   Barely pours out its radiance;
Fear makes her breast tremble,
She's scared to look behind her,
   Fear clouds her eyes . . .
The little flame crackles,
And a cricket, the midnight messenger,
   Dolorously cried out.

Propped up on her elbow,
   Svetlana is barely breathing . . .
There . . . someone knocked lightly
   With the lock—she listens;
Timidly, she looks into the mirror:
   It seemed as if someone's bright
Eyes were gleaming
   Behind her shoulders . . .
Fear took her breath away . . .
Suddenly a sound reaches her—
   A quiet, light whisper:
"I am with you, my beauty;
The heavens have been tamed,
   Your murmur has been heard!"

She looked back . . . her sweetheart
   Stretched his arms out to her.
"My joy, light of my eyes,
   For us there will be no more separation.
Let us ride! The priest is already waiting in the church
   With the deacons and deaconesses;

The choir is singing a wedding song;
    The church glows in candlelight."
A sweet look was her answer;
They go to the wide courtyard,
    To the wooden gates;
Their sleigh awaits them near the gates;
The horses are impatiently tearing away
    Their silken bridles.

They got in . . . All the horses took off at once;
    Their nostrils give off smoke;
A blizzard rose up from their hooves
    Over the sleigh.
They gallop . . .everything is deserted all around;
    Svetlana sees the steppe,
The moon is a misty circle;
    The glades barely shine.
Her prophetic heart trembles;
The maid timidly says:
    "Why have you grown silent, my darling?"
With not even a word does he answer her:
He looks at the moonlight
    Pale and despondent.

The horses hurry along the knolls;
    They trample the deep snow . . .
There, off to the side, the lonely
    Temple of God is visible;
A whirlwind opened the doors;
    A crowd of people are in the church;
The bright light of the chandeliers
    Grows dim from the incense;
A black coffin is in the middle;
And the priest drawls out:
    "Be taken by the grave!"
More than ever the maiden trembles;
The horses go by; her sweetheart is silent,
    Pale and despondent.

Suddenly they were surrounded by a snowstorm;
    The snow is falling heavily in tufts;
A black raven, with wings whistling,
    Hovers over the sleigh;
The raven caws: *grief*!
    The hurried horses
Keenly look into the dark distance,
    While lifting their manes;
A little flame glimmers in the field;
A quiet little corner was visible,
    A little hut buried under the snow.

The swift steeds hurried off even faster,
Ploughing up the snow while running
    Right up to it, all of them together.
They went tearing along . . .and in a flash
    They disappeared from view:

It was as if the horses, sled and
    Bridegroom never existed at all.
All alone, in the dark,
    Abandoned by her sweetheart,
The young maid is in a terrible spot;
    A storm, a blizzard surrounds her.
She can't turn back—there are no traces . . .
She sees a light in the cottage:
    Here she crosses herself;
While saying a prayer she knocks at the door . . .
The door shakes . . .it squeaks . . .
    And opens quietly.

What's this? . . There's a coffin in the cottage;
    It's covered with a white linen cloth;
The Savior's face shows at its foot;
    A small candle burns before the icon . . .
Ah! Svetlana, what's wrong with you?
    In whose dwelling place did you find yourself?
The mute inhabitant of the empty
    Hut was dreadful.
She enters all atremble, all in tears;
She fell into the dust before the icon,
    And prayed to the Savior.
And with a cross in her hand,
Under the saints in the corner[3]
    She hid timidly.

Everything grew still . . .no more blizzard . . .
    The candle smolders weakly.
Sometimes it sheds a trembling light,
    Sometimes it darkens . . .
Everything is in a deep dead sleep,
    A dreadful silence . . .
Hark, Svetlana! . . There is a
Light murmur in the silence.
Then she looks: a bright-eyed dove,
White as snow,
    Quietly fluttering,
Flew to her in the corner;
It quietly settled on her breast
    And embraced her with its wings.

Again it's quiet all around . . .
    Then it seems to Svetlana
That under the white linen
    The corpse is stirring . . .
The pall fell away; the corpse
    (His face is gloomier than the night)
Is now completely visible—he has a wreath upon his
                      brow
    His eyes are shut.
Suddenly . . .his closed lips groan;
He tries to slide
    His cold hands apart . . .
But how's the young maid? . . She is trembling . . .

Her end is near...but
    The little white dove is not sleeping.

It roused itself, it unfolded
    Its light wings;
It flew off to the corpse's chest...
    Deprived of all of his strength,
He groaned and then began
    To gnash his teeth dreadfully
And began to shine his terrible eyes
    Upon the young maid...
Again his lips were pale;
And his eyes rolled back to reveal their white sides,
    Death was depicted...
Look, Svetlana...O Creator!
The corpse is her dear sweetheart!
    Ah!.. then she woke up.

Where am I?.. She's all alone
    In the *svetlitsa* near the mirror;
The light of dawn is shining
    Through the thin curtains of the window;
A noisy rooster is beating its wings,
    Meeting the day with its song;
Everything sparkles...Svetlana's spirit
    Is troubled by the dream.
"Ah! What a horrible, terrible dream!
It bodes no good—
    Only a bitter fate;
Secret gloom of days to come,
What do you promise my soul,
    Joy or grief?"

Svetlana sat down near the window
    (Her breast ached terribly);
From the window the wide road
    Is visible through the mist;
The snow gleams under the sun,
    A fine steam grows crimson...
Hark!.. a resonant bell
    Thunders in the empty distance;
Snowy powder lies on the road;
Zealous horses and a sleigh
    Are rushing along, as if on wings;
Closer; look, they're already at the gates;
A stately guest goes to the porch...
    Who? Svetlana's fiancé.

Svetlana, then was your dream
    A prophet of torment?
Your sweetheart is with you; he's still the same
    After the test of separation;
The very same love is in his eyes,
    As are the very same pleasant glances;
The very same dear speeches
    Are on his sweet lips.

Open up, temple of God;
Loyal vows,
    You fly up to the heavens;
Gather, young and old;
After you clink your ringing cups, sing
    In harmony: many years to them!

My beauty, smile
    Upon my ballad;
There are many marvels in it
    But very little sense.
Your gaze makes me happy,
    And I don't want glory;
They taught us that glory is smoke;
    The world is a sly judge.
Here's the meaning of my ballad:
"Our best friend in this life
    Is faith in God's providence.
The law of the Creator is good:
Here unhappines is a false dream;
    Happiness is the awakening."

Oh, you, my Svetlana,
    Don't be aware of these dreadful dreams...
Creator, may you be her shelter!
    Don't let the wound of sorrow
Or the shadow of passing sadness
    Ever concern her;
Her soul is like a clear day;
Ah! let the hand of calamity
Rush right past her;
May her whole life be as bright
    As the pleasant lustre
Of a little stream in the lap of a meadow;
May all the gaiety that was hers in the past
    Be the friend of her days.

1808-12

Notes

1. Zhukovsky lists several ways that the girls told fortunes.
2. A small bright room in the upper portion of a house.
3. Every house had a special corner set aside where icons hung. People burned candles in front of them. Here Svetlana takes refuge.

P. A. KATENIN

The Murderer

In the village of Zazhitnoe there is a wide courtyard,
    A wooden hut, with
A *svetlitsa*, a high tower, and
    A whitewashed chimney.

This rich house does not lack anything;
    Neither bread nor wine,
Neither soft, patterned, decrepit furniture,
    Nor a treasury of gold.

The owner, the *starosta*[1] of the area,
    Was born an orphan,
Without kith or kin or friends,
    But only with poverty.

And the stout lad would have lived with it forever,
    Had not a peasant taken pity on him:
The old man took him home and raised him
    Like his very own son.

A major road goes through the village;
    He kept an inn,
And with God's help
    His profits grew quickly.

But how can you save yourself from evil people?
    It's a misfortune to be poor;
It's even worse to be rich, always on guard
    Against more bitter injury.

Once, toward evening,
    Some merchants came to spend the night,
And harnessed their cart
    To go off early in the morning.

They argued about the bill for awhile,
    And then they took off from the courtyard;
But this time the landlord himself
    Lay strangled on the *sleeping shelf*.[2]

An alarm went up in the house; with some witnesses
    They caught up with them, and found
That they had taken the landlord's belongings
    Along with their own.

They didn't say a word in their own defense,
    And for their punishment,
The criminal court sent them to Siberia
    To work the copper mines.

But meanwhile, they prayed for him and committed
    The old man to the grave forever;
Along with the property, his stepson
    Received the rank of *starosta* in the village.

But what are ranks, money, glory,
    When your soul aches?
Then neither honors, nor amusements,
    Nor life itself are good.

Thus he struggled with all the strength he had
    For almost ten years;
Neither his wife nor his children were dear to him;
    The whole wide world grew hateful.

He wanders alone in the forest all day long,
    He avoids meeting anyone,
And all night long he doesn't tear his eyes away
    From the window, and constantly looks through it.

Especially when a hot day
    Dies out into a clear night
And a bright moon shines in the sky—
    Then he doesn't give up for a minute.

Everyone is asleep; but he alone sits down
    Near the window sill.
First he starts to laugh, then he gets embarrassed
    And looks at the moon.

His wife has noticed his habits
    And she became frightened of her husband,
But she doesn't understand what puzzles him
    And asks that he explain.

"Master, why don't you sleep at night?
    Or is the night too long for you?
And why do your eyes stare at the moon
    As if it were an enemy?"

    "Be quiet, wife, it isn't a woman's affair
        To know all of a man's secrets:
It would be considered daring to tell you;
        You couldn't bear not to chatter it about."

    "Ah, no! as God is my witness,
        I won't say even the tiniest word;
Only tell me everything, my benefactor,
        From the beginning to the end."

    "Let it be then—I'll tell you and come what may;
        You remember the old man;
Although suspicion fell on the merchants,
        I was the one to get the old fool off my hands."

"How could it have been you!"—"Just this way: it
                    was in summer,
I remember, just like now.
Not long before sunrise;
        The door stood open.

I went into the hut, the old man
        Was sleeping soundly on the shelf;
I put the noose on him, but at the wrong moment,
        I touched him with the knot.

The old fool woke up and saw that it was bad!
        No one else was in the house.
'Since it does not astonish you to kill me,
        Then strangle me.

But mark my words: a villain
        Will not forever be cheated of his punishment;
There is a witness out there; he sees even
        When no people are about.'

He said that and pointed through the window,
        I jerked up with all my strength.
I frightened myself a bit with the thought
        That he was threatening me with someone.

I glanced out, but only the infernal
        Moon was looking at me.
And it hasn't stopped—and it's been
        Ten years since that day.

But enough now! Aren't you silent, bold one!
        I don't fear you thus;
Stare like a barn owl, and grin with rat's teeth,
        Just keep it to yourself."

At this point the *starosta* again looked
        At the moon with an ironic smile;
Then, not saying a word,
        He lay down and fell asleep.

But his wife doesn't sleep: her fear and conscience
        Don't give her any peace.
She takes her frightful tale to the judges,
        And they send for the murderer.

He contradicted himself out of fear.
        But this was God's work,
And, not able to bear up under the punishment,
        He died trying to carry it out.

God's punishment scours about after a villain;
        Let him deceive the people,
But God will seek out the guilty one—
        That's the moral of my song.

Notes

1. Village elder.
2. A broad sleeping berth near the ceiling.

Olga
(From Bürger)

A tearful dream disturbed Olga,
A vague progression of evil dreams:
"Beloved sweetheart, have you deceived me?
Or are you no longer among the living?"
Sharing the glory of Peter's army,
He went with it to Poltava;
But he doesn't write even a word or two:
Is he still alive and healthy.

The Swedes fell in battle,
The Turk was beaten without a fight,
And the desired fruit of victory—
Peace—was brought back to Russia;
And to the sound of bells,
With wreaths, songs, tambourines,
And trumpets, the host returned to Russia
To rest from all their labors.

And a mob of people were all about;
The old, the young—everyone is running
To see how the conquerors
Are returning from their campaign;
Everyone came to meet them on the road;
They cry out: "Hello! Praise God!"
Ah! but only Olga's greeting
Gets no response from anyone.

She searches, she asks; it's bad:
There hasn't been any word of him for a long time;
They don't know whether he is alive or not; it's a wonder!
It's as if he disappeared without a trace.
Right here, after dissolving in tears,
She beats her breast;
And after she prostrates herself on the damp ground,
She tears at the black curls on her brow.

Her mother hurriedly rushed towards her:
"What are you doing? What's wrong with you, my light?
Can your sorrow really be inconsolable?
Is God not with us?"
"Ah, my own, everything is lost;
There is no more joy in the world.
God himself has offended me:
Only sorrow, sorrow is left for poor us!"

"It's God's will! The Creator is
Our helper in all things.
He is the bearer of joys and blessings;
Pray to him, my light."
"Ah, my dear, everything is empty;
God has sent me evil sorrow,
God has no pity on our requests.
Only sorrow, sorrow is left for poor us!"

"Listen, daughter! in the distant Ukraine,
Perhaps your fiancé
Has already circled the wedding lectern
With another beautiful maiden.
What is the loss of a traitor?
Sooner or later—he will pay,
For he will never escape
Divine judgment."

"Ah, my dear, everything is lost,
There is no hope—not even a trace;
There is no more joy in this world;
What's the wide world to me if I'm all alone?
It's worse than the grave, it's worse than hell.
Death is the only . . . the only consolation;
God has no pity on our tears:
Only sorrow, sorrow is left for poor us!"

"O Lord! forgive this unfortunate creature,
Don't judge a madwoman;
Lead to repentance
A mind that isn't privy to her words.
Daughter, don't be excessively sad,
Fear suffering, recall your faith:
A stranger to sin will find
A heavenly bridegroom."

"Where, then, my dear, is torture more vicious?
Or where is the limit to suffering?
It's hell for me when I am separated from my betrothed;
When I'm with him—it's paradise for me everywhere.
I fear neither death nor hell.
Death alone is my only comfort.
When I'm away from my sweet one, the world is
                                        unbearable.
There is no bliss anywhere."

Thus she sobbed all day,
She cursed divine Providence,
She wrung her white hands,
She tore at her black hair;
And the clear sky grew dark,
The red sun set,
Everything settled down peacefully,
The bright stars lit up.

But the maiden cries bitterly,
Tears are rolling down her face;
And suddenly someone gallops along the field,
Someone, a rider, dismounts near the porch;
Hark! it grows noisy beyond the door,
Hark! its knocker begins to sound out;
And a familiar voice suddenly
Calls out to Olga: "Arise, my darling!

Open up quickly and noiselessly.
My sweet, are you sleeping in the dark?
Are you thinking tearful thoughts?
Do you have laughter or sorrow on your mind?"
"My sweet one! it's you! how late at night it is!
I cried my eyes out
Over you with bitter tears.
How did God bring you to us?"

"We gallop in the fields only at night.
I came for you from the Ukraine;
I left there late
To take you with me."
"Ah, come in, my darling!
A cold wind whistles in the fields;
You will warm yourself, my bridegroom,
Here in my embraces!"

"Let it whistle, let it heave,
Let it do what it wants, it's time for us to go.
My raven-hued steed is seething for flight,
I must not await the morning here.
Get up, come on, sit behind me,
My raven-hued steed will take us there in no time;
We still have a hundred versts to go: it's time
To be off to our nuptial couch."

"Ah, what a road at night!
And we have to ride a hundred versts!
The clock is striking . . . fear God:
It's only half-an-hour 'til midnight."
"The moon is shining, it's good for riding;
I soon will ride as a corpse:
Before morning I'll get you
Right to our nuptial couch."

"How do you live? tell me honestly;
What is your house like? big? tall?"
"My house is a dug-out." "How is it inside?" "Crowded."
"And our bed?" "It's made of six boards."
"Will your bride settle down in it?"
"There's enough room for the two of us.
Get up, come up and sit behind me:
Guests are waiting for me and my bride."

Olga got up, went out, and sat
Behind her groom on the horse;

She wrapped her white arms
All around his body.
The rider and the maiden rush along,
Like an arrow, like a sling, like a bird;
The steed runs, the earth shakes,
Sparks beat out from under its hooves.

On the left, on the right, on all sides
Dry land and water fly behind
Them, past their eyes; under the horse's
Hooves, bridges thunder.
"The moon is shining, it's good for riding
I soon will ride as a corpse.
Are you afraid, my little light, to sleep with a corpse?"
"No . . . why make mention of the dead?"

What are those sounds? What is that singing?
What is that raven's cry in the gloom?
A sad ringing! a burial!
"We give the body over to the earth."
Up closer, they see a priest with his congregation
Carrying a coffin, the whole choir is singing.
The approach is slow, heavy,
The song is incoherent and wild.

"Why are you howling out of place?
The time for burial will come;
I am bringing my bride for her wedding crown,
Everyone follow me there!
Near the bed in which I sleep,
Clergy! sing the wedding verses to me;
Priests! show up for work and
Bless us for sleep."

They grew silent, the coffin disappeared,
Suddenly everyone obeyed his words,
And everyone ran quickly
After them, right in their tracks.
The rider and the maiden rush along,
Like an arrow, like a sling, like a bird;
The steed runs, the earth shakes,
The sparks beat out from under its hooves.

To the right, to the left, on all sides,
Mountains, dales and fields—
Everything flies behind them; under the horse's
Hooves the earth runs.
"The moon is shining, it's good for riding,
I soon will ride as a corpse.
Are you afraid, my little light, to sleep with a corpse?"
"Enough of making mention of the dead!"

An execution pillar: above them beyond the clouds
The moon glimmers timidly.
The dance of someone's dirty scum
Is visible all around.

"Who's there! scum! get behind me!
Run behind me with the crowd,
So that to the sounds of your dancing, I,
More joyfully will lie down next to my wife."

Singing a plaintive song, the scum
Tear after the rider,
Just like a gusting whirlwind
Which started to make noise in a damp pine forest.
The rider and the maiden rush along,
Like an arrow, like a sling, like a bird;
The steed runs on, the earth shakes,
Sparks beat out from under its hooves.

To the right, to the left, on all sides
Meadows and forests fly behind them;
Everything flashes before their eyes:
Stars, clouds and skies.
"The moon is shining, it's good for riding;
I soon will ride as a corpse.
Are you afraid, my little light, to sleep with a corpse?"
"Ah! why do you mention the dead!"

"Steed of mine! the cocks have begun to sing.
Be careful that the sun not rise,
That the mountain tops not begin to whiten.
Rush along like an arrow shot from a bow.
Our long trip is ended, ended.
The nuptial couch is ready.
I rode as quickly as a corpse,
And finally arrived."

Violently straining, the steed
Galloped at the stone fence;
With the crack of a whip
The hinges and lock suddenly fell from the door.
The steed went to the fence; a cemetery was there,
The eternal dwelling place of the dead;
The gravestones shone
In the pale rays of the moon.

Just for a second what does Olga
See before her? a marvel! fright!
Like ashes, the rider's armor
Completely crumbles into dust;
Head, face, hands, body—
All turns deathly pale on her sweetheart.
And he already stands with a scythe,
A frightful, skeletal frame of bones.

The raven-hued steed reared on its hind legs,
Began to neigh in a wild voice,
He struck the earth, fell down,
And the bridegroom disappeared.
A wailing sound rose high into the ether;
There was gnashing deep beneath the earth;

Olga, frightened, mindless,
Was immobile and silent.

Here infernal spirits danced over
The dead girl by the light of the moon:
And hummed to her in a drawling manner
In the aerial heights:
"Don't go to God's judgment seditiously;
Bear the sorrow, even if it pains the heart.
You were punished in the flesh;
May God forgive your sinful soul."

1816, 1831

I. I. KOZLOV

The Monk
A Kievan Tale

Beautiful friend of bright days gone by,
Trusty friend of days both gloomy and grim,
The cause of all my thoughts, both sad and happy,
My wife and mother of my children!
Here is my song, whose sad sound
In times of nocturnal insomnia used to
Captivate me and trouble my soul
With a certain unseen force.
O, how many times I cried over the strings
When I sang of the suffering of the Monk,
And of the sorrow of his soul, deceived by dreams,
And of the blaze of passions stirring hearts!
My soul grew to know his soul:
I wandered with him in the darkness of strange forests;
From his native Dniepr shores
A familiar melancholy came over me.
Perhaps it would be so sweet for me not to dream;
Perhaps it would be so harmonious for me not to sing!—
Like my Monk, I have long since buried
All my youthful passions in my breast;
And like him, I have substituted
All earthly joys with celestial hope.
It's not for me to see the day with golden sunsets,
Or the roses of spring, or the faces dear to my heart!
Already in the prime of my life, I am, among the living,
Like a cold shade come from indifferent tombs.
But troubled by that heavy shadow, I direct
A restless swarm of tender thoughts
To the two children whom you cherish
And to you, almost dearer to me than they.
I live in you,—and my dream is sweet!

My fascination is always with me.
So in the dark night a flower, the beauty of the fields,
Pours out its fragrance, invisible to the eye.

17 September 1824
St. Petersburg

I

Beyond Kiev, where the wide Dniepr
Seethes and roars in its steep banks,
Near a grove on a high hill
There stands a cloister of monks;
A battlement encircles it,
With four towers at the corners
And in the middle is God's temple
With its gilded domes;
A row of cells, a dark passage,
A chapel at the holy gates
With a miracle-working icon within,
And off to the side a spring of very cold water
Murmurs like a healing stream
Under the shade of an ancient linden tree.

II

There is an evening gloom in the misty field;
The sunset is already fading in the heavens;
No song is heard in the meadows;
No herds are seen any more in the valleys;
No horn begins to sound in the forest,
No one goes by,—only occasionally
A small bell just barely rings out
Along the high road;
And on the Dniepr there already are no more lights
On the boats of the fishermen;
The midnight moon has ascended
And the bright stars burn;
Glades, groves, waters sleep;
On the tower the appointed hour has struck;
The cloister is deep in sleep;
All around there is peace and quiet.
In a distant cell the light of an icon lamp
Barely shines; and in this cell
A Monk, a young sufferer,
Is ending his dreary days.
Losses, passions and grief
Have traced their horrible mark
On his sullen brow;
There is a storm in the depths of his heart,
His fate is covered by darkness:
No one knows from where he comes
Or who he is. But, at odds with himself,
A fateful secret torments him.
He arrived one night during a storm;

Since that time he has remained in the cloister,
He mournfully led the life of the Monks,
He shunned everyone, he hid from everyone,
His odd appearance frightened everyone,
The Monk did not speak with anyone,
But in the depths of his sad soul
Something horrible was noticeable.
At the solemn hour of prayer
He also sang a song of praise . . .
But often howls of painful torment
Broke into the holy sounds!
In the dark of night
He never could find peace in his cell,
And in his long robe,
Like an apparition, he would wander among the graves;
Now immobile, he awaits the end:
An ailment tortures the Monk.

III

With a look of tender emotion, the Father Superior
Holds the cross of salvation before him,—
And he who is suffering painfully sighs:
He turned, he trembled,
Twice he quietly raised himself slightly,
Twice he tried to begin to speak;
It seemed that he was afraid
To recall a certain terrible dream,
And timidly he looked around queerly.
Monk, Monk, do you really
Still remember those former dreams! . .
But he overcame the fear of the grave,
His fading strength caught fire;
He grabbed the elder by the hand
And this is what the sufferer said:

IV

"Father, among you I am a sullen stranger,
Perhaps I disturbed your salutary
Meditations and the peace of
The holy cloister with my melancholy.
Here is my secret: in the spring of my days
I already knew all the grief of life;
I grew up as a homeless orphan,
I never saw any familial caresses;
The joys of childhood flew by,
Scarcely touching me:
When children my age were playing,
I was already sunk in thought;
A pure and beautiful flame
Burned in vain in my youthful breast:
I had no one to love!
Alas! Fearing the cold disdain
Of unfriendly people,
I had to hide

The agitation of a passionate heart,
And the first ardor of my soul;
My youth blossomed sadly,
I looked at the world shyly,
I did not know what joy was;
From the very years of adolescence,
Not sharing love with anyone,
I lived unsociably in silence,—
And a severe, simple life
Seemed comforting to me.
I loved to wander among the forests,
To chase after beasts all day,
To swim across the wide Dniepr;
I loved to play with danger,
To laugh impudently at life,—
I had nothing to lose,
I had no one with whom to part.

V

But soon from the shores of the Neva
A soldier all covered with gray hair
Came to live out his days among us,
Under the shade of native oaks.
He lived in his own village with his wife,
And with them lived a seventeen-year-old daughter . . .
O elder! the coffin is before me . . .
The light of God darkens before my eyes! . .
She had not been in this world for very long . . .
But I still live through her alone . . .
She alone is in my dreams
Both on earth and in the heavens! . .
Holy father, it's no use for you
To know all about her now,
I do not want to name her! . .
Just pray for the unfortunate soul!
Fate brought us together by chance;
Her beauty captivated me;
She gave her heart to me,—
And her mother and father betrothed us.
The garlanded marriage lectern awaited us;
All of my former grief was now forgotten,—
And marvelling in loving rapture,
I blessed the Creator.
Was it so long ago that, mournfully withering away,
My young life was a burden to me?
Was it so long ago that, crushed by cold melancholy,
My soul languished?
And suddenly heaven gave me the chance
To live, to feel completely,
To cry sweet tears,
And to see joy never dreamed of!
With what holy innocence,
Through her ardent soul,
She poured bliss onto me!
And what mortal under the moon

Could love her as much as I?
My dream came true in her;
The whole secret world of my soul—
And I, the creation of her love,
I came to life again through love for her!

VI

But again fate became embittered;
Again I was doomed to misfortune.
Somehow, suddenly, to our ruin,
A distant relative appeared;
He was a cornet in the Polish army;
A villain, he betrayed honor.
First he himself insidiously flattered her
In order to enter into a marriage with her;
He wanted to rob, to oppress—
He was contemptible, and with a smile of reconciliation
He sought only revenge.
O my father! sincere ardor
Is an exalted gift of the blessed heavens;
No, a sacred flame does not burn
In a soul clouded by vice.
Stars are not visible in a misty haze:
Love is a holy thing on earth
For him who loves!.. Ah, but separation
From our own dear mother
Was decreed by fate!
She was unexpectedly struck down
By a painful ailment ... We sobbed,
We surrounded her death-bed with prayers;
The inevitable hour came:
Our own dear one was passing away from us.
It is still now before my eyes,
As it was on the dreadful night of separation;
With the tears of warmest faith
The earthly mother blessed
Her sobbing daughter
And, having taken the holy face
Of the pure maiden into her trembling hands,
Turned her over to her heavenly mother.
With the demise of the mother, the villain
Began to seek revenge more boldly;
He slandered; with a malicious trick
He conquered the weak soul—
And the old man went back on his word:
The long-wished-for marriage was nullified.
Deceived by low slander,
He thought, the merciless father,
That he could tear asunder
The bonds of ardent hearts; and the young daughter,
Embracing his knees,
Poured out a flood of tears in vain;
But neither their wrath, nor threats,
Nor vengeance scared me;
I despised the villain, carried off the daughter,
And secretly married her.

VII

Perhaps you, holy father,
Accuse me of impudence;
But, just elder, you do not know,
You have not known fateful passion.
You see the trembling of my heart,
And the deathly cold, and my hot breath,
And my pale face, and my dull gaze,
My madness, my shame,
And sin, and blood—here is a passionate flame!
Here is the horrible trace of my love!
But let my fate be still more terrible:
She was ...she was mine!
O, how we shared our life together!
Comforted by our fortune, and
Finding within ourselves the whole world,
How ardently we loved one another!
She was dear when she was vividly tender,
In pensive melancholy she was even more dear;
To my joy, she blossomed;
With her my soul was brighter.
A year swept by like a charming dream.
I knew that I would soon be a father;
We dreamed sweetly of the future
And together we got our hopes up
That our angry parent would forgive us.
But avid spite does not sleep:
At a dangerous time the news reached us
That all of our hopes were taken away,
And that the daughter was already cursed by
                                        her father ...
The horrible deceit succeeded—
The villain killed the unfortunate girl:
I buried the mother with our infant.
And I...the cause of it all!...Stood—alive!
Over that grave, where my son lay
With my dear sweetheart ...
Holy father!
What happened with me afterwards—
I do not know: suddenly my reason
Was clouded over by some kind of darkness;
I only remember that day and night
I wandered about the high road, I
Fell; when I came to
I was lying in a squalid hut.
I had no sense of my misfortune, no strength;
I got through life by suffering,
And the agitation in my heart died away;
My languid face showed
Not sorrow, but fear and astonishment;
All of the past slumbered in my soul;
But by chance my wedding ring
Flashed into my eyes ...
. . . .

VIII

I abandoned our deserted land;
Alone, in despair, in tears,
With an orphaned soul, I rambled
In distant thickets and forests.
For seven years gloomy gorges and
Mountains listened to
My wailing, my howling and my reproaches.
Sullen, sorrowful, wild,
I tormented myself with my former dream;
I sobbed for what was gone.
Nocturnal shadows, mountain torrents,
The whistle of a storm, the wailing of the winds
Secretly became one with my black meditation,
With my unquenchable melancholy;
And grief became an enjoyment,
A holy relic of former days;
It seemed to me that through my torment
I was not completely parted from her.

IX

Where the heart loves, there it suffers,
And our merciful God is there:
He gives us a cross, but in that cross
Sends us hope.
After seven difficult, terrible years
A comforting light flashed before me.
Once during the night, I
Was sitting sadly over a river;
And the starry-fiery firmament of the sky,
And the quiet shimmering of the moon,
And the murmur of the leaves, and the lapping
Of the waters made silver by the moon—
All involuntarily captivated my soul.
Everything in this world of bliss enthralled me
With its secret beauty.
My shattered spirit awoke:
'Creator of all things! My infant
With my unforgettable darling
Live in your holy land;
And perhaps I will be with them,
And there they will be mine forever!..'
The miracles of love were understood:
My heart trembled with hope,
With some secret anticipation;
I lifted my face to the heavens,
I dared to question them with my tears ...
And I perceived that this serene ocean
With its imperishable stars
Was given to me as an answer.
Since then, my father, I have found
Consolation in my calamity,
And I hoped to gain union with her
In suffering through this painful cross.

As before, I still shed tears,
But their hope delights me,
And quiet sorrow has replaced
My severe grief.
Burning with faith, I forgot
My misfortune and the villain:
With the infant in heaven she appeared
To my heart in heavenly dreams.
I raised my soul to her—
And my thoughts were filled with only one thing:
I wished to be as pure as she,
And part joyfully with life;
But I wanted to die
In my native land.
I began to pine in foreign hills;
I wanted to have a final glance
At our graves, our valleys,
I wanted to see the land, imbued with her presence,

And our little country home, and garden.
And the dark blue waves of the Dniepr,
And the church on the hill, where their dear
Ashes sleep in the shade of the birches,
And see how the sunset blazes
Over their quiet grave.

X

Ah, what happened with my soul,
When in its holy beauty
The face of my native Kievan fields
Suddenly opened up before me.
As before, they were growing green,
The waves of the Dniepr resounded just the same,
The very same forest still grew dark in the distance,
They were singing the very same songs over the
                                    stubble of the fields,
And everything was just the same in my native land,
Except that she alone was not there!
Everywhere there were familiar valleys,
Streams, knolls and plains
In charming, dear silence.
From all sides they appeared to me
Along with my bright years;
But I, a stranger in my own country,
Greeted them with tears,
Dismal melancholy
And a poisoned soul.
I walked; day yielded to evening;
And soon the village temple of God
Appeared before my frightened eyes;
Beside myself I went nearer
To that grave where my son, my wife ...
My whole life was buried.
I stepped lightly, as if I feared
To interrupt their eternal sleep.

I stopped a painful moan in my breast
So that I would not disturb their peace.
My sad spirit did not dare to give in to
Its troubled passions.
It seemed to me that over their grave
I breathed in holy air.
Something marvelous happened to me,
And with unearthly hope
I quietly bent my knee,
Prayed, cried and loved . . .
Suddenly I heard a rustle beyond the bushes;
I look, and what face meets mine?
A reaper with his young sweetheart
And a cart laid over with sheaves;
And I see that among the sheaves
There sits an infant with crimson cheeks,
Wearing a garland of cornflowers.
Involuntarily I trembled:
'I had it all, I lost it all,
We were not allowed to live for each other.
My dear darling is in the damp earth,
And my infant is not wearing flowers—
Worms in the grave are eating him away.'
In tears I unconsciously threw
Myself on his grave;
My heart burned;
The melancholy of my soul killed my strength.
Kissing the turf, I dug up
With my greedy hands
That earth where I would lie with them;
I grumbled in wild insanity;
I dreamed of something frightful;
I was scarcely breathing; just as in a painful
Dream, everything flowed together in murky darkness;
Already sensation of life stopped,
And I lay among the graves
More dead than the cold corpses.
But the fresh air, the dampness of the night
Brought the sufferer back to life again;
My breast heaved a sigh, my eyes opened.
My languid stare wandered all around:
Everything was quiet, covered with a haze,
The moon barely shone in the mist,
And the midnight wind barely rustled
The grass of the graves.

XI

I got up and with a bowed head
Went across the glade
With hurried steps; beyond the bushes
The road twisted under the hill;
Almost unconscious, without a goal
I followed my nose;
From behind the bushes someone on a horse
Was coming right at me.

I myself do not know by what fate,
But suddenly . . . I see before me
By the trembling lustre of the moon,
The murderer of my son and wife.
I went on, forgetting the whole world,
I didn't think I would find him;
I didn't want to seek revenge on him;
But he, the perpetrator of my separation,
He was there where my dear ones lie in their graves,
When tears of frenzy were still
Quivering in my eyes . . .
My conscience knows, and God sees:
I wanted to forgive—but forgive I couldn't.
I betrayed blessed hope,
I recalled all that had gone before—
And I grabbed his horse by the bridle:
'Villain, did you recognize me?'
He looks timidly, is surprised,
He attempts to bare his sabre;
Alas! I had my dagger with me . . .
And all bloody, he fell from his horse.
It hadn't yet become light;
Beside myself, I go back;
Both the graves and the fields are silent,
Everything was dozing before the dawn,
Only a rumbling from afar rushed by,
As if a horse galloped without a rider;
I withdrew unfeelingly.
Everything that happened seemed to me
To be like something frightful in a dream.
Suddenly the bell for matins rang out . . .
The church was glowing with holy fires,
But the heavens—were glowing with eternal stars,
And the light of the moon turned
The quiet graves with their crosses into silver.
The inviting bell rang,
But I stood and I looked,
I did not dare to enter the bright church . . .
How could I pray now, and for what?
What should I wait for at the altar?
Could I really hope to be united
With her in holy love forever?
How could purity combine with
The turbulent passions of a murderer?
How could I embrace an angel in heaven
With bloodied hands?!

XII

I entered your cloister,
I sought tears of repentance,
Alas, I, a sinner, ruined
The blessed hopes of my heart!
At one time, with faith,
Hour by hour I rejoiced in my calamity:
Now—it's terrible to live until the grave!

And beyond the grave—an eternity without her!
My father, I thought that among you
I could alleviate heaven's anger with tears;
I thought that fasting, prayer and toil
Would find forgiveness for my guilt;
But even in the cloister of salvation
I hear the familiar noise of storms;
My former emotions have awakened,
And my heart is full of former thoughts.
Wearied by despair,
I see her irresistible image all around.
She is in my mind, she is in my utterances,
She is in the prayers on my lips;
My ardent heart strives toward her,
But it fears to disturb the holy shade
In the lap of peace.
O, believe that when I was not stained with blood
I breathed with a pure love,
I knew how to forget about earthly concerns:
I thought about living with her in heaven.
Now, with one destructive blow,
I am separated from her up there,
Again I burn with an insane fire
Darkened by wild melancholy.
Here, on the straw, in a cold cell,
I shed tears before the cross;
I wither, suffer, love,
I dry up in dreary grief.
All hell, all the fury of passions,
Boil again in my breast,
And, the sacrifice of my turbulent sufferings,
My criminal sobbing
Disturbs the sacrament of the night.

XIII

Yesterday—midnight strikes—fear of the grave
Destroyed my last strength,
And with incomprehensible melancholy
I poured out my sufferings
Before the holy icon;
I beseeched the merciful one
To forgive my bloody sin,
To accept my tears of repentance.
Suddenly there was something overshadowing me
                              from above,
It was as if it illuminated my soul
And frightened sinful me;
My father, with a secret holiness
My icon lamp cast a trembling, pale ray
Languidly into my poor cell.
Covered with a white shroud
She appeared before me,
And her black eyes glowed
Brighter than the stars of an autumn night.
Oh no, this was not a phantom of a dream,

And not a deception of imagination!..
Holy father, there was no doubt!
Her shroud fell off of her
And it was, believe me...she!
She was charming, young!
Her smile was unearthly!
And her dark curls ran down
From her forehead to her lily-white bosom,
And I thought that her lips
Were whispering of the dear past;
The very same love was in her eyes,
And our infant was in her arms,
'She!.. I am forgiven by heaven!'
And tears gushed out like streams.
Beside myself, I rushed at her,
Grabbed her and pressed her to my breast...
But her heart does not beat,
The captivating shade is quiet;
The implacable one drifts again
To a mysterious canopy;
My greedy hands were trembling,
And were embracing only the air;
Deceived by a dream, they
Alone were flattened to my breast.
'Are my prayers really rejected?
Are you really a messenger of banishment?
Or, at this terrible hour of death,
Did my still faithful friend
Want to look at her doomed friend
For the last time?'..."
And the Monk fell from my bed onto his kness
And his voice of suffering quieted down;
His face grew alive, began to sparkle:
"You are here again!.. the end of separation!
You are calling!..mine!..always!..everywhere!..
O, how bright!..to him!..to you!.."

XIV

Two days, two nights he languished,
And cried bitterly, and prayed;
On the third day the holy father
Calls the peaceful cloister together;
The last hour is already flying
Over the youthful, sinful head.
In a group the monks entered
Their brother's cell, carrying candles,
And brought a white shroud...
And a wooden coffin was behind the doors.
Mournful was the languid song of those
Praying for the peace of his soul;
By the dim gleam of the burning candles,
The appearance of their black cassocks was mournful.
The holy father read the prayer for
The dying over the monk.
When the fateful minute

Ended his sad destiny,
He, blessing the decaying dust,
Gave the order to strike the bell . . .
And the ringing resounded three times
Over the midnight waves,
And news about the deceased was carried
Far by the surging river.
The prophetic ringing quickly reached a cave
Where a just monk was trying to save himself:
"A deceased person!"—the old man whispered,
Opened the lectern and took out his beads;
The peaceful dream of a fisherman
In his hut by the shore was interrupted by it.
A babe in arms began to cry;
A half-awake mother blesses him,
Begins to compose a prayer,
And quietly rocks the cradle—
And in front of the smouldering fire
She falls again into a deep sleep.
And at his time a wayfarer and his dear wife
Were crossing a field,
They chased away their horror
Into the dark night with a jolly song;
Only the ringing resounded—and they
Crossed themselves, embraced,
More sadly went on hand in hand . . .
And the sound died out in the darkness of the night.

1824

E. A. BARATYNSKY

Eda

Why are you shy with me,
My sweet little friend, my little Eda?
Why, why does my conversation terrify you
When we are alone?
Believe me, I don't have a crafty soul;
There, far away in my native country,
I have a kind sister.
A sister of wondrous beauty;
I am tenderly, tenderly loving with her,
And you resemble her.
It's been a long time . . . what can be done? . .
But such is the lot of regiments!
It has been a long time, Eda, since I
Have seen my happy native land,
Since I have kissed my sister!
Her face resembles yours, but may your heart
                              resemble hers too.
Don't let my dream fail,

And with your love,
Remind me of her love!
You are dear to me. Gaiety, torment—
I thirst to share everything with you.
Don't go away, give me your hand!
Trust in me, sweet friend of mine!

With a smile both insinuating and flattering,
So spoke a handsome hussar
To the Finnish girl, Eda. Rus' was
His fatherland. Not so long ago
The itinerant lot of regiments
Led him into the Finnish mountains.
A severe land: its beauties
Frighten and amaze one's eyes;
Stone mountains have plunged
Onto stone mountains there;
Their capricious masses grow dark blue
As they reach up into the heavens;
Pine forests rustle on them;
Waterfalls stormily stream from them;
There the vale does not gladden the eye,
It is flooded with granite lava.
A pyramidal granite cliff, with
Its peak clothed in sad moss, stands
Like an enormous guard over it.
Your gaze wanders over the decrepit cliffs;
The foreigner is filled with a vague thought:
Are not the gloomy ruins
Of an ancient world lying before him?
Until now in this happy remote spot,
The simple daughter of a simple father,
With her beauty of face and beauty of soul,
Young Eda shone.
There was no one more beautiful in the mountains:
A tender flush upon her cheeks,
A floating figure and golden hair
In careless ringlets about her shoulders,
And eyes as pale-blue
As the Finnish skies.

The day died out, gilding the cliffs.
In front of her hut,
Her face clear and untroubled,
The young maiden was sitting all alone.
He sat down modestly beside the modest maid,
He meekly struck up a conversation with her;
She did not think of stopping it,
But in languid pensiveness
She listened with a weak heart:
Thus a rose of the first spring days
Trusts the faithless rays of the sun;
Feeling a warm breeze, it
Opens its fragrant bud
To its caresses,
And does not foresee the chilling cold,

The killing cold, ready to breathe on it.
Her hand already lay a long time
In the hand of my hussar:
In sweet oblivion, she did not
Take it away from him.
He pressed the poor girl to his heart:
Then the maiden wanted to raise to him
A glance of reproach, even of anger,
But her glance did not express anger.
Bright gaiety shone
In her childlike eyes,
And finally the Finnish girl
Answered him in words such as these:
        "I have already loved you for a long time;
And why not? You are good-natured,
Always thoughtfully obedient
To my slightest whims.
At times they were annoying:
You love me, this I see:
My soul is thankful.
You are dear to me: don't I always
Rush to please you?
Every morning I bring you
Flowers; I gave you
A ring; I was always made
Gay by your gaiety;
I grew sad when you were sad.
What of it? Even in this I sinned:
We are strictly, strictly forbidden
To make friends with you. They say
That all of you are treacherous, malicious;
That maidens ought to avoid you,
That you will somehow ruin us;
That one is lost when one falls in love;
And I've thought many times that you,
Perhaps you will ruin me?"
        "I am your undoer, Eda? I?
Then let Our Heavenly Judge
Send me any punishment at all!
No, no! On this I kiss you!"
        "What? Why? How ashamed I am!"
The young maiden says.
It's already late. She is ready
To stand and flee in indignation.
But he holds her: "Stop! two words!
Stop! Your eyes are stern:
Can I have offended you?
Oh no, stay; forgive a moment
Of forgetfulness, a minute of playfulness!"
"I am not angry; just let me go!"
"Your eyes are full of insult,
And you cannot lie with your face:
Allow me, in the name of peacemaking,
Allow me to kiss you again."
"Leave me alone!"
        —"My beautiful friend,

You will mercilessly send me
To horrible oblivion
Just for a childish whim!
But you won't understand my suffering!
And such is your love!
My sweet friend, one kiss!
One—or I won't believe in it!"

        And the poor girl sighed
And quietly turned
Her sweet face to him,
A face which hitherto was averted from him.

        How he controlled himself!
With what languid, and at the same time,
Seemingly modest slowness,
Was he able to leave the mark of
His kiss on her. What feeling
He poured into her young breast with it!
Even cold art can
Master such a kiss.
Ah, Eda, Eda! Why,
For such a long moment,
Did you drink of the passionate oblivion
In its damp flame?
Now your soul is full
Of anxiety for your vague desire,
Now you won't close your eyes
In refreshing drowsiness;
Dreams, hitherto unknown to you,
Will fly down to your bed.
And for a long time your hot bed
Will not give you peace.
Spring playfully began to grow light
On your rosy stones,
And the moss on them is bright green,
And the little bird began to sing gayly,
And a silvery brook brightly runs
Along your granite couch,
And in the morning the forest
Smells of a cool fragrance from the east.
There beyond the mountain a dale hides,
There flowers are already turning into many colors;
Already the incense of cherry trees
Streams there in the clean air:
Magic spring frightens you
With its sweet bliss.
Don't listen to the mellifluent little bird!
Waking up from sleep, don't turn
Your face from the porch to the morning coolness,
And don't go to the beautiful dale,
But, above all, do
Run after your hussar!

        Sleep has already embraced the wilderness;
A clear moon rose over the mountain,

Blending its crimson light
With the last purple of the sunset;
A double, trembling shadow
Of black firs reclines,
And transparent night replaces
The imperceptibly dimming day.
It's already late. The young maiden,
With burning cheeks, rises
Quietly, and not raising her eyes,
Goes slowly into her corner.

    At one time good little Eda
Was carefree, gay:
At one time she looked everyone
In the eye brightly and affably:
What then could change her?
And what then so suddenly invested
This morning with the dusk of night?
She is distracted, sad,
And adds nothing to any conversation;
No longer do her eyes contain any
Distinct greetings for anyone as they did before.
Questions wait long for her answer,
And often this answer is strange;
First her cheeks are hot, then they are colorless,
And the fruits of secret grief,
Fresh traces of burning tears,
Are often noticeable on them.

    The careless lodger
Started to play too many tricks:
She would place her finger to her lips,
This way to warn him with a smile.
And whenever he would give her
Some cheap bit of finery,
The Finnish girl would run to her mother
To boast about her wonderful new dress,
And in the meantime would run to thank him
With a gay curtsy. Occasionally
She would playfully splash cold water
On her sleepy friend, quickly run away,
And loud laughter would be heard for a long time.
He would be summoned with a sweet joke
By his little one, to be a companion
Of her labors and of her joys.
Whether the sun was rising or whether
The shadow of night lay down on the drowsy hills,—
The pretty girl would cordially say
Good day and good night.

    Where is that time? Now in his presence
She is somehow shyly embarrassed
By her movements;
And now there is no sign of any
Gay jokes; the maiden doesn't even
Begin insignificant conversations with him,

As if he has turned into her enemy;
At times to make up for it she could not tear her
Pensive eyes away from his eyes.
At times to make up for it, when they were alone,
The poor girl, all aflame,
Would press herself to the hussar's breast,
And full of ruinous passion,
She herself would turn her lips
To meet his kisses;
But in the sleepless night, all alone,
Alone with her fake repentance,
Terribly agitated,
Frightened for her soul,
She would whisper despondently: "What's to
                  become of me?
With every day I grow sadder and sadder;
Ah, where are you, my soul's peace!
Where will I go for you!"
And childlike tears flowed
Involuntarily from her eyes.

    She lived not without surveillance.
Her father, a stern old man,
Partly penetrated her heart.
He did not take his suspicious gaze
Off the unfortunate maiden.
He followed her;
And he might have espied something,
But only the young jokester
Once did see and hear how the old grumbler
Angrily walked back and forth
In his room, how later
He forcefully banged the table
With his fist and resolutely said
To poor Eda, pale and trembling
Before him: "Trust me,
It will turn out badly for you with this hussar!
In vain do you always meet him
Around corners. Now
You are happy to listen to the scoundrel.
Learn the worst. Misfortune
Will fall on a fool. Then my
Anxiety will not be great:
Let anyone put my customs to shame,
But I won't have a strumpet for a daughter."
Quietly wiping away sad
Eda's tears, her mother
Meekly said: "What's to grumble about?
Until now she was
So submissive to us.
What is she guilty of now?
You sin when you insult the poor girl."
"Yes," he said, "pet her,
But I've already spoken my piece."

The next day, in her room,
When it was already evening,
Eda sat all alone with her
Familiar grief. The Holy Bible
Lay before her.
Bent over with her brow upon her hand,
With a distracted finger
She distractedly leafed through
Its crumpled pages
And flew off in involuntary thought
To those days of her purity of heart.
He approached her with a sullen face,
Sat down in silence, and in silence clasped
His chest with his arms in the shape of a cross;
Signs of hidden, heavy torment
Showed in him. Finally:
—"My duty," said the conniver,
"Demands a separation from you.
For the last time I come
Now to hear your sweet voice,
To see your eyes so dear to me:
The dusk of night will cover the earth
And will separate us forever.
It's your stern father's fault:
I heard his reproaches;
No, no, my love for you
Will not inflict new sorrow!
Farewell!" Pale, barely breathing,
She listened to the hussar.
"What are you saying: Is it possible? Now?
And forever, my beloved . . ."
—"I will flee from here; but in my soul
I will remain here in the wilderness dear to me.
With you I loved to see
These very streams, these very mountains;
With heavenly joy I raised my
Eyes to this very sky;
Away from you the light of day
Can no longer gladden me!
I gave vent to an unfortunate love
And trusting it, ruined
All the beauty of future days
For a fleeting moment, a beautiful moment.
But listen! A short time is left to us:
Afraid of jealous eyes
Following us everywhere,
Until now we met in passing
And in stealth. Don't be insulted
By my entreaty. At parting
Allow me, allow me to have
A tranquil meeting with you!
As soon as the cover of night descends
And your people close
Their heavy eyes
In deep sleep until the dawn,
I will come to the quiet refuge

Of my beloved: oh, dismiss
Your maiden's fear and for a minute
Draw back your annoying lock!
In sad silence I will cling
To your lips, o life of mine,
And in a farewell kiss
I will leave you my soul."

The maiden glanced at her seducer
With regret; herself not knowing why,
She didn't dare
To trust him:
Some misfortune threatened her;
A certain fear pierced through her;
Her heart said vaguely
That his tongue was lying.
The holy book, still lying
In front of her as it had before,
Reminded her of her duty.
After he pressed her to his
Heaving chest, she said,
"No, no, why do you play
With my simplicity so maliciously?
Or aren't there enough sins yet?
Still, will I still bend
A willing ear to the voice of temptation?
Leave me alone, sly spirit!
Leave me without new pangs of remorse."

But his opponent really almost
Helped him: he poured out his
Murmurs with such force, he expressed
His sorrow so bitterly that
The sweet maiden began to feel sorry for the hussar:
And tears fell in heavy drops
From her eyes.
And at the same time the cunning one
Showered both reproaches and entreaties upon her.
—"Why do you delay? Moments are precious!"
He finally approached her:
"Give me your word!"—"How can I give you
My word when I am grieving with all my soul?"
She said, "Take pity on me!
I can barely control myself!
And that I know!" Quickly and passionately
He pressed her to his breast.
"I will be there; wait for me!" he said;
He said this and quickly disappeared.

Already the hills and fields
Are covered in heavy blackness.
After sharing a humble supper
With her unpretentious parents,
The maiden entered her own corner;
She glanced pensively at the door:
Believe that the nocturnal guest is dangerous;

Her timid conscience whispered,—
And her door was bolted.
She wound her golden curls
In soft little papers;
Somehow she managed to remove
Her clumsy daytime garb;
She freed her heavily panting
Breast from its lacing;
She lay down and intended to sleep.
It is already late, midnight, but
Sleep does not close her lashes:
"He will knock now,
Why did I lock the door?
Indeed I am capricious.
I will let him in: you know my beloved
Will spend a moment here with me,
Then he will leave here forever."
Thus thinks the maiden and then
Quietly rises from her bed,
Walks to the door with trepidation
And her hand is already touching
The fateful bolt;
Now she slowly takes her hand away.
Then again she draws her hand to it;
The iron moved: All of the
Unhappy maiden's blood froze,
And grief wrung her heart.
But then a strange hand
Shook the door: "Beautiful friend,
Eda, do not be afraid; it is I."
And, losing her breath in confusion,
Full of an unknown heat,
My poor maiden
Was already in the hussar's embrace.

    Alas! he got his desired
Victory that night:
Poor little Eda, you could not
Overcome your intoxicated feelings!
Dawn turns the heavenly sphere crimson.
False ecstasy has disappeared;
And with it has flown away the ghost of happiness;
The abyss of misery has opened:
You cry tears of sorrow
Following right on your tears of passion!
Ashamed of glowing daytime,
On the edge of your fateful bed,
You sit with bowed head.
Look at your young friend!
Heed him: no, no, he will not
Endure a terrible separation from you;
All of his days and nights are for you:
Your father will not scare him:
He will allay all suspicions,
He will deceive vigilant eyes;
You will be his for as long as he lives . . .

All of this is in vain: she does not heed him,
She does not lift her eyes to her friend,
She closed her silent lips
While casting an unseeing gaze on the ground;
To her, the conversation of her friend
Is just like the wind senselessly whistling
Through the gorges of the Finnish mountains.

                    * * *

Not for long, beautiful maiden,
Did you avoid your seducer,
Languishing with dismal sadness.
Again you yielded to your heart:
A tender love forgave
A perfidious, merciless love.

In a hurry did day follow day.
The young maiden was already
Submissive to the hussar in all things.
Like a tame fallow deer, she
Followed him everywhere. Sometimes
A thick canopy of a sleepy oak
Welcomes them as a couple in the mid-day heat;
Sometimes a drowsy pine forest summons them,
Sometimes mountain grottoes invite them
Into the dusk of sweet benevolent bliss.
But more often they met
In a deep, neighboring valley;
On a thick, rustling canopy
Over the quickly flowing stream,
They sat down on the grass.
Occasionally in languid idleness,
Her lover places his carefree head
On the submissive maiden's knees
And closes his eyes in light sleep.
She quieted her breathing and listens to
The breathing of her friend;
She waves annoying midges away
From him with a branch of a tree;
She plays with his wavy hair
With her childlike fingers.
Sometimes when the moon rises,
And the wild country drowses beneath it,
She receives him on her bed
In her own secluded refuge.

    But my tender maiden
Suffers with secret sorrow.
Once at their usual time,
Near the waters of their favorite brook,
They sat quietly.
In quiet oblivion her lover
Gazed at the bright streams
Running playfully before him.
Into its swift current he somehow threw

A little flower plucked along the way.
The young maiden sighed;
Inclining her head to her friend, she whispered,
"So shall you throw me
To my ruin, caressing
Me and cherishing the moment."
Gently beautiful lips
Smiled a sweet smile,
But grief also had its effect:
And involuntary tears
Appeared on her eyelashes.
She wiped them with her scarf
And trying to look
More merrily at her friend, said:
"Farewell, senseless melancholy!
Today my life is sweet,
Today I am your friend,
And tomorrow you will be with me.
And then another day, and it's quite possible
That with God's help, I will not
Live until our fateful separation!"

More than once did she embarrass
Her lover with her innocent tenderness,
And occasionally awoke in him
Pity and even remorse;
But more and more often he grew weary
Of her melancholy love
And he summoned the moment of parting;
Already to him it was like a moment of happy freedom.
Not in vain did he summon it!

Again the violent Swede
Does not observe the treaties;
He wants to test anew the unequal
Destiny of military confrontations with the Russians.
Advance guards have already
Crossed beyond the fortress of Kyumen.
War, War! The next day will be
The day of fateful parting.

The young maiden has no more tears.
With a dead face and a dead soul
She looks at the bustle of
Marching formations: an end to it all!
The alarmed conniver does not dare
To rest his eyes on her.
The night closed in. Everything has
Subsided into a deep sleep. For the
Last time he goes to his sad darling.
He whispers words of comfort to her.
He kisses her in vain—
She listens, devoid of feelings,
And lets him kiss her,
But meekly, indifferently!
All of her dreams have run away.

They passed an oppressive night
In silent sadness.
Already the radiance of the day calls him to go;
Already they are leading an eager
Horse to the young soldier;
Already he is mounting. With dull eyes
She stands in the doorway
Of her empty hut.
Farewell, poor maiden!
He has already galloped away
Along a distant road. Your eyes can
No longer make him out beyond the hills...
After she knelt down, she first
Lifted her arms to the heavens,
Then she reached out after him
And plunged her face into the dust
With a silent moan of mortal agony.

Winter's cold froze over the streams,
And like mountains of ice
They hang down from the granite mountains
Over their own rapids.
Here and there rocks, raising their heads
From under their snowy garb,
Grow dark beyond other rocks.
The sky has disappeared into the
Gray and wavy gloom. Winter
Blizzards begin to make a noise, begin to howl.
And what about my poor maiden?
The fire of her eyes has gone out;
There is not even a shadow of the former Eda in her:
She grows exhausted in the flower of her days,
But tears and reproaches are foreign to her.
Pale as the winter sky,
Lost in the silence of hopeless sadness,
She sits motionless at the window;
She sits and dejectedly listens to
The rebellious howl of the storm,
And dreams: "My sweetheart is not with me;
You have become hateful to me, sad world!
Will I wait out my end or not?
When, when will you, blizzard,
Wipe away my light traces from the face of the earth?
When, when will my grave
Give me its refuge in deep sleep,
And when will the raging winds
Pile a high snowdrift on it?"

There is a cemetery. Hills
Squeeze other hills, crosses squeeze other crosses there,
The eyes find it all monotonous;
A narrow fence surrounds them
(Among the bushes it is barely visible,
Built of round stones);
The grave of my maiden
Has lain beyond it for quite some time.

And who looks for it now?
Who visits it with tender grief?
All around everything is empty, everything is quiet;
At times only the wind whistles
And stirs the juniper.

1824

A. S. PUSHKIN

RUSLAN AND LYUDMILA

DEDICATION

For you alone, enchanting beauties,
Queens of my spirit, for your sake
Did I convert to scribal duties
Some golden leisure hours, and make,
To whisperings of garrulous ages,
Once-on-a-time my faithful task.
Accept them, then, these playful pages;
And no one's praises do I ask
From fate, but shall be pleased to thank it
If one young girl should love, and pine,
And peep, perhaps beneath her blanket,
At these unshriven songs of mine.

An oaktree greening by the ocean;
A golden chain about it wound:
Whereon a learned cat, in motion
Both day and night, will walk around;
On walking right, he sings a ditty;
On walking left, he tells a lay.

A magic place: there wends his way
The woodsprite, there's a mermaid sitting
In branches, there on trails past knowing
Are tracks of beasts you never met;
On chicken feet a hut is set
With neither door nor window showing.
There wood and dale with wonders teem;
At dawn of day the breakers stream
Upon the bare and barren lea,
And thirty handsome armored heroes
File from the waters' shining mirrors,
With them their Usher from the Sea.
There glimpse a prince, and in his passing
He makes a dreaded tsar his slave;
Aloft, before the people massing,

Across the wood, across the wave,
A warlock bears a warrior brave;
See Baba Yaga's [1] mortar glide
All of itself, with her astride.
There droops Kashchey, [2] on treasure bent;
There's Russia's spirit...Russian scent!
And there I stayed, and drank of mead;
That oaktree greening by the shore
I sat beneath, and of his lore
The learned cat would chant and read.
One tale of these I kept in mind,
And tell it now to all my kind...

CHANT THE FIRST

The lore of ages long gone by,
In hoar antiquity compounded.

A ducal wassail-chamber high;
By stalwart sons and friends surrounded,
Vladimir-Sun [3] sat feasting there;
To valiant Prince Ruslan his fair
Young maid in wedlock he was linking,
And from a heavy tankard sinking
His mead in honor of the pair.
Our forebears were no hasty eaters,
Not speedily, you would have found,
The jars and silver pledging-beakers
Of wine and ale went foaming round.
High cheer of spirit they would pour them,
The spume rose lisping to the brim,
With gravity the bearers bore them
To guests and deeply bowed to them.

Now speeches merge in hum and hubbub;
Abuzz the revelers' gay round;
When tuneful singing of a sudden
Blends with the gusli's nimble sound;
A hush descends; all hark Bayan,
The sweet-voiced bard, for praise to sound them
Of fair Lyudmila's grace, Ruslan,
And of the garland Lel had wound them.

But overwhelmed by fiery passion,
Ruslan takes neither drink nor ration;
Upon his heart's-love fixed his gaze,
He is now sigh, now scowl, now blaze,
And gnaws away, impatience mounting,
At his moustache, each moment counting.
With brow beclouded, untoward,
About the clamorous wedding-board
Three other youthful knights are seated;
Their sulking leaves the ladle bare,
The bumpers of their circling cheated,
They take no pleasure in the fare.
They do not hear the bard Bayan;

Their troubled gaze is downward bent:
They are the rivals of Ruslan;
Deep in their luckless hearts is pent
Of love and hate a venom blent.
One is Rogday, the valiant lord
Who clove wide open with his sword
The bounds of Kiev's fields of gold;
The next—Farlaf, poltroon conceited,
In toping contents undefeated,
But in the sword-clash less than bold;
Fierce young Ratmir, intently brooding,
The Khazar khan, is last, not least:
All three are pale of cheek and moody,
No feast to them, this merry feast.

And now it ends. The diners, surging,
Arise, in noisy swarms converging,
All gazing at the newly wed:
The bride looked down, her color altered,
As if her modest spirit faltered,
The happy bridegroom cheered instead.
But nature lies in shadows huddled,
The hush of midnight drawing on;
The boyars, lately mead-befuddled,
Made their obeisance and are gone.
The groom, in rapturous elation,
Lets his enflamed imagination
Caress his lovely, bashful fair;
While, secret rue his heart o'erstealing,
The Duke confers with tender feeling
His blessing on the youthful pair.

And here they lead the bridal maiden
To couch her on the marriage-bed;
And Lel, as other lamps are fading,
Lights his nocturnal torch instead.
Now readies Love his gifts to lovers,
Long-cherished hopes are winning home;
And downward sink the grudging covers
Upon the rugs of Eastern Rome...
Can you not hear the lovelorn whispers,
The dulcet sounds of kisses there,
The gently intercepted lisping
Of final shyness?...Tokens fair
Of ecstasy beforehand given,
The groom now tastes it...Flash! By glare
Of lightning, thunderpeal, is riven
The dusk, the flame dies, smoke is drifting,
All's sunk in sooty murk, all shifting,
Ruslan struck senseless in the gloom...
Then all died down, a voice half broke
The fearsome silence, twice resounding,
A shape from out the depths of smoke
Loomed darker than the haze surrounding...
The chamber hushed in mute repose,
The bridegroom, terrified, arose,

Cold sweat still coursing down his face;
His trembling fingers, chill and stark,
Went out to probe the soundless dark...
Woe! of his lovely friend no trace!
He seizes but on empty air,
Dense gloom: Lyudmila is not there—
Snatched in a nameless power's embrace.

Ah, if love's martyrdom condemns
A sufferer to hopeless passion,
Though sad his lot, he still, my friends,
May live to bear it in some fashion.
But let embrace, past endless years,
Close on your love and feel her in it,
The goal of longing, pining, tears,
And have the bride of but one minute
Snatched off and lost forever...I
For one, my friends, would rather die!

Ruslan, though, worse for him, is living.
What did the Great Duke have to say?
Crushed by the fearful tiding given,
To fury at Ruslan a prey,
"Where, where's Lyudmila?" asked he, trembling,
Dread glare of wrath upon his brow.
Ruslan is deaf. "Sons, vassals all!
Your former merits I recall,
Take pity on an old man now!
Well then, which one of you engages
In quest to save my daughter's life?
His exploit shall not lack for wages:
To him—yes, villain, wail and writhe!
Not man enough to guard his wife!—
Lyudmila's hand I hereby proffer,
With half my ancestors' domain.
Who, sons and noble friends, will offer?..."
"I!" spoke the brokenhearted swain.
"I!" "I!" Rogday's cry reinforces
Those of Farlaf and glad Ratmir.
"Straightway we saddle up our horses;
We'll ride the world through; do not fear,
Our Sire, a lengthy separation;
We'll fetch her from the earth's four ends!"
The aged prince to them extends,
By anguish bowed unto prostration,
In wordless gratitude his hands.

All four emerge—Ruslan appearing
Half dead from misery, and grim,
The thought of his lost consort searing
His soul and mortifying him.
And now they mount their mettled horses;
Along the Dnieper's smiling courses
They canter on in dusty swirls;
In haze afar their image furls;
And lost from sight are horse and man...

But long the Great Duke gazes, scanning
The face of the now empty land,
His anxious thought the distance spanning.

Ruslan pined mutely, in a limbo
Where memory and sense are lost.
Behind him rode, one arm akimbo,
Head arrogantly sideways tossed,
Farlaf, puffed up and all-defiant.
He crows: "It almost came too late,
This quest at large—I couldn't wait!
How soon will they bring up a giant?
Then, ahh...let streams of gore be poured,
The pledge that jealous ardors merit,
Rejoice, exult, my faithful sword,
Rejoice, exult, my steed of spirit!"

The Khazar khan, who clasped already
Lyudmila in his mind's embrace,
Was fairly dancing in the saddle,
Youth's fervent spirits in him race;
Hope lighting up his gaze with cheer,
He now streaks on in full career,
Now falls to curveting, now teases
His eager stallion, makes him rear,
And charge the hillocks as he pleases.

Grim is Rogday and mute—what squeezes
His idly jealous heart is fear,
Fear of a dark fate that awaited;
He feels the most unease of all,
And oftentimes his scowl of hatred
On Prince Ruslan will darkly fall.

Throughout that day the rivals travelled
By Dnieper's bank a common trail,
Till shades of night from orient levelled
The sloping banks and filled the vale;
Deep Dnieper lies in mist; the horses
Must needs be rested now and fed.
On yonder a broad highway crosses
A highway wide that slopes ahead.
"Here it is time to part," they voted,
"And chance the fated aftermath."
Each charger then, by steel ungoaded,
In freedom chose its random path.

What now, Ruslan, our luckless farer,
Alone in desert hush? It seems
Lyudmila and that night of terror
Are but the stuff of distant dreams.
Bronze helm on brow more tightly pressing,
From mighty hands the reins dismissing,
You walk your steed amongst the fields,
And in your soul there slowly yields
Faith to despair—hope barely glimmers.

But there! A cave before him shimmers
With light within. Straightway he marches
Beneath its brooding vaults and arches,
With very Nature jointly raised.
He entered moodily, and gazed:
There sits an elder, bright of dome,
Of tranquil mien and whiskers white,
A lamp before him sheds its light
Upon an open parchment tome,
Which he is diligently reading.
"I bid you welcome here, my son,"
He hospitably greets Ruslan.
"I whiled my twilight age away
In here these twenty years preceding;
Now I have lived to see the day
Which I have long anticipated.
This our encounter, son, is fated;
Sit down and hear what I shall say.
From you Lyudmila has been wrested;
Your hardy spirit, sorely tested,
Would flag; yet woe will swiftly flee;
Brief is your clash with destiny.
Pluck up your faith and hope, serenely
Brave all, do not despond; fare forth,
And brace your heart and sword more keenly
To carve a pathway to the North.

Know then, Ruslan: your foul offender
Is the magician Chernomor,
The northern ranges' dread commander,
Fair maidens' predator of yore.
Not ever has his mansion's splendor
Been pierced by human gaze before;
But you, vile artifices' ender,
Shall beard the malefactor, and—
He is to perish by your hand.
No more than this may I uncover,
My son: your future, understand,
Henceforward is your own to govern."

Crouched at the elder's feet, the knight
Now kissed his hand in exultation.
The world before his eyes turned bright,
Forgot his spirit's sore vexation.
Then he bethought himself; again
Upon his flush a cloud descended.
"That qualm—I know its cause—be ended,"
The elder said, "For it is vain
And easily dispelled. Your terror
Is of the grizzled wizard's love;

But calm yourself, you are in error,
It has no force to harm your dove.
He plucks the stars from heaven's reaches,
He whistles, and the moon will quake,
But what the law of eons teaches

That all his magic cannot shake.
That jealous palpitating warder
Of his unyielding locks and gates
Is but an impotent marauder
To the sweet captive that he baits.
About her chambers mutely slinking,
He execrates his fate unblest . . .
But goodly knight, the sun is sinking,
And you are much in need of rest."

[Unable to sleep, Ruslan asks the old man to relate the
tale of his life. After the old man tells of his adventures,
they notice that it is now morning and time for Ruslan to
resume his quest. In the next canto we find out that
Rogday goes off into the forest. On the other hand, Farlaf
sleeps the morning away and is just settling down to eat
near a brook when a knight gallops up. Rogday is the
knight who comes upon the lazy Farlaf. Rogday plans to
kill the man near the brook until he finds out that it is
merely Farlaf. He then rides off and meets an old crone,
who gives Rogday the directions that lead him on further.
Rogday ends up fighting and dying in a duel with Ruslan.
The crone also tells Farlaf to give up the quest and go
back to his place in Kiev.]

But reader! What about our maiden?
Let's leave the horsemen for the nonce;
We'll soon be back there, but before,
It's more than time now to be turning
To the fair prisoner and learning
Her fate with dreaded Chernomor.

Indecorous comrade-in-arms
Of my disorderly invention,
I took the liberty to mention
How one dark night Lyudmila's charms
Were whisked away at one fell stroke
From eager hands in swathes of smoke.
Now, at the time—distressful plight!—
The fiend's inexorable might
Had swept you off the bridal pillows,
Spun like the whirlwind up and out,
And through black air and foggy billows,
Sped to his mountainous redoubt—
You, reft by the revolving vastness
Of nerve and sense, revived—in dread,
Still speechless, tremulous, half-dead—
In the enchanter's fearsome fastness.

Thus, standing by my cabin door
Once in the summer time, I saw
The chicken-run's majestic pasha
Pursue one of his harem, rush her
About the yard, with outspread wings
In sensuous ecstasy already
Embrace his love; but aerial rings

Are drawn above him, shrewd and steady;
Pernicious stratagem in train,
The village poultry's ancient bane,
The gray kite hovered—veered to lunge,
And struck the yard with lightning plunge.
He soars up, spirals high, and passes
To far-off shades of safe crevasses,
Grim talons in his luckless prey.
Grieved at the murderous foray,
No less by chilling terror shattered,
The rooster vainly calls his love . . .
All that he sees is drifting fluff,
On drifting breezes slowly scattered.

The princess labored until morn
In throes of dreamlike indecision,
As one who in a nightmare vision
Lies paralyzed—until at dawn
She rose, her waking mind unsealing,
Excitement mixed with nameless fear;
Her soul seeks flaming heights of feeling,
Gropes for a someone, senses reeling:
"Where is my spouse," she lisps, "my dear?"
She calls—and would recall the sound,
And gazes fearfully around.
Where is her chamber gone? Instead
The captive maiden's limbs are spread
On swells of down; above her hovers
A splendid silken canopy;
The tapestries, the quilted covers
Are patterned, tasseled broidery;
Brocaded tapestries abounding;
In clusters rubies wink and blaze;
And golden censers, all surrounding,
Diffuse an aromatic haze;
Enough, though . . . luckily I needn't
Describe this realm of magic thrall:
Scheherazade, my antecedent
To those purlieus, has done it all.
But rich appointments go unheeded
If our true love is not on call.

Three girls, of comeliness entrancing,
In charming light attire advancing
Upon the princess, with profound
Obeisance curtsied to the ground.
Then, all inaudibly, one darted
Up to Lyudmila, light as air,
And with ethereal fingers started
To braid our maiden's golden hair
(An art spent nowadays on curls),
Then pressed on her pale brow and parted
Fair hair a diadem of pearls.
With modestly averted glances
The second maiden now advances;
A sarafan of azure dims

The splendor of Lyudmila's limbs;
A filmy veil descends, enfolding
Her shoulders, breast, and tresses golden,
Like mist at dawn in gauziness.
Begrudging covers now caress
Enchantments fit for Eden's dwellers,
And flimsy slippers lightly press
Those feet of which the gods are jealous.
The third girl hands her, last to linger,
A belt of pearl-encrusted skeins,
The while, invisibly, a singer
Diverts her with her merry strains.
Alas—her heart derives no easing
From sarafans or pearly bands,
From songs or entertainments pleasing
Or jeweled clasps for golden strands.
Unseen, the looking glass might borrow
The glory of her form, her dress;
She, eyes cast down and motionless,
Persists in silence and in sorrow.

(Those who have gleaned the truth of ages
From heart's most dark and private pages,
Emerge confirmed in the belief
That if a lady, deep in grief,
Through tears, by stealth, in spite of reason,
Decorum, common sense, or season,
Does not still look into the glass—
She must be in a hopeless pass.)

Lyudmila, lonesome and forlorn,
Not knowing what to do, is drawn
Up to the latticed window yonder,
And lets her glances sadly wander
Across that vastness far and drear.
All speaks of death. The snowy highlands
For glaring carpets glitter near,
Whence, like immense and changeless islands
Of craggy white, the peaks protrude
And in eternal stillness brood.
No smoke from cottage chimneys stealing,
No snowy path a wanderer gropes,
No hunting pack's melodious pealing,
No horn-notes thrill these desert slopes.
At most you see a whirlwind sailing
That emptiness with dismal wailing,
And on the skyline's sallow gray
Denuded forests sadly sway.

In helpless tears, Lyudmila stands
And thinks, face buried in her hands:
"God—what awaits me, wretched mortal?.."
She pushed against a silver portal;
It opened with a tuneful sound,
And the astonished maiden found
A park: far more enchanted ground

Than all the pleasances, we read,
Were roamed by pastoral Armide,
Than terraces King Solomon
Or dukes of Tauris sported on.
The world of green about her harbors
Palm avenues, and laurel banks,
And myrtle trees in fragrant ranks,
A wealth of swaying, rustling arbors,
With cedar spires superbly towering,
And orange groves, part gold, part flowering.
Their shapes in tranquil pools revive;
Hills, glades, and valleys all around
In fervent spring's renewal thrive;
The cooling airs of May run throbbing
Along the wonderstricken ground,
In shades of trembling foliage sobbing
The Chinese nightingale is found.
Slim adamantine founts aspire
With merry splashing to the sky:
Beneath are statues to admire
That seem alive...if Phidias' eye,
Whom Pallas and Apollo taught,
Had seen them gleam there in the drizzle,
He would have dropped his magic chisel,
At first enchanted, then distraught.
On marble barriers led to shatter
In winking arcs of nacreous flash,
Plunge waterfalls, foam up, and scatter;
While brooks in shade of birch and ash
With lazy ripples barely splash.
Like shelters from the verdant brilliance
For cool and quiet here and there,
There wink ethereal pavilions,
And eager roses everywhere
Lend flush and fragrance to the air.
Yet my Lyudmila, feeling tragic,
Walks by it all but does not see;
The gloss and luxury of magic
Have lost the charm of novelty.
She strolls, not caring whither bound,
And walks the garden all around,
And has her fill of bitter weeping,
At times with stricken glances sweeping
The sky's impenetrable vaults.
The lovely eyes abruptly brighten:
A finger on her lip, she halts;
It seems, a thought to tempt and frighten
Has struck her...An escape she fears
Lies open: high above her, clinging
To facing boulders, there appears
A bridge across the fall—and wringing
Her hands, disconsolate, she nears
And stares into the foaming eddy
In tears, resolved to end it all;
Brow clutched, breast beaten, she is ready—
But does not jump into the fall
And goes on walking after all.

But tiring soon, our charming captive
(So long outdoors and on her feet),
Stopped, dried her tears, and grew receptive
When something in her murmured "eat?"
She sat and looked about—how easy!
For whoosh! an awning rustles down
To shelter her, all dim and breezy;
An exquisite repast is laid,
The setting sparks with crystal glitter;
From quiet depths of leafy shade
Clear runs of harp-notes trill and titter.
The princess marveled much at this,
In private, though, took it amiss:
"Torn from my love, imprisoned, friendless—
Why should my stay on earth be endless?
Ah, jailer, whose pernicious lust
Would now indulge me, now torment me—
Your evil might cannot prevent me
From choosing death: I can! I must . . .
I have no stomach for your tents,
Your tedious songs, your blandishments—
I want no meals, no tunes, no meeting,
I'll die amidst your opulence!"
The princess thought, and—started eating.

Lyudmila rose; which action banished
From sight the sumptuous repast,
The awning next, the music last,
Till all the sorcery had vanished.
Alone again, she roams the gardens,
From grove to glade she strays, forlorn,
Serenely through her sapphire stardoms
Selene, queen of night, is borne.
On every side the vapors thicken,
With streamers weaving hill to hill;
And she, abruptly slumber-stricken,
Feels lifted by an unknown will,
Which wafts her through the air and eases
More airily than vernal breezes
Through vesper incense of the rose
Her form across the chamber sill
Back on her couch, more gently still—
Her couch of mourning, bed of woes.
In come, once more, the three young girls
And, bustling, set about their service
Unrobing her of gown and pearls;
But their expressions, sad and nervous,
Their downcast, taciturn constraint,
Speak unavailing reprimands
To Fate, a wordless shared complaint.
We hasten on: by tender hands
The slumbrous princess is undressed;
Sweet with the charm of careless ease,
In but a snowy-white chemise,
She beds herself at length for rest.
Obeisance rendered, heavy-hearted,

The maidens hastily departed
And gently pressed the portals to.
And now—how does our prisoner do?
Shakes like a leaf, her breathing stilled,
Eyes black with fear, her bosom chilled;
A fitful slumber leaves her troubled;
She strains to penetrate the gloom,
Unstirring, watchfulness redoubled:
Her heartbeat in the pitch-black room
Thrums in that silence of a tomb.
The darkness whispers . . . now she hears
A creeping sound behind her curtain;
And now . . . oh horror! steps, for certain—
She hides in pillows to her ears . . .
A noise outside her door. The night
Was rent apart by sudden beaming,
The door became a shaft of light,
And wordlessly, majestic-seeming,
With scimitars unsheathed and gleaming,
A long twin file of moors appeared,
Most solemn of expressions wearing,
On pillows sedulously bearing
An equal length of silver beard.
And chin in air, there stalks behind it,
With measured gravity highminded,
A hunchbacked dwarf of haughty mien;
A tall tarboosh protects the sheen
Upon his skull, completely shaven—
Those whiskers' launching place and haven.
He is quite near now! Like a streak
Lyudmila hurtles through the curtain
And flies to clutch the grizzled freak
With nimble fingers by the turban;
With shaking fist she gives a tweak,
And, terrified, lets out a shriek
That all the moors are deafened quite.
The startled hunchback cringes, winces,
Turns paler than the frantic princess,
His hands clapped on his ears in fright;
He tried to run away, but tangled
In his own beard, fell down, half strangled
Got up, fell down; he lurched and swerved.
The dusky train of thralls, unnerved,
Broke up and buzzed and whirled and wrangled,
Then picked the wizard off the mat
And whisked him off to be untangled,
Leaving Lyudmila with his hat.

* * *

[In Canto Three Naina comes to Chernomor's aid. He goes to Lyudmila, but discovers that she has disappeared.]

Well, reader mine, shall I relate
Just where our lovely one had flitted?

All night she had bethought her fate
In moist-eyed wonderment and—tittered.
The beard still awed her, but the dwarf
No longer was a dreadful rumor:
She knew him, and he was a laugh—
And terror sits but ill with humor.
The rays of morning slanting nearer,
Lyudmila, rising to the dawn,
Had her regard obliquely drawn
Into a lofty limpid mirror.
From lily shoulders golden strands
Unthinkingly she culled and parted,
Unconsciously by careless hands
A glossy braid was somehow started.
Then, in a corner, unawares
She came upon her first day's clothing;
She sighed, and dressed, and, struck with loathing,
Gave way again to quiet tears.
Her eyes, however, did not leave
The faithful glass in her emotion;
And then she happened to conceive
A frivolously girlish notion:
To try for size the wizard's hat.
All private in her habitat,
No prying eyes—what could it matter?
What sort of headgear does not flatter
A girl of seventeen, at that?
And trying on is always fun!
She turned the hat: now backward slanted—
Down on one eyebrow—level—canted—
And front-to-back she put it on.
Just then—oh, miracles of yore!
Lyudmila vanished from the mirror;
She turned the hat back, ventured nearer.
Her image met her as before;
She turned it back—a void once more—
She took it off—back in somehow!
"Too bad, my spellster friend, too bad!
What price the great magician now?
This should dispose of you, my lad!"
The maiden, flushed with wicked pleasure,
Put on the hat of the old lecher
And turned it backward as she had.

      Back to our hero, though. I blush
To have dilated long and late
On moors and whiskers and tarboosh,
Abandoning Ruslan to fate!
Fought off the onslaught of Rogday,
He slowly rides through drowsing forest
Down to a valley broadly terraced
Beneath a lustrous morning sky.
He cannot help a shudder, sighting
A grim tableau of ancient fighting.
Bleak desolation: everywhere
Shine bleaching bones—now here, now there

Stray armor rusting in the field,
A broadsword, clutched in bony fingers,
A gorget, a corroded shield;
Weed-grown, a shaggy helmet lingers,
Within, a shrunken death's-head fraying;
A knight's entire skeleton
Lies where he fell, still mounted on
A steed unfleshed; spent lances, graying,
Rise slanted from the softened site,
In peaceful ivy garlands swaying.
No sound appears about to alter
This spectacle of torpid blight;
The sun from its empyreal height
Illuminates the vale of slaughter.

      The prince looks all about with groans,
And murmurs, heavy-eyed and sighing:
"Oh field of battle, field of dying,
Who planted you to brittle bones?
What host in bloody battle-gear
Last stamped on you, whose noble prancer?
Who sank on you with glory here?
Whose prayers did the heavens answer?
Why have you fallen mute and yield
To rank oblivion's choking grasses? . . .
What if from time's black grip, o field,
Not I, not anybody passes?
What if some hillock mute and grim
Becomes the grave of Prince Ruslan,
And bardic music of Bayan
Strikes up no memory of him?"

      But a knight-errant needs a sword,
And armor-plating never harmed him;
So presently Ruslan recalled
That combat had of late disarmed him.
He strides about the battlefield;
'Mid bones with creepers interwoven,
In rustling piles of cuisse and shield,
Of sword and helmet bent and cloven,
He seeks a suit of mail or chain.
Then woke the steppe from numb abandon,
With clash and clatter shrilled the plain,
He picked a buckler, half at random,
A ringing horn, a helmet trim—
A sword alone eluded him.
All kinds of carvers leaned and lay,
But all were flimsy or too short;
He was a fine substantial sort,
Not like the knights of latter-day.
In want of exercise and fun,
He picked a lance of steel for play,
Then pulled an iron tunic on
And thus continued on his way.

The ruddy western flares are paling
Above an earth to slumber soon;
From bluish swathes of vapor sailing
There now ascends a golden moon.
The steppe is shadowed, dark the track,
From it across nocturnal gloom
Ruslan, bemused, sees, deeper black,
Far off a massive hillock loom;
There something fearsome seems to snore.
He rides up closer, close—and hears:
The mound is breathing, it appears.
He looks and listens as before,
In perfect calm, his heart unflagging;
But, nervous ears erect and wagging,
The horse digs in his heels and quakes;
His stubborn head flung high, he shakes,
His bristling mane on end with fright.
Beneath the moon, no longer clouded,
The mound, in gauzy vapor shrouded,
Before the prince's eyes turns bright,
Revealing a portentous sight . . .
How bring it home to mind or sense?
It is a living head—immense,
Its massive eyelids closed in slumber;
It snores; from the prodigious rumble
The helmet rocks, its windblown plume
Fades out aloft in shadowy gloom.
In frightful comeliness, inert
Above the darkened prairie towering,
With overwhelming silence girt,
This desolation's guardian louring
Looms awesomely in front of him,
A misty hulk with menace grim.
Ruslan, incredulous, would close
With this gargantuan repose
And break it, if he might with profit.
He rode a watchful circuit of it
And, speechless, stopped before the nose.
Its nostrils with a spear-tip teased,
The head raised up its lids and shivered,
Then quickly puckered up and sneezed . . .
A whirlwind rose, the prairie quivered,
Dust swirled; from whisker, brow, and lash
A tumbling swarm of barn-owls crash;
From slumber waken brush and weed,
An echo-sneeze—the dauntless steed
Rears, neighs, speeds off on flying feet;
The rider barely keeps his seat.
And then a voice behind them thundered:
"Hoy, foolish knight, where have you blundered?
Come, let's enjoy our rendezvous!
I gobble cheeky boys like you!"
Ruslan looked back, by proud if painful
Exertion reined his steed about,
And gave a laugh, his voice disdainful.
"What do you want?" the head cried out.

"What kind of visitor, God rest me,
Fate sends on purpose to molest me!
Run, while you can without a fight!
I'm going back to sleep, it's night,
Good-bye!" The knight, with indignation
Responding to this rude address,
Exclaimed in angry reprobation:
"Subside, you boom of hollowness!
Have you not heard the true refrain:
A giant skull, a midget brain?
I ride and ride, straight down the middle,
And when I strike, I do not fiddle!"
At this, dumbfounded by his daring,
The head, with pent-up fury glaring,
Swelled up; the bloodshot eyes resembled
Live embers with their scarlet gleam;
The lips, all flecked with lather, trembled,
While ears and mouth were wreathed in steam—
And suddenly, its cheeks dilated,
It fell to blowing at our knight;
In vain his steed, its chest inflated,
Head straining sideways, eyes closed tight,
Tried to press forward unabated
Through all this whirlwind, rain, and night;
Exhausted, terrified, half-blinded,
Once more it flings its legs behind it
And flies for cover out of sight.
Once more the hero, stoutly tackling
The head, is blown away, alack!
That monster, for its part, is cackling
Behind him like a maniac
And shouts: "Prince Charming! Hero! Clown!
You are not off?? Don't let me down!!
Tut, tut, he's running like a stag!
And you a champion fighter! Hear me,
Give me one teensy slap to cheer me,
Before you've ruined your poor nag!"
With this, the thing, for illustration,
Struck out its tongue and gave a leer;
Ruslan, concealing his frustration,
With silent menace weighed his spear.
His arm propelled it, sinews pliant,
The chilly iron hissed, defiant,
And quivered in the shameless tongue;
And blood came weltering in torrents
Where from the frantic maw it hung.
The head, from pain, surprise, abhorrence
In a profoundly chastened mood,
Its crimson color fading, chewed
On steel; still seething, but subdued.
Thus on our stage you see at times
One of the Muse's lesser mimes,
From unexpected hissing deaf,
No longer know stage-right from left;
He pales, forgets his lines, sweats rivers,
His head droops to his chest, he shivers,

And with a gulp comes quite unglued
Before the hooting multitude.
To profit by the state of nerves
Which grips the head, our gallant serves
And, hawklike, swoops to the attack.
His doughty right hand, raised above,
Deals with its heavy armored glove
The giant cheek a frightful thwack;
The steppe re-echoed with the crack,
Which carnadined its dewy heather
Both far and wide with bloody lather.
The head was rocking—teetered back,
Half wheeled, fell down, and started rolling,
Its iron helmet loudly tolling.
Look! on its recent base or source
A sword of chivalry lay glinting.
The joyful prince with quick resource
Took hold of it, and followed, sprinting,
The head along its blood-daubed course,
Intent (of all uncouth ideas)
On lopping off its nose and ears.
The falchion is already raised,
Already starting down and swishing—
When suddenly he hears, amazed,
A plaintive moan of meek petition . . .
He drops the sword-arm, harks intently,
His wolfish wrath subsiding gently;
The vengeful soul is given pause,
Is mollified by mild entreating;
So in the vale the snow-bank thaws
Beneath the blazing noon-sun's beating.

"You have returned me to my senses,"
Confessed the head in contrite tone;
"I offered you unjust offences,
As your right hand has amply shown.
To your command I am obedient;
But you, o noble knight, be lenient!
Worth your compassion is my plight.
I too was once a gallant knight!
In bloody fray I met no other
To equal me in pluck and brawn;
And happy me—had I not drawn
The rivalry of my young brother!
You, Chernomor, with craft and spite
Did all my dire misfortunes wreak!
The family escutcheon's blight,
A dwarf from birth, a bearded freak,
From early childhood he had smarted
To look at me, so tall and whole,
And in his wickedness had started
To hate me for it in his soul.
I had been always something simple,
Though tall of stature; and that wretch,
While not much bigger than a pimple,
Is devilish smart—and vile to match.

To my discomfiture, besides,
In his outlandish beard resides
Of sorceries some fateful junction;
Dismissing all humane compunction,
While yet the beard remains intact,
He shrinks from no unholy act.
Thus in fraternal accents warm—
"A word with you," one day he pleaded,
"Do not refuse—your gifts are needed
A weighty service to perform.
Beyond the mountains (say my parchments)
Upon a placid ocean beach,
Sequestered under dungeon archments,
A sword is kept—of fearful reach!
I am apprised by magic sources
That through the will of hostile forces
This sword shall know both you and me:
It would undo us both forever;
From me it is ordained to sever
My beard, from you—your head. You see
That it is vital we acquire
This tool of injury and shame!"
"Well, on with it—who's hanging fire?"
I told the midget, "I am game,
To the four corners of creation,"
On my right shoulder flung a pine,
And on my left, for consultation,
I set that viper kin of mine
And started on the long, long road.
Good luck would have it, as I strode,
That all, as if to spite the curse,
Went prosperously just at first;
Beyond far heights of orient sloping
To sea, we found the fateful crypt;
With my bare hands I tore it open,
And the sequestered sword I gripped:
But not secure! Fate willed it, rather,
That we fell out with one another—
Nor was it over small reward!
But over who would own the sword.
I argued, he flared up, we gave
As good as got—till he invented
An underhanded trick, the knave,
Grew calm and outwardly relented.
"Let us break off this painful scene,"
Said Chernomor with pious mien,
"Which but dishonors our accord;
Both sense and heart to peace impel us;
Let us appeal to Fate to tell us
Who is the owner of his sword.
Let's hug the earth, start listening;
(How truly malice makes you clever!)
And which is first to hear a ring,
Let him possess the sword forever."
With this he crouches, ear to ground,
And I fool that I am, believe him;

I lie there, hearing not a sound
And gloating how I will deceive him—
But foully was myself undone!
The villain, when I could not see,
Rose soundlessly, stole up to me
Upon my blind side, straightened, spun,
And like a gale the blade hissed to it—
Ere I could look to my defense,
I had no head with which to do it.
Some supernatural influence
Preserved the head both life and sense.
In briars lies my ribwork rigid,
My bulk is rotting uninterred
In distant land by man unheard;
This part of me the evil midget
Transferred to this forsaken land,
Where ceaseless watch I was to stand
Upon the sword you took today.
Oh, knight! I see the fates preserve you:
Take it, and stoutly may it serve you!
Should chance decree that on your way
You meet this feeble-bodied charmer,
And feel in best of form and armor,
Avenge his treason and foul play!
This will rejoice my soul and save me,
Then I shall leave the earth content—
Nor in my gratitude resent
The unforgotten slap you gave me."

[In Canto Four Ratmir travels south and finds himself in a harem, where the women divert his atten-
tions. Ruslan rides to the north and has various trifling adventures along the way. In the meantime Lyudmila
is playing hide-and-seek, using her captor's hat. But
Chernomor traps her by pretending to be Ruslan.

In Canto Five Ruslan captures Chernomor and
forces the magician to lead him to Lyudmila. However,
Ruslan finds her in an enchanted sleep. Ruslan gathers
her up and sets out with Chernomor and Lyudmila. On
the way Ruslan again encounters the Giant Head, who
can now die in peace. The three go on and settle down in a
wooded valley. Here Ruslan meets Ratmir, who is now a
recluse fisherman.

Meanwhile Naina returns to Farlaf and guides him
to the spot where Ruslan and Lyudmila are asleep. Farlaf
stabs Ruslan three times and leaves him to die. He then
rides off, taking Lyudmila with him.

Canto Six begins with a picture of the dead Ruslan
and the trapped Chernomor. The dwarf peeks out from
the saddlebags in which he is trapped, sees that Ruslan is
dead, and prematurely thinks that he is free. Meanwhile
Farlaf returns to Kiev with Lyudmila. Farlaf lies about
the way he found Lyudmila, who still sleeps on in
enchanted dreams. To add to Lyudmila's father's trouble,
the enemy Pechenegs assault the city.]

Beyond the steppelands' torrid reaches,
Beyond a chain of savage mountains,
The home of winds, of thundering gales,
A realm which even brazen witches
Are loath to tread when daylight fails,
Deep in a dale two magic fountains
Have broken from the valley bed:
The one with *living* water gushing,
And down the boulders gaily rushing,
The other charged with waters *dead*.
There all is silent, nothing stirs,
With cooling breath, a stillness hushing
The sough of hundred-year-old firs
Undwelled by birds. No roe-fawn dares
To drink here; for twin spirit forces,
Mute in the very womb of calm,
Since earth spun off the Father's palm
Have stood on guard above these sources . . .
Two empty flagons in his hands,
The hermit came; the guardians started,
They broke their immemorial stance
And, filled with holy fear, departed.
The hermit, bending over, hung
The jars into the virgin waters;
He filled them full, and straightway swung
By sightless airways to those quarters
Where by a barrow, stark and cool,
Ruslan lay in a crimson pool.
The sage bent over him and sprinkled
Upon the corpse the drops of death:
Which made its gashes, raw and wrinkled,
Close up, and spread a rosy breath
Of comeliness; and next he sprinkled
The drops of life upon the form;
And resurrected, vital, warm,
Athrob with eagerness and vigor,
Ruslan stands up again, a figure
Of dazzling youth, who keenly eyes
The clear of day, while bygone rigor
Fades like a dream, a dim surmise . . .
He is alone, though! Where's his bride?
Fears freshly banned return to hound him;
He starts: the sage is by his side
And gently lays his arm around him:
"Foiled, son, is infamy accursed,
And bliss awaits—fulfilled your mission;
A bloody banquet calls you first;
Your sword is bid to spread perdition.
When gentle peace restores the land,
You take this ring before Lyudmila;
The spell of evil will be banned,
Its touch against her brow will heal her.
Your countenance will rout the foe,
Peace will descend, and malice perish.
Prove worthy of your bliss, and cherish
Our friendship, knight! Your hand . . . for lo!

It is beyond the grave we twain,
Not sooner, are to meet again."
He spoke—and vanished as he told him.
Our hero, speechless with delight
To be restored to sound and sight,
Threw out his arms as if to hold him,
But did not hear a further sound;
Deserted are both air and ground.
Alert, the dwarf still bagged astraddle,
Ruslan's proud steed, in fighting vein,
Rears up and neighs and shakes his mane:
Now mounts the prince, now grips the saddle,
Now charges forward hale and bold
Across the fields, across the wold.

What aspect offers, while he speeds,
Beleaguered Kiev? Battle-tense,
The people on its eminence
With horror scan their crops and seeds,
On battlement and turret station
In tremors bide the visitation.
The houses keen with mournful airs;
Pale fear has hushed the thoroughfares.
Next to his daughter, bowed and gray,
Vladimir stayed behind to pray:
His stalwart army, knights and yeomen
And paladins, prepares the foemen
A deadly, decimating fray.

The day had come. The raiders swarmed
Down from the hills in waves unformed;
The teeming plains, like seething cauldrons
Rolled forth indomitable squadrons
To lash the walls like surf the coast.
In Kiev, trumpets, banners flurried,
Defenders formed in ranks and hurried
To meet the reckless surging host.
They clashed—and slaughter raged unbridled.
Forescenting death, the war-steeds sidled
As sword and armor clashed head-on;
A cloud of arrows whirred and spun;
With blood the fields began to run.
The hordes plunged forward hell for leather,
Now mounted squadrons crashed together,
Each tightly locked fraternal rank
Hacks at the foemen, bank by bank.
Here's pawn and horseman, slashing, jolting,
There frightened chargers wildly bolting,
There's carnage, close-in, leg to leg,
A Russian falls, a Pecheneg,
The second maced, the first upended
By feathered death swift as a bird;
A heavy shield has crushed a third,
And maddened horses' hoofbeats end it . . .
Both sides outfought the light to gain
The battle-day, but neither could;

Behind the bleeding mounds of slain
The fighters tumbled where they stood.
And firm the armored sleep they slept;
But seldom from the field of horrors
The groan of fallen men was swept,
Or prayers of the Russian warriors.

There paled at length the shade of morn,
The ripples silvered in the water;
The day of destiny was born
On heaven's misty eastern quarter.
The skies unveiled themselves of night,
And hills and forests flushed with light.
But still in bonds of slumber sealed,
Inertly lay the battlefield.
Abruptly, loud alarums shattered
The silence in the hostile part,
Outcry and challenge, weapons clattered,
Unnerving to the Kiev heart.
The throngs crowd forward helter-skelter
And see amongst the foe, afar,
Steel-clad and flashing like a star,
A mounted warrior, in a welter
Of carnage, stabbing, slashing, keening
The strident horn in his careening . . .
It was Ruslan. He raked the raiders
Like bolts of God the infidel;
The dwarf behind him still, he fell
Upon the terror-struck invaders.
Whereso his saber flashed, where steed
Had borne him in its angry darting,
There heads and shoulders started parting,
Ranks shrieked and sank like swathes of weed.
At once the martial sward appears
Bestrewn with bodies maimed and redded,
Still breathing, trampled down, beheaded,
And piles of armor, arrows, spears.
The battle sounds, the trumpet's wail
Sent armored Slav platoons with thunder
Of hooves upon the hero's trail
To slaughter . . . Infidel, go under!
Wild fosterlings of fell incursion,
The Pechenegs, in panic, wheel;
They call their scattered cobs to heel;
Averse to further armed exertion,
Down dusty fields in shrieking hordes
They flee the flash of Kiev swords,
But all are sentenced to perdition,
A sacrifice to Slav renown;
Kiev exults . . . But on to town
The mighty prince pursues his mission.
The sword of vengeance in his right,
His brazen armor running gore,
His lance-tip like a streak of light,
His crest the pelt of Chernomor,
He seeks, all hope re-animated,

The ducal house through roar and shouting;
The populace, intoxicated,
With chants of homage crowds about him.
Now high in hope, he penetrated
Where wrapt within her wondrous spell
The sleeping maid was said to dwell.
The Duke sat at her feet, his head
Bowed low in sorrow and suspense.
He was alone; his friends had sped
To battle in the town's defense.
Alone Farlaf, averse to war,
Despising bellicose alarms,
Was standing vigil at the door,
Aloof from adversary arms.
The instant that he knew the prince
His blood ran cold, his stare grew senseless,
Pale terror froze his countenance,
He crumpled to his knees, defenseless . . .
The wage of treason, earned long since,
Was due! Ruslan remembers, clutches
The gift ring, takes a rapid pace
And with a trembling movement touches
The placid slumber-cradled face . . .
And lo! the petals drew asunder,
The flower-eyes opened, shining bright;
She sighed, as if in musing wonder
About so lingering a night.
It was as if she felt the trace
Of some dim nightmare—then she knew him.
And gave a gasp, cried out, and drew him
Into the bliss of her embrace.
His soul in fiery transports throbbing,
Ruslan stands dear and blind and numb;
The noble ancient overcome,
Caressed his long-lost children, sobbing.

How shall I end my endless drone?
Of course, my dearest, you have guessed it!
The ancient's groundless wrath was flown:
At Ruslan's feet and at his own
Farlaf in abject shame confessed it,
His foul and murderous stratagem;
The happy bridegroom pardoned him;
The dwarf, his magic mischief ended,
Was added to the Court supply;
Vladimir, toasting evils mended,
Sat in his wassail-chamber high,
By all his dearest ones surrounded.

The lore of ages long gone by,
In deep antiquity compounded.

1818-20

Translator's Notes

1. The best known of the Russian witches. Pushkin gives her a free ride here, but tradition has her paddle a mortar with a pestle and sweep behind her with a broom.

2. Kashchey or Koshchey, usually called "deathless," in fairy tales and byliny, plays the role of a grasping guardian of treasure hostile to the hero. So does the serpent or dragon, and they often interchange roles in parallel versions of tales. Although Kashchey is mentioned in the preface, it is Chernomor who takes his part in the poem, and Naina, who significantly adopts a serpent's guise, seconds him in defending the treasures—Lyudmila and the Beard. But Kashchey is a far more durable nuisance than Chernomor. To kill him, one must find the island of Buyan (cf. Pushkin's *Tsar Saltan,* from under a green oak tree dig up an iron casket, wherein a hare, in which a duck, wherein an egg. If this egg be squeezed, the ogre will feel a mortal agony; if squashed, it will be his death.

3. The folklore embodiment of Vladimir I Svyatoslavich, Prince of Novgorod (970-979) and Great Prince of Kiev (979-1015), in-law of the East Roman Emperor and Christianizer of Rus'.

THE GYPSIES

Across the Bessarabian plains
A noisy gypsy band is wending.
By river's edge as twilight wanes
They camp in torn tents at day's ending.
How free and cheerful is this field
Beneath the skies, how calm their dreaming;
Through wheels of wagons half concealed
By carpets, fires are brightly gleaming;
A family is gathered round
Preparing supper, horses grazing
On open land, while on the ground
Behind the tent a tame bear's lazing.
The steppe's alive: concerns arise
As every family occupies
Itself with travel preparations,
The women's songs, the children's cries,
An anvil's clangorous vibrations.
But now a sleepy peace surrounds
The camp of nomad gypsy forces,
And in the steppe there are no sounds
But barking dogs and neighing horses.
Now everywhere they've doused the light,
And all is calm, the moon's rays shimmer
Alone from out the heav'nly height
And make the quiet campsite glimmer.
But one old man is not in bed;
He sits before the coals instead,

And warmed by their last heat, he gazes
Off to the distant field ahead
Enveloped in the night's damp hazes.
He's waiting for his daughter, gone
To wander in the field. The straying
Young girl is used to freely playing.
She will return; but night comes on.
He knows the moon will soon abandon
The clouds that distant skies enfold—
No sign yet of Zemfira; and in
The tent the old man's meal grows cold.

But here she is. Behind her presses
A youthful man whose face is not
Familiar. Now the girl addresses
The gypsy, "Father, I have brought
A guest. Behind a hill I sighted
Him walking through this desert land.
He wants to join our gypsy band;
So for the night I have invited
Him here. His name's Aleko, he
Is on the run—the law pursues him.
He wants to follow after me.
I'll be his faithful friend—I choose him."

Old Man

I'm glad. Beneath our tent you may
Remain till morning comes or stay
Still longer, do not rush to go. It
Is up to you. I'm ready now
To share both roof and bread. See how
We live—our lot—and get to know it—
Our poverty and freedom show it.
Tomorrow at first light of dawn
We'll take the wagon, set out rolling;
You choose whatever work you care
To: Hammer iron or take the bear
And, singing, through the towns go strolling.

Aleko

I want to stay.

Zemfira

He'll be mine. Who
Should ever try to drive him from me?
But now it's growing late . . . the new
Moon hides; the fields are wrapped in dew,
And slumber soon will overcome me.

———

The old man roams as dawn is breaking
With light steps round the quiet tent.

"Get up, Zemfira: time for waking!
Arise, my guest! The night is spent!
Now leave your pleasure-bed!" And surging
Around him come the gypsies then,
Tents taken down, wagons converging
To set out on the road again.
Now everything is moving when
The crowd across the steppe has started.
Small children playing games are carted
In baskets placed on donkey backs;
Husbands and wives, girls, boys come after,
Both young and old march in their tracks;
The shouts, noise, gypsy songs and laughter,
The roaring of the bear, his chains
That ring with an impatient clatter,
A mixture of bright ragged dress,
Old men's and children's nakedness,
The howl of barking dogs, the chatter
Of buzzing bagpipes, wagons' squeak—
Life in a wild, disordered fashion,
But filled with lively restless passion,
So different from the joys we seek—
Dead pleasures of a blank existence,
A slave chant's tedious persistence!

———

The youth looked sadly at the plain
Now emptied of its population
And yet this sorrowful sensation
He wasn't able to explain.
Black-eyed Zemfira stood beside him,
Now he was free, no one need guide him.
The sun shone gaily overhead
With noonday radiance abounding;
What sets the young man's heart to pounding?
And what is there for him to dread?

The small bird of God's creation
With a carefree life is blessed;
Knows no worry or vexation
As he winds his sturdy nest;
He sleeps till red dawn is breaking
On a branch the whole night long,
Hears the voice of God, and shaking
Out his wings, pours forth his song.
After nature's beauty, spring, the
Heat of summer will pass by—
And late autumn days will bring the
Gloom of fog and stormy sky:
Men, grown bored with life, are grieving,
But the small bird flies away
To warm distant countries, leaving
Till spring brings a better day.

Just like this bird, so he, forever
An exile in migration, never

Had known a nest so safe, could not
Become accustomed to the thought.
Wide-ranging his peregrination,
Each place a lodging for the night,
While every day from dawn's first light
He left to God's determination,
And no amount of trepidation
His heartfelt idleness could blight.
In glorious hours there hovered o'er him
A star that lured him magically;
And sometimes there appeared before him
The chance for fun and luxury;
And even thunder rarely grumbled
Above his solitary head;
On fine days, or when storm clouds rumbled,
He slept, unworried, free from dread.
He lived, unheedful of the power
Possessed by fate, crafty and blind;
But God! What passions every hour
Played in his docile soul and mind!
With what great turmoil have they bubbled
From deep in his exhausted breast!
How long have they been calm, untroubled?
Just wait! They'll waken from their rest.

———————

Zemfira

Tell me, my friend, don't you regret that
You've cast so many things aside?

Aleko

What have I lost?

Zemfira

            Could you forget that?
The home to which you once were tied.

Aleko

What is there to regret? Existence
In stifling towns, a slave's subsistence,
Surpasses your imagining!
There people crowded behind fences
Don't breathe fresh air as day commences
Nor scent of meadows in the spring;
Ashamed to love, afraid of thinking,
They trade what freedom still remains;
Their heads in front of idols sinking,
They beg for money and for chains.
What are the things I have forsaken?
The prejudice and treachery,
The mad pursuit of courses taken
By crowds, or shining infamy.

Zemfira

But there huge palaces impress us,
And colored carpets can be found.
There games and noisy feasts abound,
And how rich are the maidens' dresses!

Aleko

Noise of the towns seems gay, it's true,
But without love there is no pleasure,
The girls . . .much lovelier are you
Than they, although you must make do
Without rich clothes, pearls, and such treasure!
Don't ever change, sweet friend! And I . . .
I have one single aspiration,
To share with you as time goes by
My leisure, love, and exile's station!

Old Man

You love us, though you weren't born here,
But lived among a wealthy nation.
To one used to such ostentation
Our freedom is not always dear.
We have a legend we've protected:
Once long ago to us there came
A citizen the czar directed
To leave his home. (His strange surname
Can be no longer recollected.)
His life already had been long,
But young and lively was his spirit—
He had the wondrous gift of song,
Like water sounds to all who'd hear it—
Now everybody loved this good
And gentle man, who made his dwelling
Upon the Danube's banks and could
Enchant the people with his telling
Of tales; not much he understood,
Was timid like a child, unable
To work, and so the others would
Snare fish and wild beasts for his table;
And when the winter winds began
To howl, and rapid streams froze over,
They took care of the saintly man
And wrapped him in a woolly cover;
But with a life so poor and humble
The old man never could fit in;
He'd wander, pale and pining, grumble
That he'd been punished for his sin,
By God's wrath he was castigated . . . .
He waited to be liberated.
From sadness given no relief,
He walked along the Danube, crying,
As he recalled, in bitter grief,
His home far in the distance lying.

And finally when he lay dying
He made the last of his requests,
That his unhappy bones be carried
Southward—in death still restless guests
On foreign soil—and there be buried.

Aleko

Such then comprises your sons' fate,
O Rome, O famous empire! Poet
Of love, of gods, to me relate
What glory is, how shall we know it?
A voice of praise, the grave's low din,
A sound that runs through generations?
Or else a wild gypsy's narrations
That in a smoke-filled tent begin?

Two years have passed. The population
Of gypsies wanders peacefully;
And as before at each location
Finds peace and hospitality.
The bonds of education spurning,
Aleko is as free as they;
And without cares, regrets, or yearning
He passes each nomadic day.
His former life he has refused to
Recall; unchanged, he now is used to
The gypsy life he calls his own.
He loves their nightly rests, inactive
And carefree days, and finds attractive
Their speech's plain, sonorous tone.
The bear, his tousled tent-guest, making
Escape from his own den, cavorts
Throughout the steppe, in hamlets, taking
Roads that approach Moldavian courts.
Before a wary crowd convening,
He dances badly, roars and gnaws
The tiresome chain around his paws;
The old man beats a tambour, leaning
Upon his staff, Aleko sings
And leads the bear, his steps directing,
Zemfira makes the rounds, collecting
The people's willing offerings.
Night falls at last; the uncut millet
The three companions now prepare;
The old man sleeps—and all is still . . .it
Is dark and quiet everywhere.

The old man tries to warm his frigid
Blood in the sunny rays of spring;
Of love his daughter starts to sing.
Aleko hears, grows pale and rigid.

Zemfira

Husband old and severe,
Cut me, burn me, your wife:
I am strong; I'll not fear
Either fire or the knife.

I despise you, and I
Have contempt for you; I
Love another, and will
Love this one till I die.

Aleko

Be still. These wild songs I don't care for.
Your singing's tiresome to me.

Zemfira

So what? That's none of my affair, for
I sing to please myself, you see.

Burn me, cut with a knife;
I'll be silent, the same;
Husband old and severe,
You will not learn his name.

He is fresher than spring,
Hot as summer and such
A young man, and so brave!
And he loves me so much!

How I gave my caress
When the hour was late,
How we laughed at the thought
Of your aging gray pate!

Aleko

Be still! It's time this song was ended . . . .

Zemfira

So you have comprehended me?

Aleko

Zemfira!

Zemfira

You may be offended,
Since I sing for you specially.

She goes out singing. The old husband remains.

Old Man

Yes, I recall the song's creation
In our own time, and that among
Us as a form of recreation
Since bygone days it has been sung.
Camped on the steppes of the Kagula,
Rocking our child in pale firelight
Once long ago my Mariula
Would sing it on a winter's night.
Now hour by hour within my mind the
Remembrance fades of years gone past;
But in my memory left behind, the
Fond strains of this one song will last.

———————

Night comes; the azure heavens glisten
Beneath the southern moon's bright light.
Zemfira in a state of fright
Awakes the old man: "Father, listen!
Aleko in his sleep is quite
Alarming, groans and sobs all night."

Old Man

Don't bother him in this condition.
There is an old Russian tradition:
Now in the middle of the night
A household spirit gains admission,
Constricts the sleeper's breath; he'll go
Before the daylight comes. Sit tight.

Zemfira

He's whispering my name so clearly.

Old Man

He seeks you in his dreaming, for
Of all things he loves you most dearly.

Zemfira

His love has now become a bore,
Disgusting; and my heart is seeking
Its freedom...Quiet! Hear him moan?
There is another name he's speaking....

Old Man

What name?

Zemfira

            You hear? A husky groan,
He grinds his teeth! How terrifying!
I'll go and wake him....

Old Man

            No use trying,
Don't drive the nighttime sprite away—
He'll leave....

Zemfira

            Now he's begun to stir, he
Is calling me...I'd better hurry—
You go to bed—no need to stay.

Aleko

And where were you?

Zemfira

            I was just passing
The time with Dad. You frightened me:
Some kind of spirit was harassing
You—your soul seemed in agony;
Asleep, you gnashed your teeth, while calling
My name aloud.

Aleko

            I dreamed of you.
I saw such visions—how appalling!
It seemed as though between us two...

Zemfira

Don't credit these hallucinations.

Aleko

All my beliefs have come apart:
The dreams, and your sweet protestations
Of love. I don't believe your heart.

———————

Old Man

Foolish young man, why do you sigh
And languish here with such persistence?
We have bright skies, a free existence,
And lovely women. Please don't cry:
You'll kill yourself with all this bother.

Aleko

But she has ceased to love me, father.

Old Man

She's still a child. Don't be depressed
Or melancholy, I implore you:
Your love is hard and painful for you
While woman's heart—she loves in jest.
Just look at how the free moon rambles
Beneath the heaven's distant crest;
And all of nature as it ambles
Along, by its bright light is blessed.
It passes on, illuminating
Each cloud it visits on the way—
From cloud to cloud, unhesitating,
It moves, but never stops to stay.
Who'll tell the moon to cease her ranging
Throughout the sky, to hold one place?
Who'll tell a girl to be unchanging
And one man only to embrace?
Console yourself!

Aleko

How she could love me!
When everything was calm and still,
The evening hours she would fill
While bending tenderly above me!
And full of childish gaiety
How many times she would delight me
With her dear lisp, and could excite me
With her sweet kisses—instantly
She'd drive away my bleak dejection!
And now? She is disloyal to me!
She's grown cold, lost her old affection.

Old Man

Now here's a story you should know:
It happened to me long ago.
The Danube's borders were not threatened
In that past time of which I tell—
(You see, the sorrow lingers yet, and,
Aleko, I recall it well.)
We feared the sultan's mighty powers;
The pasha over us held sway
From out of Akkerman's high towers—
I was quite young; and in that day
My soul with joy was always boiling;
And not a single graying hair
Amidst my curly locks was coiling—
Among our lovely maidens there
Was one in whom my heart delighted
As in the sun. I long admired
Her, till my ardor was requited . . . .

Alas, how soon my youth expired,
Just like a shooting star expended!

But you, O time of love, extended
A briefer time: in just one year
My Mariula's love had ended.

We met one day as we drew near
Kagula's streams, a congregation
Of gypsies, strangers who'd prepared
Their camp near ours and two nights shared
With us our mountain habitation.
They left the third night, did this throng,
And Mariula went along,
Our little baby girl forsaking.
I slept in peace, but found on waking
My love was gone! I searched the place,
I called to her—there was no trace.
Zemfira cried, longed for her mother,
I started weeping—since those days
I've never wanted any other;
All girls disgusted me; my gaze
Did not find one to give me pleasure,
And I have never shared my leisure
And lonely days with anyone.

Aleko

But why is it you didn't run
Right then to seize one so ungrateful
And plunge a knife into her hateful
And wily heart for what she'd done?

Old Man

But what, my friend, would be the reason?
Young love, like birds, you can't restrain.
Joy comes to each one in his season;
What has been will not be again.

Aleko

I'm not like that. No, I would never
Surrender up my rights! O no!
I'd have revenge upon my foe.
I'd seek him out and if I ever
Should come across him sleeping there
Above the sea's abyss, I swear
I'd show the wretch no mercy, hurling
Him helpless deep into the whirling
Blue waves without timidity;
His sudden terrified sensation
On waking I'd reproach with glee
And long would the reverberation
Of his steep fall be sweet to me.

———

Young Gypsy

One kiss...just one more...I entreat you.

Zemfira

My husband's jealous: I can't stay.

Young Gypsy

One farewell kiss...till I next greet you.

Zemfira

Good-bye, and meanwhile stay away.

Young Gypsy

Tell me—when's my next chance to meet you?

Zemfira

This evening, with the first moonlight,
Behind the grave mound which you see there....

Gypsy

She'll cheat me! She won't come tonight!

Zemfira

I see him! Run!...Dearest, I'll be there.

———

Aleko is asleep. His dreams
Are strange, disturbing to him; such is
Their force that in the dark he screams,
Extends a jealous hand and touches
Not his Zemfira, but instead
Cold pillows meet his timid clutches—
And then he knows his love has fled....
He listens—but no sound comes to him....
He trembles as fear rushes through him,
In him now flow both heat and chill;
He gets up, from the tent emerges,
And roams the camp—his terror surges;
All is at peace; the fields are still;
It's dark above; clouds are concealing
The moon. The starlight barely shines.
Beneath the dew a trail's outlines
Toward the distant mounds are stealing:
Impatiently he follows on
The trail down which Zemfira's gone.
The distant roadside grave has whitened
Before him as he seeks his goal....

He drags his weak legs onward, frightened
By strange forebodings in his soul.
His lips and knees in trepidation
Begin to tremble as he nears,
And then...is this hallucination?
Above the defiled grave he hears
Low whispers, two shapes he can see now.

First Voice

It's time...

Second Voice

Not yet...

First Voice

Dear, I must flee now.

Second Voice

No, no, don't go, let's wait till day.

First Voice

It's late.

Second Voice

How timidly you love me.
A minute!

First Voice

You'll be the death of me.

Second Voice

One minute!

First Voice

What if I'm away
When he wakes up?...

Aleko

I've wakened. Stay!
Don't both rush off now, I implore you;
This place will make a good grave for you.

Zemfira

Run, darling, hurry...

Aleko

No, don't run!
Where do you flee, my handsome one?
Lie down!

Plunges a knife into him.

Zemfira

Aleko!

Gypsy

I am dying . . . .

Zemfira

Aleko, you have killed him! See:
Stains from his blood completely cover
You. Why'd you do it?

Aleko

Let it be.
Now breathe the passion of your lover.

Zemfira

Enough! I do not fear you. I
Curse what you've done. Your terrifying
Threats don't scare me—don't bother trying . . . .

Aleko

Then die yourself!

Stabs her.

Zemfira

In love I die . . . .

———

The east shone bright, as daylight hovered.
On a gravestone behind a hill
With knife in hand and clothes blood-covered,
Aleko sat in morning's chill.
He wore a horrible expression;
Two bodies at his feet lay still.
The gypsies in a sad procession
Walked round him in a state of dread.
They dug a grave, and a progression
Of women gently kissed the dead

Ones' eyes in sorrowful succession.
The old man sat alone and, dazed,
Upon his murdered daughter gazed,
Numbed by his heartache and depression;
They lifted up the youthful pair
And carried them away from there
To where the earth's cold lap embraced them.
Aleko watched . . . . When they had raised
The last handfuls of earth and placed them
Upon the graves, he bowed his head
And sank into the grass then, lurching
From off the rock where he'd been perching.

Then, drawing near, the old man spoke:
"Leave us, proud man! We're untamed folk;
We have no laws; it's not our practice
To torture or to kill—we hate
Laments and blood. Your murderous act is
A thing we cannot tolerate . . . .
You weren't born to live in this fashion,
Your *own* freedom's your only passion;
Your voice will now fill us with fear:
We, meek and kind, don't comprehend you,
You're bold and cruel—don't stay here,
Leave us. Farewell, and peace attend you."
He spoke—the camp prepared for taking
Their leave from this vale, dreadful place,
Where they'd made their night's habitation.
Soon they were gone without a trace;
But still there stood in isolation,
By a rude carpet half-concealed,
One wagon in the fatal field.
Just so sometimes before the waking
Of winter, as the dawn is breaking,
There rises up a flock of cranes
That past its season yet remains
And with a cry goes flying madly
Southward, but one who feels the sting
Of someone's deadly bullet, sadly
Is left, suspended by his wing.
Upon the dark cart night came stealing,
But inside no one moved to light
A fire; beneath the wagon's ceiling
No one was sleeping through the night.

Epilogue

Thus through the special magic power
Of lyric poetry, I see
Those bright and gloomy days—they flower
Within my clouded memory.

Once in that region where the clangor
Of warfare for so long was shrill,
Where Turk and Russian clashed in anger
Over their boundaries, where still

Our old two-headed eagle proudly
Of bygone glories clamors loudly,
Above an old camp boundary,
Roaming one day, I chanced to stumble
Upon a group of gypsies, humble
Sons of a peaceful liberty.

Behind these people unencumbered
By any occupations, I
Would wander, share their meals, and by
Their homely blazing fires I slumbered.
I loved to hear them as they came
Marching along with joyous singing—
And on my lips there long kept ringing
Dear Mariula's tender name.

But even here there is no gladness,
Poor sons of nature! For there dwell
Beneath your ragged lodgings sadness
And painful dreams you cannot quell.
Misfortune even here has found you,
Within your desert nomads' tents,
And urgent passions still surround you;
Against fate there is no defense.

1824

THE TALE OF THE GOLDEN COCKEREL

In the realm of Threeteenseventy,
Commonwealth of Thriceleventy,
Lived the famous Tsar Dadón.
Fierce he was from boyhood on,
And when scarcely more than twenty
Wrought his neighbors wrongs aplenty.
Aging now, he changed in mind,
Would give up the warlike grind
For a life serene and festive.
But his neighbors, growing restive,
Caused the grizzled Tsar alarm,
Dealing him a world of harm.
To protect the tsardom's borders
From the raids of bold marauders,
He was forced to raise and post
An unconscionable host.
Field commanders, never drowsing,
Still would scarce have finished dousing
Flames at left when, ho! at right
Hostile banners hove in sight.
These fought off, some visitation
Came by sea. The Tsar's frustration
Drove him wild enough to weep
And forgo the balm of sleep.
Who could thrive when thus infested?

So he pondered and requested
Succour from a gelding sage,
Planet-reckoner and mage;
Sent a runner to implore him
And the magus, brought before him,
From beneath his ample frock
Drew a golden weathercock.
"Let this golden bird," he chanted,
"High atop the spire be planted,
And my clever Cockerel
Be your faithful sentinel.
While there's naught of martial riot,
He will set his perch in quiet;
Let there be on any side
Signs of war to be espied,
Of some squadron border-poaching,
Or some other ill approaching,
Straight my bird upon the dome
Will awaken, perk his comb,
Crow and veer, his ruff a-fluffing,
Point where harm is in the offing."
Rapt, the Tsar allowed the sage
Heaps of gold for ready wage.
"Such momentous boon afforded,"
He rejoiced,"shall be rewarded
By a wish, to be fulfilled
Like my own as soon as willed."

Cockerel atop the spire
Started guarding march and shire,
Scarce a danger reared its head,
Up he perked as though from bed,
Slewed about, his collar ruffled,
To that side and, wings unshuffled,
Crew aloud "Keeree-kookoo!
Reign abed, your guard is true."
Kings, the Tsar's domains investing,
Henceforth never dared molest him:
Tsar Dadon on every hand
Hurled them back by sea and land!

One year, two, the shrewd informant
Had been roosting all but dormant,
When one morning they broke in
On Dadon with fearful din.
"Tsar of ours! The realm's defender!"
Cries the household troop's commander,
"Majesty! Wake up! Alert!"
"Eh?...what's up?...Is someone hurt?"
Drawled the Tsar amid a double
Yawn, "Who is this? What's the trouble?"
Answered him the Captain thus:
"Hark, the rooster's warning us;
Look below and see the people
Mill in fear, and on the steeple
See the rooster, ruffle-fleeced,

Crowing, pointing to the East."
"Up! No time to lose!" their Master
Spurred them on, "Mount horses! Faster!"
Eastward thus a force he sped,
With his eldest at its head.
Cockerel gave over screaming,
And the Tsar continued dreaming.

Seven days go by and more,
But no message from the corps:
Has the march been rough or quiet—
Naught to tell it or deny it.
Cockerel goes off once more!
Tracking down the elder's corps,
Rides the younger with another
To the rescue of his brother.
Presently subsides the bird;
And again no more is heard!
And again the people, troubled,
Wait a week, their fears redoubled.
Yet again the cock is heard,
And Dadon sends out a third
Host, himself commander of it,
Though unsure what this might profit.
Day and night the columns wind,
Then it preys upon each mind:
Not a camp or battleground,
Not a warriors' burial mound,
Is encountered near or far.
"Strange and stranger," thinks the Tsar.
One week gone, the country changes,
Rising, high through hills and ranges,
Then, amid the peaks ahead,
Look! a silken tent is spread.
Wondrous hush enfolds the scene
Round the tent; a gaunt ravine
Cradles hosts in battle rent.
Now Dadon has reached the tent . . .
Staggers backward: sight appalling,
Hard before his eyes lie fallen,
Stripped of helm and armor chain,
Both his noble princes slain,
Pierced each by the other's charge;
And their wandering mounts at large
On the mead all stamped and scored,
On the bloodied meadow-sward . . .
"Boys . . .my boys . . ." the father groaned,
"Strangled both my hawks," he moaned,
"Life is forfeit—woe is me . . .
Here were killed not two but three."
Wail of men and master merges
Soon resound with heavy dirges
Gorge and cliff, the mountain's heart
Shakes. Behold, the curtains part
On the tent . . .The prize of maidens,
Queen of Shamakhan, in radiance

Lambent like the morning star,
Quietly salutes the Tsar.
Silenced by her brilliant gaze
Like a nightbird by the day's,
Numb he stands—her sight outstuns
Aye! the death of both his sons.
Now she looked at him, beguiling,
Swept a graceful bow and, smiling,
Took his hand and drew him on—
To her tent came Tsar Dadon.
At her table did she seat him,
To all sorts of victuals treat him,
And for rest his body laid
On an othman of brocade.
Thus full seven days he lavished,
All enslaved by her and ravished,
On delight and merriment
In the royal maiden's tent.

At long last, though, forth he sallied,
His surviving forces rallied,
And, the maiden in his train,
Led his army home again.
Rumor started to outspeed him,
Tales of hap and no-hap breeding . . .
Throngs of subjects small and great
Swirl beyond the city gate
Round the coach of Tsar and Empress,
Fabled Shamakhanian temptress;
Tsar Dadon salutes them there . . .
All at once he is aware
Of his friend, the wise old eunuch,
In his white tarboosh and tunic,
Snowy-thatched now, like a swan.
"Father mine," exclaimed Dadon,
"Hail! How fare you? At your leisure
Come and speak; what is your pleasure?"
"Tsar!" replied the aged mage,
"Now we square desert and wage.
For the aid I once accorded,
You recall, I was awarded
My first wish—to be fulfilled,
Like your own, as soon as willed.
Let this maid be what I won,
This young queen of Shamakhan."
"What?" Dadon fell back, amazed.
"What possessed you? Are you crazed?
Does some wicked demon ride you?
Have your wits dried up inside you?
What's your game, in heaven's name?
Pledge I did; but all the same
There are limits, well you knew;
And—what use is she to you?
Kindly lodge it in your head
Who I am! Why, ask instead
For my mint, a magnate's sable,

Stallion from the royal stable,
Half my tsardom if you please!"
"No, I wish for none of these!
Just you give me what I won,
This young queen of Shamakhan,"
Piped the sage in former fashion.
"No!" the Tsar spat, in a passion;
"You yourself have brought this on!
You'll have nothing! There! Be gone
While you're in one piece! I say!
Drag the scarecrow from my way!"
Whitebeard wanted to pursue it,
But with some, you're apt to rue it;
With an angry scepter blow
Tsar Dadon has laid him low,
Not to breathe again.—The city
Gave a shudder, but our pretty:
"Ha-ha-ha" and "hi-hi-hi,"
Not a pious thought, you see.
Tsar Dadon, though greatly flustered,
Smiled at her, as soft as custard,
And proceeded cityward.
Then a tiny sound was heard,
And in sight of all the people,
Look! The cock whirred off the steeple,
Swooped upon the coach of state,
Perched upon the monarch's pate,
Fluffed his ruff and pecked and clink!
Soared aloft . . . Without a blink
Tsar Dadon slid off his seat,
Gave a wheeze and stretched his feet.
Gone the empress sight unseen,
Just as though she'd never been.
Tale of sense, if not of truth!
Food for thought to honest youth.

1834

The Bronze Horseman

Introduction

Upon the bank by barren waves
He stood and pondered mighty thoughts
While gazing outward to the sea.
The river broadly flowed before Him.
Alone, a poor boat raced along,
And on the mossy, swamp-lined shore
Black huts were outlined here and there,
The shelter of the wretched Finn.
A forest, through the mist untouched
By rays of mist-enshrouded sun,
Was rustling round about.

Thought he:
From here our might will menace Sweden,
For here a city will be built
To spite our neighbor's arrogance.
Here nature has decreed that we
Will hack a window into Europe
And stand on strong legs near the sea.
Then here on unfamiliar waves
All flags will come to visit us,
And we will feast in spaciousness.

A hundred years went by and out
Of forests dark and marshes dank
A city rose, a noble beauty,
The wonder of all northern lands.
Where once the Finnish fisherman,
Sad stepson of the wilderness,
Alone stood on the river's bank
And outward cast his ragged net
Into the somber, secret depths;
Today upon the bustling shore
Great palaces and towers crowd
In forms of graceful symmetry,
And scores of ships from all the earth
All strive to reach the prosperous port.
The Neva has been clothed in granite
And bridges hang above her flow.
The river's islands have been veiled
In gardens of green emerald.
Now time-worn Moscow has grown dim
Beside the youthful capital
Just as a purple-mantled widow
Seems pale beside a new young queen.

I love you, Peter's proud creation.
I love your profile's austere grace,
The mighty current of the Neva
Between her granite covered banks,
The fretwork patterns of your fences,
Transparent, twilit, pensive nights.
Their moonless luster fills my room.
I read and write without a lamp.
I love your massive, dozing streets,
Deserted, clear beneath the glimmer
Of the Admiralty spire.
The dark of night can never hide
The golden shimmer of the sky.
For as one twilight fades away,
Another hastes to follow it
And gives night but a half an hour.
I love your cruel winter's frost,
The bite of cold, unstirring air.
I love the running of the sleighs
Beside the Neva's pale expanse,
The rosy cheeks of little girls,
The glitter and the cheerful chatter

And the clatter of the balls,
And when the bachelors are feasting,
The hissing of the foaming glasses,
The punch's dancing, bluish flame.
I love the lively militance
Of drills upon the fields of Mars,
The uniform and ordered beauty
Of infantry and cavalry,
The graceful rippling of the banners
Come back from victory in rags,
The radiant bronze of soldiers' helmets
Shot through and through in battle's heat.
I love, defiant capital,
The thunder of your fortress guns
When into the imperial house
The northern empress bears a son,
Or when again triumphant Russia
Rejoices in her foe's defeat,
Or when the ice-encrusted Neva
Breaks out and travels to the sea,
Exulting in the flush of spring.

Display your splendor, Peter's city,
And stand, unshakeable, like Russia;
Let even conquered elements
Now make their peace with you;
Let Finnish waves fore'er forget
Old hatreds, ancient bondage, too;
Don't let their unavailing spite
Awaken Peter from eternal sleep!

It was an awful time, my friends.
The memory of it is still fresh,
And for you now I will begin
To tell about those woeful days.

Part One

November breathed its autumn cold
Upon the gloom of Petersburg.
The restive waves splashed noisily
Against the fence that rimmed the river.
The Neva writhed convulsively
As a sick man beset by fever
Lies tossing in his restless bed.
Already it was late and dark.
Rain beat at windows angrily.
The wind blew howling mournfully.
Then from his round of visiting
Evgeny hurried to his home.
That's what we'll call our story's hero.
The name has such a pleasing sound,
And toward it my pen's long been friendly.
His family name we need not know
Although perhaps in days gone by
It shone beneath Karamzin's pen.

But now the name has been forgotten
By worldly men and idle gossip.
Our hero lives in Kolomna.
He works, is shy, and does not grieve
For his departed ancestors
Or for the unremembered past.

Upon arriving home Evgeny
Took off his clothes and went to bed.
He tried but could not fall asleep,
His mind disturbed by many thoughts.
He thought about his poverty
And of the trouble it would be
To earn both freedom and esteem.
If only God would multiply
His fortune and his intellect.
He thought about those lucky idlers
Who had no great intelligence
And yet their lives flowed by so smoothly
Untroubled by a need to work,
While he had worked two years already.
He also thought about the weather
And how it still had not grown calm.
Evgeny knew the Neva's bridges
Already must have been removed
And he would not see his Parasha
For at least a day or two.
At that Evgeny deeply sighed
And, like a poet, set to musing:
"Get married? Me? Why shouldn't I?
It would be very hard, of course.
But . . . so what! I'm young and healthy.
I'll labor night and day, if need be.
I'll find a way to build myself
A humble and uncluttered home
And there I'll make a peaceful life
With Parasha, who'll be my wife.
A year will pass, perhaps another.
Then I'll obtain a better post,
And I'll hand over to Parasha
The care of children and household.
And so we'll live for all our lives
Until we come to death together.
Our grandchildren will bury us."

Those were his thoughts as cheerless night
Weighed heavily upon his mind.
He wished the dismal wind would wane
And that the rain would cease to beat
So angrily against the windows.
He finally closed his sleepy eyes.
But look, the foul night's mist is thinning.
Pale morning's light already comes.
O dreadful day.
                    All night the Neva
Strained toward the sea against the storm,

And yet the river could not vanquish
The frenzied folly of the tempest.
At last she could no longer struggle.
The morning saw upon her banks
Great swarms of people there assembled
To gaze in awe at spray and mountains
And foaming crests of wrathful waves.
But then the Neva's flow was blocked
By strong winds blowing off the gulf.
In anger whirling back she swept
Her islands drowning in the wake.
The tempest grew more furious,
The restless Neva thrashed and roared
And like a cauldron steamed and boiled.
Then all at once, a maddened beast,
She pounced upon the helpless city.
All ran away, and all around
Was suddenly left desolate,
And suddenly the waters rushed
Into the subterranean vaults,
As the canals in coursing torrents
Poured towards the iron gratings, and
Petropolis emerged like Triton
Immersed in water to the waist.
Assault! Attack! The angry waves
Like thieves climb into broken windows.
Careening boats crash into panes.
Now hawkers' stalls beneath wet shrouds,
Remains of cabins, logs and roofs,
And goods of frugal merchants' trade,
Debris from bridges smashed by waves,
Belongings of pale poverty,
And coffins from a washed-out churchyard
Float through the city's flooded streets!
The people see the wrath of God,
And they await their punishment.
Alas! Everything will perish.
Where will more food and shelter come from?
The late tsar in that dreadful year
In glory governed Russia still.
He strode out on the balcony
And spoke in sorrow and confusion:
"Not even tsars can overcome
The anger of God's elements,"
And thoughtfully through mournful eyes
He looked upon the tragedy.
Broad rivers flowed throughout the streets
And changed the city's squares to lakes.
The palace seemed a dismal island.
He spoke again—From end to end
Through nearest streets and farthest went
His generals on his command
Amid the stormy waters' peril
To save the panic-stricken people
From drowning in their flooded homes.

On Peter's square there stands a building
Upon the corner newly raised
There on the high-set portico
With paws outstretched as if alive,
Stand two lions mounting guard.
Astride one of these marble beasts
Evgeny sat throughout the flood.
He did not stir, a dreadful pallor
Upon his face. He feared, poor man,
Not for himself. He did not notice
As greedy waves washed at his feet
Nor how the rain lashed at his face
Nor when the wildly howling wind
Rose up and swept away his cap.
Filled with despair his eyes were fixed
As if glued to one distant point.
Like mountains there from stormy depths
The angry waves arose and broke.
The storm was there, and there the water
Was laden with debris . . .My God!
Alas! so close to raging waves
Almost beside the very gulf
There stand the shabby fence, the willow
And tiny cottage, where they live,
His love Parasha and her mother.
His dream . . .or is he dreaming this?
Or can it be that all our lives
Are nothing but an empty dream,
The heavens' sneering at the earth?

And the poor man, as if bewitched,
As if chained to the marble beast,
Cannot climb down! While all around
Is swirling water, nothing more!
And back turned towards the wretched man,
He towers in unflinching height
Above the agitated Neva
With arm extended into space—
The idol on his proud bronze steed.

Part Two

But finally sated with destruction
And tired of her shameless riot,
The Neva dragged her waters back,
Admiring her mutiny
And dropping booty carelessly.
A robber, thus, with vicious band
Bursts fiercely into a small village,
Destroying, killing, crushing, looting;
Screams, gnashing, swearing, violence,
Alarm and wails . . .Weighed down by plunder,
Afraid that they might be pursued,
The tired bandits hurry home
Their booty dropping on the way.

The waters dropped. The pavements opened.
His soul transfixed by hope and fear
Evgeny hastened in distress
Toward the scarcely humbled river.
Still in the flush of victory
The waters boiled maliciously
As if a fire burned beneath them.
While froth still covered swelling waves.
The Neva breathed in heavy gasps
Just like a foaming, panting steed
That has just galloped back from battle.
Evgeny looks. He spies a boat
And toward it runs as to a treasure.
He hails the boatman. For a fee
The carefree boatman soon agrees
To ferry him across the waves.

The skillful oarsman labored long
To navigate the stormy waves
While at each swell the tiny boat
Rose up and tottered at the peak,
About to plummet to the trough
And cast the daring voyagers
Into the waters—Finally
They reached the shore.
                        The wretched man
Runs madly down the well-known street
Until he comes upon the spot
That once was so familiar to him.
But now he cannot recognize it.
Before him all has been destroyed,
This house torn down and that demolished,
Some buildings twisted, some collapsed,
Still others shifted by the waves.
As if it were a battlefield
The ground is strewn with sprawling corpses.

Evgeny, comprehending nothing,
Exhausted by his suffering,
Runs headlong to his destiny,
Awaiting him unknown as if
Enclosed in an unopened letter.
He runs into the neighborhood.
The bay is there. The house stands near . . .
What's wrong?
              He stops, steps back, then forth.
He looks, then walks, then looks again.
He finds the place the house should stand.
The willow's there. The gate was here.
It seems the waves have pulled it down.
The house is nowhere to be seen.
Then, full of dark foreboding, he
Continues walking, walks in circles
And mumbles loudly to himself.
Then suddenly he strikes his brow
And bursts out wildly into laughter.

At last the dark of night descended
Upon the trembling capital,
But people did not go to bed.
They talked at length among themselves
About the past day's happenings.

Through the weary, leaden clouds
The light of morning flickered down
Upon the silence of the city
And could not find a single trace
Left by the past day's tragedy.
The harm was veiled by crimson dawn
And order was again restored.
With cold insensitivity
The masses walked upon the streets
So recently freed by the waters.
Emerging from their past night's shelters,
Officials hurried to their jobs.
The fearless merchant, not despairing,
Opened up his plundered cellar
And counted up his heavy losses
For which he planned to wreak revenge
By preying on his fellow men.
Small boats were carried out of courtyards.
Count Khvostov, heaven's favored poet,
Already sang with deathless lines
The sorrow of the Neva's banks.

Alas! my poor, grief-torn Evgeny . . .
Bewildered by the dreadful shocks,
His rattled mind could not hold up.
The roar of the rebellious Neva
And of the winds rang in his ears.
Unspeaking, full of awful thoughts,
He wandered tortured by some dream.
A week went by and then another.
He did not go back to his room,
And when the period was up,
The landlord let the empty chamber
To a poor poet, and Evgeny
Did not go back to fetch his things.
By day he wandered aimlessly.
By night he slept upon the wharf.
He lived on bits passed out of windows.
His threadbare clothes grew torn and tattered.
Bad children threw stones at his back
And coachmen hit him with their whips
As sometimes he walked off the curb
Into the street and blocked their paths,
But nothing did he seem to notice.
The noise of his inner unease
Drowned out all other sounds around him,
And so he dragged his wretched life,
Not beast nor man, not this nor that,
Not dweller on the earth nor ghost . . .

One night he slept upon the wharf.
The summer days inclined toward fall.
A biting wind blew over him.
Dark waves were splashing on the pier;
They grumbled, beating at smooth steps
As do petitioners before
The door of an indifferent judge.
The poor man woke. The night was dark.
A cheerless drizzle filled the air,
And in the distance through the gloom,
A sentry shouted to the wind . . .
Evgeny started. He recalled
The past disaster vividly.
He sprang up and began to wander.
He stopped and slowly trained his eyes,
With savage fear upon his face.
He found himself beneath the columns
Of a large building. On its porch
With paws outstretched, as if alive,
Stood the lions mounting guard,
And straight before him in dark height
Upon the massive, fenced-in rock,
The idol with extended hand
Sat astride his proud bronze steed.

Evgeny winced, and in his mind
The dreadful images grew clear.
He recognized again the place
Where once the flooding waters played
And where the preying waves had thronged
In angry riot all around him,
The marble lions and the square,
And he whose towering head of bronze
Unmoving loomed in evening's gloom,
The tsar whose fatal will had built
His capital so near the sea.
How awful is his mist-veiled form!
What thoughts are mirrored in his face!
What power latent in his frame!
Where are you galloping, proud steed,
And where will you set down your hooves!
O mighty lord of destiny!
Did you not thus on chasm's brink
In height with iron bridle raise
Proud Russia rearing on her haunches?

Around the idol's pedestal
The wretched madman circled once.
He fixed his savage looks upon
The face of Him who once had held
Dominion over half the world.
Emotion swelled within his breast.
He laid his fevered brow against
The cooling iron of the fence.
His eyes grew misty, and a spark
Shot through his heart. His blood boiled up.

His face grew darkly menacing
Before the proud and heartless giant.
Then, gritted teeth and fingers clenched,
As if an evil force controlled him,
"Just wait, proud miracle creator,"
Evgeny whispered angrily
And in his fear began to tremble,
"I'll get revenge!" Then all at once
He burst into a frantic run.
It seemed to him the awesome tsar
A fleeting moment seethed with anger;
It seemed his face was slowly turning . . .
Across the empty square he runs,
And as he runs, he hears behind him,
Like rolling thunder rumbling,
The powerfully resounding gallop
Of hooves upon the trembling pavement.
By pale moonlight illuminated,
His hand extended toward the sky,
The Horseman races after him
His steed at a resounding gallop.
And all night long the madman ran
No matter where his feet would take him.
But everywhere the dread Bronze Horseman
With heavy tread behind him galloped.

Whenever since that time he chanced
To walk upon the statue's square,
Confusion showed upon his face,
And he would haste to press his hand
Against his heart as if to stop
The pain of inner suffering.
He would remove his worn-out cap
And lower his embarrassed eyes.
Then timidly he would pass by.

A tiny island can be seen
Across the waters from the shore.
From time to time a fisherman
Who's late returning with his net
Will land and cook his supper there,
Or an official in his boat
Out for a Sunday promenade
Will visit the deserted isle,
Where nothing grows, not even grass.
The flood in play had carried there
A battered cottage, which remained
Above the waves like a black bush.
Last spring they ferried it away.
The hut was empty and demolished.
My madman lay across the threshold,
And on that very spot his corpse
Was buried for the sake of God.

1833

M. Yu. LERMONTOV

THE LAY OF THE MERCHANT KALASHNIKOV

Greetings to you, Tsar Ivan Vasilevich!
It is to you we fashion our song, O Tsar,
Of your best-liked *oprichnik*,
And brave Kalashnikov, the merchant.
We made our song in the old way,
We sang it to a psaltery's tune, to say
Nothing of chanting and recitation.
Good Christians were entertained by it
And the *boyar* Matvey Romodanovsky
Poured us each a heady cup of wine
And his pretty wife, moreover, gave us
A present on a silver tray—
A towel embroidered with silver thread.
We feasted for three days and nights;
All listened, and shouted for our song again.

I

It is not the bright shining sun we see;
Nor is it the light-dazzled clouds.
Rather, it is the proud seated Tsar
Ivan Vasilevich crowned in gold,
His loyal myrmidons seated behind,
His loyal *boyars* and princes in front.
His *oprichniks,* like satellites, sit to each side.
The Tsar revels to God's greater glory
And so parties to his heart's content.

Now smiling he commands his servants
To fill his golden cup once more
With the sweet red wine he favors
And likewise to fill his henchmen's cups.
They drink well, and praise the Tsar's name.

Except, that is, for one fine warrior,
A surly youth who would not hoist
The golden cup up to his lips.
His face drooping in the shadow
Of his head, he stared abjectly at the floor,
His mind vexed by a single thought.

The Tsar bunched his mighty brows at this
And drew a bead upon the youth,
Just as a circling hawk, looking down,
Spots a hapless, blue-gray dove.
Still the youth refused to raise his head.
So in a fit the Tsar brought down his staff
With such force that its iron tip
Whanged into the rough-hewn floor.
Nevertheless the youth sat as before.

So from his threatening nimbus the Tsar spoke
And the youth was lifted from his reverie.

"You there, my brave Kiribeyevich,
What disloyal notions are you hiding?
Do you envy our pomp and circumstance?
Are you tiring of your long service?
When the moon appears, the stars rejoice
That heaven's road glows beneath them,
Yet if only one star conceals its face,
It will fall to earth a cinder.
It is not right for you, Kiribeyevich,
To scorn the Tsar in the midst of his joy—
For aren't you a Shuratov by birth,
And reared by Malyuta as her son?"

Then the *oprichnik* answered the Tsar,
Bowing obsequiously at the waist:
"My liege and sovereign master, Ivan Vasilevich!
Don't glare so at your worthless slave
If wine won't extinguish his heart's fire
Nor constant feasting lighten his thoughts.
If I angered you, Sire, bid them
Remove me and chop off my head;
It is a burden to my shoulders anyway
The way it sinks by itself to the ground."

The Tsar Ivan Vasilevich answered him this way:
"What could sadden such a young man as you?
Is your brocade caftan wearing thin?
Or your sable cap now crumpled up?
Does your purse no longer jingle with gold?
Has your once-sharp sword grown dull?
Or your horse lame? Was he poorly shod?
Has the merchant's son knocked you down
In a brawl by the Moscow River?"

Kiribeyevich looked up, tossing his head
And curly hair, and answered proudly:
"Sire, no man alive can knock me down,
Neither *boyar*'s nor a merchant's son!
My stallion's never picky-footed,
And my sword's as bright as mirror glass.
On holidays, Sire, by your pleasure
I can boast of fashion as rich as any.

When I go riding on my mount
Up and down the river bank
With my silken sash around my waist
And my velvet cap with sable trim·
Sitting jauntily on my curly head,
The young girls and wives materialize
By their gates and stare at me
And speak *sotto voce* each to each.
Only one of them averts her face
And covers it with a silken veil.

"Search every inch of Holy Russia, Sire,
And you'll never find such a one as she.
She moves swan-like wherever she goes,
Her look's as pretty as a dove's,
Her voice has a nightingale's timbre.
In her cheeks twin roses bloom
As fresh as in Aurora's face.
Bright ribbons twine her braided hair
Which falls in generous blonde folds
Around her shoulders, and reaches
Finally, to lie on her pretty breast.
She was born and reared in a merchant's house
And her name is Alyona Dmitrevna.

"When I look at her, I grow faint
And enervated, my arms hang limp
And my eyes see spots, then dark.
My Tsar, I grow afraid that I
Will go through life alone.
My horse looks like nothing now.
Silk and finery hold no interest.
Even money—I don't care for that.
Whom, after all, would I share it with?
Who would delight in my prowess?
Whom would my fine clothes impress?

"Let me transfer to the Volga steppe.
Let me lead a Cossack's life!
I'll lose my dazed head in fighting:
A Tatar's sword'll slice it off.
Those infidels will grab my sword
And my lively horse for themselves,
My rich Circassian saddle too.
Crows will peck my sockets clean.
Gray rains will lick my bones.
My dust will blow across the plain
To the steppe's end, unconsecrated."

Then, laughing, the Tsar answered him like this:
"My faithful servant, I'll ease your pain.
Your Sovereign will come to your grief's aid.
Here, my ruby ring and pearl
Necklace that delights everyone . . .
Find a matchmaker and through her
Send these gifts to your fair one,
Your lady Alyona Dmitrevna:
And if she consents, hold a wedding feast;
If not, be calm and let it pass."

All hail to you, Tsar Ivan Vasilevich!
Today your cunning slave has tricked you!
The best part of the truth he's hidden:
He's neglected to say his fair lady's
Married, and to a merchant yet!
Married in our Holy Mother Church
By rites of God and Christian law.

Drink up, boys, and sing!
We'll tune up the psaltery
And drive away your cares.
We'll sing again for Tsar and Lady!

II

A young merchant sat in the marketplace,
The handsome, tall Stepan Paramonovich
Of the house called Kalashnikov.
His silken wares were well displayed
And he counted coins in little piles.
Sometimes he solicited in a positive
Voice, but had no luck. The rich *boyars*
Passed by: they did not look in
And no one gave him any business.

In the church vespers have rung
And sunset glows on the Kremlin domes.
The slate-gray clouds move into place
Overhead, driven by a noisy wind.
Soon the market crowd disperses
And the merchant Stepan Paramonovich
Shuts his stall with an oak-plank door,
Turning an elaborate key in the lock,
And nearby, tethered to a chain,
He sets on guard a seething mastiff
And, lost in thought, departs for home
And wife across the Moscow River.

He soon arrives at his storied house,
And bafflement steals over him, for there
Is no wife as usual to greet him home.
The table's empty, nor is there a cloth
And before the icon a single candle
Flickers. He calls his old servant woman:
"Tell me, Yeremevna, where has
Your mistress gone—she is not here.
Where's Alyona Dmitrevna, my wife?
And my children, have they grown tired
Of games, all that incessant noise,
And been put early to their beds?"

"Dear Master, Stepan Paramonovich,
What I will tell you is strange.
Alyona Dmitrevna went to vespers
But now the priest and wife are back.
They've lit candles and sit at dinner
But my mistress has not yet returned.
The children, grown fretful and tired,
Are not asleep at all, but cry
For their mother, and will not stop."

Then a frightful thought rose in the heart
Of the young merchant Kalashnikov.
He stood at the window and stared

Fixedly at the snow-dusted street.
The snow continued softly and steadily,
Erasing the tracks of passers-by.

Suddenly he hears the door slam
And the sound of hurried footsteps.
He turns and sees—Good Lord!—
His young wife standing in the door.
Bare-headed and white as the snow,
Her hair messed up, the plaits undone;
In her eyes a crazy look,
And her white lips speaking nonsense.

"And where have you been, my little wife?
Wandering in some market or court?
Why has your hair come so unfixed
And your dress been pulled to shreds?
Are you wandering back surfeited
On the orgy of some *boyar*'s son?
It was not for this we married,
I can tell you, by the holy shrine
And exchanged rings on our wedding day.
I'll jail you in your very room
And hinge your freedom in with iron.
You'll never see the sun again
Nor slander my good name."

Hearing this, Alyona Dmitrevna
Grew pale and shook like an aspen leaf.
She wailed and sobbed and down
Her cheeks ran rivulets of tears.
She sank to her husband's knees, imploring:

"O my lord, bright sun of my sky,
Hear me out—or kill me now!
Your words stab me like a dagger
And threaten to split my heart in two.
I don't fear a cruel, physical death
Or endless slander, but your rejection,
My husband, petrifies my soul.

"When I was leaving church tonight
I thought I heard the sound of steps
Behind me in the snow. I turned
And saw a man running after me,
And at that my knees became rubber.
I pulled my veil down tight,
But he grabbed my hands
And whispered to me in a low voice:
'What are you afraid of, my pretty one?
I'm no highway robber or crook,
But a bodyguard of the Tsar himself.
I'm Kiribeyevich of Malyuta's house.'
These words made me even more frightened.
My head went round and my eyes dimmed.
He squeezed me, and he kissed me too.

He held me closer and whispered,
'Speak, and tell me what you want,
My love; answer, and it's yours!
Is it pearls or gold your heart lusts for?
Brocade or silk? Will you take that
From me? I'll fit you like a princess.
You'll be the envy of all Moscow's wives.
Don't let me die a wretch's death,
Unrequited in the love I want.
Let me love you now, before we part.'

"He kissed me forcibly, my lord,
And even now, even here in my house,
His contemptible kisses scorch my face,
For I could see the neighbors' wives
Staring and sniggering from their gates.

"At last I twisted my arms away
From his grip and ran for home
Leaving my embroidered shawl—your wedding gift—
And my veil in his molester's hands.
I was blameless, and he shamed me.
Now when shall I ever show my face,
Such gossip will trail after me?

"My husband, shield me from the liars
And their withering mockery.
Who is left for me to trust but you,
Who else turn to for help?
Were it not for you I would be
An orphan—my parents are dead,
My mother and father both in the grave . . .
Of my brothers the elder ran away
Never to be heard from again
And the younger's a child, as you know,
Both in years and mentally . . ."

So Alyona Dmitrevna trailed off
And cried and cursed her circumstance.

Then the merchant Stepan Paramonovich
Sent word for his brothers to come
Quickly, and they came and bowed to him
And when they spoke, they spoke alike:
"We come expressly for you, brother,
So tell us truly what is the matter
That we've been roused so late
And summoned on a frosty night?"

"Listen, brothers, and I'll tell you all.
A real misfortune has fallen on this house.
The Tsar's *oprichnik*, one Kiribeyevich,
Has thrown mud on our honor and name.
Such disgrace is intolerable to my soul
And the evil unendurable to my heart.
Tomorrow there will be a fight

Before the Tsar, beside the Moscow River.
I'll fight His Majesty's *oprichnik*
Till I can draw my breath no more.
If he should kill me, then you, brothers,
Must come and fight for truth's sake
And honor, and do so without fear.
You both are younger and stronger than I.
Your hearts and souls are blameless of sin;
Thus the Lord may be merciful."

Then his two brothers said as one:
"Wherever the wind goes in the sky's vault
The clouds go quickly because they obey.
When the blue-winged eagle cries for
His young to follow to the battlefield
Where the carcasses lie scattered about,
They come without delay to the feast.
Brother, you are like a father to us.
What you ask of us we will do.
We'll stand by you assuredly."

Drink up, boys, and sing!
We'll tune up the psaltery
And drive away your cares.
We'll sing again for Tsar and Lady!

III

Over great and gold-domed Moscow,
Over the Kremlin's white stone walls,
Morning rises in her scarlet robe
From beyond the hills and creeps
Up over the housetops, driving
Back the clouds without exception.
Her tresses flow out across the sky,
And her face bathes in snow so white
She is like a young beauty at a mirror
Beholding herself back in the sky.
Why are you awake, bright morning?
And why are you rejoicing?

From all over ancient Moscow
Warriors came and other fighting men
To see the fight at the river bank
And such amusements as a holiday meant.
The Tsar came, and his retinue,
His *oprichniks* and his *boyars* too.
He commanded them to stretch a chain
Made of silver overlaid with gold
In order to measure the frozen river
For a suitable place to fight.
Then the great Tsar Ivan Vasilevich
Commanded his heralds in a mighty voice:
"Gather, you brave boys and fighting men,
And fight for our paternal pleasure.
Come gather around the boxing ring.

Who wins his match the Tsar will reward.
Who loses God will forgive!"

Wordlessly Kiribeyevich stepped up,
Bowed low to the Tsar and flung
His velvet cloak down from his shoulders.
Waiting there with hand on hip
He straightened his red hat and stood
Until the challenger showed himself.
The heralds shouted out three times
But no one took up the challenge.
Instead they stood, nudging and whispering.

Suddenly the crowd parts silently
And the merchant Stepan Paramonovich
Of the Kalashnikov house and name
Steps out, and everyone can see him.
He bows reverently to the Tsar,
To the Kremlin fortress and the churches
And lastly to the Russian people.
His eyes, burning with a falcon's stare,
Drill the young *oprichnik* standing there
And he takes his place before his rival:
He pulls on the gloves he'll box with,
Pulls his heavy shoulders back
And strokes his beard meditatively.

Then the *oprichnik* spoke and said,
"Tell me, whose is your house
And what's your name. Tell me,
For how else will I know how
The priests should say their prayers
And whose corpse I'll boast of after."

Stepan Paramonovich answered him this way:
"My name is Stepan Kalashnikov.
I was sired by an honest man.
I have always lived by God's Commandments,
Never having brought shame to another's wife,
Nor skulked along like a cat burglar.
I've never hid from the light of day.
There's one thing you've said that's true:
The priests will bend over one of us
And say Mass by noon tomorrow at the latest.
And one of us bragging with our cronies
Will feign modesty of his victory.
Now I don't fight you for the show
Or a joke, you heathen bastard,
But to fight until one of us is killed."

Kiribeyevich, at this speech, turned gray
As spring snow, and all at once
His bright eyes grew dim.
A chill electrified his spine
And words he'd prepared he left unsaid.

Now without another word the rivals
Circled, and so the fight began.
Kiribeyevich landed the first blow;
Roundhousing his gloved fist, he pounded
Stepan Paramonovich square on the chest.
The merchant reeled back and staggered a bit;
On his chest there hung a copper crucifix,
A relic from Kiev, and this cross
Had penetrated his chest from the blow.
From below it, like dew, blood appeared,
And he said to himself, this merchant,
"What's to be *will* be, it's certain.
But I'll stand for what's right to the end!"
And he steadied himself in order to strike
And winding up, with all his might,
He hit his rival with a strong right cross,
Punching him full on the side of the head.

From the *oprichnik* came a little moan,
He swayed a moment from side to side,
Then toppled over onto the ice
Like a fresh-cut pine tree in a copse
That an axe cuts down from the roots.
He fell and lay quiet, for he was dead.

At this spectacle the mighty Tsar
Was overcome by a spluttering rage.
He knit his brows and stamped his feet
And commanded his men to seize and bring
The merchant before him instantly.

So spoke the great Tsar Ivan Vasilevich:
"Tell me the truth, for I want it:
Did you or did you not intend to kill
My most loyal and trusted bodyguard,
My *oprichnik*, Kiribeyevich?"

"I will tell you the truth, my Tsar,
I fully intended to exact his life,
But I cannot tell you why I did so—
God alone will know why I did...
So execute me, Sire; order my head laid
On the block to await the butcher's axe.
But I pray you, Tsar, show clemency
To my widow and my little children
And be merciful to my faithful brothers."

"It's a good thing, brave merchant,
That you who are so fierce a boxer
Have answered so truthfully to me.
I will provide a grant for your
Widowed wife and your children.
Moreover, never throughout the land of Russia
Will your brothers pay a tax again.
As for you, fierce heart, your head
Will go down on the block by my command.

I will have the blade especially sharpened;
I'll dress the headsman to the nines
And I'll have the great bell toll for you
So that all Moscow will know
The Tsar's generosity and good will."

Crowds stream into the market square
While the bell begins its sad discourse
And its mourning sounds throughout Moscow.
On an incline where the scaffold rises
In a blood-red, ruby-studded blouse
The headsman struts and swings his axe
And rubs his hands—beside himself
With impatience—for his victim, the merchant.
And so the brave Kalashnikov embraces
His brothers and kisses each goodbye.

"My brothers, you are dear to me.
Let me hug you now, for very soon
You and I will part, as I will die.
Give greetings to my wife Alyona Dmitrevna,
Greet the house our parents reared us in,
And salute our relatives and friends.
Afterwards pray for me in our holy Church,
Pray for the deliverance of my sinful soul!"

And thus he was put to death.
It was a cruel death, and a shameful one.
The headsman raised his polished axe
And the head wobbled off the butcher block.

They buried him beyond the Moscow River
In an open field where three roads coming
From Tula, Ryazan and Vladimir intersect.
They heaped some topsoil on his grave
And on that a cross made out of maple.
Now the winds will not calm down.
They sing over his anonymous mound,
Bypassing the graves of Christian folk.
And when codgers pass, they cross themselves,
When youths pass, they walk head-high,
When virgins pass, they dab a tear,
When minstrels pass, they sing a song.

You brave boys!
You good singers!
You strong and happy voices!
As you began well, so must you end.
Sing what is praiseworthy, honorable and just!
To the generous *boyar* his glory!
To the lady wishes and fame!
And glory too to all good
Christians!

1837

The Demon
An Eastern Tale

Part I

1.

A mournful Demon, outcast spirit,
Flew high above the sinful earth,
And memories of his finest days
Began to crowd before his eyes;
Of days, when in his home of light,
Pure Cherub then, he also shone,
And when a meteor in flight
Did love to greet him with a smile
So tender—and to get one in
Return; when through eternal mists,
Athirst for knowledge, he pursued
A roving train of caravans
Of stars all scattered out in space;
When he still loved and still believed,
Creation's happy first-born son!
He knew not spite, he knew not doubt;
A cheerless row of fruitless years
Still could not cause his mind unease . . .
And much, much more . . . but now he had
No strength to recollect it all!

2.

The outcast wandered endlessly
O'er desert worlds without asylum;
One century another chased,
As minute follows minute
In a monotonous parade.
And while he ruled a trivial earth,
Without enjoyment spread the seeds
Of evil, but this art of his
Met no resistance anywhere—
And evil soon began to pall.

3.

And o'er the high Caucasian peaks
The one cast out from Eden flew:
Beneath him Kazbek, like a diamond's edge,
Did glitter 'mid eternal snows;
And darkening so far below,
Just like a crag, that nest for snakes,
The radiant Daryal meandered;
And, leaping like a lioness
With shaggy mane along her spine,
The Terek roars—and mountain beasts
And birds, which circle in the azure heights,
Attended to the speeches of
Its icy waters; golden clouds
From southern climes, for many miles

Accompanied it to the north;
And clustered crowds of rocks all filled
With enigmatic drowsiness
Kept nodding over it,
While following its flashing waves;
And castle towers on the rocks,
All menacing, watched through the mists—
Like giant sentries at their post
To guard the gates of Caucasus!
And all around, God's whole creation
Was wild and wondrous; but the proud
And haughty spirit viewed his God's
Creation with a scornful eye,
And nothing was reflected on
His lofty brow.

4.

And then before him living beauties
Of yet another canvas bloomed:
The valleys of luxurious Georgia
Were spread like carpets in the distance;
Oh, happy, splendid corner of the world!
With poplars shaped like pyramids,
And ringing streams that run along
The bottom formed of multi-colored stones;
Rose bushes in which nightingales
Still sing of beauties, unresponsive
To the sweet voices of their loves;
And sycamores form canopies
Of branches thick with ivy crowns,
Where during scorching times of day
The timid deer can hide in caves;
The lustre, life and noise of leaves,
The sound of voices hundredfold,
The breathing of a thousand plants!
And noon's voluptuous heat,
And nights forever damp
With aromatic dew,
And stars as bright as eyes
And glances of young Georgian maids! . .
But nature's glow could not arouse
Within that sterile, exiled breast
New feelings or new powers, yet
Could wake cold envy from its sleep;
And all before him that he saw,
He either hated or despised.

5.

Gray-haired Gudál built for himself
A lofty house, a courtyard wide . . .
It cost the long-obedient slaves
So many tears, a lot of toil.
From morning on lie shadows from
Its walls on slopes of nearby peaks.
And in the rocks are hewn some steps
Which make a path from corner tower

Right to the river; flitting down
Those very steps, Tamára goes,
Young princess veiled in white,
To fetch some water from Aragva's banks.

6.

And ever did this gloomy house
In silence watch the valley from its cliff;
But now a giant feast is under way—
Zurnás[1] ring out, the wines flow fast—
Gudal has pledged his daughter's hand
And called his clan to celebrate.
While on the roof spread out with rugs
The young bride sits among her friends:
Their leisure hours slip by amid
The games and songs. The distant peaks
Already hide the semi-circle of
The sun; and clapping hands to keep
The time, they sing—the youthful bride
Takes up her tambourine.
And there she is. Above her head
She twirls it in her hand. And suddenly
She darts about much lighter than
A bird, then stops and looks around—
Her misted eyes begin to shine
From under lashes, full of envy;
And first she lifts her coal-black brows,
Then suddenly she slightly bows,
And then her little foot divine
Slides by and floats along the rug;
And full of childlike joy, she smiles.
A moonbeam which does now and then
Play lightly on the waves
Could scarce compare with her sweet smile,
So lively, just like youth—and life itself.

7.

I swear by the North Star, and by
The rising and the setting of the sun,
That never any earthly tsar
Or any shah of golden Persia
Had kissed such eyes as hers;
No splashing fountain in a harem
Did ever on a torrid day
Pour out its pearly dew to bathe
A figure such as hers!
Nor yet did any mortal hand
Caress so sweet a brow,
Unplait such hair as hers;
Not since the time when earth lost Eden,
I swear, no beauty such as this
Did bloom beneath the southern sun.

8.

She danced, and danced for one last time.
Alas! what would tomorrow bring

To freedom's frisky child,
To her, Gudal's own heiress, but
The mournful lot of slavery.
A fatherland 'til now so strange,
A family as yet unknown.
And often secret doubts arose
To cloud her features once so bright;
Her each and every movement was
Composed and filled with much expression,
So full of sweet simplicity
That if the Demon, flying past,
Had at the time but glanced her way,
Then, recollecting former ties,
He would have turned—and caught his breath . . .

9.

The Demon had caught sight of her . . . and felt
Quite suddenly within himself
Ineffable emotions which
Rushed by. And sounds of heaven filled
The wasteland of his muted soul—
Again he knew the sacredness
Of beauty, love and kindliness! . .
And he enjoyed the charming scene
For quite a while—and then his dreams
Of former happiness slid by
Before him in a lengthy chain,
As if they were linked star to star.
And held in place by unseen power,
He grew acquainted with new sadness;
Emotions suddenly began
To speak a language once his own.
Was this some sign of his rebirth?
Within his mind he could not find
Temptations of perfidious words . . .
Forget?—God granted no oblivion,
Oblivion he would not accept! . .
. . . .

10.

When he wore out his own good steed,
Near twilight time the bridegroom sped
Impatiently to nuptial feasts.
With fortune's help he came upon
The bright Aragva's green-hued banks.
And burdened heavily with gifts,
Just barely moving step by step,
A caravan of camels gleams;
Stretched out behind him on the road,
Their little bells keep ringing out.
For he, the lord of Sinodal,
Now leads the precious caravan.
His graceful form was belted tight;
His saber's mountings, dagger's too,
Were shining 'neath the sun; and on
His back he wore a carved, notched gun.

The wind was playing with the sleeves
Of his *chukhá*[2]—which is all trimmed
Around with golden lace.
His costly saddle is embroidered
In colored silk; the bridle's tassled.
The horse beneath him, all in foam,
Is of a priceless, golden hue.
Swift foster-child of Karabakh,
It fearfully moves back its ears,
And snorting, looks askance from its steep ledge
Down to the foam of racing waves.
The shoreline path is dangerous
And narrow! Cliffs are on the left,
The deep, rebellious river's on the right.
It is already late. On snowy heights
The rosy glow's gone out; mists rose . . .
The caravan picked up its pace.

11.

Look, there's a chapel near the road . . .
For many years here rests in God
A certain prince, now canonized,
But slain by a revenging hand.
Since then whenever travelers
Would hurry off to holidays
Or wars, they always offered up
A zealous prayer at the chapel;
And then that prayer would protect
Them from a Moslem dagger.
But when the daring bridegroom scorned
The custom of his ancestors,
The crafty Demon set upon
Him with a clever, lying dream:
Thus in his thoughts, and under dark
Of night, he kissed his bride's sweet lips.
Then suddenly two men sprang up,
And more—a shot!—what is all this? . .
And rising on his ringing stirrups,[3]
He pulled his sheepskin cap down to his brows,
But the brave prince said not a word;
A Turkish gun flashed in his hand,
He cracked his whip—and like an eagle
He rushed ahead . . . a shot again!
A wild cry and hollow moan
Tore down into the valley's depths—
The battle didn't go on long:
The timid Georgians ran away!

12.

And all grew still; massed in a crowd,
From time to time the camels gazed
In horror at the riders' corpses;
And in the quiet of the steppe
Their little bells rang hollowly.
The splendid caravan was sacked.
And night birds drew their circles o'er
The bodies of the Christian men.

No peaceful grave awaits them there
Beneath the monastery stones,
Wherein their fathers' dust was buried;
Their sisters, mothers covered with
Long hanging veils won't come
From distant parts to visit graves,
To grieve, to wait, to supplicate! . .
Sometime a zealous hand will build
A cross in memory of them
Along the road, above the rock;
And ivy, growing thick in spring,
Will circle it caressingly
Within its emerald net;
And turning off the tricky road,
Quite often will a tired pedestrian
Rest under God's own shade . . .

13.

The horse takes off as fast as any deer;
It snorts and roars as if to war;
Then suddenly it checks its gallop,
And listens to the wind
While it dilates its nostrils wide;
Then all at once it strikes the earth
With ringing calks upon its hooves;
And flapping back its tousled mane,
Flies off completely unaware.
A silent horseman sits on it!
At times he bounces in the saddle.
He's pressed his head against the mane.
But he no longer tugs the bridle,
His feet have slid into the stirrups.
But bloody streams flow wide; they are
Already seen on his *shabrack*.[4]
O dashing, speedy steed, you bore
Your master from the fray just like a shot.
But in the darkest hour, a spiteful
Assetian bullet brought him down.

14.

Within Gudal's own house they wept and moaned,
The people crowded in the yard:
Whose overheated horse rushed in
And fell on stones right near the gates?
Who was this lifeless rider?
The wrinkles on his darkened brow
Preserved the traces of alarms of battle.
His arms and clothes were all in blood;
His hand was lifeless as he held the mane
He clutched in final, frantic grasps.
Bride, not for long did your own eyes
Watch out for your young groom:
He kept his princely word,
He hurried to the nuptial feast . . .
Alas! no more will he
Sit on his dashing steed.

15.

God's punishment like thunder flew
Upon this carefree clan!
Then poor Tamara sobbed as she
Fell down upon her bed; tears flowed
In steady streams. And shallowly,
Laboriously, her chest gasped out for air;
And then it was as if she heard
Above her some bewitching voice:
"Don't cry, my child! don't cry in vain!
Your tear won't fall upon the mute
Dead man as if it were life-giving dew:
It only clouds your bright-eyed gaze
And burns your virgin's cheeks!
He's far away, he's unaware,
He does not value grief;
A heav'nly light caresses now
His incorporeal gaze;
He hears the songs of paradise . . .
What are life's petty dreams,
The moans and tears of some poor maid
To one who dwells above the skies?
Oh, no, my earthly angel, trust
Me that the destiny of just
A single mortal's worth
Mere seconds of your precious grief!
　　　In the empyrean ocean
　　　Harmonies of all the planets
　　　Sail on silently in mists,
　　　Rudderless, without a sail:
　　　Fibrous flocks of clouds one
　　　Cannot capture walk along and
　　　Leave no traces there among the
　　　Boundless fields of heaven.
　　　Hours of parting, hours of meeting
　　　Bring no joy, no grief to them; they
　　　Wish for nothing from the future,
　　　Don't regret the past. And on the
　　　Agonizing day of sorrow
　　　Simply think of them a little;
　　　Be as carefree, unconcerned with
　　　Moral destiny as they are!
As soon as night begins to cover
Caucasian summits with its pall,
As soon as earth, enchanted by
Some magic charm, grows hushed and mute;
As soon as wind begins to stir
The withered grass atop the rocks,
And little birds that hide within
More gaily flutter in the gloom;
And as it swallows greedily
The dew of heavens, under vines
Of grapes a nighttime flower blooms;
As soon as a still, golden moon
Begins to rise beyond the peaks
And glances at you on the sly—

Then I shall start to fly to you;
I'll visit you until the break
Of day, elicit golden dreams
Upon your lashes so like silk . . ."

16.

And in the distance all his words
Grew still, as sound died after sound.
She started, then she looked around . . .
An inexpressible confusion
Now rose within her breast; no fright,
No sorrow, ardor, ecstasy—compared
With it. And suddenly her feelings seethed
Within; her soul tore off its chains,
A flame raced through her veins.
It seemed to her that even now
His novel, wondrous voice rang out.
And just before the morning came,
Long-sought-for sleep closed tired eyes;
A strange prophetic dream
Disturbed her sleepy thoughts.
Aglow with beauty quite supernal,
A hazy, silent stranger came
And bent his head to where she lay;
His eyes looked down upon her face
With so much love, with so much sadness,
It seemed as if he pitied her.
This was no angel heaven-sent,
Her guardian divine:
No crown of iridescent beams
Of light adorned his curly hair.
This was no dread, infernal fiend,
No vile or martyred soul—oh, no!
He looked just like the radiant evening sky:
Not day, not night—not gloom, not light!

Part II

1.

"Ah, father, father, quit your threats,
You musn't scold your own Tamara;
I'm crying; can't you see the tears;
They're not the first I've shed.
A crowd of grooms will hurry here
From distant lands; it's all in vain . . .
There is no dearth of brides in Georgia;
But I shall never be a wife! . .
Oh, don't rebuke me, father, don't;
You see yourself that day by day
I fade, a victim of some toxic spite!
A cunning spirit still torments
My life with dreams I can't resist;
I perish—still they press me down!
So let your senseless daughter live
Within a holy cloister's walls;
Our Savior will defend me there,

I'll pour my sorrow at His feet.
No joy exists for me on earth . . .
I'll live within a gloomy cell;
A darkened world of holy things, so like
An earthly coffin, welcomes me . . ."

2.

And her relations took her to
A lovely cloister far away;
They clothed her youthful breast
Within a humbling hairshirt vest.
But even in her convent garb,
It could have been some rich brocade,
Just as before, the lawless dream
Kept beating still within her heart
Before the altar all aglow
With candles burning bright. Amid
The solemn songs, between her prayers,
She often heard the well-known speech.
Beneath the gloomy church's dome,
Sometimes without a sound or trace,
A well-known image floated through
The weightless haze of incense smoke;
As silent as a star, it shone,
Enticed, called out to her . . . but—where? . .

3.

The holy convent hid itself
Within the coolness of two hills.
It was surrounded by long rows
Of sycamores and poplars—but
When in the gorge night lay in rest,
The icon lamp of our young sinner
Gleamed through the windows of her cell.
And under shade of almond trees,
Where rows of mournful crosses stood,
Those silent guardians of the tombs,
Light birds in chorus practiced songs.
And springs with icy waves made noise,
And gamboled on the stones beneath
An overhanging rock; like friends,
They flowed together in the gorge,
And rolled on even farther 'mid
The bushes and the frosted flowers.

4.

The mountains loom up in the north.
In presence of Aurora's morning glow,
When dark'ning puffs of smoke
Appear within the valley's depths,
And, turning to the east,
Muezzins make their call to prayer;
When trembling voices of a bell
Resound and raise the convent from its sleep;
And at this solemn, peaceful hour,
As our young Georgian maid descends

The steeply sloping mountain side to fetch
Some water in an elongated urn,
As if they formed a lambent-lilac wall,
The summits of the snowy chain
Make silhouettes against the sky;
But at the sunset hour
They dress in reddish shrouds;
Among them, slicing through the clouds,
His head held higher than all others' stood
Kazbek, Caucasian tsar almighty,
In turban and brocaded cloak.

5.

But filled with sinful thoughts,
Tamara's heart's indifferent
To these pure ecstasies. Before her now
The world is dressed in gloomy shade;
Within it all becomes for her
Mere pretext for more torment—
Both morning's ray and gloom of night.
Sometimes, when coolness of
A sleepy night embraces earth,
Bereft of reason she falls down
Before a sacred icon
And cries; and in nocturnal silence
Her heavy sobbing catches the
Attention of a passerby.
He thinks: "Some mountain spirit chained
Within a cave is languishing away!"
And straining his keen sense of hearing,
He spurs his worn-out horse ahead . . .

6.

Replete with yearning, trepidation,
Tamara often sits close by
Her window, lost in lonely contemplation,
Her watchful eyes fixed on a distant spot,
And sighing, waits the whole day through . . .
Then someone whispers: he will come!
For not in vain did he appear to her,
His eyes all full of sorrow,
His wondrous speeches full of tenderness.
She languishes for many days,
Herself not knowing why:
She wants to pray to saints on high,
Her heart can only pray to *him*;
This constant battle wearies her,
She lies upon her bed of dreams—
The pillow burns, she chokes, she's scared,
She starts, then trembles head to toe;
Her breast and shoulders are aflame,
She has no strength to breathe, her eyes mist up,
Embraces greedily seek out responses,
And kisses melt upon her lips . . .
. . . .
. . . .

7.

When evening's shadows had already dressed
The hills of Georgia with an airy shroud,
Obedient to his passion's habit,
The Demon flew down to the cloister.
But for a long, long time he dared
Not violate the holy refuge or
The peace. There was a moment when
He seemed to be in readiness
To leave behind his cruel design.
He wandered lost in thought close by
High walls: and from his steps, without
The wind, leaves trembled in the shade.
He raised his eyes: her window shone
Illuminated by an icon lamp;
She's long been waiting for someone!
And now amid a total hush
Harmonious clanging of *chingárs*[5]
And sounds of songs resound about;
But then those sounds poured out
Like measured tears, one then another;
The song was very tender, light
As if it had been written up
Above, for those still on the earth!
Could not an angel who had yearned
To meet again his long-lost friend
Have flown down here by stealth
To sing to him about the past,
To ease his suffering?..
At last the Demon understood
The ache of love, its agitation;
He wishes to retreat in fear ...
He cannot stir his wings!
A miracle! a heavy tear
Slides from his eyes which have grown dim ...
Until today close by this cell,
There is a stone all burned right through
By someone's tear as hot as flame,
By some inhuman tear!

8.

And he walks in, prepared to love,
His soul receptive to good will;
He thinks the long-desired time,
The era of new life, has come at last.
His haughty soul became acquainted
With vague, expectant trepidation
And fear of mute uncertainty
As if they'd never met before.
How evil that foreboding was!
He enters, looks around—before
Him stands a cherub, God's own messenger,
The lovely sinner's guardian.
His brow is all aglow, his lips—
A shining smile; his wings protect
Her from the foe within their shade;

A ray of beatific light
At once deprived the tainted eyes of sight,
In place of any sweet-voiced greeting
A painful reprimand rang out:

9.

"O restless spirit, wanton spirit,
Who called you to this midnight gloom?
Your worshippers are not now present,
And here 'til now no evil ever breathed;
Don't let your sinful footsteps pave
A path to my beloved one
Or to my holy place.
Who called you here?"
                              In answer then
The cunning evil spirit grinned
Ironically; his countenance
Grew red, suffused with jealousy;
Again within his soul the poison of
An ancient hatred reawakened.
"She's mine!" he said ferociously—
"Leave her alone! for she is mine!
Protector, you appeared too late;
You are no judge of her, of me.
For I've already placed my seal
Upon a heart all filled with pride;
This holy place is yours no more
It's I who love and rule here now!"
With saddened eyes the angel glanced
Upon the poor, lost victim, then
He flapped his wings and slowly sank
Within the ether of the sky.
. . . .

10.

Tamara
Oh! Who are you? your speech is dangerous!
Did hell or heaven send you here?
What do you want?

Demon
   You're beautiful!

Tamara
But tell me, who are you? Respond . . .

Demon
I am the one you noticed once
In midnight silences, the one
Whose thoughts once whispered to your soul,
Whose sorrows you so vaguely guessed,
Whose image you perceived in dreams.
I am the one whose look destroys all hope;
I am the one whom no one loves;
I am the scourge of all my earthly slaves,
I am the tsar of conscious liberty,

I am the foe of heaven, nature's evil;
But yet you see—I'm at your feet!
With tenderness I've brought for you
A silent prayer full of love,
The torments I first knew on earth,
And my first tears. Oh! hear me through—
Have pity! You could send me back
To goodness, heaven too—with just a word.
And there I would appear, all dressed
Up in a sacred shroud made of
Your love, just like a newborn angel
Adorned in new magnificence;
Oh! only hear me out, I pray—
I am your slave—it's you I love!
As soon as I caught sight of you—
I secretly began to hate
My power, immortality.
Against my will I envied now
Man's joy on earth, so incomplete;
It pained me not to live like you;
I feared to live apart from you.
An unexpected light began
To glow again more vividly
Within my bloodless heart. And, serpent-like,
The sorrow at the bottom of
An ancient wound began to stir.
Without you what's eternity to me?
The boundlessness of my domain?
They're simply empty, ringing words,
A spacious temple—but without a god!

Tamara

Just leave me be, o cunning spirit!
Be still, I won't believe a foe . . .
The creator . . . Alas! I can't
Begin to pray . . . My weakened mind
Is filled with venom that destroys!
Now listen, you will ruin me;
Your words are poison, full of fire . . .
But tell me, why do you love me!

Demon

You ask me why, my beauty, why?
Alas, I do not know! . . Filled with
New life, I proudly tore the crown
Of thorns right off my sinful head,
And flung my past straight to the dust:
My heav'n and hell are in your eyes.
I love you with unearthly passion,
In ways you'll never, ever love,
With all my rapture, all the might
Of my immortal thoughts and dreams.
Since time began your image was
Engraved within my very soul;
It rushed along before me in
The deserts of unbounded space.

So long disturbing all my thoughts,
Your dear, sweet name rang out to me;
My blissful days in paradise
Were lacking only you.
Oh! if you could but understand
How bitter is the languor of
My life; to suffer, take delight
While century into century flowed,
Expect no praise for evil done,
Nor get rewards for any good;
To live for self, to bore oneself
In this eternal battlefield
Without a triumph, with no peace!
To pity always, but not want,
To know it all, to feel it all,
To see it all, despise it all,
And all on earth to try to hate! . .
And from the time that God himself
Did curse me; since that very day,
Forever cold were all the ardent
Embraces of the world of nature;
The universe grew dark before me;
I saw the wedding costumes of
The stars, well-known to me for ages . . .
They flew right by in crowns of gold;
What of it? for each one of them,
My former brothers, knew me not.
Then in despair I called to those
Who were like me, poor exiled souls;
Alas! their evil faces, looks
And words did I myself avoid.
And then in fear I flapped my wings,
Took off . . . but whither, for what reason?
I do not know . . . my former friends
Rejected me; like Eden's pair,
For me the world grew mute and still.
Thus does a damaged boat without
A sail, without a rudder, float
Along the currents' free caprice,
Of final destination unaware.
Sometimes at early morn, a patch
Of thundercloud, all growing dark
In azure heights, dares not to stop
Alone in any spot, but thus
It flies without a goal; it leaves no trace,
And God alone knows whither, whence!
But not for long I ruled mankind,
And not for long did teach them sin,
All that was noble I defamed,
And censured everything of beauty;
And not for long . . . with ease I quenched
Their flame of purest faith forever . . .
But were those fools and hypocrites
Alone deserving of my toils?
I hid within the mountain gorges,
And like a meteor began

To roam the gloom of darkest night . . .
A lonely wanderer rushed off,
The closeness of my fire led him astray,
And falling with his horse into
A chasm, he called in vain—he left
His bloody prints along steep walls . . .
It wasn't long before these bleak
Amusements ceased to feed my spite!
In battling mighty hurricanes,
So often raising up the dust,
All dressed in lightning and mist,
I loudly rushed into the clouds,
Into rebellious elements,
To muffle murmurs of my heart,
Escape the thoughts that wouldn't flee,
The unforgettable—forget.
What is a tale of painful losses,
Travails and toils of mortal crowds
Of generations past and those
To come, before a single minute of
A pain I can't acknowledge here?
And what of men? their life and toil?
They have passed through, they will pass through . . .
They have some hope—a judgment fair;
He may forgive, could censure too!
My sorrow just goes on and on
And on; like me it has no end;
It will not sleep in any grave!
It first caresses like a snake,
Then burns, whips out just like a flame,
And like a stone it presses on
My thoughts—so indestructible
A grave of hopes and passions lost! . .

Tamara
But why should I your sorrows know,
And why should you complain to me?
For you did sin . . .

Demon
            Against you, though?

Tamara
But they might hear us!

Demon
            We're alone.

Tamara
But God!

Demon
        Won't cast a glance at us;
He cares for heaven now, not earth!

Tamara
But punishment, the pains of hell?

Demon
So what? I'll be there at your side!

Tamara
Whoever you may be, chance friend—
Destroying peace forevermore,
With secret joy, against my will
I listen, sufferer, to you.
But if your speech is trickery,
But if you are concealing lies . . .
Oh! mercy, please! What glory's yours?
What can my soul be worth to you?
Can heaven love my soul much more
Than all of those you did not note?
For they, alas! are lovely too;
As here, their couches maiden-pure
Are ruffled not by human hand . . .
No! give me now your fateful vow . . .
And say—you see: I suffer now;
You see how female are my dreams!
Against your will you now embrace
The fear that dwells within my soul . . .
You understand, you know it all—
So certainly you'll pity me!
Give me your vow, swear to renounce
Your evil whims from this day forth.
Are there no sacred promises,
No longer any sacred vows?

Demon
I swear by earth's first day of life,
I swear, too, by its very last,
I swear by punishment's disgrace,
By triumph of eternal truth.
I swear by bitter pain caused by my fall,
By my short dream of victory;
I swear by our first meeting, then
By threats of parting once again.
I swear by crowds of spirits, by
My brothers subject now to me,
By swords of angels so impassive
And of my ever-watchful foes;
I swear by heaven and by hell,
By earthly holy things, by you;
I swear by your most recent glance,
And by your tear, the very first,
And by the breath upon your gentle lips,
And by your waves of silky hair;
I swear by suffering and bliss,
I swear by love of mine for you:
That I renounce my old revenge,
That I renounce my bitter thoughts;
Henceforth insidious flattery's venom
Will not again disturb my brain;
I want to make my peace with God,
I want to love, I want to pray,
I want to trust in good again.

I'll wipe away from off my brow,
Now worthy of you, traces of
The fire of heaven with repentant tears—
And let the world, serenely dumb,
Just fade away without me there!
Believe me: only I 'til now
Did understand and rank you high:
I've chosen you my holy thing,
I laid my power at your feet,
And I await your gift of love
And grant eternity for just
A moment of your time.
Believe, Tamara, I'm steadfast
And great—in love as well as hate.
As ether's independent son,
I'll take you to a land above;
And you will be *tsaritsa* of
The world, as well as my first friend:
You will begin to look at earth
Without regret or interest;
There where no happiness is real,
No beauty everlasting keeps,
Where only punishment and crimes abound,
Where people live for petty passion,
Where people know not how to love
Or hate without their fears and dread.
Or don't you know how fleeting love
Of people for each other is?
Arousal's for the blood of youth—
But days run by and blood grows cold!
Who can stand up to separation,
Temptation of a new-found beauty,
To boredom and to weariness,
And even willfulness of dreams?
No! you must know, it's not for you;
My friend, you're not marked out by fate
To wither, mute, in crowded spheres
Of jealous coarseness, like a slave
Among the craven and the cold
Dissembling friends and foes alike;
[Among] those sterile hopes and fears,
[Among] those empty, painful toils!
You will not sadly fade away
Beyond high walls, not knowing passion,
Amid your prayers, while equally
As far from God and man as you can be.
Oh no, most beautiful creation,
You are ordained for other things;
A different suffering waits for you,
And depths of other ecstasies;
So leave, then, all your former longings,
[And leave] the poor world to its fate:
And in return I shall reveal
To you the gulf of proud cognition.
Right to your feet I'll lead a crowd
Of spirits who are in my service;

To you, my beauty, I shall give
Attendants light and magical;
For you I'll rip the golden crown
Right off the rising morning star;
I'll take some midnight dew from blooms;
And with this dew I'll sprinkle it;
I'll wind a ray of rosy sunset
All ribbon-like around your form;
I'll fill the air surrounding us
With purest whiffs of perfumed scents;
And constantly I shall caress
Your ears with wondrous songs to hear;
And I shall build luxuriant halls
Made out of amber, turquoise stones;
I shall sink to the ocean's floor,
I'll fly out right beyond the clouds,
I'll give you everything on earth—
Just love me—do! . . .

11.

And lightly he
Did touch with his own ardent lips
Those lips of hers, lips all atremble;
He answered all her supplications
With speeches bursting with temptations.
His mighty eyes looked into hers!
He burned her. In the gloom of night
He simply glittered over her,
As fascinating as a dagger.
Alas! the evil spirit triumphed!
The fatal poison of his kisses
Did instantly pass through her breast.
An agonizing, horrid scream
Disturbed nocturnal quietness.
All things were in it: suffering, love,
Reproach with final supplication,
The hopelessness of her farewell—
Farewell to her young life itself.

12.

But at that time the midnight guard,
Alone, all hushed, with iron gong,
Completing normal rounds once more,
Meandered 'round the steep-cut wall;
And near the youthful maiden's cell
He checked his measured step, and with
His hand poised o'er the iron gong,
He stopped, his soul all in confusion.
And through the silence all around,
It seemed to him that he did hear
A willing kiss upon two pairs of lips,
A short-lived scream, a weakened moan.
And then and there suspicious doubt
Pierced through the old man's very heart . . .
But yet another moment passed
When all grew still; and from afar

A gentle breath of wind
Brought with it murmurs of the leaves.
A mountain river mournfully
Was whisp'ring with its darkened banks.
In fear he hurries to read through
The prayers of God's holy servants,
To chase from his own sinful mind
The witchcraft of an evil spirit;
As in a dream, with shaking fingers
He crosses first his troubled breast;
Then silently, with quickened steps,
Continues on his normal route.
. . . .

13.

As sweet as any sleeping Peri,
She lay within her coffin boards;
The languid color of her brow
Was whiter, purer than her shroud.
Her eyelids lowered for all time . . .
But who, o God, would not have said
Her eyes beneath were merely sleeping,
Or, miracle, were only waiting for
The morning star, perhaps a lover's kiss?
But uselessly a morning ray,
In golden streams, slid over them;
In vain, in mute despondency,
Her kinfolk's lips kissed over them . . .
No! Nothing has the power to
Tear off [dread] death's eternal seal!

14.

Tamara's holiday attire
Had never been, in happy days,
So many-colored or so rich.
The flowers of her native gorge
(For ancient rites demand it so)
Pour forth their fragrance over her
While hands now dead clasp onto them
As if to say farewell to earth!
And nothing in her peaceful face
Alluded to her dying hour,
Its flames of passion, ecstasy;
And all the features of her face
Were filled with beauty likened to
Cold marble, alien to expression,
Devoid of feelings and of reason,
Mysterious as death itself.
A smile so strange congealed upon
Her lips, where first it quickly flashed.
It spoke to all attentive eyes
Of much that was quite sorrowful:
In it there was a cold disdain
Found in a soul prepared to fade,
A final thought's expressive phrase
Of mute farewell to all the earth.

A worthless gleam of former life,
[A life] which seemed so much more dead
Than eyes forever closed in death,
With more despair than any heart could hold.
So at the solemn sunset hour,
When melting in a sea of gold,
The chariot of day steals off,
Caucasian snows, for just a second,
Preserve their rosy play of lights
And penetrate the distant darkness.
But half-alive this very ray
Meets no reflection in the desert,
Lights up no path for anyone
From high upon its icy peaks! . .

15.

Relations, neighbors in a crowd
All set upon their mournful way;
And tearing out his ringlets gray,
And mutely striking at his breast,
One final time Gudal sits high
Upon his white-maned steed; then the
Procession can set off. Three days,
Three nights their journey will drag out:
A peaceful haven was cut out
For her among old forebears' bones.
One of Gudal's progenitors,
A thief who preyed on wanderers
And towns alike, when sickness struck
Him down and when the hour of penitence
Arrived, to pay for all his sins,
He promised God to build a church
On summits of those granite rocks,
Where only songs of storms are heard
And whither only black kites fly.
And soon among Caucasian snows
A solitary temple rose,
And once again the evil man's
Old bones there found eternal peace;
And then this rock, so dear to clouds
Transformed into a graveyard scene:
But could its dwellers long deceased
Be really warmer nearer to
The skies? . . Their final dreams grew much more still
The further that they were from men . . .
In vain! for dead men never dream
Of sorrows, joys of former days.

16.

Far out in blue ethereal space
A holy angel flew on golden wings,
And carried off in his embrace
The sinful soul from earth.
He chased away her doubts
With speeches sweetly full of hope,
And with his tears he washed away

All traces of her suffering, faults.
And from afar already sounds
Of paradise came to their ears—
And suddenly—across their path
The hellish spirit rushed from the
Abyss. He was as mighty as
A noisy whirlwind and he flashed
Like streaks of lightning while he said
In proud and reckless insolence, "She's mine!"

Tamara's sinful soul did press
Itself to his protecting breast,
While muting horror with a prayer.
Her fate hung in the balance,
Before her once again he stood,
But, God!—who could have known him now?
He gazed with such malicious eyes,
So full of all the deadly poison of
A hatred which would never know an end,—
The coldness of the grave fanned out
From his impassive face.

"Begone, you gloomy spirit, source of doubt!"
Responded heaven's messenger—
"You've celebrated long enough;
The hour of judgment's now at hand—
God's verdict is correct and good!
The days of testing have gone by;
The chains of evil fell from her along
With earthly trappings subject to decay.
But look! We've waited such a long, long time
For her! Her soul was one of those
Whose life was just a moment of
Intolerable agony
Of unattainable delights:
The Maker wove the living fiber of
Their lives out of the finest air,
They were not made to live on earth,
And earth was made, but not for them!
She has atoned for all her doubts,
She's paid the cruelest price . . .
She suffered and she loved—it was
Her love that opened paradise!"

The angel gazed severely at
The tempter standing there,
And joyfully he flapped his wings
And plunged right into heaven's light.
And the defeated Demon cursed
His former, reckless dreams;
And once again he was alone
In all the universe, alone
And proud, as he had been before,
Without a chance of hope or love!

———————

And on a rocky mountain slope
Above the valley of Koyshaur,
Still stand until this very day
The merlons of an ancient ruin.
And legends are still full of tales
About them, all too frightening for a child . . .
The silent monument so like a ghost,
A witness to those magic days,
Shows black among the trees.
Below, a mountain village spreads about,
The earth grows green and flowers bloom;
Discordant droning of the voices down
Below die out, while caravans, their bells
All ringing, come from distant lands,
And, rushing down right through the mist,
The river shines and foams.
And jesting nature has her fun,
In sunshine, coolness and in spring,
In life forever young,
Just like a carefree child.

But gloomy is the castle now,
Which in its turn served out its years,
Just like a poor old man who has
Outlived his friends and his dear family.
And only hidden creatures now
Await the rising of the moon:
Then they have time to celebrate, be free!
They buzz, they run from every side.
A grey-hued spider, new recluse,
Spins out the first threads of its web;
A green-hued lizard family
Quite joyously plays on the roof;
And then a cautious snake crawls out
From its dark nook and slithers to
The flagstones of the ancient porch,
Then suddenly it twists into three rings,
Then like a lengthy band lies flat
And shines just like a sword of steel,
Forgotten in the field of ancient battles,
Now useless to a fallen hero! . .
All's wild: nowhere is any trace
Of years gone by: the hand of time
So long and carefully has swept
Them all away. And nothing here
Reminds one of the famous name
Gudal, or of his daughter dear.

And on the spot where earth has claimed
Their bones, preserved by sacred power,
Upon a steep stone peak, the church
May still be seen among the clouds.
And at its gates there stand on guard
Two blackened stones of granite,
All capped with hoods of snow;
And on their breasts instead of coats

Of mail, eternal ices burn.
And sleepy, massive snowslides frown,
While hanging down around the ledges;
They look like waterfalls which once
Were trapped in ice quite suddenly.
And there a blizzard walks patrol
While blowing dust from grey-hued walls;
It first strikes up a lengthy song,
Then calls out to the sentinels;
From far and wide the news is heard
That in that land there is a wondrous church;
But only eastern clouds crowd 'round
To hurry there to pray; but now—
For many years no one at all
Has mourned for them while sitting near
The stones that mark the family plot.
The rocks of gloomy Kazbek stand
As greedy guardians of their loot,
And man's eternal grumbling can't
Disturb the scene's eternal peace.

1841[6]

Notes

1. An instrument which somewhat resembles bag-pipes.

2. An outer garment with folded sleeves.

3. The Georgians use stirrups that are like slippers made of ringing metal.

4. A saddlecloth made of goatskin, probably of Turkish origin.

5. A type of guitar.

6. Lermontov began working on this poem as early as 1829 and at least six other versions, mostly incomplete, exist. The 1838 version is complete. I chose the final version, probably finished in 1841, for the source of my translation. See M. Yu. Lermontov, *Izbrannye Pro-izvedeniia v dvukh tomakh,* vol. II, (M.-L.: Sovetskii pisatel', 1964) for the final text (pp. 277-308) and variants (pp. 441-520). This edition is part of the series, *Biblioteka poeta, bol'shaia seriia.*

PROSE IN RUSSIA: 1790-1841

Н. Гоголь

PROSE IN RUSSIA 1790-1841: INTRODUCTION

Up until the time of Karamzin there was no *real* literary prose tradition in Russia. The prose that did surface in the eighteenth century consisted largely of translations or blatant imitations of foreign models. And except for a few tales, prose genres only began to develop during the reign of Catherine the Great, who wanted Russia to have its own journals in the mode of Addison and Steele's *Tatler* and *Spectator*. The heyday of the journals ended, however, when Catherine began to feel the bite of their satire. One notable figure who rose to prominence during this era was Nikolai Novikov (1744-1818), a journalist and writer of tales. Novikov's journals were primarily the ones that directed their sting at Catherine; she closed them down. Neoclassicism and Lomonosov's table of genre and language, both of which placed novels and tales in the lower echelons of literature, also discouraged the development of prose writing in the eighteenth century.

In spite of these conditions, prose did appear in Russia before the 1790s, all of it based on Western European literature. Two names which are associated with fiction before Karamzin are Fyodor Emin (1735-70) and Mikhail Chulkov (1743-92). The first is known primarily for his long epistolary novel *The Letters of Ernest and Doravra* (1766), modelled on Rousseau's *Julie, ou La Nouvelle Héloïse*. Mikhail Chulkov's novel *The Comely Cook, or the Adventures of a Debauched Woman* (1770) is a Russian version of *Moll Flanders*. Chulkov is a bit more skillful than his contemporaries and shows some advances in narrative technique and manipulation of time.[1] Perhaps the only other name that need be mentioned is Pavel Lvov, the author of a Russian version of Richardson's *Pamela*, called *Russian Pamela, or History of Maria, A Virtuous Peasant Girl*. These works are notable not so much for literary style as for the new sensibility they introduced to Russian readers.

It is precisely the mood of the "new sensibility," the reaction against the Enlightenment's emphasis on pure reason, that set the stage for Karamzin. The novels of the West in the mid-eighteenth century shifted attention from the aristocracy to the middle class, with its own set of standards and morality. Human values and worth were not based on birth and wealth alone. Relativism, revolt against strict hierarchy in all spheres, developing social consciousness, growth of emotional self-consciousness, and reliance on feelings all led to the cult of freedom and the individual—and the era of Romanticism. This period, then, was the transitional stage from Neoclassicism to Romanticism.

It is in this light that we look at Karamzin's prose and examine its importance in the development of Russian literature. Before Karamzin began writing his tales, he wrote a travel account of his journey to the West, *Letters of A Russian Traveler* (1791-1801).[2] He filled these letters with his own philosophical ideas and his comments on life in foreign lands. According to one critic Karamzin's travel book contains a mixture of the two types of travel literature popular at the time: Sterne's, which concentrates more on the sentiments, mood and personality of the narrator; and Charles Dupaty's, which is "a mixture of ethnographic, historical, and geographical material with the addition of dramatic scenes, lyrical digressions, moral and social observations."[3] Karamzin's book followed Dupaty's more than it did Sterne's. The main charm of the *Letters* for the reading public, though, was Karmazin's elegant, sweet, clear, musical language.

Besides the letters Karamzin wrote a number of tales, of which the most famous, though not necessarily the best, is "Poor Liza."[4] The story was so popular that people actually paid visits to the spots where Liza lived and died.[5] Although the story with its flood of emotions and simplistic characters and situations may seem silly to the modern reader, it did not seem silly at all to the readers of the late eighteenth century. While on the surface the story may seem simple and unsophisticated, close study reveals its merits as a work of real literary value.

The most lasting value of "Poor Liza" is its language. On one level the story demonstrates Karamzin's theory that Russian literary language should follow the dictates of the literary salon: it is neither too "high" with Church Slavonicisms, archaic conjunctions, meandering syntax, nor too "low" with coarse vulgarisms. On another level the language corresponds to the themes; in order to create a euphonious prose "Karamzin emphasized the sentence's rhythm and balance, its melody and intonation, all of which provided a harmonious accompaniment to the concrete semantic meaning."[6]

More than just the prose is balanced; the entire story is set within a symmetric frame. Note how the descriptions of the monastery in the beginning and of Liza's cottage near the end are similar, with groans resounding around the deserted sites.[7] In the first passage the groans and atmosphere of decay and ruin foreshadow the events of the story, while in the second the groans invite us to remember Poor Liza's corpse in the grave.

Karamzin also uses nature to evoke moods and emotional responses. Throughout the story nature descriptions parallel the moods of the characters, especially Liza's and the narrator's. Karamzin uses a stock device of the period, the pathetic fallacy, to imply that nature itself is part of Liza's drama and that it cares for her. In one famous passage, for example, the heavens thunder when Liza gives herself to Erast.

Karamzin's characters are part of the Romantic convention and are barely developed in the story. Liza's mother is almost a background figure and Erast and Liza fall into the already hackneyed pattern of doomed lovers of different social classes; of the three, Erast has the most complex personality, yet he remains decidedly flat. We do find out that he builds his expectations of life from his reading and that he is a decidedly weak fellow who seems, however, to be genuinely sorry for Liza's plight.

Perhaps the only character whose personality shines through is the narrator. He is a man of feeling, has a sense of morality, believes in the afterlife and in God, is impatient with impetuous behavior, and is concerned with Liza. In short, he appears to be exactly the type of man Karamzin thought would make a good writer—a pure, moral man, the only type who could write the kind of literature that could have a positive influence on his readers.

The narrator/author of "Poor Liza" does not want his readers to miss the theme of the story; for this purpose he speaks in two voices, his own and Karamzin's. In an excellent analysis of Karamzin's narrators, Roger Anderson explores these two voices and examines their roles in the tales.[8] According to Anderson, in order to control the reader the narrator establishes verisimilitude through details of real people and real places. He is involved with the characters—he has met Erast—but is not a part of the action. He narrates the events and then describes his own feelings and reactions to them.

In contrast to the voice of this emotional narrator is the rational and ironic voice of the "author," who intrudes with his digressions.

> Whereas as narrator he generates a sense of helpless melancholy about the human condition, as philosophizing author he draws clear moral standards against which character behavior is explicitly judged. By introducing principles of moral justice into the work, Karamzin provides an element of stability amidst the emotional foundering of characters and, to some extent, the narrator as well.[9]

The author/narrator also introduces the themes of the melancholy state of the human condition and the belief that happiness exists beyond the grave.

These themes are not new, but Karamzin's treatment of them is. The appeal of Karamzin's stories is that he hones away the hundreds of pages so common in the novels of the eighteenth century and conveys the same ideas in a concentrated, and therefore more emotionally charged, form. In this way Karamzin influenced his age and the years to follow. He ushered in the age of short forms, in which stories, elegies, epigrams and lyrics took precedence over long odes and dramas.

In 1803 Karamzin abandoned his literary career to devote the rest of his life to his *History of the Russian State.* But many others were there, eager to take up where Karamzin left off. Unfortunately, most of them simply imitated him; fortunately they are now forgotten.

Prose began to flourish in the 1820s, but only in the thirties did it become more original. John Mersereau dates the Romantic period in Russian prose as approximately 1815-40.[10] In his study he points out differences among Romantic writers but also offers the following "unifying norms" in their prose:

> 1. The fictional world is represented through metaphoric means (as opposed to Realism's representation through metonymic means).
> 2. The dominant narrative mode is telling (as opposed to Realism's means of showing). That is, a narrator primarily recounts events rather than presenting dramatic scenes of the events themselves.
> 3. Primacy of plot and setting (as opposed to Realism's primacy of character, with emphasis upon psychologization).
> 4. In Romantic fiction there is evidence of an author-narrator voice, with frequent intrusions into the action by this voice (as opposed to the absence of authorial voice in Realist fiction).
> 5. Romantic fictionists seemed quite concerned with providing a motivation or justification for their stories, that is, to explain the genesis of their tales[. . .] On the other hand, Realists were concerned with motivating the inner details of their fiction.
> 6. The psychology of Romantic characters was often completely arbitrary; this arose partly because characters had to be subordinated to intrigue. Realists present characters whose psychological condition is motivated and consistent.
> 7. Romantic fictionists were concerned with the exotic in all forms, and this was manifested by bizarre settings, both temporal and spatial. Realists tended to deal with mundane contemporary experience.
> 8. The implausibile or even the supernatural were quite permissible in Romantic fiction, whereas Realist fiction is usually bound by rules of probability and totally excludes the supernatural.[11]

Favorite genres also unify the period; these include historical novels, society tales, travel notes, anecdotes, hussar tales, novels of manners, confessions, adventure stories, supernatural tales and *Künstlernovellen,* i.e., stories whose heroes are artists or writers. These, then, are "Romantic" genres.

In the early twenties a man who was eventually to become one of the chief representatives of Russian Romanticism appeared on the literary scene; he was Alexander Alexandrovich Bestuzhev-Marlinksy (1797-1837), a prose writer and poet whose life was as flamboyant as his prose tales.[12] Born in St. Petersburg of an ancient family, he was educated at home; he knew French, English, and German fluently, as well as Caucasian dialects. Bestuzhev read a great deal and was a dazzling member of the social set. He embarked early on a military career and soon achieved great success. His life was full of drama in all spheres of his activity: court, literary and military. Among other deeds, Bestuzhev led his Moscow regiment to revolt on December 14, 1825, was exiled to Siberia and the Caucasus, became a friend of mountain bandits, was the suspected murderer of his alleged adolescent mistress, possibly was a spy, and died in battle. His death became a legend in itself.[13]

Bestuzhev began his literary career in 1819 with an attack on Shakhovskoy and Katenin which caused a sensation because of its "flamboyance of style and vicious wit."[14] He was one of Russia's first literary critics and started the trend of yearly reviews of literature with his "Glances."[15] He also engaged in literary polemics as an advocate of the "new style" and in his linguistic analyses of Russian took on almost every one of the literary "old believers." He was an opponent of "servile imitation of the French" and a defender of *narodnost'*[16] in literature.

Bestuzhev's style in the fictional sphere is also full of "pyrotechnics." His style, known as *Marlinism,* is an example of extremism in Romanticism. Its chief characteristics are hyperbole, torrid passions, exclamatory tones, declamations, rhetoric,[17] heavy use of "epithet, striking metaphors, and a very pronounced overlay of authorial comment."[18] Bestuzhev-Marlinsky's stories, especially those of his second period, are known for their authenticity of detail, exotic local color, and rich pictures of the Caucasian landscape.

Bestuzhev-Marlinsky's works fall into two periods: pre- and post-Decembrist uprising. During the first period, when he published under his own name of Bestuzhev, he mainly wrote historical and Byronic society tales (of men and their passions).[19] The "hussar" stories belong to this group. In 1830 super-romantic stories attributed to someone named Marlinsky began to appear in the journals. These stories fall into three categories: sea stories, tales of horror, and stories of the Caucasus.[20] It was only years later that people realized Marlinsky was Bestuzhev's pseudonym.[21]

"An Evening on Bivouac" dates from Bestuzhev's first period; it appeared in 1823. A hussar tale based on the same ideals as Davydov's poetry, this story is actually a skillfully wrought, tightly structured work of art. As Leighton has noted, three anecdotes are set in a frame where soldiers are sitting around a fire and telling stories. The efficient structure of the tale, with its good transitions and its contrasts between serious and humorous tones, saves the stories, he says. Leighton further points out the witty dialogue and swift repartee as excellent media for Bestuzhev's manipulation of language.[22]

There is, I think, even more tightness in the structure of this tale and more subtlety in Bestuzhev's narration than Leighton implies. The use of a frame to "justify" stories was old hat in the Romantic age, yet Bestuzhev manipulates his frame more naturally than most. He begins by describing the artillery in the background and adds enough details to set a realistic scene of soldiers settling down after a day on the battlefield. At the end of the story the concluding portion of the frame is short, almost abrupt. As opposed to the beginning, where "in the distance from time to time artillery shots could be heard . . .," the concluding portion is a call to battle when "suddenly there was a shot, another, a third." Here three distinct shots lead to action and the tale actually comes full circle.

The tale begins only after action has stopped—even the conversation has dwindled. Into this scene charges Olsky, who begins a new cycle of "action," the telling of anecdotes. The process begins with bombast, proceeds to wishful thinking and ends in a reflective mood where the men again fall silent. Then the shots ring out and the men are once more called to action on the field. There is a nice symmetry to the tale: action, shots, silence, action (story-telling), silence, shots, action.

Within this frame the anecdotes themselves also form some interesting patterns. Olsky's adventure tale is as blatantly overblown as his language; similes, metaphors and hyperboles tumble out as quickly as his actions. In contrast, Lidin's anecdote is the briefest of the three and, as he tells us, is "filled . . .with mere feelings instead of adventures." But in some ways Lidin's story also has an air of mystery about it. He says that his anecdote is interesting to him alone since it concerns his dreams and wishes. Yet it almost seems as if he lists his improbable desires as a humorous sop to his listeners, for Lidin may or may not have really been dreaming; he keeps this mystery to himself.

In contrast to Olsky and Lidin, Mechin is more meditative. His anecdote shows how he changed from an impetuous dreamer to a man with "a sorrow in his soul." The implication is that Mechin has really lived while Olsky must find his adventures in the newspapers and Lidin can only dream. Mechin's anecdote also combines elements of the first two: impetuous adventures and feelings, but his are tamed down, first by the outside influence of a friend and then by his own maturation. In Mechin's anecdote we also see flamboyant language, with rhetorical exclamations and similes, but Mechin uses that language in a reflective manner which tones it down a bit, and he introduces his anecdote more subtly than Lidin.

Both Mechin and his anecdote are microcosms of the entire tale "An Evening On Bivouac." The tale moves from bombastic, perhaps literarily based, false emotion in Olsky's story to Lidin's false-sounding anecdote. Then we hear Mechin's anecdote, which is not only a true story, but evokes *true emotions* in all of the men at the end. His narration of the anecdote follows the development of the theme of truth vs. falseness in the story.

Mechin begins to tell the story of a medallion, about which the others have been wondering for a while. When he finally produces the medallion, no one is able to see the face of Sophia S. on it. An enemy, shooting at Mechin, has shattered Sophia's face depicted on the enamel. The state of the medallion may be a foreshadowing of Sophia's fate. The object of Mechin's love, Sophia marries his rival, someone richer than Mechin, but she perishes because of this marriage. Her shattered portrait is surrounded by diamonds—an obvious sign of wealth.

Falseness is at first hidden in Mechin's anecdote. Only gradually do we learn that Sophia is false to Mechin, that the certain "captain" deceives Sophia's family about his wealth and motives for marriage, and that Vladov hides the truth about Sophia from his best friend. In the end it turns out that Mechin can take the truth, while Sophia cannot, for Mechin arrives too late to save her. But Vladov is always there, always offering the truth to Mechin, who first refuses it and then acknowledges it.

Vladov plays a pivotal role in helping Mechin grow up. He first tries to persuade Mechin not to marry Sophia by telling him to be careful in interpreting Sophia's sighs ("...what makes you so sure the princess is sighing from love and not a tight corset, that she gazes into your eyes for your sake and not to admire herself in them?") and not to rush into marriage. After the duel Vladov does not tell Mechin everything, but waits until he knows his friend can handle the truth.

When Mechin finds out the final outcome of the duel, he wants to take the shot that is due him (cf. Pushkin's "The Shot"), but Vladov calms him down. At first Mechin is inconsolable, but then finds partial consolation in Vladov's constant friendship—a feeling more exalted than his early passion for Sophia. In the end, when he sees Sophia again, Mechin is surprised that he truly loves rather than hates her. Mechin through his suffering has grown from a boy who feels superficial passion to a man who feels true love.

In a later tale, "Ammalat-Bek" (1831), Marlinsky's characters are more developed, and the tale is longer and more varied. It is a compendium of Romantic elements: letters, Ammalat's diary/confession, adventure, an exotic setting with ethnographic details and local color, travel impressions and a love story. But it is also an ironic character study of the conflict between two men from different worlds who want to trust and understand each other, but cannot because of their different cultural backgrounds.

The main narrator is an unexceptional stylized Marlinsky, but both Ammalat and Verkhovsky tell portions of their story; thus, "Ammalat-Bek" is a tale with three points of view. All three narrators are Romantic characters, especially the impetuous rebel Ammalat and the "dreamy escapist"[23] Verkhovsky. Ammalat is impuslive, daring, and good, but also cruel, crafty and brutal. Even though Marlinsky is sympathetic to his Caucasian hero, he does not gloss over his faults. In the very first chapter we see Ammalat needlessly beat his horse to death; we also see him betray his pledge to the Russians by allowing Akhmet-Sultan to murder a Russian soldier in his tent. We see him flee rather than face the consequences of his actions. Because of Ammalat's youth and inexperience, Ahmet can manipulate him to act in a manner that eventually destroys the young bek.[24]

Verkhovsky is the civilized contrast to this "noble savage." He is a later version of Mechin, but Verkhovsky is too sensitive and innocent for his own good. He is naive in his treatment of Ammalat and is completely devoid of the cunning which is a necessary element of the Caucasian's personality. Verkhovsky's main failing is his attempt to treat Ammalat as a European rather than accept him on his own terms. Instead of a comedy of errors, "Ammalat-Bek" is a tragedy of misunderstandings.

As Leighton points out, the tragedy is personal and individual. Ammalat sees Verkhovsky's "honesty as either a superior form of guile or a weakness" and doubts that Verkhovsky can understand his passions.[25] Ammalat's second assessment of Verkhovsky is certainly true. We see the fatal result of this mistrust when Ammalat murders his protector in imagined revenge. The real irony of the tale occurs when Verkhovsky's brother kills Ammalat and unwittingly avenges the death of his older brother.

What makes this book interesting is the advance Marlinsky has made in characterization and development of psychological analysis. "The themes of a-wakening of the consciousness of a primitive man, confrontation between the man of nature and the man of civilization, individual freedom, and the resentment of one man in the face of another's selfless generosity are unexpectedly sophisticated themes for Russian literature of the 1830's."[26]

"Ammalat-Bek" is remarkably advanced when you compare it to a novel which appeared only two years earlier. *Ivan Vyzhigin* (1829) may be the most tedious novel ever written and it is difficult to understand its immense popularity in Russia when it first appeared. Mersereau thinks that this novel of Faddey Bulgarin's (1789-1859) was so popular with the lower and middle classes because it satirizes the upper classes.[27] He is probably correct. Nevertheless it is still hard to imagine that wading through hundreds of pages of sanctimonious drivel was the only way the masses could thumb their noses at the elite.

The open hostility in the novel is just one of Bulgarin's negative traits. Bulgarin was the son of a Pole who took part in Poland's national freedom movement. He entered the Cadet Corps in Petersburg in 1789 and later was wounded in battle while fighting against an Uhlan regiment. At one time Bulgarin served with, and deserted, a Polish legion fighting with Napoleon against Russia. After the war he settled in Petersburg, where he engaged in publishing enterprises and in editing journals. From 1822-25 he edited the journals and almanacs *Northern Archive, Literary Leaves,* and *Russian Thalia,* in which he published parts of Griboedov's *Woe from Wit.* He also worked with Ryleev on the *Northern Star.*[28]

Even though Bulgarin was associated with Griboedov and Ryleev, he never was under suspicion after the Decembrist Revolt because he was probably an agent for the Third Section. It is rumored that he even betrayed some of his Decembrist friends to the authorities. Bulgarin worked in the Ministry of Public Education and had a very successful career in government service until he died.

Bulgarin is most remembered for his journalistic work in the twenties and thirties on the Petersburg newspaper *Northern Bee,* a reactionary publication which endorsed "autocracy, orthodoxy, and nationalism"; in it he systematically attacked all of the major writers of the time, including Pushkin, Gogol, Lermontov, and Belinsky. He also was not above informing on them to the authorities. Mirsky sums up Bulgarin's character by saying that "during the reign of Nicholas I he acquired the reputation of a vile sycophant whom all honest men abhorred. He was a clever, but essentially vulgar, journalist."[29]

This analysis could easily be a description of one of the villains in *Ivan Vyzhigin,* but Bulgarin has neither Mirsky's imagination nor his sense of style. The novel is a picaresque, first-person narrative which tries to prove *à la* Richardson and Fielding, but without the latter's comic tone, that virtue is its own reward. The events follow a strict chronological order, although the characters do relate their own past histories through Ivan's filter of memory. The characters are all flat stereotypes, either good or bad, who find themselves in unbelievable coincidences due to tortuous twists in the story—all predictable by that time. To distinguish the villains from the heroes, Bulgarin gives them names like Mr. Virtue and Mr. Thief. But even the "good" characters are unsympathetic and no one (at least now) cares about any of them. In fact even the main hero elicits no sympathy, but is actually rather dumb and gullible. Ivan's own stupidity usually lands him in all kinds of troubles and he never seems to learn any lessons from his experiences until the last page or two.

The entire novel is as contrived and clichéd (scar on shoulder recognition scene) as the ending. One gets the impression that Ivan falls into as much trouble as he does merely to give Bulgarin a chance to vent his spleen against every class, character type, and institution which does not suit his fancy.

Another novel which came out in 1829 also exhibits some of the same deficiences as *Ivan Vyzhigin:* flat characters, conventional story, and mechanical inclusion of ethnographic and historical details. However *Yury Miloslavsky* by Mikhail Zagoskin (1789-1852) is a much more enjoyable novel to read. There is romantic interest and a hero who faces a real moral dilemma, one which challenges his divided loyalty to the Polish tsar and Russian land and people.

Perhaps the somewhat dramatic quality of the novel is due to the fact that Zagoskin began his literary career as a dramatist. Even though he was born into a family of nobles, he received a bad education at home. He fought in the Napoleonic War, was wounded and decorated. In Petersburg, he got to know Shakhovskoy and began his long association with the theatre. After his first play, a one-act comedy called *The Prankster,* came out, Zagoskin continued working in the area of light comedy and vaudeville. After 1820 he moved to Moscow and continued working in the theatre until 1842, when he was made director of the Kremlin's Armory.

Besides plays Zagoskin wrote a number of historical novels after the success of *Yury Miloslavsky* in 1829, but those other novels were never very popular. Zagoskin and Lazhechnikov are probably the two most famous of the "Walter Scottists" of this era. Some critics place Lazhechnikov's works on a higher level because of his better knowledge and depiction of the historical periods he describes.

Zagoskin's *Yury Miloslavsky* is set in the Time of Troubles when the Poles occupied Russia. The story tells of the struggle for power and Russia's final victory. It concentrates on the revolt which started in the town of Nizhny and was successful due to the combined efforts of Minin and Pozharsky. Pushkin thought that the novel had minor flaws but in general did "transport" readers back to the era. (See below for Pushkin's review.) Mirsky thinks that "in spite of its conventionality, crude nationalism, cardboard pyschology, and lack of real historical color, it is a very good romance of its time."[30]

Zagoskin tries to inject historical local color by describing buildings, gardens and courtyards. Often after these descriptions the narrator interjects nostalgic comments comparing "the good old days" with modern times. The former usually are better—in his opinion. Zagoskin also makes sure his characters are dressed in the typical period costumes. The descriptions usually appear before a new character arrives on the scene and thus place the characters in their normal milieu.

Zagoskin also tries to recreate an older type of language. For example, everyone addresses each other in familiar (*ty*) rather than formal (*vy*) forms. In addition, he laces his prose with Polish expressions and a lot of proverbs. In between dialogue the narrator's formal prose greatly contrasts with the folksy tone of his characters. His sentences tend to be rather long, with many subordinate clauses; however, they are usually well-balanced, with many repeating syntactical patterns. Sometimes the rhetoric flows into the long speeches of the heroes, but generally it stays in the narrator's domain. The narrator does not try to hide the fact that he is telling a story; he often introduces new chapters with statements like "We left our heroes . . .," "While Yury is asleep, let's see . . .," "We now ask the reader to accompany us . . ." and "The order of our narration demands that we go back a little."

The hero, Yury Miloslavsky, the son of a Russian patriot, took an oath of loyalty to the Polish tsarevich, Vladislav, but not to his father, King Sigismund. That oath is a cause of great pain for Yury, because he dearly loves his country and wants the Russians to regain control of their own land. Love for an unknown girl he used to see in church also plagues Yury. It seems that he will never be happy and will never marry, so Yury takes an oath to become a monk after the war. This oath leads to further complications in his life. Zagoskin does a fairy good job of conveying Yury's pain but stops there. Yury is not a complex character and has a simplistic, naive view of life. He never solves his problems but does eventually leave them behind, after a monk releases him from his two oaths of loyalty and chastity. The results are predictable: Yury marries and becomes a hero.

In contrast to this solemn youth, a fun-loving, adventurous, crafty, humorous Zaporozhets Cossack, Kirsha, provides some light moments in the novel. His tricks save him from a cruel fate. Kirsha more than once saves the day for Yury and even manages to bring Yury together with his beloved "girl in the church." His exposé of a sorcerer and his apprentice at a local wedding begins a chain of events that leads to this reunion. In addition to Kirsha many standard characters people the pages of the novel: the faithful retainer Aleksey, the old, loving nanny, the holy fool, and the villainous Poles, the worst of whom is Kruchina-Shalonsky, father of Nastenka—the girl in the church, another lifeless female character from the seventeenth century.

In 1830 Pogorelsky's (Aleksander Perovsky, 1787-1836) novel *The Convent Girl* came out and treated Russian readers to a girl quite different from the flat, usually lifeless, "Poor Liza" model. Perovsky was the illegitimate son of the very influential Count A. K. Razumovsky.[31] After a luxurious early life with his mother, Perovsky left for Moscow and the university in 1805, and in two years not only completed his course work, but also earned his Ph.D. in botany. He defended his thesis in three separate speeches in three different languages: French, German and Russian. Perovsky subsequently entered government service in Petersburg, but returned in 1810 to Moscow, where he became a friend of Vyazemsky and Zhukovsky. An early "Karamzinist," he was one of the organizers of the Society of Lovers of Russian Literature at Moscow University. In 1812 he returned to Petersburg and fought in the war against Napoleon. He worked in Dresden as an adjutant to a general and there became acquainted with the works of E. T. A. Hoffmann, who influenced his first book.

In 1820 Perovsky became a member of the Free Society of Lovers of Russian Literature. While still in government service he translated Horace. In 1822 he went home after the death of his father and there wrote his best novella, "The Lafertov District Poppyseed Cake Vendor," a "horror" tale of a witch-like old woman and her companion, a cat, who later turns into a handsome man. Perovsky later included this work in his novel, *The Double, or My Evenings in Little Russia* (1828). He spent his last years living with his sister A. A. Tolstaya and educating his nephew, A. K. Tolstoy. He died in Warsaw on his way to a cure for his stomach ailments.

The Convent Girl first began to be serialized in 1830 in Delvig's *Northern Flowers*;

the second part came out in 1833. Critics generally agree that part two is not as good as the first volume. The characters, including Anyuta, revert to older, more sentimental models and the events become more clichéd.

The Convent Girl was called the "first successful novel of contemporary provincial morals in opposition to the reactionary novel of Bulgarin, Ivan Vyzhigin."[32] Pogorelsky's works have characteristics that span a forty-year period. He can be called a Karamzinian sentimentalist because of the emotional style which occurs in some of his works. But the fantastic element of The Double is closer to the brand of Romanticism associated with the influence of Tieck and Hoffmann. Pogorelsky introduced the principles of Romantic Irony and the Romantic Grotesque into his work. His moral tone connects him with V. F. Odoevsky (see below) and his use of colors definitely fits into the Romantic style. His use of local color (Ukrainian is thrown into some of the dialogue in The Convent Girl) is also typically Romantic.

Some of the characters in the novel are also stock types: the villain-rogue Pryzhkov, the hero Blistovsky, the gypsy culled from literature models, the provincial girls who speak French. Some of the situations in the novel are also already clichés from both foreign and domestic literature. The kidnapping of Anyuta, a mysterious hut in the forest, the expectation that a young man is a suitor of one young lady when he in reality has come to ask for the hand of another (Perovsky uses this twice), an orphan at the mercy of a cruel guardian, and mockery of provincial French are all old hat, even in 1830.

What is new is Perovksy's attempt to construct a plot as well as tell a story.[33] He fractures time with flashbacks and a reordering of events in order to provide motivation for the actions of the story. The narrator's decision to describe Anyuta's life in Petersburg only *after* we see her reactions to Barvenovo is quite crafty. Not only does the contrast between the two places partially justify Anyuta's reaction, but it also calls our attention to the motive of these reactions and guides the reader into understanding them. Perovsky's narrator gets out of the picture early, lets the main character tell part of her story in letters, then relates the story of Anyuta himself. However, Anyuta has told him her own story, thus establishing the "truth" of what the narrator relates. The narrator is intrusive and interrupts the story to relate his point of view about the characters of Anyuta, Blistovsky, Auntie Anna, Dyundik and the others. He also drops hints to the reader along the way. For example, his broad hints about the irregularity of Anyuta's father's will prepares us for its being a forgery.

The narrator's intrusive quality performs two functions in The Convent Girl: it manipulates the reader by trying to introduce suspense into the narration and provides comic relief, thus lightening the tone of the book. The comedy in the book is very broad, sometimes bordering on the slapstick. At one point the wife of Anyuta's guardian Dyundik eavesdrops on a conversation between him and Blistovsky. Dyundik angrily rushes out of the room in mid-sentence and smacks Marfa Petrovna (who had her ear glued to the door) on the forehead with the door. In another scene involving the Dyundiks, Marfa Petrovna falls from her chair and dies from anger when she learns that Blistovsky and Anna have married. If this were not silly enough, Marfa Petrovna's last words to Dyundik are an older equivalent of the slang phrase, perhaps not too crassly rendered as "Buzz off, Bozo!" However, Dyundik tells everyone her parting words are "Farewell, my darling." Dyundik cannot resist hypocrisy.

Perhaps the best comic episode in the novel occurs when Blistovsky meets the

Dyundik girls who speak to him in a language they imagine to be French. What makes this scene so convincing is that Blistovsky actually *does not* understand what the girls are saying. Their mutual dismay is humorous and natural.

The narrator's interruptions not only inject humor but also build suspense. In his attempt to construct a plot the narrator usually interrupts the action to give background information. Others have certainly done this before Perovsky, but he normally interrupts an adventure in the middle, at its most exciting part. We read the next chapter to find out what happens in the one after that. The most extreme example of this device is Perovsky's delay of three years between the publication of the two volumes.

The Convent Girl is built on contrast; the most obvious example is Perovsky's pairing of antithetical types. He shows the great difference between Anyuta's true guardian, Auntie Anna, and her legal one, Dyundik; Anyuta's two suitors, Blistovsky and Pryzhkov; and the daughters of the two guardians. When Blistovsky comes to visit Barvenovo, Auntie's estate, cousin Praskuta thinks he has come to pay court to her. When she finds out that he has actually come for Anyuta, Praskuta takes to her bed and her health deteriorates. Nevertheless she never wishes evil upon Anyuta and even warns her against going off with Dyundik. On the other hand, Blistovsky's "rejection" of Vera Dyundik, who also thinks he has come for her, leads to all of Anyuta's troubles.

Blistovsky and Pryzhkov are conspicuously antithetical characters in every way, and Perovsky uses one incident in particular to reveal a basic difference between them. As soon as Blistovsky asks for Anyuta's hand and Anna Andreevna gives her blessing, he asks whether he can call her auntie. She consents and Blistovsky treats auntie with great respect and affection. Conversely, when Blistovsky runs into Pryzhkov at the fair, the latter is making fun of a "respected" old lady, criticizing her clothes and her wrinkles. Blistovsky is shocked when he finds out that this "respected lady" is Pryzhkov's grandmother; his shock later turns into anger when he observes Pryzhkov getting ready to spray the old woman with a gadget akin to a squirt gun! Here we can see something more serious behind Perovsky's use of slapstick humor.

The best contrast in the book exists between the narrator and Anyuta, who acts as a secondary narrator in her letters and as the source of our travelling narrator's tale. The narrator's language is much more formal and literarily rhetorical than Anyuta's. He uses long sentences, parallel constructions, subordinate clauses and a great many participles and gerunds instead of more conversational relative clauses. Anyuta's letters to Masha, on the contrary, are lively and informal. Her sentences are short, full of dashes, exclamation points and ellipses. She almost never uses participles. Of course now this contrast seems only logical and expected, but in 1830 in Russia it was a narrative breakthrough of sorts. What is also interesting about our two narrators is the fact that they do have something in common: they both address their readers, are clearly writing for specific audiences, and are both "travelling" narrators—or at least both of their narrations begin with accounts of their travels. In addition, both writers want to be sure that their readers do not misinterpret their remarks. In the excerpts printed in this anthology you can see where after listing all of the shortcomings of the people and the estate, Anyuta goes on to plead with Masha not to think badly of any of them because all of the people are so *dear*. The main narrator does the same thing. He refers to Anyuta's letters and goes on to belabor the point that in spite of what she found at Barvenovo, she took it all in her stride like the spunky girl she is: "Anyone else in her place," etc.

Anyuta *does* take everything in her stride and her reaction to the realization that Barvenovo in Little Russia bears no resemblance at all to the elegant Tsarskoe Selo near Petersburg is one of embarrassment at her mistake. After she admits this mistake to Masha, Anyuta continues her description of the Ukraine with obvious interest, almost with delight. Perovsky cleverly puts his "local color" into the mouth of his young heroine as she sees it for the first time. How much more natural and innovative is this device than the stilted artificial descriptive interruptions of his predecessors! The main narrator merely complains throughout his travels about stationmasters, the peasant hut and the bugs which keep him awake all night. Of course, none of this is new to him.

Anyuta's letters also reveal something relatively new in Russian prose—an attempt at character development. Anyuta begins to round out as a character in the first half of the novel. From her letters we indirectly find out that she is capable of lasting emotion, relies on love, is not afraid of putting herself in a bad light, has a sense of humor, is naive, and generous. Later on in the story, when she refuses to marry Pryzhkov, we also find out she has a mind of her own. She also turns the tables on Dyundik. He tells her that her father's will states that she will be cursed if she marries a man without Dyundik's approval. But when he tries to get her to marry Pryzhkov, Anyuta uses that same will in her snappy retort:

> "Klim Sidorovich! Don't you talk to me about father. In the will which you showed me, it states that I may not marry without your consent. If that really was his wish, then I do obey it...but it's not stated there that I must accept the man you choose, and so I earnestly request that you forever deliver me from similar proposals. I want to carry out my father's will, not yours.[34]

Not only is Anyuta crafty and spunky, she is adventurous as well. While the entire Dyundik family is scared silly of an "apparition," Anyuta takes a note from him and then goes to her room to read it. She does scream though, loudly enough to wake up the family. Later when she receives another note, an escape plan, she complies without a second thought and steals off into the gloomy forest. Clearly Anyuta is more interesting than most of the characters we have thus far encountered. She may not yet be a fully developed, psychologically real human being, but Anyuta and Perovsky were on the right track.

Perovsky makes innovations in the novel, but still relies on the old-fashioned device of the frame narrative. Writers used the frame to justify the telling of their stories and to verify the authenticity of their tales. At this stage prose writers in Russia still did not have the self-confidence simply to begin telling a story without any preamble. Pushkin would do this in "Queen of Spades," but only after he had also written *The Tales of Belkin* within a frame. Perovsky, however, goes to greater lengths than anyone else to establish the authenticity of the story. Not only has he met almost all of the characters, he has married one of Auntie Anna's daughters, visits Anyuta regularly, and even lives close to everyone. I may be attributing too much subtlety to Perovsky, but isn't it possible that he is making fun of the function of the frame device itself?

Perovsky may or may not be poking fun at a romantic cliché, but Vladimir Fyodorovich Odoevsky (1804-69) is clearly laughing at and satirizing another phenomenon of his age—girls who do not speak Russian and who willingly give up any trace of individuality they might have. We see this in one of Odoevsky's fantastic stories, "A Tale of Why It Is Dangerous for Young Girls to Go Walking in a Group along Nevsky Prospect" (1833). Odoevsky is a remarkable representative of his age.[35] He was born in Moscow into a family of impoverished nobility. Odoevsky's mother was a serf and he was very close to her. He attended the nobleman's Pensionat of Moscow University and later worked in the Ministry of Justice. During that time Odoevsky began to publish music reviews and, as a trained Schellingian,[36] he took part in the activities of the *Lyubomudry* group, with their interest in native Russian literature and German philosophy; with Kuchelbecker he edited in 1824 the miscellany *Mnemosyne.* In 1826 he moved to Petersburg, where he held various offices until 1846, when he became director of the Rumyantsev Museum. Odoevsky was also well known in his time for his literary salon, which met on Saturdays.[37] His salon was noted for its high cultural level, various interests and wide sphere of acquaintances. People gathered there for evenings of literature and music.

Odoevsky himself was a man of many talents and interests, which we see in the various themes of his stories: politics, Russian supremacy over the West, Russian messianism, anti-utilitarianism, anti-slavery, the "boundaries of knowledge, the meaning of science and art, sense of human existence, atheism and belief, education, government rule, the function of individual sciences, madness and sanity, poetic creation, logic."[38] These many themes show up in his numerous short stories, on which his fame mainly rests. The types of stories he wrote are as numerous as his themes: satires, fantasies, children's stories, society tales, *Künstlernovellen,* and anti-utopias. The *Künstlernovellen* discuss the role of the artist in society as the one creature who is the link between humans and the higher realms. Society naturally scorns him since it is occupied with the petty concerns of the *beau monde.* Odoevsky further dissects "polite society" and all of its empty occupations in his society tales, such as "Princess Mimi." Some of his stories are satirical, but almost all investigate serious themes and the importance of philosophy. His collection *Motley Stories* appeared in 1834, and *Russian Nights* in 1844. The latter is a collection of dialogues in the Platonic mode.

"A Tale of Why It Is Dangerous . . ." exists on a less exalted plane than *Russian Nights* and is a fantasy/satire against the pernicious influence of society "mamas" and foreign culture on young Russian girls. In this story Odoevsky takes a "homogenized" Russian beauty and turns her into a doll under a glass jar, who nods her head along with all of the other dolls in the window of a shop in which objects, foreign and fantastic, are sold.

Odoevsky makes his point—that the women of Petersburg have no individuality—in a number of ways. In the first paragraph he uses the simile, "like nuns in a nunnery" to indicate that, like nuns, they only go out with companions. But the simile becomes more pertinent when we remember that at that time all nuns dressed alike. Another of Odoevsky's double-edged comments concerns the "mamas," whom he obliquely compares to crows. One girl gets left behind because the mamas can count only to ten. On the surface Odoevsky's comment is merely another gibe at the mamas, but it also reflects on the young girls. Are they all so interchangeable that their own mothers cannot even tell them apart—or even notice that one is missing? It is not surprising then that no one bothers to pick up the doll at the end. Who would want someone so commonplace that even her mother does not realize she is missing?

Odoevsky also underlines his point by not giving the girls names and by describing them as being "one more beautiful than the other." But which is which?

Odoevsky is less subtle later in the story when the "foreign sharper" makes a dozen hats and dresses, all cut out of the young girls' own clothes. Odoevsky's anti-West sentiments are painfully clear in his depiction of the foreigners in the "infidel sharper's" employ: a brainless French head, a German nose with donkey-ears and a tightly-packed English torso. This motley foreign quartet works together to extract everything that is naturally Russian from the child; they even cut out her Russian heart. After they have transformed her into a doll they put her under a glass bell, presumably to protect her from dust. However, this image implies more than that.

In the first part of the story the mamas get all of the blame, in the next part the foreigners receive their share. At the end Odoevsky links the two pernicious influences together when he says, "And who is guilty of all this? In the first place, the foreign infidels who spoil our beauties, and then the mamas who cannot count higher than ten. Here is the moral for you." But the two are indirectly linked earlier through the image of the bell. Before the girls and their mamas enter the shop, they attract a lot of attention on Nevsky Prospect. However, no one can approach the girls because "in front was a mama, at the rear a mama, in the middle a mama . . ." These protective parents isolate and shelter the girls just as the glass bell covers the unfortunate girl/doll in the shop.

We should not be surprised by what happens to the girl, for all of the wares in the "infidel-sharper's" store are of a magical design. The long list of items for sale prepares the scene for fantastic occurrences. Moreover, the events take place in Petersburg, a city connected with strange events in Russian literature.[39]

Petersburg, and more specifically, the Petersburg *beau monde* come under attack in the society tales of the day. One of the most famous examples of this genre is Odoevsky's "Princess Mimi" (1834). This story is an advance over much of the literature we have thus far examined. Gone is the "frame," and "Princess Mimi" begins right in the middle of a ball with a conversation between the two main characters—the victim, Baroness Dauerthal and her slanderer, Princess Mimi. Odoevsky displays more narrative self-confidence when he stops the action at the most exciting part and interjects the preface to the story along with a discourse on the trials of writing novels. This is certainly not a new device; it conjures up the shade of Laurence Sterne and *Tristram Shandy,* and is a good example of Romantic Irony, the device through which the narrator reminds the reader that, after all, he *is* reading fiction.

This use of Romantic Irony is also a reminder of the main theme of the story, appearances vs. reality. Early in the story we meet the "guardians of morality" who search for the Baroness' mythical lover. When they cannot determine who he may be, they decide to hold her up as an example because they agree that "her art of preserving outward decorum was equal to the highest morality."[40] In a long digression a gentleman in a carriage lashes out against these "guardians of morality" and exposes them for what they are. But in an ironic tone the narrator remarks as he begins the next chapter: "Fortunately, few people shared the unknown orator's ferocious opinion about today's society, and therefore its petty affairs flowed on in their usual way without interference."

In another ironic touch the real affair between Countess Rifeyskaya and Granitsky goes unnoticed, except by the Baroness, who views it with relief. She thinks it will divert attention away from her. But she is wrong. The Baroness cannot do anything right and the "guardians of morality" interpret her innocent acts maliciously. The lengths to which these vile people go in their avoidance of truth are most clearly evident in the climax of the story. Inwardly gloating at the Baroness' blush when she asks for a ride home, Princess Mimi expects to find Granitsky waiting for the Baroness in the carriage. Imagine Mimi's shock when she meets the Baron and not Granitsky. This should end all gossip, but it does not. Even when faced with the truth, society prefers to accept the lie.

This theme appears again in the scene between the baron's younger brother and his aunt. Even though the young baron enumerates all of Granitsky's sterling qualities, the aunt prefers to accept society's assessment and demands that the young baron defend his brother's honor. The result of this conversation is the tragic duel in which Granitsky perishes. The ultimate irony of the duel is that when the young baron realizes that there is no truth to the rumors, and the two reconcile, they both decide to go on with the duel to keep up appearances.

Thus seven lives[41] are ruined so that the petty jealousy of Princess Mimi can be gratified. Yet this vicious woman is but a symptom of the decaying, diseased Petersburg society. Even though we cannot condone Princess Mimi's actions, we can understand them through Odoevsky's psychological probing of his spiteful heroine. Because she did not marry, Princess Mimi had to find some way to stay in the society without which she had no life. Princess Mimi is also a victim of Petersburg society and its superficial, hypocritical standards of human worth.

Another society tale also appeared in 1834, but one of a much higher artistic caliber: Pushkin's "The Queen of Spades." This story is a literary masterpiece. Pushkin wrote some prose throughout his career, but it was only after 1830 that prose captured most of his attention. In the famous "Boldino Autumn" of 1830, one of the most productive times of his life, Pushkin wrote his *Tales of Belkin,* five stories supposedly written by Belkin, a landowner whose life story appears in the frame introduction. They are all short, terse, unadorned, and thoroughly entertaining. After 1831 Pushkin mainly wrote prose; among the works of these last years of his life are the following: "Egyptian Nights," a story about poetry, inspiration, and the poet's attitude to himself and society; *Dubrovsky,* an unfinished robber novel; *The Captain's Daughter,* probably the only good historical novel of the era (about the Pugachev rebellion); and "The Queen of Spades," a fantastic society tale.

Pushkin's prose covers most of the themes of Romanticism, yet it is usually realistic in tone and classically balanced in style. His prose, especially "The Queen of Spades," takes us up to the age of Realism. Already in this story Pushkin begins to debunk Romantic myths. At first reading, the story is a typical ghost story with a secret formula to success at cards, an apparition who gives the hero a secret, a winking corpse as well as a winking queen of spades. Hermann is also a Romantic hero, a man with a mysterious past, with "at least three crimes on his conscience." He also resembles Russia's ultimate Romantic idol, Napoleon. But a close reading of the story reveals that all of the "fantastic elements" have rational explanations.[42] The mysterious solution—three, seven, ace—has been in Hermann's mind all along.[43] These numbers appear on almost every page in one way or another. The story is not about the supernatural; it is a psychological exploration of a monomania that leads to madness. Pushkin's narrator even states quite plainly what is driving Hermann mad when he says, "Two fixed ideas cannot exist together in moral nature, just as two bodies cannot occupy one and the same place in the physical world."

The monomania that drives Hermann insane causes him to see winking cards and corpses. Uncharacteristic behavior, in this case heavy drinking, explains Hermann's apparition—or hallucination. Also, as John Mersereau has pointed out, Pushkin's apparition is a parody of the romantic ghost, for the old woman appears, "softly shuffling her slippers."[44] Mersereau shows how "The Queen of Spades" refutes the Romantic idea that there is refuge in madness. The Russian critic Shkovsky notes that "of all the people linked with the name of Napoleon this is the most unromantic . . ."[45] Shklovsky sees Hermann as unromantic because he is "a virtuous German, a German bourgeois."[46]

The details in the story not only debunk Romantic fantasy, but also add a classical balance to the structure. Proffer shows how certain details are repeated and "if a theme is mentioned once, it will be repeated, however briefly, in the story."[47] These details include roses in powdered hair, mention of "children, grandchildren and great-grandchildren," and the countess' movement left to right.[48]

Pushkin's manipulation of time also plays a key role in underlining Hermann's madness. Since Pushkin's style is so sparse, every word counts. So does every reference to time. At the beginning of the story references to time are very precise. In the first chapter we find out that the men sat down to supper at five in the morning and left the table at quarter to six. One can chart the exact chronology of each event. However, precise references to time end after Hermann learns the secret of winning at cards. As Hermann becomes more disoriented, time references become more hazy and imprecise. It is also interesting that many of the events in the story occur at intervals of one, three and seven days.

Time references are not the only precise feature of the story. Precision is one of the many features of Pushkin's prose. Abram Lezhnev summarizes the qualities of Pushkin's prose.

> Laconism, lack of embellishment, concreteness, business-like character of the metaphors and similes, rapidity of sentence, dynamism, a tendency to the "noun-verb" type, quickness of tempo, evenness and restraint in intonation—these are the basic features of Pushkin's style.[49]

"The Queen of Spades" is a model example of this style.

Two years after "The Queen of Spades" Pushkin wrote an account of his travels to the Caucasus in *A Journey to Arzrum*. In this work "he reached the limits of noble and bare terseness."[50] These travel notes are short, restrained and honed of all superfluities. Pushkin appreciates the beauty of the mountain scenery but does not fall into rapture over every mountain stream. Romantic excess so normal in other travel notes does not appear in *A Journey to Arzrum*. Early in the journey Pushkin even says, "Soon one's impressions are dulled. Hardly a day had gone by, and the roar of the Terek and its monstrous waterfalls, its cliffs and precipices no longer attracted my attention." Compare that to Marlinsky's descriptions in *Ammalat-Bek*.

During his literary career Pushkin gradually tended more and more to Realism and rejected Romantic excesses. The touch of reality shows through in *A Journey to Arzrum*. Instead of romanticizing the native elements, Pushkin is frank in his assessment of the natives' stupidity, the primitive conditions, the awful food, the stench, the discomfort of the trip, and the dirth of Circassian beauties so praised in prose and poetry. One critic even demonstrates quite convincingly that *A Journey to Arzrum* is a parody of Romantic literature in general and Pushkin's own Byronic tales in particular.[51] In *Journey* Pushkin took his already lean prose and almost scraped it to the bone until it had a cold and elegant tone inimical to that of most Romantic literature.

Probably no one's prose contrasts with Pushkin's more than Gogol's; its style has been summed up as "polysyllabically unelegant." Gogol is a phenomenon in Russian literature. People are still trying to understand him. Nikolai Vasilievich Gogol (1809-52) was born in the Ukraine, the son of petty gentry. His father was a versifier and wrote for the Ukrainian puppet theater (*vertep*); his mother was a confirmed hysteric. Gogol was probably the most poorly educated of Russian writers and did not excel in school, where he read works of German Romanticism and eighteenth-century Russian poetry. In 1829 he went to Petersburg, where he wrote and published his poem *Hans Küchelgarten.* After the critics panned it, Gogol bought up all the copies and left the country. Back in Petersburg he bungled an actor's job, got into the civil service, began to write and even got a job as a teacher of history. He did not distinguish himself in that field.

In 1831 he published his *Evenings on a Farm near Dikanka,* a collection of stories narrated by Rudy Panko. The stories show the influence of Tieck, Hoffmann, and Ukrainian folk tales; they contain elements of comedy, tragedy, lyricism, and demonology. He did not publish anything important until *Mirgorod* (more stories set in the Ukraine) came out, followed by *Arabesques* in 1835. His next work, "Taras Bulba," is a historical tale about the Cossacks. The last work he wrote before he left Russia in 1836 was the play, *The Inspector General.* He spent most of the next twelve years abroad, mainly in Rome; but he also wandered about Paris and Germany. Gogol visited Russia only twice during that period. In 1842 his great novel *Dead Souls* as well as "The Overcoat" were published. The last four or five years of Gogol's life are riddled with contradictions. He went through several spiritual crises until he died a terrible death in 1852.

Gogol's style, which is as complex as his personality, includes all levels of language, even Church Slavonic, parodistic use of bureaucratese and journalistic phrases. His prose is noted for its high-pitched rhetoric, syntactical complexity, use of many tropes and figures of speech (especially the simile), a lot of sound play, and poetic rhythm. One can even scan passages of his prose just like poetry. Gogol also uses this style for a humorous effect. In fact lack of grammatical and syntactical logic is one of his main comic devices.[52] Others include hyperbole, metonymy, parody, slapstick, funny names and patent impossiblities. His early works are colorful, but in his works after "Nevsky Prospect" the settings become cloudy, rainy, and gloomy.

A gloomy, snowy St. Petersburg scene is one of the characteristics of the "Natural School,"[53] a term Bulgarin first used in a derogatory manner to describe Gogol; for Belinsky it became synonymous with Realism. Other traits of the "Natural School" include concentration on physiognomy—usually insulting; comparisons of humans to animals; detailed descriptions of the trivial and low; "crooked-tonguedness," i.e., use of many particles and prepositions; stupid, illogical conversations with numerous swear words; average and below average characters; and use of schematic pairs of characters.[54]

Gogol's characters never develop, but are really caricatures, often grotesque, who are recognized through their leit-motifs. Many peripheral characters pop in and out of his stories, never to be seen or mentioned again. His young women are almost always idealized and unappoachable; consequently, love stories are rare.

"The Portrait" is uncharacteristic of Gogol's style. The version which came out in 1842 (translation included below) is much less Romantic than the 1835 version which appeared in the collection *Arabesques*. The later redaction lacks typical "Gogolian hyperbole and humor."[55] But the 1842 edition is important as a statement of Gogol's aesthetic theories and as a defense of his misunderstood works, *Dead Souls* and *The Inspector General*; some portions of the story are somewhat autobiographical (Gogol's slowness in writing and his life in Rome).[56] "The Portrait" is a very solemn statement of Gogol's belief in the artist's moral responsibility.

The artist must sacrifice himself in order to aid in the salvation of humanity. He must not betray his mission; for once he prostitutes himself for material rewards, the artist loses all chance of self-redemption. Hence Chertkov's own despair when he realizes what he has done to himself by abandoning his early ideals.

The artist must reveal truth to mankind, but never without beauty. He has within him the power to transform things that are trivial and low, to make them valuable through the process of his art.[57] For through this process the artist can use things that are low and base to teach man to look at himself and not to judge others before his own soul is pure. Gogol believed that because the poet is closer to God he must be purer than other mortals. Gogol uses Father Gregory as his example of the true artist and puts his own philosophy into the monk's speeches to his son. Father Gregory unwittingly profaned his art by allowing the anti-Christ, the devil, to roam the world for fifty years. But through prayer, sacrifice, and the painting of holy icons, the monk wins back his salvation.

Not so Chertkov. At first he is, or appears to be, one of those true artists: "His old greatcoat and drab clothes indicated that here was a man who was dedicated to his work to the point of self-sacrifice . . . ." He scorns bad art and even asks what use such art can be to people. When he sees the painting of the old man, it is the artist's talent which attracts him and compels him to spend all his money to own it. Then when Chertkov sees the eyes, he is so frightened he runs off without the money or the portrait. He fears the portrait and the apparition until he gets the money and moves to a new apartment—all according to the old man's advice. Only then "the life-like quality of the eyes no longer seemed so frightening . . ." After that his luck changes.

Chertkov realizes what he has lost when he sees the painting done by the young Russian artist who has just arrived from Italy. The description of this true artist loosely parallels the early Chertkov: "he suffered poverty, humiliation, even hunger, and with rare self-sacrifice he scorned everything and was insensitive to all but his beloved art." This young man's picture evokes emotional responses, tears, from the gallery visitors.

When Chertkov runs out in tears, he is crying for all that he has lost—his talent, integrity and salvation. He goes out, buys great art works and destroys them after he finally realizes he will never produce a great work of art. Through these acts Chertkov "deprived people of those holy, beautiful works in which great art raised the veil from heaven and showed Man the part of his inner world which is so full of sounds and holy secrets." He does the work of the devil.

At first glance it seems surprising that as late as 1842 Gogol was still writing of those ideals of German philosophy, especially Schelling's, that were by this time out of general favor. But the story is just a further step in the evolution of ideas Gogol never relinquishes and later develops in his *Selected Passages from a Correspondence with Friends.*

The age of Romanticism was drawing to a close and one of its most representative writers helped to usher it out. Mikhail Lermontov began writing prose about 1829 and for three years experimented with three plays in prose.[58] They are obviously Romantic, full of high drama and overblown passions. In 1835 he wrote *Masquerade,* a drama in rhymed iambic lines of different length. Lermontov's first real prose piece, *Vadim* (1832), is ostensibly an unfinished historical novel about the Pugachev rebellion. It is really a story of an ugly hunchback who murders to avenge his father and pursues his sister Olga with incestuous intent. In this work Lermontov is still searching for a prose style and therefore the writing is highly imitative. Shevyryov describes it as an "intermediate form between poetry and prose."[59] Eikhenbaum says it "is something like a narrative poem in prose."[60]

Lermontov's next attempt at prose, the unfinished society tale *Princess Ligovskaya* (1835-36), shows real growth in his prose style and tends to the lucidity of *A Hero of Our Time.* Indeed, this unfinished work, whose hero is the forerunner of Pechorin, clearly anticipates Lermontov's great novel.

A Hero of Our Time moves Russian literature into the age of Realism. Its themes, characters, setting, genres (travel notes, Caucasian tale, adventure story, society tale, fantastic story) and form—a frame plus five tales—are Romantic; its clean prose and psychological probing of the main character Pechorin mark it as an early work of Russian Realism. The structure of the novel, with its fracture of time sequence and multiple narrators, functions as a complex device to reveal Pechorin's character. The point of view moves from a narrator who has never met Pechorin, to an old army officer who considers Pechorin his friend, to Pechorin himself, who in his diary reveals his innermost thoughts and feelings. In this novel Lermontov has created some of the first round characters in the great tradition of the rich portrait gallery called the nineteenth-century Russian novel.

Then why "Shtoss"? Why read an unfinished fragment of a projected Petersburg novel? The answer is that this little story may not be what it seems. On the surface the story falls back into a Romantic pattern with fantastic events, ethereal spirits, quest for beauty, and retreat to insanity. But one critic views "Shtoss" not as a Romantic story, but as a parody of Romantic tales. In his article, "Lermontov's *Shtoss:* Hoax or Literary Credo?" John Mersereau looks closely at the details and discovers that in this work Lermontov was writing a parody of Gogol's Petersburg stories ("Nevsky Prospect," "Notes of a Madman," and "The Portrait") and Pushkin's "The Queen of Spades."[61] Mersereau argues that in "Shtoss" Lermontov rejects the Hoffmannesque/fantastic elements of Romanticism as well as its glorification of madness.[62] Lermontov takes those themes and makes them prosaic. After a convincing argument Mersereau comes to the following conclusion: "The particular combination of disparate elements that *Shtoss* represents seems to make sense only if we see it as an antiromantic work following the direction indicated earlier by Pushkin in *The Queen of Spades.*"[63] To use Apollon Grigoryev's term, the "drift" away from Romanticism was in the air. So if Pushkin and Lermontov knew that the age of Romanticism was over, I certainly shall not argue with them.

Notes

1. For a detailed description see J. G. Garrard, "Narrative Technique in Chulkov's *Prigozhaia povarikha,*" *Slavic Review* 27 (1968), pp. 255-63.

2. Another travel work of great importance is Alexander Radishchev's *Journey from Petersburg to Moscow.*

3. Henry M. Nebel, Jr., *N. M. Karamzin* (The Hague: Mouton and Co., 1967), p. 154.

4. My sources for the discussion of Karamzin's prose are Nebel (see note 3), Roger B. Anderson, *N. M. Karamzin's Prose, The Teller in the Tale* (Houston: Cordovan Press, 1974), and Carl R. Proffer, "Poor Liza" in his *From Karamzin to Bunin* (Bloomington: Indiana University Press, 1969), pp. 1-4.

5. This phenomenon resembles the "Werther craze" in Germany when young men dressed like Goethe's hero and even committed suicide in imitation of him.

6. Nebel, p. 130. A detailed analysis of a passage from the story occurs on pp. 128-31.

7. Anderson, pp. 78-80.

8. Anderson, pp. 73-85.

9. Anderson, p. 82.

10. John Mersereau, Jr., "The Chorus and Spear Carriers of Russian Romantic Fiction," in *Russian and Slavic Literature,* ed. Richards Freeborn, R. R. Milner-Gulland and Charles A. Ward (Columbus: Slavica Publishers, Inc., 1976), p. 38.

11. Mersereau, pp. 39-40.

12. My discussion is based on Lauren Leighton, "Marlinsky " *Russian Literature Triquarterly* 3 (Spring 1982), pp. 249-68 and Lauren Leighton, *Alexander Bestuzhev-Marlinsky* (Boston: Twayne Publishers, 1975).

13. Leighton, "Marlinsky," p. 249.

14. Leighton, *Bestuzhev-Marlinsky,* p. 14.

15. After Bestuzhev, Küchelbecker, Belinsky and even Apollon Grigoryev continued the trend.

16. Leighton, *Bestuzhev-Marlinsky,* p. 253.

17. Leighton, *Bestuzhev-Marlinsky,* p. 116.

18. Mersereau, p. 41.

19. Leighton, "Marlinsky," p. 258.

20. Leighton, "Marlinsky," p. 262.

21. Leighton, *Bestuzhev-Marlinsky,* pp. 29-30.

22. Leighton, *Bestuzhev-Marlinsky,* pp. 87-89.

23. Leighton, *Bestuzhev-Marlinsky,* p. 112. The rest of my discussion is based on Leighton's more detailed analysis on pp. 111-16.

24. Leighton, *Bestuzhev-Marlinsky,* p. 114. See this source for a much more detailed analysis of the relationship between the two.

25. Leighton, *Bestuzhev-Marlinsky,* p.114.

26. Leighton, *Bestuzhev-Marlinsky,* pp. 115-16.

27. Mersereau, p. 51.

28. Mersereau, p. 50.

29. D. S. Mirsky, *A History of Russian Literature,* ed. and abr. Francis J. Whitfield (New York: Alfred A. Knopf, 1966), p. 120.

30. Mirsky, p. 115.

31. N. L. Stepanov, "Anton Pogorelsky," in Anton Pogorelsky, *Dvoinik, ili moi vechera v Malorossii—Monastyrka* (Moscow: Khudozhestvennaia Literatura, 1960), pp. 3-22.

32. Stepanov, p. 7.

33. Philip Edward Frantz, "A. A. Perovskij (Pogorelskij): Gentleman and *Litterateur,*" Diss. University of Michigan 1981, pp. 115-20.

34. Pogorelsky, *Monastyrka,* pp. 307-8.

35. I draw my information on Odoevsky from Ralph Matlaw, "Introduction" in V. F. Odoevsky, *Russian Nights,* tr. Olga Kashansky-Olienikov and Ralph E. Matlaw (New York: Dutton and Co., Inc., 1965), pp. 7-20; Simon Karlinsky, "A Hollow Shape: The Philosophical Tales of Prince Vladimir Odoevsky," *Studies in Romanticism* (Summer 1966), pp. 169-82; and M. Aronson and S. Reyser, *Literaturnye kruzhki i salony* (Leningrad: Priboi, 1929).

36. Mersereau, p. 43.

37. Aronson, p. 281.

38. Matlaw, pp. 14-15.

39. For example, a statue of Peter the Great comes alive in Pushkin's *Bronze Horseman,* and a nose gets a life of its own in Gogol's "Nose."

40. Later Tolstoi's heroine, Anna Karenina, receives society's censure not for her affair, but for her lack of discretion.

41. The Baroness, the Baron, his brother, his second, Granitsky, his second, and Countess Rifeyskaya.

42. Carl R. Proffer, "The Queen of Spades" in *From Karamzin to Bunin,* p. 8.

43. Proffer, p. 10.

44. John Mersereau, Jr., "Lermontov's *Shtoss*: A Hoax or Literary Credo?" *Slavic Review* 21 (1962), p. 294.

45. V. B. Shklovsky, from *Notes on Pushkin's Prose* in *Russian Views of Pushkin,* ed. and tr. D. J. Richards and C. R. S. Cockrell (Oxford: Willem A. Meeuws, 1976), p. 189.

46. Shklovsky, p. 189.

47. Proffer, p. 8.

48. Proffer, pp. 8-9.

49. Abram Lezhnev, *Proza Pushkina* (Moscow: Khudozhestvennaia Literatura, 1966), p. 78. Quoted in Proffer, p. 8.

50. Mirsky, p. 120.

51. Anthony Olcott, "Parody as Realism: the *Journey to Arzrum,*" *Russian Literature Triquarterly* 10 (Fall 1974), pp. 245-59.

52. Alexander Slonimsky, *Tekhnika komicheskogo u Gogolia* (Petersburg: Akademiia, 1923).

53. Among others, early Dostoevsky, early Turgenev and Pisemsky.

54. Viktor Vinogradov, *Gogol i naturalnaia shkola* (Leningrad, 1925).

55. Carl R. Proffer, "Introduction," in N. V. Gogol, *Arabesques,* tr. Alexander Tulloch (Ann Arbor: Ardis, 1982), p. 10.

56. For an explanation of Gogol's revisions see Carl R. Proffer, *The Simile and Gogol's "Dead Souls"* (The Hague: Mouton, 1967), pp. 183-200, especially pp. 195-97 for the autobiographical elements.

57. Proffer, *Simile,* p. 186.

58. For analyses of Lermontov's prose see John Mersereau, Jr. *Mikhail Lermontov* (Carbondale: Southern Illinois University Press, 1952) and B. M. Eikhenbaum, *Lermontov,* tr. Ray Parrott and Harry Weber (Ann Arbor: Ardis, 1981).

59. Quoted in Eikhenbaum, p. 147.

60. Eikhenbaum, p. 147.

61. Mersereau, *Shtoss,* pp. 280-95.

62. Mersereau, *Shtoss,* pp. 284-86.

63. Mersereau, *Shtoss,* p. 295.

PROSE IN RUSSIA: 1790-1841

N. M. KARAMZIN

Poor Liza

Perhaps no one who lives in Moscow knows the environs of the city as well as I, because no one spends as much time in the fields as I, no one wanders about on foot more than I—without plan, without goal—wherever my nose leads me through meadows and groves, across hill and dale. Each summer I find pleasant new places or new beauties in the old ones.

But the most pleasant place for me is the one where the gloomy Gothic towers of Si . . .nov Monastery rise up. Standing on this hill you can see almost all Moscow to the right—the terrible mass of houses and churches which strikes one's eyes in the form of a majestic *amphitheater:* a marvelous picture, especially when the sun is shining on it, when its evening rays burn on the countless golden cupolas, on the countless crosses rising up to the sky! The fluffy, dark-green, flourishing meadows stretch out below, and beyond them, over yellow sands flows the clear river ruffled by the light oars of fishing dories or gurgling under the rudders of heavily laden barges which sail from the most bountiful areas of the Russian Empire and supply ravenous Moscow with grain. On the other side of the river one can see an oak grove beside which numerous herds graze; there, sitting in the shade of the trees, young shepherds sing simple, doleful songs and thus shorten the summer days which are so monotonous for them. A little farther, in the thick green of ancient elms, glitters the goldcapped Danilov Monastery; even farther away, almost on the edge of the horizon, Sparrow Hills look blue. On the left one can see spacious, grain-covered fields, small woods, three or four hamlets, and in the distance, the village of Kolomensk with its tall castle.

I often go to this place, and I almost always greet spring there; I go to the same place in the gloomy days of autumn to grieve along with nature. The winds howl frightfully against the walls of the deserted monastery, between the graves overgrown with tall grass and through the dark passageways to the cells. There, leaning on the ruins of the tombstones, I heed the dull moan of times which have been swallowed up in the abyss of the past—a moan at which my heart shudders and trembles. Occasionally, I enter the cells and imagine the men who lived in them— and pictures! Here I see a gray elder on his knees before a crucifix and praying for the quick removal of his earthly chains, because all pleasures in life have disappeared for him, all of his feelings have died except the feeling of sickness and weakness. Over there—a young monk with a pale face and languishing gaze is looking at the field through the window-grating; he sees joyous birds freely swimming in the sea of air, he sees them and bitter tears pour from his eyes. He is languishing, withering, drying up; and for me the doleful tolling of the bell heralds his untimely death. Occasionally I examine on the portals of this temple representations of the miracles which took place in the monastery: here fish fall from the sky for the nourishment of the inhabitants of the monastery which has been besieged by numerous enemies, there an ikon of the Virgin Mary is putting the enemy to flight. All of this renews in my memory the history of our fatherland, the sad history of those times when the fierce Tatars and Lithuanians plundered the environs of the Russian capital with fire and sword, and when unhappy Moscow, like a defenseless widow, looked to God alone for help in her ferocious calamities.

But most often I am drawn to the walls of Si...nov Monastery by the memory of the lamentable fate of Liza, poor Liza. Oh! I love those things which touch my heart and make me shed tears of tender grief!

About a hundred and fifty yards from the monastery wall, by a small birch grove in the middle of a green meadow stands an empty cottage without doors, without windows, without a floor; the roof has long since rotted and caved in. In this cottage thirty years ago lived beautiful, dear Liza with her mother.

Liza's father was a rather well-to-do settler because he loved work, tilled the land well, and always led a sober life. But soon after his death the wife and daughter were impoverished. The lazy arm of the hired worker worked the field poorly, and the grain stopped growing well. They were forced to rent their land—and for an extremely low rate. Besides this, the poor widow, almost constantly shedding tears over the death of her husband (for even peasant women know how to love!), got weaker day by day and could not work at all. Only Liza—who was fifteen when her father died—only Liza worked day and night, without any mercy for her tender youth, without mercy for her rare beauty; she wove flax, knitted stockings, picked flowers in the spring, and gathered berries in the summer—and she sold them in Moscow. The kind, sensitive old woman, seeing her daughter's tirelessness, often pressed her to her weakly beating heart, called her God's mercy, her provider, and the joy of her old age; and she prayed God that He reward her for all she was doing for her mother. "God gave me hands to work," Liza said, "you fed me with your breast and took care of me when I was a baby; now it is my turn to take care of you. Only stop grieving, stop weeping; our tears will not bring father back to life." But often tender Liza could not hold back her own tears—oh! She remembered that she had a father and that he was no more, but to comfort her mother she attempted to conceal the sadness of her heart and to seem calm and happy. "In the next world, dear Liza," the grieved old woman would answer, "I will stop weeping in the next world. There, they say, everyone will be happy; I surely will be happy when I see your father. Only I don't want to die now—what will happen to you without me? Whom can I leave you to? No, let God arrange a place for you first! Perhaps we'll soon find a good man. Then, blessing you, my dear children, I will cross myself and calmly lie down in the damp earth."

Two years passed after the death of Liza's father. The meadows were covered with flowers and Liza went to Moscow with lilies of the valley. In the street she met a well-dressed young man of pleasant appearance. She showed him the flowers and blushed. "Are you selling these, Miss?" he asked with a smile. "Yes," she answered. "And how much do you want?"—"Five kopecks."— "That's too cheap. Here's a ruble for you." Liza was surprised; she dared to glance up at the young man—she blushed even more, and lowering her eyes to the ground, she told him she would not take the ruble.—"Why not?"—"I don't need extra."—"I think that beautiful lilies of the valley picked by the hands of a beautiful girl are worth a ruble. But since you won't take it, here are five kopecks for you. I would like to buy flowers from you all the time; I would like for you to pick them only for me." Liza gave him the flowers, took five kopecks, bowed, and wanted to leave; but the stranger stopped her by the arm.—"Where are you going, Miss?"— "Home."—"And where is your home?" Liza said where she lived—said it and left. The young man did not want to hold her, perhaps because passers-by had begun to stop, look at them, and smirk treacherously.

When she got home Liza told her mother what had happened to her. "You did well not to take the ruble. Perhaps he was some bad man . . . ."—"Oh, no, mother! I don't think so. He had such a kind face, such a voice . . . ."—"Still, Liza, it's better to feed yourself by your own labors and not to take anything free. You still don't know, my dear, how evil men can offend a poor girl! My heart is always in my throat when you go to the city; I always put a candle before the ikon and pray the Lord God for Him to save you from any misfortune and harm." Tears appeared in Liza's eyes; she kissed her mother.

The next day Liza picked the last lilies of the valley and again went to the city with them. Her eyes were quietly looking for something. Many people wanted to buy her flowers, but she answered that they were not for sale, and she looked from one side to the other. Evening fell; she had to return home, and the flowers were thrown into the Moscow River. "No one will possess you!" said Liza, feeling a kind of grief in her heart. The next evening she was sitting by the window, spinning and singing plaintive songs in a soft voice; but suddenly she jumped up and cried out, "Oh!" The young stranger was standing by the window.

"What's wrong?" asked her frightened mother, who was sitting beside her. "Nothing, mama," Liza answered in a timid voice, "I just saw him."—"Who?"—"The man who bought my flowers." The old woman glanced out the window. The young man bowed to her so courteously, with such a pleasant expression, that she could think nothing but good of him. "How do you do, my good old woman!" he said. "I am very tired; would you have some fresh milk?" Obliging Liza, without waiting for her mother's answer, perhaps because she knew it in advance, ran to the storeroom, brought a clean pot covered with a clean wooden plate—she grabbed a glass, washed it, and dried it with a white towel, filled it and handed it through the window, but she herself kept looking at the ground. The stranger drank up—and nectar from the hands of Hebe could not have seemed more tasty to him. Everyone will guess that after this he thanked Liza and thanked her not so much in words as in looks. Meanwhile the good-hearted old woman managed to tell him about her woe and comfort—about her husband's death and the fine qualities of her daughter, about her love of work and tenderness etc. etc. He listened to her attentively, but his eyes were—is it necessary to say where? And Liza, timid Liza occasionally would glance at the young man; but lightning does not flash and disappear in a cloud as fast as her blue eyes turned to the earth when they met his glance. "I would like," he said to the mother, "for your daughter not to sell her work to anyone except me. Then there will be no reason for her to go to the city so often, and you will not be forced to part with her. I can drop by on you myself from time to time." At this point joy flashed in Liza's eyes, joy which she wanted vainly to conceal; her cheeks burned like the sunset on a clear summer evening; she looked at her left sleeve and picked at it with her right hand. The old woman willingly accepted this proposition without suspecting any bad intention in it, and she assured the stranger that the cloth Liza wove and the stockings she knitted were exceptionally good and wore better than any others. It was getting dark, and the young man wanted to leave. "But what is your name, good and kind sir?" asked the old woman.—"My name is Erast," he answered.—"Erast," said Liza softly, "Erast!" She repeated the name five times as if trying to memorize it. Erast said good-bye to them and left. Liza followed him with her eyes, but her mother was sitting in meditation, and then, taking her daughter by the hand, said to her, "Oh, Liza! How kind and good he is! If only your fiancé were like that!" Liza's heart kept fluttering. "Mama! Mama! How could that happen? He's a gentleman, but among the peasants . . . ." Liza did not finish her sentence.

Now the reader should know that this young man, this Erast, was a fairly rich nobleman with a decent mind and a good heart, good by nature—but weak and flighty. He led a carefree life, thought only of his own pleasure, sought this in worldly amusements, but often did not find it: he was bored and complained about his fate. At the first meeting Liza's beauty made an impression on his heart. He often read novels and idylls; he had a rather lively imagination and often he transported himself mentally to those times (real or unreal) when, if we are to believe poets, all people wandered carefree across meadows, went swimming in pure springs, kissed like turtledoves, rested under roses and myrtle, and passed all their days in happy idleness. It seemed to him that in Liza he had found what his heart had long been seeking. "Nature is calling me into its embrace, to its pure joys," he thought, and he decided—for a while at least—to abandon high society.

Let us turn to Liza. Night fell—the mother blessed her daughter and wished her sweet dreams, but on this occasion her desire was not fulfilled: Liza slept very badly. She imagined the new guest of her soul—the image of Erast—so vividly that she awoke almost every minute, awoke and sighed. Liza got up before the rising of the sun, went to the bank of the Moscow River, sat down on the grass, and feeling despondent, she looked at the white mists which trembled in the air and, rising upwards, left glittering droplets on the green coverlet of nature. Silence reigned everywhere. But soon the rising luminary of the day awakened all creation: groves, hedges came to life, little birds fluttered and began to sing, flowers raised their little heads in order to drink in the life-giving rays of light. But Liza kept sitting despondently. Oh, Liza, Liza! What has happened to you? Until now, waking up with the birds, you were as merry as they were in the morning; and a pure joyous soul shone in your eyes as the sun shines on drops of heavenly dew; but now you are pensive, and the general joy of nature is alien to your heart. Meanwhile a young shepherd was driving his herd along the bank of the river, playing his pipes. Liza fixed her gaze on him and thought: "If the one who occupies my thoughts now had been born a simple peasant shepherd—and if it were he that was driving his herd past me now: oh! I would bow to him with a smile and say pleasantly: 'How do you do, kind shepherd! Where are you driving your flock? And here grows green grass for your sheep, and here there are red flowers from which you can plait a garland for your hat.' He would glance at me with a caressing look—perhaps he would take my hand . . . . A dream!" The shepherd playing his pipes walked past and disappeared behind a nearby hill with his flock.

Suddenly Liza heard the sound of oars—she glanced at the river and saw a boat, and in the boat was Erast.

All her veins began to throb, and of course this was not from fear. She got up and wanted to leave, but could not. Erast jumped out onto the bank, approached Liza, and her dream was partially fulfilled: for *he glanced at her with a caressing look and took her by the hand* . . . . And Liza, Liza stood with lowered eyes, with fiery cheeks, with a trembling heart—she could not take her hand away from him, could not turn away when he came close to her with his pink lips . . . . Ah! He kissed her, kissed her with such ardor that the whole universe seemed to her to be blazing in fire! "Dear Liza!" said Erast. "Dear Liza, I love you!" And these words resounded in the depths of her soul like an enchanting heavenly music; she scarcely dared believe her ears and . . . . But I abandon my brush. I will say only that in this moment of rapture Liza's timidity disappeared—and Erast discovered that he was loved, loved passionately by a new, pure open heart.

They sat on the grass in such a way that there was not much space between them—they looked into each other's eyes, and talked to each other: "Love me!" And two hours seemed an instant to them. Finally Liza remembered that her mother might get worried about her. They had to part. "Oh, Erast!" she said, "Will you always love me?"—"Always, dear Liza, always," he answered.—"And can you swear to me that this is true?"—"I can, darling Liza, I can."—"No, I don't need an oath, I believe you, Erast, I believe you. Could you deceive poor Liza? That couldn't be."—"It couldn't, it couldn't, dear Liza!"—"How happy I am, and how mama will cheer up when she learns that you love me!"—"Oh, no, Liza! There's no need to tell her anything."—"Why not?"—"Old people are suspicious. She will imagine something bad."—

"That couldn't happen."—"Still, please don't say a word to her about it."—"All right. I must obey you, even though I don't want to hide anything from her." They said good-bye, kissed for the last time, and promised to see each other every evening either on the bank of the river or in the birch grove, or somewhere near Liza's hut—only they would definitely, unfailingly see each other. Liza walked away, but her eyes turned back a hundred times to Erast, who was still standing on the bank and watching her.

Liza returned to her cottage in a completely different mood from the one in which she had left. Her heartfelt joy revealed itself on her face and in her movements. "He loves me!" she thought, and she was enraptured by the thought. "Oh, mama! What a beautiful morning! How joyous everything is in the field! Never have the skylarks sung so well, never has the sun shone so brightly, never have the flowers smelled so good!" Leaning on her crutch the old woman went out into the meadow to enjoy the morning which Liza had described in such exquisite colors. Indeed, it seemed to her extremely pleasant: her dear daughter had cheered up all of nature for her with her own cheer. "Oh, Liza," she said, "How good everything is with the Lord God! I am in my sixties, and I still cannot look upon the Lord's works enough. I cannot see too much of the pure sky which resembles a high tent, or of the earth which is covered by new grass and new flowers every year. It must be that the Heavenly King loved man very much when he decorated this world so well. Oh, Liza! Who would want to die if we did not sometimes have grief? Apparently it has to be like this. Maybe we would forget our souls if tears never dropped from our eyes." And Liza thought: "Ah! I will forget my soul before I forget my dear friend!"

After this, Erast and Liza, fearing not to keep their word, saw each other every evening (when Liza's mother went to bed) either on the bank of the river or in the birch grove, but most often under the shade of hundred-year-old oaks (about a hundred and seventy yards from the hut), oaks which shaded a deep, clear pond that had been dug in ancient times. There, through the green branches, the rays of the moon often silvered Liza's light hair, with which zephyrs and the hand of her dear friend often played; often these rays illumined a glittering tear of love in the eyes of tender Liza—which Erast always dried with a kiss. They embraced—but chaste, shy Cynthia did not hide from them behind a cloud: pure and sinless were their embraces. "When you," said Liza to Erast, "say to me 'I love you, my friend!', when you press me to your heart, and glance at me with your tender eyes, oh! then I feel so good, so good, that I forget myself, I forget everything except—Erast! Wonderful! It is miraculous, my friend, that I could live calmly and merrily without knowing you! Now that seems incomprehensible to me, now I think that without you life is not life, but sadness and boredom. Without your eyes the bright moon is dark, without your voice the singing nightingale is dull, without your breath the breeze is unpleasant to me."

Erast was enraptured by his shepherdess—thus he called Liza—and seeing how much she loved him, he seemed more amiable to himself. All of the glittering amusements of high society seemed insignificant to him in comparison to the pleasures with which the passionate *friendship* of an innocent soul nourished his heart. With revulsion he thought about the despicable voluptuousness with which he formerly sated his feelings. "I am going to live with Liza as a brother with his sister," he thought, "I will not use her love for evil and I will always be happy!" Foolish young man! Do you know your own heart? Can you always answer for your impulses? Is reason always the tsar of your feeling?

Liza demanded that Erast often visit her mother. "I love her," she said, "and I wish her good, and it seems to me that seeing you is a great blessing for anyone." Indeed, the old woman always cheered up when she saw him. She liked to talk to him about her late husband and to tell him about the days of her youth, about how she met her dear Ivan for the first time, how he fell in love with her and in what love, what accord he lived with her. "Ah! We could never look at each other enough—right up to the hour when ferocious death cut him down. He died in my arms!" Erast listened to her with unfeigned pleasure. He bought Liza's work from her, and he always wanted to pay ten times more than the price which was set by her, but the old woman never took extra.

Thus passed several weeks. One evening Erast had been waiting for his Liza for a long time. Finally she came, but was so unhappy that he was frightened; her eyes had turned red from tears. "Liza, Liza! What has happened to you?"—"Oh, Erast! I've been crying!"—"About what? What has happened?"—"I must tell you everything. A suitor is courting me, the son of a rich peasant from a neighboring village; mother wants me to marry him."—"And you agree?"—"Cruel man! Can you ask about that? Yes, I am sorry for mother; she cries and says that I do not want her to have peace, that she is going to be tormented at death if she does not marry me off while she's alive. Oh! Mother doesn't know that I have such a dear friend!" Erast kissed Liza, said that her happiness was dearer than anything on earth to him, that after her mother's death he would take her to his house, that he would live with her never to part, in the country, and in the sleepy forest, as if in paradise. "But you cannot be my husband!" said Liza with a quiet sigh. "Why not?"—"I am a peasant."—"You insult me. Most important of all for your friend is the soul, a sensitive innocent soul—and Liza will always be dearest to my heart."

She threw herself into his arms—and this was to be the hour when her purity would perish! Erast felt an unusual agitation in his blood—never had Liza seemed so exquisite to him—never had her caresses touched him so strongly—never had her kisses been so flaming—she did not know anything, did not suspect anything, did not fear anything—the dark of the evening fed desire—not a single little star shone in the heavens—no ray of light could illuminate the error.— Erast feels himself trembling—Liza too, not knowing why—not knowing what is happening to her . . . . Ah, Liza, Liza! Where is your guardian angel, where is your innocence?

The error took only a minute. Liza did not understand her feelings, she was astonished and began asking questions. Erast was silent—he searched for words and did not find them. "Oh, I am afraid," said Liza, "I am afraid of what has happened to us! It seems to me that I am dying, that my soul . . . no, I cannot say it! . . . you're silent Erast? You are sighing? . . . My God! What is this?" Meanwhile, lightning flashed and thunder rolled. Liza began to tremble all over. "Erast, Erast!" she said. "I am terrified! I am afraid that the thunder will kill me like a criminal!" The storm raged threateningly, rain poured from black clouds—it seemed that nature was lamenting Liza's lost innocence. Erast tried to calm Liza and he walked her to the cottage. Tears were rolling from her eyes when she said good-bye to him. "Oh, Erast! Assure me that we will be happy as before!"—"We will be, Liza, we will be!" he answered.—"God grant it be so! I cannot disbelieve your words; after all I love you! Still, in my heart . . . . But enough! Farewell! Tomorrow, tomorrow we will see each other."

Their meetings continued, but how everything changed! Erast could no longer be satisfied just by innocent caresses of his Liza, just by her glances full of love, just by the touch of her hand, just by a kiss, just by pure embraces. He desired more, more, and finally, he could desire nothing—and he who knows his heart, he who has meditated on the quality of his tenderest pleasures will of course agree with me that the fulfillment of *all* desires is the most dangerous temptation of love. For Erast Liza was no longer the angel of purity who had formerly flamed in his imagination and enraptured his soul. Platonic love had given way to feelings of which he could not be *proud* and which were not new for him. As for Liza, having given herself to him completely, she lived and breathed only in him; in everything, like a lamb, she submitted to his will and she supposed that her own happiness was in his pleasure. She saw the change in him and often said to him: "You were in better spirits before; we were calmer and happier before, and I wasn't so afraid of losing your love before!" Sometimes parting from her, he said to her: "I cannot come to see you tomorrow Liza, I have important business." And every time Liza sighed at these words.

Finally she did not see him for five days in a row and she was greatly disturbed: on the sixth day he came with a sad face: "Dear Liza, I must say farewell to you for a while. You know that we are at war; I am in the service, my regiment is going on a campaign." Liza turned pale and almost fainted.

Erast caressed her, said that he would always love dear Liza, and that he hoped on his return he would never part from her again. She was silent for a long time, then she burst into bitter tears, grabbed his hand, and glancing at him with all the tenderness of love, she asked: "Can't you stay?" "I can," he answered, "but only with the greatest ignominy, the greatest stain upon my honor. Everyone will despise me; everyone will shun me as a coward, as an unworthy son of the fatherland."—"Oh, if it's like that," said Liza, "then go, go where God commands! But you could be killed."—"Death for the fatherland is not terrible, dear Liza."—"I will die, as soon as you are no longer on earth."—"But why think that? I hope to return to you, my friend."—"God grant it be so! God grant it be so! Every day, every hour I will pray for it. Oh, why is it I do not know how to read or write! You would inform me about everything that happens to you, and I would write to you about my tears!"—"No, spare yourself Liza, spare yourself for your friend. I do not want you to weep without me."—"Cruel man! You can think of depriving me of this consolation too! No! When I have parted from you I will stop weeping when my heart dries up."—"Think about the pleasant minute when we will again meet."—"I will, I will think about it! Oh! If only it would come soon! My dear, kind Erast! Remember your poor Liza who loves you more than herself!"

But I cannot describe everything that they said on this occasion. The next day was to be their last meeting.

Erast wanted to say good-bye to Liza's mother, who could not hold back her tears when she heard that her *kind handsome gentleman* had to go away to war. He forced her to take some money from him, saying: "In my absence I do not want Liza to sell her work, which according to our agreement belongs to me." The old woman showered him with blessings. "God grant that you return to us safely," she said, "and that I see you again in this life! Maybe by then my Liza will find herself a suitor who pleases her. How I would thank God if you came to our wedding! And when Liza has children, you know sir, that you must be their godfather! Oh! I want so much to live until then!" Liza was standing beside her mother and did not dare to glance at her. The reader can easily imagine what she was feeling at this moment.

But what did she feel when, having embraced her for the last time, having pressed her to his heart for the last time, Erast said: "Farewell, Liza! . . ." What a touching scene! Like a scarlet sea the dawn was spreading across the eastern sky. Erast was standing under the branches of a tall oak tree holding in his embrace his pale, languid, bereaved friend who, bidding him farewell, said farewell to her own soul. All nature attended in silence.

Liza sobbed—Erast wept—he left her—she fell—she got up on her knees, raised her hands toward the sky, and watched Erast who was walking away, farther—farther—and, finally, disappeared—the sun rose and poor, abandoned Liza lost her feelings and consciousness. She came to—and the world seemed doleful and sad to her. All of the pleasures of nature had disappeared for her along with the one who was dear to her heart. "Oh!" she thought, "Why have I been abandoned in this wasteland? What is preventing me from flying after my dear Erast? War does not terrify me; I am terrified only without my friend. I want to live with him, to die with him or to save his precious life with my death. Wait, wait my dear! I will fly to you!"—She already wanted to run after Erast but the thought: "I have a mother!"—stopped her. Liza sighed and, bowing her head, walked toward her cottage with soft steps.—From that hour her days were days of melancholy and grief which she had to hide from her tender mother: and her heart suffered all the more! It found relief only when Liza, isolating herself in the depths of the forest, could freely pour forth her tears and moan over being parted from her dear one. Often the sad turtledove joined its plaintive voice to her moaning. But sometimes—although extremely rarely—a golden ray of hope, a ray of comfort brightened the darkness of her sorrow. "How happy I will be when he returns to me! How everything will change!"—At this her eyes brightened, the roses on her cheeks grew fresh, and Liza smiled like a May morning after a stormy night.—About two months passed in this way.

One day Liza had to go to Moscow in order to buy some rosewater with which her mother treated her eyes. On one of the big streets she met a magnificent carriage, and in that carriage she saw—Erast. "Oh!" Liza cried out and she rushed toward him, but the carriage drove past and turned into a courtyard. Erast got out and was going to go onto the porch of a huge house, when suddenly he found himself in Liza's embrace. He turned pale—then, not answering a word to her exclamations, he took her by the arm, led her into his study, locked the door, and said to her: "Liza! Circumstances have changed; I am engaged to be married; you must leave me in peace and forget me for your own peace of mind. I loved you, and I love you now, that is, I wish all the best for you. Here is a hundred rubles—take it," and he put the money in her pocket. "Allow me to kiss you a last time—and go home."—Before Liza could come to her senses he led her out of the study and said to his servant: "See this girl to the street."

At this minute my heart is surging with blood. I forget the man in Erast—I am ready to curse him—but my tongue does not move—I look at the sky, and a tear rolls across my face. Oh! Why am I not writing a novel instead of a sad, true story?

So Erast deceived Liza in telling her that he was going into the army?—No, he was in fact in the army, but instead of fighting with the enemy, he played cards and lost almost all of his estate. Soon peace was concluded, and Erast returned to Moscow burdened with debts. He was left with only one way of correcting his circumstances—marrying a rich, middle-aged widow who had been in love with him for a long time. He decided on this and moved into her house after devoting a sincere sigh to his Liza. But can all of this justify him?

Liza found herself in the street and in a state which no pen can describe. "He, he drove me out? He loves someone else? I am lost!" These were her thoughts, her feelings! A cruel fainting spell interrupted them for a while. A kind woman who was walking along the street stooped over Liza, who was lying on the ground, and tried to bring her to; the unhappy girl opened her eyes, got up with the help of this kind woman, thanked her, and began walking without knowing where. "I cannot live," thought Liza, "I cannot! . . . Oh, if only the sky would fall upon me! If only the earth would swallow up a poor girl! . . . No! The sky will not fall, the earth will not shake! Woe is me!" She left the city and suddenly found herself on the bank of a deep pond in the shade of the ancient oak trees which several weeks before had been the silent witnesses to her raptures. This reminiscence shook her soul; the most terrible, heartfelt torment was depicted on her face. But in a few minutes she was lost in thought—she looked around her, saw the daughter of a neighbor (a fifteen-year-old girl) walking along the road; she called to her, took the ten imperials out of her pocket and giving them to her said: "Dear Anyuta, dear friend! Take this money to my mother—it is not stolen—tell her that Liza is guilty before her, that I have hidden from her my love for a certain cruel man, for E . . . . Why know his name? Tell her that he betrayed me—ask her to forgive me—God will be her helper—kiss her hand as I am kissing yours now—say that poor Liza told you to kiss her—say that I . . . ." At this point she threw herself into the water. Anyuta screamed, began to cry, but could not save her; she ran to the village—the people gathered and they pulled Liza out, but she was already dead.

In this way one who was beautiful in soul and body ended her life. When we are *there* in the new life, we will see each other; I will recognize you, tender Liza!

She was buried near the pond under a somber oak, and they put a wooden cross on her grave. I often sit here in meditation leaning on the receptacle of Liza's dust; the pond ripples before my eyes; the leaves rustle above me.

Liza's mother heard of the terrible death of her daughter and her blood turned cold from horror—her eyes closed forever.—The hut was deserted, the wind howls in it and superstitious villagers, hearing the noise at night say: "The dead girl's moaning there, poor Liza is moaning there!"

To the end of his life Erast was unhappy. Having learned of Liza's fate, he could not find solace and he considered himself a murderer. I made his acquaintance a year before his death. He himself told me this story and led me to Liza's grave.—Now, perhaps, they have already become reconciled!

A. A. BESTUZHEV-MARLINSKY

An Evening on Bivouac

> ...scarce the dawn appears,
> Each into the field goes flying,
> Each with cap tipped over ears,
> Skirted cloaks like whirlwinds playing,
> Horses seething 'neath their men,
> Sabres whistle, foes go falling,
> And the battle ends—Again
> In the night the bucket's swinging.
>
> *Davydov*

In the distance from time to time artillery shot could be heard scathing the left flank of the overrun enemy, and the evening sky flared as if from summer lightning. Huge fires flamed up over the field like stars, and the shouts of soldiers and foragers, the creak of wheels, the neighing of horses imparted vivid life to the hazy picture of a military camp. The advance posts had fallen to the squadron of the Hussar Regiment commanded by Colonel Mechin. After setting up the picket line and giving orders for the horses to be fed across it, the officers settled down around the fire to drink tea. After guard duty it is a joy for the unscathed to chat about this and that while the cup makes the rounds, to praise the brave and poke fun at the careful etiquette shown by others toward cannon barrages. The conversation of our advance-post officers had already dwindled perceptibly when cuirassier lieutenant prince Olsky sprang down from his horse before them.

"Greetings, friends."

"Welcome, prince! We've been wondering when you would show up. Where have you been all this time?"

"Need you ask? At my usual place at the front of my unit, chopping, flailing about, winning out—but for that matter even you hussars proved today you don't wear your mantles on your right shoulders. My thanks to you. But first, sergeant major! have my donets put up and fed—he hasn't had a thing to eat but gun smoke today."

"I hear you, your radiance . . . ."

"My radiance doesn't hear or heed a thing until he's downed a bit of glintwine, without which he is neither radiant nor dark. Pour me a glass."

"By all means!" replied Captain Struisky, "but let me warn you, the goblet is dear—you'll have to pay off with an anecdote."

"Hundreds, if you wish! It's cheap at the price. I'm full up on anecdotes and I'll tell you one of my latest, something happened to me. To the health of brave men, comrades!"

"A short while back we had to get by somehow without a crumb of provisions for three days. Thanks to you and the cossacks, every place we looked was as empty as my pockets, and what's worse, heavy cavalry isn't allowed to forage. What to do? My hunger was increasing all the more in that from the French line could be heard the harmonious mooing of oxen—answered by the plaintive echo of my own empty belly. I was lying there beneath my cloak, pondering the vagaries of this world, chewing on a dry crust so moldy it could have been used for the study of botany, so stale I had to cram it down my throat with a ramrod. Suddenly a most happy idea dawned on me. On the spur of the moment was foot in the stirrup and—forward march!

'Where are you off to on your dashing Beauty?' asked my comrades.

'Wherever fancy takes me.'

'What for?'

'To dine or die!' I replied in a tragic voice, and putting the spurs to my horse to give the impression of being carried, I took off like a bird and disappeared from the sight of my astounded comrades. They considered me as good as dead. Galloping past the Russian picket line, I fastened the handkerchief that used to be white in my youth to my sword, and set off at full speed.

'*Qui vive?*' a voice rang out from the enemy picket line.

'*Parlementaire russe!*' I replied.

'*Halte là!*'

A sergeant rode toward me with his pistol cocked.

'Why are you here?'

'For a chat with your detachment commander.'

'Where is your trumpeter?'

'He was killed.'

My eyes were blindfolded, I was led away on foot, and in three minutes I had already guessed by the aroma that I was alongside the officers' hut. 'A good sign,' I thought to myself, 'just in time for supper.' The blindfold was removed and I found myself in the company of a colonel and some eight gentlemen, officers of the French horse-chasseurs. Perhaps I should mention here that I am hardly a backward sort of fellow.

'Messieurs!' I said quite jauntily bowing, 'I haven't eaten in almost three days, and knowing that you have more than enough I decided, in accord with the code of chivalry, to pin my hopes on the magnanimity of foes and drop in on you for dinner. I am firmly convinced that no Frenchman would jest with my freedom. After all, will France win very much if it captures a cavalry lieutenant, all of whose knowledge and actions end at the point of his broadsword?'

I had not deceived myself: my escapade was to the liking of the French. They feted me through the evening, filled my food case to the top, and we parted good friends, promising at our first meeting to split one another's skulls with great enthusiasm.

"Wasn't that in print somewhere?" sarcastically asked staff-captain Nichtovich, who had the reputation of a relentless critic in the regiment.

"If it was in print, it would have been news to you!" retorted Olsky.

"And after what affair did it happen?"

"After the same one in which you were wounded in the heel."

The staff-captain choked on his drink and pulled at his mustache, searching vainly for a swift retort. On this occasion, however, his wit failed him.

"Don't you have something to tell us, Lidin?" asked the colonel, turning to an officer who was absentmindedly puffing at a pipe that had gone out a long time ago.

"No, colonel! Not a thing. My novel is amusing to me alone, filled as it is with mere feelings instead of adventures. And I must confess, you have just knocked a most magnificent castle in the air to the ground. I was dreaming that I had been promoted for distinction to staff officer, that I had just snatched a 'St. George' from the very jaws of an enemy cannon, that I had just returned to Moscow decorated with wounds and glory, that my second uncle once removed, who is older than the Zodiac of Dandarah, had died with joy, and I, newly rich, was just throwing myself at the feet of my dear, incomparable Alexandrina!"

"Dreamer, dreamer!" said Mechin. "But who is not, at one time or another? Who has believed more than I in a woman's love and fidelity? I shall tell you of an event in my life which, my dear Lidin, may serve as a lesson to you, if those who are in love can learn from another's experience. And for you, gentlemen, I will mention in advance that this is the story of the medallion about which I promised to tell you some time ago. Lend an ear!"

"About two years before the present campaign Sophia S. was attracting all the hearts and lorgnettes of Petersburg. Nevsky Boulevard seethed with pining admirers when she went for a stroll, benefit performances were a certain success whenever she dropped in at the theater, and at balls one had to do some jostling just to catch a glimpse of her, let alone enjoy the honor of a dance. Curiosity impelled me to learn a bit more about her, vanity provoked me to win Sophia's attention, and her charm, her educated mind and her kind heart enchanted me forever. In short, it is said, and I believe, that love flies on the wings of hope: I fell head over heels in love with the princess. You are aware, my friends, that nature instilled in me searing passions which carry me to rapture in times of joy, to frenzy or despair in times of adversity. Judge for yourself, then, what bliss was mine at signs of marked reward. I wandered around in a delirium of idylls, I imagined that life without her was unbearable, all the more so in that Sophia's parents were casting favorable glances in my direction.

I was living at that time with my best friend, retired Major Vladov, a man of most noble principles, ardent character, but cold reason. 'You are making an ass out of yourself,' he would inevitably retort in response to my raptures, 'choosing a bride from such a brilliant circle. The princess's father has more debts and whims than money, and your estate won't last long with a woman accustomed to luxury. You will tell me she can be re-educated to your liking, she is only seventeen years of age. But on the other hand, what prejudices her upbringing has instilled in her! Everything is possible as regards love, you will assure me, but what makes you so sure the princess is sighing from love, and not from a tight corset, that she gazes into your eyes for your sake, and not to admire herself in them? Believe me, at just those moments when she is so tenderly discoursing on frugality, on the joys of domestic life, her thoughts are yearning after feminine frills, or a carriage with white wheels in which she can shine at Ekaterinhof, or a new shawl for which you will be dragged off on weary visits so she can show off. My friend! I know your heart, which is so easily stricken by trifles, and in the princess I see a charming, a most pleasing woman, but a woman who loves to live in society and for society, and who is hardly likely to sacrifice so much as a cotillion for your sake, let alone the life of the capital when finances or obligations of service call you off to the army. Reproaches will be followed by deathly indifference, and then—farewell, happiness!'

I scoffed at his words, for by then I had come to know Sophia's favor, and every day I found new merits in her, with each hour my passion grew. Not that I was in a hurry for an understanding: I wished the princess to love me not for my uniform, or for my mazurka, or for my witty words, but for myself, without any poses. At last I reassured myself on this score, and I made my decision.

On the evening I planned to make my proposal, I danced with the princess at the ball of Count T. and was as happy as a child, filled with raptures of hope and love. A certain captain, reputed at the time as a model of fashion, became vexed that Sophia would not deign to dance with him and permitted himself some quite immodest expressions at her expense, standing behind me, and sufficiently loudly. He who dares insult a lady imposes on her cavalier the obligation of taking vengeance for her, even should he be completely unacquainted with her.

When I overheard these witticisms at the princess's expense, my temper flared and I could scarcely contain myself until the close of the quadrille. Explanations were not long forthcoming. Mr. Captain thought to worm his way out of it with jests, claimed he did not remember his words. 'But unfortunately, my esteemed sir, I have a very good memory. You will either beg my lady's pardon on your knees, or tomorrow at ten o'clock, willingly or unwillingly, you will meet me on the Okhta.'

As you know, I am not fond of duels for form's sake: we faced off at five paces, and his first shot, aimed by blind luck, dropped me in my tracks. Some Spanish poet or other—I don't recall his name—has said that the first blow of the apothecary's mortar is already the knell of the funeral bell: the bullet went straight in close to the lungs. St. Anthony's fire threatened to burn my heart to cinders, but Lesage and Molière not withstanding, I managed to recover, with the aid of physicians and plasters, in a month and a half. A wan face is very endearing, but in order not to make my appearance before the princess like a corpse, I restrained myself for a few days and did not fly off to the princess's dacha until I was fully recovered. My heart was beating with a renewed life: I envisioned my joyful reunion with Sophia, her anxiety, the proposal, matrimony, the first day of its . . . . Filled with raptures of hope I fly up the staircase, into the ante-parlor—and my ears are smitten by the sound of the princess's loud laughter. I must confess, I was taken aback. What! The very Sophia who used to pine if she did not see me for two days is having a good time after I suffered my deathbed for her sake! I paused before a mirror—I thought I heard my name mentioned, something about Don Quixote; I entered—a young officer was leaning over the back of her chair and saying something to her in a low voice, and in quite friendly fashion at that, so it seemed to me. The princess was not in the least embarrassed: she inquired after my health with cool solicitude, treated me like an old acquaintance, but quite obviously preferred her guest, for she had no wish to understand either my glances or my allusions to what had once been. I could not begin to imagine what this could mean, was unable to understand the reason for such matter-of-fact coolness. In vain did I seek in her eyes that clear anxiety which makes reconciliation so sweet: there was not so much as a spark or a shadow of love in them. Pride set a fire in my blood, jealousy tore my heart asunder. I seethed, bit my lips, and fearful lest my feelings burst forth in words, I decided to leave.

I don't even remember where I galloped among the fields and swamps in a pouring rain; at midnight I returned home without my hat, unconscious. 'I pity you!' said Vladov, coming to meet me, 'but—forgive the reproach of friendship—did I not foretell that the princess's home would be your Pandora's box? Be that as it may, a strong disease requires strong medicine— read this.' He handed me an engagement announcement—the princess's betrothal to my opponent! . . . Fury and revenge, like lightning, flooded my blood. I swore to shoot him, according to the code of the duel (I was still due my shot at him), so that the crafty woman would not be able to triumph with him. I determined to have it out with her, to reproach her . . . . In a word, I flew into a stormy rage. My friends, do you know what the thirst for blood and revenge is like? I tasted it on that terrible night! In the silence I could hear the seething of the blood in my veins: first it would smother my heart with a surge, then it would cool to ice. I envisioned ceaselessly the roar of the pistol, the fire, the blood and corpses.

It was almost morning before I fell into a deep sleep. I was awakened by an orderly of the minister of war—'Your grace, please report to the general!' I jumped up with the thought that surely I was being called to account for the duel. I reported. 'His Majesty, the Emperor,' the minister began, 'has ordered the selection of an able officer to carry important dispatches to General Kutuzov, commander-in-chief of the Army of the South. I have appointed you, make haste! Here are the packets and travel permits. My secretary will note the hour of your departure in the post-horse registry. Have a good journey, Mr. Courier!' A stage was standing at the door and I was three stations down the postroad before I realized what had happened. My magnanimous Vladov was riding with me.

And it was then that I learned that friendship consoles, but does not restore the heart, and the long road, contrary to general belief, only bruised, without allaying, my feelings. The commander-in-chief received me with marked affection and finally persuaded me to remain with the standing army. Contempt for life led me to thoughts of suicide, but Vladov touched me with his advice and tender concern. He who advises life is always eloquent, and he saved me from two murders, my name from ridicule. 'I knew everything,' he told me, 'but didn't dare tell you when you were ill. Seeing that the secret was out, and knowing your frenzied nature, I rushed to the secretary of the minister of war, a friend of mine, and requested, implored, that you be sent on courier duty. Time is the best advisor, and now admit it—is your enemy worth the smoke? Is your darling worth the fuss? She who chose for her fiance a man without honor and principle, merely because he is fashionable, because her mother noticed a zero more than you have in the fine-sounding titles of a man who could lose a diamond portrait of his fiancée, her gift to him, in a card game with me?' And he handed me this medallion."

The colonel removed it from his bosom and showed it to the officers.

"I'll saw my head off with a dull rock if I can see anything!" shouted Olsky. "The whole enamel facing is smashed to smithereens!"

"Providence," continued the colonel, "spared me from death on the banks of the Danube to serve my fatherland a bit longer: a bullet smashed against Sophia's portrait, but did not spare it. A year went by, and the army, after the conclusion of peace with the Turks, advanced to intercept Napoleon. Anguish and the climate had broken my health: I requested a month's leave to the Caucasus to seek healing waters for my health, the water of life for my spirit.

On the day following my arrival I accompanied a local doctor on his rounds. 'You will meet,' the doctor told me as we approached one little house, 'a beautiful person who is wasting away, victim of a marriage of convenience. Her parents sang her a pretty song of the joys of luxury, a grievous vanity enticed her into the snares of a socially brilliant scoundrel, and deceived by a momentary whimsy of the heart, she threw herself into his clutches. And what came of it? Her aunties and her mama, having sought wealth in a fiance, found only vainglory, immense debts, and depravity. He had sought a dowry, and when deceived by promises, showed the blackness of his true character in his own turn: he tormented his wife with caustic reproaches, drove her to consumption by his behavior, and finally, having gambled and dissipated everything away, threw her over and besmirched her reputation in society. Now she has come here to die beneath the warm skies of the Caucasus.' I was hesitant about disturbing her with my visit. 'Oh, no!' the doctor said, 'as a matter of fact, consumptives die on their feet, and I make it a practice to while away my patients' time with distractions when it is impossible to prolong their lives with medicine.' Chatting thus, we entered the room. It was Sophia! . . .

There are some feelings and scenes which are inexpressible. I had thought I hated Sophia; I had convinced myself that if fate ever led me to an encounter with her I would repay her treachery with cold contempt; but when, instead of a proud young beauty, I beheld an unfortunate victim of society, with dimmed eyes, with a deathly pallor in her face, I realized how much I loved her. All proprieties vanish on the brink of the grave, and when Sophia came to her senses her hand was moist with my tears and kisses. 'You do not curse me, Viktor? You forgive me? . . .' she said in a heart-rending voice. 'Noble soul . . . . You take pity at seeing me so cruelly punished for my thoughtlessness. Now I shall die in peace.'

Life, like an expiring lamp which flutters from a breath of air, revived in her so that for several days she was something of her former self. But how terrible it was for me to behold Sophia's destruction, to hear her breathing steadily decline, to feel the torments she bore with such angelic fortitude! . . . She expired—without complaint, blaming herself for everything. My friends! I have endured much suffering, but not one torture in the world compares to the torment of seeing a beloved one die. It is dreadful even to recall it . . . . Sophia died in my arms!"

The colonel was unable to continue. The touched officers were silent, and a tear even rolled from beneath the captain's eyes, fell down over his mustache and vanished in his silver cup of glintwine. Suddenly there was a shot, another, a third. The cossacks from the outposts rushed past the squadron.

"How is it? Are there many of the enemy?" the captain asked hastily, springing onto his circassian.

"As far as the eye can see, your honor," replied a cossack sergeant.

"Bridles ready! Mount up!" commanded the colonel. "Flankers! Check your pistols. Sabres ready! Move out by threes to the left! At a trot! March!"

Ammalat-Bek: A Caucasian Tale (excerpts)

Dedicated to N. A. Polevoy

Slow to Offend—
Quick to Avenge!

I

It was *juma*.[1] Not far from the town of Buynaki, an extensive settlement of Northern Dagestan, a Tatar youth rode up to participate in races and trick riding, that is, he came riding in for an equestrian competition with all the attendant heroics found in these parts when it comes to man and horse. Buynaki lies upon two outcroppings of a steep mountain precipice. From the road which winds from Derbent to Tarki, and off to our left a bit, the crest of the Caucasian mountains rises high above, as though supported by the forest's many trunks. To our left, sprawling out like a meadow, the shore stretches gently into the waters of the Caspian. The sea, eternally lapping the beach, rolls in like mankind itself come to play upon the firmament. The spring day was drawing toward evening and all the town's inhabitants, called out surely more by the freshness of the evening air than by idle curiosity, left their dwellings and gathered in crowds along both sides of the road. Women without veils, in colored scarves rolled into turbans upon their heads, in long silk gowns drawn up to the length of short *arkhaluki* (tunics), and in wide-cut pants,[2] sat in rows as lines of children formed in front of them. The men congregated in circles. They stood, sat on their haunches,[3] or sauntered around in groups of two or three. Elder men smoked tobacco from small wooden pipes. Happy chatter was heard all around, and at times the clang of horseshoes and the cry *"Kach, kach!"* (Watch out!) from riders preparing for their races rose above the throng.

Dagestan nature is fine in the month of May. Millions of glowing roses just like sunsets spill in red from the cliffs. The air wafts with their scent. Within the green dusks of the evening copse, no nightingale could ever fall silent. Almond trees, resembling cupolas, stand ablaze in silver bloom; about them tall vines entwine their leaves in spirals. Towering over all with their long, sinewy trunks, they look like Muslim minarets. Wide-shouldered oaks, old warriors indeed, stand on guard between the poplar and plane trees; and bushes gather in clumps around them like children at their knees. Yet this low-lying green seems prepared to uproot itself and flee the summer heat, making for the high mountains. Here, playful herds of rams, mottled with pinkish spots; there, bullocks stubbornly muddying themselves in the mire around the fountains or for hours on end lazily butting horn against horn; yes, and here and there about the mountainside stately steeds stand, unfurling their manes in the wind, proudly prancing, then racing off over the hills—these are the frames of each Muslim settlement. You might imagine that on this *juma* the outskirts of Buynaki are even more lively than usual, for it was a special occasion summoning a picturesque mixture of folk. The sun set its gold onto the gloomy walls of each flat-roofed hut, clothing them in the garb of multiple shapes, and even managing to bestow upon them a pleasant appearance ... Ahead of them galloped a rider, raising dust along the road. The mountain crest and the limitless sea bestowed grandeur on this picture, and all nature breathed warmth and life.

"He's coming! He's coming!" a voice from the crowd rang out. Everyone stirred.

The riders, who until then had been conversing with each other (having dismounted for that purpose) or who had scattered about the field, now leaped upon their steeds and tore off to meet the train of carts descending from the mountain ridge: Enter now Ammalat-bek, the nephew of the Tarkovsky *shamkhal,*[4] with his retinue. He was clothed in a black Persian blouse (*chukha*) embroidered with gold lace; the free-hanging sleeves spilled behind his shoulders. Under his vest a Turkish shawl wound around *arkhaluki* made from brightly colored material. Red outer pants were tucked into green boots adorned with high thick heels. His weapons, a blade and pistol, blazed silver and their gold engraved letters shone brightly. The handle of his sword was encrusted with precious stones. This Lord of Tarkov was not only tall and stately, but also a youth with an open face. From under his cap black *zilfliary* (locks) twined behind his ears . . . a fine moustache shaded his upper lip . . . his eyes shone with proud friendliness. He was mounted on a pure red stallion, which stormed beneath him like a whirlwind. Shirking both the customary and the fashionable, there was a light Cherkes saddle with silver below the pommel, tooled stirrups of black damask steel cut with gold engravings, rather than the circular Persian shabrack sewn from silk. Twenty *nukers,*[5] on dashing racers and dressed in blouses shining with lace, tossed back their caps and galloped behind in a wild display. The people rose respectfully before their bek and bowed, placing their right hands on their right knee. Rumor and rumble of approval flowed before him from woman to woman.

Having ridden up to the southernmost boundary of the field of competition, Ammalat came to a halt. Honored personages, old men supported by staffs, and the village elders of Buynaki surrounded him, attempting to receive a word of greeting. But Ammalat did not deign to turn his attention on anyone in particular and with a cold civility responded in monosyllables to the flattery and bows of his attendants. He waved his hand—the signal for the race to begin.

***

[As the competition commenced] Ammalat was approached by Safir-Ali, his *emjek,*[6] the son of one of Buynaki's many impoverished beks, a young man handsome in appearance and attractive for his simple, gay, happy manner. He had grown up with Ammalat and therefore spoke informally with him. He leaped from his horse, bowed his head and said, "Nuker Memet-Rasul has run your old, cropped *zherebets*[7] stallion hard and is now forcing him to jump a ditch seven strides wide."

"And he won't jump?" the impatient Ammalat shouted. "Now! right this moment! Bring the steed to me."

He met the horse in the middle of the road and, without stepping into the stirrup, leaped onto the saddle and flew off to the cavernous ditch cut deep into the land. He charged up, squeezed his knees to signal the horse to jump . . . but at the very edge the tired old steed, knowing not to depend on its failing strength, suddenly turned aside. Ammalat had to circle back around.

The second time, having been soundly whipped, he reared to jump, but settled back down, became obstinate and stomped his forehooves.

Ammalat exploded.

In vain Safir-Ali attempted to calm Ammalat so he would not punish the once glorious steed who in many battles and on long journeys had lost the resiliency of his legs. Ammalat heard no word and urged the horse with blows from his bare sword. Thrice they galloped toward the crevice, and when this third time the old steed tried with all his might but again dared not leap, Ammalat beat him so soundly about the head with the handle of his sword that the horse crumbled to the earth without a breath in him.

"For your faithful service," Safir-Ali muttered, gazing upon the dead stallion. "Can this be considered a just reward?!"

"This is the reward for disobedience!" Ammalat asserted, eyes ablaze.

Seeing their bek's wrath, all fell silent and stepped back. The valiant riders continued their feats upon the field.

Then suddenly the cadence of Russian drums came; Russian bayonets flashed from behind a hill. It was a company of the Kurinsky infantry regiment sent to Akusha, a town recently up in revolt at the instigation of Shah-Akhmet-Khan, the banished ruler of Derbent. This particular company was charged with the mission of guarding a wagon train along the mountain road connecting Derbent and Akusha. The company commander, Captain ***, rode ahead with a young officer. Before reaching the competition the drummers beat the tattoo to fall out; the company halted, packs were dropped, arms stacked and a temporary camp (meaning they would light no fires here) was organized.

In 1819 the arrival of a Russian detachment could not have been a surprise to any Dagestan resident; yet even today it brings them no great pleasure. Their fanaticism guarantees that they see in the Russian an eternal enemy. But they know he is powerful and wise, and thus they have taken to abusing him in secret, hiding their hostility behind a facade of good will.

At this same moment, and from the other end of the field, a rider of average height and athletic build approached the Russians. He was dressed in mail, helmet, and was fully armed for battle. Five *nukers* rode behind him. By their dusty clothes and sweaty, foaming steeds it was clear they had just completed a long journey of little rest. The first horseman, having checked the soldiers carefully, rode at an easy pace past their stacked weapons, brushing them and knocking them over. Following their leader, the *nukers* did not ride around but rode daringly straight over the fallen rifles. The guard, who had been shouting at them to keep their distance as they approached, grabbed the armored rider's steed by the reins; a crowd of soldiers, angered by the Muslim's bold disdain, gathered to heap abuse upon him.

"Halt! Who goes there?" was not only the guard's exclamation but his query.

"Obviously you're a new recruit if you cannot recognize Sultan-Akhmet-Khan Avarsky,"[8] the armored rider answered coolly as he wrenched the guard's hand from the reins. "It appears that last year at Bashli[9] I gave you Russians something to remember me by. Translate that to him," he said to one of his *nukers*. The Avarian repeated his words quite distinctly in Russian.

"It's Akhmet-Khan! Akhmet-Khan!" the soldiers responded. "Grab him! Take him! Make him pay for the Bashli massacre. The scoundrel hacked our wounded to pieces!"

"Back, you cur!" Sultan-Akhmet-Khan shouted in Russian at a rank and file soldier who had grabbed the reins again. "I am a Russian general!"

"A Russian traitor is more like it!" shouted a chorus of voices in response. "Take him to the captain, drag him to Derbent to Lieutenant Verkhovsky."

"I'd rather go to hell with the likes of you," Akhmet-Khan responded with a disdainful sneer. Then suddenly he reared his steed, swung left, right, and then whirling fully round, cracked his whip and was gone. With a shout the *nukers,* intent upon their master's every move, raced after him, knocking down a group of soldiers to open a path of retreat for themselves. A hundred paces away the khan slowed to a walk and neither looked back nor changed the sour expression on his face. He fingered his bridle absentmindedly. A crowd of Tatars . . . caught his attention. Upon seeing the khan each bowed with respect, hand raised to forehead.

"And you poor bullocks look on . . . as the Russians laugh in your faces. They deride your customs, trample your faith underfoot, and you wail like old ladies instead of avenging yourselves as men should! Cowards! Cowards!"

"But what can we do?!" many voices cried out. "The Russians have cannons and bayonets . . . !"

"And you mean to say you don't have weapons; where are your daggers? It's not the Russians who are brave, but you who are cowardly. Shame on the Muslim peoples: the Dagestan saber shakes in fear before the Russian knout. You fear the cannon's roar, but not the Russian's reproaches. The Russian military book of rules is more sacred to you than a chapter from the Koran. Siberia frightens you more than hell . . . Is this how your forefathers behaved? Is this how your fathers bethought themselves? They neither counted their enemies nor calculated whether or not it would be effective to fight force with force. They fought bravely. They died gloriously. And, tell me, what is there to fear? Do the Russians have armored bodies? Don't their cannonballs have fuses? Think of the scorpion—we catch them by the tail which carries death!!! Is it not the same?!"

This speech excited the crowd. Tatar pride was awakened. A restless confusion began to grow, and the crowd circled tightly around a small group of Russian soldiers nearby.

Sultan-Akhmet-Khan chose to absent himself from the imminent, but insignificant, fight he had instigated. He rode from out of the crowd's midst, leaving two *nukers* behind to continue the Tatar's spirit of vengeance. He left with the others for Ammalat's *utakh*. [10]

"Conquer!" Sultan-Akhmet-Khan greeted Ammalat-bek, who had come out to meet the khan at the door.

This typical Cherkes greeting was pronounced with a significant look. Upon kissing his guest in greeting, Ammalat inquired, having noticed the look:

"Is this a joke or a prediction, dear guest of mine?"

"That depends on you," the khan responded. "The sole heir to the title *shamkhal* needs merely to draw his blade to . . ."

"To have nowhere to sheathe it again, khan? My unenviable lot is this: it is still best to rule Buynaki than to hide in the mountains like a jackal who holds a title which can no longer command attention nor demand obeisance."

"No, not like a jackal, Ammalat, but like a lion. And from the highest mountains the lion rides in vengeance to find eternal sleep in his forefathers' mansion. No, Ammalat, it is better to die in glorious battle!!"

"And would it not be better to awaken from such a dream altogether?"

"Why? To be blind in sleep to what must be mastered when awake? The Russians, for obvious reasons, regale you with roses and sing you to sleep with fairy tales; and another steals the golden flower from your own garden." [11]

"And what can I do with my small powers?"

"Powers are in one's soul, Ammalat! . . . Just dare, and all others will bow down before you. Do you hear?" Sultan-Akhmet-Khan uttered these words as shots rang out in town. "That is the voice of victory!"

Safir-Ali ran into the room with an alarmed look upon his face. "Buynaki is up in arms," he shouted hurriedly. "A force has surrounded the Russians and has started a crossfire with them."

"Good-for-nothings!" Ammalat cried out, tossing his weapon over his shoulder. "How dare they rise up without me? Come on, Safir-Ali, in my own name we must kill the first who dared disobey me."

"I've already tried to cool them," Safir-Ali exclaimed, "but no one will listen. Sultan-Akhmet-Khan's *nukers* are keeping them at it. They say he counseled, even commanded, that they attack the Russians!"

"Have my *nukers* really said so?" asked the khan.

"Not only have they said so, they've been encouraged by your example," Safir-Ali responded.

"Well, then, I am quite satisfied with them," Sultan-Akhmet-Khan muttered. "What brave lads!"

"What have you done, khan?" Ammalat shouted with chagrin.

"What you should have done long ago."

"How can I justify myself before the Russians?"

"With lead and steel . . . The deck is afire; fate is working on your behalf. Swords are bare, so let us go too and hunt the Russians . . ."

"They are here already!" the Russian Captain shouted as he and ten others strode past the uneven ranks of Tatars into the Buynaki leader's dwelling.

Confused by the sudden revolt for which he might be considered the responsible party, Ammalat met his angered guest in a hospitable way.

"Enter in peace," he greeted the Captain in Tatar fashion.

"I shan't trouble myself as to whether it is in peace I have come to you," the Captain responded, "for I know already. I see with my own eyes that I am not met in peace in Buynaki. Your Tatars, Ammalat-bek, have dared shoot at the company of soldiers who are as much mine as yours, not to say the property of our tsar!"

"In truth of fact, it is quite stupid for them to *shoot at* the soldiers," the khan said, disdainfully stretching out upon some pillows, "when they should be killing them."

"Here is the cause of it all, Ammalat," the Captain uttered with wrath, pointing at the khan. "Without this impudent scoundrel not a single hammer would have been cocked in Buynaki! And you are a fine fellow, Ammalat-bek . . . You call the Russians your friends and take our enemy into your quarters as if he were an honored guest to whom you give shelter as to a comrade and whom you honor like a friend. Ammalat-bek! In the name of the commanding general, I demand that you give him over to us!"

"Captain," Ammalat responded, "a guest in a Tatar house is no less than sacred. Turning him over would be to commit a great sin which would rest forever on my soul. It would be an unredeemable disgrace. Respect my request; respect our customs."

"I shall tell you in my turn—recall Russian law, recall your duty. You have sworn allegiance to our Russian ruler, and that oath commands that you not take pity upon one of your own if he is a criminal."

"I would sooner hand over a brother than a guest, dear Captain! It is not your place to judge what and how I have promised to fulfill my oath to the Russians. My guilt is to be judged in the court of Allah before the pashas! . . . Let fate protect the khan in the open field, but within my shelter, under my roof, I am bound to be his defender, and so I shall be!"

"You shall answer for this! You shall answer for this traitor!"

The khan silently lay in repose during this argument, proudly puffing smoke from his pipe. But when he heard the word "traitor"— his blood boiled; he jumped up and indignantly rushed the Captain.

"A traitor, you say?" he shouted. "It would be better to say that I would not be a traitor to those to whom I am beholden by loyalty. The Russian pasha has given me a rank of general, the *sardar* (*gosudar*) [tsar] has wooed me, and I have been faithful as long as I was not required to do something impossible or debasing. And suddenly I am asked to send to Avaria my very own troops so that a fortress might be built. And what name would I deserve were I to forsake the blood and sweat of the Avarians, my own brothers!? And even if I were to attempt the same, do you really think that I could succeed? Thousands of free men's daggers and bullets would pierce my heart, the heart of their betrayer; the very mountain walls would tumble down upon my head. I refused the Russians' friendship, but yet was not your enemy; and what was the reward for my good will? for my sound advice? I was personally, viciously, insulted in a letter penned by one of your generals when I was the very one who had given him good advice and cautioned him—and his impudence, his not listening to me, cost him dearly in Bashli . . . I spilled a veritable river of blood in revenge of a few drops of abusive ink. Now this river divides me from you into eternity."

"That blood cries out for revenge!" the Captain shouted angrily. "And you shall not escape, villain!"

"Nor shall you," exclaimed the fiery khan, thrusting his dagger into the Captain's stomach as the latter raised a hand to take him by the collar.

The mortally wounded Captain fell with a moan to the carpet.

"You have ruined me," Ammalat uttered, clasping his hands together in dismay. "He is not only a Russian, but a guest in my house."

"There are offenses which cannot be housed under one's roof," the khan muttered darkly. "Fate has cast the dice; there is no time to wonder now; lock the gate, protect your own, and smite the enemy!!"

"An hour ago I had no enemies . . . And now I have nothing with which to ward them off. I have neither powder nor ball; the people are running amuck in the village . . ."

"The folk have scattered already!" Safir-Ali shouted in despair. "The Russians are riding into the mountains after them. They are almost here as well!"

"So, ride with me, Ammalat," the khan ventured. "I am off to Chechnya to set up our line of defense . . . What shall be, God knows, but there is bread for you to eat in our mountains! Come with me!"

"I shall!" Ammalat said decisively. "My sole survival is in flight . . . There's no time for protestations or reproaches now."

"Bring my steed! Six *nukers* come with me!"

"And I as well," uttered Safir-Ali with a tear in his eye. "And I will go with you willingly even as your slave if you want."

"No, my dear Safir-Ali, no! You remain here to watch over the people and to protect my home. Bear my greetings to my wife; take her to her father's. Don't forget me! Farewell!!"

They had hardly galloped out one gate when the Russians forced entry at the other.

II

The khan rode in silence, apparently lost in unpleasant thought. Ammalat-bek was held by his own dark ruminations. The clothes of each rider bore traces of a recent skirmish—their mustaches were scorched from pistol fire, and smatterings of others' blood were dried upon their faces. The proud gaze of the khan seemed to challenge both fate and nature to do him battle; a gloomy smile of discontent with a hint of disdain pulled back the corners of his lips. But on Ammalat's pale face there was imprinted only a grim languor. With half-closed lids he seemed unable to lead his horse. Now and then a moan broke from him; he had sustained a wound to his arm during the skirmish. The uneven gait of his Tatar steed, unaccustomed to the mountain paths, intensified his pain.

***

Skirting a small mountain settlement, they spent the night below the mountain peaks, nourishing themselves on a fistful of grain and the traditional honey biscuit without which mountain tribesmen rarely set off on a journey. They had long ago left behind the northernmost arm of the mountains near Koisa, a town they had passed by means of the bridge near Ashirte. So, too, they had quit the Koysubulintsy land with its naked Salatay ridge. The unbeaten path they took to keep from the guarded highways lay amidst deep forests and along slopes so steep that it took one's breath away in terror. They began to ascend the last rise, the one which finally separated them from the south. Here were the lands of Khunzakh, or Avaria, the khan's kingdom. The forest receded, then too the scrub brush in the rocky plain on the high mountain pass where only clouds and snowstorms wander. The mountain's incline was so steep that the riders had to wind their way, now left, now right, in switchbacks up to the mountain crest. The khan's stallion, accustomed to the rocks and crags, carefully and unfailingly strode from boulder to boulder, testing each with its hoof to see if it might not hold. With confidence it slid down the precipices on its hindquarters. But Ammalat's proud, fiery *zherebets*, native of the easy, rolling Dagestan hills, grew excited, spun and continually lost its footing. Spoiled by the good life in Dagestan it could not hold up under the physical pressures of a two-day march under the hot sun by day, in the cold of the mountain ranges at night, along the sharp declivities, and nourished merely by the meager grasses found here and there among occasional fissures in the rock. It snorted heavily as it mounted higher and higher. Sweat ran in rivulets from its chest. Its wide nostrils puffed fire, and foam boiled about its bit.

"Allah Bereket!" Ammalat shouted upon attaining the summit. From here a grand view of Avaria opened before him. Then suddenly his exhausted steed slumped to the earth beneath him, blood bursting from its opened mouth. His final breath broke the saddle strap.

The khan rushed to help the bek free himself from the stirrups. But with horror he noticed that his efforts only tore the bandages from Ammalat's wound. Blood poured forth anew. Yet it seemed the young man was insensitive to his own pain. His tears flowed over the loss of his trusted racer . . . Thus one drop does not just fill, but brings the cup to overflowing.

"You shall no longer bear me as a feather in the wind," he spoke. "Neither shall you bear me in the dusty clouds of the race, hearing behind us the familiar cries of dissatisfaction from our rivals and the happy shouts from the throng. Nor shall you carry me again into the intense flame of battle; and worse yet, you shall not even once be able to test yourself in the iron rain of Russian cannons. With you I have earned the glorious stature of a true horseman. Why should I now survive you and that suddenly distant glory?" He bowed his head to his knees and drew still. The khan dressed his wound. After a long silence Ammalat raised his head.

"Leave me, Sultan-Akhmet-Khan," he said decisively. "Leave an unfortunate to his own fate. The road is long and I am done in. Remain with me and you shall perish for naught. Look at the eagle flying above us; it senses that my heart is soon to die within its claws . . . thank God. It is better to find the aerial grave of a great bird's nest than to lay down my dust for the foot of some Christian to tread upon. Farewell, do not tarry."

"Shame on you, Ammalat. You are quitting the fight over nothing. True, it is a setback that you are wounded and that your horse has fallen! But the wound shall heal long before your wedding day. And a steed much better than this shall be found. Think now, Ammalat, Allah has prepared more than misfortunes for you. In the flower of your years and in the greatness of your mind it is a sin to despair so. Sit astride my steed and I shall lead you on. By nightfall we shall be home. We must move on now, for time is precious!"

"For me there is no longer any time left, Sultan-Akhmet-Khan . . . I thank you with all my heart for your brotherly care, but I shan't avail myself of it any longer . . . Leave me to the mercy of fate. Here, on these inaccessible heights, I die freely and with satisfaction . . . For what is there in life to draw me back to it? My parents lie in the earth, my wife is deprived of her sight, my uncle and father-in-law crawl in Tarki before the Russians; in my homeland, giaours feast on my inheritance, and I am now a mere exile from my own home; I have even fled from death in our recent battle. I do not want to live, for I do not deserve to!"

"Don't speak such rubbish, dear Ammalat. Your fever certainly explains such talk. But we have been created to live longer than our fathers; you may yet find another three wives if one has been insufficient; if your father-in-law has been unkind to you, then remember that your bloodline is good. For this alone you must live. For the dead neither power is needed, nor victory necessary. Our sacred duty is to avenge ourselves on the Russians. Return to life if only for that. And if we have lost a battle, it is not the whole war. Today the victory is theirs, tomorrow ours. Allah bestows happiness, but man creates his own glory, not by happiness but by firm conviction . . . Take heart, Ammalat . . . You are wounded and weak; I am strong by dint of habit and not tired in the least by our flight. Sit upon my steed and together we shall vanquish the Russian more than once!"

Ammalat's face flamed. "Yes, I shall live to seek revenge!" he cried out, "a revenge that is subtle, direct and unmistakable. Believe me, Sultan-Akhmet-Khan, if only for this I accept your magnanimity! Henceforth I am yours . . . I bow at your father's grave; I am in your debt! Guide my every step, command where my blows shall fall. And if ever, lost in the petty comforts of a comfortable life, I forget my oath to you, recall this moment to me, recall to me these airy heights: Ammalat-bek will awaken and his dagger will strike as lightning."

With one arm holding the wounded youth in the saddle, the khan carefully began to descend from the bare peak. Time and again rocks slipped from under his legs and rushed downward, or the steed slid down atop the slippery granite. They were therefore quite glad upon reaching the moss line. Little by little, crooked, knotty shrubs began to mark the mountain's green shroud, now wafting from fissures in large fans, now spilling down from clefts in long strands that looked like ribbons and flags. Finally they rode into a dense forest of hazel, then oak and cherry, and lower yet, plane trees and *chundar*. The many shapes, the wealth of flora, and the magnificent hush of the leafy forest inspired a sudden, unbidden reverence for the untamed forces of nature. Now and again from out of the night gloom, like morning itself, a field would glisten, aglow with a glorious carpet of flowers untrampled by human foot. Here the path ducked into a thicket, there cut past a mountain face, below which in some dark depths flashed and splashed a stream, now foaming between boulders, and then quietly flowing along the rocky bottom of a small pool beneath the shade of a barberry bush or a sweetbriar. Pheasants, their rainbow tail feathers glittering, slipped in flight from shrub to shrub; wild doves whirled about the cliffs, now in a flying sheet of light or in a column ascending straight to the sky; sunset poured its ethereal purple on them, and thin clouds quietly darkened in the crags; everything breathed with an evening's cool, totally unfamiliar to those who inhabit the lowlands.

Our travellers were already near the village Akokh, which lay behind a small mountain of Munzakh (Avaria). A ridge of insignificant height divided them from this settlement . . .

***

Only the khan's knowledge of the mountains saved the travellers from a momentary fall into the river Uzeni below the steep decline. Ammalat saw almost nothing before him. The double veil of night and fatigue clouded his eyes. His head whirled as they attained yet another ridge. As if in a dream, he stared blankly at the khan's gates and its guard tower. With an unsure leg he stepped to the ground within the courtyard amidst the shouts of retainers and *chelyadintsy,* and when he had barely crossed the lattice threshhold of the khan's harem his spirit quickened momentarily. Then a deathly paleness threw its snow upon his afflicted face. Worn out by the journey, a great loss of blood, by hunger and a deep, heartfelt languor, the youthful bek fell unconscious upon the oriental rug.

III

Amongst the mountain tribes there grow the most effective medicinal herbs, particularly for healing broken bones and wounds. But no herb or compress could heal Ammalat as fast as the presence of a dear young girl of the tribe, Seltaneta, Sultan-Akhmet-Khan's daughter. With a pleasant hope he slept, for in his dreams he was assured of seeing her; when awake he reveled in the joyful knowledge that he would see her by day . . . His strength returned quickly and with his strength his interest in Seltaneta grew in equal measure. Ammalat was married, but as often occurs in the East, merely at family convenience. He never saw his bride before their wedding and afterwards found nothing attractive in her, nothing which might have aroused a sleeping heart. Later she became blind, and this event even more surely cooled a relationship based upon Asian sensibilities. Family discord between him and both his father-in-law and uncle even more surely separated the couple. Recently they rarely saw each other. Is it then a surprise that after such discord our young man, fiery by nature and self-willed by habit, had suddenly become inflamed by a new love? To be with her was his greatest pleasure, to await her appearance the most delectable occupation. Just hearing her voice would cause him to shudder; each sound, as though the sun's own rays, penetrated his soul. His sensitivities came to feel more like pain, but a pain so exquisite that he wished to prolong it into eternity. Little by little the young couple's acquaintance deepened into friendship . . . They were continually together. The khan often traveled into the depths of Avaria on business, to mete out punishment, and on military duty. Then he would leave the bek to the gentle and quiet care of his wife. He clearly saw Ammalat's inclination toward his daughter and in secret was glad of it; it aggrandized both his public and personal image, for a relationship with a bek who has a birthright to a *shamkhalstvo* put in his control a thousand means of deterring the Russians.

***

And so the summer passed. One day the khan, embracing Ammalat, said to him:

"Glory unto you. Jembulat, a renowned warrior from Malaya Karbarda, has summoned you to attack the Russians with him. You must now avenge the honor lost in our previous battle. Time cannot be wasted; tomorrow, before dawn, you must depart."

No matter how vexing this news was to Ammalat, steeling his heart, he nevertheless answered that he would gladly go. He felt strongly that the name of this great warrior, Jembulat, was sure of success.

But Seltaneta visibly whitened and bent her head like a flower upon hearing this ominous news of an imminent parting. Her gaze, fixed constantly on Ammalat, revealed her misgivings, the painful foreboding of ill.

"Allah!" she cried out in grief, "Again these raids, again these murderous games! When shall the blood cease its endless flowing?!"

"When the mountain streams run white with milk, when the sugar cane waves on our snowcapped summits," the khan muttered behind an ironic grin.

IV

Recently mountain tribesmen in large numbers have begun to fall only upon peasant villages because of the risk of heavy losses. The tribesmen, daringly to be sure, raid deep into our territory to steal herds of our horses. This transpires only rarely without a fight. The most adventurous *uzdeni* (Avarian warriors) try to participate in such raids in order to earn honor among each other; such honor is something they prize even more highly than the glory gained by some daring feat while hunting.

In the fall of 1819 the Kabardintsy and Chechentsy, emboldened by the absence of the Russian general, Ermolov, gathered one and a half thousand strong to attack a small village across the Terek, to pillage it, take prisoners and drive off the horses.

The leader of this enterprise was the Karbardinets prince Jembulat. Ammalat-bek, arriving at the prince's camp with a letter in hand from the khan, was received warmly. True, they performed no ritual of welcome for Ammalat, but this is because they have no sense of rank in their army; a fleet-footed steed and one's own passionate nature command one's place in battle. [After a raid] they would break into small groups, and head along barely visible paths to a friendly *aul*, where they could hide until night. By dusk all the detachments would arrive there. It goes without saying that the villages in the *aul* would greet their fellow countrymen with open arms, but [today] Jembulat, not trusting a ritual display, had placed the settlement under guard and warned the inhabitants that whosoever might attempt to inform the Russians would be hacked to pieces. The majority of *uzdeni* went their separate ways, to the homes of blood brothers, or to relatives, but Jembulat himself, with Ammalat and his trusted riders, remained in the open air next to a fire while their tired horses reposed for the morrow. Jembulat, prone on a felt cloak and arms folded, considered tomorrow's strategy. Far, however, were Ammalat's thoughts from the field of battle. How sorrowfully did his heart contract in separation from his Seltaneta. The sound of the metal strings of a mountain balalaika *(komus)* accompanying a doleful voice broke Ammalat's reflections. A Karbardinets began to sing a song of old:

> Upon Kazbek great clouds swoop down
> In the shape of mountain hawks...
> A flying line of *uzdeni* shocks
> Them from atop the mountain crowns;
> Higher, higher, on steeper ground
> They gallop on; the Russians face defeat!
> And their whole trail's a bloody heap.
>
> The troop's pursuit is underway.
> Sword and bayonet fall hot;
> Death is dealt by grape and shot.
> Strength's no safety in the fray.
> "Flee, *uzdeni,* don't be caught!"

You fire on in disarray,
Your forest fortress far away.[12]

Lest at the Russian's hand we die
A Mulla falls upon his knees—
Like an arrow to the skies
His prayer to blessed Allah flies.
Sent out into the heavens, seas,
In rhythm with the Mulla's bows:
"Il Allah, don't forsake us now."

All salvation seems to flee.
Then suddenly from forest dear
Like heaven's manna warriors near,
Lower, closer, wonderously—
A miracle is made, 'tis clear.
Safe now are the Mussulmen
Within their leafy forest's den.

"That is how it was in days of old," Jembutat said with a smile. "When our elders believed more firmly in prayer and when God heard them more often. But now, friends, our hope is in your own courage. Our miracles are to be found in the blades of our swords, and we must wield them effectively if we are not to bring shame upon ourselves. Listen, Ammalat," he turned, twisting his mustache, "I shan't hide from you that tomorrow's battle may be quite hot. I've just learned that Colonel Kotsarev has gathered his regiment; but where he is, how large an army he has, no one seems to know."

"The more Russians, the better," Ammalat responded calmly. "More Russians, fewer misses."

"And likewise, the more difficult a victory."

"For me this matters little, even if our final triumph takes one hundred years. I long for vengeance. I seek glory."

***

Jembulat gave a whistle which was then repeated down the line: in a trice the entire band congregated. Many *uzdeni* from surrounding villages, considered by the Russians to be peaceful, had attached themselves to the band. Having discussed with them where best to cross the Terek, the warriors moved toward the shore in silence. Ammalat-bek could not help but be amazed at the silence maintained not only by the riders but by their horses! Nary a whinny nor a snort. As if wary themselves, the horses stepped lightly over the ground. They flew quickly like a silent cloud, suddenly gained the Terek, which at the chosen spot was cut by a small promontory, and from which a rocky reef stretched to the other shore. The water this time of year is not high and thus a crossing was possible; despite this fact, however, a detachment of the band went upstream to cross in deeper water where they might lead the Cossacks to believe they had found and rebuffed a raid.

***

The raid went off perfectly; it caught the Russians completely by surprise.

***

Dawn came, the fog lifted and disclosed a picture both splendid and horrifying. The band was hauling off captives, some bound to stirrups, others tied to saddle straps. Thunderous weeping, unrestrained moans and wails of grief drowned out their joyous cries of victory. Burdened by the spoils, slowed in their march by ambling herds of horned cattle, they crept back to the Terek. The prince and his best riders, dressed in armor and helmets which shone brightly and flowed like water, swarmed round the procession, like lightning from a blue-grey storm cloud. In the distance and on all sides border-guard Cossacks galloped, threw themselves behind great oak trees and bushes and began an intense crossfire with the stout lads sent back to protect the rear. Here and there shots burst into flame; occasionally a Cherkes fell from his horse. In the meantime, just as the first Cossacks managed to herd a portion of the cattle across the Terek, a dusty cloud and a loud thunder of horses brought news that a mighty counterattack had already been mounted against them. About six hundred warriors led by Jembulat and Ammalat turned their mounts to repulse the attack and to buy time for their men to ford the river. Without any of our military precision, with shouts and blood-curdling screams, they rushed headlong upon the Cossacks. Watch! Not a single weapon was drawn from the backslung holster, not a single blade shone in any man's hand: Cherkes warriors do not pull their weapons until the very last moment. And so it was now; having traversed thirty yards at a gallop, they grabbed their arms and fired, riding at full tilt. They tossed their discharged weapons into their left hands and struck with their swords. The Cossacks, however, answering with might and main, retreated. Taking heart in their success, the mountain warriors gave chase, but only to be enticed into a trap, one they themselves had so often used! The Cossacks led them into the forest edge, where men of the 43rd regiment were hidden. As if from the very ground itself, clusters of footsoldiers arose, bayonets bent forward, and a sharp firefight ensued. Rushing about in vain, the mountain warriors attempted to gain a small wood and attack our Russian men from behind. But our artillery arrived just in time to decide the matter. The experienced Colonel Kotsarev, Chechen bane that he was, and a man whom they feared for his bravery but respected as much for his integrity and selflessness, this Colonel Kotsarev led the fight so well that success could not be considered in jeopardy at any time. Cannon scattered forest animal and bird; grape shot peppered the fleeing *uzdeni*. It was an utter defeat. Two cannon balls pounded the promontory; Cherkes warriors were blown into the water from the shore; the whole length of the river was flooded with their bodies. With a roar, shot hit the foaming waves and with each retort several horses turned belly up, drowning their riders. It was sad to see the wounded clinging to the tails and reins of others' steeds, pulling them under, saving no one and killing more by their panic; it was terrible to see the weary warriors fighting by the steeply banked shore, struggling to crawl free, and falling into the insatiable, abysmal current which carried them away, swallowing them whole. The bodies of the dead floated amidst the half-alive, and blood-red streaks, like an asp, wound in and around the white water. Smoke rolled over the Terek, and in the distance the snowcapped peaks of the Caucasus, covered by black clouds, threateningly enclosed the field of battle.

***

Jembulat and Ammalat-bek fought desperately, twenty times unhorsed, falling twenty times more, worn out with fatigue, but not yet vanquished. With a hundred fine lads they swam across the river, rushed headlong, tethered their horses, and fired at the other shore. Thus occupied, they recognized too late that up river, Cossacks had crossed and were waiting to cut them off. With a joyous cry the Russians surrounded them. Death was now unavoidable.

"Well, Jembulat," said the bek to the Kabardinets, "our fate is sealed! Do as you see fit, but I shall not give up alive. Better to die from a bullet than from the Russians' damnable fetters."

"And do you think," exclaimed Jembulat, "my hands were made for tying?! Allah preserve me from such infamy! The Russians might capture my body, but my soul? Never! Brothers, comrades!" he shouted to his men, "Happiness has forsaken us, but our Damask swords shall not. Sell your life dearly to the giaours! He is not victorious who merely wins the fight, but he who wins glory. And glory is his who values death more highly than captivity!"

"Let us die! Die gloriously!" shouted one and all, thrusting their daggers into their horses' ribs to deprive the Russians of the spoils. Then, pulling the carcasses into a circle, they lay behind them, preparing to meet the charging Russians with steel and sword.

Now the Cherkes warriors leapt up with a wild cry, spent their last shot, and, shattering their rifles on the rocks, threw themselves at the Russians with bare blades . . . All fell to the Russian bayonet.

"Forward, behind me, Ammalat-bek," shouted the ferocious Jembulat, rushing into what was to be his last fight. "Forward! Death is our freedom."

But Ammalat could not hear his cry: a blow to his head from behind had thrown him to the ground, covered in blood amongst the dead.

V

A Letter from Colonel Verkhovsky to His Fiancée
Derbent to Smolensk, October 1819

***

You command me, that is, you wish me to describe my life day by day, hour by hour . . . Oh, what an insignificant and boring manuscript it would be if I were to take up this task. You know full and well, unkind woman, that I cannot be said to be living when I am without you . . . . My existence is merely the disappearing trace of a chain once dragged across this inhospitable soil. My military duties alone, tiresome as they may be, at least divert me and cut my time shorter. Thrown into a climate murderous to one's health and into a society which suffocates the soul, I find in my comrades people who at least can understand my thoughts. Yet I long to find one who can sense my deepest feelings. I hoped I might find such a one amongst the Asian population. But no. Everyone around me is either so uncultured and wild or else so culturally refined and narrow-minded that I am gripped by anguish and vexation. One could sooner wrest fire from a rock than substantial intercourse from our way of life here. But your every wish is sacred to me, so I shall set forth, albeit summarily, the dreary details of the week just concluded: it has turned out to be somewhat more colorful than the others.

I have already written you that we are returning with the general from our march into Akusha. We have fared quite well: Shah-Akhmet-Khan has flown to Persia. We have burned scores of villages, fired their crops, grains, and eaten the infidels' rams. When at long last the winter snows drove these unruly natives from their inaccessible heights, they bowed their heads before us and returned hostages to us. We have captured the high mountain fortress "Storm." We are now dispersed to our sundry winter quarters; my own regiment is back in Derbent. The day after our arrival the General wished to bid us all farewell; he is heading off on another march. We gathered at our adored leader's. Aleksei Petrovich jokes with everyone like a comrade-in-arms and instructs us much like a father. He is not frightened to show himself to us from an intimate perspective.

***

As we chatted among ourselves an officer from the Cossack troops arrived with a missive for the General from Colonel Kotsarev. Having read the report, Aleksei Petrovich mopped his brow.

"Kotsarev has clipped the tribesmen in fine order," he said to us. "These rotters made a raid across the Terek, moved far behind our lines, and sacked a village. But we took their captives back in a counterattack; the foolish tribesmen laid their lives down out of ignorant bravado."

The Cossack captain, having been asked how that battle had gone, ordered prisoners to be brought forward who had been wounded in battle then restored to health. Five were placed before the General.

A cloud passed before Ermolov's brow when he saw them; his eyes glazed and his eyebrows tightened.

"Scoundrels!" he shouted at the *uzdeni*. "Three times you have taken an oath not to plunder, and three times you have broken your oath. And what is it you want? Fields? Cattle? Defense of the one and the other?! Oh no, you want to steal from the Russians to make names for yourselves, to gain the spoils to be had by insidiously inciting the Cherkes warriors to attack our villages! Hang them!" he said thunderously. "Hang them by their own ropes . . . No wait! Let them cast their lot: Freedom shall be given to the fourth man. Let him return to his fellows and tell them that I come to teach them to keep their word and to curb them in the manner I see fit."

The *uzdeni* were led away. But one Tatar bek remained behind. Only then did we turn our attention to him. He was a young man, around twenty-three, of extraordinary beauty, lean, much like the Apollo Belvedere. He bowed slightly to the general when the general approached, raised his hat, but instantly resumed his proud, cool bearing. Unalterable submission to fate was imprinted on his face.

The general looked him straight in the eyes with his own mighty orbs . . . . The bek showed nothing, did not even lower a lash.

"Ammalat-bek," Aleksei Petrovich finally said, "do you not remember that you are a Russian subject? The Russian law stands above your head?"

"I would never have forgotten it," the bek answered, "had I found therein a defense of my own rights. I would not now be standing before you a criminal had my hand not been forced."

"Ungrateful child!" the general exclaimed. "Your father, and you yourself, have been at war too long with the Russians. Yet had we been Persians, your family would now be less than dust. Our sovereign, however, has been kind enough not to place you in prison. Instead he has allowed you to rule. And how have you repaid this kindness?! By clandestinely sowing discord and then openly revolting! And that is not all: you took in and hid in your home a sworn enemy of Russia. Then you allowed him, before your very eyes, to disembowel most ignobly a Russian officer! Nonetheless, if you had only laid a submissive head before me I would have forgiven you, taking into consideration your youth and understanding the inevitabilities of your customs. Instead you flew into the mountains, and with Sultan-Akmet-Khan you defied the Russian borders and were again defeated, only to join with Jembulat in yet another attack. Certainly you are aware what fate now awaits you."

"I am aware," Ammalat-bek answered coldly. "I shall be shot."

"No, a bullet is too decent a death for a thief," the angered general shouted. "On the shaft of an overtuned bullock cart we shall stretch your neck beyond breaking—this is the reward you deserve."

"It makes no difference to me that I die, only that I die quickly," Ammalat responded, "I ask but one favor, and that is not to torture me by some long, drawn-out proceeding; this would be a death thrice over."

"You deserve death, you impertinent man, one hundred times over! But I promise you, in one way or another, tomorrow you shall no longer exist . . . ."

The handsome lad's lot moved everyone . . . I decided to put in a word on Ammalat's behalf, if only to gain some relief for him. I pushed open the tent flap and quietly approached the gloomy Aleksei Petrovich. He was sitting there alone, both arms resting on an incomplete report to the tsar. Aleksei Petrovich had known me as an officer back home. I had met him in battle on the Kulmskoe field. He had always been kind to me, and my sudden intrusion did not surprise him. Smiling knowingly, he said:

"I see, yes, I see, Evstafy Ivanovich, that you have come to ask a favor. I can tell because you usually march boldly in. But now it's on tiptoe. You needn't. I'm sure you're here about Ammalat."

"You're right," I answered. I did not know how to begin.

***

"A generous heart inspires a reasonable mind," I muttered.

"A dutiful man's heart, my dear friend, must listen to the mind. Of course, I can stay Ammalat's execution, but I must punish him . . ."

***

Seeing the general's vacillation, I began to speak with greater conviction.

" . . . He is young, and Russia may yet find in him a faithful servant. Generosity never works in vain."

Aleksei Petrovich shook his head.

"I have done many ungracious things in my life . . ." he began, and then trailed off. "But that is how it had to be. I release him with no restrictions. That is not my way. Thank you for helping me decide to be good and still not appear to be weak. But mark my words: you want to take him under your care. Do not trust him; never warm a snake on your breast."

I was so intoxicated with my success that, thanking the general, I ran to the tent where Ammalat-bek was being kept. Three guards surrounded him. A lantern shone. I entered and the prisoner was lying on a cot; tears were shining in his eyes. He did not hear me approach, so deeply was he lost in his thoughts. Who, indeed, is pleased to give up life?! I was delighted that I could bring him joy at such a painful moment.

"Ammalat!" said I, "Allah is great, and the tsar is forgiving. He is giving you your life! . . . There is only one condition: you must live with me . . . You shall be as a friend to me, like my own brother."

The Asian was beside himself. Tears poured from his eyes.

"The Russians have conquered me!" he cried out. "Forgive me, Colonel, that I have thought unkindly of you and your brothers. From this moment on I am a faithful servant of the Russian tsar, a true friend to all Russians both in my soul and with my sword . . ."

I am sure, dearest Maria, that you shall preserve one of your sweetest kisses for me in reward for this affair. Always, whenever I act magnanimously, I comfort myself with the thought that my Maria will praise me for it. But when will this be, my priceless one? Fate is our stepmother. I know your anguish persists in our separation. But the general will not allow me a leave of absence. I am not deeply angry, but I am somewhat vexed by this . . .

We have been in Derbent for three days now. Ammalat lives with me. He is silent, sad, prone to wild fits, but his fear is a distraction for me. He speaks Russian quite well; I've set him to learning grammar. His intellectual capacities are unusually strong. In time I hope to make of him a wonderfully cultured Tatar.

(The conclusion of the letter does not concern our subject.)

***

A Portion of a Letter from Colonel Verkhovksy to His Fiancée
(Six months later; Derbent to Smolensk)

***

Why is our Ammalat so sorrowful, so sorrowful, and distraught? He has made such immense progress that he requires no further educating, no further teaching! Yet when we touch on abstract matters, his mind, so to speak, makes use of a short-barrelled weapon which may shoot with power and accuracy up close but not at a distance. But is it his mind which is insufficient here? Is his attention perhaps pulled by something else? . . . With a twenty-three-year-old, it is not too difficult to imagine just what this something else is. Sometimes he seems to listen attentively to my words. But I put a question to him and it's as if he's dropped from the clouds. At other times I find tears streaming from his eyes; but if I inquire, he neither sees nor hears. Then last night something happened. He was drifting along in a quiet sleep, dreaming, when the word *Seltanet, Seltanet* (power, power) broke from his lips. Can it be that a love of power is the cause of his suffering? No! No! Another passion moves his soul and runs riot in Ammalat's mind. Can I really doubt the clear signs of a sublime Angst—love?! He is surely in love; passionately in love. But with whom? Oh, I shall find out, mind you. Friendship is as prying as a woman.

VI

Excerpts from Ammalat-bek's Diary Translated from Tatar

. . . Have I been sleeping up until now, or am I now dreaming? . . . So this is what this new world is called: thought! . . What a beautiful world. For so long you were dark and mysterious to me, like the Milky Way, which, it is said, is made up of thousands of shining stars! From out of the gloom and fog I seem to be ascending to a mountain top of knowledge. With each step my vision widens and expands . . . I breathe more freely, I gaze into the sun's eyes . . . and below my steps the clouds storm about! Vexatious clouds! From below you obscure the sky, and from above you efface the earth!

I am amazed that the simplest questions "why" and "how" have never occurred to me before . . . Now I am held captive between the covers of a book, trying to make sense of its mysterious markings . . . Verkhovsky leads me toward knowledge, giving me the tools to do so. As a young swallow with its mother, I try out new wings with Verkhovsky . . . The distance and the inaccessible heights of wisdom amaze but do not frighten me. The time will come when I shall wing all about this heavenly vault . . .

Since Verkhovsky and his books have begun to teach me to think for myself I have become happier. Not long ago a stormy steed, a steel saber, and a wicked rifle gave me great joy; the toys of a child . . .

***

What good is there in understanding the forces of nature when I cannot alter my own soul, guide my own heart! I am taught by science how to hold back the very sea itself, yet I cannot hold back my own tears!

***

I am still young, so I now must ask what friendship is. I have a dear friend in Verkhovsky; kind, true, attentive. But I myself am no friend! I feel (and I reproach myself for this) that I do not treat him as I should, as he deserves. Am I at fault here? In my soul, there is room only for my Seltaneta. In my heart there is no other feeling but love for her.

* * *

Can I be taught to see without light? Can I breathe without air? Seltaneta is my light, my air, my life, my very soul!

***

VII

From Colonel Verkhovsky's Letters to His Fiancée
April, Derbent

. . . [Ammalat] has now lived with me for one and a half years but until today he had not opened himself to me. Yet he loves me and sees clearly that I desire to know the secrets of his heart—not from idle curiosity, but from heartfelt sympathy. And now, at last, he has told me everything . . .

***

We were about to mount up when a moan broke from the tribesman I had wounded. He opened his eyes, raised up slightly, and in a pitiful voice begged us not to leave him to the forest animals. [Ammalat and I] rushed to his aid. To Ammalat's amazement he recognized in the man one of Sultan-Akhmet-Khan Avarsky's *nukers.* When asked how he had fallen into a band of thieves, he responded:

" . . . The Khan sent me to a neighboring village, Kemek, with a message to give to the renowned *gakim* (doctor) Ibragim to obtain from him some sort of herb. It is said that this herb releases, as if by magic, any ill from the body. To my great horror [the robber] Shemardan captured me as I was on my way . . ."

"You say you were originally sent for a medicine?" asked Ammalat. "Who was it for? Who is ill?"

"Our Khanum, Seltaneta, is at death's door . . ."

" . . . Colonel," Ammalat cried out, grabbing me by the hand. "Fulfill one sacred wish: let me gaze upon my Seltaneta even if it is for the last time."

"Upon whom, my friend?"

"Upon my priceless Seltaneta, Khan Avarsky's daughter, whom I love more than life, more than my own soul . . . She is ill, dying, may even now be dead. I am losing time speaking to you in vain! . . ."

He fell upon my breast, suffocating with anxiety, weeping without tears, unable to speak a single word.

There was no time now to suspect him of treachery, and still less to imagine why it would be wrong to let him ride over to our enemy. There are circumstances in life when propriety disappears into the dust; I felt that Ammalat now found himself in just such circumstances. Against my own misgivings I decided to let him go. Whosoever from purity of heart makes another beholden to him may soon collect his due twice over—this is my trusted motto, my firmest guide. I embraced the anxious Tatar, and our tears flowed together.

***

VIII

Ammalat's boisterous, unexpected arrival disturbed the doleful gathering of those present at Seltaneta's.

* * *

"Is it you, is it really you?!" she cried, extending a hand to him. "Allah Bereket! Now I am satisfied! I am happy," she uttered softly, leaning back upon her pillows.

A smile lit her mouth, her lashes fell, and again she slipped into her former unconsciousness.

* * *

Ammalat's appearance had a salutary effect on the invalid. What the mountain doctors had been unable to accomplish occurred now from happenstance . . . After a long, gentle sleep she awakened with her former strength, with refreshed senses.

"I feel so light, mama," she said to the *khansha,* looking about gaily, "as if I am made of air."

* * *

The next day Ammalat was allowed to visit the convalescent girl.

* * *

Tears gushed from his eyes [upon seeing her], but remembering at last that he was not alone, he pulled himself together and raised his head. But his voice refused to utter a word. Only with an effort could he say:

"We have not seen each other for so long, Seltaneta!"

"And almost parted eternally," Seltaneta responded.

"Eternally?" Ammalat uttered in a half reproachful voice. "And you could think such a thing, believe such a thing? Is there not another life, one in which grief is not known, where there is no parting from either family or from those dear to you? Had I lost the talisman of my happiness, with what disdain would I have thrown from myself these rusty, wearisome bonds of being. I would hardly have felt required to battle ever again with my fate!"

"It's a pity that I did not die," the Seltaneta exclaimed. "You so bewitchingly describe the other side, it seems you are already prepared to fly to it."

"Oh no, live! Live a long life! For happiness, for . . ." 'Love' was what Ammalat wished to say, but he blushed instead and fell silent.

Satisfied now with her heart's return, little by little the roses of health returned to the cheeks of the young girl. Everything followed its usual course.

The khan did not query Ammalat about battles, marches or the deployment of the Russian army . . .

* * *

Once . . . the lovers sat eye to eye. Resting her head upon his shoulder, Seltaneta inquired:

"*Aziz* (my heart), are you suffering, are you languishing here with me?"

"Oh, do not speak ill of him who loves you more than the heavens," Ammalat replied. "For I have experienced the hell of parting and cannot think of it without growing sad. It would be easier a hundred times over to part with life than with you, my dark eyes."

"Yet you think of parting . . . that means you must want to."

"Do not poison my wounds with doubt, Seltaneta. In your life you have only known how to bloom like a rose, to flutter like a butterfly; in your life to do your will has been your sole obligation. But I am a man. I am a friend to another; fate has linked me to an unbreakable chain of gratitude in return for his kindness. This chain pulls me back to Derbent."

"Duty! Obligation! Gratitude!" Seltaneta pronounced each word sadly, bowing her head. "How many golden and glorious words you have acquired from him by which to hide, as with a shawl, your disinterest in remaining here with me. Are you saying now that you have not already given your soul in love to me, in a love greater than any friendship? You did not have the right to give it again to another! Oh, forget your Verkhovsky, forget your Russian friends and your Derbent beauties! . . ."

* * *

"No, Seltaneta, I cannot, I may not, remain here . . . I have more than once spoken to Akhmet-Khan about my hopes [for us], but the answer is always: 'Swear to be the Russians' enemy and then I shall listen to your request.' "

"Say farewell to hope, then."

"And why farewell to hope, Seltaneta. Why not say together 'Farewell, Avaria.' "

Seltaneta shot a meaningful glance at him.

"I do not understand you," she said.

"Love me more than anything on this blessed earth, more than your father and mother and beloved homeland. Then you shall understand me. Seltaneta! I cannot live without you. But I am not allowed to live with you . . . . If you love me, let us flee together!"

"Flee?! The khan's daughter flee?! Like a prisoner, a criminal?! This is too horrid! It is unheard of!"

* * *

At four in the afternoon, the usual hour for repast among Muslims, Sultan-Akhmet-Khan was often gloomy and ferocious. From beneath his darkened brow his eyes flashed forth untrustingly; they rested upon his daughter for a long time, and then on his young guest . . .

After the customary washing of hands after the meal, the khan called Ammalat outside into the large courtyard. There, two saddled horses awaited them. A group of *nukers* were already mounted and ready.

"Let's go test the courage of my new young falcons," the khan said to Ammalat. "The evening is glorious, the heat has fallen, and we can surely catch a bird or two by nightfall."

The khan rode next to the bek, a falcon on his arm. To the left, along the steep slope, an Avarian was clinging, throwing a hooked pole into a cleft and then, hanging from this attachment, climbing higher and higher. On his waist was tied a bag which held seeds; a long rifle hung from his shoulders. The khan stopped, pointed him out to Ammalat, saying:

"Look at that old man, Ammalat-bek. At risk of life and limb he seeks a tuft of earth on that naked mountain side to sow there a mere handful of wheat. With his own bloody sweat he plants the seeds. And just as often, he pays with his blood for the protection of his cattle from the incursions of both man and beast. His land is poor, but just ask him why he loves his homeland, why he wouldn't trade it for your cloudy fields below, for your abundant pastures in the lowlands? He'd say, 'Here I do what I wish; here I bow to no man. These snows, these naked heights protect my will.' And it is this will of his that the Russians would take from him, just as they have taken it from you. You have become a Russian slave, Ammalat!"

"Khan, you know that it is not Russian bravery, but Russian kindness that has won me: I am no slave, but their comrade."

"Then a hundred times worse for you, and a hundred times more shameful! Here is the heir of a *shamkhal* who seeks the silver sword knot[of the Russian army], takes pride in the fact that he is a colonel's servant!"

"Let your words die, Sultan-Akhmet-Khan! I am beholden to Verkhovsky for more than my life: friendship's union has joined us together! . . . I gave my promise to return, and I shall keep it!"

"Is this final?"

"Yes. Final. And time now to do so."

"The sooner the better. I once knew you, and you me, although from afar. Offense and flattery aside, I shall not hide from you that I have always wanted you to be my son-in-law. I was glad when Seltaneta fell in love with you. Your captivity delayed my plans for a while. Your long absence, rumors of your change worried me. And then you appeared, and all appeared to be as it had been. But you did not bring us your heart of old. Nonetheless, I hoped that you would return to your former ways, but I deceived myself, bitterly deceived myself! It is a pity, but what can now be done? I cannot have a son-in-law who serves the Russians!"

"Akhmet-Khan! Once I . . ."

"Let me finish . . . Your boisterous arrival, your frenzy at the ill Seltaneta's door, revealed to everyone your affection, your secret desires. Throughout the mountains they praised you, calling you my daughter's betrothed . . . But now, with the union broken, it is time to sow new rumors. For my family's good name, for my daughter's peace of mind, you must leave us. Now! This is necessary, and cannot be altered. Ammalat! Let us part good friends. But *here* we can meet each other only as relatives, and in no other way. May Allah return to you your true heart and lead you back to us an inseparable friend. Until then, farewell!" With these words the khan turned his horse and rode off at a full gallop back to his retinue.

Had thunder from the heavens fallen upon the silent Ammalat, he would not have been more downcast, nor more frightened as by this unexpected assault. The dust had long ago settled on the khan's tracks. Ammalat still stood motionless on that spot, darkening now in the sunset's glow.

IX

One evening a strange Tatar came into the headquarters, looked about disdainfully, and with a low bow laid his sandals before Ammalat-bek. By Asian custom this signaled a desire for a private word. Ammalat understood, nodded, and both went outside. The night was dark, fires had been extinguished, and the guard line had been set far forward.

"We are alone here," Ammalat told the Tatar. "Who are you and what do you require?"

"My name is Samit. I am a Derbent resident and a member of the Sunni sect. I am presently serving in a detachment of Muslim horsemen. My message is more important to you than it is to me . . . *The hawk does not love the mountains.*"

Ammalat shuddered, then looked disbelievingly at the messenger. These were the words which Sultan-Akhmet-Khan had written him in code before.

"What do you mean 'does not love the mountains!'" he responded. "There are many lambs for the hawk in the mountains, *and for man great lodes of silver.*"

"*And damask steel for warriors.*"

Ammalat took the messenger by the arm.

"Is Sultan-Akhmet-Khan well?" he asked quickly. "What news have you brought from him? Have you seen his family recently?"

"I am sent to ask, not to answer. Will you follow me?"

"Where? Why?"

"You know who sent me—that is sufficient. If you do not believe him, then do not believe me . . . If you don't wish to run your head into a noose tonight, then tomorrow I shall tell the khan that Ammalat did not dare leave the Russian camp."

The Tatar hit the mark with this remark.

* * *

Samit led Ammalat between the brush above the river. Having covered half a verst among the rocks, they began to descend. They inched along the steep ledge in continual danger of falling, grabbing onto sweetbriar roots for safety, and finally, after much difficulty, they landed at a narrow opening into a small cave at water level. It was awash with a once-rapid current that now flowed gently. Stalactites and stalagmites quivered in a firelight that burned within the depths of the cave. Therein, Sultan-Akhmet-Khan lay upon a carpet and seemed to be waiting patiently while Ammalat gazed about in the thick smoke which swirled around him. A cocked weapon lay on the Sultan's knee. The feathers of his cap played in a wind which blew from a fissure behind him. He raised himself in greeting as Ammalat approached with a hearty hail.

* * *

" . . . You must know, Ammalat, that a rider sent to Ermolov was detained on his way to beg the general to condemn you, to show no mercy to you, whom your mentor considers a traitor. This Russian was ready to betray you with a kiss had he only been able. When you are absent he barely hides his hatred of you."

"Who dares drown me while I am under Verkhovksy's protection?"

"Listen, Ammalat. Let me tell you a story: to escape wolves, a ram ran into a kitchen, glad at his luck to find refuge in the embraces of some minions. In three days he was in the cauldron. This is your story, Ammalat! It is time to open your eyes. The man whom you consider your best friend is least hesitant to betray you. You are surrounded, lost in treachery. My sole desire has been to warn you. Seltaneta's mother-in-law to be has led me to believe . . . that you shall be sent away, never to return . . . I suspected as much, but upon investigation I learned that there is more to it than I had expected. Today I captured a *shamkhal nuker* in whom Verkhovsky entrusted his insidious plans; with some encouragement I learned from him that the *shamkhal* is giving five thousand *chervontsy* to have you removed . . . Verkhovsky is not positive you should be killed, wishing instead to send you to Siberia . . . forever. The matter is not yet decided—death or exile—and tomorrow the division is going from house to house, including yours in Buynaki, to bargain either for your blood in death or for your sweat in hard labor. They're making up false documents as evidence. They may poison you with the wheat produced by your own people; or they shall bind you, bemoaning their fate in a great golden grief as you are led away in chains."

* * *

"Revenge! Revenge!" cried the bek. "Merciless revenge! Unending suffering to the hypocrites!"

* * *

"Ammalat, first, if you are to find revenge you must strike by your very side and destroy your worst enemy: you must kill Verkhovsky [and bring me his head]."

"Verkhovsky!" Ammalat stuttered, stepping back. "Yes! He is my enemy, though once he was a friend who saved me from an ignominious demise."

"Only to send you into an ignominious life of exile!"

"Yes, this is necessary. But what will good people say of me? What shall my conscience say in its wailing response at such a wicked act?"

* * *

The khan disappeared.

Ammalat stood there for a long time, possessed and devoured by new, horrible feelings. At last Samit mentioned that it was time to return to the camp. Not knowing how he had got there or where he was, he followed his mysterious guide to the shore, found his horse, and . . . rushed to his tent. There all the tortures of the soul's hell awaited him. Heavy is the first night of a maddening fever, but more horrific still is the first night of villainy's own bloodcurdling thought.

X

An Excerpt from Colonel Verkhovsky's Letter to His Fiancée
(From a Camp in the Settlement Kyafir-Kumyk, August)

... Ammalat is in love! Oh, how in love he is!! Never, even in the very heart of my own fiery youth, did my love reach such proportions. I burned like a censer ablaze with the sun's own rays. But Ammalat!? He is blazing hot, like a ship struck by lightning on a storm-tossed sea. With you, Maria, we have more than once read Shakespeare's *Othello*. Only this violently passionate Othello conveys the nature of Ammalat's tropic heat. He often, and at great length, speaks of his Seltaneta. As for myself, I love to entice him into venting his firebreathing eloquence. Now it is a troubled waterfall disgorged from within a deep cave, and then a flaming sink hole boiling with oil. And how his eyes shoot forth veritable stars, and how his cheeks dance in the colors of summer lightning! How beautiful he is then! There is nothing ideal about him, but for this reason his earthiness is so magnificent, so captivating. Delighted and touched myself, I hold the rapture-exhausted youth to my breast. There he sighs, lowers his eyes, bows his head, as if embarrassed to look upon the mundane world (not to mention upon me), presses my hand, and, with an unsure gait, strides away. After such a scene you cannot get a single word from him for the rest of the day.

* * *

Upon our return from Khunzakh, Ammalat became even more morose than usual; he has been so the last few days. In silent suffering he seems to be concealing the most lofty, the most gentle and sensitive feeling (one, by the way , which brings man closer than anything to the Blessed in life) as if it were some disdainful weakness of some horrible crime. He asked, convincingly too, to go once more to Khunzakh to gaze again upon his beauty. But I refused, and I refused for his own good. I've already written Aleksei Petrovich about my "pet" and he has ordered me to bring him with me to take the waters. Aleksei Petrovich will be there too and wishes to send a missive to Sultan-Akhmet-Khan which will stand both Russia and Ammalat in excellent stead ... Oh, how happy I shall be in Ammalat's happiness! He will be beholden to me for the sublime life he will have in Russia. When we arrive back home, we shall come straight to see you. I shall have him kneel before you and shall say to him, "Worship her! If my heart were not suffused with love for Maria, I am sure your Seltaneta could no longer claim your heart."
Yesterday I received a pass from the general. A magnanimous man! He gives wings to good tidings. All is in order, my dear and precious one. I am coming to see you at the spa! I only need take the regiment back again to Derbent and I am off to see you!

XI

A bitter poison of calumny inflamed Ammalat's very innards ... Here is what Ammalat wrote, attempting to release his soul's anguish as he prepared to perform the perfidious deed:

Midnight.
Why, Sultan-Akhmet-Khan, why did you throw a lightning bolt into my breast? A brotherly friendship; then a brother's betrayal; and now fratricide ... What ghastly extremes! And between them but one single step, one solitary moment ...

I cannot sleep. I can think of nothing else. I am forged to this thought like a criminal to a storm-tossed log. The bloody sea rolls on, splashes and storms about me, and above only lightning flashes . . . No stars . . . My soul is like a bare precipice where birds of prey fly in consort with evil spirits, dividing their prey and readying themselves for the next kill. Verkhovsky! Verkhovsky! What did I do to you?! Why do you wish to tear the star of my freedom from the heavens? Is it because I loved you so tenderly?!! And why do you sneak about like a thief, telling lies, sowing bad seed, defaming me? You could have said to me directly: "I require your life." And I, without a murmur, would have given it . . . laying my life down like Abraham's son. Had you only sworn on my life, I would have forgiven you. But to see my freedom stolen from me, and Seltaneta, as though burying me alive! Villain! And yet you breathe?! Not for long . . .

* * *

XII

. . .Verkhovsky awakened Ammalat, raised his head and said to him: "Ready yourself. You're coming with me."

Such unfortunate words . . . thoughts of treachery and of his exile charged through Ammalat's being in a fiery jolt.

"With you?" he responded with an evil smirk, "with you to Russia? Oh, doubtless I shall, if you yourself are going there!"

* * *

In violent anger he sped off at a gallop to have time to ready his weapon, suddenly turned back toward the colonel, passing by once and then riding rapidly in circles around him. With each stride the flame of his madness intensified. It seemed to him as though the wind were whipping by his ears, buzzing "Kill! Kill! This is your enemy! Remember your Seltaneta . . ." He took his trusted rifle from off his shoulder, cocked it, and emboldening himself with a wild shriek, rushed with bloodthirsty intensity at his doomed sacrifice.

All this time Verkhovsky suspected nothing wrong. He peacefully watched Ammalat's riding and imagined that what he saw was no more than an Asian custom of showing off prior to leaving on a long journey.

"Fire away, Ammalat-bek! Hit the mark!" he shouted to the murderer as the latter bore down upon him at a full gallop.

"What better mark than the breast of an enemy!" Ammalat-bek answered, aiming carefully. At ten paces he pulled the trigger! . . . The shot rang out . . . Silently and slowly the colonel slipped from his saddle. His frightened steed, widening its nostrils and shaking its mane, sniffed the rider in whose hands the reins were quickly freezing. Suddenly Ammalat was over the body, rearing on his steed's hind legs. Ammalat leapt off, and, leaning on his smoking rifle, gazed coldly a few moments upon the face of the deceased, as if proving to himself that he does not fear this unmoving sight, extinguished eyes, thickening blood . . . It was difficult to know, impossible to guess, what whirlwind blew within Ammalat's breast at this moment . . .

* * *

An alarm went along the front lines, soldiers and Don Cossacks responded quickly to the shot. But they arrived too late. They could neither prevent the vicious crime nor catch the fleeing murderer. Within five minutes the bloody body of the treacherously killed colonel was surrounded by a crowd of soldiers and officers. Disbelief, disgust and anguish were written on each man's face. The grenadiers, resting on their bayonetted weapons, wept uncontrollably. Their heartfelt tears flowed in streams upon their beloved and brave superior.

XIII

For three days and nights Ammalat wandered the mountains of Dagestan. As a Muslim, even in those villages controlled by the Russian command, he was amidst people from whom thieving, brigandage, and daring escape earned the highest respect; he was, therefore, safe from pursuit. But could he possibly flee his conscience? Neither his mind nor his heart could justify his bloody deed, and the image of Verkhovsky falling from his horse relentlessly came before his eyes either opened or closed. This more than anything else embittered and vexed him. An Asian who has strayed but once from the path quickly oversteps the bounds of common decency. The khan's behest that he, Ammalat, not appear before him without Verkhovsky's head rang in his ears. Unable to confide his evil intentions to his *nukers,* he decided to ride to Derbent alone, entirely alone, across mountain, field, and stream.

The godforsaken and gloomy night had just cast its crepe wings over the seaside mountain ridges of the Caucasus when Ammalat quit the ravine laying behind Derbent's citadel, the Naryn-Kale fortress. He mounted the ruins of a tower which once had guarded the Caucasian wall that stretched across the vast mountain range. He tied his horse at the foot of the burial mound from which Ermolov had stormed Derbent when he was but a lieutenant in the artillery. Knowing where government servants were buried, he could make his way directly to the Russian's cemetery. But how was he to find his Verkhovsky's fresh grave in the darkness of night? No stars in the sky; clouds upon the mountains; a wind from the high ridges, like a nocturnal fowl, was striking the forest with its wings; an involuntary shudder coursed through Ammalat at the very border of the quick and the dead, the latter whom he was daring to disturb. He cocked an ear. The sea raged, crashing upon the flagstone at the shore, then withdrew. The long, drawn-out "On guard!" of the watchmen suffused the air about the city walls, and jackals howled in response. Then all but the flowing whine of the wind fell silent. How many times he and Verkhovsky had kept vigil on such nights!—But where was he now? And who lowered him into his grave? And now his murderer was here to behead the corpse of recent friendship, to outrage the remains. Like a graverobber he had come to steal the spoils concealed therein, to quarrel with the jackals over the remains.

* * *

"Human feelings," Ammalat spoke, wiping cold sweat from his brow. "Why do you inhabit a heart which has forsaken its humanity? Away! Away! Am I afraid of removing the head from a corpse whose life I myself have already taken? It is no loss to it; but for me it is the single treasure with which to buy my Seltaneta. Stay, weary mind—dust is not sentient!"

With a trembling hand Ammalat lit a torch of dried grasses and went to seek the new grave. Some reddish earth and a large cross revealed to him the colonel's final resting place. He yanked the cross out of the earth and with it began to dig into the mound; he rent the as-yet-unhardened brick vault and tore open the coffin's lid. The flaming grass, flashing and sputtering, cast an uneven, blood-blue light upon the object. Bending over the body, the murderer, more pale now than the corpse, gazed upon the deathly form. He forgot why he had come here. His head whirled from the stench of decay. His heart turned over at the sight of the worms which squirmed out from under the funeral gown. Quitting their horrid work and frightened by the light, they tried to crawl away, winding themselves together in a knot and hiding under one another! Then at last, steeling himself, he raised his dagger once, twice, thrice . . . yet each time his hand, grown numb, missed the mark. Neither revenge, nor pride, nor even love—in other words, no single passion of his which had moved him to kill the man earlier—could now bestow on him the courage to perform this nameless, godless act of mutilation. Turning the head back to reveal the neck, in a dark forgetfulness reminiscent of sleep, Ammalat began to chop Verkhovsky about the neck . . . On the fifth blow head separated from body. With ineffable disgust he tossed it into the sack he had thought to bring beforehand. Then he rushed out of the tomb. Up until now he had managed to conquer himself. But when, with his terrible treasure in hand, he began to scurry up and out of the grave, the stones and brick gave way with a sudden jolt beneath his feet, and he, covered in muck and sand, fell back upon Verkhovsky's violated remains. Presence of mind abandoned the desecrator. It seemed to him that the flame of his torch enveloped him, that hell's own spirit world, dancing and howling in laughter, wound about him . . . With a labored groan he tore himself upward, crawled out unconsciously from the narrow grave and began to run, fearing even to look back. He jumped onto his steed and drove it relentlessly on, taking no heed of mountain or ravine. And each bush which caught at his clothes seemed to him the dead man's hand pulling at him; and each rustling of the leaves and each howl of the jackal cried with the anguished voice of his twice-defiled friend.

* * *

Toward evening on the third day, Ammalat reached Khunzakh. Trembling with impatience, he leapt from his exhausted horse and took the fateful sack from his saddle knot. The khan's courtyard was filled with warriors. Riders in mail were walking about or lying along the walls on carpets. They spoke together only in whispers . . . Both their drooping brows and their gloomy visages foretold that Khunzakh was truly in the grip of a most terrible grief. *Nukers* ran hurriedly to and fro. No one questioned Ammalat or led him into the grounds. Indeed, no one paid the least attention to him. At the doors to the khan's bedroom sat Surkhay-Khan-Jinka, the sultan's adopted son. He was weeping bitterly.

"What does this mean?" Ammalat asked in alarm. "You? Who even in your youth would never drop a tear! Why is it you are weeping?"

Surkhay silently pointed to the door, and in utter confusion Ammalat crossed a threshhold which would decide for him the remainder of his life.

A scene which shook the young bek's heart to the core presented itself to his eyes. The khan lay upon a mattress in the middle of the room, disfigured by a ravaging disease. Invisibly, but unmistakably, death hovered over him. The slowly extinguishing gaze of the dying man showed clearly that he was facing death in utter terror.

***

Nonetheless, Ammalat remained untouched by this scene, consumed as he was by his own singular desire. With a firm step he approached the khan and said to him in a loud voice:

"Greetings, khan! I have brought you the gift you sought of me, a gift fit to drive death from your door and to bring the dead back to life. Prepare the wedding! Here is what you sought in trade for Seltaneta—Verkhovsky's head!" And with these words he emptied the sack at the khan's feet.

The bek's familiar voice awakened the khan only for a moment from his last living dream; he raised himself with great effort in order to gaze upon the gift. A shudder ran through him like a wave as his eyes fell upon the skull.

"Let him who dares regale a dying man with such a horrid sight consume his own heart," he sputtered in barely audible condemnation. "I must now make peace with my enemies, and not . . . Oh, pain! Give me some water, water . . . Of all the moments in life, why have you fed me boiling oil at this one, Ammalat-bek? Ammalat! I damn you! . . . curse you into eternity!"

This effort wasted the khan's last drops of life. He fell back upon the pillows a breathless corpse.

***

Ammalat stood as though struck by lightning.

***

"Seltaneta! For you I have done that by which I now lose you . . . Fate so commands—let it be so! But tell me, have you truly lost your love for me, do you indeed despise me for this?"

His familiar and dear voice touched her heart. Seltaneta raised lashes glistening with tears, raised her eyes filled with grief, but upon seeing Ammalat's frightening, blood-suffused visage, she covered her face again with her delicate hands. She pointed at her father's body, then at Verkhovsky's head, saying firmly:

"Farewell, Ammalat. I pity you. And I cannot be yours out of pity."

Speaking these words, she fell unconscious upon her father's body.

Ammalat's innate pride mixed now with his fiery blood and flowed into his heart. The bek's spirit was charged with bile.

"So this is how I am received here!" he uttered, throwing a disdainful glance upon the woman. "So this is how an oath is fulfilled in this house. I am happy that my eyes have been cleared. I was too callow, too naive, when I valued the passing love of a flighty young girl . . . I see that here, with Sultan-Akhmet-Khan's death, pride and hospitality have died as well."

He exited proudly.

***

And where did Verkhovsky's murderer go? Where did he drag out his miserable existence? No one knew. Rumors swept Dagestan that he was living with Chechentsy and Koysubulintsy, that he had lost his looks and health, and even his courage. But who could say definitely? No one. Little by little talk of Ammalat ceased, although his evil betrayal is yet fresh in the minds of both Russian and Muslim communities in Dagestan. Even today his name is pronounced by no one unless it be with recrimination.

XIV

The Battle of Anapa, 1828

* * *

From the very outset of the battle not a single tribesman dared venture close to the Russian line, save one: the Russians gazed in amazement at the stately Cherkes warrior on a white horse who calmly rode back and forth before our lines. Everyone recognized in him the same rider who at noon leapt our front trenches in an effort to encourage the Cherkes youths to strike the Russians from behind. Splashing about and rumbling, the shot peppered the ground all about him. His steed champed at the bit. But he? He coolly glanced at the battery, rode past them as if they were firing nothing at him but flowers. The artillerists gnashed their teeth in vexation at the rider's bravado. Shot after shot tore the earth and air, but he remained unharmed. It was as if he were enchanted.

"Fire a cannon ball at him!" cried a young artillery officer who had just arrived from the corps school. He more than anyone was most vexed by each miss. He said to his gunner, "I want to get that braggart so badly. I'd almost load the cannon with my own head. Grapeshot does not seem to be doing the trick, so let's leave off. A cannon ball will hunt this guilty one down."

So saying he . . . aimed the weapon through his scope and, calculating the exact moment when the rider would reach the point within his sights, stood up and gave the fateful cry, "Fire!"

For a few moments smoke covered the battery in dark gloom . . . It cleared off . . . a frightened steed sped off—and below it the bloody body of the rider dragged along with one foot caught in the stirrup.

***

That night when all had fallen still, the young artillery officer sat over his half-dead captive attentively examining him in the half-light of his lantern. A reptilian trace of anguish, well-marked grooves upon the cheeks, deep wrinkles on the forehead, earned not by time but by exhausted passion, and bloody scars disfigured a handsome face whereon some unknowable, torturous pain, something surely more horrible than death, had etched itself . . . The officer could not withhold an involuntary shudder. The prisoner sighed deeply. With an effort he raised a hand to his forehead, opened his heavy eyelids, and muttered some incomprehensible sounds and disconnected words . . .

"Blood . . ." he spoke, gazing upon his hand. "All in blood! Why did they place *his* bloody shirt on me? . . . Even without it I am already swimming in blood . . . Why do I not drown in it? . . . How cold it is today . . . Once it inflamed me . . . yes, and that was hardly better. It was so stifling on this earth . . . and so cold in that grave! . . . How horrible to be a corpse! . . . I am a fool. I have sought death . . . Oh, let me return to the good earth! . . . Let me live, even if only one more day, if only one more short hour! . . . What is that? What? 'Why did I hide another in the grave?' you whisper . . . Find out for yourself who is in it! Find out for yourself how it is to die! . . ."

A spasm broke his delirium; an indescribably terrible moan rent the sufferer's breast. He fell into a wearisome oblivion in which the soul lives on only to suffer longer.

The officer, touched to the quick, raised the poor fellow's head, pressed cold water to his forehead and wiped his temples with alcohol. This brought him to his senses. He slowly opened his eyes, shook his head several times, as if wishing to shake the cloud from his lashes, and then looked intently upon the officer's pale face, only faintly illuminated by the weak light of the lantern's fluttering candle. And then suddenly, as if by a magic force, he raised himself up from his bed with a penetrating cry . . . His hair stood on end, his entire body was shaken by a feverish chill. His hands sought to push something from himself . . . His face expressed an indescribable horror.

"Your name?!" he finally shouted, turning to the young man. "Who are you? A messenger from the grave?"

"Why, I am Verkhovsky," the youth responded.

This shot straight into the prisoner's heart.

* * *

It was awful to view the disfigured face of the man as death suddenly consumed him.

"He truly must have been a great sinner!" Verkhovsky said quietly to the translator who stood next to him. He, too, shuddered involuntarily.

"A titanic villain," the translator added. "I'm convinced that he was a deserter from our side. I've not heard a mountain tribesman speak Russian as well as this prisoner. Let me look at his weapon to see if there is any insignia on it by which we might know him."

So saying he unsheathed the dead man's dagger and with curiosity held it toward the lantern. He read and then translated the inscription:

"Slow to Offend—Quick to Avenge!"

"A brigand's code, to be sure," Verkhovsky said. "Oh, poor brother Evstafy. It was to such wild barbarity, to such a distorted sense of honor that you fell in sacrifice!"

The good lad's eyes filled with tears as he remembered his brother's treacherous death.

"Is there anything else inscribed?" he inquired.

"Here, it seems, is the name of the dead man himself," the interpreter responded. "It is: Ammalat-bek!"

Author's Notes

1. *Juma* corresponds to our day of rest. Here are the names of the days of the Mohammedan week: *shambi* (Saturday), *ikhshamba* (Sunday), *dushamba* (Monday), *seshamba* (Tuesday), *chershamba* (Wednesday), *pkhan-shamba* (Thursday), *juma* (Friday).

2. Although in truth of fact there is no difference between men's *shalvari* and women's *tumani* (pants), it would be considered a great offense if you were to say that a man is wearing *tumani,* or a woman *shalvari.*

3. For Asians, the usual form of sitting on the streets or before elders. Thus, N. M. Karamzin erred significantly when translating the words from the Volhynian chronicler, "Zle te, Romane, na kolenekh *pred* khanom sedishi" as "Khudo tebe, Roman, na kolenyakh stoish pered khanom." Of course, sitting on one's haunches was not to the Galician prince's pleasure; but it was not as demeaning an act as the historian supposes.

4. The first *shamkhals* were relatives and deputies of the Damascus halifs. The last *shamkhal* died upon returning from Russia. With him a useless title ended. His son, Suleman Pasha, now rules his inheritance as any one would his own meager private property.

5. *Nuker*—the usual name for attendants, or retinue. More to the point, however, this is the same title given the ancient Scottish Henchman. He is to be found at all times and everywhere with his sire; he waits at table, cuts and tears the master's food with his hands, and so forth.

6. *Emjek*—brother of the breast, from the word meaning wetnurse. Among the Caucasians this kinship is more sacred than that of flesh and blood; anyone would put his life before that of his *emjek*. Mothers attempt to become linked to important families by this means. The boy is brought to the other's mother; she feeds him at her breast; the ritual is fulfilled, and an unbreakable bond between the coevals is initiated.

7. *Zherebets*—a superb breed of horse from Persia.

8. The brother of Hussein-Khan Jemutaysky, he became khan Avarsky upon marrying the only heir to the Avarsky *khanstvo,* the former khan's widow.

9. Our company of 3,000 was surrounded by 60,000 mountain natives, including Avarians, Koysubulintsy and others. At night the Russians broke through the net but suffered heavy losses in so doing.

10. House in Tatar is *ev; utakh* means quarters; and barn is used to refer to almost any building.

11. Word play is the stock-in-trade among the Asians. *Kuzylgyullar* means roses, but the khan alludes also to *kusyl,* money.

12. There have been few times when we have been able to rout the mountain warriors from the forest. Thus, they consider the forest their most effective stronghold. This song is translated almost word for word.

F. V. BULGARIN

Ivan Vyzhigin (excerpts)

Plot Summary: Volume I

The novel begins with a description of a male Cinderella type known as the Orphan, who turns out to be Ivan Vyzhigin. Ivan (Vanya) lives a life in the Gologordovsky ("bare-pride") household without love and caresses; the dog is loved more than the boy. One day little Vanya delivers a note to an officer and the boy's fortunes change. The consequences of this note are many: Petronella Gologordovskaya and the officer, Milovidin ("sweet appearance"), fall in love and elope without her father's blessing; their money runs out quickly; Milovidin goes to his uncle for more and leaves Ivan to the mercy of a Jew at whose tavern they were all staying.

After a cliched description of the Jew's crookedness and Ivan's growing unhappiness with his life, the Skotino ("cattle") family take Ivan home with them. While he is running an errand for them, his fortunes change yet again and the first of too many coincidences occurs. A young woman catches sight of Vanya and asks about a scar on his shoulder. Her protector, a wealthy prince, comes for the boy, who goes to live with his aunt Adelaida Petrovna. We then get to see Ivan's transformation into a spoiled brat, albeit a talented, intelligent and precocious one, ripe for the influence of nasty Vorovatin ("thief").

Vorovatin appears and teaches Ivan such vices as lying and card-playing. Meanwhile Aunt Adelaida takes up with Grabilin ("robber"), who changes the atmosphere in the household to one unbearable for Ivan. So Ivan bares his soul to Vorovatin and also hints about his late, rich, noble father. Vorovatin introduces Ivan to Grunya, and they fall in love. At this crucial point Grunya's family moves to Orenburg, but Ivan and Vorovatin go after her. Again Ivan's fortunes change, but not for the better.

In a series of misadventures the following events take place: Vorovatin steals Ivan's money; Ivan finds Grunya, learns that her house is a "man-trap," overhears her scornfully describing him to another suitor, falls in a swoon, almost loses his mind, and wakes to find himself in a Khirghiz camp; Ivan finally recovers from his illness—only to find himself the slave of the Khirghiz prince, Arsalan Sultan.

We hear of Arsalan's visit to Petersburg (city vs. natural life) and then see how wonderful life is in the steppe. We are given all of the details of life on the steppe, it seems. Meanwhile Ivan is promoted to Arsalan's military attendant; he learns to ride a horse like a native; gets close to the prince; saves his life in a war; and has a reunion with his first benefactor Milovidin, who is a prisoner in another caravan.

Milovidin tells the story of how his uncle's housekeeper cheated him of his money and how he led an "irregular" life in Italy with a young Russian countess. The two Russians (Ivan and Milovidin) set off for home after Ivan receives his freedom and other rewards from Arsalan. They arrive in Russia without passports, but with the goods. Naturally, they get swindled, but they also get to meet the provincial police official, who turns out to be an honest man! Amidst all of their adventures and ceaseless discussions about various subjects, including commerce, they visit a jail and meet a wretched prisoner, Vorovatin's former crony. He dies that night, taking with him to the grave the secret of the identity of the countess who is trying to destroy Ivan.

Volume II

This volume begins with a section about landowners and is full of pro-Russian, anti-foreign sentiment. Ivan and Milovidin meet the perfect landowner, Mr. Rossiyaninov ("Russian"). Their adventures take them all the way back home, where Ivan is reunited with his aunt, now a pock-marked hag. She finally tells her story and we all find out that she is really Ivan's mother and the Hussar Miloslavsky was his father, although no proof of his paternity exists. Ivan, his mother and Milovidin all live together peacefully until Ivan decides to enter the military. But before he leaves, he and Milovidin go on a round of visits and pay their final call at the home of Milovidin's cousin, Anita. This gives the narrator a chance to engage in a long diatribe against society life. But then something worse than society appears on the scene—actresses, one of whom just happens to be Grunya.

Ivan goes to the theater, sees Grunya, gives her money and their "romance" begins anew—to the tune of 10,000 rubles. Ivan goes that far into debt all for the love of a tart. In order to survive, Ivan learns how to cheat at cards and then becomes deeply involved with swindlers. And the money rolls in.

In the meantime Ivan's mother enters a convent and Milovidin finds Petronella; they reconcile. Milovidin then finds out about the death of his uncle's housekeeper and goes to Kiev to make amends with the old man.

Things are not so good for Ivan. Upon returning home from a house party, he finds a policeman waiting for him. The policeman tells Ivan that Grunya swindled people and that she has left for Paris with a Frenchman. The policeman, who turns out to be honest, stays to dinner and convinces Ivan to change his ways. So Ivan decides to marry and through a matchmaker meets the merchant family Moshnin ("moneybags"). Ivan goes to a party and is smitten with the wrong daughter. He then joins the army, wins distinction in the war, returns to Moscow, retires from the service and moves to Petersburg.

In addition to all of the other things wrong with Petersburg, Vorovatin is there and tries to compromise Ivan. In the midst of this, Ivan meets a young woman, Olga, yet another poor, unfortunate orphan. It turns out that Olga too is a victim of Grabilin, who was her grandmother's husband and deprived her mother of her rightful inheritance. Ivan becomes her protector and falls in love with her. But since the course of true love cannot yet run smoothly, Ivan is arrested and put to jail for some unknown offense. Anita and Olga sustain him throughout.

Now it is time for Ivan's deliverer and he appears in the character of Pyotr Petrovich, the honest police official of the provinces. He clears Ivan and deals with Vorovatin, who finally tells Pyotr Petrovich the whole story of Ivan's background and of his rightful inheritance as son of Prince Miloslavsky. But this puts Ivan in the middle of a lawsuit and provides an opportunity for a diatribe against lawyers and the law.

Because of the costs of a lawsuit, Ivan must go to usurers. At this point we find out (Vyzhigin mercifully spares us the details) that Ivan wins his case. Ivan and Olga marry, Grabilin returns Olga's inheritance, and the newlyweds live happily, with Pyotr Petrovich as a daily visitor. We find out the fate of the other characters as well. Bulgarin closes Ivan's adventures with a statement that sums up the tone of this bombastic novel: "Critics will forgive my faults for the sake of my good intentions, and see that the bad is here introduced for no other purpose than to throw more splendor on the good."

Ivan Vyzhigin*

Chapter XX

> A landowner, like whom, God grant, there were more in Russia!—Like priest, like people.

By our good conduct and the favorable representations of Pyotr Petrovich, we gained the good opinion of the *Capitan Ispravnik,* who sometimes called upon us, invited us to drink tea with him, and allowed us to take excursions outside the town. One day, when we were at his house with Pyotr Petrovich, the conversation turned upon the difficulties which the country police meet with in keeping order over a wide stretch of country, in a thinly peopled district, intersected with impassable morasses and woods. "Catch a vagrant who can," said the *Capitan Ispravnik,* "if a landowner and his peasant choose to conceal him! You would require a thousand rank and file to catch a single individual in a wood which covers one or two hundred versts!" "The landowners have a great trust to answer for before their Maker, their emperor, and their country, for everything which is done within their possessions," said Pyotr Petrovich. "On a landowner depends all the happiness, the morality, the education, and the prosperity of his peasants; consequently, on the naked gentry collectively depends all the morality, education and prosperity of the whole of Russia. The government places no obstacles to bar the progress of the nobility to education and prosperity. No affectionate father cares more for the education and happiness of his darling son than the Russian emperors care for the Russian noblesse. But why should the Russian nobility behave like the man in the parable who hid his lord's talent in the earth? The nobleman having received it should divide it, should increase among his people their attachment to the throne, their love of their country, and excite them to morality by his own example." "That is all true," said the Sheriff; "but, in the opposite case, the nobility will be like the barren fig-tree of which mention is made in Luke's Gospel (chapter xiii). A nobleman, as the favorite son of an affectionate father, ought to employ himself all his lifetime in fulfilling the will and good intentions of the common father of Russia. A nobleman who lives on his own estates, should esteem himself as much in actual service as if he sat at the imperial council-board, or was commander-in-chief of the forces. A nobleman is the head police-officer on his estate, collector of the emperor's taxes, overseer who apportions the district rates, judge of equity among his peasants, guardian of their health and property, and director of the parish-school." "Excellent, excellent, Pyotr Petrovich!" exclaimed the *Capitan Ispravnik,* rushing to embrace Virtutin and adding, "That is as it should be; the district-police would then be a real executive power, which could enforce order and regularity where it was wanted, by the power of law, in cases where persuasion had no effect!" "It will be so in the course of time, at the ripening of the fruits of education, the seeds of which are so uninterruptedly sown by our wise monarchs; when we shall have a sufficient number of first-rate Russian teachers for the education of our youth in the Russian fashion, not after the manner of the French or English." "These Russian foreigners have long been a bone in my throat," said the *Capitan Ispravnik.* "I have more respect for a French cook or an English coachman than for a Russian bit of a Knyaz,[1] who apes Lords and Marquisses in their whims and singularities. There came, not long ago, to live on his estate here, a young weather-cock who had left the service, conceiving himself ill used because his commanding officer had told him that he was not fit to occupy a distinguished situation, he not being able to write three lines logically and grammatically. Slabogolovin [weak-in-the-

---

*This is from a translation published in London by Whittaker, Treacher and Co. and in Edinburgh by H. Constable in 1831. The name of the translator is not noted.

head] had read some French pamphlets upon politics with the assistance of his governor, and as he subscribed to some English newspapers, he fancied himself a great politician, and born to be a lawgiver to his country. Along with the fumes of champagne, he had filled the heads of his blind companions with rules of philanthropy and wisdom out of Voltaire's *Philosophical Dictionary,* and passed for a liberal, an orator, and a stickler for the rights of man. After taking this false step on the road of ambition, he came to his estate——, and do you know what was the end of his philosophy?" "Doubtless he began to establish country schools, and exert himself for the improvement of his peasants," said Milovidin. "You have not hit the nail on the head," said the *Capitan Ispravnik,* laughing. "The Government which cares for the welfare of its subjects in reality, though not in empty words, was obliged to take into its own hands the guardianship of the property of this eloquent orator of the human race, owing to his barbarous treatment of his peasants and destructive management of his estates. Listen to bawlers of this stamp after a sumptuous dinner, or of an evening amongst a crowd of young people: they will treat you to a dissertation on the happiness of mankind or on legislation; but at their own houses, and in every place under their control, they are would-be Bashaws. The real friend of mankind does not cry out nor bawl against the laws of the land or established order, but contenting himself with things as they are, does as much good as is in his power; and much good can be done always and everywhere,[2] if there be only an inclination to do it! Among us, the practice of good must be brought to much greater perfection before we meddle with theory. Do you know what I would propose, Pyotr Petrovich? Take these gentlemen to our friend Aleksandr Aleksandrovich Rossiyaninov. You will see what people among us are hidden under a bushel; I will give you my own horses. Move about, gentlemen, you have had a long stay in our little town!"

Next morning we set out on our visit to Mr. Rossiyaninov, who lived on his estate which was twenty-five versts[3] distant from the town. At the distance of fifteen versts, we observed an astonishing difference in the cultivation of the fields. In low places, trenches were everywhere cut to let off the water. The fields were properly measured off and manured; and the meadows were free from mole-heaps and useless bushes. On the brink of a winding rivulet, a paved descent was formed from the pasture, so that the cattle might drink without getting wet or muddying the water. The road on both sides was planted with trees; bridges were erected everywhere, and boggy parts of the road covered with spars. "You can see," said Pyotr Petrovich, "that we have entered the possessions of an orderly man." On arriving at the village, Milovidin clapped his hands with admiration, and exclaimed: "Look what the whole of Russia could be and should be!" Well-finished wooden *izbas* [huts] were erected in single rows on both sides of the road. The windows were embellished with graven ornaments, and the courtyards all enclosed with high railings and with neat gates and roofs. The houses were placed at some distance from each other, as a precaution against fire. Between the houses were little gardens with fruit trees. Behind the courtyards were orchards, and at their extremity, barns. At the end of the village stood a fine stone church, shaded with tall lime trees. The priest's house was distinguished by its clean and neat appearance. Beside the church were some pretty little buildings for the use of the community. In one of them was established an infirmary and apothecary's shop; in another a hospital for the maintenance of the friendless, the infirm and the aged; in a third, the village storehouse and shop, containing such wares as are indispensable to peasants, as well as the first necessaries of life; in the fourth, the village school and *slovesnoy* court.[4] At the edge of the village was a smithy, and in the middle a large well. The peasants of both sexes had a healthy appearance, and the young women were distinguished for their beauty, the natural consequence of contentment.[5] We met on the street neither dirty children, nor ragged women, nor drunken men. The peasants' horses and cattle were of an excellent breed, and the machines and implements for agriculture were all in good order. We entered into one peasant's house in order to have a glimpse at their domestic economy. The house had a cellar, and was divided into two halves, one with a chimney, the other without one. The first, which was composed of three divisions, was occupied by the family; in the second they baked bread, boiled the victuals for themselves and drink for the cattle, dried their wet clothes when they returned from work in bad weather and the like. "I know some landowners," said Milovidin, "who, seized with a foreign mania, took it into their heads to build German houses for Russian peasants, and to require of them as much cleanliness as in Germany. That is an absolute impossibility in this country, and not only does not add to the happiness of the peasant, but is a great encumbrance to his life. Our climate and local circumstances require a different structure of our houses than in Germany and England. It is impossible to build large stone houses for the peasants among us, because, in the first place, it is not everywhere that we have materials for that purpose, and in the second, because it costs more, and our peasants do not live in large families and therefore have no necessity for a number of rooms, which must be heated in the greater part of Russia eight months in the year. Without a smoky *izba* it is even difficult for a Russian peasant to live in our moist and cold climate in the northern governments: without it he would have no place to dry himself. The wish of doing good frequently brings no advantage if it is carried into effect without a knowledge of local circumstances. In this respect, Mr. Rossiyaninov seems to understand his business." On the porch,[6] we saw *lapti*.[7] "That still has an air of barbarity," said Milovidin. Pyotr Petrovich examined them with more attention, and said: "These are not *lapti* but *shmony,* that is to say, coverings for the feet made of hemp. The use of *lapti* is less advantageous, as they require a great deal of wood."[8] "When do your peasants wear *shmony*?" he inquired of a man whom he met: "I see that on the street they are all in boots." "When they go a fishing, my son: in the meadows during the hay harvest, and in wood-work, they save the boots; and the feet too are not so comfortable in a boot as they are in *lapti* made of well-tarred twine." "Do you see that they make use of this sort of shoes only during work, and they are really much better adapted for this purpose than the wooden shoes of the French and German peasants. If the peasant amidst contentment has not given up the use of such a covering for his feet, it is a proof that it is useful and suitable for him."

Around the peasant's courtyard was a shed, where carts, sledges, ploughs, and harrows stood, and where they stabled the horses occasionally. At the end of the yard was a cowhouse and stable, and beyond the house, a vapor-bath. I asked the mistress what they used for light in the winter time. "Our neighbors," she replied, "the peasants of other masters, burn splinters of wood, father, but we light our izbas with lamps supplied with hemp oil. You see, we have not to buy the hemp oil, my son; for every woman among us makes her oil from the seed."—"Have you a drinking-house in the village?" asked Milovidin. "God forbid, my worthy fathers!" replied the woman. "In old times when our former *barin*[9] was alive, there was a drinking-house here: so our peasants got drunk regularly on holidays, and were out of sorts on working days. But, now, thank God, there is an end to that. And our parson, God save him, tells us in church that it is a great sin to get drunk, and our surgeon tells us that spirits shorten one's life, and our master forbids us to drink, and hates drunkards; so drunkenness is at an end, and both man and money are better housekeepers. It is a different matter at Easter, or a marriage, or a christening: then we brew beer, and our *barin* himself gives us spirits. In our autumn and winter work, our *barin* also orders the laborers to drink a glass of vodka, but no more than one apiece. God save him; he is a real father and no *gospodin.* "

Five versts beyond the village, on the high bank of a river, stood the manor house, built of wood on a stone foundation, painted green, with a red roof. Behind the house a large garden extended towards the river. Around the courtyard were various establishments for domestic purposes. The symmetry of the parts showed the skill of the architect, and the want of ornament was fully compensated for by the neatness and solidity of the building. At the entrance, we were met by a servant dressed neatly, though very plainly. He said that his master had gone into the fields, but his mistress was superintending her daughters' lessons. We were met in the antechamber by the landlord's oldest son, a youth sixteen years of age, who begged us to wait without impatience till his mother had finished what she was doing. The youth's tall figure, rosy cheeks, and good address showed that as great pains had been taken with his physical as his moral education. Pyotr Petrovich, who was an intimate acquaintance of the family, proposed that we look through the rooms and garden. The landlord's son Alyosha undertook to be our guide. Passing through three salons and a hall which were distinguishable for nothing but their uncommon neatness, we entered Mr. Rossiyaninov's study. It was a large room, around which were disposed immense shelves full of books in Latin, Greek, French, German, Italian, and Russian. In the middle of the room were three tables; on one lay newspapers and periodicals; on another, papers in manuscript; and on the third, newly received books. In another room which was attached to the study, there were shelves containing physical instruments, a chemical apparatus, and models of various machines; on the tables stood globes, and one side of the hall was hung with geographical maps. A small case with shelves contained within it a collection of minerals. "This is like Europe!" said Milovidin. From there we went into the garden, which contained neither artificial ponds which contaminate the air by their poisonous exhalations, nor dearly built bridges on dry land, nor grotesque summer houses of a barbarous architecture, nor new ruins. The garden was filled with fruit trees and different berry bushes, distributed very tastefully. Nut and lime-tree groves afforded an agreeable retreat in hot weather, while a large alley round the garden, shaded with high trees, served as a promenade. On plots of grass were erected swinging ropes and different things to amuse children. At the end of the garden, on the south side, there was a greenhouse, not a large one, but well constructed. "That is another luxury," said Milovidin. "A luxury which is not only pardonable, but even useful," replied Pyotr Petrovich. "What can be more agreeable to an inhabitant of the north than the products of more favored climates? The very contemplation of the diversity, riches, and liberality of nature elevates the soul and brings the creature nearer to the Creator.—Amidst these products of various regions, thought descends upon the earthly globe. I will say more—why should we deprive ourselves of the satisfaction of raising the tender fruits which nature has denied our northern climate? This is not the repletion of a shameful gluttony, but the satisfaction of a pardonable curiosity. Besides, it appears to me a much more commendable occupation to raise the fruits of the earth than to keep a variety of living creatures under restraint and hurt the weaker animals." All of a sudden a voice was heard behind us: we saw a man of a cheerful and healthy countenance, in a leather cap and green camblet surtout, who was making his way toward us. It was the landlord himself. "How do you do, my friend," he said, stretching out his hand to Pyotr Petrovich, who presented us to him, and in a few words related our proceedings. "I have already heard in part," added our landlord: "you will often be obliged here to listen to what you do not wish to hear. Walking newspapers are among us in greater circulation than printed ones. If one wishes to know the truth, he should only believe the hundredth part of the provincial news. I was told that two Russian gentlemen had arrived from India through the Kirghizian *steppe,* where one had been a reigning prince and the other his minister, and that they had brought with them whole barrels of ducats and bales of shawls. I am persuaded that, if this news reaches another government, one of you will be transformed into the great Mogul, and the other into some terrible warrior.—Your treasures will be magnified to millions of ducats and barrels filled with diamonds. But I beg you to enter the room—it is dinner time."

On entering, the worthy landlord presented us to his wife and two daughters, of whom the elder was fourteen and the younger twelve years of age. Their son was ten years old. To our astonishment, the lady of the house addressed us in Russian, and was dressed very plainly, although she was receiving for the first time guests who passed for *millionaires*. The landlord also presented to us his childrens' teachers, a Frenchman, Monsieur Instruit, and a German, Herr Hutman, whom he called his friends. It appeared to me singular that Mr. Rossiyaninov, whom Pyotr Petrovich described as extremely patriotic and an enemy of foreign education, should keep in his house foreigners to teach his children. Pyotr Petrovich perceived my astonishment from the oblique glances which I cast on the foreigners, and communicated my observations to the landlord. Mr. Rossiyaninov took me and Milovidin into another room, and said: "Don't be astonished, gentlemen, that I employ foreigners in the education of my children. To deliver youth unconditionally into the hands of foreigners is our greatest folly, which has been the source of all sorts of mischief to the Russian nobility: it is this which has made it almost a foreign colony in Russia, hardly knowing their mother tongue, nor its customs, nor its history, but taught from their infancy to love everything that is French and English, and despise everything that is Russian. But to employ foreigners under the supervision of parents is proper and commendable, if the people selected for that purpose are of a respectable moral character and behavior, and not seekers of adventures and charlatans. Without a knowledge of foreign languages a man can never acquire that refinement which is peculiar to Europeans. Other nations have got before us in the march of intellect, and have more means of keeping continually ahead of us in the career of science. To translate everything worthy of attention and curiosity which appears in foreign countries would be impossible. To contrive from the resources of our own minds everything which has already been discovered and invented would be ridiculous, so that it is necessary to adopt the easiest means of acquiring the immense empire of knowledge, and those means are an acquaintance with foreign languages. By knowing them, you become a citizen of the world: you must agree that you must first become a *man* before you are either a Frenchman or a Russian. I love Russia more than my life. I wish its happiness more than I do that of my own children, and am willing to sacrifice for her my own life and that of my children, my property, and all my earthly comforts; but it does not follow from this that I ought not to love foreigners, nor avail myself of the products of their minds and ingenuity. That would be a barbarism worthy of a Turk, a Chinese, or an Algerine. The first objects in the education of my children are the learning of their mother tongue, with the history and statistics of Russia; and my first and chief endeavor is to impregnate the minds of my children with an unlimited attachment to everything pertaining to their native country. That is my part of the business. Amidst all this I do not conceal from them that we have not yet arrived at that degree of refinement which is found in other nations: but, on the other hand, I excite a desire in their minds to improve their country, by the propagation of everything that is good and useful. The domestic education of my oldest son is now finished, and I intend next winter to send him to the university." We were called to the table, and Mr. Rossiyaninov put an end to his explanation.

The dinner consisted of four courses, prepared with taste and in abundance. The wine did not run over the brim, as they say; but after each course, every one of the company, except the children and ladies, had a large glass of excellent wine poured out for them.—Besides there were decanters of water, small beer, *kvass,* cider, and wine made of apples and berries which was an excellent drink, and sparkled like champagne, appearing to me much more agreeable than real wine. For a dessert we had beautiful ripe fruit. In addition to Mr. Rossiyaninov's family, the two teachers and ourselves, at the table were two retired officers, two old women, distant relations of the landlady and the parish priest. I observed with satisfaction that all the guests without exception were served alike, both in regard to eating and drinking. That is not always the case with gentlemen who give poor people a place at their table. Mr. and Mrs. Rossiyaninov, on the contrary, behaved to all with extreme civility, nor did the landlord show his wit at the expense of the poor people who enjoyed his hospitality. During dinner the conversation was of a general nature. After it was finished, we all went into the garden, and, waiting for coffee, took our seats under the shade of some dense lime trees. All at once the tears trickled from Milovidin's eyes. He drew upon him the attention of all, as well as their sympathy, and rather disconcerted our hosts. "You are melancholy," said the lady of the house. "No, madam; these are tears of contrition and not of melancholy. I am enraptured with your family happiness, the prosperity of your peasants, and the well-ordered condition of your estate, and rejoice that you are Russians." The landlord squeezed Milovidin's hand, and added, "What you say is true: we, or at least I, am happy in my family." Mrs. Rossiyaninov, in place of an answer, tenderly embraced her husband, and the children threw themselves about his neck, exclaiming, "Papa, you comprise all our happiness and all our joy!" One of the retired officers squeezed Mr. Rossiyaninov's hand; the other looked up to the heavens and crossed himself; the females went to kiss the hands of the worthy couple. An old servant who was bringing in coffee shed tears in silence. Mr. Rossiyaninov's heart was touched. "You see now whether I am happy," he exclaimed. "Can there be a greater bliss than that of being loved by worthy beings. Do not think, however, that my happiness has cost me much trouble. No! it is the kindness of Providence, for which I shall never cease to return thanks. I have endeavored only to fulfill my duty as far as I have been able, nothing more. If you have any curiosity, I will relate my history to you in a few words.

"My father was an officer in the navy and married for love, without having any means to support his family besides his pay. He remained in the service till he attained the rank of general, and owing to these circumstances could not give me and my sisters a splendid education. He attained riches by his bravery, taking some rich prizes in the Turkish war. His shattered constitution would not allow him to remain longer in the navy: he retired, bought this property, consisting of five hundred souls, and settled in the country. My sisters married as soon as their parents were able to give them a sufficient dowry. I entered the Guards, but had the misfortune to hurt myself in a fall from my horse, and was obliged by the doctor's advice to retire from the service. I was then no more than nineteen years of age. I was advised to live some years in a warm climate, to regain my strength and take the benefit of the mineral waters. I employed that time in educating myself, went through a regular course of study in the university of Bologna, and afterwards completed my education in Paris. Returning to my native country with renewed health and fresh accomplishments, I wished to be useful to my country in the civil service. At that time I had the misfortune to lose my parents, and was left a solitary individual in the world. After serving some years in a petty occupation, and seeing that neither my endeavors nor my zeal, nor, I may venture to say, capacity and higher abilities than those of my colleagues, were of any avail to raise me above the common herd, I began to cool in my zeal for the public welfare. An old friend of my father's, to whom I complained of my fate, cured me of my error, and pointed out to me the true road to happiness. "My dear friend!" said he to me one day, "you have no family connections, and do not belong to the number of those children of fortune whose entire value consists in the name; consequently you will always be doomed to support on your shoulders, amidst the chancery dirt which lies at the foot of the hill of fortune, the incapacity of others, that it may be crowned by your services. You must wait for some extraordinary opportunity, one of those fortunate configurations of the heavenly bodies described in the calendars, before the rays of the sun penetrate through the thick atmosphere of nepotism and shine upon you, a gentleman of no family. There are exceptions, I do not dispute; but to wait for such a chance requires an iron patience, which you do not possess. What is it that you seek? It is to be useful to your sovereign and country, is it not? You have the means in your own hands. You have five hundred peasants. Dedicate yourself to their happiness. Believe me, you would not have a long time to wait before the happiness of five hundred males, and probably as many females, would be dependent upon you. You are well-instructed, you have read and travelled much, and consequently have many capabilities for managing your estate, making your peasants happy, and what is more, being an example to others. Economy is not difficult, and your *starost* [village elder] with his own knowledge of local circumstances will be more useful to you than two courses of agronomy. The chief thing is to keep your expenses within your income, and to apply the balance which remains in your favor in the improvement of your own property, and of the condition of your peasants. Keep your wants within bounds, restrain your desires, and you will have a surplus revenue: apply this to what is useful, and it will bring you contentment, comfort, and happiness!" Like a man blind from his birth, who, when he first recovers his sight after a successful operation, is enchanted with the view of objects of which he had no previous conception, I recovered the use of my mental faculties through the prescription of my real friend. This is his daughter!" added Mr. Rossiyaninov, pointing to his wife. "I married, left the service, and settled on my estate. My father being old and infirm at the time when he retired to the country, could take no part in the management of his estate, and left it to me in the same condition as he had bought it. The fields were most wretchedly cultivated, the peasants in poverty, and in a half-savage state as regarded their moral condition. In the course of twenty years, with God's assistance, and the strenuous endeavors of myself and my wife, we have succeeded in bringing our property to the state in which you see it. I had no independent capital and carried on my improvements entirely from my income, by degrees, working as fast as I could without too much haste, and building upon a solid foundation. God has blessed my exertions. Now all the young people on my estate know how to read and understand their duty to God, the emperor, their master, and their equals. Without letters, gentlemen, it is impossible to implant morality in the minds of the people, or to give them a due conception of the duties which conduce to their real happiness. People cannot be instructed by the mere sense of hearing, and by dint of repeated practice, as poodles are drilled. Before a man can be instructed, he must be able to read: what he reads he will recollect, and besides, the time employed in reading is no misspending of what might be applied to more useful purposes; for the greater part of uninstructed people spend their leisure hours and days in irregularity. My peasants soon understood that I had their good in view, and assisted me in my object with heart and soul. In this I was also greatly indebted to our worthy clergyman, who, in the midst of all his poverty, behaved in such a manner that the peasants could not but respect him. He took no participation in their drinking bouts and amusements, but visited them only when he went to give them spiritual assistance, advice, admonition, or to perform his clerical duty. The reverend pastor ate his bread by the sweat of his brow, working with his own hands a small plot of ground; except for his legal provision, he would never take anything from the peasants. He settled disputes, never in his own person giving occasion for dissatisfaction; he never allowed in his presence any improper jokes, nor gave occasion for any himself. In a word, father Simeon was and is such a man as a parish clergyman should be—gentle, abstemious, humane, and serious in his behavior. You saw him at dinner, gentlemen. His condition is now improved, along with the condition of us all. I reckon it the first duty of a landowner to raise the clergyman to such a state that he can live independent of the peasants; he will not till then be respected by his parishioners, but can *then* proceed without fear in correcting their moral conduct.

"Following the advice of my father-in-law, I began the management of my estate, not after the English or German fashion, but after a fashion suitable to our climate, soil, and manners. I did not carry out any innovations on a great scale, till I had made repeated trials of their effects upon a small scale. At last we finished our buildings, improved our fields, and nothing remains for us to do now but to maintain what we have done."

We passed our time in the company of the worthy Mr. Rossiyaninov and his family in the most agreeable manner, and at sunset, departed for town, not, however, without being earnestly pressed by the landlord and landlady to remain. I made haste to return, as the next day was that on which the post would arrive, and I was quite impatient for letters from Moscow. We promised to come another time and spend several days with the worthy Aleksandr Aleksandrovich, and left him with a melancholy heart, as if we were leaving our father's house. When we got beyond the gate, Milovidin crossed himself, and raising his eyes to heaven, exclaimed: "God bless Russia, and grant her many more such landowners."

Translator's Notes

1. *Knyaz* is the highest title of Russian nobility, and corresponds to Duke in English, but is generally translated "Prince." As titles are extended to the whole family of those who possess them, it may be easily conceived that there is a considerable number of such princes in the Russian empire.

2. A maxim borrowed from the experience of one of the most celebrated nations of antiquity: see Exodus, chapter V.

3. A verst is two-thirds of an English mile.

4. Literally *court of words,* because in the ordinary courts of law the pleadings are carried on in writing. In towns the police majors preside at these courts of words, but when the subject contested amounts to more than eighteen rubles (about fifteen shillings sterling), their jurisdiction ceases. [In today's currency this amount is worth approximately five pounds British, or ten dollars American.—CR]

5. If the happiness of the laboring classes is to be measured by their physiognomy, the Russians will not stand high on the European scale.

6. A porch, or *seni,* as it is called in Russian, is almost indispensable to prevent the loss of the heat created by the stove.

7. Bark shoes plaited in the same way that list shoes are made in this country, but much clumsier: they are the covering for the feet most commonly used by the Russian peasants.

8. Being made of the bark of young birch trees.

9. One of the appellations given by the Russian peasants to their proprietor.

M. N. ZAGOSKIN

Yury Miloslavsky

Plot Summary, Part I

The novel begins with a description of Russia during the Time of Troubles. We first see two men lost in a snowstorm: Yury Miloslavsky and his servant Aleksey. They find and save an almost frozen Cossack, Kirsha. The three of them arrive at a tavern just as a conversation about politics among a soldier, merchant, and police agent is coming to a close. Since the tavern is crowded, Kirsha plays a trick on the trio by telling them that a fourth person among them is a criminal. This scares them away and Yury, Kirsha and Aleksey have a place to stay for the night.

The next morning an obnoxious Pole arrives and orders everyone about. Yury forces the fat Pole to eat an entire goose. After this Yury and Aleksey leave and Kirsha promises to follow. When Kirsha catches up with Yury, he tells his new friend that the Poles are after them. Yury and Aleksey leave and Kirsha remains behind to fight the ten Poles. Naturally Kirsha wins.

We return to Yury (see excerpts below). We find out how he came to love a girl in Moscow and that he is now on an errand from Pan (Mr.) Gonsevski to the house of Kruchina-Shalonsky. He is then to go to Nizhny to see what kind of treachery is going on against the Polish tsar. After Yury sees Shalonsky and leaves, the old man secretly calls his aide Omlyash. He then calls in the nanny to ask after his daughter, Nastenka, whom he wants to marry off to Gonsevski (a favorite of the king) in order to get honors for himself. When he hears of Nastenka's sad state, he calls for a wizard. Yury is now in his room daydreaming of Russia and a girl he has seen in church. Unbeknownst to Yury, the girl in Moscow loves him too and she just happens to be Shalonsky's daughter Nastenka.

Meanwhile Krisha escapes and hides in the home of a local sorcerer. Here he overhears the sorcerer and a woman plotting to dupe guests at a wedding reception. Kirsha goes to the wedding and exposes the plot. The locals take him for a better sorcerer. While Kirsha is telling tales of his journeys, someone summons him to Shalonsky's to try to cure Nastenka. This he does by telling her about Yury. The payment he asks from her father is that she not go to Moscow for six months and six days, thus delaying the girl's wedding to Gonsevski.

The next scene is a description of a gathering of Poles and local gentry. Here Yury appears, exposes the fat Pole from the tavern as a liar but refuses to toast King Sigismund. A *yurodivy* (a holy fool) comes in and disrupts the party. After he leaves, the music and fun begin.

Part II

On his way to question Shalonsky about Yury, Kirsha overhears a plot to ambush his young friend. After considerable delay and a number of adventures, Kirsha does meet up with Yury and Aleksey. Together they avoid the ambush. Kirsha also tells Yury about Nastenka. Before they part and Kirsha leaves them, the *yurodivy* appears and warns Yury of danger.

The next section describes the beginning of the revolt in Nizhny, the big demonstration where the butcher Minin rouses the crowd's patriotic fervor in urging them to go to war against the Poles. In the midst of all this Yury meets an old man who talks to him about the young man's father. In despair Yury goes to the shores of the Volga and meets Minin, who turns out to be the stranger at the inn whom we met at the beginning of the novel. They go to a meeting of the town elders, where Yury delivers his message from Gonsevski. They all jump on him for being a traitor, but Minin gives him a second chance. Yury then shows himself to be the true patriot he really is. Yury and Aleksey leave town but are ambushed by Shalonsky's men, who kill Aleksey.

Part III

Four months later a weary traveler meets a band of Cossacks. In this group is Kirsha, who recognizes the traveler as Aleksey! He tries to find out what happened to Yury. Aleksey tells how he was saved by a fisherman, but how he fears that Yury was cut up and thrown in the Volga, all because of the treachery of Turenin, at whose house Yury made his patriotic speech.

Kirsha goes off to find Yury. Meanwhile the scene switches to a conversation between Turenin and Shalonsky. Kirsha and his Cossacks arrive on the scene, save Yury, and put Turenin and Shalonsky into a dungeon.

Yury goes on to a monastery, where he tries to become a monk. But the abbot instead releases Yury from his vow to serve the Polish prince. Now Yury is free to fight with the Russian patriots. However, after the war he will return to the monastery according to the vow he took at the grave of St. Sergey. Yury then falls in with the priest Eremey, to whom a mob brings a young girl as captive. She turns out to be Nastenka, who sees Yury and thinks he took part in the murder of her father. She finds out that he did not. In order to save the girl, Eremey marries her to Yury and the newlyweds sneak off while the crowd drinks.

Meanwhile we find out that Shalonsky is not dead. He is saved by a passerby who turns out to be the *yurodivy*. The latter gets Shalonsky to repent on his deathbed through a Christian outpouring of love. In the meantime Yury is taking Nastenka to a monastery where she will be safe. On the way there Yury tells her of his vow and that he cannot be her husband.

After he leaves her Yury joins the battle, in which he is wounded. The Russians win. Kirsha finds Yury and brings the monk Avraamy to see him. They find a loophole and open the way for Yury to marry Nastenka in deed as well as in name. Later the Russians march triumphantly into the Kremlin.

Yury Miloslavsky

Part I, Chapter 7

We left Yury and his servant Aleksey in plain view of a whole crowd of Poles who thought that these two were their rightful booty; but they soon realized that they had miscalculated. In a few minutes our travelers lost sight of them. The incessant curves and turnings of the road, which often narrowed to the point where the two riders could not travel side-by-side, helped them conceal themselves from the pursuit of the horsemen, who in crowding together at the narrow places, got in each other's way and were unwillingly forced to stop. After they galloped for a few miles, our travelers began to rein in their horses and soon the total silence that surrounded them as well as the faintly audible, distant clatter of horses' hooves, convinced them that the Poles had turned around and that they had nothing to fear.

"Well, sir," said Aleksey, "our Lord had mercy on us!"[1]

"But poor Kirsha?"

"Yury Dmitrich! He's a nimble young fellow . . . And how could they ever catch him in such a dense forest?"

"But what if he's wounded?"

"Merciful God! I suppose he'll survive!"

"I'd give a lot to be able to believe that. Well, Aleksey, have you no shame? You suspected Kirsha of treachery . . ."

"I repent, sir, I sinned against him; but now I think . . ."

"What's that?"

"That he is not a *Zaporozhets*."[2]

"There are good people everywhere, Aleksey."

"And you, sir, very likely call even the Poles good people."

"Certainly; I know many I would wish to be like."

"And just like them pursue wayfarers in order to rob them?"

"A gang of Russian robbers or a crowd of Polish camp servants[3]—what does either one prove? No, Aleksey, I respect the brave and noble Poles. There will come a time when they will recall that in their veins flows the blood of our ancestors, the Slavs; perhaps our grandsons will embrace the Poles as their own brothers, and the two strongest lines of the ancient rulers of the entire north will merge into one great and invincible people!"

"Don't get angry, sir, but since you lived with those Poles you have become too wise and speak so beautifully that I don't understand one little word. But as you please, God only knows what lies ahead; but now it would be good if those uninvited guests took themselves back where they came from. Your dead father—God grant him the heavenly kingdom!—would not have let you think that way. After the death of our mistress, your mother, you were left alone with him—the apple of his eye—but nevertheless he used to say that it would be easier for him to see you, his only son, in an early grave than as the servant of a Polish king or the husband of a faithless Polish girl!"

"Husband! . . ." Yury repeated in an undertone, and a deep sorrow appeared on his face. "No, my kind Aleksey! The Lord did not grant me to be the husband of the one who touched my heart: so it's obvious that it's my fate to languish as an orphan forever."

"Oh sir, sir! More than one star shines in the sky, and there is more than one fair maiden in Holy Rus.[4] Are you still constantly thinking of that dark-eyed young *boyarina*[5] whom you used to see in Moscow at the Church of Our Savior of the Pines? You chose not to find out just who she was; you put it off and put it off and then she disappeared, vanished. For that matter, I say, should a youth such as you, sir, pine away from grief because of it? Just send out a call that you want to get married and you'll have to protect yourself from all of those wives, and perhaps . . . who can tell? . . . [there will be so many of them that] you won't be able to ride around the group of prospective brides, even with a horse . . . And you won't have to look, but you'll find your dark-eyed beauty."

"Wed to another! . . . No, it would be better never to see her than to see on her finger a wedding band which she exchanged with someone else!"

"What God ordains, will be. But now, sir, that's not the issue: what road should we take now? There are two of them here: into the forest on the right, out of the forest on the left . . . Oh, but fortunately here comes a fellow carrying brushwood. Hey, over here fellow! Which road will take us to the estate of the boyar Kruchina-Shalonsky?"

When he heard this formidable name the peasant doffed his hat, bent to the waist to the travelers and silently pointed to the left. After a half hour our travelers rode out of the forest and a long row of low huts built on the banks of a small river rose before their eyes. A wide cross-street led to a church; along the other side of the river on the slope of a hill rose the wooden roof and beautiful toll house[6] of the boyar's home, enclosed by a high paling like a fortified stockade. Around the manorial courtyard were scattered the huts of manor serfs, the stable, kennel, and large stockyard. All of these buildings with their annexes, storerooms and enclosures took up so much space that at first glance one would think it was a second village no smaller than the first. After they crossed the bridge secured by thick piles, our travelers climbed the hill and entered the vast courtyard of the boyar. The front facade of the main building was more than fifteen *sazhen*s[7] long, but the height of the house was as great as its length. Small square windows with red frames and many-colored shutters were separated by wide piers. At the end of the left side of the house there was a porch with an enormous awning held up by wooden pillars that were formed like today's carved balusters used sometimes for decorating the exterior of houses. On the right side of the house there adjoined a two-story tower which had almost twice as many windows as the other parts of the house. Along both sides of the fence were built long tables, a kitchen, cellars with a high pigeon coop; and in the center of the yard stood a hanging swing. We should point out to our readers that the proud boyar Kruchina was renowned for luxury and that for a long time already he had been reproached for his imitation of foreigners and for his obvious contempt for the simple customs of his ancestors; therefore a description of his house cannot give a true understanding of the way of life of the Russian boyars of that time. Their houses didn't astound anyone with their vastness or splendor: a large room called a *svetlitsa*[8] was separated from the dark hut by a spacious and warm *seni*[9] in which lived the housemaids; because of this they got the name of "*seni* girls." Sometimes a narrow and steep stairway led from the passage to the tower; around the house they built a cellar, stables, storerooms and bathhouses. That's a short but rather faithful description of the houses of the boyars and nobles of that time who strictly adhered to the old Russian proverb "A hut's not pretty because of its stoop, But pretty because of its soup."[10]

Going across the courtyard Yury noticed that major preparations were going on: servants were running back and forth; in the kitchen a blazing fire burned; several cooks bustled about a slaughtered bull; all of this led Yury to the conclusion that the boyar Kruchina was expecting guests. Those menials whom Yury encountered as he rode up to the porch looked at him in amazement: his crumpled and threadbare *okhaben*[11] in which he was wrapped from head to toe, Aleksey's unattractive clothes—in short, none of this warranted the impudence of the unknown guest who, contrary to the custom of simple folk, did not get off of his horse, but rode on horseback into the courtyard of the proud boyar. After he handed his horse over to Aleksey, Yury ascended the sloping staircase into a vast front room. Along the walls on wide benches sat about twenty serfs dressed in colored caftans; neatly hanging coats of mail, *berdyshi,*[12] bludgeons, sabres, and guns were the only decoration on the bare walls of this room. One of the servants, not rising from his place, asked Yury in a gruff voice whom he needed.

"The boyar Timofey Fyodorovich," answered Yury.

"And who sent you?"

In place of an answer Yury threw off his *okhaben*. His richly laced caftan and valuable sabre had a stronger effect on these ignoramuses than did Yury's noble appearance: they promptly jumped down from their benches and the one who asked the first question, now bowing politely, said that the boyar had not yet arisen and would it please the guest to wait; then he invited him to go into another room. Yury followed the servant into a vast square room, in the midst of which stood long oaken tables; along the walls were benches covered with gaily colored rugs. More than an hour elapsed and no one appeared. Since he had nothing to do, Yury began to inspect the portraits on the walls; these were fairly good according to the style of painting of the time. Almost all of them depicted Poles and one of them showed the Polish king in his crown and royal purple. The portrait was half-length, and the king was depicted leaning with his elbow on a table on which were lying a sceptre with a two-headed eagle and the crown of Monomakh,[13] holy to all Russians. Yury shook with indignation while he read the inscription in Polish: "Sigismund—Polish king and Russian tsar." Not even thinking about the consequences of this, his first rash action, he stretched his arm to tear the portrait from the wall, when suddenly the doors from the inner rooms opened and a neatly dressed man of about thirty walked into the room. After greeting Yury and announcing himself as one of the boyar's *znakomtsy,*[14] he asked what need the traveler had of the master.

"I must talk myself to Timofey Fyodorovich," answered Yury.

"He has no time: he is dispatching a messenger to Moscow."

"I myself have come from Moscow and I've brought him a document from Pan Gonsevski."

"From Pan Gonsevski? Oh, that's another matter! I beg your pardon! I will immediately report to the boyar. But permit me to ask: while you were there, perhaps they got the news in Moscow about the Polish king's glorious victory?"

"Which victory?"

"So you don't know? Smolensk was taken."

"Is it possible?"

"Yes, yes, that nest of rebels is now in our hands. The boyar, Timofey Fyodorovich, yesterday received a document from his friend, Andrey Dedeskin, a native of Smolensk who helped the king capture the city . . ."

"And probably wasn't rewarded as he should have been for such service?" said Yury, who hid his indignation with difficulty.

"Oh no! He is now in the king's good graces."

"I don't believe it: Sigismund does not tolerate traitors in his presence."

"What do you mean! What kind of traitor is he! When they took the city, the traitors and rebels all locked themselves up in the cathedral; beneath it was a powder magazine. They set fire to themselves and every last one of them perished. It serves them right! . . . But don't get angry, I'll go and inform the boyar about you."

"Loyal people of Smolensk!" said Yury when he was left alone. "Why couldn't I have perished along with you? You laid down your lives for your country, but I . . . I swore allegiance to the one whose father is ravaging the Russian lands like a fierce enemy!"

A loud cry ringing out in the courtyard distracted his gloomy thoughts for a minute; in the middle of the yard several servants were pouring water all over some hideous old man; shaking from the cold, grimacing and jumping about in a very strange fashion, the unfortunate creature was bellowing in a preposterous voice. Kind, sensitive Yury could not at all have figured out what this cruel joke meant if the loud laughter in the next room had not suggested to him that this was one of boyar Shalonsky's amusements. The loathing he felt for the master of the house doubled at the sight of this inhumane sport which finished when they dragged onto the tables the old man, blue from cold and barely alive. On the heels of this *funny* sight that very same boyar's *znakomets* walked in and invited Yury to go along with him. Crossing a small room, his guide opened doors covered in red cloth and led him into a room whose walls were covered with Dutch gilded leather. In front of a large table on a high carved chair sat a man of about fifty. A pale face bearing the stamp of strong unbridled passions; a sparse hoary beard and gray eyes which, glaring out from under a scowl, were ready to flare up with rage at the slightest contradiction—all of this taken together presented an appearance not in the least attractive. Hair shaved in the Polish fashion and a sash wound low around a long damask caftan gave him the appearance of a rich Polish *pan*;[15] but at the very same time a *feryaz*[16] with golden tabs worn unbuttoned over his caftan brought to mind the magnificent clothes of Russian boyars. It wasn't difficult for Yury to guess that he was seeing the boyar Kruchina before him. Bowing politely, he gave him Pan Gonsevski's letter which was tied with a silk ribbon.

"Have you been gone long from Moscow?" asked the boyar as he unrolled the letter.

"Eight days, Timofey Fyodorovich."

"Eight days! What a fine messenger my future son-in-law chose! Well, young man, if you were serving me and not Pan Gonsevski . . ."

"I serve only the Russian tsar, Vladislav," Yury interrupted coldbloodedly.

"Indeed! Well then, who are you, loyal servant of tsar Vladislav?" Kruchina asked derisively.

"Yury, son of the boyar Dimitry Miloslavsky."

"Dimitry Miloslavsky's! . . that stubborn, bitter enemy of the Poles? . . . And you're his son? . . . Well, it's all the same! . . . Sit down, Yury Dimitrich. How strange that Pan Gonsevski didn't find someone besides you to send to me."

"I undertook to deliver this document to you out of friendship."

"The son of the boyar Miloslavsky calls the Polish prince Russian tsar . . . calls Gonsevski his friend . . . Remarkable! So, has your father lost his mind?"

"He's been gone from this world a long time."

"So that's it! . . . Don't censure me, Yury Dimitrich: I will read what Pan Gonsevski writes in his letter to me."

Yury noticed that as he read the letter the boyar gradually got more sullen, annoyance and impatience showed on his face.

After he had read the letter, he said, "No, you're not going to divide the property with them! If it were up to me I'd wipe them out completely! I will plough and sow the place where that thieving god-forsaken little town stands! . . Here is what Gonsevski writes to me in his letter," he continued as he turned to Yury. "He heard a rumor that those tireless Nizhny-Novgorodians are stealthily recruiting an army, and so he desires that I send you to Nizhny to find out what's going on there and if it's possible, to force the main instigators to obedience, promising them the king's mercy. He says he's [Yury] the son of a Moscow boyar who is known for his hatred of the Poles; therefore his example can make these dunces understand. So when the son of Dimitry Miloslavsky kisses the cross [in allegiance] to the Polish prince, it will already be obvious that that is the way it should be."

"I am ready to carry out Gonsevski's commission with joy," answered Yury, "for I am sure in my heart that the election of Vladislav will save our fatherland from final destruction."

"Yes, yes," interrupted the boyar, "Pacify the rebels! Convince them! Wait until all these Nizhny cities belong to them, and then try to quiet them down. No, gentlemen Muscovites! We shall suppress the recalcitrants—not with tender words but with fire and sword. Gonsevski sent Pan Tishkevich here with a regiment; but you won't scare them with that. If only he had listened to me and sent a larger army; then Nizhny would have been razed to the ground a long time ago!"

"It's no fun, my lord, to cut off your left hand with your right; there's no joy in raising Russian against Russian. And how much Christian blood has been shed! Thousands of Orthodox believers lie dead near Moscow. And are not the prayers of those whose hands are covered with the blood of their brothers, not repugnant to Our Lord God?"

The boyar Kruchina gazed intently at Yury and with a mocking smile asked him when he planned on becoming a monk? and for what reason did he hook a sabre on his belt instead of rosary beads?

"The enemies of Russia already know that I know how to use a sabre, my lord," said Yury, "but only the Lord himself knows whether I will have the reward of being allowed to be a monk."

"And do you really think, you tender-hearted emissary of Gonsevski," continued the boyar, "that the people of Nizhmy will be as merciful to you and won't dare to do away with you, a traitor and servant of the Polish king?"

"And they would have done their part justly if I, Yury Miloslavsky, were a servant of the Polish king!"

"Oho, what a swell!.. You're really talking of high-blown matters!" said Kruchina, knitting his thick brows.

"Yes, my lord," continued Yury, "I serve not the Polish king but the Russian tsar, Vladislav."

"But isn't Sigismund his father?"

"His, but not ours. So thinks all Moscow, so think all Russians."

"Not so fast, young man, not so fast! Don't speak for everyone. You are still very young, you have no right to teach your elders; we know better than you what is most fitting for Russia. Today you'll rest, Yury Dmitrich, but tomorrow at daybreak you will set off on your journey: I'll give you a document for my acquaintance, the boyar, Istoma-Turenin. He lives in Nizhny, and I ask you to confer in all things with this man, who is wise and also experienced in such matters. First let them swear an oath only to Vladislav; but then . . . whatever God wills! It's not a long leap from the son to the father..."

"No, my lord, only when the Russians change completely."

"Fine, let's talk about that later. Just keep in mind Yury Dmitrich, that in a powerful storm it is not the small child, but the experienced helmsman who steers the damaged ship. But I have things to attend to . . . so, don't judge too severely . . . . Good-bye for now! Has Gonsevski lost his mind!" continued the boyar, following Yury out with his eyes, "to send me this youngster who continuously goes on and on about Vladislav and even about his fatherland! It's obvious that they're at their wit's end in Moscow! Fine, my young man! You'll go to Nizhny, and whatever you have on your mind, you won't fool me: you'll dance to my tune, or..."

The boyar whistled and asked the servant who entered whether his groom Ormlyash had returned from the city.

"He's just alighted from his horse, sir," answered the servant.

"Tell him not to show himself to anyone, but to come to me secretly through the garden gate and to be ready for departure. Go!.. And call Vlasevna to me."

In a few minutes an old woman of about sixty walked into the room; she was dressed in a silk *shushun*[17] and crimson cap edged in fur. After praying to the icon, she bowed low to the boyar and having calmly folded her arms, she awaited the bidding of her master in respectful silence.

"Well then, Vlasevna," asked the boyar, "are you going to make me happy? How's Nastenka?"

"The same, little father, Timofey Fyodorovich! She doesn't eat anything, she doesn't sleep at all; all night she dashes about the room, everything makes her sad—she herself doesn't know about what! I have asked her: 'What's wrong with you, my little one, what's wrong with you, my joy? What's to be done with you?' 'It hurts, mummy,'—that's the only answer; and only God knows what hurts!"

The boyar became thoughtful. A bad citizen can hardly be a good father; but even wild beasts love their children; however, the ambitious boyar saw in her a future wife of a favorite of the Polish king; for him she was the surest means to honor and power, which comprised the only object of all of his secret thoughts and impatient desires. He was quiet for a few minutes and then asked whether she had made use of the drugs the Polish doctor left for her before his departure for Moscow.

"Eh, eh, little father Timofey Fyodorovich," answered the old woman, shaking her head. "It seemed as if she got worse from those drugs. If you please, my lord, be angry with me if you wish, but I'm convinced that Anastasya Timofeevna got sick for a reason. No, my dear, she's not ailing without cause."

"What do you think, Vlasevna, is she ruined?"

"Ruined, little father, God sees that she is ruined!"

"I find that hard to believe; well, if nothing helps, then we can do nothing: go and have a talk with Kudimych."

"Even without your order, sir, I've already thought about having a word with him; they're even saying that allegedly some traveler here outdid Kudimych. So can't you order him, Timofey Fyodorovich, to appear before you? He's in the village now, feasting with the young people at Foma the bailiff's place."

"All right, go get him, let him look Nastenka over. And tell him: if he helps her, he can ask me for whatever he wants; but if he makes her worse, even though he's a wizard, he won't save himself . . . I'll flog him to death! . . Now go," continued the boyar as he rose, "In an hour, or maybe before that, I'll come to you to have a look at the invalid myself."

In the meantime the nobleman whose task it was to entertain Yury walked through the rooms and led him into a large chamber where there were several beds without curtains.

"Right here," he said, "rest the boyar's guests. Wouldn't you like to settle down or have a bite to eat? A man on the road always feels like eating."

"Thank you," answered Yury, "I'm not hungry, but I would like to rest."

"So I won't stand in your way, my lord; lie down and take a nap; dinner will be late today. Timofey Fyodorovich wants everything to be in shape to entertain Pan Tishkevich, who is arriving today with his regiment. Have a good sleep, Yury Dmitrich! And now I'll go and see whether they took care of your horses."

When he was left alone, Yury went to the window that had a view of the garden, or as they said then, kitchen garden; in our times it would not deserve such a humble name. Fifty-odd thick lindens, two or three patterned orchards of fruit trees, a large pond full of fat carp, a lot of currant and raspberry bushes and several beds of vegetables—that's what today's beautiful paths, pavilions, cascades and other surprises have replaced. It seemed to Yury that someone was walking in the garden along the fence between the bushes. He would not have paid any attention to this if the person had not resembled a wolf who wants to steal past in such a way that no one notices him; he walked along the snowdrifts because the position of the path in the garden was much too visible; he looked around in all directions, almost shyly. Because of the distance Yury could not examine his face, but he noticed that he was tall and built like a *bogatyr*. Because he wished to rest just for a little while, Miloslavsky lay down without undressing on one of the beds. In spite of his fatigue, he could not fall asleep for a long time: an inexplicable sorrow lay like heavy lead on his heart; all of his bright dreams, all of his joyous hopes for the freedom and happiness of his fatherland—everything that filled his soul with ecstasy was replaced by some kind of gloomy foreboding. The words of the boyar Kruchina, but most of all the taking of Smolensk, proved to him that the election of Vladislav had not put an end to Russia's calamity. Civil war, the triumph of the enemy and finally, the horrible truth of the enslavement of the fatherland rose in his imagination. Gradually the heart of the fiery youth beat stronger, the blood stirred in his veins; but fatigue overcame him: his eyes were closing, his dreams were clothing themselves in truth, and visions bore Yury into the first capital of the Russian tsardom. It seemed to him that the entire sky was covered with a heavy mist; that he, along with a crowd of bitterly weeping, ragged citizens of Moscow, went up to the Armory; that a red banner with the image of a one-headed eagle was unfurling. Yury glances away in horror . . . and here in front of him is the ancient Cathedral of the Savior of the Pines: the church doors are open wide, he walks in, and who is there hurrying to meet him? . . *She!* A quiet, barely audible whisper reaches his ears: "I have waited for you a long, long time, my betrothed! Let's hurry . . . the priest is ready; he is waiting for us at the lectern; let's go!" In quiet ecstasy Yury presses her hand to his heart . . . and they're already standing side by side . . . they are being handed the wedding candles . . . Suddenly a wild cry rings out at the door. A crowd of Poles bursts into the interior of the cathedral, and laughing unrestrainedly, they surround the bride; Yury looks for his sabre—it's not there; he wants to hurl himself at the villains, but his numb limbs won't obey. And with a cry of despair, without any strength at all, he falls on the cold church rostrum, loses his senses and again, as if waking up from a dream, he sees himself in the middle of Red Square.[18] Clear skies are above him . . . people throng all around . . . there is joy on everyone's face . . . quiet, charming singing rings out in the churches; in the distance towards the northeast the rising sun appears through a thin mist out from behind the walls of a holy cloister . . . *She* is near him again; there's a wedding band on her right hand . . . with a glance full of ineffable tenderness, she says to him: "Joy of my days, my darling! look, do you see the Russian sun rises? . . . Soon, soon our dear motherland will sparkle in its bright rays! . . . Look, it's chasing away the rest of the storm clouds, which in the distance darken in the west like a funeral pall . . ." But suddenly Yury again sees Polish soldiers, again he hears cries of despair . . . *She* again disappears and all alone, like a miserable orphan, he wanders along the deserted Moscow streets; or then in agonizing anguish he sits among feasting enemies and hears with horror the loud exclamations: "Long live Sigismund, Polish king and Russian tsar!"

Part III, Chapter 7

At ten o'clock at night on the very day when, because of an extraordinary coincidence, Miloslavsky broke the vow he made the night before—to devote the rest of his days to the single life—some poor traveler in a tattered gray caftan walked quickly along the Great Moscow road situated along the slope of a deep ravine overgrown with a dense forest. After he passed over a long and narrow bridge thrown across a thin water meadow, the traveler entered onto a small glade cut by a diagonal road. It was a moonlit night and in spite of the thick shade of the trees, it was easy to distinguish all objects. After he reached the crossroad, the traveler stopped, shuddered and stepped back in horror: lit by the full moon, the whole right side of the glade was covered with heaps of dead bodies. Struck by this unexpected sight, the traveler stood motionless in one place for several minutes, when suddenly a weak, barely audible moan reached his ears, and at that moment it seemed to him that in the midst of this large pile of bodies, at the very spot where the diagonal road went out onto the glade, with effort someone raised his head, sighed heavily and dropped it back on the ground. Going a little closer the traveler saw that this unfortunate person, covered with deep wounds, was the only one out of all of them who still preserved some signs of life. At the same time that the philanthropic stranger, who ostensibly wished to help the wounded man, thoughtfully bent over him, he moved again and turned his face to the side and the moon illuminated it.

"Oh righteous God!" cried the stranger, who stepped back and crossed himself, "it is he! it's that arrogant and powerful boyar!.. And so some of your longsuffering is fulfilled, Lord!... But he's breathing... he's still alive... Oh, if only this unfortunate creature could make his peace with you! But how can I bring him to?.." added the traveler after he glanced around. "The forester's hut isn't far from here... I'll try there..."

He raised up a bit the wounded man, whom the reader has probably already recognized as Kruchina-Shalonsky, put him over his shoulders, and bending under the load, went along the diagonal road; at the end of the road a scarcely noticeable, dim fire flickered through a thicket of trees.

At almost the very same time Miloslavky and his wife were riding out of Kudinov's village; their escort the Tatar Temryuk rode in front of them and Aleksey and a servant girl behind them. While they could still hear loud cries and joyous songs, Anastasia observed a deep silence, and shuddering at every new, joyous exclamation which echoed behind them, she nestled up to Miloslavsky with trepidation. But when everything grew silent about them and when the pale glow from the blazing bonfires, around which feasted the rowdy crowd of what seemed to her to be her executioners, began to die out gradually, she began to breathe more freely and finally said in a timid voice full of charm:

"You are silent, Yury Dmitrich!.. Utter just one little word... Ah! one tender word from you, one greeting from you could lighten an unfortunate orphan's grief."

"Anastasia!" answered Yury in a quiet voice, "I'm an orphan myself and is it my place, when I am so bitter and wretched, to comfort you in your misfortune, when there is no comfort for me in all the wide world?.. Oh, the Lord did not unite you and me for joy!"

"Not for joy!.. No, Yury Dmitrich, I don't want to anger God: with you, even sorrow will be a joy to me. You would still not have known, nor would have ever known, if you were not my husband now, that I have loved you for a very long time. Asleep and awake, I was never away from you... you were always my betrothed. When that villainess, anguish, wearied my heart, I thought of you; and your image, like a comforting angel, poured consolation into my soul. Now you are mine, and if you also love me..."

"Do I love you!.." cried Miloslavsky, "You!.. Oh, Anastasia! do you remember, in Moscow, at the Church of Our Savior of the Pines? I didn't know who you were when I saw you for the first time, but my heart began to throb from joy... It seemed to me that I met you after a long separation, that I knew you for a long time... that I couldn't help but know you! Unfortunate creature! I forgot everything... forgot that I was standing in God's temple... an unfinished prayer died on my lips... No! I sinned even more: in my madness I prayed not to the images of the holy saints... Anastasia! I saw only you! Thus did I anger the Lord and so I must bear my bitter lot without a murmur; but you were praying, Anastasia! God's paradise burned, shone in your eyes, which were turned to the holy icons... I saw clearly: no earthly thoughts clouded your soul... the awful sin of profanation of a holy object does not burden you... For what reason, then, is the Lord punishing both of us?"

"Don't sin, Yury Dmitrich! What's the purpose of this rash grumbling. The Almighty visited us with grief, we are both orphans; but has He really abandoned us forever? And should we tempt His mercy at the very moment when He, feeling pity for us, has joined us forever?"

"Forever!" repeated Yury in a low voice, "Oh, Anastasia!"

"Yes, my dear, loving friend! only death can separate us . . . Give me your hand, joy of my days, my darling! . . It's true, isn't it, that you will never abandon your Anastasia . . . Do you feel," she continued in a voice full of ineffable tenderness, pressing Yury's hand to her bosom, "do you feel how my heart beats? . . It lives through you! And if someday you stop loving me . . ."

"Never! Never!" whispered Yury, covering her trembling hand with ardent kisses.

"My priceless one! . . My deliverer! . . Oh, how sweet my life has become again! This is your gift, my sweetheart! it all belongs to you! . . Oh! tell me yet again that you love me!"

"More than anything in the world!" cried Miloslavsky, who momentarily forgot the whole horror of his situation.

"And you can grumble against Divine Providence? . . and I dare to call myself an orphan when you are my husband? . ."

Yury shuddered as if he had just awakened from a deep sleep.

"Your husband! . ." he repeated, quickly jerking away his hand in horror.

"What's wrong with you, my sweet friend?" asked Anastasia in a timid voice.

Yury did not answer at all.

"You are silent? . ." she continued, "Oh, talk, Yury Dmitrich, tell me in what way I could have angered you?"

Miloslavsky finally answered, "Anastasia, I won't grumble . . . I resign myself to the will of the Almighty; but we are unlucky, my friend, very unlucky!"

"Not while you call me your wife . . . while I belong to you . . ."

"But do you know, ill-fated orphan . . . Oh well! why put it off! . . why torment you with slow death! . . Anastasia! . . I am not your husband!"

"You're not my husband? . . But didn't you circle the marriage lectern with me? . . Didn't I exchange this ring with you? . ."

"In order to save you I had to do it; but I cannot be anyone's husband."

"You can't?"

"No, Anastasia! Yesterday, over the grave of St. Sergius, I swore to leave the world and vowed that at the end of the battle, I would don the robes of a monk."

"Merciful God! . . O cruel person, why then didn't you let me die?"

"Listen to me, Anastasia, and don't judge me!"

Yury began to relate how he had loved her, not even knowing who she was; how an unfortunate incident revealed to him that his stranger was the daughter of the boyar Kruchina; how, having lost hope of being her husband and bound to the oath which prevented him from rebelling against the enemies of his fatherland, he decided to renounce the world; how he took the vow of a monk and obeying the will of his mentor Avraamy Palitsyn,[19] set off from the Trinity Monastery to fight near Moscow's wall for the orthodox faith; finally how he arrived at the village Kudinovo and why he had to call her wife. With unusual firmness she heard out his entire story; but when he finished, she muffled herself in her veil, began to sob, and bitter tears flowed like a river from her eyes. Yury continued to ride silently near her; several times he wanted to renew their conversation, but the words died on his lips; and what could he say to comfort the unfortunate, bitter orphan?

In the distance a fire gleamed; Termyuk stopped his horses and, turning to Yury, said:

"Do you see, my lord? . . there, beyond those trees? . . that's the Khotkov monastery. Methinks you can get there now without an escort; the road is direct; and it's time for me to rest. I haven't closed my eyes once in two whole days."

Yury let his escort go and within a quarter of an hour our travelers arrived at the monastery gates. They knocked for a long time until the gateskeeper heard; finally the gate opened and a monastery servant, rubbing sleepy eyes, asked in an angry voice:

"Who's there?.. What kind of nightowls are you?..." But recognizing Anastasia, he cried from joy and ran to inform the Father Superior about her. The travelers got down from their horses. Anastasia was silent. Yury was silent too; but when the gates opened a few minutes later and they had to part, all of their resolution disappeared. Anastasia fell sobbing on Miloslavsky's chest.

"Farewell, my deliverer!" she said sobbing, "good-bye forever!"

"Forever!.. No, Anastasia!" cried Yury, holding her in his arms, "when we both awake from our heavy earthly dream to life everlasting, then we will see each other again!... And there where neither tears nor sighs exist, there—o sweet friend!.. I will call you wife again!"

Anastasia tore from his embrace. The heavy gates creaked, the metal lock started to bang shut, the doorkeeper slammed the gates; and after he jumped on his horse, Yury darted off in a whirlwind from the walls of the cloister in which he had buried his earthly happiness in a silent grave forever.

For a while let's leave Yury, who hurried off to drown his agonizing sorrow in blood—his own or his enemies'; and let's go to the hut, where, showered with curses and branded with the disgraceful name of traitor, the onetime strong and famous boyar, now a homeless sufferer forsaken by the whole world, fought against death. Half sunk in the earth, lit only by a single wax candle-end which burned before the icons, the forester's hovel was at the moment the last earthly dwelling of the rich boyar Kruchina, who was used to living in tsarist splendor. A few pieces of straw thrown on the bench replaced his luxurious downy bed, and instead of a crowd of submissive slaves, one poor beggar, covered in rags and tatters, sat at the head of his bed. Sighing heavily, the dying man came to from his unconsciousness and opened his eyes; for a few minutes his weak lifeless sighs left him motionless; finally he gradually began to distinguish objects around him. With great effort he raised his hand and silently lifted it to his lips, which were clotted over with blood. The beggar gave him a cup of water; having slaked his thirst, the boyar uttered in an indistinct voice:

"Where am I?"

"In the hut of a kind man," answered the beggar.

"Who is speaking to me?"

"It is I, Fyodorych, Mitya..."

"Where are my servants?"

"Your servants!.. Poor fellow!.. You freed them all, Fyodorych!"

"Where is my daughter?"

"What?.. then she, the dear one, was with you?.. My sweetheart!.. Well, Fyodorych, misfortunes never come singly!"

"Oh, I'm beginning to remember ... murderers!.. So ... they murdered her!.. villains! But I'm still alive?.. Why?.. For what reason?"

"What do you mean, why, Fyodorych?.. Just think it over well. They surely didn't catch your daughter unawares: like a pure little dove she was always ready to accept her bridegroom.[20] But what would you have even begun to do, unfortunate creature, if God had not been merciful and had not given you time to put yourself in order and even to break off with your friends? And look around, Fyodorych, look how many of them are right behind you! pride, malice, dishonesty, murder, and all kinds of profanity ... Eh, Fyodorych! don't destroy yourself, my dear, repudiate these friends, don't take them with you! You know, the doors to heaven aren't large—you won't crawl through them with such a crowd!"

Shalonsky's pale cheeks flushed; it seemed as if all of his strength returned; he raised himself halfway up and, fixing a wild look at Mitya, said in a hard voice:

"What are you talking about, *yurodivy?*[21] What do you want from me?.. Repentance?.. No!.. it's too late for that!.. If everything I believed in as a child is true, then my sentence has been decided a long time ago!"

"Oh, Fyodorych, Fyodorych! Who told you that?"

"Yes, if of two roads I chose one and walked along it all of my life, then can I really turn again at the crossroads just before death?"

"Can you?" interrupted Mitya, and his eyes glistened with an unusual fire, and the timid grandeur of a righteous man showed forth on his brow, which expressed only openheartedness and peace. "Can you?" he repeated in an inspired voice: "Insignificant, frail creature! Is it for you to set limits to God's mercy? Is it for you to measure the infinite love of the creator for his creation?.. So! given over to slyness and deceit, nourished with innocent blood, from your youth you walked the path of lawlessness; they bemoan your acts in heaven; but you are worse than the thief who, dying, said, 'Remember me, lord, when you are in your kingdom!' And scarcely had these words flown out of the mouth of the murderer, when his name was already inscribed in heaven! Washed in the blood of the Savior, his soul had scarcely disappeared on high when the Redeemer himself already hurried to meet him! Turn your grieving face to our father, wish only to be together with Him and He will already be with you and will already be in your soul!.."

Just as a weary traveler, faint with thirst on a hot day, swallows greedily each drop of beneficent rain pouring on his head, so too the dying man listened to his comforter's words, full of Christian love. The boyar's heart, long buried in crime, began to beat in repentance; with every new word of the *yurodivy,* his face changed, and finally the last, terrible struggle of vice, bitterness and strong passions was depicted on his pale half-dead face—the struggle with his soul, now pierced with the first light of heavenly paradise.

"How is this!" he said after an extended silence, "you, whom I banished from my home in disgrace... at whom I swore, whom I showered with curses... who should hate me... desire my eternal ruin..."

"Your ruin!.. Ah, you don't know... you have not yet partaken of the sweetness of Christian love, my lord ... Your ruin!.. Let the Lord take the rest of my days in exchange for one moment of your spiritual repentance! But what am I saying ... insane person that I am! Is my insignificant sacrifice needed in order to move to mercy Him, who is infinite love ... who is already filling your soul, my lord?.. So I see the paradise of the Most High in your dimming eyes! Are you crying?.. Cry, my lord, cry! These tears ... oh, great the heavenly emissaries!.."

Who can describe the feelings of a dying sinner when God's finger touches his soul? He saw all of the abomination of his former deeds; they were repugnant to him, he hated himself; however, hope and love, not despair, filled his soul.

"Merciful God!" he cried out, pouring forth streams of tears, "why can't I prolong my disgraceful life?.. Why can't I, sick, suffering, covered with sores, rejected by all, scorned by everyone, why can't I blot out even a hundredth part of my serious transgressions in prolonged repentance!.."

"They are already gone, my lord!" said an ecstatic Mitya, "your tears washed them away... the first tears of a repentant sinner... oh! what joy, what celebrations they are preparing in heaven, when even I, a cursed, unworthy sinner, hiding pride and vanity under these poor tatters, cannot find the words to express my joy!"

Weakened by this severe spiritual shock, the boyar Kruchina lowered himself onto his bed; the precursor of imminent death, a feverish chill, ran through all of his body . . .

"Mitya, Mitya!" he said with a catch in his voice, "my end is near . . . I am growing weak! . . . If my daughter has not perished, find her and take her my sinner's blessing . . . I feel that the lamp of my life is going out . . . Oh, if only I could die the death of a Christian, like an orthodox believer . . . If only the Lord would consider me worthy . . . No, no! . . Is a murderer and villain worthy to touch with his unclean lips . . . oh, my guardian angel! Mitya! . . pray for a repentant sinner!"

Suddenly someone knocked at the window.

"Who's there," asked Mitya.

"A priest from the village of Nikolsky," answered an unfamiliar voice.

"A priest," cried the *yurodivy.*

"Yes, my kind man! I'm going somewhere to perform the rites for the dying, and I lost my way; could you take me to the main road?"

"Do you hear, Timofey Fyodorovich? Do you still doubt God's mercy! Come in, father, there is also a dying man here."

"Mitya!" cried Kruchina, "raise me up! help me get up . . . No, leave me . . . I feel enough strength within . . ."

The boyar raised himself up, his face turned a vivid red, his greedy eyes, turned to the door of the hut, burned with impatience . . . The priest entered, and in a few minutes the meek joy and peace of a righteous man were depicted on the renewed face of one who has made peace with heaven: the Lord allowed him to say the prayer: "Today, Son of God, accept me as one of yours." He joined his redeemer; and when his eyes closed forever, Mitya honored his "dust" with a final kiss and said in a quiet voice:

"Farewell, Timofey Fyodorovich! rejoice in the heavenly kingdom, you who were chosen for the glorification of ineffable divine mercy! You lived like a villain and ended your life like a just man . . . Happy is your fate: the great mystery of redemption was acted out over you! . . ."

Translator's Notes

1. Aleksey calls Yury *boyarin,* that is, nobleman. I render this as "sir."

2. A Cossack.

3. Servants of a low order.

4. Rus' is the ancient name for Russia.

5. A noblewoman.

6. The word Zagoskin uses here is *terem,* which means tower. However, during ancient times *terem* also meant toll-house.

7. A Russian measure of length equal to 2,134 meters.

8. A small, bright room in the upper floors of a house.

9. A cool sleeping room used especially in the summer.

10. Literally the proverb is: "A hut is not pretty because of its threshold, but is pretty because of its *pirogi.*" *Pirogi* are pastries filled with various foods such as meat, cabbage, mushrooms and even fruit. I changed the translation in the text to convey the rhyme of the original.

11. Old Russian roomy outerwear which resembles a caftan and has a square turned-down collar and long, straight, often folded sleeves.

12. An ancient side-arm, a battle-axe with a blade shaped like an elongated half-moon, mounted on a long pole.

13. The crown of early tsar, Vladimir Monomakh, and a sign of the office of tsar.

14. At that time poor nobility who lived in the boyar's home were called *znakomtsy*: they ate at the boyar's table and engaged him in domestic conversation. (*Author's note.*)

15. In old Poland the title of someone in the nobility. It now is the Polish equivalent of "mister."

16. Ancient Russian, loose outerwear for both men and women. It had no collar and was gathered at the waist.

17. A piece of ancient Russian woman's clothing resembling a loose top, short fur jacket or even a sarafan, but without a collar and hanging sleeves.

18. The Russian word for red [*krasny*] earlier meant beautiful.

19. A monk at Trinity Monastery during the Time of Troubles and a chronicler of that era.

20. Death.

21. A holy fool. People believed that the fools' feeblemindedness was a sign that they were God's chosen people and that they had special powers.

A. A. PEROVKSY-POGORELSKY

The Convent Girl

Plot Summary

Instead of supplying a foreword, the narrator tells us that he is on a trip, and adds for the reader who may want to know where he is going, that he is on his way to a neighbor's to be godfather at his child's christening. On the journey he has trouble with a stationmaster, gets soaked to the skin and must spend the night in a peasant's hut. The bugs keep him awake and he needs something to read. He looks around and finds a packet of letters from a schoolgirl at the Smolny Institute to her friend Masha. A woman traveler (Anyuta) left them behind. (See below, chapter 2.)

The narrator tells us Anyuta's life story. Her mother died in childbirth and her father makes the nasty, fake benefactor, Klim Sidorovich Dyundik, her guardian. After her father dies Anyuta goes to live with her aunt, and Klim Sidorovich forgets about her. But Aunt Anna Andreevna sends Klim the will in which Anyuta's father makes him the girl's guardian. Klim thinks of the advantages of taking the child in (namely, he can brag that he is bringing up a poor orphan), but his wife, Marfa Petrovna, is against the idea. They finally decide to send her to Smolny Institute in Petersburg. Aunt Anna is unhappy, but the alternatives are worse. So Anyuta goes off to Petersburg and we see her at school and at her friend Masha's house.

By way of contrast we next see her back in the Ukraine with her aunt and cousins and find out more about her romance with Blistovsky. (See below, chapter 6.) Just as the family is sitting down to celebrate Anyuta's engagement, Auntie remembers that only Klim Sidorovich can grant Anyuta permission to marry. She decides to send him a note, but Blistovsky decides to go in person to ask for Anyuta's hand. Blistovsky realizes that he knows Klim Sidorovich and has doubts about a felicitous outcome. He promises to tell us why.

He recounts Blistovsky's adventures at a horse fair some time before. A gypsy leader is trying to sell horses, but Blistovsky sees nothing of value until, on his way out, he spots a fine group of horses. But Klim Sidorovich tries to talk him out of buying the horses and begins instead to tell Blistovsky about his daughters and their proficiency in French (what juxtaposition!). When Blistovsky finally goes back for the horses, he finds out that the gypsy has already bought them for someone else. He then goes to dinner at Dyundik's.

At dinner the girls speak a variety of French comprehensible to them and their teacher alone. Blistovsky doesn't understand a word. Later at a meeting, the girls hear Blistovsky speaking French and they think that he is making fun of them. The next day Blistovsky "exposes their French" to Dyundik, who fires their teacher.

Back at the fair we hear many stories that have nothing to do with Anyuta. Blistovsky gets into a fight with a character named Pryzhkov because the latter squirts water at an old lady. After the fight Blistovsky learns that Pryzhkov is Marfa Petrovna's nephew. Blistovsky flees, loses his way, and finds himself in the camp of a gypsy who confesses to having bought those fine horses at the fair for Klim Sidorovich.

This flashback takes us to the moment when Blistovsky arrives at Klim Sidorovich's front porch. The Dyundiks think he has come for Vera, their daughter. They even try to ward off Pryzhkov. But trouble breaks out when Blistovsky asks for Anyuta's hand. Needless to say, he goes back to Barvenovo empty-handed. So ends part one.

Klim Sidorovich next pays a visit to Barenovo to take Anyuta home with him. Everyone stalls him for a bit, and Auntie says that she will go along with him and Anyuta. But Praskuta, her daughter, is sick; so Auntie must stay behind. The night before departure, Praskuta warns Anyuta not to go. But Anyuta does go off with Klim and Klara Kashparovna, the neighbor who brought Anyuta back to Barvenovo from Petersburg.

The welcome Anyuta receives is a real contrast to her homecoming at Barvenovo. Marfa Petrovna is decidedly cold. She begins to machinate against Anyuta by sending Klara away, inviting Pryzhkov to dinner, and generally making the young girl very unhappy. Klim Sidorovich shows Anyuta the will, which states that Anyuta is cursed if she marries against Klim Sidorovich's wishes. (Here the narrator hints broadly that this part of the will is a forgery.) Anyuta reluctantly gives in and goes to her room. That night Anyuta hears a sound outside her room and is faced with an apparition which hands her a note. It turns out to be a letter from Klara.

Because of this occurrence and the fact that the "apparition" killed their dog, the Dyundiks decide to go off to a secret hut in the forest. They also try to get Anyuta to consent to marry Pryzhkov, but she says that she need not do that because the will does not tell her whom to marry.

We next see them all—Anyuta, Dyundiks, Pryzhkov, servants—at a spooky hut in the forest. They spend a few days there but everyone is jumpy. One night Anyuta gets a note planning her escape. It turns out that the note is from Pryzhkov, who wants to carry her off. Anyuta runs away, but her screams are to no avail. Pryzhkov chases her, someone throws a sack over his head, he lets go of Anyuta, who tries to run away. But then somebody grabs her and she faints.

Now we go back to Aunt Anna Andreevna. They all wonder why Anyuta is gone so long. They really panic when Klara returns alone. The next day Blistovsky arrives and he and Auntie decide to go after Anyuta. Because of the help of a couple of *dei ex machina*—the gypsy and the ex-French tutor—Blistovsky rescues Anyuta and takes her home.

Before he leaves us, the narrator ties up the loose ends: Marfa Petrovna reads the news of Anyuta's marriage and dies of anger; Klim Sidorovich stays at home ready to regale visitors with stories of his non-existent hospitals; Pryzhkov hangs himself in Paris (probably) because of gambling debts; Anyuta and Blistovsky live happily; Auntie visits often and treats Anyuta's two boys as if they were her own grandchildren; Klara practically lives with the Blistovskys; the travelling narrator lives happily with his wife Agafya Alekseevna, known to us as Gapochka. Praskuta is not yet married but there is reason to believe she will be soon. The French tutor is teaching again and his only sorrow is that the narrator won't let him teach his sons French. Blistovsky obtains the gypsy's freedom from Klim Sidorovich and the gypsy is doing well at fairs and markets and often visits the narrator's family.

The Convent Girl

Chapter II: "Continuation"

First Letter

Oh, Masha, sweet Masha! Here I've already spent a whole week at my aunt's in Little Russia[1] and haven't grown used to it at all! What lies ahead in my future—I don't know!—but now it seems to me that I will never get used to this kind of life or to these people! Asleep and awake I dream of Petersburg, and the Neva, and the institute,[2] and you, my sweet friend! and R**, and S**, and F**, and all of you kind, unforgettable dear little friends of mine! Ah, Masha! write to me; do not forget that we promised to love each other forever, even when we were in *mocha shades!*[3] And then how many times did we renew our promises when we were in *blues* and *whites*! Don't forget this, my Masha! And now I have need of your friendship even more than ever before; I feel completely alone here; the whole world seems to have abandoned me, or maybe I am living in another world!—But you still really don't know why I'm so sad here, do you?

During the whole journey from Petersburg to Barvenovo, though I constantly thought about the institute, nevertheless I pondered over my imminent meeting with my relations with pleasure. I so wanted to see my aunt and my *cousines*.[4] (By the way, here I'll call them my cousins.) I fancied that my auntie would be like A**, but I imagined my cousins in the following way: the elder one like N** (who has now entered the teachers' school), the younger one like you, my Masha, or at least like R**. How I was mistaken in my calculations!

We arrived in Barvenovo rather early in the morning.

"This is Barvenovo!" said the woman whom they sent [to fetch] me in Petersburg; [she said this] with a very merry expression on her face.

I hurriedly stuck my head out of the carriage to see as quickly as possible this Barvenovo which was so praised along the way . . . Oh, Masha! I'm ashamed to confess . . . I thought that Barvenovo would even be a litttle like Tsarskoe Selo[5] or at least like Kamenny Island;[6] but instead of that—would you believe?—not even a little, little bit like them! I saw a great number of low, small houses: instead of roofing, blackened straw was thrown about on top any which way . . . None of them had chimneys, Masha, but others hung over so on one side that it was frightful to look . . . The streets were narrow, crooked and dirty!

"So this is Barvenovo!" I thought and my heart began to pound exactly the way it did at the institute right before an examination. Children and women were running out of their little houses: the former wore tattered shirts, but the latter were also wearing almost nothing but shirts, only here they wear a type of apron—in a red, blue and green checkered pattern. They bowed low (to me or the carriage—I don't know); and the men who were there also removed their caps and bowed. You probably think, dearest Masha, that the peasant men here are just like the coachmen in Petersburg or perhaps like the Finns who sell butter there? Absolutely not. They wear long white caftans and the same kind of caps . . . I haven't seen any hats here at all; but their heads, *ma chère,* are completely shaved, only a topknot is left. However, they seem to be *so kind!*

We rode across a narrow dyke and across a bridge which was still narrower and besides had no railings; we turned to the left and rode into the courtyard, right up to the porch. The courtyard was full of people; they were all running behind the carriage and crying out: "Here's our little lady, here's our little lady!" The women and children who had followed us from our very arrival in the village, stopped at the street and watched us through the gates. On the porch stood a tall, fat, gray-haired little lady wearing a large man's cap and a red woolen skirt; a calico kerchief, which scarcely covered her shoulders, was thrown about her neck. Masha! her feet, her feet were bare! She gave me her hand, kissed me right on the mouth and said: "Wonderful, Galechka! How you have grown!"[7]

Masha! don't show anyone my letter: this lady was—my aunt! (Here no one calls me Anyuta . . . auntie and my cousins call me Galechka, some of them call me little miss, but others all call me Ganna Trokhvymovna,[8] after my father. They say that it's all the same whether I'm Anyuta or Galechka, but I don't like it . . . please, sweet Mashenka, don't ever call me Galechka.)

We went into a room, not very large, but tidy and in order: I would have liked it had it not been so low: it felt stuffy to me! My cousins ran in almost right after her. "And these are my daughters," my aunt said to me, "this is Praskuta and this is Gapochka!"

They were in morning dress, that is, their hair was tied with a wide black ribbon and they were wearing black coats, no corsets and—please Masha! don't tell anyone!—large leather boots! However, they are *so kind!* I especially like Gapochka. They look very much alike and are not bad-looking, but are too fat and rosy-cheeked. In the whole institute there is no one as fat and rosy-cheeked as my cousins.

We very quickly got to know each other. God knows how happy they were that I arrived. They asked about Petersburg, about the institute, about the balls—even I grew tired of my tales. Then I had to show them all of my dresses—if only you could have heard them here! They don't like the fashionable new sleeves; and they really shouldn't wear gossamer sleeves; their arms are so red! Most of all they liked my feathered hat—you know, the one from Mme Xavier! They have many more clothes than I, but only tasteless ones! They have enough pearls and diamonds, but all in old settings. I advised auntie to send them to Petersburg to Monsieur Duvalier or to Rempler, but she doesn't want to hear of it. "What are you saying, Galya!" she said to me, "you've gone off your head!" (It seems that in local dialect this means: you've gone crazy.)

After dinner my cousins took me around the farm. They showed me the winery, mill, granaries. storehouses, and the barn where they fatten the pigs. Masha! how fat they are! My cousins know farming well; they say that I must also learn about it . . .

More than anything, I've had enough of the language in which they express themselves here. Can you believe that I understand almost nothing? Early yesterday evening I was sitting in my room and reading a book; on the porch auntie was conversing with the distiller. Don't you know what a distiller is, Masha? It's a Jew who makes wine. They were talking a lot about *barda* . . . I didn't understand anything, but only heard auntie say: "Save the *barda,* save the *barda!"*—and the Jew answered, "Why wouldn't I save it, ma'm; the *barda* is beautiful, the *barda* is excellent!" In Petersburg I read the works of Zhukovsky and remembered that he talks about bards . . . in my distracted state, I somehow imagined that the *barda,* whom they so praised, had to be the wife of some bard or poet . . . and as soon as the distiller left, I ran up to auntie and asked her to introduce me to the *barda.* "And what would you make of it!" auntie replied. "I reckon that some people warsh with *barda* so that their hide gets white . . ." Ah, Masha! how ashamed I was when I found out what *barda* really is! Here *barda* is something other than it is in Petersburg: here that's what they call the sediment which remains on the bottom when they make wine!

But perhaps you didn't understand auntie's words? If I translate them into Russian, this is what she told me: "But what would you do with it? I heard that people wash with *barda* to get their skin whiter..." Warsh, in Little-Russian means wash, and they call my skin—hide. Masha!

But I think you've enough of my letter and Little Russian speech. The next time I'll write to you as if auntie speaks Russian. Farewell, dear Mashenka! greet R** and S** and kiss F** for me. I'll write you with the next post.

P. S. I forgot to tell you that auntie doesn't walk barefoot all day, and that my cousins wear boots only in the mornings, especially when the courtyard is muddy. They usually dress quite properly for dinner: auntie wears a dark silk kerchief on her head, almost like our merchants' wives, only in a different style; and my cousins have enough dresses and almost are all new, only the waists are too short and they always go around without corsets. I offered them mine, but they don't fit—too narrow. Farewell, dearest Mashenka!

Second Letter

Well, another week has gone by since I arrived here, dearest Mashenka. O Petersburg! I shall never forget you. What a difference between Petersburg and Barvenovo! I succeeded in getting acquainted with our neighbors—and rather quickly at that. Here it's not like it is in the capital, Mashenka: when you're introduced to someone here, no one takes it lightly! Guests usually come around ten o'clock in the morning and stay until quite late at night, and sometimes even to the next day. Here you can't take a long time getting acquainted! You sit together from morning 'til night, going over everything that's in your soul. *A propos, ma chère!* how many souls [serfs] do you have? I still don't know, and you yourself have perhaps never thought about it? Here it's the first or second question people ask when you get introduced; I can tell you how many souls each of our neighbors has. This is the way I found out I have three hundred of them, and about fifty of those have run away; only I still haven't been able to find out, *ma chère,* where they've run off and why.

At first these conversations seemed very strange to me; but now I'm starting to get used to them. In general the people here are all *so kind,* and I'll be very sorry if you, on the basis of my first letter, don't grow to love them. Everyone here loves and pampers me; and as soon as they learned that I had just arrived from Petersburg, neighbors, one after another, began to visit us. Each day there are guests and my head is going around in circles. And Masha, you just can't imagine how much they eat here. In the morning they drink tea and eat zwieback and sweet rolls; then in about two hours they have breakfast; then they eat lunch; after that they have an afternoon snack; then they drink tea, and finally they have supper. Don't think that I'm joking, Masha. After supper they pass around raisins, almonds and various jams. In addition to that my cousins chew on roasted nuts all day; I can't understand why their teeth aren't all broken!

Auntie loves me very much and I love her too; I requested that she not wear a man's cap in the morning and that she not walk barefoot. She didn't get angry at that; however, she didn't pay attention to me either. "My mama and grandmama and great-grandmama wore caps," she answered, "and I have been used to doing the same since I was a young child; and so now, in my old age, I cannot adopt your fashions. And the reason you saw me barefoot—why, you yourself are guilty; I was so overjoyed when you arrived that I forgot to put on my stockings!"

Auntie did not tell me this the way I am writing it; but I promised you that I wouldn't use Little Russian in my letters; you probably wouldn't understand a word—I hardly understand it! And it's true, *ma chère,* that since then I haven't seen auntie barefoot: in the mornings she walks around in woolen stockings, but, truth to tell, without shoes.

How impatiently do I await a letter from you! Every time that our Jew comes back from town (every landowner here has his own Jew), I run to meet him . . . It seems to me that I'm in such a state that I'll kiss him when he brings a letter from you! Ah, Masha! You really haven't forgotten me, have you? No, that can't possibly be! We've loved each other for so very long!

Farewell, sweet Mashenka! May God be with you! I can't write you a lot today since we're going to a ball at the local cornet's (it's a type of rank): I promised to fix my cousins' hair in the Petersburg style and they are wearing corsets for the first time today; we somehow sewed them. Farewell, Masha!

Third Letter

Thank you for your letter of June 5, my sweet, dearest Masha! How glad I was to get it! How happy I am that you haven't forgotten me! How long the mail takes! If I were the tsar, every day couriers would go back and forth from Petersburg to Barvenovo and from Barvenovo to Petersburg.

Ah, Masha! last week I wrote to you that I was going to a ball . . . How many new things have happened to me since then! If you only knew! but I'll tell you everything in order.

It was very gay at the ball . . . It began at six o'clock and we danced almost 'til dawn . . . They don't know French quadrilles here at all, Polish dances, Scottish dances, simple quadrilles—it seems that's all—and they're not at all like Madame Didelot taught us! We danced a mazurka, but not very well! My partner was the arithmetic teacher from the local district school. He stamps his feet a lot and his boots smelled terribly of tar. I don't like this odor, but auntie and my cousins say that it is very good for one's health. This teacher is supposed to be the best of the local dancers and he seems to quite believe this himself. You know how in a mazurka your partner grabs you by the waist with one hand and twirls you around himself—he hurled me so forcefully that I flew far away from him and almost fell. Auntie says that I'm the one to blame because my waist is so thin that they don't know how to grasp it.

Mashenka! do you know Blistovsky, who serves in the guards in Petersburg? His rank is staff-captain; he has two crosses:[9] one in his buttonhole and one on his neck, and he also has a white medal on a blue ribbon. His name is Vladimir Alexandrovich. He was educated by some *abbé* Nikol. He is tall, has curly brown hair, blue eyes, like yours, and his mustache, *ma chère,* is not large, but more beautiful than any other I have ever seen! His disposition is quiet and modest and he has a very kind heart. He says that he often saw you on Nevsky Prospekt and once at a ball; I don't remember whose. He knows your brother well and is on friendly terms with him. If you don't know about him, then please, *ma chère,* find out about him. I really, really need to know about his character; and write to me with the first post. Do you hear, *ma chère,* please don't forget, with the first post!

He has a thousand souls here in the neighborhood; he comes here to buy horses for his regiment; it seems that they call this "on remount service"? You can find out about him quite easily: just ask about an officer who went to Little Russia on remount service.

I met him at the ball. When the teacher hurled me to one side, I would have fallen if Blistovsky hadn't caught me. The teacher was very ashamed—he apologized by saying that he was wearing new boots which he forgot to coat with chalk, and that he didn't want to dance anymore. In order not to disrupt the mazurka, Blistovsky took his place. Ah! Masha! how nicely he dances and how easy it is to waltz with him! You can't imagine!

It seems, Masha, that he likes me very much. At least that's what he told me that very night at the ball. But maybe he was only joking. You know, they say that does go on among young people! However, he seems so modest that he probably isn't like the others in this respect.

He came to see us the next day after the ball. Praskuta thinks he came for her sake because he danced an entire Polish set with her; and then he gave her her shawl when we were leaving. But that can't be! Right, Masha? I'll tell you frankly, in secret: I know that it's not for her that he comes. Yesterday, when we went out for a stroll—to gather mushrooms—he told me quietly that he comes to see me and even—Masha! please don't tell anyone about this—he asked my permission to talk to auntie . . . I didn't answer him at all . . . Write me, *ma chère,* did I do well not to answer him? Just so that he didn't think that I was angry at him!

Blistovsky plays the flute very well and sings. He has a very, very pleasant voice. Yesterday he accompanied me when I played the clavichord and then we sang a duet . . . Auntie doesn't like Italian music very much. Praskuta and Gapochka also sing, and they sing quite willingly, but they never took lessons. They don't like to sing Little Russian songs in front of guests, and [these songs] are all very beautiful . . . Instead this song is very fashionable here: *Who could love as passionately as I love you,* and also: *Of all the flowers, I loved the rose most.* Auntie also sometimes sings: *I am going off into the wilderness* and *The morning sun has risen, Mashenka has come to me.*

Auntie found out only three days ago that I sing. Blistovsky was over; at his request I sat down at the clavichord and sang: *Di tanti palpiti.* Auntie listened impatiently.

"What language is that?" she asked when I stopped. "Your voice is good, but what kind of song is it when you can't understand a word? Did they teach you in that institute to sing only French and German? Lizaveta Filippovna! please sing that little song they sent you from Kiev! Now, that I like: it is both tender and full of feeling!"

Lizaveta Filippovna sat down at the tambour. (This is a certain noblewoman who sometimes visits us for a few days.) She looked sideways at Blistovsky, blushed, lowered her eyes to the tambour and began to sing the little song from Kiev. She has a beautiful voice, Masha; only Blistovksy says that he likes mine better. I'll try to get the song from Lizaveta Filippovna and I'll write it down for you, letter by letter, preserving the Little Russian. This is how it starts:

     Duty behooves me to part with you,
     Honor behooves me to forget you.[10]

This song should really be Russian; but here they pronounce Russian words so strangely that it's often impossible to understand. You probably won't guess, for example, that [the second line] should mean the same as *behooves me to forget you*; but here everyone is convinced that this is pure Russian.

I will also send you the notes to this song, dearest Masha!

The voice part is nice enough, but I don't know how you'll like the words. They can drive you crazy here. This is the favorite song of local society.

Farewell, dear Mashenka; don't forget to find out about Blistovsky and answer me with the first post. I embrace you a thousand times in my thoughts.

* * *

After arriving in the village of N**, immediately after the service and mutual congratulations, I began to inquire about the author of the letters. My friend only had to read the first letter to guess who wrote it.

"This is my relation," he said with a pleased look on his face; "a beautiful and most gracious woman who unfortunately is slightly ill and therefore could not come to the christening. You must meet her; she was educated at Smolny Institute, she is very intelligent, kind and enjoys the respect of everyone in the district. Someday I will tell you her adventures, which are not at all ordinary. Allow me to read these letters and show them to my wife. She's known her from the time of her arrival from Petersburg."

I handed him the letters and he began to read them with visible pleasure, but after he read them to the end, he thought it over for a while and gave them back to me.

"Didn't you want to show them to your wife?" I asked.

"Yes," he answered, a little confused, "but it would be better to leave them for another time."

I looked at him in surprise.

He noticed this and continued, "Listen, I'll tell you quite frankly the reason why I don't want to show these letters to my wife. The Lizaveta Fillippovna who is mentioned in the third letter is my wife. You know what women are like, even the kindest ones! She, of course, loves her very much, but in the face of this . . . I wouldn't want . . ."

"I understand! . ." I answered and hid the letters in my pocket.

Soon thereafter I personally met the author of the letters. She told me the stories of all the adventures of her life and allowed me to publish them. A few other people, who also played a role in these adventures, filled in the parts missing from her stories and in this way the book, which is here presented to the public, was composed.

Chapter VI: Return to Little Russia

From Anyuta's letters, featured in the second chapter of this book, it is already known to the readers into what state of surprise Anyuta fell, when, upon her arrival at Barvenovo, she found everything in a state different from what she had assumed it would be. Anyone else in her place probably would have lost all of her spirits and would have spent day and night in tears, or probably would have looked with annoyance and contempt at her auntie and cousins, and would finally have become odious to all of her relations and friends. But Anyuta was not like that: imbued wih good morals and trained to be modest, she would never have even thought to laugh at others because they were not dressed like her, nor would she scorn those whom chance had deprived of a secular education. Because of this everyone loved and respected her; her cousins did not envy her advantages and her auntie was lost in admiration of her. Although Anyuta always thought of Petersburg with regret, humbly obeying the dictates of fate, she sincerely intended to grow accustomed to the new situation in which she found herself. And when she found out about her auntie's good qualities and about the ardent love she had for her; and then when she found out from strangers how, when she was left an orphan by the death of her parents, Anna Andreevna took her in with maternal tenderness; then all comparisons between her aunt and the school inspector and between her cousins and school friends were effaced from her grateful heart. Through experience itself she learned that neither clothing nor an outer glow make up the worth of a person; and having come to love her relations sincerely, she even began to find pleasure in the rural life which had seemed to her so unpleasant those first days.

However, like any honest historian, I find that I need to inform the reader that another situation, quite independent of her auntie's good qualities, contributed not a little to the added attractions of country life in Barvenovo in Anyuta's eyes. Staff-Captain Blistovsky, whom she had seen at the cornet's ball, made a strong impression on her inexperienced heart, made for the tenderest feelings. At first she didn't realize this herself; it seemed to her that she liked him more than the others only because his manners reminded her of her beloved Petersburg. In her naive inexperience she did not even note the effect she had on Blistovsky, and his effort to make her like him, she attributed to simple courtesy. The delusion about her own heart under which she found herself grew stronger when she found out that Blistovsky recently had come from Petersburg, where he even saw Masha; and so it seemed so natural that she liked to talk with him more than with others. After her return home from the ball, Blistovsky never left her thoughts; but since these thoughts of him were usually interspersed with remembrances of Petersburg and Masha, she was still left in error for a long time about her heart's true feelings.

Meanwhile Blistovksy, more experienced than she, was convinced at his first sight of Anyuta that the happiness or unhappiness of his entire life would depend on her. He had lived in Petersburg a long time, he had spent time in foreign lands, and he had often come to Little Russia, where a considerable part of his estate was situated; however, neither in Petersburg, nor in Little Russia, nor anywhere else had any girl made such an impression on him as had Anyuta.And he didn't think that this impression was the effect of her beauty alone! Of course, her tall, stately figure, large blue eyes shaded by her long dark lashes and, in general, all of her charming appearance filled his eyes; but rarely before had his heart beat more strongly at the sight of a similar figure, similar eyes! In his life he often met girls whom he liked for their beauty; but never before had he found in one so much gentleness and good nature, such a dear and innocent smile, such captivating expression in all of her features. After he began a conversation with her, he was struck by her sensible opinions, and even her very naivete and her ignorance of the world gave her a certain unusual charm. "No!" he thought, "such looks could not be deceiving!" And he vowed to himself to use all of his power to gain her love.

Since Blistovsky had a strong, decisive disposition, was rich besides, and had no parents, he depended completely on himself. He intended not to put off for long any decision concerning his fate, to get to know Anyuta better and at the first chance, to talk it over with her. And so on the day after the ball he set off for Barvenovo.

In Little Russia in those homes where they have not yet succeeded in exchanging ancient Russian hospitality for modern society decorum, one does not need a lot of time to get to know a household well and to be accepted as one of the family. Of course it is true that a rich, single guards officer in the provinces is always accepted very well; but if you examine carefully the reasons for this reception, then it is not difficult to discover that often it is not guided by hospitality alone. I myself had the chance to see in a few homes how they pamper a young man while he is still single and how they receive him soon thereafter when he turns up already married in the very same house. The disparity between those receptions was striking, although in that short time the young man had not changed at all, either in appearance or spirit. But be that as it may, auntie—as we already know—does not belong to the group of people of fashionable discrimination, and therefore received Blistovsky with her normal cordiality, not worrying at all about the reasons for his visit. Anyuta became overjoyed when he unexpectedly came into the room, and still under her naive delusion, did not think to hide her pleasure, supposing that she was happy only for the chance to talk about dear Mashenka! Praskuta's heart also began to beat hard: she thought he had come for her and she blushed all over!

We shall not weary our readers with an elaboration of the tale which is already familiar to them from Anyuta's letters. Blistovsky came to Barvenovo almost every day, and each day discovered new virtues in his beloved and each day he loved her more. A few times he requested Anyuta's permission to talk with her auntie, but he could not get a decisive answer. Finally, after he received her consent, he wasted no time in taking advantage of it.

It was just before evening. Auntie was sitting in the gazebo, put together out of lathes around which hops and red beans were entwined; she was listening attentively to the steward, who was reporting to her on the successes of the harvest . . .

"Welcome, Vladimir Alexandrovich," she said. "Wouldn't you like to learn about farming? This year we have a good crop of corn thanks to our merciful God! About seven rubles a *dessiatin,* [11] and in a spot closer to the village, and there's still more! And what will the yield of the threshed corn be? I only fear that our hemp will be ruined by the weather like our neighbor's was. They say that all of Ivan Ivanovich's [hemp] is gone, as if it had been mowed down. Up 'til now the Lord has been merciful to us; but what does the future hold!"

Vladimir didn't care about the hemp or about the corn, but he had to wait until auntie's conversation with the steward came to an end. For a long time he listened to her discourse about the harvest and about the threshing, about the buckwheat, oats and hemp, about the repairs the winery really needed, and so on. Impatience born of love made this conversation seem to him to be longer than it really was, and he crossed himself from joy several times when the steward received his last orders and directions, kissed his mistress' hand and bowing low, left the gazebo.

"Excuse me, Vladimir Alexandrovich," said auntie, "I completely forgot that it's not fun at all for you to listen to me going on about my farming cares. But don't get angry; you know you're no stranger here! Why did you leave the young ladies? You haven't quarreled with them already, have you?"

"I came to talk to you privately, Anna Andreevna! My fate depends on you—the happiness or unhappiness of my whole life."

"The Lord's power is with us, what's happened to you? What kind of influence can I, a tiny person, have on your fate? Or are you joking with me, Vladimir Alexandrovich?"

"I couldn't be further from jokes, auntie! But first would you allow me to call you this always?"

"And why not, my dear fellow?—please, if it gives you pleasure! But what's wrong with you?"

"Auntie! I love Anyuta! make me the happiest of mortals: agree to give me her hand!"

"So that's what this is all about!" said auntie, drawing out the words as she grew thoughtful. This proposal came totally unexpectedly, although for some time Blistovsky's visits were becoming highly remarkable. We already explained to the readers that Anna Andreevna did not belong to that group of people who refuse hospitality in any form at all, and that is why at any other time Blistovksy could have come to her house several times and it would never have occurred to her to keep an eye on him and try to see whether he was in love with one of the young ladies. But this time a certain incident turned her attention to the frequent visits of the young officer.

For some time auntie had noticed that Praskuta was completely transformed. She became sad and pensive; the lively rosiness in her cheeks began to disappear and her eyes often seemed to be full of tears. At first auntie imagined that Praskuta was unwell, and ignoring her protestations, gave her various herbs and medicines to drink from her home pharmacy; but they did not end the sickness. Praskuta became more and more pensive and sad and auntie grew more and more worried about her! Finally, for all of her simplicity, auntie began to grasp that Praskuta's strange sickness had some connection with Blistovsky. On the very same day when Vladimir asked for Anyuta's hand in marriage, auntie observed her daughter anew and grew still more convinced of her hunch. Her eyes did not miss that Praskuta alternately grew pale and blushed, even when from afar she heard the familiar sound of Blistovsky's carriage; but when the carriage began to get closer to the porch, Praskuta got up from the tambour and hurried out of the room.

"Where are you going, Praskuta?" asked Anna Andreevna.

"I have something to do, mama!" answered Praskuta and it seemed to auntie that tears shone in her eyes when she looked back desperately as she was leaving the room.

For some time poor Praskuta had noticed the mutual love of Vladimir and Anyuta.

And so that is what auntie was thinking about after she heard Blistovsky's proposal! She loved Anyuta just as ardently as her own daughters, but at the same time she could not be indifferent to Praskuta's plight. She imagined what a blow the news of Vladimir's engagement would be to her—and her heart broke at the thought that the happiness of one of her daughters accompanied the unhappiness of another. Finally Anna Andreevna's constant hope in God's providence gave her courage. She thought, "God is merciful and will not abandon us. Praskuta is still young enough to fall in love with another! And Anyuta certainly will be happy with such a good man as Vladimir Alexandrovich!"

Meanwhile Blistovsky was sitting on pins and needles; he could not understand the reasons for auntie's perplexity and imagined that she perhaps had some doubts about him. However, auntie quickly brought him out of his anxiety.

"Vladimir Alexandrovich!" she said in a voice trembling with tender emotion—"I think you are a good and honorable man and hope that Galechka will be happy with you. Take her; I bless you from the bottom of my heart!"

Vladimir, beside himself with joy, fell on Anna Andreevna's neck. He kissed her hands, called her his dearest, kindest, nicest auntie and immediately wanted to run to Anyuta.

"Wait just a bit!"—said auntie, greatly moved; "let me wipe away my tears; let's go together!"

The gazebo was very close to the house, but for Vladimir, who had to go slowly with auntie, the way seemed unbearably long.

"It seems that you are walking purposely slower than usual, aren't you, auntie?" he said.

"But it seems to me," she answered laughing, "that today you are walking faster than usual."

"Anyuta, my Anyuta!" he cried out, after he entered the room where she and Gapochka were sitting on the sofa. He grabbed her hand ardently and fell at her feet. At first Anyuta grew confused, paled and did not know what she should do. But after she looked about desperately and saw that her auntie was standing in front of her with a merry smile, she guessed by some instinct what this meant. Unbeknownst to her, her head involuntarily fell on Vladimir's shoulder and their lips united in a tender kiss.

Soon everyone in the house knew that Anyuta was engaged and they came to congratulate her. And even Praskuta found out about it; she wanted . . . to come down, but she lost heart! She told everyone that she was sick, wrapped up her head and went to bed. Anna Andreevna went to her; she did not propose giving her any medicines, but only embraced her tenderly, cried over her quietly, and blessed her, not saying a word. Then she returned to Anyuta and tried to be merry.

Teatime arrived. Anyuta sat at the table and Vladimir settled down nearby so that he could help her. On the lovers' faces were clearly depicted the feelings which filled their hearts. On that day Anyuta did not pour the tea as artfully as she usually did and her kind auntie repeatedly reproved her for her absentmindedness. Meanwhile Vladimir could not take his eyes off her and in his ecstasy did not notice that she forgot to put sugar in his cup. He gave himself over to sweet dreams of the future; at times he imagined he had already married Anyuta, that his young wife was pouring tea in his own house and that auntie had come to visit them. His thoughts flew still farther away . . . Suddenly Anna Andreevna hurriedly jumped up from her chair, put her cup on the table and cried out:

"Ah, I'm a fool! Forgive me, Lord! What did I do? Galechka, my dear! I'm guilty before you; I'm guilty before both of you! How could I agree to Vladimir Alexandrovich's proposal! My God, my God! What can I do now?"

Vladimir got frightened and also jumped up from his place. Anyuta looked at Anna Andreevna in astonishment and did not say a word. No one understood what had happened to auntie, who meanwhile continued her exclamations, obviously completely disturbed. Finally Vladimir went to her and took her hand:

"Please, auntie! What's happened to you?" he said.

"I completely forgot about Klim Sidorovich! It's true we've not seen hide nor hair of him for so long! as if he vanished without a trace. Nevertheless, I know, my dears, that he is alive and well, forgive me, Lord!"

Vladimir and Anyuta still did not understand auntie.

"What Klim Sidorovich?" both of them cried out almost in one voice.

"He's your guardian, Galya! to whom your deceased father—grant him the heavenly kingdom!—entrusted you before his death and upon whom you depend. Without him we cannot decide anything; and I, an old fool, completely forgot about him. We must write to him; but until we receive an answer from him—don't get angry, children!—I must take back my word!"

Anyuta had hardly ever heard about Klim Sidorovich, and not having had any dealings with him, scarcely remembered his name and even less did she think about what influence he could have on her fate. Now for the first time in her life she heard that her deceased father had put her under Dyundik's care. Vladimir was also amazed that Anyuta had a guardian, and although he could not suppose that this guardian would interfere with his marriage, but foreseeing that a correspondence with him could delay his happiness, he grew very distressed at this new revelation. In this frame of mind he decided to see whether they could proceed without Klim Sidorovich's help.

"Auntie!" he said, "It seems to me that you are getting quite upset for no reason at all. If Anyuta's guardian hasn't made anything known about himself for so long, this is a sign that he doesn't care about her, and in that case there is no need to ask his permission. You have taken the place of her parents and we don't need anyone's consent except yours."

"Quiet, my good fellow, quiet! It's true that I think of Anyuta as my very own daughter; and it's also true that Klim Sidorovich doesn't think about her very much—but I'm not rebuking him! Since my cousin Trofim Petrovich closed his eyes, did this so-called guardian ask about her even once? but nevertheless, a father's will is God's will. Tell me, Anyuta, my pet: if your deceased father were alive, would you obey him?"

"You surely don't doubt that, auntie!"

"No, my pet, I don't doubt it! So, if you would obey him if he were alive, than how much more should you respect his will now that he's no longer in this world. Aren't I telling you the truth, Galechka? No, Vladimir Alexandrovich! Your will has nothing to do with anything now! You must ask Klim Sidorovich!"

They had to submit to auntie's demands! Vladimir himself felt that she was perfectly correct and that without the approval of the guardian appointed by Anyuta's father it would not be proper to ask for her hand. And so they proposed to write to Klim Sidorovich with the first post and, until they received an answer from him, to tell no one about what had happened that evening. Auntie calmed down after she realized that she undoubtedly would get a favorable reply, for the guardian could have no reason at all to refuse. However, in spite of the fact that the others also shared auntie's hope, the gaiety of the evening was somewhat spoiled by this unexpected complication.

In those first minutes Vladimir was so struck by auntie's reaction that he did not even think to inquire in more detail about this newly discovered guardian. But when it came to reckoning just when he would be able to have an answer, and when he then found out that the guardian lived in the Poltava district, the thought suddenly came to him that this could be the very Klim Sidorovich whom he had met last year. And when he learned that his last name was Dyundik, then all of his doubts disappeared; but this discovery did not cheer him up even a little. He knew Klim Sidorovich and Marfa Petrovna quite well, and certain particular circumstances set him thinking that they would not hurry with an answer to his letter.

This thought disturbed him greatly. After pacing pensively across the room a few times, he finally decided to go himself to the Poltava region in spite of the unpleasantness of parting with Anyuta for at least a week.

"Auntie!" he said, when he had firmly decided to do this, "it seems to me that it would be best if I went myself to Anyuta's guardian."

"Yes, of course, Vladimir Alexandrovich! Go with God! And meanwhile we will take care of your Anyuta most diligently. And so I won't need to write a long letter which, truthfully speaking, I don't very much like to do. Yes, in truth, I would not know how to describe you well; and now you can meet him yourself and he will see what kind of fiancé my Galechka got for herself."

"But I already know him, auntie! last year I saw him fairly frequently in Romny."

"So much the better! That means he won't have to think it over very long and you will return to us even sooner. Well, thank God, all's for the best! And I never would have imagined that you know him. Just look how lucky that is! When do you intend to go?"

Vladimir looked at Anyuta and shuddered at the thought that he had to leave her; finally, gathering his courage, he said:

"I think I'll go tomorrow, auntie! The sooner I leave, the sooner I shall return!"

"Well, then, I'll get my little letter ready for tomorrow!"

And in fact, on the next day, near evening, a wagon with a dashing troika rode up to the low porch of auntie's house. Vladimir bade everyone farewell, firmly pressed Anyuta to his heart, not paying attention to Anna Andreevna's admonitions; then he clambered up on his vehicle and galloped off at full speed. Auntie, Anyuta and Gapochka stayed on the porch and watched him until the dust raised on the road by his galloping troika settled down.

Auntie's house felt deserted after Vladimir's departure, and for a long time the peaceful inhabitants of Barvenovo could not get used to his absence. Everywhere reigned despondency, compounded still by everyone's unease about Praskuta's sad situation; but in praise of the latter, I must say that the news about the complication in regard to Anyuta's betrothal did not make her in the least bit happy.

Meanwhile, until Vladimir finds himself on the great Poltava highway, we shall relate to the readers why his recollections about his former acquaintance with Klim Sidorovich had such a powerful and unpleasant effect on him. But for this we must move back in our minds a whole year before the time we described in this chapter.

Notes

1. The Russians called the Ukraine "Little Russia."

2. Masha was a student at the fashionable Smolny Institute for noblewomen in St. Petersburg. In the translation I sometimes refer to it simply as the institute.

3. Colors of uniforms and dresses the girls wore.

4. Russians use two terms for cousin, one more fashionable, the other more colloquial. Anyuta makes the distinction here.

5. A fashionable village, the site of the lyceum which Pushkin attended.

6. An island near Petersburg, once a retreat for the wealthy.

7. She says this in Ukrainian.

8. Her real name is Anna Trofimovna.

9. Decorations for valor and service.

10. This is in Ukrainian.

11. A Russian measure of land area equal to 2400 square sazhens (a sazhen equals 2,134 meters) or 1.09 hectares.

V. F. ODOEVSKY

A Tale of Why It Is Dangerous for Young Girls to Go Walking in a Group along Nevsky Prospect[1]

> "I beg your pardon, Madame! You wish to leave us already? With your permission I shall accompany you."—"No, I do not wish that such a courteous gentleman should cause himself any labor on my part."—"Madame, you are surely jesting."
> *Manuel pour la conversation par Madame de Genlis*, p. 275

Once upon a time in Petersburg the sun appeared; a whole bevy of young girls was walking along Nevsky Prospect; there were eleven of them, neither more nor less, each one more beautiful than the next; and three mammas of whom, unfortunately, the same could not be said. The pretty little heads twirled around, the tiny feet tapped against the smooth pavement, but they were all bored: they had already grown weary of looking one another over, they had long since grown weary of discussing everything with one another, they had long since grown weary of laughing at one another and were completely bored to death with one another; but all the same they held each other's hands, not leaving one another, like nuns in a nunnery; such is the established custom with us: a young girl is dying of boredom, but she does not give her hand to a man unless he has the joy of being her brother, her uncle or, what of course would be an even more enviable good fortune,—eighteen years of age: for "what will the mammas say?" Oh, these mammas! Some day I shall fix them! I shall do away with their ancient tricks! I shall pick to pieces their rules of etiquette, I shall prove to them that they have not been written by nature, have not been ratified by the mind! They interfere in the affairs of others, while our young girls become ever so bored and wither and wither away until they begin themselves to resemble the mammas, although in their hearts they are not at all like the mammas! Just you wait! I shall deal with you!

Be that as it may, our bevy flew along the Prospect and frequently encountered passers-by who stopped in order to gaze upon the beauties; but approach them no one would—and how could they? In front was a mamma, at the rear was a mamma, in the middle a mamma—terrible!

Here on Nevsky Propect a newly arrived sharper has put out a glistening shingle! Through the windows gleam vaporous clouds, all the colors of the rainbow are scattered about, golden satin flows like a waterfall through the velvet and darling little dolls, all swathed in down, nod their dear little heads beneath crystal bells. Suddenly our first pair comes to a stop, turns about and skips onto the iron steps; the second pair follows, then the third, and finally the entire shop is filled with beauties. For a long while they sorted and they admired—and that was not all: the owner was so nimble, with blue spectacles, in a stylish jacket, with large side-whiskers, he exerted and overexerted and almost burst himself; and he talked and he traded, applauded and abused, and collected and counted out the money ceaselessly, he unfolded and unrolled before my beauties; first a gossamer of cobwebs with a scattering of butterfly wings; then timepieces that could be laid on the head of a pin; then a lorgnette of the eyes of a fly through which it is possible to see instantly everything that is happening all around; then a silk lace which melts from the touch; then slippers made of dragonfly feet; then feathers woven from ewe's fur; then mercy me! rouge that leapt impetuously to the cheek. Our beauties might have spent a century in here had it not been for the mammas! The mammas gathered their wits, shook their bonnets, wheeled to the left in a circle, and coming out on the steps, wisely began to count in order to be certain that all the beauties had come out of the shop; but as misfortune would have it (they say that the crow can only count up to four) the mammas could only count to ten: it was hardly wise that they completed their count and made for home with ten young girls, observing the previous order and etiquette, but having forgotten the eleventh in the shop.

Hardly had the bevy moved on than the foreign infidel immediately bolted the door and turned to the beauty; and he took everything away from her; the hat, the shoes, the stockings, and left only (the cursed devil!) a skirt and blouse; he seized the wretched girl by the braid, put her on the shelf and covered her with a crystal bell.

Grasping his pen-knife and taking the hat into his hands with extreme dexterity he carved out from it in a thrice the dust that had come flying up from the pavement; he cut and he cut, and out of nowhere there appeared in his hands two hats, one of which almost flew off through the air when he placed it on a peg; then in the same careful manner, he cut out patterned flowers in the material the hat was made of and thus he created yet another hat; then once again—and a fourth hat emerged on which there was only the outline of flowers; then again—and a very plain hat emerged; then again and again—and all in all he accumulated twelve hats; the cursed devil did exactly the same with the dress, and with the shawl and with the shoes, and with the stockings, and he produced everything in twelves which he carefully placed in a box with foreign stampings . . . and all this, I assure you, he accomplished in the course of a few minutes.

"Do not weep, my beauty," he coaxed in his broken Russian accent. "Do not weep! It will still do for your dowry!"

When he had finished his work he added:

"Now it is your turn, my beauty!"

With these words he waved his hand and stamped: all the clocks struck thirteen, all the chimes began to ring, all the organs began to play, all the dolls began to prance, and out of a tin of powder popped a brainless French head; out of a tin of tobacco a German nose with the ears of a donkey; and out of a bottle of soda water a tightly packed English torso. All of these esteemed gentlemen sat down in a circle and goggled at the magician.

"Woe!" cried the sorcerer.

"Yes, woe!" replied the brainless French head, "Powder has gone out of style!"

"That is not the trouble," grumbled the English torso, "I've been thrown out of doors like an old empty sack."

"Even worse," whined the German nose, "people ride me like a horse, and what's more, put the spurs to me."

"That is not the problem!" objected the sorcerer, "That is not the problem! It's much worse—Russian girls no longer wish to be foreign dolls! This is the real woe! Let it continue—and the Russian will think that in fact they are not."

"Woe! Woe!" all the infidels cried in a single voice.

"It behooves us to think up a new hat for them," said the head.

"To instill in them the rules of our morality," continued the torso.

"To give them in marriage to our brother," asserted the sensitive nose.

"All this is fine!" replied the sorcerer, "But it will not do! Now things are not what they used to be! A new remedy is needed for a new woe; it behooves us to turn to cunning!"

He thought and he thought, this sorcerer; finally he waved his hand once again, and before the gathering there appeared a tripod, pickling brine and a retort; and the villains fell to work.

Into the retort they squeezed out a multitude of Mme de Genlis's novels, Chesterfield's letters, several moldy sensations, an embroidery frame, Italian roulades, a dozen new contredanses, several computations from English moral arithmetic, and out of all this they extracted a kind of colorless and dispirited liquid. Thereupon, the sorcerer opened the window, passed his hand through the air of Nevsky Prospect and seized a whole handful of city slander, rumors and tales; finally, out of a drawer he extracted an enormous bundle of papers and with savage delight he showed them to his colleagues; these were fragments from diplomatic letters and excerpts from letter-writing manuals in which were contained assurances of "deepest respects" and "yours sincerely's"; all this the villains, leaping about and laughing, fell to mixing with their devilish concoction: the French head huffed up the flame, the German nose stirred and the English torso pounded away like a pestle.

When the liquid had solidified, the sorcerer turned to the beauty; he fetched the poor trembling creature out from under the glass bell and set to cut out of her (the villain!) her heart! Oh! How the wretched beauty suffered, how she struggled! How firmly she clung to her own innocent, her own passionate heart! With what Slavic courage she resisted the infidels. Soon they were in despair and prepared to abandon their undertaking, but the sorcerer, sensing victory, seized some old mamma's bonnet, tossed it on the coals and when the bonnet began to smoke, the fumes stupefied the beauty.

The villains took advantage of the moment, out of her they drew her heart and dropped it into their devilish concoction. For a long, long while they stewed the wretched heart of this Russian beauty, stretching it and puffing it up, and when they had glued it back into place, then the beauty allowed them to do with her whatsoever they desired. The accursed infidel seized her round cheeks, her tiny little feet, her delicate hands and with his penknife set to scraping the fresh Slavic color from them and carefully collecting it in a tin with the label *rouge végétal*; and the beauty became oh so white, like a snow-bird; the taunting villain was not satisfied with this: with a small sponge he wiped all the whiteness from her and squeezed it into a phial with the label *lait de concombre,* and the beauty became yellowish-brown; then to her tiny neck he attached a pneumatic apparatus, turned it on—and her neck collapsed forward and dangled on the bones; then with tiny pincers he forced her mouth open, seized the tongue and twisted it in such a fashion that it was unable to pronounce a single Russian word properly; finally he tied her into a narrow corset, tossed some kind of unbecoming fleece over her and set the beauty out in the cold in the window. Hereupon, the infidel grew calm; the brainless French head leaped into the tin of powder with a laugh; the German nose sneezed with pleasure and returned to the tobacco tin; the English torso was silent, merely stomping on the floor with joy, and he too wound his way into the bottle of soda water; and everything in the shop returned to its former order, with the exception that it now had one more doll!

Meanwhile time flew and flew; shoppers came into the shop, they purchased cob-webbed gossamer, lorgnettes made of flies' eyes and admired the dolls. Then one young man's gaze fell upon our beauty, he became thoughtful, and in spite of the fact that his comrades laughed at him he purchased her and took her home with him. He was a solitary fellow, of a quiet nature, he loved neither noise nor fuss; he stood the doll in a prominent place, dressed and shod her, kissed her tiny little feet and admired her like a child. But the doll's Russian spirit was soon felt: she found his hospitality and kind-heartedness very pleasing indeed. Once when the young man was deep in thought and seemed to have forgotten about her, she began to rustle and prattle; amazed, he approached her, took off the crystal bell, and looked: his beauty of a doll was still a doll. He attributed this to the work of his imagination and again fell into thought and began to muse to himself; the doll became angry: once again she fell to rustling, hopping, crying and knocking against the bell, now as though to burst out from under it.

"Are you really alive?" the young man said to her, "if indeed you are alive, I shall love you more than my own soul; now prove to me that you are alive, utter at least a tiny word!"

"Perhaps," the doll said, "I am alive, really alive."

"What! You can speak as well?" exclaimed the young man, "What joy! Is this not some delusion? Let me be certain once more, speak to me about something! . . "

"And what should we talk about?"

"About what? In the world there is goodness, there is art! . ."

"What need have I of them!" replied the doll, "all that is quite boring!"

"What do you mean? Why is it boring? Could it possibly be that it has never occurred to you that in the world there are thoughts, sentiments? . ."

"Ah, sentiments, sentiments? I know," uttered the doll, "sentiments of deepest respect and sincerity whereby I have the honor of being, dearest sir, humbly at your service . . ."

"You are mistaken, my beauty: you are confusing conventional phrases which are exchanged every day for that which constitutes the eternal, fixed adornment of man."

"Do you know what they say?" the beauty interrupted him, "one girl took a husband, but another man is playing up to her and she wants to get a divorce. How shameful!"

"How does this concern you, my dearest? Better you think of how much there is in the world of which you know nothing; you do not even know that sentiment which is called love; which penetrates the entire being of a person; the soul lives by it, it is the progenitor of heaven and hell on earth."

"When a lot of people are dancing at a ball, then it is cheerful, when there are few, it is so boring," responded the doll.

"Ah, it would have been better had you not spoken!" cried the young man, "you do not understand me, my beauty!"

And in vain he attempted to bring her to reason: if he brought her books—the books remained uncut; if he spoke to her of the music of the soul—she answered him with an Italian roulade; if he showed her the painting of a glorious master—the beauty would show him an embroidery frame.

And the young man resolved each morning and evening to go to the crystal bell and say to the doll: "In the world there is goodness, there is love; read, study, dream, dissolve in music; not in the phrases of society, but in the soul of sentiment and thought."

The doll was silent.

Once the doll fell into deep thought and she thought for a long while. The young man was in ecstasy when suddenly she said to him, "Well, now I know, I know; in the world there is virtue, there is art, there is love, not in the phrases of society, but in the soul of sentiment and thought. Be assured, dearest sir, of my sentiments of sincere virtue and passionate love with which I have the honor of . . ."

"Oh! Cease, for God's sake," screamed the young man, "if you do not recognize either virtue or love, then at least do not debase them by linking them with false, silly phrases . . ."

"What do you mean I don't know!" cried the doll wrathfully, "nothing suits you, you thankless wretch! No, I do know, I know quite well: *in the world there is virtue, there is art, there is love,* just as there is the respect with which I have the honor of being . . ."

The young man was in despair. Meanwhile the doll was overjoyed at her new acquisition; no hour passed that she did not cry: "*There is virtue, there is love, there is art,*" and she did not interpolate her assurances of profound respect: if it was snowing—the doll would state: "*there is virtue!*"—if she was brought dinner—she shouted: "*there is love!*"—and soon it reached the point that these words became unbearable to the young man. No matter what he did: whether he spoke with rapture and entreaty, whether he proved coldblooded, whether he became furious, whether he mocked the beauty—all the same there was no way she could attain the understanding of the difference between the words she had memorized and the commonplaces of society; in no way could she grasp that love and virtue could be for some purpose other than the conclusion of a letter.

And frequently the young man would exclaim: "Ah! It would have been better had you not spoken!"

Finally he said to her:

"I see that I cannot bring you to reason, that you cannot attach to the cherished and sacred words of goodness, love and art any meaning except that of respect and faithfulness . . . How can we go on like this! It is painful for me, but I do not blame you for this. But listen to me, everyone in this world must do something; you can neither think nor feel; I cannot transfer my soul into you; therefore take charge of the house in the ancient Russian fashion—tend the table, do the accounts, be obedient to me in all things; when you deliver me from the mechanical occupations of life, I shall love you, true, not as much as I would have loved you had our two souls become one, but all the same, I shall love you."

"What kind of a housekeeper am I" shouted the doll, growing angry and beginning to weep, "Is this the reason you purchased me? You bought me—so cherish, dress and console me. Why should I bother with your soul and your housekeeping! You see I am faithful to you, I have not run away from you—so be grateful, my hands and feet are weak; I love and want to do nothing, not to think, not to feel, not to care for the house—and your business is to amuse me."

And in fact, so it was. When the young man was occupied with his doll, when he dressed, undressed her, when he kissed her feet—the doll was both peaceful and good, although she never said anything; but if he forgot to change her hat, if he ever became occupied with his own thoughts, if he ever took his eyes from her, the doll would begin to pound against her crystal bell as though she were going to run away. Finally his patience was exhausted: whether he picked up a book, whether he sat down to eat, or lay down on the couch to rest—the doll would bang and scream like a living person, and would give him no peace, day or night; and his life became not life, but hell. Then the young man was seized with anger; the unfortunate wretch did not know what sufferings the poor beauty had borne; he did not know how strongly she had clung to that heart instilled into her by nature, with what pain she had surrendered to her tormentors or teachers—and then once, only half-awake, he cast the doll out the window; for this all the passers-by condemned him, yet none picked up the doll.

And who is guilty for all this? In the first place, the foreign infidels who spoil our beauties, and then the mammas who cannot count higher than ten. Here is the moral for you.

1833

---

1. Intelligent people will not accuse the author of any vulgar patriotism for this humoresque. He who understands the value of western enlightenment will also understand its abuses. [Author's note.]

Princess Mimi

1

The Ball

La femme de César ne doit pas être soupçonnée.

"Tell me, with whom were you dancing just now," said Princess Mimi, taking by the arm a certain lady who had finished the mazurka and was passing by the Princess.

"He once served with my brother! I have forgotten his name," Baroness Dauerthal answered in passing, and, being tired, rushed to her seat.

In the general commotion which usually accompanies the end of a dance this short conversation passed unnoticed by those who were standing around.

But this conversation set the Baroness to thinking—and not without reason. The Baroness, though already married for a second time, was still young and beautiful; her courtesy, splendid figure, and chestnut-colored silken locks attracted a crowd of young men to her. Each of them involuntarily compared Eliza to her husband, a hoarse old Baron, and to each of them it seemed that her languorous, moisture-laden eyes spoke of hope: only one experienced observer found in those dark, azure eyes not the flames of bliss, but simply that southern indolence which, in his opinion, unites so strangely with northern impassivity in our ladies and which constitutes their distinctive character.

The Baroness knew all her superior points: she knew that for everyone her union with the Baron was something impossible, an offence to propriety, something absurd; she also knew that at the time of her wedding people in town said she had married the Baron for his money; she liked never leaving the dance floor at balls, never having time at evening parties to sink into thought, always having several ready companions for a horseback ride, but never did she allow herself so much as a glance which would betray a preference for one person over another, nor strong excitement, nor strong joy, nor strong sorrow—in a word, nothing of the sort which might set her soul in motion: besides, whether from a feeling of duty, or from some sort of unnatural love for her husband, whether she wanted to prove that she had not married him for his money, or whether it was simply that the above-mentioned observer's remark was accurate, or else, whether out of a combination of all these reasons—the fact is that the Baroness was as faithful to the Baron as her pet Beauty was to her: she went nowhere without her husband, even asked his advice about her attire: the Baron, for his part, did not doubt Eliza's attachment to him, allowed her to do whatever she pleased, and calmly gave himself up to his favorite pastimes: in the morning he would take snuff, in the evenings he would play whist, and in the intervals he would bustle about in quest of awards. Virtuous ladies in the city had long been seeking the object of the Baroness's tenderness; but when they got together for a genreal consultation to decide the question, one lady would name one young man, a second another, a third a third, and the whole thing would break down during the argument. In vain would they go over all the young men in society: as soon as they agreed on one, he would either up and marry or begin to chase after someone else—the result was sheer despair! Finally the female guardians of morality became bored with such incessant failures: they found that the Baroness was merely taking time away which they could spend keeping other ladies under surveillance; they unanimously decided that her art of preserving outward decorum was equal to the highest morality, that she ought to be held up as an example to other ladies, and they postponed the Baroness' business pending any special circumstances which might arise.

The Baroness knew that Princess Mimi belonged to this moral estate, she also knew that this estate belonged in turn to that terrible society whose offshoots have penetrated into all classes. I am revealing a great secret; listen to me; everything that is done on earth is done for a certain anonymous society! It is the parterre; other people are the stage. It holds in its hands authors, musicians, beauties, geniuses, and heroes. It condemns people to life and death and never changes its sentences—even if they should run contrary to reason. You can easily recognize the members of this society by the following signs: others play cards, but they watch the game; others marry, but they come to the wedding; others write books, but they criticize; others give a dinner, but they judge the cook; others go off to battle, but they read military reports; others dance, but they stand near the dancers. The members of this society immediately recognize each other everywhere—not by special signs, but by a sort of instinct; and each of them, before even listening attentively to the matter at hand, will already be supporting his comrade; any member who takes it into his head to *do* something on this earth is deprived on the spot of all the advantages attendant upon his rank, he enters into the common group of defendants and can in no way have his rights returned! It is well known that the most important role in this trial is played by those people for whose existence on earth it is quite impossible to find a reason.

Princess Mimi was the soul of this society, and this is how it happened. I must tell you that she had never been a beauty, but in her youth she was not unattractive. At that time she did not have a well-defined personality. You know what feelings, what thoughts can be developed by the education women receive: embroidery, a dance instructor, a little cunning, *tenez-vous droite,* and two or three anecdotes related by grandmother as reliable guiding principles for this life and the next—there you have the extent of the education. Everything depended upon the circumstances which Mimi was to encounter upon her entrance into society: she could have become either a good wife and a good mother of a family or that which she had now become. At that time she even had suitors; but nothing ever worked out: she herself did not like the first one; the second one had not risen to the higher ranks and did not please her mother; both mother and daughter very much liked the third, the betrothal was announced and the day of the wedding set, but on the eve of the wedding they found out to their amazement that he was a close relative, and everything fell apart. Mimi fell ill from grief and nearly died; she did, however, recover. After that no suitors appeared for a long time; ten years passed, then another ten; and Mimi grew old and ugly, but giving up the idea of marriage was awful for her. How could she possibly give up the idea which her mother dinned into her head at family conferences, the idea about which her grandmother had spoken to her on her deathbed? How could she give up the thought which was the favorite topic of conversation with her female friends, the thought with which she awoke and fell asleep? It was awful! And Princess Mimi continued to go out—always with new plans in her head and despair in her heart. Her position had become unbearable; everyone around her had either married or was in the process of getting married; the little coquette who yesterday sought her patronage would herself speak today in a patronizing tone—and no wonder: she was married! This one had a husband decked out in stars and ribbons! Another's husband played a grand round of whist. Respect passed from the husbands to their wives: wives had a voice and power by virtue of their husbands; only Princess Mimi remained alone, without a voice and without support. Often at a ball she did not know which group to join—the single girls or the married women—and no wonder: Mimi was unmarried! The hostess greeted her with cold civility, looked at her as at an extra piece of furniture, and did not know what to say because Mimi was not married. And here and there people would be congratulating someone, but not Mimi—instead it was always someone who was getting married! And what quiet whispers, inperceptible smiles, obvious or imagined mockery were aimed at the poor woman who either lacked the art or had too much nobility to sell herself into marriage! poor woman! Every day her self-respect was insulted; with every day a new humiliation was born; and—poor woman!—every day vexation, spite, envy and vindictiveness little by little corrupted her heart. At last her cup ran over: Mimi saw that if not by marriage, then by other means one must support oneself in society, give oneself some kind of significance, occupy some kind of place; and craftiness—that dark, timid, slow craftiness which makes society hateful and little by little destroys its foundations,—this social craftiness developed to full perfection in Princess Mimi. There appeared in her an activity of a special sort: all her minor abilities took a special direction; even her unfavorable position was turned to her advantage. It could not be helped! One had to support oneself! And now Princess Mimi, a spinster, began to insinuate herself into the society of girls and young women; as a mature woman she became a favorite companion in the profound discussions of old, respected ladies. And it was just the right time for her! Having spent twenty years waiting in vain for a suitor, she did not think about domestic cares; occupied by a single idea, she strengthened in herself an inborn aversion to the printed word, art, to everything which is called feeling in this life, and she turned completely to the spiteful, envious surveillance of others. She began to know and understand everything that happened before her eyes and behind her back; she became the supreme judge of fiancés and fiancées; she became accustomed to discussing every rise in place or rank; she acquired her own patrons and protégés; she began to remain wherever she saw that she was interfering; she began to listen wherever people spoke in whispers; finally,—she began to speak of the general corruption of morals. It could not be helped! One had to support oneself in society.

And she attained her goal: her petty, but constant, ant-like application to her business, or rather, to the business of others, gave her real power in drawing rooms; many people feared her and tried not to quarrel with her; only inexperienced young girls or youths dared to laugh at her faded beauty, her frown, her fervent sermons against the present age, and her annoying habit of arriving at a ball and leaving for home without waltzing even once around the room.

The Baroness knew all the power of Princess Mimi and her terrible court; though pure, innocent, cold, and self-assured, she did not fear its prosecution; up to now the circumstances of life themselves had helped her to avoid it; but now the Baroness found herself in a very difficult situation. Granitsky, with whom she had just been dancing, was a handsome, well-built young man with thick, dark sideburns; he had spent almost his whole life in foreign lands, where he had made friends with the Baroness' brother; the Baroness' brother was now living in her home, and Granitsky was staying with her brother; he was acquainted with almost no one in town; every day he dined and went out together with them; in a word, everything was drawing him and the Baroness together, and she knew what a marvellous love affair could be built by a virtuous soul on such an advantageous foundation. This thought occupied her at the time she was dancing with the young man, and she involuntarily plunged into thought, seeking in her head a means of defending herself from the malicious gossip of virtuous ladies. The Baroness recalled with vexation that Princess Mimi's sudden question, which came so close to the subject of her reflections, had embarrassed her—something which was probably not concealed from the penetrating gaze of the scout; it seemed to her that there had been something special in Princess Mimi's voice when she asked the question; furthermore, she noticed that just after that the Princess began to speak heatedly with an old lady sitting next to her, and that both women, as if in spite of themselves, alternately smiled and shrugged their shoulders. All this ran through the

Baroness' head in an instant and at the same moment gave birth to an idea: to accomplish two things at once—both to divert suspicion from herself and to win the Princess' good will. The Baroness began to search for Granitsky with her eyes, but she could not find him. There was a reason for that—a very important one.

At the other end of the house was located a sacred room to which the men did not have access. There an enormous, brightly illuminated mirror reflected light blue silk curtains: it was surrounded by all the caprices of whimsical fashion; flowers, ribbons, feathers, curls, rouge— everything was strewn over the tables as in Raphael's arabesques; on a low divan lay rows of bluish-white Parisian shoes—this reminder of pretty little feet—and they seemed to be bored in their solitude; a little way off, under a light veil, were draped across the back of an armchair those mysterious inventions of culture which a prudent woman does not reveal even to him who has a right to her complete frankness: those elastic corsets, laces, garters, incomprehensible starched handkerchiefs suspended on a little cord or tied across the middle, and so forth and so on. Only Monsieur Ravi, with his magnificent topknot which looked as if it had been moulded from china, in a white apron, with curling tongs in his hands, had the right to be in this female inner sanctum during a ball; Monsieur Ravi was not affected by the magnetic air of the female dressing room which causes a tremor to run along the body of another man; he paid no attention to the luxurious impressions remaining in female garments which ancient sculptors, dampening the veil on Aphrodite, understood so well; like the chief of a sultan's harem he coolly dozed in the middle of all his surroundings, thinking neither about the significance of his name nor about what such a room suggested to his ardent compatriots.

Before the end of the mazurka one young lady, having said a couple of words to her dancing partner, fluttered into this room unnoticed by others, showed Mr. Ravi her uncurled tress, Mr. Ravi went out for other curling tongs, in one instant the young lady tore off a scrap of paper, quickly took a slender pencil out of a notebook, propped her little foot on the divan, rested the paper on her knee and wrote a few words, squeezed the note into an unobrusive ball, and when Mr. Ravi returned, complained about his slowness.

At the end of the dance, when several unfinished conversations lingered in the air, preoccupied dancers ran from corner to corner after ladies, ladies lazily examined their lists of partners, and even motionless figures surrounding the dancers changed their places in order to give some sign of life—at that moment of disorder this same lady walked past Granitsky: her smoke-colored shawl flew off her glowing shoulders, Granitsky picked it up, the lady bent forward, their hands met, and the wadded-up paper remained in the young man's hand. Granitsky's face did not change expression. He remained a short while on the same spot, carefully adjusted the glove on his hand and then, complaining about the heat and his own tiredness, walked quietly away to a remote room where several gamblers sat in sweet isolation at a card table. Fortunately one of them announced to Granitsky that he had lost his bet. Granitsky stepped to the side, took out his wallet and, as if looking for money in it, read the following words which had been written hastily by a familiar hand:

"I didn't have time to warn you. Don't dance with me more than once. It seems to me that my husband is beginning to notice . . ."

It was impossible to make out the rest of it.

By the right of indiscretion granted to storytellers we will announce who had written this note. Granitsky had known its author before she was married; she was his first passion; at that time they had sworn eternal love to each other, though various family considerations opposed their union—this was in Florence. They soon separated; Granitsky remained in Rome; his Lydia was taken away to Petersburg by her mother, who gave her in marriage, willy-nilly, to

Count Rifeysky. Be that as it may, the old lovers, having met again, recalled their former vow: a flame flared up from beneath the ashes; they decided to make up for lost time and to take revenge upon society for its willfulness by triumphantly deceiving it.

Granitsky brought the Count a whole armful of letters, recommendations, gifts, parcels, etc.; he managed in Petersburg itself to render him some sort of service and in his home he finally became almost a member of his family.

Obedient to the ruler of his heart, he returned to the hall and began to look around for some female acquaintances who could help him finish off the evening. At that moment the Baroness came up to him and asked whether he would like to be introduced to a dancing partner. Granitsky accepted her offer with the greatest joy; she led him up to Princess Mimi.

But the Baroness had made a mistake in her calculations: the Princess flared up, claimed to be ill, declared that she did not want to dance, and when the embarrassed Baroness withdrew, said to the old lady sitting beside her:

"Where on earth did she get the idea of foisting off her friends on me? She wants to use me to screen her own stratagems. She thought that it would be difficult to guess . . ."

There was a whole world of malice in these few words. How the Princess wanted someone to come up to invite her to dance! With what joy would she have shown the Baroness that it was only her Granitsky with whom she did not want to dance! But the Princess unfortunately did not manage that: and for the duration of the ball she, as usual, did not get off her chair and returned home with plans for a most cruel revenge.

Do not suppose, however, dear and gentle readers, that the Princess' anger toward the Baroness was brought on by nothing more than momentary vexation. No! Princess Mimi was a very reasonable woman, and had long since taught herself not to be carried away without reason by a movement of the heart. No! Eliza had long, long ago inflicted a heavy offense upon Princess Mimi; in the last period of her travels from ball to ball Eliza's first husband had seemed to be a quasi-suitor of the Princess'; that is, he did not feel the same revulsion toward her that other men did; the Princess was certain that had it not been for Eliza, she would now have the pleasure of being married, or at least of being a widow—which would give no less pleasure. And all in vain! The Baroness appeared, won over the admirer, married him, was the death of him, married another—and still pleased everybody, caused men to fall in love with her, and knew how never to leave the dance floor, while Princess Mimi was still single and time was running out! Often at her toilette the Princess would gaze with secret despair at her overripe charms: she would compare her own tall figure, her wide shoulders, and her masculine looks with the Baroness' soft little face. Oh, if anyone could have seen what was going on in the Princess' heart at such moments! What appeared in her imagination! How inventive it was at that moment! What a wonderful model she would have been for a painter who wanted to depict a wild islander tearing to pieces a captive who had fallen into her hands. And all this had to be contained under a tight corset, conventional phrases, and a polite exterior! All the flames of hell had to be let out only as a slender inconspicuous thread of fire. Oh, it is horrible, horrible!

In these moments of grief, sorrow, envy, and vexation, a comforter appeared to the Princess.

It was the Princess' maid. The maid's sister worked for the Baroness. The sisters often got together, and when each in turn had berated her mistress, they would get down to relating domestic occurrences to each other; then, after they had returned home, they would transmit the news they had gathered to their mistresses. The Baroness would die from laughter while listening to the details of Mimi's toilette: how she suffered while having her corset tightened around her ample waist, how she whitened her rough hands which had turned blue from tension; how she used various means to fill out her right side which had a slightly unnatural slant to it, how for the night she tied to her scarlet cheeks!—raw cutlets!—how she plucked excess hairs from her eyebrows, touched up the grey ones, etc.

The news which the Princess received was much more important: the Baroness herself was responsible for that: there was almost nothing to tell about her, and Masha—that was her servant's name—was involuntarily forced to resort to inventions. There is truth in the ancient, time-tested saying that a person is always the cause of his own misfortunes!

When the Princess returned from the ball Masha noticed that something special had happened to her mistress (although the Princess was always out of sorts at such a time): it seemed to Masha that the Princess was already fidgeting with the shoes, jars of cream, bottles, and other things which the Princess had the habit of dispatching—dispatching—how can this be said more politely?—dispatching in a direction parallel to the floor and perpendicular to the lines ending at the maid's face. Does this seem rather vague? . . The poor girl, in order to avert the storm, did not fail to resort to her only defence.

"I was at my sister's today, ma'am," she said. "The things that go on there, your excellency!!"

Masha had not made a mistake. The Princess' face brightened in an instant; she was all ears; and Masha was still talking to the Princess long after the noise of the city had started up. She told her about how the Baron often left home, and at that time a newcomer would sit with the Baroness, they would arrange to go to the theater together, to be together at the ball, etc., etc.

The Princess could not get to sleep for a long time, and when she did fall asleep she constantly awoke because of various dreams: she dreamed that she was getting married and already standing before the pulpit, everyone was congratulating her—suddenly the Baroness appeared and dragged her fiancé away; in another dream the Princess was examining her wedding dress, trying it on, admiring it—the Baroness appeared and tore it into tiny pieces; now the Princess was lying in bed wanting to embrace her husband—but the Baroness was lying in the bed and laughing; in another the Princess was dancing at a ball, everyone was carried away by her beauty, saying that she was dancing with her fiancé—but the Baroness tripped her and she fell to the floor. But there were also more comforting dreams: the Baroness appeared in the form of a maid—the Princess scolded her, hit her with slippers, and snipped off her hair; then she appeared in the form of a large black poodle,— the princess ordered it thrown out and watched through the window with pleasure as the footmen threw stones at her enemy; then in the form of embroidery cloth—the Princess pricked it with a big sharp needle and made stitches in it with red cloth . . .

And do not blame her for this, but blame, bewail, curse the perverse morality of our society. What is to be done if the ony goal for a girl in society is to get married!—if from the cradle on she hears the words: "When you're married." She is taught dancing, drawing and music only in order to get married; she is dressed up and taken out into society; she is forced to pray to the Lord God to help her get married as soon as possible. That is the limit and the beginning of her life. That *is* her life. What is there to be surprised about if every woman becomes her personal enemy and if the first quality she seeks in a man becomes *marriageability*. Beware and curse—but not the poor woman.

II

The Round Table

On cause, on rit, on est heureux.
Romans francais

Under the cover of peace and quiet,
in the circle of one's family . . .
Russian Novels

On the next day after dinner, Princess Mimi, her younger sister Maria (a young widow), the old Princess (the mother of both), and a couple of intimates in addition sat as usual at the round table in the drawing room and, in expectation of whist partners, studiously applied themselves to their embroidery.

The Princess was a very old and respected lady; in all her long, long life it was impossible to find a single act, a single word, a single feeling which was not strictly in keeping with propriety; she spoke French very purely and without mistakes; she maintained to a full degree the severity and hauteur expected of a woman of good breeding; she did not care for abstract discussions, but she could keep up small talk for days on end; she never took upon herself the unpleasant obligation of standing up for someone against general opinion; you could be certain of not meeting anyone in her home at whom people would look with distaste or whom you would not meet in society. In additon to that the Princess was a woman of unusual intelligence: she was not at all wealthy and gave neither balls nor dinners; but in spite of that she managed to navigate so skillfully among intrigues, surround people so skillfully with her nieces and nephews, granddaughters and grandsons, so skillfully inquire about one person and abuse another, that she acquired general respect and, as they say, established herself on a firm footing.

In addition to that, she was a very charitable woman: in spite of her inadequate resources, her drawing room was lit up every day, and officials of foreign embassies could always be certain of finding in her home a fireplace or a card table at which to pass the time between dinner and a ball; raffles for the poor often took place in her home; she was always buried in concert tickets from her daughters' teachers; she took under her wing anyone who was recommended to her by a respectable person. In a word, the Princess was a good, sensible, and charitable woman in all respects.

All this, as we said, gave her the right to general respect: the Princess knew her own value and loved to exercise her right. But of late the Princess had begun to feel bored and vexed with everything; whist and people, people and whist still enlivened her somehow, but before the game began she could not (in the family circle, of course) conceal her involuntary depression, and would suddenly reveal some sort of hard-heartedness, some sort of petty hatred for everything around her, some sort of absence of all cordiality, some sort of revulsion toward any good turn, even some sort of revulsion toward life. How could she help complaining about fate? Why was there such injustice? Why had this respected lady been so poorly rewarded? For, I assure you, this petty Byronism of the Princess' arose not from recollections of any former secret transgressions, not from repentance, oh, no, not from repentance! I have already told you that in the course of her whole life the Princess had never allowed herself to do anything which other people did not do; she was as innocent as a lamb; she could confront the events of her earlier life without hesitation—they were clean as glass—not a single little spot. In a word, I can in no way explain to you the source of the Princess' depression. Allow that riddle to be solved by those respected ladies who will or will not read me, and let them explain it to their grandchildren, the hope of the new generation.

And so the Princess sat at the round table in the midst of her family. O family round table! Witness of domestic secrets! What has not been confided to you? What do you not know? If a head were added to your four legs, you could be compared to our wise describers of mores who so correctly and sharply attack a society inaccessible to them and whom I so vainly strive to imitate. A mild frankness usually begins at the round table; a feeling of vexation, suppressed at another time, begins to display itself little by little; egoism leaps out from under the embroidery in full, luxuriant colors: now the manager's accounts and the disorder of the estate come to mind; then the overpowering desire to marry or to be given in marriage is disclosed; now some failure, some moment of humiliation comes to mind; then they complain about their very closest friends and about people to whom you seem to be devoted heart and soul; here daughters grumble, the mother grows angry, sisters reproach each other; in a word, here all the little secrets which are carefully concealed from society's gaze are made obvious. As soon as the bell is heard everything disappears! Egoism hides behind smoke-colored bodices, smiles appear on everyone's face, and the bachelor entering the room looks with tender emotion at the friendly circle of the dear family.

"I don't know," the old Princess was saying to Princess Mimi, "why you go to balls when you complain every time that you are bored . . .that you don't dance . . . Going out costs money, and it's for nothing. The only thing that happens is that I stay home alone without even a game of whist . . . Just like yesterday! Really, it's time for all this to end: after all, you're beyond thirty, Mimi—for heaven's sake get married quickly; at least then I'll be calmer. Really, I'm not in a condition to keep you in clothes . . ."

"I think," said the young widow, "that you yourself, Mimi, are to blame for much. Why this continual look of contempt on your face? Judging by your face, when anyone comes up to you, one would think you had been personally offended. You really are frightful at a ball . . . you antagonize everyone."

Princess Mimi. And really, why should I hang on the neck of everyone I meet, like your Baroness? Should I mince and prance and show every little boy my gratitude for the fact that he does me the honor of leading me in a contredanse?

Maria. Don't talk to me about the Baroness. Your behavior towards her yesterday at the ball was such that I don't even know what to call it. It was unprecedented impoliteness. The Baroness wanted to do something nice for you and brought you a partner . . .

Mimi. She brought him to me in order to conceal her own amorous intrigues. That's a marvelous favor!

Maria. You love to interpret everything in a bad light. Where did you notice these amorous intrigues?

Mimi. You are the only one who doesn't see or hear anything! You, of course, as a married woman, can afford to scorn the opinion of society, but I . . . I value myself too much. I don't want people to start saying the same things about me that they say about your Baroness.

Maria. I don't know! But everything they have said about the Baroness up to now has turned out to be false . . .

Mimi. Of course, everyone is mistaken! You are the only one who is right! . . I can't get over your ability to stand up for her. Her reputation is already made.

Maria. Oh, I know! The Baroness has many enemies, and there's a reason for that: she is beautiful; her husband is ugly; her kindness attracts crowds of young men to her.

Mimi flared up and the old Princess interrupted Maria:

"To tell you the truth, I'm not at all pleased about your acquaintance with the Baroness; she doesn't know how to behave at all. What are all these continual riding parties and picnics? There isn't a ball at which she doesn't twirl; there isn't a man whom she doesn't treat as a brother. I don't know what you call all this in the present age, but in our time such behavior was called indecent."

"But we're not talking about the Baroness!" objected Maria, who wanted to deflect the conversation away from her friend, "I'm talking about you, Mimi: you really drive me to despair. You speak of the general opinion. You don't really think that it is favorable to you? Oh, you are entirely mistaken. Do you think that it's pleasant for me to see that people fear your tongue like fire, that they stop talking when you approach a group? They tell me—me—your sister, to my face about your gossip, about your malice; you hint to a husband about his wife's secrets; you tell a wife about her husband; the young people simply hate you. There isn't a single prank of theirs that you don't already know about and haven't already roundly condemned. I assure you that with a personality like yours you will never get married!"

"Oh, I care very little about that," answered Mimi. "It's better to stay a spinster all my life than to marry some sickly cripple and drag him from ball to ball until he dies."

Maria flared up in turn and was preparing to answer, but the bell rang, the door opened, and Count Skvirsky entered; he was an old friend, or—what amounts to the same thing—an old whist partner of the Princess'. He was one of those lucky people whom one cannot help envying. He was busy his whole life and the whole day: in the morning he had to give nameday greetings to someone, buy a design for Princess Zizi, find a dog for Princess Bibi, drop in at the ministry for the news, make it in time for a christening or a funeral, then to dinner, and so on and so forth. For fifty years Count Skvirsky had been planning to do something serious, but he put it off from one day to the next, and because of the daily hustle and bustle he had never even managed to get married. Yesterday and thirty years ago were the same thing for him: fashions and furniture changed, but drawing rooms and cards are the same today as yesterday, and will be the same tomorrow as today—he was already displaying his calm, imperturbable smile to a third generation.

"The heart rejoices," Skvirsky said to the Princess, "when one comes into the room and looks upon the dear circle of your family. Nowadays there are few such harmonious families! You're all together, always so cheerful, so satisfied, and one sighs involuntarily when recalling one's own bachelor corner. I can honestly assure you—let other people say what they want— but as far as I am concerned, I think that unmarried life ..."

Skvirsky's philosophical discourse was interrupted when a card was offered him.

In the meantime the Princess' drawing room had soon filled up: there were husbands for whom their own house is a sort of Kalmyk tent, suitable only for a night's lodging; and those dear young people who come to your house in order to have something to say at the next one; and those whom fate, in defiance of nature, has drawn into the flywheel of drawing rooms; and those for whom the simplest visit is the consequence of profound calculations and the textbook for a year's intrigue. There were also those people for whom Griboyedov himself could not find any other descriptive name than Mr. N. and Mr. D.

"Did you stay long at the ball yesterday?" Princess Mimi asked one young man.

"We danced some after supper."

"Tell me, how did the comedy end?"

"Princess Bibi finally succeeded in fastening her comb ..."

"Oh! Not that ..."

"Ah, I understand! .. The tall figure in the black dress coat finally made up his mind to start a conversation: he brushed against Countess Rifeyskaya's hat and said, 'Excuse me.' "

"Oh, that's still not it . . . So you didn't notice anything?"

"Oh, you're talking about the Baroness?"

"Oh no! I hadn't even thought about her. Why did you start up about her? Are they really saying something about her?"

"No, I haven't heard anything. I only wanted to guess what you meant by your question."

"I didn't mean anything."

"Then what comedy are you talking about?"

"I was talking about the ball in general."

"No, say what you like, there is something going on here! You spoke in such a tone . . ."

"That's society for you! You are already drawing conclusions! I assure you that I wasn't thinking about anyone in particular. But since you mentioned the Baroness, did she dance a long time after I left?"

"She didn't leave the dance floor."

"She doesn't take care of herself at all. With her health . . ."

"Oh, Princess, you're not talking about her health at all. Now I understand everything. That Colonel of the Guards? . . That's it, isn't it?"

"No! I didn't notice him."

"Really? I must remember whom she danced with . . ."

"Oh, for heaven's sake, stop it! I'm telling you that I wasn't even thinking of her. I'm so afraid of all this gossiping and all these rumors . . . People in society are so malicious . . ."

"Just a moment, just a moment! Prince Peter . . . Bobo . . . Leidenmuntz, Granitsky?"

"Who is that? That new person, the tall one with dark sideburns?"

"That's the one."

"It seems that he is a friend of the Baroness' brother-in-law?"

"That's the one."

"So his name is Granitsky?"

"Tell me, please," said a lady who was playing cards and listening attentively to Mimi's words, "what sort of a person is this Granitsky?"

"The Baroness takes him everywhere," answered the Princess' neighbor at the ball.

"And today," noted a third lady, "she had him on display in her theater box."

"That could only happen with the Baroness," said the Princess' neighbor. "God knows what sort of person he is! Some sort of apparition . . ."

"It's really ture that God alone knows what sort he is! He is some sort of pseudo-Jacobin, or *un frondeur* in any case; he doesn't know how to live. And what nonsense he talks! The other day I started to persuade Count Boris to take a ticket for our Tselini, and this—what's his name—Granitsky began telling within earshot about some sort of insurance company that was to be set up against concert tickets . . ."

"He is not a good person," many people remarked.

"Don't let the Baroness hear that!" said Mimi.

"Well, now I understand!" the young man interrupted her.

"Oh, no! I swear to God I only meant that this conversation would be very unpleasant for her; he is a friend of their household . . . And for any . . ."

"Allow me to interrupt you once more, because I'll tell you what you wanted to know. After supper the Baroness danced with Granitsky without stopping. Oh, now I understand everything! He didn't leave her side: if she left a scarf on a chair, he brought it to her; if she was warm, he came running with a glass . . ."

"How malicious you are! I didn't ask you a thing about that. It's hardly surprising that he's looking after her! He is almost a relative to her, he lives in their home . . ."

"Oh! He lives in their home! What cocksureness there is in that Baron! Don't you think?"

"Oh, for heaven's sake, stop it! You are forcing me to say things that are not in my head: with you one immediately turns into a gossip, and I—I fear that so much! . . . God save me from making remarks about anyone! . . And especially the Baroness, whom I so love . . ."

"Yes! That's true! . . The Baroness' husband doesn't take any interest in her: she, poor thing, sits at home, always alone . . ."

"Not alone!" objected the young man, smiling at his own wit.

"Oh, you interpret everything in your own way! The Baroness is a very moral woman . . ."

"Oh, let's be just!" remarked the Princess' neighbor. "We don't need to condemn anyone; but I don't know what rules the Baroness observes. I don't know—somehow a conversation started up about *Antony,* that awful, immoral play; I couldn't sit through it, but she took it into her head to defend the play and to assure us that only such a play can halt a woman at the edge of ruin . . ."

"Oh, I confess," remarked the Princess, "everything that is said, done, and written in our age . . . I understand nothing!"

"Yes," answered Skvirsky, "I will say that as far as I am concerned, I think that morality is essential; but enlightenment is also . . ."

"There you go again, Count!" objected the Princess. "Today everyone repeats over and over again: 'enlightenment, enlightenment!' No matter where you look there is enlightenment everywhere! They're enlightening the merchants and enlightening the peasants, and in the old days there wasn't any of this, and everything went along better than it does now. I judge in the old-fashioned way: they say enlightenment, but if you take a look, you see that it's depravity."

"No, excuse me," answered Skvirsky, "I don't agree with you. Enlightenment is essential, and I'll prove it to you as easily as two times two makes four. What, then, is enlightenment? Well, take my nephew, for example: he graduated from the university, knows all the sciences— both mathematics and Latin—he has a diploma, and all roads are open to him—both to a Collegiate Assessorship and to something even higher. Allow me to say that there is enlightenment and there is enlightenment. Take a candle, for example: it burns, and without it we wouldn't be able to play whist; but if I take it and put it up against the curtain, the curtain catches fire . . ."

"Please mark that down," said one of the players.

"What I'm saying?" asked Skvirsky, smiling.

"No, a rubber!"

"You reneged, Count! How could you?" Skvirsky's partner asked with irritation.

"What? . . Me? . . Reneged? Oh good heavens! . . Really? Well, that's enlightenment for you! . . Reneged! Oh, good heavens, I reneged. Yes, that's exactly what I did!"

Now it became impossible to make anything out: everyone started talking about Skvirsky's misfortune, and all comments, all interests, all feelings concentrated on that subject. Taking advantage of the general commotion, two guests left the room unnoticed: one of them seemed to have just arrived to make a place for himself, the other was taking him around to drawing rooms to get him acquainted. Vexation and derision were apparent on the face of one of them; the other one calmly and attentively scrutinized the stairsteps along which they were ascending.

"It was preordained that I should meet up with that good-for-nothing!" said the first one. "That Skvirsky is an old acquaintance—I knew him in Kazan—how he carried on there! And he's still holding forth! And about what? About morality? And what's most remarkable of all is that he believes what he says. Remind him that he completely ruined his nephews who were under his guardianship—then see whether he's in a position to ask what relation that has to morality. Tell me, please, how can you accept such an immoral person into society?"

His companion shrugged his shoulders.

"What am I going to do with you, my friend!" he answered, taking a seat in the carriage. "If you don't know our language—study, study, my friend: it's essential. We have shuffled the meanings of all words, and to such an extent that if you call a person immoral who cheats at cards, slanders a close friend, takes over someone else's estate, you won't be understood, and your choice of adjective will seem strange; but if you give rein to your heart and mind, extend your hand to a victim of the prejudices of high society, of if you refuse to open your door to anybody and everybody, you will immediately be called an immoral person, and that word will be understandable to everyone."

After a silence, the first continued:

"Do you know that I find your brilliant, huge parties much more bearable? There people at least say little, everyone has a decorous appearance—as if they were human: but Lord deliver me from their family circles! The moments of their domestic frankness are horrible, disgusting—even to the point of curiosity. The old Princess—a judge of literature! Count Skvirsky—the defender of enlightenment! Really, after all that you feel like being an ignoramus!"

"However, there was some justice in the Princess' words! You yourself must agree—what is the literature of today? Incessant descriptions of tortures, evil deeds, debauchery; incessant crimes and more crimes . . ."

"Excuse me," answered his companion, "but people talk that way who haven't read anything except the works of contemporary literature. You, of course, are convinced that it is ruining social morality, aren't you? As if there were something to ruin, my dear friend! Since the middle of the eighteenth century everything has been ruined so carefully that there's nothing left for our age to ruin. And is it only contemporary literature that can be reproached for that sin? For every really immoral contemporary work I'll show you ten from the eighteenth,. seventeenth, and even the sixteenth century. Now nudity exists more in words, in those days it existed in fantasy and in fact. Just read Brantome or even Tredyakovksy's *Voyage to the Isle of Love:* I don't know a Russian book more immoral than that one; it's a handbook for the most shameless coquette. Nowadays they wouldn't write such a book in favor of sensual pleasures; nowadays an author, contrary to the ancient rule, *'si vis me pleurer,'* blasphemes and laughs in order to make the reader weep. All today's literary nudity is the final reflection of the real life of the past, an involuntary confession of old sins, the tail of an ancient lawless comet by which— do you know what?—by which one can judge that the comet itself is moving off beyond the horizon, since he who writes no longer feels. Finally, contemporary literature, in my opinion, is a punishment sent from on high to the icy society of our age: the quiet pleasures of poetry are not for it, the hypocrite! It is not worthy of them! . . . And perhaps it is a beneficent punishment: inscrutable are the decisions of the human mind! Perhaps our age needs this strong remedy: perhaps, by incessantly shocking society's nerves, it will awaken its sleeping conscience in the same way that bodily suffering can bring a drowned person back to consciousness. Since I have been in our society I have come to understand contemporary literature. Tell me, in what other way, with what poetry could it interest such a being as Princess Mimi? With what masterful catastrophe will you touch her heart? What feeling could be comprehensible to her except revulsion—yes, revulsion! That is perhaps the only path to her heart. Oh, that woman really horrified me! While looking at her I dressed her in various garments, that is I developed her thoughts and feelings logically, I imagined to myself what such a soul would be like in various circumstances in life and I straightaway arrived . . . at the bonfires of the Inquisition! Don't laugh at me: Lavater used to say, 'Give me one line of his face and I'll tell you about the whole person.' Just find for me the degree to which a person likes gossip, likes to find out and relate family secrets, and all under the guise of virtue, and I will define for you with mathematical accuracy the extent of his immorality, the emptiness of his soul, the absence of any thought, any religious or noble feeling. There is no exaggeration in my words: I could cite the church fathers, for example. They had a profound understanding of the heart of man. Listen to the bitter pity with which they recall such people: 'Woe unto them on the Day of Judgment,' they say, 'better that they should not know the holy of holies than to set up a throne to the Devil in its midst.'"

"Have mercy, brother! What's the matter with you? That really seems to be a sermon."

"Oh, excuse me! Everything that I saw and heard was so vile that I had to get it off my chest. However—tell me, did you not hear Princess Mimi's conversation with that hired dancer?"

"No, I didn't pay any attention."

"You? A man of letters? . . . But in that dear society conversation was the embryo of a thousand crimes, a thousand calamities!"

"Ah, my friend! They were telling me at that time a more interesting story—about how one of my colleagues made a career . . ."

The carriage stopped.

III

The Consequences of Family Conversations

> I speak, you speak, he speaks,
> we speak, you speak, they speak.
> *The Works of . . . ?!*

Fortunately, few people shared the unknown orator's ferocious opinion about today's society, and therefore its petty affairs flowed on in their usual way without interference. And in the meantime, unnoticed by anyone, that sort of superstition which is called time was moving onward.

Countess Rifeyskaya, who had been friendly with the Baroness for a long time, had tried to get even closer to her since Granitsky's arrival: they were seen together both on walks and in the theater; the Baroness knew nothing about Granitsky's earlier acquaintance with the Countess; true enough, she noticed that they were not indifferent to each other, but she considered it the usual, momentary flirtation which people sometimes take up in their spare time because of having nothing to do. Should I tell you? The Baroness, subconsciously, even rejoiced at her discovery: it seemed to her a sure defense against the attacks of her female enemy.

But Granitsky and the Countess conducted their affairs with a special artistry acquired through long experience: they knew how to be absolutely indifferent to each other in society; while talking with other people about absolutely extraneous matters, they knew how to indicate to each other a place of rendezvous or to communicate various precautionary measures; they even knew how to laugh at each other opportunely. Their ardent glances met only in the mirror; but they did not lose a single moment: they would seize every instant when others' eyes were distracted by any sort of object. During a momentary departure from a room, from the theater—in a word, at any convenient opportunity whatsoever, their hands would merge, and often their long constraint would be rewarded with a kiss of love inflamed by their mockery of public opinion.

Meanwhile the seeds scattered by Princess Mimi's expert hand grew and multiplied like those miraculous trees of the virgin Brazilian forest which spread out their branches, and each branch drops to the earth and becomes a new tree and again pierces the earth with its branches, and more and more trees . . . And woe betide the careless traveller who finds himself caught in these countless entanglements! A young chatterbox related the conversation with Princess Mimi to another chatterbox; the latter told his mama, mama told her friend, and so on. Mimi had arranged just such a labyrinth around herself; the old Princess had hers; the Princess' old neighbor at the ball also had hers. All these labyrinths grew and grew; finally they met, intertwined, strengthened each other, and a thick net enveloped the Baroness with Granitsky, just like Mars with Venus. On this occasion all the tongues in town which could twitter began to twitter—some out of a desire to convince their listeners that they were not party to such sins, others out of hatred for the Baroness, others in order to have a laugh at her husband, and others simply out of a desire to show that they also knew the secrets of the drawing room.

Granitsky, busy with his own strategic movements with the Countess, and the Baroness, calmed by her discovery, were not aware of the storm which was ready to burst over their heads: they did not notice that their every word, their every movement was noticed, discussed, and interpreted; they did not know that a court of law, composed of bonnets of every possible fashion, was perpetually in session before their eyes. When the Baroness addressed Granitsky in a friendly way without any ceremony, the court decided that she was playing the role of innocence. When, because of some concurrence of circumstances, she happened not to say a word to Granitsky in the course of an entire evening, the court found that this was done in order to divert general attention. When Granitsky spoke to the Baron, that meant that he desired to lull the poor man's suspicions. When he kept silent, that meant that the lover did not have the strength to overcome his jealousy. In a word, no matter what the Baroness and Granitsky did, whether he sat next to her at the table or not, whether he danced with her or not, whether the Baroness was kind to her husband in company or not, whether she went out with him or not—everything served the idle court as confirmation of its conclusions.

And the poor Baron! Had he known what tender interest ladies took in him, had he known all the virtues they discovered in his person! His habitual somnolence was proclaimed the inner suffering of a passionate husband; his stupid smile a sign of unfeigned good will, in his sleepy eyes they found profundity of thought; in his passion for whist—a desire not to see his wife's infidelity or to maintain outward decorum.

Baroness Dauerthal once met Princess Mimi at the home of a common friend. It goes without saying that they rejoiced greatly, pressed each other's hand in a friendly fashion, asked each other a countless multitude of questions and both sides left them almost unanswered; in a word, not a shadow of enmity, not a shadow of a recollection of what had happened at the ball—it was as if they had increasingly been true friends all their lives. There were few guests in the drawing room besides them—only an old princess, a young widow—Mimi's sister, Mimi's old and habitual neighbor at balls, Granitsky, and two or three other people.

Granitsky had trailed through various drawing rooms all day in order to see his Countess, and not having found her anywhere, he was bored and indifferent. It was very unpleasant for the Baroness to meet Princess Mimi, and the old princess felt the same way about the Baroness. Only Mimi was happy for the convenient opportunity to observe the Baroness and Granitsky in close company. Because of all this an unbearable tension was produced in the drawing room: the conversation wandered constantly from subject to subject and constantly broke off. The hostess dragged out old news because everything possible had been said about the new, and everyone looked at her, obviously without listening. Mimi was triumphant: while speaking with others, she did not miss a single word of either the Baroness' or Granitsky's, and in every word she found keys to the hieroglyphic language customarily employed in such cases. She attributed Granitsky's obvious indifference either to a little quarrel between the lovers or to the aroused suspicions of the husband. And the Baroness! Not a single movement of hers escaped Mimi's observation, and every movement told an entire story with all the details. In the meantime the poor Baroness, as if guilty, turned away from Granitsky: now she would scarcely reply to his words, then she would suddenly address a question to him: she could not restrain herself from occasionally glancing at Princess Mimi, and often, when their sidelong glances met, the Baroness suffered involuntary embarrassment, which was made even greater by her anger at herself for her embarrassment.

After a while Granitsky looked at the clock, said that he was going to the opera, and disappeared.

"We really broke up that rendezvous," Princess Mimi said to her inseparable neighbor. "Just the same, they won't be able to conceal their tracks."

Granitsky had hardly left when a servant announced to the Baroness that the carriage for which she had long been waiting had arrived.

At that moment a vague thought ran through Princess Mimi's mind: she herself was hardly aware of it—it was the dark, aimless inspiration of malice—it was the feeling of a person who stakes a hundred to one in the sure hope that he will not win.

"I have a terrible migraine!" she said. "Please, Baroness, allow me to use your carriage to get to my home down the street: we have given our driver the evening off."

They looked at each other and understood each other. The Baroness guessed by instinct what was going on in Princess Mimi's soul. She likewise had no definite idea about the latter's intentions; but she herself took fright without knowing why; it goes without saying that she easily agreed to Mimi's proposal, but she blushed, and blushed in such a way that everyone noticed it. All this happened a hundred times faster than we have been able to relate it.

There was a strong snowstorm outside; the wind kept blowing out the streetlamps, and it was impossible to distinguish a person two steps away. Wrapped in her coat from head to toe, Mimi, with trepidation in her heart, leaned on two footmen as she mounted the steps of the carriage. She had hardly taken two steps when a large masculine hand from inside the carriage suddenly grabbed her arm, helping her to enter. Mimi threw herself back, screamed—and it was nearly a scream of joy! She ran headlong back up the stairs, and beside herself, choked by varied emotions that had flared up in her soul, she rushed to her sister Maria, who had run out of the drawing room, along with the other ladies, on hearing Mimi's scream, which had resounded throughout the house.

"Now you can talk!" she whispered to her sister, but in such a way that everyone could hear. "Now defend your Baroness! In her carriage . . . she has . . . Granitsky! Advise her at least to arrange her rendezvous more carefully and not subject me to such shame . . ."

The Baroness arrived to see what all the noise was about. Mimi became silent and as if unconscious, threw herself into a chair. While the Baroness vainly asked the Princess what had happened to her—

the door opened and—

But excuse me, kind sirs! I think that now is the most appropriate moment to make you read the—

Preface

C'est avoir l'esprit de son âge!

Some time ago the custom arose, and has already fallen into decline, of writing a preface in the middle of a book. I consider the custom excellent, that is, very useful for an author. It used to be that an author went down on his knees, begged, and implored his reader to pay attention to him; but the reader scornfully turned a few pages and coldbloodedly left the writer in his humiliating position. In our age of justice and calculation the writer in his preface forces the reader to his knees and begs for the denouement; then the author, with an air of importance, dons his doctoral robes and proves to the reader why he ought to remain on his knees—all this with the innocent intent of forcing the reader to read the preface. Have it as you wish, but this is an excellent means, since anyone who has not read the preface knows only half the book. Therefore, kind sirs, go down on your knees, read, and read with the greatest attention and with the greatest respect, because I am going to tell you what all of you have long known already.

Do you know, my dear readers, that writing books is a very difficult business?

That the most difficult books for a writer are novels?

That the most difficult novels are those which must be written in Russian?

That of the novels written in Russian, the most difficult are those in which the mores of contemporary society are described?

Omitting a thousand reasons for these difficulties, I will mention the thousand and first. This reason—excuse me!—*pardon!*—*verzeihen sie!*—*scusate!*—*forgive me!*— this reason is that our ladies do not speak Russian!!

Listen to me, dear ladies: I am not a university student, not a schoolboy, not a publisher, neither A, nor B; I do not belong to any literary school and I do not even believe in the existence of Russian letters; I myself rarely speak Russian; I express myself in French almost without errors; I speak the purest Parisian dialect—blurred "r's" and all: in a word, I, a respectable person—I assure you that it is indecent, shameful, and shameless not to speak Russian! I know that French has already begun to go out of use, but what unclean spirit prompted you to replace it not with Russian, but with the accursed English language, for which one must break his tongue, clench his teeth, and thrust out his lower jaw? And because of that necessity, farewell to the pretty little mouth with pink, fresh little Slavic lips! It would be better not to have one at all.

You know as well as I that in society strong passions are at work—passions from which people turn pale, turn red, turn green, become exhausted, and even die; but in the highest levels of the social atmosphere these passions are expressed in a single phrase, a single word, a conventional word which, like the alphabet, it is impossible to translate or invent. A novelist who possesses so much conscience that he cannot allow himself to pass off the Eskimo language as the language of society must have absolute command of this social alphabet, he must catch all those conventional words, because I repeat, it is impossible to invent them: they are born in the heat of polite conversation, and the meaning given to them at that moment remains with them forever. But where will you catch such a word in a Russian drawing room? Here all Russian passions, thoughts, mockery, vexation, the slightest motion of the soul are expressed in ready-made words which are taken from the ample French storehouse, and which French novelists use so skillfully and to which they are obliged (leaving aside the question of talent) for most of their success. How often they do without those long descriptions, explanations, and preparations which are torture for the writer as well as reader, and which they easily replace with a few worldly phrases that are understandable to everyone. Those who know something about the mechanics of arranging a novel will understand all the benefits derived from this state of affairs. Ask our poet,[1] one of the few Russian writers who really know Russian, why he used in his verses the words *vulgar, vulgaire* in their full form. This word portrays half the personality of a character, half of his situation; but to express that in Russian one would have to write two pages of explanation—and just think how demanding that would be for the writer and how much fun for the reader! That is one example for you, but a thousand could be found. And for that reason I ask my readers to take into account all these circumstances and not to reproach me if the conversations of my heroes seem too bookish for some people, and not grammatical enough for others. In the latter instance I will refer you to Griboyedov, perhaps the only writer, in my opinion, who understood the secret of transferring our conversational language to paper.

Hereupon I beg my readers' pardon if I have bored them by entrusting to their good favor these little difficulties (domestic in the truest sense of the word) and by showing the scaffolding that holds up the scenery of the novel. I am acting in this case like the director of a certain poor provincial theater. Driven to despair by the spectators who were bored by a long intermission, he decided to raise the curtain and show them in fact how difficult it is to turn clouds into the sea, a blanket into a royal canopy, a housekeeper into a princess, and a blackamoor into a *premier ingénu*. The benevolent spectators found this show more interesting than the play itself. I feel the same way.

Of course there are people born with unusual gifts for whom everything is ready—the mores, the action of the novel, the language, and the characters: if they need to depict a person of high society, or as they put it, of a modish tone—nothing could be easier! They will without fail send him to foreign climes; for the sake of greater verisimilitude in costume, they will have him not engage in work, sleep until two in the afternoon, go shopping at candy stores, and drink until dinner—champagne (of course). If they need to write a conversation as it occurs in polite society—that is even easier! Open up the first translated novel by Mme Genlis, add the words *mon cher, ma chère, bonjour, comment vous portez-vous* in the essential places, and the conversation is ready! But such accuracy of description and such faithful, penetrating vision are given by Nature to few geniuses. She treated me shabbily in this respect, and for that reason I simply ask my readers not to get angry with me if in certain of my domestic conversations I have been unable to maintain completely the coloration of high society; and to the ladies I repeat my persuasive request to speak Russian.

By not speaking Russian they are deprived of a multitude of benefits:

1. They cannot understand our compositions so well; but since in most cases one could congratulate them for that, we will skip over this circumstance.

2. If, in spite of my admonitions, they nevertheless will not speak Russian, then I—I—in the future will not write a single story for them; let them read Messrs. A, B, C, and so forth.

Certain that this threat will have a stronger effect on my female readers than any proofs, I calmly turn to my story.

And so, the door opened, and . . . the old Baron, not understanding anything about this adventure, rushed in. He had come for his wife, and since, because of some unforeseen circumstance, he intended to go somewhere with her right away, he had decided to remain in the carriage and not reveal his presence to the mistress of the house. The scream from Mimi, whom he had taken at first for his wife, obliged him to come out.

But such was the hypnotic effect prepared by rumors around the city and by all the preceding, that the whole crowd looked at him and did not believe their eyes: some time later, after a glass of water, after eau de cologne, Hoffmann drops, and so on and so forth, everyone guessed that in such circumstances the thing to do was laugh. I am certain that many of my readers have noticed in the most varied instances of life the effect of this hypnotism, which can produce a powerful conviction in a crowd for scarcely any visible reason: having been subjected to this effect, we vainly try to destroy it with reason; a blind conviction so overpowers our will that our reason involuntarily begins to seek out circumstances which might confirm our convictions. At such moments the utterance of the most absurd words exerts a great influence; sometimes the word itself is forgotten, but the impression created by it remains in one's soul and, unnoticed by the person, it begets a series of thoughts such as would never have entered one's head had that word not been spoken, and which are sometimes only very remotely connected to it. This hypnotism plays a very important role in important events as well as the pettiest incidents, and perhaps must serve as the only explanation for them. Such a case was the one at hand: the incident with the Princess was very simple and understandable, but the predisposition of all those present towards a denouement of another sort gave birth to a vague idea that the Baron was in this case some sort of *godfather*. At that moment no one was in a condition to explain to himself how this could have happened; but this idea consequently developed, became stronger, and reason together with memory found in the past a multitude of confirmations for something which was really just a solitary blind conviction.

If you only knew what a racket was raised in the city after this incident! In every corner—in a whisper or out loud—over embroidery, over a book, at the theater, before God's altar men and women talked, interpreted, explained, argued, and lost their tempers. A heavenly fire would not have produced in them as strong an impression! And all of this because it occurred to a husband to come and pick up his wife. One is truly astonished when observing such regrettable occurrences. What attracts these people to matters that do not concern them? How is it that these people, these people who are soulless, icy when it concerns the noblest or vilest deed, the loftiest or the most banal thought, the most refined work of art, the destruction of all the laws of nature and humanity—how is it that these people become ardent, wise, penetrating, and eloquent when it comes to a cross, a rank, a wedding, a family secret, or that which they squeezed out of their dry brains under the name of decency?

IV

Lifesaving Advice

> Master: "Fool! You should have done that on the side."
> Servant: "I did that, sir, I went up to him from the side."

The old Baron had a brother who was many years younger than he; he was an officer and all in all a very nice young man.

It is rather difficult to describe his character: one has to go back some distance.

You see, good people taught our fathers that one should doubt everything, calculate one's every act, avoid all systems, avoid everything useless, and everywhere seek the essential advantage, or as they said in those days, pick what was in reach and not wander off too far. Our fathers obeyed their teachers and set aside all useless things, which I shall not name in order not to seem a pedant, and they were very glad that all human wisdom confined itself to dinner, supper, and similar useful subjects. In the meantime their children grew and grew and created for themselves a system of life in defiance of good people—not a dreamy system, however, but one in which there was room for an epigram by Voltaire, an anecdote told by grandmother, a line of verse from Parny, one of Bentham's moral-arithmetical phrases, a mocking recollection of an example for samples of writing, a newspaper article, a bloody speech of Napoleon, a law based on the honor of cardplayers, and other such things on which old and young pupils of the eighteenth century subsist to this day.

The young Baron had mastered this system to perfection: he could not fall in love—for him there was something ridiculous in that sentiment; he simply loved women (all of them, with few exceptions), his hunting dog, Lepage guns, and his companions, when he was not fed up with them; he believed in the fact that two times two is four, that soon a vacancy in the rank of Captain would open up for him, that tomorrow he was supposed to dance numbers 2, 5, and 6 of the contredanse.

But let's be just; the young man had a noble, ardent, and kindly soul; but what has not been crushed by the criminal upbringing of this putrid and heavily perfumed age? Rejoice, people of calculations, doubt, and the essential advantage! Rejoice, defenders of derisive unbelief in everything sacred! Your thoughts have been scattered, you have inundated everything—both enlightenment and ignorance. Where will the sun arise which shall dry out this swamp and turn it into fertile soil?

The young Baron, wrapped up in a tight caftan, now glancing at the clock, now flipping through the pages of a French vaudeville, lay in a curved armchair in a room hung with Parisian lithographs and Asiatic daggers.

His servant gave him a note.

"From whom?"

"From the Marquise de Crequis."

"From Auntie!"

The contents of the note were as follows:

"Drop in to see me today after dinner, my dear. And don't forget, as you usually do; I have to see you about a very important matter."

"Well," the young man muttered to himself, "Auntie has probably invented yet another cousin that I'll have to lead out onto the dance floor. Oh, these cousins of mine! And where do they come from? "Tell Auntie," he said loudly, "that I'll be there. Now I want to dress."

When the young Baron Dauerthal appeared at the Marquise's, she put down her knitting needles, took him by the arm and with a mysterious look led him through a series of rooms which were distinguished by a characteristic lack of taste. When they arrived at the study, she seated him on a small sofa surrounded by pots of geraniums, balsam, mint and family portraits. The air was impregnated with eau de cologne and spermacetti.

"Tell me, Auntie," asked the young man, "what does all this mean? You don't want to marry me off, do you?"

"Not yet, my dear! But jokes aside: I must speak very, very seriously. Please do me the favor of telling me what sort of friend you have—what's his name—Granitsky, isn't it?"

"Yes, Granitsky. He's a fine young man from a good family..."

"I never heard of them. Tell me, how did you two become friends?"

"In a small town in Italy when I was exhausted, hungry, and half sick, I couldn't find a room in an inn: he shared his with me; I became ill; he took care of me for a whole week, he lent me money; I made him promise to stay at my place when he came to Petersburg; that was the beginning of our acquaintance... But what do all these questions mean, Auntie?"

"Listen to me, my dear! This is all well and good: I quite understand that a Granitsky would be glad to be of service to a Baron Dauerthal."

"Auntie, you are talking about my true friend!" the young man interrupted with displeasure.

"That is all well and good, my dear. I am not condemning your true friend—his actions towards you speak very honorably for him. But let me tell you frankly: you are a young man, you have only just entered society; you need to be careful in your choice of acquaintances. Nowadays young people are so depraved."

"I think, Auntie, no more and no less than usual ...."

"Nothing of the sort! In my time there was at least more respect for relatives; family ties were stronger then—not like now ..."

"And sometimes even too strong, dear Auntie, isn't that so?"

"That is not so! But that's not the point. Permit me to point out to you that you have acted very flightily in the case we are discussing: you met and became involved with a person that no one knows. Does he at least have a job somewhere?"

"No."

"Well, in view of that, you yourself tell me what sort of person he is! He doesn't even have a job! It's probably because he can't get accepted anywhere."

"You are mistaken, Auntie. He does not have a job because his mother is Italian, and all his property is in Italy; he cannot leave her, in fact, because of family ties ..."

"Why is he here?"

"On business for his father. But tell me, for heaven's sake, what are all these questions leading to?"

"In a word, my dear, your friendship with this person is very unpleasant for me, and you will do me a great favor if ... if you turn him out of your house."

"For goodness' sake, Auntie! You know that I obey you unquestioningly in all things, but put yourself in my place: on what grounds should I suddenly change my attitude toward a person to whom I am obliged for so much, and throw him out of the house for no particular reason? I am sorry, but I cannot bring myself to perform such an act of ingratitude."

"That's all nonsense, my dear! Romantic ideas and nothing else! There is a way, and a very polite one, of showing him that he is a burden to you ..."

"Of course, Auntie, that is very easy to do; but I repeat that I cannot take such vile ingratitude upon my conscience. I am sorry, but I cannot, I simply cannot ..."

"Listen to me!" answered the Marquise after a short silence, "you know how great your obligation is to your brother ..."

"Auntie!"

"Don't interrupt me. You know that after your father's death he could have appropriated all your property; he didn't do that, he took you at age three into his arms, raised you, put all the neglected matters into order; when you grew up he enrolled you in the service, honorably shared the property with you; in a word, you are obliged to him for everything you have ..."

"Auntie, what are you trying to say?"

"Listen. You are no longer a child and not at all stupid, but you are forcing me to say something I should not like to."

"What, Auntie?"

"Listen! First give me your word not to do anything foolish, but to act as a sensible person ought to."

"For heaven's sake, Auntie, finish saying what you're saying!"

"I have confidence in you, and for that reason I ask whether you haven't noticed anything between the Baroness and your Granitsky?"

"The Baroness? What does that mean?"

"Your Granitsky is having an affair with her . . ."

"Granitsky? . . It can't be!"

"I would not deceive you. It is true: your brother has been disgraced, his gray hairs profaned."

"But I need proof . . ."

"What proof do you need? They are already writing to me about it from Liflandia. Everyone pities your brother and is amazed that you can help betray him."

"Me? Betray him? This is slander, Auntie, pure slander. Who dared to write this to you?"

"I won't tell you that; but I'll only leave it to you to judge whether Granitsky may remain in your house. Your debt to your brother obliges you, before this liaison becomes too well known, to try in a civil way to force him to leave your house and, if possible, Russia. You understand that this must be done without raising a lot of noise; just find some sort of excuse . . ."

"Be assured that everything will be carried out, Auntie. Thank you for the information. My brother is old and weak; this is my affair, my obligation . . . Good-bye . . ."

"Stop, stop! Don't get angry! What's needed here is not anger, but coldbloodedness: promise me that you will not do anything foolish, that you will act as a sensible person ought to, not as a child."

"Oh, don't worry, Auntie. I'll arrange everything in the best possible way. Good-bye."

"Don't forget that you must act very carefully in this matter!" the Marquise shouted after him. "Talk calmly with Granitsky, don't get angry. Approach the matter from the side, indirectly . . . Understand?"

"Don't worry, don't worry, Auntie!" answered the Baron, running out.

Blood was pounding in the young man's head.

V

The Future

> . . . l'avenir n'est à personne,
> Sire, l'avenir est à Dieu.
> *Victor Hugo*

During this scene another one was taking place.

In the interior of an enormous house, behind a magnificent store, was located a small room with a single window hung with a curtain; the window looked out into the courtyard. Judging by the room's appearance, it would be difficult to guess to whom it belonged: simple plaster walls, a low ceiling, several old chairs and a mirror, in the alcove a gorgeous sofa with all the fancies of luxury, a low armchair with a curved back—all these things somehow quarreled among themselves. One of the room's doors linked it with the store via a blind hallway; the other led out onto the opposite street.

A young man briskly paced around the room; he often stopped, now in the middle of the room, now by the doors, and attentively listened. It was Granitsky.

Suddenly a rustle was heard, the door opened, and a beautiful woman, beautifully dressed, threw herself into his arms. It was Countess Lydia Rifeyskaya.

"Do you know, Gabriel," she said to him quickly, "that this is the last time we shall see each other?"

"The last time?" cried the young man. "But wait! What's the matter with you? Why are you so pale?"

"It's nothing. I got a little chilled. Because I was in a hurry to see you I forgot to put on my boots. The hallway is so cold . . . It's nothing!"

"You are so careless! You shouldn't neglect your health . . ."

The young man moved the armchair over to the fireplace, seated the beautiful woman in it, took off her shoes, and tried to warm her charming little feet by breathing on them.

"Oh, stop it, Gabriel! The minutes are valuable; I was hardly able to tear myself away from the house; I have come to you with important news. My husband has had a second stroke and,—it's terrible to say it—the doctors told me that my husband will not survive it: his tongue is paralyzed, his face has become distorted, he is terrifying! The poor man, he can't say a single word! . . He can hardly raise his hand! You wouldn't believe how sorry I feel for him."

And the Countess covered her face with her hand. Meanwhile Gabriel kissed her cold little feet, which seemed made of white marble and pressed them to his burning cheeks.

"Lydia," he said. "Lydia! You will be free . . ."

"Oh, tell me that more often, Gabriel! That is the only thought that makes me forget my situation for a moment; but there is something horrible in that thought. In order to be happy in your embraces I have to step across a grave! . . I need a man's death for my own happiness! . . I must wish his death! . . It's terrible, terrible! It turns one's heart over, it is contrary to nature."

"But, Lydia, if anyone is guilty in this, it is certainly not you. You are as blameless as an angel. You are the victim of the rules of propriety; you were given in marriage against your will. Remember how you resisted the will of your parents, remember all your sufferings, all our sufferings . . ."

"Oh, Gabriel, I know all that: and when I think about the past my conscience is quiet. God has seen all that I have borne in my life! But when I look at my husband, at his distorted face, at his trembling hand; when he beckons me toward him, me, in whom over the course of six years he has produced only one feeling—repulsion; when I remember that I always deceived him, that I am deceiving him now, then I forget what a chain of suffering, moral and physical, led me to this deceit. I languish between these two thoughts—and one does not destroy the other!"

Granitsky was silent: it would have been useless for him to try to comfort Lydia at such a moment.

"Don't be angry with me, Gabriel!!" she finally said, embracing his head. "You understand me; you have been used to understanding me since childhood. Only to you can I entrust my sufferings . . ."

And she ardently pressed him to her breast.

"But enough! Time is flying! I can't stay here any longer . . . Here is my last kiss! Now listen: I believe we will be happy; I believe that Providence will return to us what the despotism of society took away; but until that day I belong entirely to my husband. From this time on I must redeem our love and implore God for our happiness by incessant care, long nights at his bedside without sleep, and by suffering from not seeing you. Don't try to see me; don't write to me; allow me to forget you. Then I will become calmer and my conscience will torture me less. It will be easier for me to imagine myself completely pure and blameless . . . Farewell!! . . . One more thing: don't change anything in your way of life, continue to go out, dance, flirt, as if no change were being prepared for you . . . Drop in today to call on my husband, but I won't receive you: you are not a relative. And go out today and tell everyone with indifference about his illness. Farewell!"

"Stop! Lydia! One more kiss! . . How many long days will pass . . ."

"Oh, don't remind me about that anymore! . . Farewell. Be more patient than I.

Remember: there will be a time when I won't say to you 'They're coming—go away, Gabriel . . .'
Oh, it's awful, awful!"

They parted.

VI

This Could Have Been Foreseen

> "Vous allez ne rabacher je ne sais quels lieux communs de
> morale, que tous ont dans la bouche, qu'on fait sonner bien
> haut, pourvu que personne ne soit obligé de les pratiquer."
> "Mais s'ils se jettent dans le crime?"
> "C'est de leur condition."
>
> *Le Neveu de Rameau*

The young Baron Dauerthal returned home in a state of great agitation.

"Is Granitsky at home?" he asked.

"No, sir."

"Tell me as soon as he arrives."

Then he recalled that Granitsky was supposed to go to B***'s that evening.

The moments of expectation were terrible for the young man: he felt that for the first time in his life he had been summoned to an important deed; that now it was impossible to turn away with an epigram or indifference or a smile; that here he needed to feel strongly, to think forcefully, to concentrate all the forces of his soul; that, in a word, he needed to act, and to act on his own without demanding anyone's advice and without expecting anyone's support. But such tension was unfamiliar to him; he could not gather his thoughts together. His blood only flared up and his heart beat faster. As if in a dream he imagined the city's gossip; his gray-haired brother insulted and weak; his desire to show his love and gratitude to the old man; his comrades, epaulettes, swords, childish vexation; his desire to show that he was no longer a child; he thought that every crime was expiated by murder. All these daydreams flashed by in succession, but everything was dark and indefinite; he did not know how to appeal to that court which is independent of temporal prejudices and opinions and which always pronounces verdicts acccurately and correctly: his education had forgotten to tell him about that court, and life had not taught him to ask. The language of the court was unknown to the Baron.

At last the hour struck. The young man dashed to his carriage, galloped off, found Granitsky, took him by the arm, led him away from the crowd to a remote room, and . . . did not know what to say to him; he finally recalled his aunt's words, and trying to adopt a coldblooded look, said,

"You are going to Italy."

"Not yet," answered Granitsky, taking these words for a question and looking at him with amazement.

"You must go to Italy! Do you understand me?"

"Not at all."

"I want you to go to Italy!" said the Baron, raising his voice. "Now do you understand?"

"Tell me, please, what is it—have you gone out of your mind or what?"

"There are people whom I shall not name for whom any noble act is insanity."

"Baron, you don't know what you're saying. Your words smell of gunpowder."

"I am used to that smell."

"On maneuvers?"

"That we shall see."

The Baron's eyes flashed: a personal insult was in the air.

They made everyone who came into the room towards the end of their conversation promise to keep it a secret, they returned again to the hall, took a few turns around the dance floor and disappeared.

A few hours later their seconds were already measuring off the paces and loading the pistols.

Granitsky went up to the Baron.

"Before we dispatch each other to the next world I would be very interested to find out why we are shooting at each other."

The Baron took his rival aside—away from the seconds.

"That should be easier for you to understand than for me . . ." he said.

"Not at all."

"If I name for you a certain woman . . ."

"A woman! . . But which one?"

"This is really too much! The wife of my brother, my old, sick brother, my benefactor . . . Do you understand?"

"Now I understand absolutely nothing!"

"That's strange! The whole town says that you have disgraced my brother! Everyone is laughing at him . . ."

"Baron! You have been unconscionably deceived. I beg you to tell me the name of the person who deceived you."

"A woman told me."

"Baron! You have acted very rashly. If you had asked me before, I would have told you about my situation; but it's too late now, we must duel. But I do not want to die leaving you with a deception: I never so much as thought about the Baroness, here is my hand on it."

The young Baron was greatly confused during the conversation: he liked Granitsky, knew his nobility, believed that he was not deceiving him, and cursed himself, his Aunt, and all of society.

One of the seconds, an old duelist and very strict in matters of this sort, said:

"Now, now, gentlemen. It seems that everything has been smoothed over. So much the better: make up, make up; really, it's better . . ."

These words were said very simply, but they seemed to the Baron to contain mockery—or else there really was something mocking in the second's tone of voice. The young man's blood flared up.

"Oh, no!" he cried, hardly knowing what he was saying. "No, we are not even thinking of making up. We have an important explanation . . ."

The last word again reminded the young man of his criminal carelessness: beside himself, agitated by inexplicable emotions, he took his rival aside for a second time.

"Granitsky!" he said to him, "I have acted like a child. What are we to do?"

"I don't know," answered Granitsky.

"Tell the seconds about our strange mistake? . ."

"That would mean spreading rumors about your brother's wife."

"You laughed at my bravery; the seconds know that."

"You told me in such a tone . . ."

"This cannot remain like this."

"This cannot remain like this."

"People will say that at our duel we spilled champagne, not blood . . ."

"Let's try to graze each other."

They stepped to the barrier. One, two, three! Granitsky's bullet scratched the Baron's arm; Granitsky fell dead.

VII

Conclusion

> There are those who want to defend everyone and every-
> thing: they do not want to see evil in anything. These people
> are very harmful . . .
>
> *A Judgment of High Society*

Every reader has no doubt already guessed what happened as a result of all this.

As long as only men knew about the duel, they attributed it simply to Granitsky's mockery of the young Baron's bravery; rumors were varied. But when the moral ladies described by us above found out about this incident, all misunderstandings ceased: the true reason was immediately found, researched, reworked, annotated, and disseminated by all possible means.

The poor Baroness could not hold up under this cruel persecution: her honor, the only feeling which was alive and sacred in her, her honor, to which she had sacrificed all her thoughts, all the movements of a youthful heart, her honor was unjustly and irrevokably desecrated. The Baroness took to her bed.

The young Baron and the two seconds were exiled—far away from the pleasures of the social life that was the only thing which could give them happiness.

The Countess Rifeyskaya remained a widow.

There are actions which are prosecuted by society: the guilty perish, the innocent perish. There are people who sow misfortune with both hands, who arouse disgust for humanity in the souls of the high and the gentle, who, in a word, triumphantly undermine the foundations of society, and society warms them in its bosom like a meaningless sun which indifferently rises both above the cries of battle and above the prayer of the wise man.

A game of whist had been arranged for Princess Mimi—she had already refused to dance. A young man came up to the green table.

"This morning Baroness Dauerthal's suffering finally ended," he said, "the ladies here can boast of the fact that they murdered her very expertly."

"What impudence!" someone whispered.

"Nothing of the sort!" Princess Mimi objected, covering her trick, "it is not people who kill, but lawless passions."

"Oh, undoubtedly!" remarked many people.

1834

1. Need I remind the reader that the subject here is Pushkin's Onegin? [Odoevsky's note.]

A. S. PUSHKIN

The Queen of Spades

> The queen of spades signifies secret
> ill-will.
> *The Newest Fortune-Telling Book*

I

> And on rainy days
> They gathered
> Often;
> They doubled—God forgive them
> From fifty
> To one hundred,
> And they would win
> And they would note the score
> With chalk.
> Thus on rainy days
> They got down to
> Work.

Once they were playing cards at cavalry officer Narumov's. The long winter night passed unnoticed; they sat down to supper at five in the morning. Those who had won ate with big appetites; the others sat absently in front of their empty plates. But champagne appeared, the conversation livened up, and everyone took part in it.

"How did you do, Surin?" asked the host.

"Lost, as usual. It must be admitted that I'm unlucky: I play without raising the stake, never get excited; there's no way you can confound me, but I keep losing!"

"And you've never been tempted? You've never raised the bet and played the same card? Your firmness amazes me."

"What about Hermann!" said one of the guests, pointing to a young engineer. "Never in his life has he taken the cards in his hand, never in his life has he doubled the stake, but he sits with us until five o'clock and watches our play!"

"The play interests me intensely," said Hermann, "but I am not in a position to sacrifice the essential in hope of acquiring the superfluous."

"Hermann is a German: he's economical, that's all!" noted Tomsky. "But if there is someone I cannot understand, it's my grandmother, Countess Anna Fedotovna."

"How so? Why?" exclaimed the guests.

"I cannot comprehend," continued Tomsky, "how it is my grandmother does not punt!"

"What is amazing," said Narumov, "about an eighty-year-old lady who doesn't punt?"

"So you know nothing about her?"

"No! That's true, nothing!"

"Oh, then listen. You must know that sixty years ago my grandmother went to Paris and was in great fashion there. People ran after her to see *la Vénus moscovite;* Richelieu courted her, and grandmother maintains that he almost shot himself because of her cruelty.

"At that time ladies played faro. Once at Court she lost a very large amount to the Duke of Orleans on her word. When she arrived home, peeling the beauty spots from her face and undoing her farthingale, grandmother informed grandfather of her loss and ordered him to pay.

"My late grandfather, so far as I recall, was a kind of house servant to grandmother. He feared her like fire, but when he heard about this terrible loss he blew his top, brought out accounts, showed her that they had expended half a million in half a year, that they had no Moscow or Saratov estate around Paris, and he flatly refused to pay. Grandmother slapped him and went to bed alone as a sign of her disfavor.

"The next day she ordered her husband called, hoping that the domestic punishment had worked on him, but found him inflexible. For the first time in her life she reached the point of debate and explanations with him; she intended to appeal to his conscience, showing condescendingly that there are different kinds of debts and that there is a difference between a prince and a coach-maker. No use! Grandfather was rebelling. No! That's all there was to it! Grandmother didn't know what to do.

"A very remarkable man was her close acquaintance. You have heard of Count St. Germain, about whom so many marvelous stories are told. You know that he passed himself off as the Eternal Jew, as the inventor of an elixir of life and the philosophers' stone and so forth. He was laughed at as a charlatan, and in his memoirs Casanova says that he was a spy; however, in spite of his mysteriousness St. Germain had a very respectable appearance and in society he was a very genial person. To this day grandmother loves him madly and gets angry if anyone speaks of him with disrespect. Grandmother knew that St. Germain could command large sums of money. She decided to resort to him, wrote him a note, and asked him to come to her immediately.

"The old eccentric soon arrived and found her in terrible grief. She described her husband's barbarity to him in the blackest colors and said, finally, that she was putting all her hope on his friendship and kindness.

"St. Germain thought for a moment.

"'I can provide you with this sum,' he said, 'but I know you will not be calm until you repay me, and I would not want to cause you new troubles. There is another way: you can win it back.'"

"'But, my dear Count,' said grandmother, 'I am telling you that we have no money at all.'"

"'Money isn't necessary for this,' objected St. Germain, 'hear me out if you will.'"

"Then he revealed to her a secret for which each of us would pay dearly . . . ."

The young gamblers doubled their attention. Tomsky lit his pipe, took a puff, and continued:

"That same evening grandmother appeared at Versailles *au jeu de la Reine.* The Duke of Orleans was keeping bank; grandmother excused herself lightly for not bringing her debt, spun a little tale in justification, and began to play against him. She chose three cards, and played them one after the other; all three cards won and grandmother won back absolutely everything."

"Chance!" said one of the guests.

"A fairy-tale!" remarked Hermann.

"Perhaps marked cards?" put in a third.

"I don't think so," replied Tomsky gravely.

"How is it," said Narumov, "you have a grandmother who guesses three cards in a row, and you still haven't learned this cabalism from her?"

"Yes, dammit!" replied Tomsky. "She had four sons including my father; all four were desperate gamblers, and she didn't reveal her secret to any of them, even though it wouldn't have been a bad thing for them, or even for me. But here is what my uncle, Count Ivan Ilych, told me, and he assured me of it on his honor. The late Chaplitsky, the one who died in poverty after squandering millions, once in his youth lost to Zorich—as I recall—about three hundred thousand. He was in despair. Grandmother, who was always stern toward the follies of young people, somehow took pity on Chaplitsky. She gave him three cards that he should play, one after the other, and she took his word of honor that he would never play again. Chaplitsky appeared to his conqueror. They sat down to play. Chaplitsky put fifty thousand on the first card and won; he doubled, doubled again, and won back all he had lost and more . . . .

"But it's time for bed. It's already quarter to six."

Indeed, it was already getting light: the young men finished their glasses and dispersed.

II

—Il parait que monsieur est décidément pour les suivantes.
—Que voulez-vouz, madame? Elles sont plus fraiches.
A Society Conversation

Old Countess*** was sitting in her dressing-room in front of a mirror. Three maids surrounded her. One was holding a rouge pot, another—a box of pins, the third—a tall lace cap with ribbons of a fiery color. The old Countess did not have the slightest claim to beauty, which had faded long ago, but she preserved all the habits of her youth, kept strictly to the styles of the seventies, and dressed just as slowly, just as carefully as sixty years before. A young girl, her ward, was sitting at the window behind an embroidery frame.

"Hello, *grand'maman*," said a young officer who entered the room. *"Bonjour, mademoiselle Lise. Grand'maman,* I have a request of you."

"What is it, *Paul?*"

"Let me introduce one of my friends to you and bring him to you at the ball Friday."

"Bring him to me right at the ball, and introduce him to me there. Were you at ***'s yesterday?"

"Of course! It was very gay; they danced until five o'clock. How pretty Eletzkaya was!"

"But my dear! What is pretty about her? Isn't she like her grandmother, princess Darya Petrovna? . . . By the way, has princess Darya Petrovna gotten very old?"

"What do you mean gotten old," replied Tomsky absentmindedly, "it's been about seven years since she died."

The girl raised her head and made a sign to the young man. He remembered that they concealed from grandmother the deaths of her contemporaries, and he bit his lip. But the Countess received this information, which was new to her, with great indifference.

"Died?" she said, "And I didn't know it. We were appointed maids of honor together, and when we were introduced, the Empress . . . ."

And for the hundredth time the Countess told her grandson the anecdote.

"Well, *Paul,*" she said then, "help me get up now. Lizanka, where is my snuffbox?"

And the Countess went behind the screen with her maids to finish her toilet. Tomsky was left with the girl.

"Who is it you want to introduce?" quietly asked Lizaveta Ivanovna.

"Narumov. Do you know him?"

"No. Is he a soldier or a civilian?"

"A soldier."

"An engineer?"

"No, a cavalryman. But why did you think he was an engineer?"

The girl laughed and did not answer a word.

"*Paul!*" exclaimed the Countess from behind the screen, "send me some new novel, only please, not one of the current things."

"What do you mean, *grand'maman?*"

"That is, a novel where the hero does not strangle his father or his mother, and where there are no drowned bodies. I'm terribly afraid of drowned people!"

"There are no such novels nowadays. Wouldn't you like some Russian ones?"

"You mean there are Russian novels? . . . Send me one, dear sir, please send me one!"

"Good-bye, *grand'maman.* I am in a hurry . . . . Good-bye, Lizaveta Ivanovna! Why *did* you think Narumov was an engineer?"

And Tomsky walked out of the dressing-room.

Lizaveta Ivanovna was left alone; she left her work and started looking out the window. Soon, from behind the corner house, a young officer appeared on one side of the street. A blush covered her cheeks; she took up her work again and bent her head right over the canvas. At that moment the Countess entered completely dressed.

"Lizaveta," she said, "order the carriage harnessed and we will go for a drive."

Lizaveta got up from behind the embroidery frame and started picking up her work.

"What's wrong with you, my child! Are you deaf or what?" exclaimed the Countess. "Order the carriage harnessed immediately." .

"Right away," the girl replied quietly and ran into the anteroom.

A servant came in and gave the Countess some books from prince Pavel Alexandrovich.

"Good! Thank him," said the Countess. "Lizanka, Lizanka! Where are you running to?"

"To get dressed."

"Later, my dear. Sit here. Open the first volume, read aloud . . . ."

The girl took the book and read several lines.

"Louder!" said the Countess. "What's wrong with you, my dear? Have you lost your voice or what? . . . Wait . . . Push that footstool over to me, closer . . . there!"

Lizaveta Ivanovna read two more pages. The Countess yawned.

"Get rid of that book," she said, "what rubbish! Send it back to prince Pavel and have him thanked . . . . Well, what about the carriage?"

"The carriage is ready," said Lizaveta Ivanovna, glancing at the street.

"Why aren't you dressed?" said the Countess, "I always have to wait for you. It is unbearable, my dear!"

Liza ran to her room. Not two minutes had passed when the Countess began to ring with all her strength. The three maids ran in one door, and a footman in the other.

"Why is it I have to ring so long for you?" the Countess said to them. "Tell Lizaveta Ivanovna that I am waiting for her."

Lizaveta Ivanovna came in dressed in a mantle and hat.

"Finally, my dear!" said the Countess. "What kind of get-up is that? Why that? Whom are you captivating? . . . And what is the weather like? It looks as if there's a wind."

"Not at all, your Ladyship! It's very calm, madam," answered the footman.

"You always talk without thinking! Open the window. Just as I thought—a wind! And a very cold one! Unharness the carriage! Lizanka, we shall not go, there was no reason to get all dressed up."

"And that is my life!" thought Lizaveta Ivanovna.

Lizaveta Ivanovna was in fact a most unhappy creature. "Bitter is another's bread," says Dante, "and difficult are the steps of another's porch"; and who can know the bitterness of dependency better than the poor ward of an aristocratic old woman? Of course, Countess *** did not have an evil soul, but she was capricious, like a woman spoiled by society, miserly and steeped in cold egotism, like all people who have had their fill of love in their own day and are alienated from the present. She participated in all the frivolities of high society; she went off to balls where she sat in a corner all rouged, dressed in the old style, like an ugly and indispensable ornament of the ballroom; arriving guests would go up to her with low bows, as if by an established ceremony, and after that no one paid any attention to her. She received the whole town at her house, observing strict etiquette and recognizing no one's face. Her numerous servants, getting fat and growing grey in her anteroom and maids' room, did what they pleased, vying with each other in stealing things from the dying old lady. Lizaveta Ivanovna was the household martyr. She poured tea and was reproached for excess use of sugar; she read novels aloud and was to blame for all of the author's mistakes; she accompanied the Countess on her outings and answered for the weather and condition of the pavement. An allowance had been set for her, but it was never paid, while it was demanded of her that she dress like everyone else, i.e., like very few. She played a most pitiful role in society. Everyone knew her and no one noticed her; at balls she danced only when they were short vis-à-vis, and the ladies took her by the arm whenever they needed to go into the dressing-room to fix something on their attire. She was self-esteeming, keenly aware of her position, and she was looking around—waiting impatiently for a savior; but the young men, who were calculating in their frivolous vanity, did not consider her worthy of attention, even though Lizaveta Ivanovna was a hundred times more lovely than the cold and arrogant marriageable girls around whom they hovered. How many times, quietly leaving the boring and sumptuous drawing-room, she would go away to cry in her poor room, where there was a screen covered with wallpaper, a chest-of-drawers, a small mirror, and a painted bed, and where a tallow candle burned dimly in a brass chandelier!

One day—this happened two days after the party described in the beginning of this story and a week before the scene on which we stopped—one day Lizaveta Ivanovna, sitting behind her embroidery frame by the window, accidentally glanced at the street and saw a young engineer standing motionlessly with his eyes fixed on her window. She lowered her head and continued working; after five minutes she glanced up again—the young officer was standing in the same place. Not in the habit of flirting with passing officers, she ceased looking at the street and went on sewing for about two hours without raising her head. Dinner was served. She got up, began to straighten up her work, and glancing at the street accidentally, she saw the officer again. This seemed rather strange to her. After dinner she went to the window with a feeling of some disquiet, but the officer was no longer there—and she forgot about him . . . .

Two days later, going out to get in the carriage with the Countess, she saw him again. He was standing right at the entrance, his face covered with a beaver collar; his black eyes glittered from under his hat. Lizaeta Ivanovna was frightened without knowing why herself, and she got in the carriage with inexpressible trepidation.

When she had returned home she ran up to the window—the officer was standing in the same place as before, his eyes fixed on her; she walked away, tormented by curiosity and agitated by a feeling which was completely new to her.

After that not a day passed that the young man did not appear under the windows of their house at the customary hour. Unconventional relations were established between them. Sitting at her place with her work, she would sense his approach, raise her head, and look at him longer and longer every day. The young man, it seemed, was thankful to her for this; with the sharp eye of youth she saw how a quick blush covered his pale cheeks every time their eyes met. In a week she smiled at him . . .

When Tomsky asked permission to introduce his friend to the Countess, the poor girl's heart leaped. But learning that Narumov was a cavalryman, not an engineer, she regretted giving away her secret to the frivolous Tomsky with an indiscreet question.

Hermann was the son of a Russified German who had left him some small capital. Firmly convinced of the necessity of consolidating his independence, Hermann did not touch the interest; he lived just on his salary, did not allow himself the slightest whim. However, he was secretive and proud, and his comrades rarely had a chance to laugh at his excessive parsimoniousness. He had strong passions and a fiery imagination, but firmness saved him from the usual errors of youth. Thus, for example, while he was a gambler in his soul, he never took cards in his hand, for he calculated that his financial position would not permit him (as he would say) "to sacrifice the essential in hope of acquiring the superfluous"—and nevertheless he sat whole nights through at the card tables and followed the various turns of play with feverish trembling.

The anecdote about the three cards had a strong effect on his imagination and did not leave his mind all night. "What if," he thought the next evening as he was wandering around Petersburg, "what if the old Countess would reveal her secret to me? Or name the three sure cards for me? Why not try my luck? . . . Introduce myself to her, get in her good graces, perhaps become her lover; but all that will take time and she is eighty years old, she could die in a week, in two days! . . . And the anecdote itself? . . . Can it be believed? . . . No! Calculation, moderation, and industriousness—they are my three sure cards, that's what will increase my capital threefold, increase it sevenfold, and gain me peace and independence."

Reasoning in this way he found himself on one of the main streets of Petersburg in front of a house of antiquated architecture. The street was blocked with equipages; one after another the carriages rolled up to the illuminated porch. At one moment the shapely foot of a young beauty stretched out of a carriage, the next there was a rattling jackboot, and then a striped stocking and diplomatic shoe. Fur coats and cloaks flitted past the stately doorman. Hermann stopped.

"Whose house is that?" he asked the corner policeman.

"Countess ***'s," replied the policeman.

Hermann trembled. The amazing anecdote again presented itself to his imagination. He started walking around the house, thinking about its owner and her wondrous ability. It was late when he returned to his humble little corner; he could not go to sleep for a long time, and when sleep overcame him he dreamed of cards, a green table, piles of banknotes, and heaps of gold coins. He played card after card, bent the corners decisively, won constantly, raked the gold toward himself, and put the banknotes in his pocket. Waking up rather late, he sighed for the loss of his fantastic wealth, again went out to wander about the city, and again found himself in front of the house of Countess ***. An unknown force seemed to have drawn him to it. He stopped and started looking at the windows. In one he saw a blackhaired little head, apparently bent over a book or some work. The head lifted. Hermann saw a bright little face and black eyes. That moment decided his fate.

III

Vous m'écrivez, mon ange, des lettres de quatre pages plus
vite que je ne puis les lire.

A Correspondence

Lizaveta Ivanovna had barely managed to take off her mantle and hat when the Countess sent for her and again ordered the carriage readied. They went to get in. While two lackeys were picking up the old lady and shoving her through the door, Lizaveta Ivanovna saw her engineer right by the wheel; he grabbed her hand, she could not collect herself from fright; the young man disappeared: there was a letter in her hand. She concealed it in her glove and during the whole drive she neither saw nor heard anything. The Countess had the custom of asking questions constantly when in the carriage, "Who was that we just passed?" "What is the name of this bridge?" "What is written on that sign?" This time Lizaveta Ivanovna answered randomly and irrelevantly, making the Countess angry.

"What's the matter with you, my dear? Are you in a stupor or what? Can't you hear? Or don't you understand me? . . . Thank God I don't stutter and haven't lost my mind yet!"

Lizaveta Ivanovna was not listening to her. When they returned home, she ran to her room, took the letter out of her glove: it was not sealed. Lizaveta Ivanovna read it. The letter contained a declaration of love—it was tender, respectful, and taken word for word from a German novel. But Lizaveta Ivanovna did not know German and was very satisfied with it.

However, the letter she had accepted did trouble her exceedingly. It was the first time she had entered close, secret relations with a young man. His audacity terrified her. She reproached herself for imprudent behavior and did not know what to do: cease sitting by the window and cool the young officer's enthusiasm for further pursuit with inattention? Send him a letter? Answer coldly and decisively? There was no one from whom to ask advice, she had neither a friend nor a mentor. Lizaveta Ivanovna decided to answer.

She sat down at the desk, took out pen, paper, and fell thoughtful. Several times she began her letter and tore it up; first her expressions seemed too condescending to her, then too cruel. Finally she managed to write a few lines with which she was satisfied. "I am sure," she wrote, "that you have honorable intentions, and that you did not want to offend me by a thoughtless act; but our acquaintance should not have begun in such a manner. I am returning your letter to you and hope that in the future I shall not have cause to complain about undeserved disrespect."

The next day when she saw Hermann approaching, Lizaveta Ivanovna got up from her embroidery frame, went out into the hall, opened a window, and threw out the letter, depending on the alertness of the young officer. Hermann ran over, picked it up, and went into a pastry shop. Tearing off the seal he found his letter and Lizaveta Ivanovna's reply. He had expected that and he returned home, quite absorbed in his intrigue.

Three days after this a quick-eyed young girl brought Lizaveta Ivanovna a note from a dress shop. Lizaveta Ivanovna opened it uneasily, foreseeing monetary demands, and suddenly she recognized Hermann's hand.

"You've made a mistake, my dear," she said, "this note is not for me."

"Yes, specifically for you!" replied the bold girl without hiding a sly smile. "Please read it."

Lizaveta Ivanovna ran through the note. Hermann was demanding a rendezvous.

"It cannot be!" said Lizaveta Ivanovna, frightened both by the rapidity of the demands and the method which he had employed. "This is surely not written to me." And she tore the letter into tiny pieces.

"If the letter is not to you, then why did you tear it up?" said the girl, "I would have returned it to the one who sent it."

"Please, my dear!" said Lizaveta Ivanovna, flaring up at her remark, "In the future do not bring me notes. And tell whoever sent you that he should be ashamed . . . ."

But Hermann did not relent. One way or another Lizaveta Ivanovna received letters from him every day. They were no longer translated from German. Inspired by passion, Hermann wrote them; and he spoke in a language characteristic of him: they revealed both the inflexibility of his desires and the disorder of an unrestrained imagination. Lizaveta Ivanovna no longer thought of sending them back; she was infatuated with them: she began to answer them, and from day to day her notes got longer and more tender. Finally she threw him the following letter from the window:

"There is a ball at the * * * ambassador's today. The Countess will be there. We will stay until around two o'clock. Here is a chance for you to see me alone. As soon as the Countess leaves, her servants will probably disperse; the doorman will stay in the front hall, but he usually goes back into his little room. Come at eleven thirty. Go straight up the stairs. If you find anyone in the anteroom, ask whether the Countess is home. They'll tell you no, and there isn't anything you can do. You will have to go away. But you will probably not meet anyone. The maids all sit in their own room. From the anteroom turn left—keep going straight to the Countess' bedroom. In the bedroom, behind the screen, you will see two small doors; the one on the right is to the study where the Countess never goes, the one on the left is to the corridor, and a narrow winding staircase is there: it leads to my room."

Waiting for the appointed time, Hermann trembled like a tiger. At ten o'clock he was already standing in front of the Countess' house. The weather was terrible: the wind howled, wet flakes of snow were falling; the streetlights burned dimly, the streets were empty. Occasionally a cabby looking for a late fare pulled by with his scrawny nag. Hermann was standing there in just a frock-coat, feeling neither the wind nor snow. Finally the Countess' carriage was brought around. Hermann saw the lackeys carry out the old woman, hunched over, wrapped in a sable coat, and right behind her flitted her ward in a heavy cloak, hair decorated with fresh flowers. The doors slammed. The carriage rolled heavily over the crunching snow. The doorman locked the door. The windows grew dark. Hermann started walking around the empty house; he went up to a streetlight and looked at his watch; it was twenty past eleven. He remained under the streetlight, fixing his eyes on the minute hand and waiting out the remaining minutes. At exactly half past eleven, Hermann stepped on the Countess' porch and entered the brightly illuminated entrance hall. The doorman was not there. Hermann ran up the stairs, opened the door into the anteroom and saw a servant sleeping under a lamp in an ancient soiled armchair. Hermann walked past him with light but firm steps. The hall and drawing-room were dark. A lamp in the anteroom illuminated them weakly. Hermann entered the bedroom. Before a case covered with ancient ikons burned a golden lamp. Faded damask armchairs and couches with down pillows and gold trim which was coming off stood in sad symmetry around walls covered with Chinese wallpaper. On the wall hung two portraits painted in Paris by *Madame Lebrun*. One of these depicted a stout, ruddy-cheeked man of about forty, in a light-green uniform and with a star; the other was a young beauty with an aquiline nose, with her little curls combed back, and a rose in her powdered hair. Everywhere there were porcelain shepherdesses, table clocks made by the famous Leroy, little boxes, roulette toys, fans, and various feminine playthings which were invented at the end of the century along with Montgolfier's balloon and Mesmer's magnetism. Hermann went behind the screen. There was a small iron bed behind it; to the right was the door leading to the study; to the left the other one—into the corridor. Hermann opened it, saw the narrow winding staircase which led to the room of the poor ward . . . . But he turned around and went into the dark study.

Time passed slowly. All was quiet. It struck twelve in the drawing-room; one after the other the clocks in all the rooms struck twelve—and all fell silent again. Hermann stood leaning against the cold stove. He was calm; his heart beat evenly, as in a man who has decided on something dangerous but essential. The clocks struck one and then two in the morning—and he heard the distant sound of a carriage. Involuntary agitation overcame him. The carriage drove up and stopped. He heard the thump of the steps being lowered. There was a bustle in the house. Servants ran about, voices rang out, and the house lit up. The three old maids ran into the bedroom, and the Countess, barely alive, entered and sank into a Voltaire armchair. Hermann looked through a crack: Lizaveta Ivanovna walked past him. Hermann heard her hurrying footsteps on the step of the staircase. Something like a pang of conscience murmured in him and again fell silent. He turned to stone.

The Countess began to undress before the mirror. Her rose-decorated bonnet was unpinned; the powdered wig was taken off her gray and closely shorn hair. Pins scattered around her like rain. Her yellow dress, embroidered with silver, fell to her swollen feet. Hermann was witness to the repulsive secrets of her toilet; finally the Countess was in just her nightgown and nightcap: in this attire, which was more proper to her old age, she seemed less terrible and ugly.

Like all old people in general, the Countess suffered from insomnia. Having undressed, she sat down in the Voltaire armchair by the window and dismissed the maids. They took away the candles; again the room was lit by one lamp. All yellow, the Countess sat there, moving her pendulous lips, swaying back and forth from left to right. Her cloudy eyes reflected a complete absence of thought; looking at her one could think that the terrible old woman's swaying resulted not from her own will, but by the action of a hidden galvanism.

Suddenly the dead face changed inexpressibly. The lips stopped moving, the eyes became animated: before the Countess stood an unknown man.

"Don't be afraid, for God's sake, don't be afraid!" he said in a distinct and quiet voice. "I have no intention of harming you; I have come to implore you for one favor."

The old lady looked at him silently and, it seemed, did not hear him. Hermann imagined that she was deaf, and bending down right to her ear he repeated the same thing to her. The old lady remained silent as before.

"You," continued Hermann, "can make my life happy, and it will cost you nothing; I know that you can guess three cards in a row . . . ."

Hermann stopped. The Countess, it seemed, understood what he was demanding of her: she seemed to be searching for words for her answer.

"That was a joke," she said finally, "I swear to you, it was a joke!"

"This is nothing to joke about," Hermann objected angrily. "Remember Chaplitsky, whom you helped win?"

The Countess was visibly disturbed. Her features portrayed violent agitation in her soul; but she quickly fell back into her previous senselessness.

"Can you," continued Hermann, "identify the three sure cards for me?"

The Countess remained silent. Hermann continued:

"Whom are you saving your secret for? For your grandsons? They are rich without it; they don't even know the value of money. Your three cards won't help a spendthrift. He who does not know how to take care of his patrimony will still die in poverty—in spite of any demonic efforts. I'm not a spendthrift; I know the value of money. Your three cards won't be wasted on me. Well? ... "

He stopped and waited, trembling, for her answer. The Countess remained silent. Hermann got on his knees.

"If ever," he said, "your heart knew the feeling of love, if you remember its raptures, if even once you have smiled at the crying of a newborn son, if anything human has ever beat in your breast, I implore you, by the feelings of a wife, lover, mother, by everything that is holy in life, do not refuse my request! Reveal your secret to me! What is it to you? ... Perhaps it is connected to a terrible sin, to a pact with the devil .... Think: you are old, you do not have long to live—I am ready to take your sin on my soul. Just reveal your secret to me. Think: the happiness of a man is in your hands, not only I, but my children, grandchildren, and great grandchildren will bless your memory and will respect it as a holy thing...."

The old lady did not answer a word.

Hermann rose.

"Old witch!" he said, clenching his teeth. "Then I'll force you to answer...."

With this word he took a pistol out of his pocket.

At the sight of the pistol the Countess displayed strong feeling for the second time. She threw back her head and raised her arm as if warding off a shot.... Then she fell backward ... and remained motionless.

"Stop being childish," said Hermann, taking her arm. "I'm asking for the last time: do you want to identify the three cards for me? Yes or no?"

The Countess did not answer. Hermann saw that she was dead.

IV

7 Mai 18—
Homme sans moeurs et sans religion!
Correspondence

Lizaveta Ivanovna was sitting in her room still in her ball attire, sunk in deep reflection. Arriving home, she hurried to dismiss the sleepy maid who had unwillingly offered her services—she said that she would get undressed herself, and with trepidation she walked into her room, hoping to find Hermann there and wishing not to find him. With her first look she assured herself of his absence and thanked fate for the obstacle which prevented their rendezvous. She sat down without undressing and started remembering all of the circumstances which had lured her so far in such a short time. Not three weeks had passed since the time she first saw the young man through the window—and already she was corresponding with him and he had succeeded in demanding a night-time rendezvous! She knew his name only because some of his letters had been signed; she had never talked to him, had not heard his voice, had never heard anything about him ... until this very evening. Strange thing! At the ball that same evening Tomsky wanted to get revenge on young Princess Polina * * * (at whom he was mad because contrary to her custom she was flirting with someone other than him) by showing indifference: he invited Lizaveta Ivanovna and danced an endless mazurka with her. The whole time he joked about her proclivity for engineering officers; he assured her that he knew considerably more than she could suppose, and some of his jokes were so aptly aimed that a few times Lizaveta Ivanovna thought that her secret was known to him.

"From whom do you learn all this?" she asked, smiling.

"From the friend of a person you know well," answered Tomsky, "a very remarkable man!"

"Who is this remarkable man?"

"His name is Hermann."

Lizaveta Ivanovna answered nothing, but her hands and feet turned to ice . . . .

"This Hermann", continued Tomsky, "is a truly romantic character. He has the profile of Napoleon and the soul of Mephistopheles. I think that he has at least three crimes on his conscience. How pale you've gotten! . . ."

"My head aches . . . What did Hermann tell you . . . or whatever his name was? . . ."

"Hermann is very dissatisfied with his friend; he says that in his place he would act quite differently . . . I even suspect that Hermann himself has his eyes on you; at least he listens to the amorous exclamations of his friend in anything but an indifferent way."

"But where did he see me?"

"In church, perhaps: out driving! . . . God knows! Perhaps in your room, while you were asleep. He's capable of it . . ."

Three ladies who came up to them with the question *"oubli ou regret?"* interrupted the conversation which was becoming so tormentingly fascinating for Lizaveta Ivanovna.

The lady Tomsky chose was Princess * * * herself. She managed to smooth things over with him while turning an extra circle and spinning around before her chair an extra time. When he returned to his place, Tomsky was no longer thinking either about Hermann or Lizaveta Ivanovna. She wanted to renew the interrupted conversation without fail, but the mazurka ended and soon afterward the old Countess left.

Tomsky's words were nothing but mazurka chatter, but they were deeply implanted in the soul of the young dreamer. The portrait which Tomsky had outlined corresponded to the picture she herself had composed; and thanks to the latest novels this already banal character frightened and captivated her imagination. She sat with her bare arms crossed; her head, still decorated with flowers, was bent over her exposed bosom . . . . Suddenly the door opened and Hermann walked in. She began to tremble . . . .

"Where have you been?" she asked in a frightened whisper.

"In the old Countess' bedroom," replied Hermann, "I've just come from her. The Countess is dead."

"My God! . . . What are you saying?"

"And it seems," continued Hermann, "that I am the cause of her death."

Lizaveta Ivanovna looked at him and Tomsky's words rang out in her soul: *the man has at least three crimes on his conscience!* Hermann sat down on the window-ledge near her and told her everything.

Lizaveta Ivanovna listened to him with horror. So the passionate letters, the ardent demands, the audacious, stubborn pursuit—none of this was love! Money! That was what his soul thirsted for! It was not she who could slake his desires and make him happy! The poor ward was nothing but the blind helper of a robber, the murderer of her old benefactress! . . . She cried bitterly in her tormenting, belated repentance. Hermann watched her silently; his heart too was torn, but neither the tears of the poor girl nor the amazing charm of her grief troubled his stern soul. He felt no pangs of conscience at the thought of the dead woman. One thing horrified him: the irreparable loss of the secret from which he expected enrichment.

"You are a monster!" said Lizaveta Ivanovna finally.

"I did not want her death," replied Hermann, "my pistol is not loaded."

They fell silent.

Morning was breaking. Lizaveta Ivanovna extinguished the glittering candle; the pale light illumined her room. She wiped her tear-stained eyes and raised them to Hermann; he was sitting on the window-ledge, arms folded, frowning menacingly. In this position he was amazingly like a portrait of Napoleon. The similarity struck even Lizaveta Ivanovna.

"How are you going to get out of the house?" said Lizaveta Ivanovna finally. "I had planned to take you by a secret staircase, but it is necessary to go past the bedroom, and I'm afraid to."

"Tell me how to find the secret staircase and I'll go out."

Lizaveta Ivanovna got up, took a key out of the chest-of-drawers, handed it to Hermann, and gave him detailed instructions. Hermann pressed her cold, unresponsive hand, kissed her bowed head and went out.

He descended the steep staircase and again entered the Countess' bedroom. The dead woman was sitting there, turned to stone; her face expressed profound calm. Hermann stopped before her, looked at her for a long time, as if wishing to confirm the terrible truth; finally he went into the study, felt about for a door behind the tapestry, and disturbed by strange sensations, started down a dark staircase. Along this same staircase, he thought, perhaps sixty years ago, toward this same bedroom, at this same hour, wearing an embroidered caftan, his hair combed *à l'oiseau royal,* pressing his three-cornered hat to his heart, crept a lucky young man who had long since rotted in the grave, and today the heart of his ancient lover had stopped beating . . . .

At the foot of the staircase Hermann found a door which he unlocked with the same key, and he found himself in a transverse corridor which led him to the street.

V

> That night the deceased Baroness von B*** appeared to me. She was all in white and said to me: "Hello, Mr. Councillor!"
>
> *Swedenborg*

Three days after the fateful night, at nine o'clock in the morning, Hermann set off for * * * monastery, where the service for the body of the deceased Countess was being held. Though he felt no repentance, he could not completely suppress the voice of his conscience which kept telling him: "You are the old lady's murderer!" Having little true faith, he had a multitude of superstitions. He believed that the dead Countess could have a harmful influence on his life, and he decided to make an appearance at her funeral to beg her forgiveness.

The church was full. Hermann could hardly make his way through the crowd of people. The coffin stood on an opulent catafalque under a velvet canopy. The deceased lay in it, with arms crossed on her chest, in a lace bonnet and a white satin dress. Her domestics stood around it—the servants in black caftans with armorial ribbons on their shoulders, and with candles in their hands; the relatives were in deep mourning dress—children, grandchildren, and great grandchildren. No one was crying; tears would have been *une affectation.* The Countess was so old that her death could not surprise anyone, and her relatives had long viewed her as having lived past her time. A young bishop gave the funeral oration. In simple and touching phrases he described the peaceful passing of the righteous woman whose long years were a quiet, touching preparation for a Christian demise. "The angel of death found her," said the orator, "engaged in pious meditations and waiting for the midnight bridegroom." The service was completed with sad decorum. The relatives were first to go take leave of the body. Then followed the numerous guests who had come to pay their respects to the one who had been a participant in their vain

amusements for so long. After them came all of the servants. Finally an old housekeeper who was the same age as the deceased went up. Two young girls were holding her under the arms. She was not strong enough to bow down to the ground—and she alone shed a few tears when she had kissed the hand of her mistress. After her Hermann decided to approach the coffin. He bowed down to the ground and lay for a few minutes on the cold floor which was strewn with fir twigs. Finally he got up; pale as the deceased herself, he went up the steps of the catafalque and bowed . . . . At that moment it seemed to him that the dead woman glanced at him mockingly, winking one eye. Hermann moved back hastily, stumbled, and crashed backwards to the ground. They picked him up. At this same time Lizaveta Ivanovna was carried out onto the porch in a faint. This episode disturbed the solemnity of the somber ceremony for a few minutes. A muffled murmur arose among the visitors, and an emaciated chamberlain, a close relative of the deceased, whispered into the ear of an Englishman who was standing next to him that the young officer was her illegitimate son, to which the Englishman replied coldly, "Oh?"

Hermann was extremely upset all day. At dinner in a lonely inn, he drank a great deal, contrary to his custom, in hope of suppressing his inner agitation. But the wine inflamed his imagination even more. When he returned home he threw himself on the bed without undressing and fell fast asleep.

It was still night when he awoke; the moon illumined his room. He glanced at the clock—it was quarter to three. Sleep had left him; he sat on the bed and thought about the funeral of the old Countess.

At that moment someone looked in his window from the street—and immediately walked away. Hermann paid no attention to this. In a minute he heard the door to the anteroom being opened. Hermann thought that his orderly, drunk as usual, was returning from a nocturnal carousal. But he heard an unfamiliar walk: someone was walking, softly shuffling slippers. The door opened. A woman in a white dress entered. Hermann took her for his old wet-nurse and was amazed—what could bring her here at such an hour? But the white woman, gliding, suddenly appeared in front of him—and Hermann recognized the Countess!

"I came to you against my will," she said in a firm voice, "but I have been commanded to fulfill your request. The three, seven, and ace will win for you in sequence, provided that you do not play more than one card in twenty-four hours and that you never play in your life afterwards. I forgive you my death provided you marry my ward, Lizaveta Ivanovna . . . ."

With these words she turned quietly, went to the door, and disappeared, slippers shuffling. Hermann heard the door slam in the hall, and saw someone look in the window at him again.

For a long while Hermann could not come to his senses. He went out into the other room. His orderly was sleeping on the floor; with difficulty Hermann woke him up. As was customary, the orderly was drunk; it was impossible to get any sense out of him. The outside door was locked. Hermann returned to his room, lit a candle, and wrote down his vision.

VI

—*Attendez!*
—How do you dare say *attendez* to me?
—Your Excellency, I said "*Attendez,* sir!"

Two fixed ideas cannot exist together in moral nature, just as two bodies cannot occupy one and the same place in the physical world. In Hermann's imagination the three, seven, and ace quickly overspread the image of the dead woman. The three, seven, and ace did not leave his head: they stirred on his lips. Seeing a young girl he would say, "How shapely she is! A real three of hearts." Asked what time it was, he would answer, "Five minutes before the seven." Every fat-bellied man reminded him of an ace. The three, seven, and ace pursued him in his sleep, assuming all possible shapes: the three bloomed before him in the form of a luxurious plant, the seven presented itself as Gothic gates, the ace as an enormous spider. All his thoughts flowed into one: using the secret which had cost him so dearly. He began to think about resigning his job and traveling. He wanted to extort a treasure from enchanted fortune in the open gambling houses of Paris. Chance saved him the trouble.

A society of rich gamblers was formed in Moscow under the leadership of the famous Chekalinsky, who had spent his entire life playing cards and had once amassed millions by winning promissory notes and losing cash. Long experience had earned him the trust of his comrades, and his open house, famed chef, kindness, and merriness won the respect of the public. He came to Petersburg. The young people rushed to him, forgetting balls for cards and preferring the temptations of faro to the allurements of philandering. Narumov took Hermann to him.

They passed through a series of magnificent rooms filled with polite servants. Several generals and Privy Councillors were playing whist; the young men were sprawled languidly on overstuffed divans, eating ice cream and smoking pipes. In the drawing-room behind a long table around which about twenty gamblers were crowded, sat the host, keeping bank. He was a man of about sixty, of the most respectable appearance; his head was covered with silver grey; his full and fresh face displayed affability, his eyes glittered, animated by a constant smile. Narumov introduced Hermann to him. Chekalinsky shook his hand amiably, and asked him not to stand on ceremony, and continued dealing.

The round lasted a long time. There were more than thirty cards on the table.

Chekalinsky stopped after each play in order to give the players time to make their arrangements; he wrote the losses down, politely listened to their demands, even more politely straightened out a card whose corner had been bent more than once by a preoccupied hand. Finally, the round ended. Chekalinsky shuffled the cards and prepared to deal another.

"Allow me to bet on a card," said Hermann, stretching his hand out from behind a fat man, who was playing there. Chekalinsky smiled and bowed silently as a sign of his humble consent. Smiling, Narumov congratulated Hermann on the termination of his lengthy fast and wished him a lucky start.

"Stake!" said Hermann, writing the figure in chalk on his card.

"How much, sir?" asked the banker, squinting. "Excuse me, I cannot make it out."

"Forty seven thousand," replied Hermann.

At these words all heads turned at once, and all eyes were fixed on Hermann. "He's gone out of his mind!" thought Narumov.

"Allow me to point out to you," said Chekalinsky with his unchanging smile, "that your bet is high; no one here has yet staked more than two hundred seventy-five rubles at once."

"Well," objected Hermann, "will you play against my card or not?"

Chekalinsky bowed with an air of the same modest consent.

"I only wished to inform you," he said, "that, honored by the trust of my comrades, I can only play for cash. For my part, I, of course, am sure that your word is sufficient; but for the orderliness of the game and accounts I request you to put your money on the card."

Hermann took a banknote from his pocket and gave it to Chekalinsky who, cursorily examining it, put it on Hermann's card.

He began to deal. On the right lay the nine, on the left the three.

"It won!" said Hermann, showing his card.

A whisper began among the gamblers. Chekalinsky frowned, but the smile immediately returned to his face.

"Do you wish the money now?" he asked Hermann.

"If you will be so good."

Chekalinsky took several banknotes from his pocket and immediately counted them out. Hermann took his money and walked away from the table. Narumov could not get over it. Hermann drank a glass of lemonade and went home.

The next evening he appeared at Chekalinsky's again. The host was dealing. Hermann walked up to the table; the punters immediately gave him a place. Chekalinsky bowed genially to him.

Hermann waited for a new round, placed his card down with his forty seven thousand and yesterday's winnings on it.

Chekalinsky began to deal. A jack fell on the right, a seven on the left.

Hermann revealed his seven.

Everyone gasped. Chekalinsky was visibly disturbed. He counted out ninety four thousand and handed it to Hermann. Hermann took it coolly and departed that very minute.

The next evening Hermann again appeared at the table. Everyone was waiting for him. The generals and Privy Councillors left their whist to watch such unusual play. The young officers jumped up from the couches; all of the servants gathered in the drawing-room. They surrounded Hermann. The other gamblers did not place their cards, waiting impatiently to see how he would end. Hermann stood at the table preparing to punt alone against the pale but still smiling Chekalinsky. They each opened a deck of cards. Chekalinsky shuffled. Hermann took out his card and placed it down, covering it with a heap of banknotes. It looked like a duel. Profound silence reigned all around.

Chekalinsky began to deal; his hands were shaking. On the right lay a lady, on the left an ace.

"The ace won!" said Hermann and revealed his card.

"Your lady is beaten," said Chekalinsky genially.

Hermann shuddered: in fact, instead of the ace, he had the queen of spades. He did not believe his eyes, not understanding how he could have misdrawn.

At that moment it seemed to him that the queen of spades winked and grinned. The extraordinary similarity struck him . . . .

"The old woman!" he exclaimed in horror.

Chekalinsky pulled the lost banknotes toward himself. Hermann stood motionless. When he walked away from the table, noisy talk arose. "Excellently punted!" the gamblers said. Chekalinsky again shuffled the cards: the game continued as usual.

Conclusion

Hermann went out of his mind. He is in room 17 of the Obukhov hospital; he does not answer any questions, and he murmurs unusually rapidly: "Three, seven, ace! Three, seven, queen!"

Lizaveta Ivanovna married a very amiable young man; he serves somewhere and has considerable property; he is the son of the old Countess' former steward. A poor relative is being brought up by Lizaveta Ivanovna.

Tomsky has been promoted to captain and will marry Princess Polina.

A Journey to Arzrum

Preface

Recently I happened upon a book which was printed in Paris last year (1834) under the title *Voyages en orient entrepris par ordre du Gouvernement Français.*[1] The author, in giving his own account of the campaign of 1829,[2] ends his discussion with the following words:

Un poète distingué par son imagination a trouvé dans tant de hauts faits dont il a été témoin non le sujet d'un poème, mais celui d'une satyre."[3]

As for the poets in the Turkish campaign, I knew only of A. D. Khomyakov[4] and A. N. Muravyov.[5] Both were in Count Dibich's army. The former wrote some fine lyric poems at the time; the latter reflected upon his journey to the Holy Land, which had produced such a strong impression. But I have not read any satire on the Arzrum campaign.

I would never have imagined that this was a reference to me, if in that very book I had not found my name among the names of the generals of the Detached Caucasus Corps.[6] "*Parmi les chefs qui la commandaient (l'armée du Prince Paskewitch) on distinguait le Général Mouravief...*[7] *le Prince Géorgien Tsitsevaze ...*[8] *le Prince Arménien Beboutof...*[9] *le Prince Potemkine, le Général Raiewsky,*[10] *et enfin—M. Pouchkine ... qui avait quitté la capitale pour chanter les exploits de ses compatriotes.*"[11]

I confess: these lines of the French traveler, despite their flattering epithets, vexed me more than the abuse of the Russian literary journals. *To seek inspiration* has always seemed to me a ridiculous and absurd fantasy: you cannot find inspiration; it, of itself, must find the poet. For me to go to a war intending to sing the praises of future exploits would be on the one hand quite arrogant, and on the other quite improper. I do not involve myself with military opinions. That is not my affair. Perhaps the bold crossing over Sagan-Lu,[12] a maneuver by which Count Paskevich cut the Seraskir[13] off from Osman-Pasha,[14] the defeat of two enemy corps in a single day, the swift march to Arzrum, all of this, which was crowned with complete success, is perhaps extremely worthy of ridicule in the eyes of military men (such as, for example, Mr. Commercial Consul Fantanier,[15] the author of the journey to the Orient); but I would be ashamed to write satires on a famed Commander who received me affectionately in the shelter of his tent and found the time amidst his great concerns to accord me flattering attention. A person who has no need of the protection of the mighty values their goodwill and hospitality, for there is nothing else he can ask of them. An accusation of ingratitude ought not to be left unanswered, as if it were worthless criticism or literary abuse. This is why I have decided to print this preface and publish my travel notes, as *all* that I have written about the campaign of 1829.[16]

A. Pushkin

Chapter One

The Steppes. A Kalmyk Tent. The Caucasus Spas. The Georgian Military Highway. Vladikavkaz. An Ossetian Funeral. The Terek. The Darial Pass. Crossing the Snowcapped Mountains. The First Glimpse of Georgia. Aqueducts. Khozrev-Mirza. The Mayor of Dushet.[17]

... From Moscow I went to Kaluga, Belev and Orel, and added thereby an extra two hundred versts:[18] however, I did manage to see Ermolov.[19] He lives in Orel, near which his estate is located. I called on him at eight in the morning and did not find him at home. The driver told me that Ermolov visited no one except his father, a simple, devout old man, and that the only people he did not receive were the town clerks, but that everyone else had free access to him. In an hour I called on him again. Ermolov received me with his usual cordiality. At first glance I did not find in him the least resemblance to his portraits, which are usually painted in profile. A round face, fiery gray eyes, bristly gray hair. The head of a tiger on the torso of Hercules. His smile is unpleasant, because it is not natural. But when he falls into thought and frowns, he becomes handsome and strikingly like the poetic portrait painted by Dawe.[20] He was wearing a green Circassian jacket.[21] On the walls of his study hung swords and daggers, mementoes of his rule in the Caucasus. It is obvious that he finds it hard to endure his inactivity. A few times he took to speaking of Paskevich and always scathingly; he would speak of his easy victories and compare him to Joshua, before whom the walls fell at the sound of a trumpet, and instead of referring to him as the count of Erivan[22] he would call him the Count of Jericho. "If he were to attack a stupid, inexperienced, but merely stubborn pasha, for example, the pasha who was in command at Shumla,"[23] said Ermolov, "that would be the end of Paskevich." I relayed to Ermolov Count Tolstoi's[24] statement that Paskevich had done so well in the Persian campaign that the only way left for a clever man to distinguish himself would be to act slightly worse. Ermolov burst out laughing, but did not agree. "It would have been possible to save people and expense," he said. I think that he is writing, or wants to write, his memoirs. He is dissatisfied with Karamzin's *History*:[25] he would like an ardent pen to describe the progress of the Russian people from insignificance to glory and power. Of Prince Kurbsky's[26] writings he spoke *con amore*.[27] He let the Germans have their due. "In about fifty years or so," he said, "people will think that in the present campaign there was an auxiliary Prussian or Austrian army, presided over by some German generals[28] or other." I stayed with him for about two hours. He was vexed at not remembering my full name. He kept apologizing with compliments. Several times the conversation touched on literature. Of Griboedov's verse[29] he says that his jaw aches when he reads it. Of government and politics there was not a word.

My route was to take me through Kursk and Kharkov; but I turned off onto the direct road to Tiflis, thereby sacrificing a good dinner in a Kursk tavern (which is no mean trifle on our journeys); what is more, I did not have enough curiosity to visit the University of Kharkov, which is not nearly so tempting as the Kursk taverns.

The roads to Elets are terrible. Several times my carriage got stuck in mud, which was fully the equal of Odessa mud.[30] Sometimes I covered no more than fifty versts in twenty-four hours. Finally I saw the Voronezh steppes and rolled easily over the green plain. In Novocherkask I found Count Pushkin,[31] also on his way to Tiflis, and we agreed to travel together.

The transition from Europe to Asia is more perceptible with every hour: the forests disappear, the hills level out, the grass gets thicker and the vegetation richer; birds appear which are unknown in our forests; eagles sit on the hillocks that line the main road, as if on guard, and look proudly at the traveler; over lush pastures

> Herds of indomitable mares
> Wander proudly.[32]

The Kalmyks settle around the station shacks. Their ugly, shaggy horses, known to you from Orlovsky's fine drawings, graze around their tents.[33]

The other day I visited a Kalmyk tent (a wicker frame, covered with thick white felt). The whole family was about to have lunch. A cauldron was boiling in the middle, and the smoke was escaping through an opening at the top of the tent. A young Kalmyk girl, quite pretty, was sewing, and smoking tobacco. I sat down beside her. "What's your name?"—***—"How old are you?"—"Ten and eight."—"What are you sewing?"—"Trouser."—"For whom?"—"For self." She handed me her pipe and began to eat. Tea was boiling in the cauldron with mutton fat and salt. She offered me her ladle. I could not refuse and swallowed a mouthful, trying not to take a breath. I do not think that the cuisine of any other people could produced anything more repulsive. I asked for something with which to get rid of the taste. They gave me a small piece of dried mare's meat; I was happy even for that. Kalmyk coquetry frightened me; I hurried out of the tent—and rode off from the Circe of the Steppes.[34]

In Stavropol[35] I saw on the horizon the clouds that had so impressed me exactly nine years before.[36] They were still the same, still in the same spot. These are the snowcapped peaks of the Caucasian chain.

From Georgievsk I went by to visit Goryachie Vody.[37] Here I found great change: in my time the baths were in hastily built shacks. The springs, for the most part in their primitive state, gushed out, steamed and flowed down the mountains in various directions, leaving white and reddish traces behind them. We scooped the seething water with a ladle made of bark or the bottom of a broken bottle. Now magnificent baths and buildings have been erected. A boulevard lined with young lindens runs along the slope of Mount Mashuk. Everywhere there are neatly kept pathways, green benches, rectangular flowerbeds, little bridges, pavilions. The springs have been refined, lined with stone; nailed up on the walls of the bathhouses are lists of instructions from the police; everything is orderly, neat, prettified . . .

I confess: the Caucasus spas offer more conveniences nowadays; but I missed their former wild state: I missed the steep stone paths, the bushes and the unfenced cliffs over which I used to clamber. With sadness I left the spas, and set out on my way back to Georgievsk. Soon night fell. The clear sky was studded with millions of stars. I was riding along the bank of the Podkumok. Here A. Raevsky[38] used to sit with me, listening to the melody of the waters. The majestic Beshtu stood outlined darker and darker in the distance, surrounded by mountains, its vassals, and finally it disappeared in the darkness . . .

The next day we continued and arrived in Ekaterinograd, formerly the seat of the military governor.

The Georgian Military Highway begins in Ekaterinograd; the post road ends. One hires horses to Vladikavkaz.[39] A convoy of Cossacks and infantry soldiers is given, and one cannon. The mail leaves twice a week and the travelers join up: this is called an *opportunity*. We did not have to wait long. The mail arrived the next day, and the third morning at nine we were ready to set out. The whole caravan, consisting of five hundred people or thereabouts, assembled at a meeting-place. There was a drum roll. We were off. The cannon preceded, surrounded by infantry soldiers. Behind it stretched a long line of carriages, brichkas,[40] and the hooded carts of the soldiers' wives, who were transferring from one fortress to another; behind them the train of two-wheeled carts began to creak. On either side ran herds of horses and oxen. Around them galloped Nogai tribesmen in felt cloaks and with lassos. At first I greatly enjoyed all this, but it soon bored me. The cannon moved at a slow pace, the wick was smoking, and the soldiers lit their pipes from it. The slow pace of our march (on the first day we covered only fifteen versts), the unbearable heat, the scarcity of provisions, the restless stopovers for the night, and finally the continuous creaking of the Nogai carts made me lose patience. The Tartars pride themselves on this creaking, and say that they travel about like honest people who have no need to hide. On this occasion it would have been more agreeable for me to journey in not quite such respectable company. The road is rather monotonous: a plain; hills on either side. On the horizon—the peaks of the Caucasus, which every day appear higher and higher. Fortresses, good enough for this region, with surrounding trenches, which in the old days each of us could have jumped over without running; with rusty cannon, which have not fired since the days of Count Gudovich;[41] and crumbling ramparts, on which garrisons of chickens and geese roam. In the fortresses there are some shacks where with difficulty one can obtain a dozen eggs and some sour milk.

The first place of note is the Minaret fortress. On the way to it, our caravan went through a delightful valley between burial mounds, overgrown with linden and plane trees. These are the graves of several thousand who died from the plague. They were dotted with many-colored flowers which had sprung up from the infected dust. The snowy Caucasus gleamed to the right; an enormous wooded mountain rose before us; beyond it lay the fortress. All about it one can see traces of a ruined aul,[42] which used to be called Tartartub and was in its time the main village in Great Kabarda. The slender, solitary minaret bears witness to the existence of the now vanished settlement. It rises gracefully between heaps of stones, on the bank of a dried-up stream. The inner stairway has not yet collapsed. I climbed it to the platform, from which the mullah's[43] voice resounds no more. There I found several unknown names scratched in the bricks by fame-seeking travelers.

Our route became picturesque. The mountains towered above us. On their peaks one could make out barely visible flocks, crawling about like insects. We could also make out a shepherd who might have been a Russian and who, once taken prisoner, had grown old in his captivity. We came upon more burial mounds, more ruins. Two or three grave monuments stood on the side of the road. In accordance with the custom of the Circassians, their horsemen are buried there. A Tartar inscription, an image of a sword, a brandmark, all carved on the stone, have been left to predatory grandsons in memory of a predatory ancestor.

The Circassians hate us. We have forced them out of their free and spacious pasturelands; their auls are in ruins, whole tribes have been annihilated. As time goes on, they move deeper and deeper into the mountains and direct their raids from there. Friendship with the *peaceful* Circassians is unreliable: they are always ready to aid their rebellious fellow tribesmen. The spirit of their wild chivalry has declined noticeably. They rarely attack the Cossacks in equal number, and never the infantry; and they flee when they see a cannon. Even so, they never pass up an opportunity to attack a weak detachment or a defenseless person. The area is full of rumors of their villainies. There is almost no way of pacifying them, save by disarming them just as the Crimean Tartars were disarmed,[44] which is extremely difficult to accomplish because of the hereditary feuds among them and the blood vengeance. The dagger and the sword are parts of their body, and an infant begins to master them before he can prattle. For them killing is a simple bodily motion. Captives are kept in the hope of ransom, but they are treated with horrible inhumanity, forced to work beyond their strength, fed with raw dough, beaten at will, and guarded by their boys, who at a single word have the right to hack them with their child's swords. Recently a peaceful Circassian who had shot at a soldier was captured. He tried to justify himself by saying that his rifle had been loaded for too long. What can one do with such people? One must hope, however, that our annexation[45] of the Black Sea, by cutting the Circassians off from trade with Turkey, will force them to become more friendly with us. The influence of luxury may favor their taming: the samovar would be an important innovation. There is, however, a stronger means, one more moral, more in keeping with the enlightenment of our time: the preaching of the Gospel. The Circassians accepted the Mohammedan faith very recently. They were attracted by the active fanaticism of the apostles of the *Koran,* among whom Mansur,[46] an extraordinary man who had long incited the Caucasus against Russian rule, distinguished himself, and who was finally caught by us and died in the Solovetsky Monastery. The Caucasus awaits Christian missionaries. But instead of the living word, it is easier for our lassitude to pour forth dead letters and send mute books to people who are illiterate.

We reached Vladikavkaz, formerly Kapkai, the threshold of the mountains. It is surrounded by Ossetian auls. I visited one of them and found myself at a funeral. People were crowding around a saklya.[47] Outside stood two oxen harnessed to a cart. The relatives and friends of the deceased were assembling from all directions and were entering the saklya, weeping loudly and beating their foreheads with their fists. The women stood by quietly. They carried out the corpse on a felt cloak . . .

> . . . like a warrior taking his rest
> With his martial cloak around him[48]

they laid him in the cart. One of the guests took the dead man's rifle, blew the powder from the pan, and laid it alongside the body. The oxen started off. The guests rode behind. The body was to be buried in the mountains, some thirty versts from the aul. Unfortunately, no one could explain these rituals to me.

The Ossets are the poorest tribe of all the peoples who inhabit the Caucasus; their women are beautiful and, as one hears, very well disposed to travelers. At the gate of the fortress I met the wife and daughter of an imprisoned Osset man. They were bringing him his dinner. Both seemed calm and brave; however, at my approach both bowed their heads and covered themselves with their tattered *yashmaks.*[49] In the fortress I saw Circassian hostages, spirited and handsome boys. They are constantly playing tricks and escaping from the fortress. They are kept in a sorry state. They go about in rags, half naked, and in appalling filth. On some of them I saw wooden shackles. It is very likely that the hostages, once released, do not miss their stay in Vladikavkaz.

The cannon left us. We set out with the infantry and the Cossacks. The Caucasus received us into its sanctuary. We heard the muffled roar and caught sight of the Terek, which was pouring forth in several directions. We traveled along its left bank. Its noisy waves move the wheels of the low little Ossetian mills which look like dog kennels. The farther we penetrated into the mountains, the narrower the pass became. The confined Terek throws its turbid waves with a roar over the cliffs which block its path. The pass winds along its course. At their rocky base the mountains have been ground smooth by its waves. I went along on foot and kept stopping, overwhelmed by the gloomy beauty of nature. The weather was bleak: the clouds were stretched heavily around the black peaks. Count Pushkin and Stjernvall,[50] as they watched the Terek, reminisced about Imatra[51] and gave preference to "*the thundering river in the North.*"[52] But I had nothing with which to compare the spectacle before me.

Before we reached Lars, I dropped behind the convoy, having lost myself in contemplation over the enormous cliffs, between which the Terek beats with indescribable fury. Suddenly a soldier runs up to me, shouting to me from afar: "Don't stop, your Excellency, they'll kill you!" Unexpected as indeed it was, this warning seemed extremely strange to me. The fact is that Ossetian bandits, safe in this confined terrain, shoot at travelers across the Terek. The day before we crossed, they had attacked General Bekovich[53] this way, who, however, galloped past as they shot at him. On the cliff one can see the ruins of some castle: they are cluttered with the saklyas of peaceful Ossets, like swallows' nests.

In Lars we stopped to spend the night. Here we found a French traveler who frightened us with the road ahead. He advised us to leave our carriages behind in Kobi and continue on horseback. It was with him that for the first time we drank Kakhetinsky wine[54] out of a stinking *wineskin,* recalling the feasting in the *Iliad:*

And in goat-skins wine, our joy![55]

Here I found a soiled copy of *The Prisoner of the Caucasus,*[56] and, I confess, reread it with great pleasure. It is all weak, young, incomplete; but a great deal was intuited and expressed aptly.

In the morning we moved on. Turkish prisoners were working on the road.[57] They complained about the food that was given them. They just could not get used to Russian black bread. This reminded me of the words of my friend Sheremetev,[58] on his return from Paris: "It's terrible, brother, to live in Paris: there's nothing to eat; you can't get hold of black bread!"

Seven versts from Lars is the Darial post. The pass bears the same name. The cliffs stand like parallel walls on both sides. It is so narrow here, so narrow, writes one traveler,[59] that you not only see, but, it would seem, you feel the closeness. A patch of the sky shows blue, like a ribbon, over your head. Streams falling from the height of the mountain in shallow and splashing spurts reminded me of the Abduction of Ganymede,[60] that strange painting by Rembrandt. Besides, the light in the pass is completely in his style. In certain places the Terek washes against the very foot of the cliffs, and rocks are heaped up on the road like a dam. Not far from the post a little bridge is boldly thrown across the river. When you stand on it, it is as if you were in a mill. The whole bridge shakes, and the Terek roars like the wheels that move the millstones. Opposite Darial on a steep cliff one can see the ruins of a fortress. Tradition has it that it was the hiding-place of a certain Queen Daria,[61] who gave her name to the pass: a legend. Darial[62] means gate in ancient Persian. According to the testimony of Pliny,[63] the Gate of the Caucasus, which was erroneously called the Caspian Gate, was located here. The pass was locked with a real gate, made of wood, fitted with iron. Under it, writes Pliny, flows the river Diriodoris.[64] A fortress was also erected here to restrain the raids of the wild tribes; and so on. See the journey of Count J. Potocki,[65] whose scholarly research is as entertaining as his Spanish novels.

From Darial we set out for Kazbek. We saw the *Trinity Gate* (an arch, formed in the cliff by a powder explosion)—the road used to run beneath it, but now the Terek which so often changes its bed flows through there.

Not far from the settlement of Kazbek we crossed over the *Furious Gorge,* a ravine which during heavy downpours turns into a raging stream. At this time it was completely dry, and roaring in name only.

The village Kazbek is located at the foot of Mount Kazbek and belongs to Prince Kazbek.[66] The prince, a man of about forty-five, is taller than the pivot-man of the Preobrazhensky Regiment. We found him in the *dukhan* (that is the name for Georgian taverns, which are much poorer and dirtier than the Russian ones). In the door lay a big-bellied wineskin (ox fur), spreading its four legs wide. The giant squeezed some *chikhir*[67] wine out of it, and asked me some questions which I answered with the respect due his rank and size. We parted great friends.

Soon one's impressions are dulled. Hardly a day had gone by, and the roar of the Terek and its monstrous waterfalls, its cliffs and precipices no longer attracted my attention. An impatience to reach Tiflis completely overpowered me. I went past Kazbek as indifferently as I once sailed past Chatyrdag.[68] It is also true that the rainy and foggy weather prevented me from seeing its snowy mass, which in the expression of a poet "holds up the horizon."[69]

A Persian prince was expected.[70] At some distance from Kazbek we happened to meet some carriages, which made passage on the narrow road difficult. As the vehicles passed, the convoy officer announced to us that he was accompanying a Persian court poet, and at my request introduced me to Fazil-Khan.[71] With the help of an interpreter I was about to start a bombastic Oriental greeting; but how humiliated I felt when Fazil-Khan answered my inappropriate inventiveness with the simple, intelligent courtesy of a gentleman! "He hoped to see me in Petersburg; he was sorry that our acquaintance would be of short duration, and so on." With shame I was forced to abandon my pompously jocular tone and come down to ordinary European phrases. That was a lesson for our Russian tendency to make fun of others. In the future I shall not judge a person by his sheepskin *papakha*[72] and painted nails.

The post of Kobi is located at the very foot of the Mountain of the Cross, over which we now had to go. We stopped there to spend the night and began to think of how to accomplish this awesome feat: should we leave the carriages and mount the Cossacks' horses, or send for Ossetian oxen? To be on the safe side, I wrote an official petition in the name of all of our caravan to Mr. Chilyaev, who was in charge out here, and we went to sleep expecting carts.[73]

The next day about noon we heard noise, shouts, and saw an unusual spectacle: eighteen pairs of scraggly, undersized oxen, driven by a crowd of half naked Ossets, were with difficulty dragging along the light Viennese carriage of my friend O***. This spectacle at once dispelled all my doubts. I decided to send my heavy Petersburg carriage back to Vladikavkaz and to ride to Tiflis on horseback. Count Pushkin did not want to follow my example. He preferred to harness a whole herd of oxen to his brichka, which was loaded with supplies of every kind, and to ride in triumph over the snowy ridge. We parted, and I set out with Colonel Ogarev, who was inspecting the local roads.[74]

The road went through a landslide which had fallen at the end of June 1827. Such accidents usually happen every seven years. An enormous block fell down, burying the pass for a whole verst and damming the Terek. Sentries who were standing further down heard a terrible thunder and saw that the river had quickly become shallow and in a quarter of an hour completely silent and drained. The Terek was unable to burst through the landslide for two hours. But then it was terrifying![75]

We were climbing straight up, higher and higher. Our horses got stuck in the loose snow, under which little streams could be heard. I looked at the road in amazement and could not understand how any wheels could possibly ride over it.

At this time I heard a muffled thunder. "That's an avalance," said Mr. Ogarev to me. I looked around and saw not far off a heap of snow which was crumbling and slowly sliding down the steep mountainside. Small avalanches are not rare here. Last year a Russian driver was going along the Mountain of the Cross. An avalanche broke off: an awesome mass fell down on his vehicle; it swallowed wagon, horse, and peasant, rolled across the road and down into the precipice with its booty. We reached the very top of the mountain. A granite cross stands there, an old monument repaired by Ermolov.

The travelers usually get out of their carriages and walk there. Recently some foreign consul came by: he was so weak that he demanded to be blindfolded; he was led by the arm, and when the bandage was removed, he got down on his knees, thanked God, and so on, which greatly astonished the guides.

The instantaneous transition from awesome Caucasus to lovely Georgia is enchanting.

The air of the South suddenly starts to waft over the traveler. From the height of Mount Gut the Kaishaur Valley opens up with its inhabited cliffs, its orchards, and its bright Aragva, which winds like a silver ribbon—and all this in a reduced scale, at the bottom of a three-verst-high precipice along which the dangerous road goes.

We were descending into the valley. A new moon appeared in the clear sky. The evening air was quiet and warm. I spent the night on the bank of the Aragva, in Mr. Chilyaev's home. The next day I parted from my amiable host and continued on my way.

Georgia begins here. Bright valleys watered by the merry Aragva replaced the gloomy gorges and the awesome Terek. Instead of bare cliffs I saw green mountains and fruit trees around me. Aqueducts gave evidence of the presence of civilization. One of them struck me with its perfect optical illusion: the water seems to run uphill.

In Paisanaur I stopped to change horses. There I met a Russian officer who was accompanying the Persian prince. Soon after, I heard the sound of little bells, and a whole line of *katars* (mules), tied one to the other and packed in the Asian manner, dragged itself along the road. I set out on foot without waiting for the horses; and at half a verst from Ananur, where the road turns, I met Khozrev-Mirza. His vehicles were standing still. He personally looked out of his carriage and nodded to me. A few hours after our meeting some mountaineers attacked the Prince. When he heard the whistle of bullets, Khozrev leapt out of his carriage, mounted a horse and galloped off. The Russians who were with him were amazed at his courage. The fact is that the young Asian, not being used to a carriage, regarded it as a trap rather than a refuge.

I got to Ananur, feeling no tiredness. My horses had not arrived. I was told that the town of Dushet was no more than ten versts away, so I set out on foot again. But I did not know that the road went uphill. Those ten versts were worth a good twenty.

Evening fell; I went ahead, all the time climbing higher and higher. To lose one's way was impossible; but in places the muddy clay, formed by springs, reached up to my knees. I got completely exhausted. The darkness increased. I heard the howling and barking of dogs and was glad, imagining that the town was not far away. But I was mistaken: it was the Georgian shepherd dogs barking, and jackals, not unusual beasts in that area, howling. I cursed my impatience, but there was nothing I could do. Finally I caught sight of lights, and around midnight I found myself near houses surrounded by trees. The first person I met volunteered to take me to the mayor, for which he demanded an *abaz*[76] from me.

My appearance at the mayor's, an old Georgian officer, produced great commotion. First, I demanded a room, where I could undress; second, a glass of wine; third, an *abaz* for my guide. The mayor did not know how to receive me, and looked at me incredulously. Seeing that he was in no hurry to carry out my requests, I began to take my cloak off in front of him, asking his pardon *de la liberté grande*.[77] Fortunately, in my pocket I found the order for posthorses[78] proving that I was a peaceful traveler, and not Rinaldo-Rinaldini.[79] That blessed document had an immediate effect: a room was assigned to me, a glass of wine was brought, and an *abaz* given to my guide along with a fatherly reprimand for his venality, demeaning to Georgian hospitality. I threw myself down on the sofa, hoping to fall into a heroic sleep after my deed: but there was no chance of that! Fleas, far more dangerous than jackals, attacked me and gave me no peace the whole night. In the morning my man came to me and announced that Count Pushkin had safely crossed the snowy mountains with the oxen and arrived in Dushet. I had to hurry! Count Pushkin and Stjernvall visited me and suggested that we again continue together. I left Dushet with the pleasant thought that I would spend the night in Tiflis.

The road was as pleasant and picturesque, although we seldom saw any signs of habitation. A few versts form Garsiskal we crossed the Kura river on an ancient bridge, a monument of the

Roman campaigns,[80] and rode at an even trot, and sometimes even gallop, toward Tiflis, where we arrived unnoticed at about eleven at night.

Translator's Notes

1. *Journeys to the Orient Undertaken by Order of the French Government. (French.)* This was Victor Fontanier's second journey to Anatolia, published in Paris.

2. The war between Russia and Turkey of 1828-29 was conducted on two fronts: in the Balkans, and in eastern Turkey. The Russian army was under the command of Field Marshals Ivan Ivanovich Dibich-Zabalkansky ("who went across to the Balkans") [1785-1831] and Ivan Fyodorovich Pashkevich-Erivansky ("of Erivan' ") [1782-1856].

3. A poet, distinguished by his imagination, found in so many lofty deeds of which he was the witness not the subject for a narrative poem, but for a satire. *(French.)*

4. Writer, historian. In 1830 he published some poems concerning his recent stay in Adrianople, a city in the Balkans.

5. Writer on religious themes. His *A Journey to the Holy Land (Puteshestvie ko sviatym mestam)* was published in 1832.

6. The Detached Caucasus Corps was at this time (1829) largely made up of former Decembrists, i.e., participants in the officers' rebellion of December 14, 1825, and their sympathizers.

7. Raevsky's immediate superior, called Karsky ("of Kars") after distinguishing himself at the taking of that city in June 1829.

8. This is a rendition of Chavchavadze, Alexander Garsevanovich (1786-1846), the prominent Georgian poet, Griboedov's father-in-law. Born in St. Petersburg, he served as an officer in the Russian army that entered Paris in 1814.

9. Vasily Osipovich Bebutov (1791-1858) took part in the Napoleonic wars and had been Ermolov's aide-de-camp.

10. Nikolai Nikolaevich Raevsky (1801-43), commander of the Nizhegorod Regiment of Dragoons. He had been Pushkin's close friend since 1820. ("Nizhegorod" was an abbreviation for Nizhny Novgorod, the city on the Volga now called Gorky.)

11. Among the leaders who commanded it (Prince Paskevich's army) one could distinguish General Mouravief . . . Prince Tsitsevaze of Georgia . . . Prince Beboutof of Armenia . . . Prince Potemkine, General Raiewsky, and finally—M. Pouchkine . . . who had left the capital in order to sing the praises of his compatriot's exploits. *(French.)*

12. A mountain ridge in eastern Turkey.

13. The Commander-in-Chief, or minister of war, of the Turkish army. The name of this Seraskir was Salih Pasha.

14. The title Pasha was one of honor, not hereditary, and always followed the name. It denoted the highest official of a province in Turkey.

15. Pushkin uses this title ironically. It was rumored that Fontanier was a spy for the French government.

16. This was not quite true. Pushkin's journey had provided material for some travel notes, published under the title "The Georgian Military Highway" ("Voennaia gruzinskaia doroga") in 1830 in the *Literary Gazette*, and for several poems written in 1829, including "On the Hills of Georgia . . ." ("Na kholmakh Gruzii . . ."), "To the Kalmyk Girl" ("Kalmychke"), "From Gafiz" ("Iz Gafiza"), "Oleg's Sword" ("Olegov shchit"), "The Caucasus" ("Kavkaz"), "The Avalanche" ("Obval"), "The Monastery on Mount Kazbek" ("Monastyr' na Kazbeke"), and "Turkish Cavalry Soldier" ("Delibash").

17. The headlines for the five chapters do not exist in Pushkin's manuscripts. They first appear in the *Contemporary.*

18. About 133 miles. One verst equals 0.6629 miles.

19. Alexei Petrovich Ermolov (1772-1861) had been the Commander-in-Chief of the Russian army in the Caucasus before Paskevich, of whom he was strongly critical. At the time of Pushkin's visit, Ermolov was officially in disgrace.

20. George Dawe (1781-1829), English portrait painter, creator of The Military Gallery in the Winter Palace, St. Petersburg. Containing more than 400 portraits of Russian generals of the War of 1812, it also includes the portrait of Ermolov.

21. Several people of the Caucasus region are mentioned in the *Journey.* The Circassians and Ossets were mountain tribes. The Nogais and Kalmyks were nomads living on the steppes just north of the Caucasus.

22. The Russian Graf Erivansky is close to what Ermolov insists on calling him, Graf Erikhonsky (Count of

Jericho), referring to the Biblical legend of Joshua and the battle of Jericho (Joshua, VI). Throughout the work Paskevich is referred to with his title—"the Count." This is somewhat pointed, since it had been given him only in 1828, and he was well-known for his love of flattery.

23. A fortress in the Balkans (now Bulgaria), which had not fallen to the Russians.

24. Probably Fyodor Ivanovich Tolstoi (1782-1846), called "The American," because he had visited the Aleutian Islands, then part of Russian America. At this time he was serving as intermediary in the marriage negotiations between Pushkin and his future wife.—The writers Lev Nikolaevich Tolstoi (1828-1910) and Alexei Konstantinovich Tolstoi (1817-75) both belonged to this same branch of the Tolstoi family.

25. Nikolai Mikhailovich Karamzin (1766-1826), major writer and historian. His *History of the Russian State (Istoriia gosudarstva Rossiiskogo)* was published in 1818-29.

26. Andrei Mikhailovich Kurbsky (1528-83), prince, military leader, strong opponent of Ivan the Terrible.

27. *Con amore*—With love. *(Italian.)*

28. This refers to Dibich, who was German-born, but in Russian service.

29. Alexander Sergeevich Griboedov (1795-1829), diplomat and playwright. He was appointed ambassador to Persia in 1828. It may be interesting to note that Ermolov, when describing this to the poet Davydov, said that his jaws ached from chewing the verse, not reading it.

30. Odessa mud—Pushkin had spent part of his exile (1823-24) in this Black Sea port.

31. Vladimir Alexeevich Musin-Pushkin (1798-1854), son of the famous collector of manuscripts. He had been arrested in connection with the Decembrist rebellion but received only a light sentence of demotion.

32. From "Peter the Great in Ostrogozhsk" ("Pyotr Velikii v Ostrogozhske" in *Thoughts (Dumy*, 1823) by Kondraty Fedorovich Ryleev (1795-1826), poet, Decembrist. Ryleev was one of five hanged for their participation in the Decembrist rebellion, and his name was therefore not allowed to appear under this verse.

33. Alexander Osipovich Orlovsky (1777-1832), well-known Polish artist.

34. Famous sorceress in Greek legend. Odysseus and his men visited her island and were changed into swine.

35. One of a line of Russian fortresses along the southern boundaries of the Empire, built in 1777.

36. While in exile in the South of Russia, Pushkin spent part of the summer of 1820 in the Caucasus with the Raevsky family.

37. Hot Springs was also called *Kavkazskie mineral'nye vody* (The Caucasian Mineral Springs). The place Pushkin describes was later named Pyatigorsk.

38. Alexander Nikolaevich Raevsky (1795-1868), the older of the brothers, for some time Pushkin's Byronic idol. He is said to have inspired Pushkin's poem "The Demon," which was written in 1823.

39. Since 1931, Ordzhonikidze.

40. A long, open, horse-drawn carriage with a folding top over the rear seat and a front seat facing it.

41. Ivan Vasilievich Gudovich (1741-1820) had commanded the Russian troops in Dagestan and Georgia in three wars against Turkey: 1768-74, 1787-91, and 1806-12.

42. A Caucasian mountain village.

43. A teacher of Islam, religious leader.

44. The Crimea had been annexed by Catherine II in 1783.

45. The east coast of the Black Sea, conquered by Catherine II in 1783, was again declared Russian in the Treaty of Adrianople, September 1829, which concluded the war between Russia and Turkey.

46. Mansur (means: victorious; real name: Ushurma)[died in 1794], a Circassian who in 1785 proclaimed a holy war for his faith, Islam. He was captured by the Russians in 1791 and imprisoned in the Schlüsselburg Fortress, where he died. That he died at the Solovetsky monastery was just a legend.

47. A small stone dwelling.

48. In English in the original. From "The Burial of Sir John Moore" (1817) by Charles Wolfe (1791-1823), an Irish poet. The poem, greatly admired by Byron, was popular in Russia through the translation of Ivan Kozlov (1779-1840).

49. The veil worn by Moslem women.

50. Emil Stjernvall-Walleen (1806-90) was traveling to the Caucasus with his brother-in-law Count Musin-Pushkin. Stjernvall was Finnish, but lived and worked in St. Petersburg.

51. A waterfall in Finland.

52. From Stanza 72 of "The Waterfall" ("Vodopad") by Gavrila Romanovich Derzhavin (1743-1816), major Russian poet.

53. Fyodor Alexandrovich Bekovich-Cherkassy ("the Circassian") was actually Kabardinian by nationality. He came into Russian service in 1806. After the taking of Kars, he became the manager of the Pashalic of Kars.

54. From a region in the Caucasus.

55. From the *Iliad*, Book III, after the Russian translation by Ermil Ivanovich Kostrov (about 1750-90).—A more recent translation of the *Iliad* had been made by Nikolai Ivanovich Gnedich (1784-1833), published in 1829.

56. A long narrative poem published by Pushkin in 1822.

57. These Turks were prisoners of war in the on-going military operations.

58. Probably Pyotr Vasilievich Sheremetev (1799-1837), who had worked in the Russian Embassy in Paris. Pushkin met him in the Caucasus spas on the way back (August 1829).

59. The traveler Pushkin cites here in "N . . . N . . .," whose anonymous work *Notes During a Trip to the Caucasus and Georgia in 1827 (Zapiski vo vremia poezdki na Kavkaz i v Gruziiu v 1827 godu)* was published in 1829. Pushkin owned this book and used it in reworking his travel notes ("The Georgian Military Highway") into *A Journey to Arzrum.*

60. This painting by Rembrandt is in the Dresden Art Gallery, and was popular in gravures. In Greek mythology Ganymede was a beautiful boy whom Zeus abducted and made into a cup-bearer.

61. Pushkin read about this legend in *Voyage dans la Russie meridionale et particulièrement dans les provinces situées au delà du Caucase fait depuis 1820 jusqu'en 1824 (Journey in South Russia and Especially in the Provinces Situated beyond the Caucasus, Undertaken from 1820 to 1824)* by the French consul to Tiflis, J. F. Gamba (1763-1833). The book was published in Paris in 1826.

62. Persian *Dar-i-Alan* means "Gate of the Alans." This was the medieval name for the Ossets.

63. Pliny the Elder (Gaius Plinius Secundus; 23 or 24-79 A.D.), Roman historian and geographer, author of the celebrated *Historiae Naturalis XXXVII (Natural History in 37 Books).*

64. Diri odoris—"Of foul odor." *(Latin.)*

65. Pushkin read the information from Pliny in *Voyage dans les steps d'Astrakhan et du Caucase (A Journey to the Steppes of Astrakhan and to the Caucasus),* published in Paris, 1829, by Jan Potocki (1761-1815), Polish count, historian, linguist, traveler, writer. His "Spanish novels" include *Manuscrit trouvé à Saragosse (Manuscript Found in Saragossa,* 1814), also originally written in French.

66. Probably Nikolai Gabrielevich Kazbek (Kazibeg), whose family had ruled this area for generations.

67. Georgian red wine.

68. Pushkin had sailed from Kefa (now Feodosia) to Yurzuf (now Gurzuf) westward along the southern shore of the Crimea, thus passing Mount Chatyrdag, with the Raevskys in the late summer of 1820.

69. From "Half-soldier" ("Polusoldat," 1826) by Denis Vasilievich Davydov (1784-1839), a minor poet.

70. Khozrev-Mirza (1812-78), grandson of Feth Ali Shah (1771-1834). He was on his way to St. Petersburg with official apologies for the massacre of the Russian mission in Teheran, January 30, 1829, in which Griboedov, among others, perished.

71. Fazil-Khan (died 1852), Persian poet, Khozrev-Mirza's teacher. He decided to stay in Russia, and went to live and teach in Tiflis, where he also died. Pushkin wrote the following lines upon their meeting: "Both the day and the hour are blessed,/ When in the Caucasus mountains/ Fate brought us together" ("Blagosloven i den'i chas,/ Kogda v gorakh Kavkaza/ Sud'ba soedinila nas").

72. This is what Persian caps are called. [Pushkin's note.]

73. Boris Gavrilovich Chilyaev (real name: Babana Chiladze) [1798-1850], Georgian by nationality. From 1828 he was the ruler over the mountain tribes along the Georgian Military Highway. The rough draft of Pushkin's note asking for assistance has been preserved.

74. Nikolai Gavrilovich Ogaryov—Supervisor of the repair work along the roads.

75. Pushkin got the information of the large landslide from Gamba, but supplied the year "1827" himself; Gamba has 1817.

76. An old Georgian coin, at the time worth about twenty kopeks in silver. The *abaz* got its name from Shah Abbas I (1587-1628), whose image was printed on Persian coins.

77. For taking such a great liberty. *(French.)*

78. This was the *podorozhnaia* necessary for travel in the Russian Empire.

79. A well-born robber, hero of the novel by the same name of Christian August Vulpius (1762-1827), a German writer.

80. Those of Gnaeus Pompeius Magnus (Pompey the Great; 106-48 B.C.), which in 65 B.C. led to Roman hegemony over Iberia, as Georgia was then called.

N. V. GOGOL

The Portrait[1]

I

There used to be no place in front of which people stopped more than the little picture shop in Shchukin Place. This shop displayed the most heterogeneous collection of marvels; the pictures were, for the most part, oil paintings covered with a dark-green varnish and set in tawdry dark-yellow frames. Winter with white trees, a totally red evening like the glow of some conflagration, a pipe-smoking Flemish peasant with a broken arm resembling more a turkey-cock in frills than a man,—these were the usual subjects. To these must be added several engravings: a portrait of Khozrev-Mirza wearing a sheepskin cap, portraits of some generals or other wearing three-cornered hats, with crooked noses. The doors of such a shop are usually hung with bundles of those pictures which testify to the native talent of Russians. On one of them the Tsarevna Miliktrisa Kirbityevna appeared, on another the city of Jerusalem, in which the houses and churches had been unceremoniously splashed with red paint which had also caught part of the ground and two Russian peasants at prayer with their mittens on. There were usually few buyers for these works, but on the other hand there were onlookers in droves. Even now, probably, some debauché of a servant is yawning in front of them, holding tureens of dinner from the inn for his master, who, doubtless, will not be taking his soup very hot today. There is probably some soldier, a flee-market cavalier, also standing in front of them, with a few penknives for sale; a peddler-woman from Okhta with a small box of shoes. Everyone expresses admiration in his own way: peasants usually prod with their fingers; the cavaliers put on stern faces; the servant boys and apprentices laugh and tease each other with sketched caricatures; the old servants wearing their frieze greatcoats stop and stare, simply to have something to gawk at for a while; but the young Russian peddler-women hurry instinctively to hear what the people are chattering about and to see what it is they are looking at. At such a moment the young artist Chertkov stopped in front of the shop as he was passing by. His old greatcoat and drab clothes indicated that here was a man who was dedicated to his work to the point of self-sacrifice and who had no time to worry about the state of his clothing, which is always a source of mysterious attraction for the young. He stopped in front of the shop and at first laughed inwardly at the hideous pictures; finally he was overcome by an involuntary state of meditation: he began to wonder who would need such works. That the Russian people should gaze at Eruslans, Lazaryches, at eating and drinking bouts, at Foma and Erema—nothing of this seemed surprising to him: the depicted subjects were very simple and could be understood by the people; but where were the purchasers of these multi-colored, dirty daubings in oils? Who needs these Flemish peasants, these red and blue landscapes which betray certain pretensions to a somewhat higher level of art, but in which art's low degradation is expressed? If only these were the labors of a child yielding to some unconscious urge; if only they did not contain any trace of correctness or even the first basic principles of automatic drawing, if only everything in them were pure caricature but with some effort, some urge to produce a likeness of nature shining through,—but nothing of the sort can be detected in them. The dimwittedness of old age, a mindless whim or, rather, an involuntary urge had guided the hands of their creators. Who had labored over them? And it was one and the same person who had labored, without doubt, because the same colors, the same style, the same skilled, practiced hand, which belonged rather to a coarsely manufactured automaton than a man, was evident in them. He nevertheless continued to stand in front of these grimy pictures and stare at them without noticing that meanwhile the little picture shop's proprietor, a gray-complexioned man of about fifty wearing a frieze greatcoat and with a long-unshaven chin was telling him that: "The pictures are all first-class and have just arrived from the exchange, the varnish is still not dry and they've not yet been framed. Look for yourself, I promise you'll be pleased with them." These beguiling words all flew straight into one of Chertkov's ears and out the other. Finally, to encourage the proprietor, he lifted several dusty paintings from the floor. They were old family portraits whose descendants were scarcely likely to be traced. Almost automatically he began to wipe the dust off one of them. A slight flush spread across his face, the kind of flush which betrays a secret satisfaction with some unexpected discovery. He began to rub it impatiently with his hand and could soon see a portrait which bore the strokes of a master's brush, although the paint had faded and turned black. It was the portrait of an old man with a somewhat agitated or even malicious expression on his face; there was a smile on his lips, a sharp, malignant smile accompanied by a certain look of horror; the flush of illness was faintly discernible on his wrinkled and distorted face; his eyes were large, dark and dim; but at the same time a certain vivacity was detectable in them. The portrait seemed to depict a kind of miser who had spent his life guarding his money chest, or one of those unfortunates who all their lives mar the happiness of others. His face, generally speaking, had preserved the distinct impression of a southern physiognomy. Swarthiness, hair as black as pitch, but streaked with gray—none of these characteristics is found among the inhabitants of the northern regions. There was an air of incompletion about the whole portrait, but if it had been completed it would have driven an expert crazy guessing how a perfect work of Van Dyck could have found its way to Russia and ended up in this little shop in Shchukin Place.

With his heart pounding the young artist put it to one side and began to rummage through the others to see if he could find any more like it, but the remainder comprised a completely different world and merely showed that the former was only a guest who had inadvertently stumbled on them. Finally Chertkov inquired about the price. The pushy dealer, deducing from Chertkov's attentiveness that the portrait was worth something, scratched behind his ear and said: "Well now, ten rubles wouldn't be too much." Chertkov put his hand in his pocket. "I'll give eleven," said someone behind him.

He turned around and saw that a crowd of people had gathered and that some gentleman in a raincoat had been standing in front of the picture, just like him. His heart began to pound and his lips started quietly trembling, like those of a man who senses that the object of his quest is about to be taken from him. Looking attentively at his new purchaser, he drew slight comfort from the fact that the man's clothes were little better than his own, and he said in a shaking voice: "I'll give you twelve rubles, the picture's mine!"

"Shopkeeper! Mark that picture down to me, and there's fifteen rubles for it!" said the buyer.

Chertkov's face shuddered convulsively, he caught his breath and said involuntarily, "Twenty rubles!"

The dealer rubbed his hands with glee, seeing that his customers themselves were doing his bargaining for him. The crowd of people around the buyers increased, having smelled out an ordinary sale being converted into an auction, which never fails to capture the interest of onlookers. The price was soon knocked up to fifty rubles. In near-desperation Chertkov shouted out, "Fifty," and then remembered that fifty rubles was all that he possessed and part of that would have to go on his rent, and besides, he needed to buy paints and a few other essentials. At this point his adversary yielded: the sum, it seemed, was beyond his means too—and the picture became Chertkov's. Taking a bank-note out of his pocket, he threw it in the dealer's face and eagerly went to seize the picture; but suddenly he jumped back from it, struck by fear. The dark eyes of the depicted old man stared at him in such a life-like, yet at the same time deathly, manner that he could not help being frightened. It seemed as though by some inexplicable power a part of life had been retained by them. Those eyes had not been drawn; they were alive, they were human eyes. They were motionless, but to be sure they could not have been more terrifying if they had moved. A certain primitive feeling—not fear, but that inexplicable sensation which we experience when something strange occurs to illustrate the disorder of nature, or rather, a certain insanity of nature—that very same feeling elicited a cry from almost all of those present. Chertkov moved a trembling hand over the canvas, but the canvas was quite smooth. The effect produced by the portrait was universal: the people rushed back out of the shop, horror-struck; the client who had competed for it with him retreated timidly. At this time dusk was beginning to thicken, it seemed, in order to make this unbelievable phenomenon even more frightening. Chertkov could not force himself to stay any longer. Not daring even to contemplate taking the picture with him, he ran out onto the street. The fresh air, the noise on the pavement, the chatter of human beings seemed to refresh him for a moment; but his soul was still oppressed by some burdensome feeling. However much he directed his glance at the objects surrounding him on all sides, his thoughts were still preoccupied with the single unusual phenomenon. "What is this?" he wondered to himself, "is it art or some supernatural sorcery which ignores the laws of nature? Does there exist a line to which higher knowledge leads a man but, once he has crossed it, he grasps something not created by human effort and tears something live out of the life which animated his model? Why is it so terrible to cross over this line, which is the borderline of the imagination? Or does reality finally follow the imagination, the impulse—that awful reality which knocks imagination off its axis as if by some external shock, that terrible reality which presents itself to a man thirsting after it when he, wishing to discover that which is beautiful in man, arms himself with a surgeon's knife, cuts through to the inner self, and sees that which is so repulsive in man? It's incomprehensible! So astoundingly, so horrifyingly life-like! Or is too close an imitation of nature as sickening as a dish which is too sweet to the taste?" With such thoughts in his head he went back to his little room in the little wooden house on Vasilevsky Island, Row 15, in which, scattered all around, lay his immature sketches, careful and precise copies of antique works of art, which showed the artist's efforts to master the basic laws and inner dimensions of nature. He gazed at them for a long time, and finally his thoughts flowed one after another and began to express themselves almost in words—so keenly aware was he of what he was thinking!

"I've been slaving away over this dry, skeletal work for a year now! I've been trying my very best to discover just what wonderful gift it is that great artists possess and which appears to be the fruit of a moment's sudden inspiration. At the slightest touch of their brush a man appears—willful, free, just as he was created by nature; his movements are animated, unrestrained. It comes to them in a flash, but I have to slog away all my life; all my life examining the boring bases and essentials, devoting my whole life to colorless work which does not in the least correspond to my feelings! They are faithful copies of the originals; but just let me try to produe something of my own—and it goes all wrong: the leg looks odd and unnatural; the arm won't rise so easily and freely; I'll never be able to capture the turn of the head as naturally as they do, and the thoughts, and those indescribable scenes . . . . No, I'll never be a great artist!"

His thoughts were interrupted by the entrance of his manservant, an eighteen-year-old youth wearing a Russian smock, with a rosy complexion and red hair. Without further ado he began to pull Chertkov's boots off, while the latter was engrossed in his own thoughts. This youth in the red smock was his lackey, his model; he cleaned his boots, idled away the time in his little ante-room, wiped up the paints and filthied the floor with his muddy boots. After removing his master's boots, he threw him his dressing-gown and was just going out of the room when suddenly he turned his head and said loudly, "Should I light the candle or not, sir?"— "Light it," answered Chertkov distractedly.—"And the landlord came by," the grubby manservant said, as if in passing, honoring the commendable tradition among all people of his profession of mentioning the most important thing only as a P.S. "The landlord came by to say that if you don't pay him his money he'll sling all your pictures out the window along with your bed."

"Tell the landlord not to worry about the money," Chertkov answered, "I've got the money." With that he went over to his coat pocket, but suddenly remembered that he had left all his money with the shopkeeper in exchange for the portrait. He began inwardly reproaching himself for his stupidity in running out of the shop for no reason, frightened by some meaningless event, taking with him neither the money nor the portrait. He decided to go and see the dealer the next day to get his money back, considering himself entirely justified in refusing such a purchase, particularly as his domestic circumstances did not allow him any extra expenditure.

The moonlight spread across his floor like a bright, white window, catching part of the bed and finishing up at the wall. All the articles and paintings hanging in his room seemed somehow to be smiling as their edges occasionally caught a little of that eternally beautiful brilliance. Just at that moment, almost by chance, he glanced at the wall and saw on it that very same strange portrait which had given him such a shock in the shop. A slight, involuntary shiver ran through his body. His first reaction was to call for his manservant-cum-model to ask him how the portrait got there and who had brought it; but the manservant-cum-model swore that nobody had called except the landlord, who had come in the morning and with nothing in his hands except the key. Chertkov felt his hair stand on end. Sitting down by the window he tried to convince himself that nothing supernatural could have taken place, and that the boy could have fallen asleep at that moment when the owner of the portrait sent it around, having located his room ahead of time by some special means. In short, he began going over all those trite explanations which we use when we want whatever has happened to have happened as we thought. He told himself not to look at the portrait, but his head turned involuntarily towards it and his glance seemed riveted to the strange picture. The old man's motionless stare was unbearable; his eyes were all agleam, absorbing the moonlight, and their life-like quality was so frightening that Chertkov automatically covered his eyes with his hand. A tear seemed to shudder on the old man's eyelashes; the bright twilight, into which the night was transformed by the sovereign moon, increased the effect; the drape slid off, and the old man's fearsome face glared out from the frame as if through a window.

Attributing this supernatural effect to the moon, whose wonderful light possesses a secret ability to endow objects with some of the sounds and colors of another world, he ordered the candle, by which his lackey was rummaging about, to be brought to him immediately; but the image of the portrait did not recede—the moonlight, mingling with the light of the candle, lent it an even more incomprehensible and at the same time strangely life-like quality. Snatching up a sheet he started to cover up the portrait; he triple-wrapped it so that it would not show through, but for all that, either as a result of his greatly agitated imagination, or because his eyes, wearied by the considerable strain, had preserved a cursory, moving image, he imagined that the old man's stare shone through the drape for a fairly long time after. Finally, he resolved to snuff out the candle and lie down on his bed, which was shut off from the portrait by a surrounding screen. He waited in vain for sleep: thoughts of the most disturbing kind dispelled that peaceful state which accompanies the onset of sleep. Depression, anguish, his landlord's demands for money, the unfinished pictures—the products of an impotent impulse, his poverty—all these things paraded in front of him in rapid succession. And when he succeeded in banishing them for a moment, the wondrous portrait crowded into and dominated his imagination, and it seemed as though its murderous eyes were gleaming through the chink in the screen. Never had he felt his soul so heavily oppressed. The moonlight, which contains so much music when it steals into a poet's lonely bedroom and dangles childishly—enchanting semi-dreams over the head of his bed—this moonlight brought him no melodious visions; his visions were delirious. At last he sank not into a sleep, but into a kind of semi-oblivion, into that depressing state in which we see with one eye the approaching dream-like visions, and with the other—the objects about us in a cloud-like haze. He saw the old man's outward form detach itself from the portrait, just as the upper layer of foam separates from a boiling liquid, he saw it rise up into the air and rush towards him, getting closer and closer, until finally it came right up to his bed. Chertkov felt his breathing stop, and he tried to sit up—but his arms refused to move. The old man's eyes shone dimly and penetrated deep inside him with all of their magnetic power.

"Don't be afraid,"—said the old man, and Chertkov noticed a smile on his lips, which seemed to sting him with derision and illuminate the dim furrows of his face with its brilliant vitality.—"Don't be afraid of me,"—said the strange phenomenon. "You and I will never be parted. You acted very foolishly: what possessed you to spend years slogging away at your ABC's when you could have been hitting the high notes in your reading long ago? You think that by means of such dedicated perseverance you'll attain artistic excellence, that you'll win and achieve something? Yes, you'll achieve something,"—and with this his face became strangely contorted and a certain immovable laughter showed up in all its furrows,—"you'll achieve the enviable right to throw yourself into the Neva from St. Isaac's Bridge, or to hang yourself with a scarf on the first nail you come across; the first dauber who buys your works for a ruble will cover it with primer so that he can paint some pretty mug on it. Get that stupid idea right out of your head! Everything on earth has to be done for a purpose. Take hold of your brush right now and draw portraits of the whole town! Paint whatever you are commissioned to paint; but don't fall in love with your work, don't sit at it day and night; time passes swiftly, and life does not stand still. The more pictures you get done in one day, the more money you'll have in your pocket, and the more fame you'll achieve. Move out of this attic and rent a luxurious apartment. I love you, and that's why I'm giving you this kind of advice; I'll give you money too, if you just come to me,"—With this the old man's face again expressed that same immobile, frightening laughter.

An incomprehensible shudder passed over Chertkov, and a cold sweat broke out on his face. Mustering all his strength he raised an arm and eventually got out of his bed. But the image of the old man dimmed, and he only managed to see him going back into his frame. Chertkov stood up, agitated, and began to pace the room. To freshen up a little he walked over to the window. The brilliance of the moon still lay on the roofs and white walls of the houses, although small clouds had now begun to move across the sky with increasing frequency. Everything was silent; occasionally there came to his ears the jingling of a carriage in which a sleeping coachman, lulled by his lazy nag, awaited his belated fare in some hidden side street. Chertkov finally convinced himself that his imagination was overwrought and was showing him the creation of his agitated thoughts in his dreams. Once more he went up to the portrait: his sheet hid it completely from view, and it seemed as if only a tiny glimmer of light was penetrating it from time to time. At last he fell asleep and slept right through until morning.

For a long time after waking he felt inside him that unpleasant sensation which overcomes a man after inhaling charcoal fumes: his head ached unpleasantly. The room was dim, and unpleasant dampness moistened the air and seeped through the cracks in his windows, which were plastered with pictures or stained with primer paint. Soon there was a knock on the door, and in came the landlord with the police superintendent, whose appearance for humble people is as unpleasant as the ingratiating face of a petitioner is for rich people. The landlord of the small house in which Chertkov lived was one of those creatures who are usually owners of houses in the Fifteenth Row on Vasilevsky Island on the Petersburg side or in a distant corner of Kolomna; a creature whose kind abounds in Russia and whose character it is so difficult to define, like the color of a worn-out dress coat. In his youth he had been a captain and a loudmouth, and had been employed in civilian matters; was a past master with the whip, was quick-witted, a dandy and a fool, but in old age he blended all these striking abilities into a sort of dull indefiniteness. He was by now a widower and retired, he no longer dressed stylishly, no longer boasted or got into fights; all he liked to do now was to drink tea and talk all sorts of nonsense over it; he would pace his room, adjusting the odd candle-end; punctually at the end of every month he would drop in on his tenants to collect the rent; he would go out into the street with a key in his hand to have a look at the roof of his house; several times he chased the house servant from the kennel where he had concealed himself for a sleep,—in a word, he was a retired man for whom, after a reckless life and joltings on the stage coach, there remained nothing but common habits.

"Have a look yourself," said the landlord, addressing the policeman, and spreading his arms out, "Please attend to the matter and explain it to him."

"It's my duty to inform you," said the police superintendent, placing his hand on the buttonhole of his uniform, "that you must pay the rent for the apartment, rent which you have owed for the last three months, immediately."

"I would be glad to, but how can I when I haven't got any money?" Chertkov answered indifferently.

"In that case the landlord must take from you property equivalent in value to the sum owed, and you must vacate the apartment this very day."

"Take anything you want," Chertkov answered, almost unconsciously.

"Many of these paintings show a pretty good talent," the policeman went on, sifting through some of them. "It's just a pity they're not finished off and that the colors don't really come to life . . . I suppose a lack of funds kept you from buying paints? And what's this picture wrapped in a piece of canvas?"

As he said this the policeman unceremoniously approached the portrait and pulled the sheet from it, because all of these gentlemen allow themselves a degree of freedom whenever they detect complete defenselessness or poverty. The portrait seemed to startle him, because the unusual life-like quality of the eyes had the same effect on everyone. Examining the picture he squeezed the frame rather hard, and as police officers' hands are alway associated with somewhat rough, manual work, the frame suddenly cracked; a small piece of wood and a jingling little bundle of gold fell onto the floor, and several shining round objects began rolling about in all directions. Chertkov made a bee-line for them and snatched out of the policeman's hands the few coins which he had picked up.

"How can you say you've no money to pay with," observed the policeman, smiling pleasantly, "when you've got so much in gold?"

"This money is sacred to me!" exclaimed Chertkov, keeping well out of the way of the policeman's expert hands, "I must keep it, these were entrusted to me by my late father. However, to satisfy you, here—this is enough for your apartment!" And he tossed a few gold coins to the landlord of the house.

Almost immediately the physiognomy and gestures of the landlord and the worthy keeper of drunken coachmen's morals changed.

The policeman began to apologize and to assure him that he was only acting in accordance with the prescribed code of procedure, and, moreover, that he had no authority to exert any pressure; and to convince Chertkov of this he offered him a pinch of snuff. The landlord assured him that he had only been joking, and assured him with such shameless invocations of the Lord as are usually used by merchants of the Gostiny Dvor market.

But Chertkov ran out and decided not to live in his former apartment any longer. He did not even have time to consider just how strange the recent event had been. When he examined the little bundle, he found that it contained more than one hundred gold coins. The first thing he did was to rent a fashionable apartment. The apartment which he acquired seemed as though it could have been specially made for him: four high adjacent rooms, large windows, all the advantages and conveniences for an artist! Lying on his Turkish sofa and looking through the unbroken windows at the swelling, rushing waves of people, he was overcome by a kind of self-satisfied oblivion and marvelled at his fate, which only yesterday had crept up on him in his attic. Unfinished and finished pictures hung everywhere on the immense, elegant walls, and among them hung the mysterious portrait which he had obtained in such a unique way. He again began to think about the reason for the unusually life-like quality of its eyes. His thoughts returned to the semi-dream he had had, and finally, to the wonderful treasure concealed in that frame. Everything led to the conclusion that there must be a story connected with the very existence of the portrait, and that perhaps even his own existence was tied up with this portrait. He jumped up from the sofa and started to examine it very carefully: there was a little drawer concealed in the frame, closed off by a flimsy piece of wood, but so skillfully contrived and matched with its surface that no one would have discovered its existence had the policeman's heavy finger not pressed that little piece of wood. He stood it up in its place and scrutinized it again. The life-like quality of the eyes no longer seemed so frightening in the bright light flooding into his room through the huge windows and the noise of the crowds thronging in the streets thundering in his ears, but there was still something unpleasant about it, and he soon attempted to avert his gaze from it. At that moment the doorbell rang, and in came a respectable-looking lady of advanced years, with a wine-glass figure, accompanied by a pretty, eighteen-year-old girl; an expensively liveried lackey opened the door for them and then remained in the hallway.

"I have come to ask a favor of you," said the lady in the caressing tone usually reserved for addressing artists, French hairdressers, and other such people who are born to insure the pleasure of others. "I've heard about your talents . . ." (Chertkov was amazed at how quickly his fame had spread.) "I should like you to paint a portrait of my daughter."

Just then the daughter's pale face turned towards the artist, who, had he been versed in matters of the heart, would have immediately recognized in it the slim-volumed story of her life: a childish passion for balls, depression and boredom at the excessive time spent waiting about before and after dinner, the urge to run around at a garden party in a dress of the latest fashion, and an eagerness to see her girl friend and say to her, "Oh, my dear, how bored I am," or to explain what alteration Mme. Sichler has made to Princess B's dress. All this was expressed in the young visitor's pale, almost expressionless face, which was slightly tinged with an unhealthy sallowness.

"I should like you to begin work right away," continued the woman, "We can give you an hour." Chertkov made a dash for his paints and brushes, picked up the already prepared stretched canvas, and settled down in his best position.

"I ought to tell you something about my Annette beforehand," said the lady, "and so to make your work a little easier. In her eyes and even in the contours of her face there has always been a certain look of yearning; my Annette is very sensitive, and, I confess, I never allow her to read modern novels!" The artist looked searchingly, but could not detect any look of yearning. "I should like you to paint her in a simple family group, or better still, alone in the open air, in green shade, with nothing to suggest that she is on her way to a ball. Our balls, I must confess, are so boring and so soul-destroying that, truth to tell, I cannot understand how one could take pleasure from attending them." But the features of both the daughter's face and the respectable lady's clearly indicated that they never missed a single ball.

Chertkov thought for a moment about how to reconcile these small incongruities and finally decided to select a prudent middle course. Moreover, the desire to overcome the problems and to be triumphant with his art, without losing any of the ambiguous expression of the portrait, attracted him. The brush threw the first misty layer onto the canvas, an artistic chaos; from this the evolving shapes gradually began to emerge. He delved right beneath the surface of his model and had already begun to capture those elusive features which, in a realistic reproduction, lend a certain character to the most unattractive model—this being the elevated triumph of truth. A certain sweet trembling began to take hold of him when he felt that at last he had grasped and perhaps was now about to express that which one very rarely succeeds in expressing. This enjoyment, which is inexpressible and wells up in one progressively, is known only to talent. Under his brush the face in the portrait seemed involuntarily to take on a color which was a most unexpected discovery for him; but the model began to fidget and yawn so much in front of him that the artist, still inexperienced, found it difficult to capture her permanent expression with so many interruptions.

"I think that's enough for the first sitting," said the respectable lady.

Lord, how awful! But his soul and strength had been roused and craved satisfaction. Lowering his head and throwing down his palette, he stood in front of the picture.

"And they told me you would have the picture completely finished in two sittings," said the lady, going up to the picture, "but you've hardly even done the rough outline. We'll come tomorrow at the same time."

The artist showed his guests out in silence and remained in a very downcast state of mind. In his cramped attic no one had disturbed him when he sat over his uncommissioned work. He vexedly moved the newly started picture away and felt like getting down to other uncompleted works. But how can the thoughts and feelings which have pierced the very soul be replaced by new ones by which our imagination has not yet had time to be captivated? Throwing down his brush, he went out of the house.

Youth is a happy time by virtue of the fact that before it lie many various roads, and that its vital, fresh soul is amenable to a thousand varied pleasures; and for this reason Chertkov found suitable distraction in no time at all. With several gold pieces in one's pocket—what is beyond the power of vigorous youth! In addition to this, Russians, and particularly noblemen or artists, possess a strange charactersitic—as soon as a coin lands in their pockets—the sky's the limit, and they don't give a damn about anything. He still had a little money left over after the money he had paid in advance for the apartment, about thirty gold pieces. And he squandered the thirty gold pieces in the course of one evening. First of all he ordered himself an excellent meal, drank two bottles of wine, and refused to accept the change; hired a smart carriage just to go to the theater which was only a few paces away from his apartment; he treated three of his friends in a café, called in somewhere else and returned home without a single kopek left in his pocket. Throwing himself on his bed he fell sound asleep, but his dreams were indistinct, and his breast as on the first night contracted as if he could feel something heavy on it; he could see through the chink in his screen, see that the image of the old man had detached itself from the canvas, and with an anxious look on its face, was counting piles of money; the gold was pouring out of his hands . . . Chetkov's eyes were smarting, and it seemed as if his senses had recognized in that gold the inexplicable delight which until then he had been unable to comprehend. The old man beckoned with his finger and pointed out to him a whole pile of gold pieces. Chertkov stretched out his hand convulsively and woke up. When he was fully awake, he walked over to the portrait, shook it, cut all around the frame with a knife, but couldn't find any hidden money anywhere; eventually he gesticulated scornfully and made up his mind to do some work, first promising himself that he would not sit too long and would not be tempted by the alluring paintbrush. Just at that moment the lady who had called the day before arrived with her pale Annette. The artist stood the portrait up on the easel, and this time his brush moved with greater alacrity. The sunny day and the bright lighting lent a particular expression to his model and a host of hitherto unnoticed delicate points in her revealed themselves. His soul was afire with determination again. He strove to capture the slightest dot or line, even the yellowishness and uneven change of color in the face of this yawning, exhausted beauty, capture it with that exactitude which only inexperienced artists allow themselves, imagining that others are as fond of the truth as they are. His brush was just on the verge of capturing the general expression of the whole when an annoying "that's enough" echoed in his ears and the lady walked over to the portrait.

"Oh, my God! What have you drawn?" she exclaimed in great annoyance. "You've made Annette all yellow; you've got some dark spots under her eyes; she looks as if she's just had a few bottles of medicine to drink. No, for God's sake, put your portrait right; her face is nothing like that. We'll be back tomorrow at the same time."

Chertkov threw the brush down in anger; he cursed himself, his palette, the delightful lady, and her daughter, and the whole world. He sat hungry in his magnificent room, without the strength to work at any of his pictures. The next day, getting up early, he seized the first painting he could lay his hands on: it was the "Psyche," which he had begun a long time ago; he stood it up on the easel, fully intending to make an effort to continue it. Just then the lady from yesterday came in.

"Oh, Annette, come and look at this!" the lady exclaimed, obviously delighted. "Oh, how life-like! What a delight! What a delight! The nose, the mouth, the eyebrows! How can we thank you for this beautiful surprise? How nice it is! What a good idea to have this hand slightly raised. I can see that you really are the great artist people told me about."

Chertkov was stunned to see that the lady had taken his Psyche for her daughter's portrait. With the shyness of a novice he began to assure her that this rough sketch was intended as a drawing of Psyche, but the daughter took this as a compliment and smile rather sweetly; her mother, too, smiled. A fiendish thought flashed through the artist's mind, a thought strengthened by vexation and malice; and he decided to take advantage of the situation.

"Permit me to ask you to sit a little longer today," he said, now addressing himself to the fair-haired young lady who was now feeling pleased with herself. "You can see that I haven't quite finished doing your dress yet, because I wanted to capture every detail of real life."

He quickly bedecked his Psyche in a nineteenth-century costume, lightly touched up her eyes and lips, and brightened up her hair before presenting his visitors with the portrait. A wad of notes and a tender smile were his reward.

But the artist stood as though nailed to the floor. His conscience was gnawing at him. He was overcome by that fastidious, sensitive concern for his reputation which is experienced by any young man who carries within his soul the dignity of talent and is forced by it, if not to destroy, then at least to conceal from the world, any of his works in which he detects imperfections, and which makes him more inclined to endure the contempt of "hoi poloi" than that of the real connoisseur. He imagined he could see an implacable judge standing before his picture, shaking his head and reproaching him for his shamelessness and lack of talent. There was nothing he would not have given, if only he could get it back! He felt like running after the lady and snatching the portrait from her hands, tearing it to shreds and trampling it into the ground; but how could he do this? Where was he to go? He could not even remember his visitor's name.

From that moment on, however, a happy transformation took place in his life. He expected his name to be blighted with ignominy, but just the opposite happened. The lady who had ordered the portrait sang the praises of the unusual artist, and our Chertkov's studio was filled with visitors, all wishing to see their likeness doubled or, if possible, increased tenfold. But the still fresh, innocent Chertkov, feeling in his soul that he was not equal to such an undertaking, and in order to make amends and somewhat atone for his crime, decided to plunge himself into his work with all possible dedication and to redouble his efforts; this was the only way he would be able to produce his objects of wonder. But his intentions met with unforeseen obstacles: his visitors, whose portraits he was drawing, were for the most part an impatient lot, always busy and in a hurry, and so his brush would hardly have begun to create something completely extraordinary when a new visitor would drop in, pompously thrust out his head, burning with a desire to see it on canvas, and the artist would hurry to finish the work all the sooner. Finally, his time was so taken up that he did not have even a single moment to devote to reflection; and inspiration, constantly stifled at the moment of conception, finally ceased visiting him. At last, in order to speed up the work, he took to limiting himself to familiar, definite, monotonous and hackneyed forms. Soon his portraits came to resemble the family portraits of the old masters which one sees so frequently throughout Europe and, even, in all corners of the world, where ladies are depicted with their arms folded on their breasts and the gentlemen in uniforms, with one hand tucked inside their jackets. At times he wished he could present a new, not yet overworked pose, which would be distinguished by its originality and relaxed manner; but, alas, anything in the works of a poet or artist which appears relaxed and unforced, far from being spontaneous, is the fruit of great perseverance. To give a new and daring expression to his art, to discover a new secret in art—for this he had to meditate at length, having averted his gaze from his surroundings and having shut himself off from life and all that is worldly. But he had no time for this, and moreover, he was too exhausted by his daily work to be in any fit state to receive inspiration; and the world which he used as a model for his paintings was too ordinary and monotonous to stir and arouse his imagination. The deeply thoughtful yet expressionless face of an office chief; the Uhlan captain's handsome yet pale uniform face with the forced smile of a Petersburg beauty; and a host of others, all typically run-of-the-mill—such were the subjects which milled before our artist every day. It seemed as if the paintbrush itself eventually assumed that colorlessness and lack of vitality which characterized his models.

The paper money and the gold which ceaselessly flashed before him finally numbed the virginal impulses of his soul. He shamelessly used the weakness of people who for an extra contour of beauty added by the artist to their pictures were ready to overlook any shortcomings, even though this beauty be detrimental to the likeness.

In the end Chertkov became a completely fashionable painter. The whole capital turned to him; his portraits could be seen in every office, bedroom, drawing-room and boudoir. Genuine artists shrugged their shoulders as they surveyed the works of this spoiled child of Fate. They tried in vain to discover a single trace of real truth, cast up by heated inspiration: there was nothing but correctly drawn faces, nearly always handsome, because the artist maintained an understanding of beauty; but there was no knowledge of the heart, passions, and habits of men—there was nothing of that which would have indicated the development of delicate taste. And some of those who knew Chertkov were surprised at this strange occurrence, because they had observed the presence of talent in his first beginnings, and they tried to solve the unsolvable problem of how one's talents could be extinguished in the full bloom of one's powers instead of developing to their full radiance.

But the self-satisfied artist did not listen to these discussions, and he gloried in his fame as he jingled his gold coins, beginning to believe that everything in the world was ordinary and straightforward, and that no such thing as revelation from on high existed in the world, and that everything necessary has to be brought under the strict order of accuracy and uniformity. He was already approaching that stage in a man's life when everything within him inspired by impulse begins to diminish, when the vigorous violin bow affects the soul more feebly and its strident notes no longer wind themselves around the heart, when the touch of beauty no longer transforms its virginal power into fire and flame, but all the burned-out feelings become more amenable to the sound of gold, and they listen more attentively to its alluring music, then gradually and imperceptibly they allow it to enfeeble them completely. Glory cannot satiate and give enjoyment to him who has stolen it and has not earned it; it produces a constant thrill only in him who is worthy of it. And for this reason his feelings and impulses all turned towards gold. Gold became his passion, his ideal, his fear, his enjoyment, his goal. The bundles of paper money grew in his coffers. And like all those to whom this awesome gift is given, he started to become boring, incomprehensible to all, and indifferent to everything. He appeared ready to develop into one of those creatures who are sometimes encountered in the world, at whom a man who is full of vitality and passion looks in horror, and to whom they appear living bodies with dead men encased in them. But nevertheless one event gave him a severe shock and completely altered the direction of his life.

One day he found a note on his table in which the Academy of Artists invited him, as a worthy member, to come and make a judgment on a painting, newly arrived from Italy, by a Russian artist who had gone there to perfect his technique. This artist was one of his former friends, one who since his earliest years had kindled within himself a passion for art; with the energetic passion of a worker he had devoted himself to it with all his soul, and for its sake he had torn himself away from his friends, his relatives, his cherished habits, and he had cast himself into an unknown land without any means of support; he suffered poverty, humiliation, even hunger, and with rare self-sacrifice he scorned everything and was insensitive to all but his beloved art.

Entering the hall he found a crowd of visitors gathered in front of the painting. The most profound silence, such as is rarely encountered among crowds of critics, prevailed everywhere on this occasion. Chertkov, assuming the meaningful expression of an expert, approached the picture—but, Lord! what was it he saw!

Pure, unblemished, and beautiful as a bride, the artist's work stood before him. Not a single trace of any desire to shine or any pardonable vanity or even the thought of showing off to the rabble—none of this could be seen anywhere in it. It excelled in humility. It was simple, innocent, divine talent, pure genius. The startlingly beautiful figures were grouped together in a perfectly natural way, freely, not touching the canvas, and startled by so many glances being directed at them, it seemed, coyly lowered their beautiful eyelashes. In the contours of these divine faces there breathed those secret phenomena which the soul does not know and cannot communicate to another; the inexpressible was serenely expressed in them; and all this was drawn so lightly, so humbly and freely that it seemed to be the fruit of a momentary inspiration which had suddenly entered the artist's mind. The whole picture was—a moment, but that moment for which a man's whole life is but the preparation. Involuntary tears were about to run down the faces of the visitors who stood around the picture. It seemed as though all tastes, all the impudent misguided digressions of taste had merged into a kind of silent hymn to a divine creation. Motionless, his mouth wide open, Chertkov stood in front of the picture and finally, when gradually the visitors and experts began to get noisy as they discussed the merits of the work, and when finally they turned to him with a request for a statement of his impressions, he came to—he tried to assume an indifferent, ordinary attitude, he tried to pass some commonplace, trite remark about state artists, and to say something to the effect that the work had some merits, and that the artist was evidently talented, but that regretfully, his ideas and the finishing touches in many places left something to be desired. But his words died on his lips, his reply was made incoherent by his tears and sobbing, and he ran from the hall like a madman.

He stood for a moment, motionless and senseless, in his magnificent studio. His whole being, his whole life were roused in an instant as if his youth had returned to him, as if the smouldering sparks of talent had burst into flame once again. God! And to have ruined all the best years of his life so mercilessly, to have destroyed and quenched the fire which, perhaps, had glowed within his breast and would by now have developed into greatness and a beauty which might have had the power to summon forth tears of amazement and gratitude! To have destroyed all this, to have destroyed it without the slightest regret! It seemed to him that at that very moment there revived in his soul the impulses and aspirations which had once been so familiar to him. He grabbed his paint brush and approached the canvas. The perspiration of effort streamed down his face; he was completely absorbed by a single desire and, one may say, was afire with a single thought: he wanted to paint the Fallen Angel. More than anything else this idea corresponded to his frame of mind. But, alas! his figures, poses, groups, and thoughts appeared unnatural and incoherent. Both his brush and his imagination had been too long concerned with one theme and this impotent impulse to break free of limits and fetters, which he had imposed on himself, smacked of error and miscalculation. He had scorned the wearying, long ladder of gradual learning and the first basic principles of future greatness. In anger he removed from his room all the paintings which bore the stamp of the deathly pallor of superficial fashion, locked the door, forbade anyone to enter, and like a passionate youth commenced his work. But alas! at every step he was stopped by an ignorance of the most basic elements, the simple, insignificant mechanism completely cooled his impulse and stood like an impassable threshold for his imagination. Occasionally the ghost of a great thought dawned on him, his imagination saw in dark perspective something which, once caught and thrown onto the canvas, might make it unique and at the same time comprehensible to every soul, some star of the miraculous shone in the unclear mist of his thoughts, because he really did nurture within himself the ghost of talent; but God! some insignificant detail, some dead rule of anatomy which a student would know—and the thought would die, the impulse of his impotent imagination was chained, unexpressed, unpainted; his brush involuntarily turned to hackneyed forms, hands folded in the same stupid manner, his heads did not dare assume any sort of original attitude, and the very folds of the clothes had a stereotyped look about them and refused to hang or drape on the unfamiliar body poses. And he could feel it, he could feel it, and see it himself! The sweat poured from him like hailstones, his lips shook and after a long pause, during which time all his inner feelings were in revolt, he applied himself again; but when one has turned thirty it is more difficult to study the boring ladder of difficult rules and anatomy, and even more difficult to attain suddenly that which develops slowly and comes only after great striving, in return for determination, for deep self-sacrifice. Eventually he recognized that awful torture which sometimes appears as a striking exception in nature, when weak talent struggles to find expression within the confines of its limits but is unable to; that torture which gives birth to something great in a youth, but which in someone who has crossed the boundary of dreams becomes a fruitless yearning, a fearful torture which makes a man capable of terrible, evil deeds. A terrible envy overcame him, envy verging on madness. A pained expression passed over his face when he saw a work which bore the stamp of talent. He gnashed his teeth and devoured it with a basilisk-like glance. At last the most fiendish plan which was ever conceived by a man developed in his mind, and with a mindless fury he hurried to put it into operation. He began to buy up all the finest works of art ever produced. When he had bought a picture for a great deal of money he would take it home to his room carefully, then hurl himself at it with the fury of a tiger, tearing it, slashing it, ripping it to shreds, and stomping on it to the accompaniment of the laughter of fiendish enjoyment. Hardly had a new work appeared, breathing with the fire of a new talent, but he would spare no effort to buy it, whatever the cost. The vast amount of wealth amassed by him provided him with all the means of satisfying his fiendish desires. He untied all his bags of gold and opened his coffers. No ignorant monster had ever destroyed so many beautiful works of art as this fierce avenger did. And people who bore within them the spark of divine knowledge, people who thirsted only for greatness, were pitilessly, inhumanly deprived of those holy, beautiful works in which great art raised the veil from heaven and showed Man the part of his inner world which is so full of sounds and holy secrets. There was nowhere a single corner where they could conceal themselves from his rapacious passion, a passion without mercy. His vigilant, fiery eye penetrated everywhere and uncovered the trace of an artist's brush even amid the dust. At every auction he attended everyone else despaired of ever procuring any artistic creation. It seemed as though irate Heaven had deliberately sent this scourge into the world out of a desire to destroy all harmony in it. This terrible passion cast a kind of terrible hue across his face; it had an almost permanently jaundiced look to it; his eyes flashed with semi-insanity; his beetling brows and permanently furrowed forehead gave him an air of ferocity and distinguished him entirely from the peaceful inhabitants of the earth.

Fortunately for the world and art, such a strained and violent way of life could not continue for long; the extent of his passions was too abnormal and colossal for his feeble strength. The fits of rage and insanity began to come more often, and eventually it turned into the most terrible disease. Acute fever, combined with rapid consumption, took such a violent grip of him that within three days he was a mere shadow of his former self. To this were added all the signs of hopeless insanity. At times it took several men to restrain him. The long-forgotten life-like eyes of the unusual portrait began to haunt him, and then his fury was horrifying. All those people who had congregated around his bed appeared to him to be terrible portraits. This portrait doubled, quadrupled before his eyes, and finally he was haunted by the idea that the walls were all hung with those terrible portraits, beaming their unmoving, life-like eyes on him. The fearful portraits looked down at him from the ceiling, up at him from the floor, and in addition he saw his room broaden and lengthen into space to make room for all these unmoving eyes. The doctor who had accepted the responsibility for treating him and was already to some extent acquainted with his strange history, attempted as best he could to discover the secret relationship between his dream phantoms and the events of his life, but could not arrive at a diagnosis. The patient understood nothing and felt nothing except his own sufferings; and he cried out and prayed in a piercing, unspeakably wailing voice, pleading for the portrait with the life-like eyes to be taken away from him, the whereabouts of which he described in such vivid detail as appeared strange in a madman. In vain they spared no effort to unearth this portrait. They searched the house from top to bottom, but the portrait was never found. Then the patient, alarmed, raised himself a little and again began to describe where it was with an exactness which indicated the presence of a clear and penetrating mind; but all searches were in vain. Finally, the doctor concluded that all this was no more than a side-effect of his insanity. Soon his life was cut short by a final, silent convulsion of suffering. His corpse was terrible. Moreover, they could find nothing more of his vast wealth, but seeing the shredded remains of the great artistic masterpieces, the value of which ran into millions, they realized the hideous purpose for which it had been used.

II

A myriad of carriages, landaus and barouches stood in front of the entrance to a house in which the belongings of a member of the breed of art-lovers were being auctioned off, art-lovers who had sweetly slumbered away their whole lives surrounded by zephyrs and cupids, and who were innocently reputed to be Maecenases who had for this reason ingenuously squandered the millions amassed by their forebears, and often even by their own former labors. The long hall was filled with the most varied crowd of visitors, who had descended like birds of prey on an abandoned body. There was a whole flotilla of Russian merchants form the Gostiny Dvor, and even from the flea-market, in their blue German dress coats. And the look on their faces was sterner, more carefree, and without that stamp of unctuous servility which is so evident in the Russian merchant. They did not stand on ceremony, despite the fact that present in the hall were a great many of those important aristocrats before whom, anywhere else, they would have been prepared to genuflect so low as to wipe off the dust brought in on their own boots. Here they were completely uninhibited. They prodded the books and pictures without ceremony, trying to assess the quality of the goods, and boldly outbid the aristocratic experts. Here were many of those visitors so indispensable to auctions, who make it a rule to attend one every day instead of taking lunch, the aristocratic experts who consider it their duty never to miss an opportunity of increasing their collection, and who can find nothing else to do between noon and one o'clock, and finally, those noble gentlemen whose clothing and pockets are so poorly lined, who appear every day, with no profit motive in mind, simply in order to observe the end results—to observe who gives more, who less, who outbids whom, and who is left with what. There were a great many pictures scattered about without any sense of order; mixed in with them were furniture and books bearing the crests of their previous owners, who no doubt did not possess sufficient praiseworthy curiosity to have taken even a glance into them. Chinese vases, marble table-tops, modern and antique furniture with curved lines, griffins, sphinxes and lions' paws, some gilt and some not, chandeliers and oil lamps—everything was just piled up, without any of the order one would find in shops. It all resembled a kind of artistic chaos. Generally speaking our reactions to the sight of an auction are rather strange: there is something reminiscent of a funeral procession about them. The halls in which they are conducted are always rather gloomy; the windows are hidden from view by furniture and pictures, and they allow no more than a meagre light to pass through; a silence is spread over everybody's face and voices: "A hundred rubles!" "A ruble twenty." "Four hundred rubles fifty kopeks"—burst forth in shrill tones from their lips, somewhat harsh to the ear. But an even greater impression is made by the funereal voice of the auctioneer, who taps his hammer and chants the funeral service over the wretched works of art gathered here in such a strange fashion.

But the auction had not yet begun; the visitors were studying the various goods thrown into a heap on the floor. Meanwhile a small crowd had stopped in front of one particular portrait: it was a painting of an old man with eyes which were so strangely life-like that one's attention was drawn to it involuntarily. It had to be admitted that the artist possessed genuine talent; even though the painting was unfinished, it bore the unmistakable stamp of a powerful brush; but with all that, the supernatural, life-like quality of the eyes gave rise to a certain amount of subconscious unfavorable criticism of the artist. People felt that there was something here which was greater than truth, that only a genius could have depicted it with such a degree of veracity, but that this genius had boldly transgressed the limit of man's freedom. Their attention was suddenly distracted by the exclamation of a visitor who was of advanced years. "Oh, that's it!" he exclaimed, gesticulating violently, riveting his eyes on the portrait. Naturally this kind of exclamation made everyone's curiosity flare up, and some of the onlookers could not restrain themselves from turning to him and saying, "You obviously know something about this portrait?"

"You're right," replied the man who had uttered the involuntary exclamation. "To be sure, I know the history of this portrait better than anyone else. Everything tells me that it must be the same as the one I wish to talk about. And as I can tell that you're all interested to know about it, I'm prepared to afford you some satisfaction."

The visitors indicated their gratitude with bows of their heads and prepared themselves to listen with great attentiveness.

"No doubt," he began, "some of you are well acquainted with the part of town called Kolomna. It has certain characteristics which sharply distinguish it from other parts of this city. The manners, occupations, conditions and habits of its inhabitants are entirely different from everyone else's. There is little of the metropolis there, but also little of a provincial town either, because the fragmented nature of a many-sided, and, if I may say so, civilized life had penetrated here too, and manifested itself in such trivia as only a densely populated metropolis can breed. It is quite another world here, and if you travel out to the remote streets of Kolomna you will, I think, feel your youthful desires and impulses leaving you. There is no bracing rainbow future here. It's all silence and retirement. The sediment from the bustling capital settles here. And indeed, retired government officials come here with their pensions of no more than five hundred rubles a year; widows who formerly lived by their husbands' labors; people of slender means who have made a pleasant acquaintance with the senate and have thus condemned themselves to living out their whole lives here; retired cooks who spend their days jostling each other in the market places, talking nonsense to the peasants in the tiny shop and grabbing five kopeks' worth of coffee and four kopeks' worth of sugar per day; and finally, there is the whole class of people whom I call ashen, who, along with their clothes, their faces and their hair, have a sort of dingy ashen appearance. They resemble a gray day when the sun fails to blind you with its gleaming brilliance, when no storm howls with thunder, rain and hailstones, and the sky is neither one thing nor the other: a mist hangs in a veil and blurs the outline of things. The faces of such people are of a rather rusty-reddish color, and their hair is tinged with red too; their eyes are almost always lackluster; their clothing also very drab and suggests that dim color you get when you mix all the paints together, and in general their whole appearance is very drab. To this class one may add the retired theater ushers, the redundant fifty-year-old titular councillors, the retired children of Mars with the pensions of two hundred rubles a year, a blasted eye and swollen lip. These people are totally devoid of any passions. They take life as it comes; they walk along in silence, paying no attention to anything and thinking about nothing at all. In their rooms they have only a bed and a bottle of pure Russian vodka which they swig each day with monotonous regularity without any flood of courage to their heads being occasioned by the strong dose, such as the young German artisan, that student from Meshchanskaya Street and unrivalled potentate of the pavement after midnight likes to give himself on Sundays.

Life in Kolomna is always the same: the rumbling of a carriage is seldom heard in its streets, except perhaps for the one carrying actors and which, with the jingle of its bells, its thunder and its rattling, disturbs the ubiquitous silence. Here almost everyone is a pedestrian. A cab rarely, lazily and almost always without a fare, crawls along, hauling a load of hay for its humble nag. The price of apartments rarely gets as high as a thousand rubles; most cost between fifteen and twenty or thirty rubles a month, and that does not include a great many corners which are let for four and a half per month, heating and coffee included. The widows of the government officials, who receive a pension, are the most respectable inhabitants of this district. They conduct themselves very correctly, clean out their apartments quite well and chat with their neighbors and friends about the rise in the cost of beef, potatoes and cabbage; there is often a young daughter to be found in their company, a silent, taciturn creature, but sometimes quite attractive; they are also often accompanied by some rather filthy little dog and an ancient clock with a mournful-sounding pendulum. These widows of government officials occupy the best rooms to be got for a rent of between twenty and thirty rubles, and sometimes even for as much as forty. After them come the actors, whose salary does not allow them to leave Kolomna. These people are free and easy, like all artists, living only for enjoyment. Lounging about in their dressing gowns, they either carve some knick-knacks out of bone or clean their pistols, or make some useful objects for the house with glue and cardboard, or play checkers or cards with visiting friends, and so while away the morning; they do the same thing of an evening, often with the addition of a bowl of punch. After these V.I.P.'s, the aristocrary of Kolomna, comes an unusual collection of smaller fry, and for the observer it is as difficult to keep a list of all the people who occupy the various nooks and crannies of a single room as it is to name all the host of insects which breed in stale vinegar. What people you'll meet there! Old women who pray, old women who drink too much, old women who both pray and get drunk at the same time, old women who make ends meet by means it is difficult to understand, who, like ants, lug old rags and linen from Kalinka Bridge to the flea market to sell them there for fifteen kopeks apiece. In a word, all the pitiful and wretched dregs of humanity.

Naturally enough, these people often experience great poverty, which prevents them from leading their normal, wretched lives; they are often obliged to seek emergency loans in order to extricate themselves from their difficulties. Then there are people among them who are known by the important-sounding name of capitalists and who can provide at various rates of interest, almost always extortionate, sums of money ranging from twenty to a hundred rubles. These people gradually amass enough funds to allow them to acquire a little home of their own. But there was a certain Petromikhali who was totally unlike the usual, run-of-the-mill usurers. Nobody knew if he was a Greek, an Armenian or a Moldavian, but his facial features at least were without doubt those of a southerner. He always went about wearing a wide Asiatic coat: he was tall of stature, with a dark, olive-complected face and beetling brows and a moustache streaked with gray—all of which gave him a rather sinister appearance. His face was completely expressionless: it was nearly always motionless and his distinctly southern physiognomy contrasted stangely with the ashen-skinned inhabitants of Kolomna. Petromikhali was totally unlike the above-mentioned usurers of this remote district of the town. He was able to lend any sum anyone might ask of him; naturally, the interest charges were also unusual. His tumbledown house with its numerous outbuildings was situated on the Kozy Marsh. It would not have been so ramshackle if its owner had been prepared to spend some of his wealth on repairs, but Petromikhali simply would not spend any money at all. All the rooms, with the exception of a small shack where he lived, were cold storerooms in which the porcelain, gold and jasper vases and any junk, including even the furniture which debtors of various grades and ranks brought as pledges, lay scattered about in piles, because Petromikhali never turned his nose up at anything and, despite the fact that he lent out his money in hundreds of thousands, he was also ready to oblige with a sum of less than a ruble. Old, useless linen, broken chairs, even tattered boots—all of this he was prepared to take into his storerooms, and beggars boldly approached him with bundles in their hands. Valuable pearls, which had perhaps once hung around the most delightful neck in the world, were locked away in his dirty, iron chest, together with an antique snuffbox which had belonged to a fifty-year-old woman, along with a diamond which had once crowned the alabaster forehead of some beautiful woman and the diamond ring of some poor government official who had obtained it as a reward for his tireless labors. But it must be pointed out that only excessive penury drove people to him. His conditions were so harsh that they made people very reluctant to approach him. But the strange thing is that the interest rates the first time did not seem excessive. By means of his strange and unusual calculations, he arranged things in such an incomprehensible way that the interest increased at a frightening rate, and even the auditing officials could not fathom his inscrutable rules, especially as they seemed to be based on laws of strict mathematical principles; they could see the increase of the total quite clearly, but they also saw that there was no mistake in the calculations. Pity, and the other emotions of sensitive men, never reached him, and no prayers could ever induce him to cancel debts or to lessen the payment. On several occasions they found on his doorstep wretched old women, stiff from the cold, whose blue faces, frozen limbs and dead outstretched arms seemed to be pleading for mercy even in death. This frequently gave rise to general indignation and the police made several attempts to investigate fully this strange man's behavior, but the superintendent of police always succeeded, under some pretext or other, in dissuading them and in presenting the case in a different way, despite the fact that they never received a farthing from him. But wealth has such a strange power that people have as much faith in it as in a government banknote. It can exert an unseen influence on all men as though they were abject slaves. This strange creature would sit crosslegged on a divan which had blackened with age, receiving his visitors without moving, except for a slight movement of the eyebrows, which served as a sign of greeting; and nobody ever heard him say anything superfluous or irrelevant. There were, however, rumors to the effect that he occasionally gave away money for nothing; demanding no repayment, but stipulating such conditions that everyone fled from him in horror, and even the most loquacious of landladies could not find strength enough to accept the proffered money, but turned yellow, wasted away and died, never having dared to reveal the secret.

There was, in this district of the town, a small house which belonged to a certain artist who at that time enjoyed renown on account of his truly beautiful pictures. This artist was my father.

I can show you several of his works, which illustrate his real talent. His life was extremely tranquil. He was one of those humble, devout painters who only lived during the religious Middle Ages. He could have achieved great fame and a vast fortune if he had made the decision to accept the large number of commissions offered to him from all sides; but he preferred to deal only with religious themes, and agreed to paint the whole ikonostasis in his parish church for a very small fee. He was often in need of money, but never contemplated turning to the awful usurer, although he could always count on being able to repay any debt later on, because he had only to sit down and paint a few portraits—and there was money in his pocket. But he was so reluctant to tear himself away from his work, so miserable when separated even for a short time from his favorite thought, that he was prepared to stay in his room starving for a few days and he would have done so always, had he not had a wife whom he loved passionately and two children, one of whom you now see before you. However, his need became go great on one occasion that he was prepared to go to the Greek, when suddenly the news spread around that the awful usurer was on the point of death. This event stunned him and he was already prepared to interpret it as being heaven-sent for the express purpose of preventing him from carrying out his intentions, when he met, breathless on his porch, the old woman who served the old usurer in three capacities—that of cook, servant and valet. The old woman who, in the service of her strange master, had completely got out of the habit of speaking, muttered under her breath a few incoherent words from which my father could only deduce that her master had some urgent need of him and was asking him to take his paints and brushes to his house. My father could not imagine why he was needed at such a time, especially with his paints and brushes, but, his curiosity aroused, he seized his case of artist's implements and set off after the old woman.

With great effort he made his way through the crowd of beggars who had surrounded the dying usurer's abode, entertaining the hope that perhaps at last, on the point of death, this sinner would repent and distribute a small part of his incalculable wealth. He entered a small room and saw, stretched out almost full-length, the body of the Asiatic, which he almost took for dead, as it lay so straight and still. At last its withered head rose a little and its eyes stared so frighteningly that my father began to shudder. Petromikhali let out a muffled exclamation and finally said: "Paint a portrait of me!" My father was amazed at such a strange request; he began to suggest to him that this was not the time to be thinking about such a thing and that he should abjure all earthly desires; that he had only a few moments of life left and thus it was time to cast his thoughts over his former deeds and repent before the Almighty. "I don't want anything. Just draw my portrait!" said Petromikhali in a firm voice, and as he spoke his face became such a mass of convulsive jerks that my father would have left for sure, if a certain feeling, which is quite innocent in an artist who is struck by an unusual subject for his brush, had not stopped him. The usurer's face was one of those which are a veritable treasure to an artist. With a mixture of fear and secret eagerness, he set the canvas on his knees, as he had no easel with him, and began to draw. The thought of using this face later on in a picture in which he wished to depict one possessed by demons which are exorcised by the potent words of the Savior, this thought made him strengthen his resolve. Hurriedly he outlined his first sketch and shades, fearing every minute that the usurer's life might suddenly come to an end, for death already seemed to be hovering on his lips. Only from time to time did he wheeze and cast his awesome, disturbed glance at the picture; finally something akin to joy flashed in his eyes, seeing how his features were taking shape on the canvas. Fearing every moment for his life, my father decided to concentrate on completing the eyes first of all. They made a very difficult subject because the feelings expressed in them were completely unusual and inexplicable. He worked at them for about an hour and finally succeeded in capturing that fire which was already guttering in the original. Feeling secretly pleased, he moved back a little from the picture to get a better view of it, but jumped back from it in horror when he saw the life-like eyes which were gazing at him. An inexplicable fear overcame him to such an extent that he, throwing away his palette and paints, dashed for the door; but the frightening, half-dead body of the usurer raised itself from the bed and seized him with its scrawny hand, ordering him to continue the work. My father swore and made the sign of the cross, saying he would not continue. Then this terrible being rolled off the bed so that its bones began to rattle. Making a supreme effort, with its eyes gleaming with eagerness and its hands clutching my father's legs, he crawled and kissed the hem of his coat and implored him to complete his portrait. But father was unmoved and only wondered at the strength of Petromikhali's will power, which had overcome even the approach of death. Finally the desperate Petromikhali, with incredible strength, pulled an old chest out from under the bed and a huge pile of gold crashed at my father's feet; seeing his still resolute firmness, he groveled at his feet and a whole stream of incantations flowed from his hitherto silent lips. One could not help feeling a certain terrible and, if one may say so, repulsive compassion. "Kind man! Man of God! Man of Christ!"—said the living skeleton in sheer desperation. "I implore you in the name of your little children, your beautiful wife, and your father's coffin, finish my portrait! Sit at it for just one more hour. Listen, I'll reveal a secret to you." With that, the deathly pallor spread across his face with even greater vigor. "But don't you ever reveal this secret to anyone—not even to your wife or your children, otherwise you will die and they will die and you'll all be terribly unhappy. Listen, if you have no pity for me, know then, that I won't ask again. After death I must go to the one I should prefer not to go to. There I am bound to undergo tortures such as you have never dreamed of; but I can stay away from there for a long while yet, even to the end of the world, if you will only complete my portrait. I found out that one half of my life will go into my portrait, if only it is painted by a skillful artist. You can see already how you've captured something of life in the eyes; you'll be able to see that lifelike quality in all my features when you've completed it. And even though my body may perish, half of my life will remain on earth and I shall avoid the torture for a long time yet. Finish the picture! Finish it! Finish it!"— exclaimed this strange creature in a heart-rending, dying voice. An even greater horror seized my father. He could feel his hair stand on end because of this terrible secret, and he dropped the brush which he, touched by the entreaties, was already just about to pick up. "Ah, so you don't want to finish drawing me?"—said Petromikhali in a wheezing voice. "Then take my portrait with you, I'm giving it to you as a gift." With these words something resembling a terrible laugh burst forth from his lips; life seemed to flicker once more through his features and a moment later only his blue corpse remained. Father did not want to touch the brushes and paints which had drawn these godless features, and he ran out of the room.

In order to dispel the unpleasant thoughts evoked by this incident, he walked about the town for a long time and returned home in the evening. The first thing he saw in the studio was the picture he had drawn of the usurer. He questioned his wife, the woman who worked in his kitchen, and the servant, but all were quite adamant that nobody had brought the portrait and that nobody had even called while he had been out. This made him think for a moment. He approached the portrait and involuntarily turned his eyes away, so overcome was he by a revulsion for his own work. He ordered it to be removed and carried up to the attic, but despite all this he was still bothered by a strange oppressive uneasiness and the presence of frightening thoughts. What surprised him most was that when he was lying in bed, the following almost unbelievable event occurred: he clearly saw Petromikhali enter his room and stop just in front of his bed. He looked at him for a long time with his life-like eyes, and then eventually began to make such terrible suggestions to him, attempting to put my father's art to such fiendish use, that the latter broke out in a cold sweat and clutched at the bed, moaning in anguish, his soul weighed down by an unbearable oppressiveness and feelings of impassioned indignation. He saw the wonderful likeness of the dead Petromikhali go back into the frame of the portrait hanging on the wall again in front of him. He decided to burn that damned artistic production of his own hands that same day. As soon as the fire was lit in the hearth he threw the picture onto its raging flames and watched with secret enjoyment as the frame, over which the canvas was stretched, exploded, and the still not dried paint sizzled; at last there was nothing left of its existence but a heap of ashes. And when it began to fly up the chimney in a light dust, it seemed as though a hazy image of Petromikhali was flying up there with it. A feeling of relief entered his soul. Feeling like a man who had recovered from a protracted illness, he turned to the corner of the room where there hung an ikon he had painted, in order to express his contrition, when, horror-struck, he saw standing before him the portrait of Petromikhali, with eyes which seemed even more life-like, so that even the children let out a scream then they saw it. This suprised my father a great deal. He decided to confess all to our parish priest and to seek his advice about what he should do in this unusual affair. The priest was a man of sound judgment and, moreover, he had a devotion to and warm affection for his calling. He was quick to answer the first summons and came to see my father, whom he respected as a worthy parishioner. My father did not even consider it necessary to take him to one side, and decided there and then, in the presence of my mother and the children, to tell him about the incredible event. But hardly had he uttered the first word, when my mother suddenly gave a muffled cry and collapsed unconscious on the floor. A strange pallor spread over her face, her lips remained open and motionless and all her features were distorted in convulsions. Father and the priest ran to her and saw with horror that she had accidently swallowed a dozen needles which she had been holding in her mouth. The doctor who came explained that there was nothing he could do to save her: some needles had become lodged in her throat, others had passed through into her stomach and intestines, and so mother had died a horrible death.

This event had a profound effect on my father's whole life. From that moment on, a moroseness took possession of his soul. He seldom bothered with his work, hardly opened his mouth to anyone and shunned all company. But meanwhile, the terrible image of Petromikhali and his life-like eyes began haunting him constantly, and my father often experienced a flood of desperate, violent thoughts at which he himself even quaked. All that settles like a black residue in the depths of the human soul and is erased and dispelled by education, by noble deeds and emulation of what is beautiful—he felt all this stirring and constantly striving to break out and allow its evil to develop to its full strength. The sullen disposition of his soul was just what was needed to make him clutch at this black side of man's nature. But I must point out that my father's strength of character was exceptional; the power he wielded over himself and his passions was beyond belief; his convictions were firmer than granite and the greater the temptation, the more he strove to resist it with all the indomitable strength of his soul. Finally, weakened by this struggle, he decided to bare his soul and reveal all and tell the whole story of his sufferings to the same priest who had usually been able to bring him some relief with his wise words.

It was a beautiful day at the beginning of autumn; the sun was shining with a fresh autumnal light, the windows of our rooms were open; my father was sitting in his studio with the worthy priest; my brother and I were playing in the adjoining room. Both rooms were on the first floor, which was a sort of attic in our little house. The door to the studio was slightly open; I glanced casually through the opening and saw that my father had moved closer to the priest and I even heard him say to him: "At last I'm going to reveal this secret . . . ." A sudden momentary shout made me turn around: my brother was not there. I went up to the window and—my God! I'll never forget what had happened: on the pavement lay the blood-covered body of my brother. While playing he must have carelessly leaned too far through the window and fallen, no doubt head first, because it was smashed to pieces. I'll never forget that terrible event. My father stood motionless in front of the window, his hands crossed and his eyes directed up to heaven. The priest was shot through with fear, remembering my mother's terrible death, and he himself then demanded that my father should keep the terrible secret to himself.

After this my father sent me to a military academy where I was to spend my school years, and he went off to take the vows of a monk in a monastery in some remote little town, surrounded by desert, where the bleak north displays nothing but a wild natural habitat. He bore all the burdensome duties of his calling with such humility and grace and conducted his life of toil with such humility, combined with the enthusiasm and ardor of faith, that it was obvious that nothing criminal could ever have the power to touch him. But the frightening image he had drawn with its life-like eyes haunted him even in this almost tomb-like isolation. The Father Superior, discovering my father's rare artistic talents, gave him the task of embellishing the church with ikons. If only you could have beheld the lofty religious humility with which he slaved over his work: in strict fasting and prayer, in deep meditation and isolation of the soul, he prepared himself for the task. He spent endless nights over his holy pictures and perhaps that is why you will seldom find such works, even by the famous artists, which bear the stamp of such genuinely Christian feelings and thoughts. In his saints there was such a divine serenity, in his penitents such grief, as I have very seldom seen in paintings done by famous artists. Finally his thoughts and impulses were directed toward depicting the Mother of God mildly stretching out her hands over people at prayer. He labored at his work with such self-sacrifice and became so oblivious of his own existence that something of the serenity introduced by his brush into the features of the world's divine Protectress seemed to have been transmitted into his own soul. At last the fearful image of the usurer ceased visiting him and the portrait ended up no one knew where.

Meanwhile, my education in the military academy came to an end. I graduated with an officer's rank, but, to my great regret, circumstances did not permit me to see my father. We were sent off immediately for active service with the army, which because of the war declared against the Turks was stationed on the border. I shall not bore you with tales about my life of marches, bivouacs and heated skirmishes; suffice it to say that the hard work, dangers and hot climate brought about a great change in me, so that those who knew me before now did not recognize me at all. My sun-tanned face, huge moustache and husky, loud voice gave me a completely different appearance. I had become a gay dog, living for today; I loved to uncork an extra bottle with a companion; I engaged in idle chatter with swarthy young girls, and loved to get up to all sorts of pranks; in a word, I was a carefree soldier. However, as soon as the campaign ended, I deemed it my first duty to visit my father.

When I drove up to the remote monastery, I was overcome by a strange feeling which I had never experienced before. I felt that I was still attached to existence but that there was something incomplete about my situation. The isolated monastery, surrounded by pale, bare nature, induced in me a kind of poetic oblivion and gave a strange, undefined direction to my thoughts, such as we usually feel in mid-autumn, when the leaves rustle under our feet and there is not a single leaf overhead, and the black branches are twisted into scanty nets; when the ravens caw high above us and we involuntarily walk faster, as if trying to gather our scattered thoughts. Many blackened wooden outbuildings surrounded the stone building. I went in beneath the long galleries, which were rotten in places and green with moss, surrounding the cells, and asked to see the monk, Father Gregory. This was the name which my father had assumed on entering the monastic order. They pointed out his cell to me.

I shall never forget the impression he made on me! I saw an old man whose pale, exhausted face seemed totally featureless and devoid of any worldly thoughts. His eyes, used to being directed towards heaven, had taken on that passionless look, permeated with an otherworldly fire, which comes to an artist only in a moment of inspiration. He sat motionless in front of me like a saint staring out from a canvas on which an artist's hand has drawn him for the people at prayer; he seemed not to notice me at all, although his eyes were turned in the direction where I had entered to come and see him. I did not as yet wish to make myself known to him and simply asked for his blessing as any pilgrim would; but how great was my surprise when he said, "Hello, Lev, my son!" This surprised me. It was already ten years since out parting and, moreover, those who had seen me more recently had not recognized me. "I knew you would come to see me," he continued, "I asked the Holy Virgin and a saint for this and have been waiting for you hour by hour, because I sense that my end is near and I wish to reveal my secret to you. Come with me, my son, and we'll pray first." We entered the church and he guided me to the large picture which portrayed the Mother of God, blessing the people. I was struck by the deep expression of divinity in her face. He lay prostrate for a long time before the image, and at last, after a long silence and a period of meditation, he and I came out.

After this my father related to me all that you have just heard from me. I believed it to be the truth because I myself was witness to the many tragic events of our life. "Now I'll tell you, my son," he added when he had finished his story, "what was revealed to me by a saint whom I saw and who was not recognized among the crowd by anyone apart from me, to whom the Merciful Creator entrusted such an ineffable blessing." So saying, my father folded his arms and turned his eyes up towards heaven, to which he was completely devoted with his whole being. And I at last heard what I am now about to tell you. You must not be surprised by the strangeness of his words: I observed that he was in that frame of mind which possesses a man who is experiencing strong, unbearable grief; when, wishing to muster all his strength, all the iron strength of his soul and finding it wanting, he turns completely to religion; and the greater the oppression of his grief, the more ardent are his spiritual contemplation and prayer. He no longer resembles that quiet, contemplative hermit who, moored to his own wasteland as though it were a long-awaited mooring place, desirous of finding rest from the world and, with Christian humility, of praying to Him who has become closer and more accessible; on the contrary, he became something immense. The fire of the spirit has not been extinguished in him, but, on the contrary, it surges forward and bursts out with greater force. Then he is turned into one great flame of religious fervor. His head is eternally filled with wonderful dreams: with every step he sees visions and hears voices; his thoughts become enflamed, his eye no longer sees anything which is of this world; all his movements, in consequence of an eternal concentration on one thing, are filled with enthusiasm. I noticed this condition in him immediately and I mention it so that the words which I heard from him won't seem too surprising to you.

"My son," he said to me after staring long and almost motionlessly into heaven—"very soon, very soon now the time will come when the Tempter of the human race, the Antichrist, will be born on earth. Terrible will that time be and it will be just before the end of the world. He is rushing on his giant horse, and terrible will be the tortures suffered by those who remain true to Christ. Listen, my son: the Antichrist has long wanted to be born, but he cannot be because the only way he can be born is by supernatural means; but in our world everything has been arranged by the Almighty in such a way that everything occurs in a natural order, and thus there is no power, my son, which can help him smash his way into the world. But our world is mere dust before the Creator. By his laws, it must be destroyed, and with every day that passes the laws of nature are becoming weaker and weaker and so the borderline holding back the supernatural is becoming easier to overcome. He is already being born now, but only a certain part of him is forcing a way into the world. He is choosing for his dwelling Man himself and is making an appearance in those people whose angel seems to have abandoned them at birth and who are branded with a terrible hatred of mankind and everything which is a creation of the Creator. Such was that amazing usurer whom I, a sinner, was audacious enough to paint with my sinful brush. It was he, my son, it was the Antichrist himself. If my sinful hand had not been so audacious as to paint him he would have departed and vanished because he could not outlive the body in which he was confined. In those repulsive life-like eyes there was a fiendish presence. You may well be surprised, my son, at the awful power of the Devil. He tries to penetrate into everything: into our deeds, our thoughts and even into the inspiration of an artist. Too numerous to mention are the victims of this Spirit of Hell which lived unseen and without any form on earth. This is that same black spirit which forces a way into us even at moments of our purest and most holy meditations. Oh, if my brush had not stopped that hellish work it would have done even more evil and there are no human powers which can resist it. For this reason it chooses that time when the greatest grief befalls us. Woe betide poor humanity, my son! But listen to what the Mother of God herself revealed to me during a holy vision. When I was working at the painting of the immaculate countenance of the Virgin Mary, I shed tears of repentance for my past life and spent a long time in fasting and prayer to be more worthy of depicting her divine features; I was enlightened, my son, by inspiration, I felt that a higher power had come to me and an angel was lifting my sinful hand and I felt my hair stand on end and my whole soul shake. Oh, my son! For that moment I would take a thousand tortures on myself! I was amazed at what my own brush had drawn. Then the immaculate countenance of the Virgin appeared to me in a dream, and I knew that as a reward for my labors and prayers the supernatural existence of this Devil in the portrait would not last forever, and that if someone would solemnly retell the story, when fifty years had passed, at the first new moon, then its power would be extinguished and dispersed, like dust, and that I may tell you all this before my death. Thirty years have now passed and twenty are still ahead. Let us pray, my son!" With this he went down on his knees and was lost in prayer.

I confess that I inwardly ascribed all these words to his fiery imagination, which had been sharpened by his constant fasting and prayer, and so out of respect I refrained from passing any remarks or making any observations. But when I saw him raise his withered arms toward heaven, and observed the deeply penitent silence of this inwardly annihilated man; the inexpressible humility with which he had prayed for those who lacked the power to resist the hellish Tempter and had thus destroyed all that was exalted in their own souls, and with what passionate self-abasement he prostrated himself as the telltale tears flowed down his cheeks, and how his features expressed a certain mute anguish—oh! then I did not possess the strength to devote myself to cold meditation and analyze his words.

Several years have passed since his death. I did not believe this story and paid little heed to it, but I was never able to retell it to anyone. I don't know why this was the case, but I can only say that I have always felt something restraining me from doing so. Today I dropped in on an auction, purely by chance, and retold the story of this unique portrait for the first time—so that I cannot but begin to wonder if there is a new moon today, about which my father spoke, because it is actually twenty years now since that time."

Here the narrator stopped and the people in the audience, who had given him their undivided attention, involuntarily turned their eyes to this strange portrait and, to their surprise, noticed that its eyes had lost all of that strangely life-like quality which had so struck them at first. And their amazement was increased even more when the features of the strange picture almost imperceptibly began to disappear as does one's breath from the surface of clear steel. Only a vague outline remained on the canvas. And when they drew nearer, they saw an unfamiliar landscape. Thus the visitors, who were already moving off, remained puzzled for a long time: had they really seen a mysterious portrait, or was it all just a dream, momentarily appearing before their eyes, which were strained by prolonged examinations of antique pictures?

1. This translation is of the re-worked 1842 version.

M. YU. LERMONTOV

Shtoss [1]

1.

Countess V. was holding an evening musicale. The finest artists of the capital were playing with their artistry for the honor of attending an aristocratic reception. Among the guests appeared several literati and scholars, two or three fashionable beauties, several young and old ladies, and one guards officer. About a dozen home-grown social lions were posing at the doors of the second drawing room and by the fireplace. Everything was going as usual; it was neither dull nor lively.

At the exact moment that a newly arrived singer was approaching the piano and unfolding her music . . . one young woman yawned, rose and went into the next room, which was empty at the time. She was wearing a black dress, apparently due to Court mourning. A diamond monogram fastened to a pale blue bow sparkled on her shoulder; she was average in height, graceful, slow and lazy in her movements; marvelous long black hair set off her still young and regular but pale face, and on that face shone the mark of thought.

"Hello, Monsieur Lugin," said Minskaya to someone, "I'm tired. Say something." She lowered herself into the wide chair by the fireplace; the man to whom she had spoken sat down across from her and made no reply. They were the only two people in the room, and Lugin's cold silence showed clearly that he was not one of Minskaya's admirers.

"I'm bored," said Minskaya, and she yawned again. "You see that I don't stand on ceremony with you," she added.

"And I'm having a fit of spleen!" answered Lugin.

"You feel like going to Italy again," she said after a short silence, "Isn't that so?"

Lugin for his part had not heard the question; he crossed his legs, unconsciously fixing his gaze on the marble white shoulders of his questioner, and continued. "Just imagine what a misfortune has befallen me! What could be worse for a person such as myself, who has dedicated himself to painting? For two weeks now everyone has seemed yellow to me—only people! It would be fine if it were objects—then there would be harmony in the general coloration—it would be as if I were walking through an art gallery devoted to the Spanish school. But no! Everything else is just as it used to be; only faces have changed. It sometimes seems to me that people have lemons instead of heads."

Minskaya smiled. "Call a doctor," she said.

"Doctors can't help—it's spleen!"

"Fall in love!" (The look which accompanied this statement expressed something like the following: "I feel like tormenting him a little!")

"With whom?"

"What about me!"

"No! You would be bored just flirting with me, and anyway—I will tell you honestly—no woman could love me."

"What about that Italian countess—what's her name—the one who followed you from Naples to Milan?"

"Well, you see," answered Lugin thoughtfully, "I judge others by my own feelings, and I'm certain that I don't make mistakes in that respect. I have in fact had occasion to awaken all the signs of passion in some women; but since I know very well that it is only thanks to artistry and habit that I am able to touch certain strings of the human heart accurately, so I do not find joy in my good fortune; I have asked myself whether I could fall in love with an ugly woman—and it turned out I could not—I am ugly—consequently a woman could not love me, that is clear; artistic sensibility is more strongly developed in women than in us men; they are more frequently and longer subservient to first impressions than we are; if I have been able to arouse in a few women that which is called capriciousness, it has cost incredible effort and sacrifice— but since I always knew the artificiality of the internal feelings I had inspired, and that I had only myself to thank for it—I have been unable to lose myself in a full, unreasoning love; a little malice has always been mixed with my passions. This is all sad, but true!"

"What nonsense!" said Minskaya, but after glancing briefly at Lugin, she involuntarily agreed with him.

Lugin's features were in fact not the least bit attractive. In spite of the fact that there was much fire and wit in the strange expression of the eyes, you would not find in his entire being a single one of those traits which make a person attractive in society; he was awkwardly and crudely built; he spoke abruptly and jerkily; the sickly and sparse hairs on his temples, the uneven color of his face, symptoms of a permanent mysterious ailment, all made him appear older than he really was. He had spent three years in Italy taking a cure for morbid depression; and although he had not been cured, he had at least found a useful means of amusement: he had taken to painting; his natural talent, which had been inhibited by the demands of work, developed broadly and freely under the influence of the vivifying southern sky and marvelous monuments of the ancient masters. He returned a true artist, although only his friends were given the right to enjoy his superb talent. His pictures were always suffused with a certain vague, but gloomy feeling: on them was the stamp of that bitter poetry which our poor age has sometimes wrung out of the hearts of its finest advocates.

It had already been two months since Lugin had returned to Petersburg. He had an independent station in life, a few relatives, and several very old acquaintances who belonged to the highest social circle in the capital, where he wanted to spend the winter. Lugin often visited Minskaya: her beauty, rare wit, and original views on things could not fail to make an impression on a man of wit and imagination. However, there was not a hint of love between them.

Their conversation ceased for a time, and they both seemed to be absorbed in the music. The singer who had dropped in was singing "The Forest King," a ballad by Schubert set to the lyrics of Goethe. When she had finished, Lugin rose.

"Where are you going?" asked Minskaya.

"Good-bye."

"It's still early."

He sat down again.

"Do you know," he said with some importance, "that I am beginning to lose my mind?"

"Really?"

"All joking aside. I can tell you this; you won't laugh at me. I have been hearing a voice for several days. From morning till night someone keeps repeating something to me. And what do you think it is?—an address. There—I hear now: 'Stolyarny Lane, near the Kokukshin Bridge, the home of Titular Councillor Shtoss, apartment 27.' And it's repeated so quickly, quickly, as if in a rush . . . it's unbearable . . ."

He turned pale. But Minskaya didn't notice.

"You don't see the person who is speaking, though, do you?" she asked absently.

"No. But the voice is a clear, sharp tenor."

"When did this begin?"

"Should I confess? I can't tell you for certain . . . I don't know . . . this is really awfully funny!" he said with a forced smile.

"Blood is going to your head, and it's making your ears ring."

"No, no. Tell me—how can I be rid of this?"

Having thought for a minute, Minskaya said, "The best way would be for you to go to the Kokukshin Bridge and look for that apartment; and since some cobbler or watchmaker probably lives there, you could order some work from him just for decency's sake, and then after you get back home, go to bed, because . . . you really are unwell!" added Minskaya, having glanced at Lugin's alarmed face with concern.

"You're right," answered Lugin gloomily. "I will go without fail."

He rose, took his hat, and went out.

She watched with surprise as he left.

2.

A damp November morning lay over Petersburg. Wet snowflakes were falling; the houses seemed dirty and dark; and the faces of passers-by were green; cab drivers wrapped in red sledge rugs dozed at their stands; their poor nags' long wet coats were curled up like sheep's wool; the mist gave a sort of greyish-lilac color to remote objects. Civil servants' galoshes pounded along the pavement infrequently; sometimes noise and laughter rang out from an underground beer tavern when a drunk in a green, fleecy overcoat and oilcloth cap would be thrown out. It goes without saying that you would encounter these scenes only in the out-of-the-way parts of the city, for instance . . . near the Kokukshin Bridge. Onto the bridge walked a man of medium height, neither thin nor stout, not well-built, but with broad shoulders, wearing a coat, generally dressed with taste; it was sad to see his lacquered boots soaked through with snow and mud, but he didn't seem to worry about it at all. His hands thrust into his pockets, his head hanging, he walked along with uneven steps, as though he were afraid to reach his goal, or as if he had no goal at all. On the bridge he stopped, raised his head, and looked around. It was Lugin. His face showed the traces of mental exhaustion; in his eyes burned a secret anxiety.

"Where is Stolyarny Lane?" in an uncertain voice he asked a passengerless cab driver who had a shag rug up to his neck and was whistling the "Kamarinskaya" as he drove past Lugin at a slow pace.

The driver looked at him, flicked his horse with the tip of his whip, and drove on by.

This seemed strange to Lugin. Enough of this, is there really a Stolyarny Lane? He descended from the bridge and asked the same question of a boy who was running across the street with a half-liter.

"Stolyarny?" said the boy. "Go straight along the Little Meshchanskaya and the first lane on the right will be Stolyarny."

Lugin was reassured. Coming to a corner, he turned to the right and saw a small, dirty lane in which there were no more than ten tall houses on each side. He knocked at the door of the first little shop; when the shopkeeper appeared, he asked, "Where is Shtoss's house?"

"Shtoss's? I don't know, sir. There is no such person here. But right next door is the house of the merchant Blinnikov, and further down . . ."

"But I need Shtoss's!"

"Well, I don't know . . . Shtoss!" said the shopkeeper, scratching the back of his neck, and then adding, "No, never heard of him, sir!"

Lugin set off to take a look at the nameplates on the houses himself; something told him that he would recognize the house at first sight, even though he had never seen it. He had almost reached the end of the lane, and not a single nameplate had coincided in any way with the one he had imagined, when suddenly he casually glanced on the other side of the street and saw above one of the gates a tin nameplate without any inscription at all.

He ran up to the gate, but no matter how hard he looked, he could not make out anything resembling a trace of an inscription erased by time; the nameplate was an entirely new one.

A yardkeeper wearing a discolored, long-skirted caftan was sweeping away the snow near the gate; he had a gray beard which had not been trimmed for a long time, wore no cap and had a dirty apron belted around him.

"Hey, yardkeeper!" cried Lugin.

The yardkeeper grumbled something through his teeth.

"Whose house is this?"

"It's sold," the yardkeeper answered rudely.

"But whose was it?"

"Whose? Kifeinik's—the merchant."

"It can't be—it must be Shtoss's!" Lugin cried out involuntarily.

Lugin's hands fell.

His heart began to pound, as if in presentiment of misfortune. Should he continue his search? Wouldn't it be better to stop it in time? One who has not been in a similar situation will have difficulty understanding it: curiosity, they say, has ruined the human race; even today it is our main, primary passion, so that all other passions can be explained by it. But there are times when the mysterious nature of an object gives curiosity an unusual power: obedient to it, like a rock thrown off a mountain by a powerful arm, we cannot stop ourselves, even though we see an abyss awaiting us.

Lugin stood in front of the gate a long time. Finally he addressed a question to the yardkeeper.

"Does the new owner live here?"

"No."

"Well, then, where does he live?"

"The Devil only knows."

"Have you been a yardkeeper here a long time?"

"A long time."

"Are there people living in the house?"

"There are."

After a short silence Lugin slipped the yardkeeper a ruble and said, "Tell me, please, who lives in apartment 27?"

The yardkeeper set the broom up against the gate, took the ruble, and stared at Lugin.

"Apartment 27? Who on earth could be living there? It's been empty God knows how long."

"Hasn't anyone rented it?"

"What do you mean—hasn't anyone rented it? They've rented it, sir."

"Then how can you say that nobody lives there?"

"God knows, nobody's living there! They rent it for a year, and then they don't move in."

"Well, who was the last one to rent it?"

"A colonel of the Engineering Corps, or something like that."

"Why didn't he live there?"

"Well, he was about to move in, but then they say he was sent to Vyatka—so the apartment's been empty ever since."

"And before the colonel?"

"Before him a baron—a German one—rented it; but that one didn't move in either; I heard he died."

"And before the baron?"

"A merchant rented it for his . . . hm! But he went bankrupt, so he left us with just the deposit ! . ."

"Strange," thought Lugin.

"May I see the apartment?"

The yardkeeper again stared at him.

"Why not? Of course you can," he answered and waddled off after his keys.

He soon returned and led Lugin up along a wide, but rather dirty stairway to the first floor. The key grated in the rusty lock, and the door opened; an odor of dampness struck them in the face. They went in. The apartment consisted of four rooms and a kitchen. Old dusty furniture which had once been gilt was correctly arranged around the walls covered in wallpaper which depicted red parrots and golden lyres against a green background; the tile stoves were cracked here and there; the pine floor, painted to imitate parquet, squeaked rather suspiciously in certain places; oval mirrors with rococo frames hung in the spaces between windows; in general, the rooms had a sort of strange, old-fashioned appearance.

For some reason—I don't know why—Lugin liked the rooms.

"I will take the apartment," he said. "Have the windows washed and the furniture dusted . . . just look how many spiderwebs there are! And you must heat the place well . . ." At that moment he noticed on the wall of the last room a half-length portrait depicting a man of about forty, in a Bohara robe, with regular features and large grey eyes; in his right hand he held a gold snuffbox of extraordinary size. On his fingers a multitude of rings glittered. The portrait seemed to have been painted by a timid student's brush: everything—the clothes, hair, hand, rings—was very poorly done; on the other hand, there breathed such a tremendous feeling of life in the facial expression—especially the lips—that it was impossible to tear one's eyes away from the portrait; in the line of the mouth there was a subtle, imperceptible curve—of a sort which is inaccessible to art, unconsciously inscribed, of course, which gave the face an expression which was alternately sarcastic, sad, evil, and tender. Haven't you ever happened to distinguish a human profile on a frosty windowpane or in a jagged shadow accidentally cast by some object, a profile sometimes unimaginably beautiful, and at other times unfathomably repulsive? Just try to transfer the profile to a sheet of paper! You won't be able to do it. Take a pencil and try to trace on the wall the silhouette which has so struck you, and its charm will disappear; the human hand cannot intentionally produce such lines: a single, minute deviation, and the former expression is irrevocably destroyed. In the face on that portrait was that inexplicable quality which only genius or accident can produce.

"It's strange that I noticed the portrait only at the moment that I said I would take the apartment!" thought Lugin.

He sat down in an armchair, rested his head on his hand, and lost himself in thought.

The yardkeeper stood opposite Lugin for a long time, swinging his keys.

"Well then, sir?" he finally said.

"Ah!"

"Well then, if you're taking it—a deposit, please."

They agreed on a sum; Lugin gave him the deposit, then sent an order to his place to have his things brought over, while he himself sat opposite the portrait until evening; at nine o'clock the most essential things had been brought from the hotel Lugin had been staying at.

"It's nonsense that they should think it impossible to live in this apartment," thought Lugin. "My predecessors obviously were not destined to move into it—that's strange, of course! But I took my own measures—I moved in immediately! And so?—nothing has happened!"

He and his old valet Nikita arranged things around the apartment until twelve o'clock.

One ought to add that Lugin had chosen for his bedroom the room in which the portrait hung.

Before going to bed Lugin took a candle and went up to the portrait, wanting to take another good look at it, and in the place where the artist's name should have been, he found a word written in red letters: *Wednesday.*

"What day is today?" he asked Nikita.

"It's Monday, sir . . ."

"The day after tomorrow is Wednesday," said Lugin indifferently.

"Just so, sir!"

God knows why Lugin became angry with him.

"Get out of here!" he yelled, stamping his foot.

Old Nikita shook his head and went out.

After this Lugin lay down in bed and fell asleep.

The next morning the rest of his things and a few unfinished pictures were brought over.

3.

Among the unfinished pictures, most of which were small, was one of rather insignificant size: in the middle of a canvas covered with charcoal, chalk, and greenish-brown primer, there was a sketch of a woman's head worthy of a connoisseur's attention; but in spite of the charm of the drawing and the liveliness of the colors, the head struck one unpleasantly because of something undefinable in the expression of the eyes and the smile; it was obvious that Lugin had resketched the head several times in different views, and that he had been unable to satisfy himself, because the same little head, blotted out with brown paint, appeared in several places on the canvas. It was not a real portrait; perhaps like some of our young poets who pine for beautiful women who have never existed, he was trying to create on canvas his ideal—a woman-angel, a whim understandable enough in early youth, but rare in a person who has had any experience in life. However, there are people whose experiences of the mind do not affect their hearts, and Lugin was one of these unfortunate and poetic creatures. The most cunning rogue or the most experienced coquette would have difficulty duping Lugin, but he deceived himself daily with the naivete of a child. For some time he had been haunted by a constant idea—one which was torturous and unbearable, all the more so because his self-love suffered as a result of it: he was far from handsome, it is true, but there was nothing disgusting about him; people who knew his wit, talent, and kindness even found his facial expression pleasant; but he was firmly convinced that the degree of his ugliness precluded the possibility of love, and he began to view women as his natural enemies, suspecting ulterior motives in their occasional caresses and explaining in a coarse, positive manner their most obvious good will. I shall not examine the degree to which he was correct, but the fact is that such a disposition of the soul excuses his rather fantastic love for an ethereal ideal—a love that is most innocent, but at the same time most harmful for a man of imagination.

On that day, Tuesday, nothing special happened to Lugin: he sat at home until evening, although he needed to go somewhere. An incomprehensible lassitude overwhelmed all his feelings: he wanted to paint, but the brushes fell from his hands; he tried to read, but his eyes flitted over the lines, and he read something totally different from what was actually printed there; he had fits of fever and chills, his head ached, and there was a ringing in his ears. When it grew dark he did not order candles brought to him: he sat by the window which looked out on the yard; it was dark outside; his poor neighbors' windows were dimly lit;—he sat a long time. Outside a barrel organ suddenly began to play: it played some sort of old German waltz; Lugin listened and listened—and he became terribly sad. He began to pace around the room; an unprecedented anxiety took hold of him: he felt like crying, laughing . . . he threw himself on the bed and burst out crying; he saw his entire past: he remembered how often he had been deceived, how often he had hurt just those very people he loved, what a wild joy sometimes flooded his heart when he saw tears which he had caused to flow from eyes now closed forever, and with horror he realized that he was unworthy of an unreasoning and true love—and it was so painful, so hard to bear!

Around midnight he calmed down, sat down at the table, lit a candle, and took a sheet of paper and began to draw something—it was quiet all around. The candle burned brightly and calmly; he drew the head of an old man, and when he had finished he was struck by the similarity between that head and the head of someone he knew. He raised his eyes to the portrait hanging opposite him; the resemblance was striking; he involuntarily shuddered and turned around; it seemed to him that the doors leading into the empty room had squeaked; he could not tear his eyes from the door.

"Who's there?" he cried out.

He heard shuffling, like slippers, behind the door; lime from the stove sprinkled down onto the floor. "What is that?" he repeated with a weak voice.

At that moment both leaves of the door began to open quietly, noiselessly; a cold breath spread through the room; the door opened by itself—it was as dark as a cellar in the room.

When the doors had opened a figure in a striped dressing gown and slippers appeared: it was a grey, stooped little old man; he moved slowly in a squatting fashion; his face—long and pale—was motionless; his lips were compressed; his grey, dull eyes, encircled by red borders, looked straight ahead aimlessly. He sat down at the table, across from Lugin, pulled out from underneath his gown two decks of cards, placed one of them opposite Lugin, the other in front of himself, and smiled . . .

"What do you want?" said Lugin with the courage that comes of despair. His fists clenched convulsively, and he was ready to throw the large candleholder at the uninvited guest.

From under the dressing gown came a sigh.

"This is unbearable," gasped Lugin. His thoughts were confused.

The little old man began to fidget on his chair; his whole figure was changing constantly: he became now taller, now stouter, then almost shrank away completely; at last he assumed his original form.

"All right," thought Lugin, "if this is an apparition, I won't yield to it."

"Wouldn't you like me to deal a hand of shtoss?" asked the little old man.

Lugin took the deck of cards lying in front of him and answered mockingly, "But what shall we play for? I want to warn you that I will not stake my soul on a card!" (He thought he would confuse the apparition with this.) "... but if you want," he continued, "I'll stake a *klyunger*.[2] I doubt that you have those in your ethereal bank."

This joke did not confuse the little old man at all.

"I have this in the bank," he said, extending his hand.

"That?" said Lugin, taking fright and looking to the left. "What is it?" Something white, vague, and transparent fluttered near him. He turned away in disgust. "Deal," he said, recovering a little. He took a *klyunger* from his pocket and placed it on a card. "We'll go on blind luck." The little old man bowed, shuffled the cards, cut, and began to tally. Lugin played the seven of clubs; it was beaten immediately. The little old man extended his hand and took the gold coin.

"Another round!" said Lugin with vexation.

The apparition shook his head.

"What does that mean?"

"On Wednesday," said the little old man.

"Oh! Wednesday!" cried Lugin in a rage. "No! I don't want to on Wednesday! Tomorrow or never! Do you hear me?"

The strange guest's eyes glittered piercingly, and he again squirmed uneasily in his seat.

"All right," he said at last. He rose, bowed, and walked out in a squatting fashion. The door again quietly closed after him; from the next room again came the sound of shuffling slippers ... and little by little everything became quiet. Blood was pounding inside Lugin's head with a mallet; a strange feeling agitated him and gnawed at his soul. He was vexed and insulted at having lost ...

"But I didn't yield to him!" he said, trying to console himself. "I forced him to agree to my terms. On Wednesday?—But of course! I must be crazy! But that's good, very good! He won't rid himself of me! And he looks so much like that portrait! ... Terribly, terribly like it! Aha! Now I understand!"

On that word he fell asleep in his chair. The next morning he didn't tell anyone about what had happened, stayed at home all day, awaited the evening with feverish impatience.

"But I didn't get a look at what he had in the bank! .." he thought. "It must be something unusual."

When midnight arrived, he rose from his chair, went out into the next room, locked the door leading into the vestibule, and returned to his seat; he did not have to wait long: again he heard a rustling sound, the shuffling of slippers, the old man's cough, and again his lifeless figure appeared at the door. Another figure followed him, but it was so indistinct that Lugin could not make out its shape.

Just as he had done the evening before, the little old man sat down, placed two decks of cards on the table, cut one, and prepared to deal: he obviously expected no resistance from Lugin; his eyes shone with an unusual confidence, as if they were reading the future. Lugin, completely under the magnetic spell of those grey eyes, was about to throw two half-imperials on the table, when he suddenly recovered his senses.

"Just a moment," said Lugin, covering his deck with his hand.

The little old man sat motionless.

"There was something I wanted to say to you! Just a moment ... yes!" Lugin had become confused.

Finally, with an effort, he slowly said, "All right—I will play with you—I accept the challenge—I am not afraid—but there is one condition: I must know with whom I am playing! What is your last name?"

The little old man smiled.

"I won't play otherwise," said Lugin, while at the same time his shaking hand was pulling the next card from the deck.

"*Chto-s*? [What, sir],"[3] said the unknown one, smiling mockingly.

"Shtoss?—Who?" Lugin's hands dropped; he was frightened. At that minute he sensed someone's fresh, aromatic breath near him; and a weak, rustling sound, an involuntary sigh, and a light fiery touch. A strange, sweet, but at the same time morbid tremor ran through his veins. He turned his head for an instant, and immediately returned his gaze to the cards; but that momentary glance would be enough to force him to gamble away his soul. It was a marvelous divine vision: bent over his shoulder gleamed the head of a woman; her lips entreated him; and in her eyes there was an inexpressible melancholy . . . she stood out against the dark walls of the room as the morning star stands out in the misty east. Life had never produced anything so ethereally heavenly; death had never taken from earth anything so full of ardent life; the vision was not an earthly being: it was made up of color and light instead of form and body, warm breathing instead of blood, and thought instead of feeling: nor was it an empty and deceitful vision . . . because these indistinct features were infused with turbulent and greedy passion, desire, grief, love, fear, and hope—it was one of those marvelously beautiful women which a youthful imagination depicts for us—before which we fall to our knees in the high emotion accompanying ardent visions, and we cry, pray, and celebrate for God knows what reason, one of those divine creations of a young soul, when, in a surplus of power, the soul creates for itself a new nature—better and more complete than the one to which it has been chained.

At that moment Lugin could not explain what had happened to him, but from that instant he decided to play until he won; that goal became the goal of his life; he was very happy about it.

The little old man began to deal. Lugin's card was beaten. His pale hand dragged two half-imperials onto the table.

"Tomorrow," said Lugin.

The little old man sighed gravely, but nodded his head in assent, and went out as he had the previous evening.

This scene repeated itself every night for a month: every night Lugin lost, but he didn't regret the money; he was certain that at least one winning card would ultimately be dealt him, and for that reason he doubled his already large bets; he suffered terrible losses, but nevertheless every night for a second he met the gaze and smile for which he was ready to give up everything on earth. He grew terribly thin and yellow. He spent entire days at home, locked in his room; he rarely ate. He awaited evening as a lover awaits a rendezvous: and every evening he was rewarded with an even more tender gaze, a friendlier smile. She—I don't know her name—she seemed to take an anxious part in the play of the cards; she seemed to await impatiently the moment when she would be released from the yoke of the old man; and each time that Lugin's card was beaten, when he would turn to her with a sad look, he would find her passionate, deep eyes fixed on him, eyes which seemed to say, "Take courage, don't lose heart. Wait, I will be yours, no matter what happens! I love you . . ." And a cruel, taciturn sadness would cast its shadow over her changeable features. And every evening, as they parted, Lugin's heart painfully contracted from despair and frenzy. He had already sold many of his things in order to sustain the game; he saw that in the not too distant future the moment would arrive when he would have nothing left to stake on the cards. He had to decide on a course of action. He decided.

Notes

1. "Shtoss" dates from February 1841. It is Lermontov's last known prose work. It may or not be finished; the title is arbitrary. Shtoss (stuss) is a game of chance belonging to the faro family—for details see Vladimir Nabokov, trans., *Eugene Onegin* (New York, 1964), vol. II, pp. 258-61.

2. A kind of gold coin.

3. *Chto-s* ("What, sir?" and pronounced *shto-s*) shtoss (the card game) and Shtoss (surname) are all pronounced identically. Here surname and question are mixed.

LITERARY CRITICISM

LITERARY CRITICISM: INTRODUCTION

Russia's literary criticism, like its literature, was in a fledgeling state at the beginning of the nineteenth century. Russia lacked both professional writers and professional critics.[1] Articles were usually personal reactions to literature with long quotations backing up the critic's appraisal that the work was good or bad. The same backwardness that the intellectuals saw in their culture, they saw in criticism—or the lack of it. But when criticism began to take its place in the journals, it too fell into certain patterns and set identifiable trends.

Karamzin, the man so influential in putting Russian literature on the road to Romanticism, also wrote some of the first criticism. His direction in criticism was "to strengthen secular literature as an institution," and in order to encourage writers, his policy was not to criticize contemporary works.[2] Zhukovsky disagreed with Karamzin, arguing that criticism of contemporaries was permissible; he even justified criticism by demonstrating its moral function: "Criticism helps form moral feeling since it calls attention to beauty in art, which is analogous to the Good (moral beauty) in nature."[3] Also Zhukovksy wrote some of the first "practical" criticism by defining genres and their rules.

Batyushkov respected technique, but also thought that the true poet lived his art; that is, life and art are inseparable. His criticism was directed more toward the poet than toward his work, a tendency which gained popularity in the Romantic era.[4]

Yet another approach to criticism emerges in the works of Pyotr Andreevich Vyazemsky, who used it as "a vehicle for satire, polemics and penetrating comments on the literary scene."[5] A strong advocate of Romanticism, he also is credited with coining the word *narodnost'*, the interpretation of which caused as many controversies as the polemics around Classicism and Romanticism.[6]

The question of nationality is related to yet another aspect of Russian criticism—the civic trend. Ryleev was the chief proponent of civic criticism which was picked up and developed by the non-aristocratic branch of professional critics, of whom Belinsky is the prime example. Along with Ryleev, Bestuzhev-Marlinsky worked on the *Polar Star* and wrote several critical articles about Russian literature. His "Glances" at Russian literature firmly established him as an important literary critic. Besides trying to resolve the meaning of nationality, Bestuzhev-Marlinsky became embroiled in the linguistic polemics between Shishkovites and Karamzinians. He brought criticism to a higher, more professional level through careful analyses of style and language.[7]

The years 1825-32 brought Russian literary criticism to "the threshold of maturity."[8] These years coincide with the growth of journalism and the appearance in the press of long, systematic surveys of literature. The bad side of criticism is that sometimes it was used for "polemics and vicious personal attacks."[9] The polemics first centered on language and morality in literature. These aspects play a role in two articles which discuss Katenin's *Olga*, a translation of Bürger's *Lenore*.

After Katenin's ballad appeared in both Moscow and Petersburg, the poet Nikolai Ivanovich Gnedich (1784-1833)[10] attacked it in a review, the translation of which appears below. Gnedich is best known for his brilliant translation of Homer's *Iliad*. He never belonged to either the Shishkovites or the Karamzinians, but he had friends in both camps. He used Church Slavonicisms and the high style when he thought it appropriate to do so, for example, in his translation of the *Iliad*; but he was also a defender of Zhukovsky.

In "About the Free Translation of Bürger's Ballad, *Lenore,* " Gnedich defends Zhukovksy's first translation, *Lyudmila* against Katenin's version, *Olga*. Gnedich mainly objects to Katenin's use of coarse language, illogical syntax and content and incorrect grammar.[11] In answer to this review, the playwright Alexander Sergeevich Griboedov (1795-1829) wrote "Concerning the Analysis of the Translation of Bürger's Ballad, *Lenore*."[12] Siding more with the Shishkov group, Griboedov stoutly defended Katenin's translation, which is really closer to the German original. In a witty manner Griboedov uses Gnedich's own argument against Zhukovsky and tries to show that Katenin's grammar is acceptable.

Questions of grammar or style do not even matter in the essay "A Word About the Poet and Poetry" (1815) by Batyushkov. Instead he deals with the life of the poet and treats poetry as a special gift for those who deserve it. For him Poetry is "heavenly fire" that mixes "imagination, feeling and dreaming." Inspiration comes only to the gifted, to those whose hearts are prepared and ready to receive it. Inspiration comes rarely and the poet cannot control it. Poets are born and must devote their entire being to poetry. They should also not live in the cities, where trivialities can distract them. To demonstrate his point Batyushkov gives "examples" of true poets who lived their art. He mainly chooses his favorite poets from Greek and Latin literature.

In his essay "About Delusions and Truth" (1820), Evgeny Baratynsky also discusses intangibles. Although not denying the validity of reason, he defends the perceptions of the world man gains through dreams and feelings. Baratynsky says there is no absolute truth and argues that a person's experiences determine what is true and what is false for him. To demonstrate this point Baratynsky describes two utterly different childhoods and shows that these result in two completely different perceptions of childhood. Yet each is true. He dismisses the superiority of old age over youth and wonders what would happen if man were born old and grew younger the longer he lived. This essay is a Romantic vision which denies the complacency of reason and endorses the world of dreams.

From these lofty philosophical heights we return to earth and the all-too-real polemics of the Romantic age. In Küchelbecker's article "On the Trend of Our Poetry, Especially the Lyric, in the Past Decade" (1824), this advocate of Shishkov and the odic tradition attacks the preponderance of elegies and epistles in contemporary literature. He tries to weigh the merits of epistles, elegies and odes against each other and expectedly comes out in favor of the ode. For him the ode soars to great heights, while epistles and elegies are too subjective and pathetically earthbound. For Küchelbecker these lower genres are not poetry. He says that no one gains anything in elegies, because they are all the same. Where is variety and richness? And while his views may all be a matter of taste, Küchelbecker's criticism of the overuse of clichés and conventions is valid. He shows that Romantics, in their repetitiveness, are guilty of the same crimes which they accuse the Classicists of committing. He ends with an appeal to the "true talents" among Russian writers to revitalize the language and literature by depending on what is national rather than merely assimilated.

Prince Pyotr Vyazemsky (1792-1878) is a spirited opponent of the Classicist view and a staunch defender of Romanticism. A poet, journalist and literary critic, Vyazemsky was a member of Arzamas and a close friend of Pushkin, whom he knew since the latter was a child. Vyazemsky came from an old noble family, but was orphaned in 1807, at which time he became a ward of Karamzin, who was married to Vyazemsky's older sister.[13]

As a champion of Romanticism Vyazemsky was both "out of date and out of tune" by the thirties.[14] And even though he outlived his contemporaries and became a bitter old man, it was in these later years that his poetry became "more significant."[15] In general his poetry is rational, cold, and witty. Perhaps Vyazemsky compensates for the impersonality of his poetry in the warm, witty correspondence he carried on with his dear friends Pushkin, Zhukovsky, and A. I. Turgenev. Vyazemsky's wit and satirical, epigrammatic style shine in his "In Place of a Foreword to *The Fountain of Bakhchisarai,* A Conversation between the Publisher and a Classicist from the Vyborg Side or Vasiliev Island," (1824). In this article Vyazemsky cleverly uses the arguments of the Classicist to show that Classical poets, especially Lomonosov, began the trend the Romantics carry on and which the Classicists deplore. The Publisher then brings up the question of nationalism; next he states that it is too early to define Romanticism since it is still in the process of evolving. The Publisher concludes with a gibe at the obtuseness of the Classicists and implies that they do not understand anything unless it is explained to them.

By 1825 the Decembrist poet Kondraty Ryleev was tired of the polemics surrounding the Classicist-Romantic controversy. In "A Few Thoughts about Poetry" he states that the terms are meaningless, and that "true self-sufficient poetry" is eternal, as are its rules. He shows how designations such as "Classical" stultify literature because "modern" writers imitate "Classical" writers rather than using them as "an encouragement." In this essay Ryleev also bemoans lack of critical judgment about original and imitative authors. He then shows how writers we designate as Classical are really Romantic. Ryleev also demonstrates how reliance on form alone can distort the integrity of the content of literature. Ryleev concludes that definitions are harmful to art—especially poetry—by limiting and inhibiting it from reaching its true heights. In this eminently rational article Ryleev argues for ideals, emotions and truths, and against slavish imitation to rules which distort those ideals.

Venevitinov's article "A Critique of an Essay of *Eugene Onegin* Published in *The Telegraph*" also takes up the issue of imitation. Venevitinov lists a number of errors in Polevoy's review of *Eugene Onegin*. The first of these is that Polevoy does not judge Pushkin on his merits alone, but in comparison with Byron. Next Venevitinov takes exception to Polevoy's methods of trying to make Pushkin look better by ridiculing the stupid questions of imagined critics of the poet. Venevitinov ends with a plea for a more positive approach to criticism and a caution not to judge a book by its first chapter alone.

Pushkin himself excelled in the art of criticism and wanted to raise its level to that already achieved in the West. Pushkin was sincere in his efforts to accomplish that goal and never balked at doing literary hack work, i.e., "write newspaper reviews of every type of book, publish and edit a journal, and answer the attacks of slanderers and the questions of fools."[16] Pushkin's reviews are usually very brief and are marked by the same qualities that distinguish his prose: lucidity, precision, an aphoristic tendency, logic and humor. His criticism runs the gamut of reviews, essays, "collections of aphorisms, letters to the editor and ... the brief note."[17] He did not hesitate to comment on his own works and also wrote many reviews of translations. In his criticism we can also find his prejudices and preferences; Pushkin hated fuzzy writing, servile imitation of rules and pomposity of theme and style. He advocated truthful analyses of characters in appropriate settings. Pushkin practiced what he preached. According to Proffer, he "avoids the common errors of literary critics ... refuses to compare unlike genres ... makes fun of those who use the opinions of characters to revile authors ... and refuses to find complexity where there is none."[18] In Pushkin's criticism we can also find his views on the role of art as well as its moral value.[19]

Nikolai Gogol also thought that art had moral value, though his views are much more extreme. As we have already seen in his story "The Portrait," Gogol believed that art is the means through which the world can be saved. In "A Few Words about Pushkin," an article in *Arabesques,* the same collection in which "The Portrait" appeared, Gogol comes back to this theme. And just like that story, "A Few Words about Pushkin" may also be an apology for Gogol's own methods and style. Gogol sees Pushkin as Russia's national poet, one who reflects "Russian nature, the Russian soul, Russian language and Russian character." Pushkin also had the ability to establish true rapport with his readers whom he delighted with his exotic portrayals of the Caucasus. However, when Pushkin left the Caucasus and began writing about the simpler, less dashing lives of Russians, his popularity began to decline. Gogol sees this as the readers' reluctance to accept as literature a simpler style and lowered subject matter. He then explores the writer's plight in the face of such rejection. Again Gogol calls upon the true artist, the great poet, to solve the problem. Gogol feels that only the great artist can look at the mundane, lowly side of life and find in it that which is unusual; he then can present this to the people without distortion. Gogol sees Pushkin as the true artist who successfully accomplished this task. Of course, since Gogol also wrote about the less elevated sides of life, his implication is that he is also a true artist.

In another article, "Petersburg Notes for 1836," Gogol concentrates on the role of theater in general and the comic playwright in particular. After a sketch of the differences between quintessentially Russian Moscow and the disparately foreign Petersburg, Gogol looks at the state of the theater to see what it can do to unify Petersburg. After demonstrating that many different classes live in the capital, he says that they all have love of the theater in common. But the theater simply cheats the people by presenting vaudevilles and melodramas with which they have no common bond. Gogol proposes that talented writers look to national songs, national dances and national types to create real drama which could unite the people. In effect, the writer should introduce the Russians to themselves; he must present a "mirror to society" in his plays. Yet again Gogol echoes the sentiments of "The Portrait" and "A Few Words about Pushkin" when he says that it takes profound talent to find the valuable buried in the ordinary.

Gogol narrows the field down more when he says that the gifted comic playwright can do that best. He even mentions *The Inspector General.* The theater can turn into a church, a place where the people can be uplifted. For Gogol laughter is good, for through it people are united. For Gogol, true comedy has both social value and aesthetic merit. Comedy can simultaneously teach and entertain the people.

By the 1830s the question of art's social responsibility became more prominent in

Russian literary criticism. This may be due to the emergence of a new class in Russia: the *raznochintsy*. Sons of priests, clerks, petty officials and other professionals, these young men would somehow find their way to the universities, get involved with other members of the intelligentsia and try to live by their wits. Most of these men were social reformers with the common goal of bettering living conditions in Russia.

The shift in emphasis in literary criticism appears as early as the mid-twenties in articles by two members of the *raznochintsy*—Nikolai Polevoi and Nikolai Nadezhdin, two of Russia's first professional critics. The most famous and most influential of the *raznochintsy* critics was Vissarion Grigorevich Belinsky (1811-48), who was responsible for the civic turn that literary criticism took in the nineteenth century. The son of a poor doctor, Belinsky entered Moscow University and became a member of the Stankevich circle. He was expelled from the university, ostensibly for reasons of poor health and "limited capabilities," but really because of a play he wrote condemning serfdom. In 1833 Belinsky became a reviewer for the *Telescope* and never quit writing reviews, literary surveys and articles until he died of consumption in 1848.

A man of integrity, Belinsky advocated justice and social reform, reading social content into all of the works he analyzed. One result of this tendency was his misinterpretation of Gogol, in whom he saw a social critic and reformer. Besides writing reviews of individual authors, he wrote several outlines of Russian literary history and annual surveys. He tried to show the development of Russian literature in all of its manifestations.

Belinsky's own education was deficient in a number of areas and he knew no foreign languages. His style was disorganized, his rhetoric confused. But Belinsky did have a knack of recognizing talent, although he certainly was not infallible in his assessments of the writers of his time. In spite of his handicaps, his works show his love of Russia and Russian literature and his exuberance and energy.

Ideologically Belinsky went through three major phases during his career.[20] Under the influence of his university circle, he first became an advocate of the German idealism popular at the time. He acknowledged the supremacy of art in its relation to the "organic whole." At that time Belinsky lived in a world of images and ideas. For a brief period (1840-41) he carried the Hegelian doctrine "All that is real is rational, all that is rational is real" to an extreme and actually became a reactionary who accepted the social order of the day.

In the last period of his life Belinsky returned to his former ideas and again became a social reformer. This period is distinguished by his literary surveys and his articles about Pushkin and *Eugene Onegin*. In these articles he recognizes Pushkin's merit as an artist and a true national poet.

Belinsky's first important work appeared in 1834 in the form of articles which comprised a series of "Literary Reveries."[21] He begins by stating that Russia has no literature, only a series of imitations of foreign writers. But Belinsky is hopeful that Russia has an extravagantly ambitious future mission to assimilate existing literature and create a new literature, a synthesis of all that has gone before.

In the next stage of his articles Belinsky defines literature. He concludes that literature is not simply published works or a collection of *chefs-d'oeuvre*, since these exist in Russia. Literature is the collection of works by artists of genius which expresses their country's national spirit. This type of literature has a natural and consistent development. To find out whether Russian literature conforms to that definition, his readers must wait for the next installments.

Belinsky then goes on to define the nature of art as the expression of the "genius" of a nation. He then expounds the Schellingian doctrines that through art man enters the world of "ideas" and loses himself in the "organic whole" of the cosmos. Thus the writer's "holy" mission is to reveal nature in all of its forms to the people. Art must reveal the idea of the universe. The best example of an artist who fulfills these goals is Shakespeare.

Belinsky now turns to Russia and a brief historical survey. During the time of Peter the Great, Russia finally began to be a part of Europe. But only the upper classes assimilated their "second-hand" literature; the lower classes remained uneducated and uninformed. Belinsky's assessment of the eighteenth century is low; he asserts that the "accepted" writers do not deserve praise or veneration—not even Lomonosov. Belinsky singles out Fonvizin and Derzhavin for praise, simply because their talents were *national*.

The early nineteenth century Belinsky sees as a period of transition. He credits Karamzin with raising the level of literary culture and sees Zhukovsky, Batyushkov and Vyazemsky as interesting minor poets. He does praise Krylov, mainly because of his "Russianness." Belinsky concludes that Russia has no literature, but her hope lies in Pushkin, a talented *Russian* poet. He also says that Russia's other hope lies in education and enlightenment.

Written in a flamboyant style, with many digressions, the "Literary Reveries" mark an important stage in the career of Belinsky and in the development of Russian literary criticism. As Belinsky became more political, his concern for aesthetics was not as strong as his concern for the social value of literature. The most influential critics who followed him concentrated on the "civic" aspect of literature and ignored its aesthetic side. According to them art had to depict "real life." Romanticism gave way to Realism.

Notes

1. Carl R. Proffer, Introduction, *The Critical Prose of Alexander Pushkin* (Bloomington: Indiana University Press, 1969), p. 4.

2. William Mills Todd, III, *The Familiar Letter as a Literary Genre in the Age of Pushkin* (Princeton, New Jersey: Princeton University Press, 1976), pp. 50-51.

3. Todd, p. 51.

4. Todd, p. 52.

5. Todd, p. 53.

6. For definitions of *narodnost'* see Lauren G. Leighton, *Russian Romanticism: Two Essays* (The Hague: Mouton and Co., 1975).

7. For a more thorough overview of Marlinsky's criticism see Lauren G. Leighton, "Marlinsky," *Russian Literature Triquarterly,* 3 (Spring 1972), 249-68.

8. John M. Mersereau, Jr. *Baron Delvig's* "Northern Flowers" (Carbondale: Southern Illinois University Press, 1967), p. 5.

9. Mersereau, p. 60.

10. Katenin did make some grammatical changes to conform with Gnedich's suggestions.

11. Gnedich belonged to an impoverished Ukrainian family and received his education in various seminaries. Plagued in youth by poverty, he also had smallpox, a disease which left him disfigured and blind in one eye. While attending Moscow University he worked as a tutor. Like his contemporaries he fell under Schelling's influence. Gnedich knew Greek and Latin well, learned some German and English, and could

read French. Before he could finish his degree, Gnedich went to Petersburg where he got a job in the Department of Public Education. At that time he became a close friend of Batyushkov and an acquaintance of other writers. After writing some verse in a Neoclassical mode, he began to compare elegies and epistles in a Romantic vein.

12. A member of the Shishkov party, this famous author of *Woe from Wit* spent time in the foreign service. His life and diplomatic career ended when he was murdered by a mob in Teheran after he was appointed Russian minister to Persia. Although he did write some lyrics and comedies, Griboedov is most renowned for his play, *Woe from Wit.*

13. Vyazemsky entered military service and served at Borodino during the War of 1812. Between 1821 and 1829 he lived at his estate, Ostafievo, near Moscow. During these years he could not get government employment, but finally did enter civil service in 1830 with a position in the Ministry of Finance. In 1856 Vyazemsky began his two-year position on the censorship board but was too lax for that appointment. From 1863 he lived abroad; he died in Baden-Baden.

14. D. S. Mirsky, *A History of Russian Literature* (New York: Alfred A. Knopf, 1966), p. 80.

15. Mirsky, p. 80.

16. Proffer, p. 10. I base my discussion of Pushkin's critical style on this essay, pp. 10-14.

17. Proffer, p. 10.

18. Proffer, p. 12.

19. See, for example, "On *The Memoirs of Samson,*" "Refutations of Criticisms," "*Vie, Poésies et Pensées de Joseph Delorme* and *Les Consolations, Poésies* par Sainte-Beuve," and "M. E. Lovanov's *Opinion about the Spirit of Literature, Foreign and Our Own.*"

20. See Mirsky, pp. 164-68 and Ralph E. Matlaw, Introduction, *Belinsky, Chernyshevsky and Dobrolyubov. Selected Criticism* (New York: E. P. Dutton & Co., Inc., 1962), pp. vii-xx.

21. As the basis for my discussion I rely on class notes and unpublished outlines from a course in Russian literary criticism taught by Edward J. Brown, Indiana University, 1967.

LITERARY CRITICISM

K. N. BATYUSHKOV

A Word about the Poet and Poetry

Poetry is that heavenly flame which, more or less, is an organic part of the human soul (that combination of imagination, sensitivity and reverie); poetry not infrequently forms both the torture and the delight of the people created solely for it. *The poet is troubled by the inspiration of genius,* said a well-known poet.[1] This is perfectly true. There exist minutes of active sensitivity: people with real talent have experienced them; artists, musicians and, most of all, poets must be quick to grasp them, for they are rare, fleeting, and often depend on health, time and the influence of external objects which are not in our power to control arbitrarily. But at the moment of inspiration, at the sweet moment of poetic fascination, I would never take up my pen if I found a heart able to feel fully that which I feel; if I could convey to it all of my secret thoughts, all the freshness of my dreams and could compel those same strings to quiver in it, those strings which produce the voice in my heart. Where can one find a heart ready to share with us these feelings and sensations of ours? There are no such hearts among us—and we resort to art to express our thoughts in the sweet hope that there are on earth good hearts, educated minds, for which a strong and noble feeling, a fortunate expression, a beautiful line and a page of living, eloquent prose are true treasures . . . "They cannot read in my heart, but they will read my book," said Montaigne[2]; and during those stormy times in France,[3] by the sound of guns, by the glow of bonfires, ignited by superstition, he wrote his *Essays* and, conversing with good hearts of all ages, he forgot his unworthy contemporaries.

Someone compared the soul of the poet at the moment of inspiration with metal made molten in a hearth; it remains for a long time in a primitive state in strong and constant heat; for a long time immovable; but when it is brought to a great heat—it glows, begins to coil, and bubbles; when it is taken from the flame—in a minute it settles down and diminishes. That is a wonderful portrayal of the poet, whom all of life should prepare for a few fruitful minutes; all objects, all feelings, all that is seen and unseen should inflame his soul and slowly bring those lucid minutes of activity closer, in order to portray so easily the entire history of our impressions, feelings and passions. Fruitful minute of poetry! how quickly you disappear, but you leave behind your eternal traces for the people who have mastered the language of the gods.

There are people, born fortunate, whom nature lavishly endowed with memory, imagination, a fiery heart, and a great intellect which knows how to give the right direction both to memory and imagination—without a doubt, these people have the gift of expressing themselves, a wonderful gift, the best possession of man; for through it he leaves behind the truest traces of himself in society and has a strong influence on it. Without it there would be nothing lasting, true, defined; and that which we call immortal on earth could not exist. Centuries pass by; memorials made by human hands are destroyed; oral tradition changes, disappears; but Homer and the holy books speak about the past. Human experience is based on them. Eternal wells, from which we draw consoling or sad truths, what gives you this durability? The art of the letter and the other, more important art—the art of expression.

This gift of expressing both your feelings and thoughts has long been subject to strict study. It is subject to invariable rules which result from experience and observation. But the very study of the rules, the continuous and persistent observation of graceful examples, is not enough. It is necessary for all life, all secret thoughts, all predilections to bow to one subject, and that subject must be—Art. Poetry, I dare say, demands the *entire person*.

I desire—let them call my desire strange!—I desire that a special way of life, a poetic *dietetics* be prescribed for the poet: in a word, that they make a science out of the life of a poet. This science would be for many scarcely less useful than all of Aristotle's rules[4] by which we learn to avoid mistakes; but we'll never learn how to create that which is graceful!

The first rule of this science should be: live as you write and write as you live. *Talis hominibus fuit oratio, qualis vita.*[5] Any other way, all echoes of your lyre will be false. For what reason did nature bring you forth? What did it place in your heart? What captured your imagination, almost against your will? Which writer were you reading when your genius trembled with ineffable joy and when a voice, the loud voice of your poetic conscience, cried out: wake up, you are a poet too! During the reading of writers of epics? And so, move away from society, surround yourself with nature: in the quiet of a village, surrounded by coarse, unspoiled customs, read the history of times past, study the sad annals of the world, learn about man and his passions, but be full of goodwill toward all men: then your thoughts will be important and majestic, the movements of your soul will be tender and passionate, but always subjugated to reason, their peaceful ruler. There is too little of that! The epic poet must completely experience *both fortunes.*[6] Like Tasso, he must love and suffer with his whole heart[7]; like Camoens, he must fight for his fatherland,[8] he must visit all countries; question all peoples, both savage and enlightened; question all monuments of art, all nature, which always speaks eloquently and distinctly to the mind that is exalted and enriched by experiences and memories. In a word, after forgetting all the insignificant profits of life and his own self-esteem, he must sacrifice everything to glory; only then will he plunge (not with the impudence of a conceited mind, but with the determination of a person carrying within his own breast the internal realization of his own strength), only then will he plunge into the stormy and vast sea of epic . . .

To live in society, to carry the heavy yoke of obligations which are often vain and insignificant, and to want to reconcile the profits of self-esteem with the desire for glory is a truly vain demand. That a way of life acts powerfully[9] and constantly on talent; of that there is no doubt. The French are an example of that: their literature, so rich in all its forms, has neither epic nor history. Their writers mostly lived surrounded by a noisy city, surrounded by all of the seductions of the court and idleness; but history and epic demand constant attention, and such importance and strength of soul which society not only takes away from a dissipated man, but also destroys completely. "Do you want to be an eloquent writer?" asks an eloquent woman writer of our time.[10] "Be virtuous and free, honor the object of your love, seek immortality and love, the gods in nature; sanctify your soul as they sanctify a church, and the angel of elevated thoughts will appear before you in all its splendor!" Charming lines full of truth! dissipated minds either will not understand you or will read you with haughty scorn.

Let's look at the lives of several poets whose names are so beloved to our heart. Horace, Catullus and Ovid lived as they wrote. Tibullus deceived neither himself nor others[11] when he told his patron Messalus that he rejoiced not in triumphs, not in the magnificence of Rome,[12] but in the peace of fields, the healthy air of forests, soft meadows, a native brook and that hut with a simple, thatched roof—the ramshackle hut in which Delia waits for him with her hair loose upon her high breasts. Petrarch was really standing, leaning against the cliff at

Vaucluse,[13] lost deep in thought when these harmonious lines flew from his lips:

> Sott' un gran sasso
> In una chiusa valle, ond' esce Sorga,
> Si stà: nè chi lo scorga
> V'è, se no Amor, che mai no'l lascia un passo
> E l'imagine d'una che lo strugge.[14]

Happy Chaulieu[15] dreamed under the branches and shady trees of his refuge at Fontenay; there he regretted the loss of his youth, the loss of the unfaithful pleasures of love. Bogdanovich lived in a world of fantasy[16] which he created when his hand drew the captivating portrayal of Dushenka.[17] Derzhavin, on the wild shores of the Suna river, washed by its seething foam, in prophetic frenzy glorified the waterfall and God.[18] And in our time, more rich in glory than favorable to the muses, Zhukovsky, separated by Bellona from his dear fields, Zhukovksy, gifted with a fiery imagination and a rare ability to convey to others a deep sensation of a strong and noble soul—in the camp of warriors, to the thunder of cannons, by the glow of his burning capital, wrote inspired lines full of fire, movement and strength.[19]

If a way of life has such a strong influence on the works of a poet, then education has an even stronger influence on him. Nothing can blot out of our heart's memory the first sweet impressions of youth![20] Time adorns them and gives them a ravishing charm. In middle age the perceived objects are weakly etched in our memory, and the soul, tired by sensations, neglects them: only passions occupy it; in old age man does not acquire [anything new], so only that which he has stored up in youth remains as his last treasure. In such a way nature unites the evening and morning of life just as the evening sunset flows into the morning sunrise during the long days of summer under our northern sky.

If first impressions are so strong in every person's heart, if they are not effaced by the whole course of his life, then they must be even stronger to preserve unfading freshness in the soul of the writer gifted with profound feeling:

> In old age it's comforting to remember years of childhood,
> The amusements, playfulness, and various objects
> Which made us happy then.[21]

If only we knew in great detail all of the circumstances in the lives of great writers, then without a doubt we could find in their works traces of their first, ever-strong sensations. The heart has its own memory. Rousseau remembered the beginning of a song which his good-natured aunt used to sing to him.[22] The young Ariosto, while staying in Florence, fell in love with a charming woman. He often visited her; he would sit for hours in profound silence, admiring the beautiful creature who embroidered with purple silk thread on silver. Impressions of those charming hands always remained in the lover's memory so strongly, that later, when telling about the battle of Mandricardo with the ill-fated Zerbino, he compares the crimson blood flowing from the deep wound of the youth to the purple tracery which the hands of the Florentine woman, white as snow, embroidered on the silver cloth.[23] Tender hearts will remember those places in Virgil where the poet talks about his dear Mantua;[24] the lives of the Roman Homer are full of reminiscences of youth; they are full of those deep, indelible impressions which plunge the reader into sweet contemplation, reminding him of his own life and the bright dawn of youth.

Climate, the look of the sky, water and earth—all of this acts on the poet's soul, which is open to impressions. We see in the songs of northern skalds and the bards of Eire[25] something severe, gloomy, wild and ever-dreamy, reminiscent of overcast northern skies and seaside mists, and of all of nature, meager with gifts of life, but always sublime, charming even in its horrors. We see the indelible imprint of climate in southern poems: a certain sweet bliss, luxury of imagination, freshness of feelings and clarity of thought, reminiscent of the sky and the charitable nature of southern countries where a person takes pleasure in a double life, compared to us, where he keeps on nourishing and pampering his own feelings, where he keeps on talking to his imagination. In vain would a native of Sicily or Naples desire to compete with the bard of Morven,[26] and, like him, describe the gloomy nature of the north; in vain would a northern poet desire to depict the luxurious valleys, cool caves, fruit-bearing groves, quiet gulfs, and Sicily's sky, high, transparent and eternally clear. Only Tasso, born under the scorching sun of Naples, could describe with such true and fresh colors the horrible drought, disastrous for the crusaders.[27] In this description, says the scholar Ginguene,[28] one recognizes an inhabitant of the south, someone who repeatedly undergoes the fatal influence of African winds, someone repeatedly exhausted by the heavy, intense heat.—Our Lomonosov, born on the shores of a noisy sea, educated in the labors of a trade fraught with danger, this amazing person was forcefully struck by nature's phenomena in the first years of boyhood: he was struck by the sun which, in the longest days of summer, just reaches the edge of the horizon when it again rises and again streams across the heavenly arc; he was struck by the northern lights, which in the northern regions take the place of the sun and pour a cold and shivering light on nature asleep beneath the deep snow. With personal pleasure, Lomonosov describes these phenomena of nature, majestic and beautiful, and duplicates them in his magnificent lines:

> The distant forests are covered by the deep,
> The merging of the skies is visible all around only from the sea.
>
> ... In the south, two hills and
> Wooded shores were revealed through the clear air.
> Between them an entry for ships opened into the gulf,
> A refuge from turbulent waters for swimmers,
> Where, whirling on the damp shores, sad Una
> Flows slowly into Neptune's embraces ...
> The star of day reached midnight,
> But did not hide its burning face in the deep,
> It seemed like a mountain on fire among the waves
> And swept the crimson brilliance out from behind the ice.
> In the middle of a most wondrous night, by the light of a clear sun,
> The tops of golden swells shine in swimmers' eyes.[29]

We will not linger over the beauty of the lines. Here all expressions are magnificent: the burning face of the sun, juxtaposed with the cold waters of the ocean; the sun, resting on the horizon, and like a burning mountain, sweeping the brilliance out from behind the ice—these are first-class beauties of descriptive poetry. The last two lines which conclude the picture are ravishing:

In the middle of a most wondrous night, by the light of a clear sun,
The tops of golden swells shine in swimmers' eyes.

But we shall note that the poet could not have written them if he had not been a witness to the wonderful phenomenon which struck the fiery imagination of an inspired adolescent and left in him a deep, indelible impression.

Notes*

1. G. R. Derzhavin, "Discourse on Lyric Poetry" (1811).

2. Batyushkov misquotes the preface to the Essays, where Montaigne really says: ". . . here they can find a few traits of my circumstances and moods, and thus more profoundly and vividly fill in the notion which they had about me."

3. The sixteenth-century skirmishes and wars between Catholics and Huguenots in France.

4. Aristotle's *Poetics*.

5. "People's speech is the same as their life." Quotation from Seneca, *Epistle 114*, line 1.

6. From antiquity: happiness and misfortune.

7. Batyushkov has in mind the legend about Torquato Tasso's love for Eleonora d'Este, the sister of the Ferrara herzog Alfonso II d'Este, which resulted in Tasso's persecution.

8. As a result of court intrigues, Camoens was sent as a soldier to Morocco and then to India.

9. Here the influence of Mme de Staël's book, *About Literature,* is evident. In this book she discusses the decisive role a nation's way of life, customs and climate play in the formation of a natural literature.

10. Mme de Staël. The quotation is from the second part of her book, *About Germany* (1810).

11. Batyushkov was unaware that some situations and characters in Tibullus' elegies are imaginary.

12. Here he is retelling the third elegy from *Book 1* of Tibullus; Batyushkov also did a free translation of it in his poem "Elegy from Tibullus."

13. Petrarch often wrote of the cliffs near his residence in Vaucluse.

14. Lines 92-96 from Petrarch's canzona CXXXV ("Qual più diversa e nova . . ."):

"Under the large cliff/In a closed valley, whence flows the Sorga,/He stands: and there is no one there at all to see him,/Except Amour, who is never even a step away,/And that image which destroys him."

15. Chaulieu, Guillaume Amfrye (1639-1720)—French poet, composer of Epicurean motifs in a melancholy tone; he was born in Fontenay and wanted to be buried there.

16. Batyushkov heard the story about Bogdanovich's "comrades" from M. N. Muravyov.

17. Bogdanovich lived in complete solitude. He had two comrades, worthy of the good-natured LaFontaine: a cat and a rooster. He spoke about them as he spoke about his friends, he told about their eccentricities, worried about their health and mourned their death for a long time. [Batyushkov's note.]

18. In his odes "The Waterfall" and "God."

19. "The Bard in the Camp of Russian Warriors" written in 1812. Bellona is the Roman mythological goddess of war.

20. See also Batyushkov's article "On Lomonosov's Character" and "Epistles to I. M. M[uravyov]—A[postol]."

21. Quotation from I. I. Dmitriev's fairytale, "Ethereal Towers."

22. See part one of Rousseau's *Confessions.*

23. See stanzas LVIII-LXVI of song XXIV of Ariosto's poem, *Orlando Furioso.*

24. In Eclogue IX, line 21; in *The Georgics* II, ll. 198-99; in *The Aeneid,* V, line 415.

25. Irish, Celtic singers.

26. Ossian.

27. See Tasso's *Jerusalem Delivered.*

28. Ginguene, Pierre-Louis (1748-1816), a French critic and author of the multi-volumed *History of Italian Literature* from which Batyushkov constantly studied and from which he formed his opinions about Tasso.

29. These are lines from the second song of Lomonosov's unfinished poem, *Peter the Great.*

*The source of these notes is K. N. Batyushkov, *Opyty v stikhakh i proze,* edited by I. M. Semenko (Moscow: Nauka, 1977), pp. 499-503. Most of the notes are Semenko's.

N. I. GNEDICH

About the Free Translation of Bürger's Ballad, *Lenore*

> *What are you wailing out of place? Your song is incoherent*
> *and wild!*
> *(Olga, Son of the Fatherland, book 24)*

Works of exceptionally talented men usually give rise to heated defenders and heated opponents, and to imitators who, with the purest motives, want to write like them; and they [give rise] to competitors—if not to say, jealous types—who write in their vein, trying to prove that their talent, which is generally respected, is not unique. These after-effects of talent are apparent even in our literature. The poems of *Mr. Zhukovsky* gave rise to many admirers and many opponents, and to imitators and competitors. We sincerely desire that his imitators, who until now only mimic him, produce something akin to *The Bard in the Camp of Russian Warriors* or *Svetlana;* but in anticipation of this—vain though it may be—how many messages to friends, in which nothing is sent except the rhyme,[how many] romances and songs which only their composers sing,[how many] ballads, unbelievable, but horrid ballads full of miracles must we read! Ah, amiable creator of *Svetlana,* how many souls will you have to answer for? What a line of murderers and corpses, hanged men and drowned men do I foresee! What a row of pale sacrifices to balladic death, and what death! Here—a beautiful girl, *when she sits, when she sleeps*—with her dear one she is dying *to life (Son of the Fatherland,* 1815, bk. 13); there—a murderer strangles an old man, ignoring the fact that a *balding* moon is gazing at him *(S. of F.,* 1815, bk. 23); here

> A beautiful maid faints,
> Falls on the damp earth,
> And her father leaves
> The wicket in a fearful rage,
>   (*Spirit of Journals,* 1816, bk. 13)

there—a *death-cap mushroom* is turned into something horrible . . . but who keeps track of all these inventions of their creators, for whom nothing is impossible, nothing is unbelievable, nothing is base! And judging by their first, bold steps, who can foresee where their imagination will lead them in this new field which has no bounds, either of truth or of taste. In fact—"only the beauties of poetry could until now excuse in this type of work (in ballads) the strange selection of subjects" (*A Lesson for Ladies' Men,* a comedy. Act I, scene 1).[1] It's necessary to spatter such rich and vivid paints in the pictures, to fill the verses with such magical charm, as for example in the ballad *Twelve Sleeping Maidens* [Zhukovsky], when they want similar ballads to be liked. "But if this type finds imitators who don't have the first-rate talent of their example and who will write only about corpses and apparitions—then our literature . . ." So I thought to myself one day while leafing through old numbers of Petersburg journals; but my thoughts were interrupted: they brought me *Moscow* journals from the city. However, that day guests distracted me from them, but I remembered them when I received the twenty-fourth volume of *Son of the Fatherland.* Going through the contents of the journals and finding, in both the *Messenger of Europe* and *Son of the Fatherland*, the poem *Olga*, I rushed to get acquainted with both *Olgas*, but at the first glance I saw that both of these *Olgas*— were one and the same old familiar *Bürger's Lenore*. But didn't *Mr. Zhukovsky* introduce us to her a long time ago? So! and after *Lyudmila* this coquette of the ballads wants to be liked again under a new name? and she suddenly appears in both capitals? and, to be sure, in new attire with new charms? I have to think that this is so; or the journalists, as if vying with each other, are hurrying to introduce her to readers. Bah! yes, it's still *Olga,* but with variations: in the Moscow journal: *why sing you out of place!* but in the Petersburg journal: *why are you wailing out of place?* Most probably this was done to please the taste of both capitals. But *Son of the Fatherland* came out later, and so I have to think that the later version is in it.[2] Let's read it. I read it, put the booklet on the table, sighed—and picked up the *Messenger of Europe*. I read and then put the *Messenger of Europe* on the table—but as luck would have it, *Mr. Zhukovsky's* poems were on that table. Should I open *Lyudmila?* Compare *Olga* with it? Does anybody need this? And would it be to *Olga's* advantage? *Lyudmila* is an original, charming, Russian poem, whose idea alone was taken from *Bürger*. The poet knew that you could make *Lenore,* a native German ballad, pleasing to Russian readers in no other way except through an imitation. But his imitation does not consist of substitution of Russian names in place of real German names of people and cities. The colors of poetry, the tone of expressions and feelings which make up the character and give physiognomies to the people, turns of speech, especially those that belong to simple dialect and distinguish the spirit of Russian folk language, were the things that transformed *Lenore* into *Lyudmila.* And since her singer has extraordinary talent, that's why I like his imitation (in spite of the German words *Hurre, hurre, hop, hop, hop* if not *Klinglingling)* more than the work of Bürger itself. It's true that there are a few absurdities in *Lyudmila,* e.g., the corpse talks so openly to *Lyudmila* about himself that his words could not lead her into error; he clearly says that his home is "A shroud, cross and six boards," and that "Their path leads to a sepulchral grave."

This destroys the act of deceiving Lyudmila and the reader at the same time; just as in Bürger, he keeps her believing him until the very end with his vague answers; he even tries to deceive her:

> Wir und Todten reiten schnell
> "We"—he says—"soon shall ride as corpses." [Gnedich's trans.]
> [We and the dead ride fast.]

Also, leaving out Bürger's pictures of the corpse's funeral, etc., indeed these pictures would be strange and, in all probability, absurd to our people, but substituting them with his own, the singer of *Lyudmila* fell into a small error:

> Do they hear the rustle of the quiet shades?
> At the hour of midnight apparitions,
> In the smoke of a cloud, all in a crowd,
>
> . . . .
>
> With their light, bright ring dance
> They twisted into an ethereal chain;
> Then they rushed after them!

These shades are beautiful, but they are totally *Ossianic* shades; but to have dashing shades in a Russian ballad! I myself wouldn't want to come across a few more errors like these in *Lyudmila;* but one needs only to close the book to forget about them. The charm of the poetry, life, movement and sweetness, the magical sweetness of the lines make up for everything! So! *Lyudmila,* after it acquainted Russian readers with the ballad form, will always be read as the original work of a native muse! Consequently, in all fairness, *Olga* should be spared comparison with *Lyudmila,* a dangerous rival; but if we must, then compare it with *Lenore.* So let's forget that *Lyudmila* exists and let's give ourselves over exclusively to our impressions of Olga's beauties.

    Olga. A free translation from Bürger. Free? Let me ask permission to doubt this. I don't dare to presuppose positively what motives compelled him to translate *Lenore* after *Lyudmila,* but if *Lyudmila* had not garnered so much just praise, then *Lenore* would hardly have appeared under the name of *Olga;* so then it seems to us that this *new* translation is not *free* in any sense. Where there's a will there's a way. But let's not dwell on this.

> A *tearful* dream disturbed Olga;
> She got up *early in the morning;*
> Has her beloved sweetheart betrayed her?
> Did he die? *ah!* I shall die!

As for me I truly would not have found anything to say against these lines, except that they—how would you say—don't reach the soul; but I ask you to listen to what malicious readers say. *Tearful dream* is a dry epithet, early in the morning is dry prose. And aren't those the same lines as in Bürger:

> Lenore fuhr um's Morgenroth
> Empor aus schweren Traumen?

> Did he die? Ah! I shall die!
> At early dawn Lenore
> Rose from her frightening dreams. [Gnedich's trans.]

> [At dawn Lenore awoke
> With a start from heavy dreams.]

Readers say that here that *ah* is bad since [it expresses] fear. But listen, amiable readers! there's no need to hurry in judging as there is in writing: first impressions are sometimes deceptive. For example, are you sure that the poet had no special intention for this *ah?* How do you know that the poet didn't want to depict, for example, how people speak when they're half-asleep—you know Olga just woke up. For such an intention—did he die? ah! I shall die—this ah! is wonderful: this line really yawns:

> The *Turk* was defeated without a battle
> And to the fatherland with wreaths—
> *With songs*—

The Turk, with songs.[3] For light verses—it's heavy, but this is small change:

The host was walking
To the ringing of bells—

But that's already not small change. It would seem that here one needs to combine poetry with logic, a syllable with grammar, although this is quite difficult for poets. But what can you do with readers? One asks, "Whenever did our armies enter cities *to the ringing of bells?*" "But if they did," says another, "then correctly it wouldn't be *to the ringing,* but *with ringing,*[4] for *to go to the ringing* or *with ringing* has the same difference as to go *to* the music or *with* music." "And so, the host marched to the ringing of the bells!" cries the third one, laughing.—Stop, tireless readers!.. What sort of great misfortune is that? It's a small mistake against logic and grammar! However, I see that if I am to listen to the judgments of such severe readers, then they will begin to take almost every couplet apart, crying out on behalf of the insult [done to] grammar or logic, taste or hearing. I won't listen to them—let them say what they want—I shall start to read alone:

Wives, children call to them
For the journey: hello! praise God!

Though truly *they call for the journey*[5] is not good, *they call: hello! praise God!* isn't said in Russian. "The Creator is a helper to everything"[6] violates grammar.

Ah, my dear, *all has disappeared!*
. . . .
Ah, my dear, *all is empty!*[7]

This is simplicity, but not poetic. *Listen, daughter!* is a very natural expression, but you might think that the mother wants to wound the daughter.

. . . in the distant Ukraine
If he isn't honoring his vows,
Your bridegroom has already
Circled the marriage *altar* with another,
. . . .
Here one must quit the *world.*

Such lines:

Although Varangian-Russian,
are really a little hard![8]

They insult sound, taste and reason. In the *Messenger of Europe,* in order to get married he walks around a *lectern,* but in *Son of the Fatherland,* an *altar.* The poet falls out of the frying pan and into the fire. We have no lectern known as a marriage lectern, but there is a funeral lectern, and we walk around the altar only during a procession. Besides, on the lips of a simple woman what does this fanciful expression mean: *the bridegroom walked around the marriage altar with another?* Isn't there something like that *in Bürger?*

... Wie wenn der falsche Mann
Im fernen Ungerlande
Sich seines Glaubens abgethan
Zum neuen Ehebande.[9]

Perhaps the disloyal one,
In the foreign land of Hungary
Renounced his faith
For a new marriage. [Gnedich's trans.]

But as soon as I pronounce the name *Bürger,* the reader will pick up his copy: "What of it," he says, "in *Bürger* it's either simpler, or more pleasant, or stronger. For example, there in the fifth couplet—these lines are strong through their simplicity":

O Mutter! Mutter! hin ist hin!
Hun [sic] fahre Welt und alles hin!
Bey Gott ist kein Erbarmen![10]

Oh Mother, Mother! all is lost!
Now lose the world and everything:
God has no mercy. [Gnedich's trans.]

Aren't these the same lines?

Ah, my dear! all has disappeared;
The world has lost its joy,
God himself has offended me.

Verloren ist verloren
[Lost is lost.]

There is no hope, there is no trace of it!" [Gnedich's trans.]

"No! that's not right, not right, not right!" says the reader. But what's this?

Lead away from sin
A mind which isn't privy to her words!

Let's look at the original.

... geh' nicht ins Gericht
Mit deinem armen Kinde!
Sie weiss nicht was die Zunge schpricht [sic];
Behalt ihr nicht die Sünde.[11]

... don't judge
Your poor child:

> She doesn't know what her tongue is saying:
> Forgive her sin. [Gnedich's trans.]

"But what does *lead away from sin a mind not privy to her words* mean?" cries the malicious reader. Does the translator propose to say that freedom of translation lies in exchanging the senseless for that which has sense? Surely—but listen, dear readers! it's already been known for a long time that you gentlemen-judges are too severe toward others. "Yes, sir, severe, and we should be severe with those who have a mind and talent, but do not learn how to use them first, but undertake everything, write down what comes to their minds and print what they write." But have mercy; suddenly you want to collate light verse, ballads, with logic, with grammar, with taste, and finally you also want to collate, couplet by couplet, the translation with the original. But didn't you see in those first couplets, the translator isn't inferior to the original in a number of couplets. Isn't this really enough? But perhaps he didn't take responsibility for those parts where he is inferior in strength and seemliness. Let's be indulgent. Let's start looking for enjoyment in the lines of the translation.

And as a matter of fact several lines could be pleasant, but they are trifles: I am not afraid of *deaths,* but right after that death is *alone,* or:

> And *suddenly* someone gallops along the field,
> *Calls to her: I'm here,* my darling![12]

These incessant small mistakes against logic or grammar, against prosody ...

> Open up more quickly, *without noise;*
> Are you asleep, my dear, in *the dark?*

We say *in the darkness.*[13] But that's not the point: the tone of the verses is generally a bit coarse for a lover, and consequently for the reader. But what can be done? *Without noise, in the dark*—they burst out for the sake of the rhyme. Both I and my poet rhyme at random!

> The bride who talks about the bed and asks:
> Will your bride settle down in it?—

is the kind of bride who does not have a place either in the original or in the translation. *Mr. Zhukovsky* sensed this. *Olga got up and ff.* is lovely, but the lines:

> The rider and the maiden gallop.
> Like an arrow, *like a sling,* like a bird!

These lines would fly, but—alas!—slings do not fly. A sling is a rope or a belt which always remains in the hands of the person casting stones with it. Surely this boldness doesn't pass for one of the wonders of the ballad? But then one would have to allow that cannons fly.

> The steed runs, the earth shakes,
> Sparks beat up from under the hooves.

Two beautiful lines, but we find them in almost the same form in *Lyudmila:*

> The steed seethes, the earth shakes,
> Sparks spray from the hooves.
> I soon will ride as a corpse.
> Darling, are you afraid to sleep with a corpse?

He is riding, but asks whether she's afraid to sleep?!—The words: *svetik* [darling—folk poetry], *vplot'* [right up to], *skoro* [quickly and efficiently—conversational], *svoloch* [scum—vulgar] and others breathe simplicity; but doesn't this kind of simplicity conflict with taste? It's true that there are many tastes, but some say there isn't any at all:

Well! to hell with good taste and intelligence! just you write and good luck!

> Straining violently, the steed
> Galloped *at the stone fence;*
> With the crack of a whip the
> Hinges and lock suddenly fell from the *door.*

What's this? the steed galloped *at the fence,* and from what door did the hinges and lock fall? But, no! my meekness is overtaxed: this couplet is really at odds with logic. *Mr. Bürger!* explain how a horse can gallop *at a fence!*

> Rasch auf ein eisern Gitterthor
> Ging's mit verhängtem Zügel
> [Rapidly toward an iron-barred gate
> It went at full gallop]
>
> (The rider) quickly jumped on the
> Latticed iron door, after he dropped the bridle. [Gnedich's trans.]

But now the situation is explained. Now I see that it wasn't the horse, but our poet who flew at the fence; rhyme carried him there: fence [*zabor*], hinge [*zapor*]. Oh, rhyme!

"Stones *shine* in the rays of the moon" is ungrammatical; one says: *by the rays.*

> The head, eyes, hands, the whole
> Body grew stiff *on* the dear one.

The eyes and hands *on* the dear one. Again ungrammatical. Oh grammar! but you're a great tyrant for poets!

> The raven-hued steed reared on his hind legs,
> *He knocked* at the earth . . .
> And forever *disappeared from their eyes.*

From whóse eyes? The knight is already a skeleton; from Olga's eyes? But

> Olga, afraid, mindless
> Is immobile and silent.
> Here they are dancing over the corpse.

What's this? Again incomprehensibility! The poet loves to mystify the reader. Olga remained immobile, and they dance over her, over her corpse? Did she turn into a pillar of salt like Lot's wife, then? Mr. Bürger, is this really your fancy?

> Lenorens Herzen mit Beben
> Rang zwischen Tod und Leben
> [Lenore's heart with trembling
> Struggled between death and life]

> Lenore's heart struggled with trepidation
> Between life and death [Gnedich's trans.]

> Nun tanzen wohl bey Mondesglanz
> Rundum ...
> Die Geister...[14]

> And by the light of the moon danced
> Around her ...
> *Spirits* ... [Gnedich's trans.]

It's clear. Pardon me, Mr. *Bürger!* You're not guilty. As she's dying, Lenore does not become a pillar; *struggling,* as you say, between *life and death,* she certainly could fall and lie there.

> Here by the light of the moon
> *Infernal spirits* dance over the corpse
> And hum in a drawling manner:
> . . . .
> Don't go to God's judgment seditiously
> . . . .
> May God forgive this sinful soul!

And here, finally, are the true marvels of the ballad! *Infernal spirits* are devils—for what else does *infernal spirits* mean? It's simple in *Bürger. Geister* are spirits and under the name of spirits we understand the souls of the dead. That's how Mr. *Zhukovsky* understood them.

> Suddenly a throng of *deceased* ones
> Stretched out of their graves.

But with *Olga's* translator, *c'est le diable qui prêche la morale*—the devils preach morality, the devils themselves pray to God to forgive the sinful soul. What kind devils he has! What fine devils he has found for his ballads! *Vivent les ballades!* And after this will anyone dare to attack them? And after this will they say to me that ballads don't have a moral goal? "Read *Olga*"—I'll cry out to each of them: in it even the devils preach morality!

Meanwhile—until I have need of these types of proofs—farewell, dear *Olga!* I won't bother you until then. But listen to some friendly advice: if you happen—and I don't wish it—to meet Lyudmila somewhere in Moscow or Petersburg, immediately abandon this malicious and proud rival: she will force you to blush, and what's worse—perhaps one of her lackeys will say to you:

> Why are you wailing out of place?
> Your song is incoherent and wild!

Farewell! My compliments.

St. Pete. region
town of Tentelevo

Translator's Notes

    1. *A Comedy against Comedy,* or *A Lesson for Ladies' Men* is a comedy by M. N. Zagoskin (1815), written in defense of A. A. Shakhovskoi's *A Lesson for Coquettes,* or *Lipetsk Waters.* (Note of the editors of the Russian text.)

    2. The publisher of *Son of the Fatherland* was obliged to note that this poem got to him about three months before that, but for some reasons it could not be printed earlier. [Gnedich's note.]

    3. The word to which Gnedich objects, Turk, is a singular form; he would have preferred the plural. This singular form does appear in formal eighteenth-century odes. He also objects to Katenin's use of a contraction, i.e., *pesn'mi* for pesnyami, a usage really no worse than the conventional poetic contraction "o'er" for "over" in English.

    4. Here Gnedich is upset about the way Katenin uses prepositions. He prefers "with ringing" *pri zvone* to Katenin's *pod zvon,* "to the ringing." In effect, Gnedich's version implies the ringing is background music to the event, while in Katenin's version, Gnedich says, it would seem that the army is walking in step to the music.

    5. Gnedich says this is simply wrong. It seems as if they are calling out to the road rather than to the men on their way in.

    6. Gnedich probably would have preferred the form of the word *ves'* (all) in the plural, where the meaning can change to everyone, i.e., not *k vsemu,* but *vsem* or *vsekh.*

    7. He thinks that "everything (all) has vanished from sight" (*vse propalo*) and "completely empty" are forms of speech of simpletons, or at least, uneducated people. But you also read these as "all is lost" and "everything is deserted."

    8. Free citation from Batyushkov's satire, "Apparition on the Shores of Lethe"—"Although their lines are a little hard,/They are sincerely Varangian-Russian." (Note of editors of Russian text.)

    9. ... As if the false man/In distant Hungary/Has given up his faith/For a new bond of marriage.[Literal trans.]

    10. Oh, Mother! Mother! Gone is gone!/May the world and everything pass away! With God there is no mercy! [Literal trans.]

    11. ... don't go to judgment/With your poor child!/She knows not what the tongue speaks/Don't keep the sin for her. [Literal trans.]

    12. Gnedich objects to the use of "suddenly" with an imperfective verb (*skachet*—he gallops), which in Russian implies duration rather than sudden action.

    13. Gnedich wants *v pot'makh* instead of Katenin's *v pot'me,* which does not exist. Katenin uses a singular form where only a plural one exists for his rhyme. There would be no difference in the meaning; in the translation I simply used "in the dark" and "in the darkness" to show some contrast.

    14. Now probably the spirits dance/round and round .../in the moonglow ... [Literal trans.]

A. S. GRIBOEDOV

Concerning the Analysis of the Translation of Bürger's Ballad, *Lenore*
Inignitas partis adversea justum bellum ingerit[1]

I read the ballad *Olga* in the *Son of the Fatherland,* and also the criticism of it, about which I have made my observations. Mr. Reviewer didn't like *Olga:* that is still not a misfortune, but he finds in it incessant mistakes against grammar and logic—this is very important provided it is just; I doubt whether it really is so; impudence carries me along further: I'll look at what kind of man of logic and literacy is the author of the review himself!

He says that *V. Zhukovsky* writes ballads as do others; consequently these others are either his imitators or his enviers. That's a little example of Mr. Reviewer's logic. Perhaps others will approve of the insulting character of his conclusions, but then what happens in literary life? Mr. Reviewer reads a new poem; it is not written as he would like; because of this he rebukes the author just as he pleases, calls him an envier and publishes this in a journal and does not sign his own name. All of this is very common and doesn't surprise anyone anymore.

The reviewer's grammar is his own, new and related to his logic; it[the grammar] in no way allows that

> To the ringing of the bells
> The host went to rest from all labor.

To enter a town *to* the sound of bells, to dance *to* music—this is said and written and confirmed by constant usage; but Mr. Reviewer doesn't like it: so, it is grammatically incorrect.

Meanwhile let's respect the whims of the reviewer, let's look at everything he doesn't like in order.

First he doesn't like ballads and repeats that in a certain comedy, "only the beauties of poetry could until now excuse in this type of work the strange selection of subjects." Strange selection of subjects, i.e., the marvelous, which permeates ballads—I confess, in my ignorance: I did not know until now that the marvelous in poetry needs pardon.

By the way, in *Olga* Mr. Reviewer doesn't like the expression *early in the morning*; he assigns it to prose: for poetry there are words much more flowery.[2]

Also the exclamation *ah!* when it bursts from the soul in these lines is not to his liking: "Did my beloved sweetheart betray me?/Did he die, ah! I shall die."

Then there's the stanza in which the return of the victorious army to the fatherland is described in such a lively manner:

> The Swedes fell in battle,
> The Turk was beaten without a fight,
> And the desired fruit of victory—
> Peace—was brought back to Russia;
> And to the sound of bells,
> With wreaths, songs, tambourines,
> And trumpets, the host returned to Russia
> To rest from all their labors.

The word *Turk,* which is often met in the model odes of Lomonosov and in the songs of the common people, is unbearable to Mr. Reviewer's fine ear, as is the contraction *with s'ngs* [songs]. This sorrow can possibly be alleviated, one need only drawl the word; but then one should drawl the entire poem; the brevity, through which the description is made so lively, would disappear; and that is what Mr. Reviewer needs: his long review proves that he does not attack through brevity.

Further on he deigns to amuse himself over the expression *Listen, daughter*—"You would think," he remarks, "that the mother wants to wrong the daughter." I submit, and certainly I'm not alone in this, that the mother simply wants to talk with the daughter.

Mr. Reviewer also doesn't like the lines:

> ... in the distant Ukraine,
> If he did not honor his vow,
> Your fiancé has already circled
> The nuptial lectern with another.

He finds that his prose is much better:

> Perhaps the unfaithful one
> In strange Hungarian lands
> Renounced his own faith
> For a new marriage.

This is the way he translates Bürger; meanwhile it's not at all obvious why this is good when the Russian verses are bad. Besides, Mr. Reviewer in no way wants the lectern to be a nuptial lectern. But from time to time he is even more capricious: in one place the epithet *tearful* seems to him to be too dry, and in another place the tone of the corpse seems to be too coarse. However I also agree with him in this; the poet is wrong, in our tearful age, even a corpse should speak in a romantic language. *Nous avons tout changé, nous faisons maintenant la médécine* [sic] *d'une méthode toute nouvelle.*[3]

This is how the lover corpse talks with Olga in the ballad:

> "We gallop in the fields only at night.
> I came for you from the Ukraine;
> I left there late
> To take you with me."
> "Ah, come in, my darling!
> A cold wind whistles in the fields;
> You will warm yourself, my bridegroom,
> Here in my embraces!"
>
> * * *
>
> "Let it whistle, let it heave,
> Let it do what it wants, it's time for us to go.
> My raven-hued steed is seething for flight,
> I must not await the morning here.
> Get up, come on, sit behind me,
> My raven-hued steed will take us there in no time;

We still have a hundred versts to go: it's time
To be off to our nuptial couch."

                      * * *

"How do you live? tell me honestly;
What is your house like? big? tall?"
"My house is a dug-out." "How is it inside?" "Crowded."
"And our bed?" "It's made of six boards."
"Will your bride be able to settle down in it?"
"There's enough room for the two of us."

The line "will your bride be able to settle down in it?" forced the reviewer to lower his eyes shyly; but in the darkness of night, when love's shyness usually disappears, should Olga not have asked such a question of her lover, with whom she is ready to share the marriage bed?— What should she do? Give herself up to meager dreams of ideal love? May God be with them, the dreamers; now whatever book you look into, whatever you read, song or epistle, dreams are everywhere, but of nature not a hair, and

Olga got up, went out and sat
Behind her groom on the horse;
She wrapped her white arms
All around his body.
The rider and the maiden rush along,
Like an arrow, like a sling, like a bird;
The steed runs, the earth shakes,
Sparks beat out from under its hooves.

It was beyond our expectations, but Mr. Reviewer liked this beautiful stanza; he only notices that the poet gave the word *sling* a meaning he considers unusual;—finally, after having written 17 pages, he has come to a fair observation. I will only say that the word *sling*, in the meaning that it has in *Olga*, can also be found in a certain place in *Zhukovsky*.

From the striking of cudgels, from the whistles of slings,
A tremulous din is heard from afar.

Zhukovsky, *Poems*, vol. I, p. 107

Then Mr. Reviewer, from having nothing to do, offers a few questions to be answered; from having nothing to do, I say, since he could very easily answer them himself, e.g., in the lines:

Violently straining, the steed
Galloped at the stone fence;
With the crack of a whip
The hinges and lock suddenly fell from the door.

The reviewer asks: from whose view?—Such questions force one to doubt whether it is really a Russian who asks them. He sent his review from the Tentelevo town of the St. Pete.

region; aren't colonists there? Perhaps he himself is a colonist? In that case I ask a hundred pardons. For an immigrant from a foreign German land, he really knows a lot of our language. But toward the end the reviewer gets extraordinarily merry. He doesn't like that

> Olga, frightened, mindless,
> Is immobile and quiet,

and he wants to drop her.—Yes, yes!—*For in Bürger,* he says, *she then could fall and lie there.* It's necessary to drop her without fail. Where did your shame disappear to, Mr. Reviewer?

But then there follows a remark which seems to the point. In the ballad the infernal spirits sing to the fallen Olga:

> "Don't go to God's judgment seditiously;
> Bear the sorrow, even if it pains the heart.
> You were punished in the flesh;
> May God forgive your sinful soul."

Precisely—hellish spirits would not plead to God to have mercy on a sinful soul, although it is that way in Bürger: however, the first three lines, in my opinion, resemble malicious reproaches, irony, much more than they do a sermon, in spite of Mr. Reviewer: but obviously it's my fate that I do not agree with him on anything. His judgments do not seem to be sound enough, but I have a small prejudice that he will probably laugh at: e.g., I think that a person who took upon himself the task of collating a Russian translation with the German original, should, by the way, know both languages well. Of course Mr. Reviewer considers this superfluous, for who well-versed in the Russian language would translate from the German:

> Rasch auf ein eisern Gitterthor
> Gings mit verhängtem Zugel.
> [Rapidly toward an iron-barred gate
> It went at full gallop]

as "he set out at full speed for the iron-latticed gates."

Some will translate this in such a fashion as Mr. Reviewer: "quickly to the iron-latticed door galloped (the rider), having lowered his bridle." In exactly the same way one could translate the French *ventre à terre* [at full speed] as *with his belly to the ground.*

In Bürger Lenore says: *Verloren ist verloren.*

But Olga in the Russian ballad [says]: "There is no hope, nothing is in sight."

The reviewer cries: *No! not right! not right! not right!* One must say, it's so, it's so, it's precisely so, it cannot be more simple or more correct, it cannot be any other way. But if you believe Mr. Reviewer, he himself would not be taking up arms against Olga, but his exacting, importunate readers surround him. They forced him to write this long criticism. I feel sorry for his readers; for isn't he maligning them?—Otherwise, why did he have to talk with them so suspiciously? *"What concerns me is that I truly would not have found anything to say against these verses, except that they do not touch my soul."* Such an incoherent answer does not satisfy anyone: with such persistent readers he should have acted more simply: he should have said to them once and for all: "My dear sirs, let's not discuss poetry, it is too wise a type of writing for us, but let's get down to the newspapers." The readers would have *dispersed,* and the useless and insulting criticism would not have filled 22 pages in the journal.

But no! Mr. Reviewer could not excuse himself: to judge obtusely, to scold—what innocent pleasure! How could he deny himself this? besides—to write in order to find one bad thing in any work is an easy victory: one needs to lay in a supply of paper, sit down and write until one is bored; one has enough—then finishes and out comes a review of the type which was written about Olga. Perhaps some won't believe me immediately; for these an experiment is the best proof:

I will take myself off to the town of Tenteleva and for a minute I will assume the mien of a reviewer, for a minute, and that certainly [I must do] because of my sins. All around me lie various compositions, both in verse and in prose; but as if by chance, *Lyudmila* has fallen into my hands. I read and then stop on the first line of the second couplet:

> Dust darkens the distance [*otdalen'e*].

One can say: Dusk darkens the distance [*dal', otdalennost'*], but that is too figurative; but *otdalen'e* means that an object is getting farther away: if one accepts that dusk darkens the distance [*otdalen'e*], then one would be able to say that it darkens the "moving away" [*udalen'e*] and the "nearing" [*priblizhenie*]. But this follows

> The military band glows—

Now I've guessed it: putting in the distance [*otdalén'e*] is used for the rhyme [band = *opolchén'e*, to rhyme with *otdalén'e*, C.R.]. Oh, rhyme . . .[4] Further:

> Where, then, Lyudmila, is your hero?

Much too pompous.

> Lyudmila, where is your happiness? [*radost'*]
> Ah! farewell *hope-sweetness.* [*sladost'*]

Hope-sweetness.—Once again for the sake of rhyme! One noun merges with another in order to strengthen its meaning, which is not necessarily contained in it. For example—maiden-beauty, lover-soldier, but hope is always sweetness. Further on the mother says to the daughter: "moaning will not raise the dead."

And the daughter replies:

> Don't invoke former days
> . . . . . .
> What's gone by is irrevocable
> . . . . . .
> Shall I recall the irrevocable?

It seems to me that they are saying the very same thing, but the intention of the poet is to force one to *state the case,* and [to force] the other [to say] that she is filled with despair. In general, how nice it is to take apart Lyudmila's words; almost all of them exude gentleness and humility; why then, it would seem, is she so severely punished? One would think that it's for her rash words; for near the end a choir of corpses howls at her:

> The murmuring of the corpses is rash,
> Your hour has tolled—etc.

But where is that horrible murmuring which draws the wrath of the Most High on her? The most God-fearing young girl will say the same thing when she hears of the death of her beloved. *The King of Heaven has forgotten us* is the strongest remark which bursts forth in her misfortune; but at the first sign of unhappiness, when she recognizes the corpse as her bridegroom, her first action is to thank God for him, and here are her words:

> Surely the King of Heaven has been *touched*
> By the anguish of a poor maiden!

Is this really the way it is in Bürger? I am opening up *Lenore.* Here is how she talks with her mother.

> O Mutter! Mutter, was mich brennt,
> Das lindert mir kein Sakrament,
> Kein Sakrament mag Leben
> Der Todten wieder geben.

> [Oh, Mother! Mother, that which consumes me,
> No sacrament can ease.
> No sacrament can give life
> To the dead again.]

Pardon me, Mr. Bürger, you are not guilty! But let's return to our Lyudmila. She grieved enough, cried enough, so, night falls.

> And the mirror of surging waters
> And the distant firmament of the heavens
> Are *enveloped* in a bright twilight.

One must not say envelopped [sic] [*oblechenny*] instead of enveloped [*oblecheny*][5]; this is a small grammar mistake. O grammar, you *are* the tyrant of poets! But hark! midnight tolls ... The corpse steals up to Lyudmila on tip-toe; of course, so that he doesn't frighten anyone.

> The knocker crashed down quietly,
> They said in a quiet whisper:
> All of her veins shivered,
> It was a familiar voice
> That spoke to her, his beloved,
> "Is my Lyudmila sleeping or not,
> Does she remember her darling, or has she forgotten," etc.

This dead man is too nice: a living person couldn't be more pleasant.

Then he suddenly recollects himself and ceases speaking in a human voice, but nevertheless says much that is superfluous, especially when you think that he was given a *short, short time* and that the *delay of a second is dreadful.*

> Let's *saddle* our horses,
> Let's *abandon* our dark cells.

Such lines:

> Although Varangian-Russian they are not,
> They really are a little flat.[6]

And they never say good-bye in a good poem.

> I started out late on my journey,
> You are mine—*be mine.*

Why is this last line dragged in?

The method the corpse uses to persuade Lyudmila to follow him is very original:

> Hark! the cries of the wilderness owl!
> . . . . . .
> Let's go, let's go . . .

It seems to me that the cry of owls is not alluring at all, but would have kept Lyudmila from this nocturnal trip. And this *hark!* is repeated too much:

> *Hark!* the cries of the wilderness owl!
> . . . . . .
> *Hark!* the midnight hour rings out!
> . . . . . .
> *Hark!* the rustling of the leaves in the woods!
> *Hark!* the whistling rings out in the backwoods!

One needs to use such exclamations much more cautiously; otherwise they lose their force. But in *Lyudmila* there are words which are repeated more than others. The corpse says:

> *You hear!* singing, people at the wedding
> *You hear!* the swift steed began to neigh.
> . . . . . .
> *You hear!* the horse gnaws the reins!

And Lyudmila answers:

> You hear? the bell is shrieking!

Finally when they have heard their fill of everything, Lyudmila's imaginary bridegroom declares to her that his home is a grave and the path to it is far away. After this I wouldn't have stayed with him even for a minute; but not everyone sees things the same way. Lyudmila grabs the corpse with a tender hand and darts away with him.

> Galloping, flying along the valleys—

On the way her companion grumbles through his teeth that he is a corpse and that:

> Their path leads to his sepulchral cell.

This absurdity has already been noted by the reviewer of *Olga*. And then what? Surely Lyudmila cried out and fainted from terror? She answers quietly:

> Why speak of the dead? Why speak of the grave?
> *The home of the dead is the womb of the earth.*

However, Lyudmila is gay enough along the way: she is greeted by pleasant shades who

> In a light bright round dance
> Wind about in an ethereal chain.

And around her

> Sing ethereal bodies,
> As if in the leaves of vine flowers
> A light breeze were beating,
> As if a little brook were flowing.

Then the corpse goes astray, using the tone of an Arcadian shepherd as he says to his horse:

> I feel the *little morning breeze.*

But let Lyudmila rush to her doom; we won't follow her any farther.

So as not to bore myself or my reader, I am casting off my mask of a captious reviewer and, in conclusion, will say a couple of words about criticism in general. If one investigates a work in order to determine whether it is good, average or bad, one must first of all look for some beauty in it. If there is none, then it doesn't pay to write criticism; if there are beautiful things in it, then one must examine what kind they are; are there many or few of them? Only by pondering this can one determine the worth of the work. This is what the reviewer of *Olga* does not know, or does not want to know.

Son of the Fatherland, 1816, part 31, No. 30

Translator's Notes

1. Injustice of the opposing side calls for a just war. [Note of editors of Russian text.]

2. He is a totally irreconcilable enemy of simplicity; I don't know how the following lines, reeking of poetic simplicity, escaped from his criticism. [Griboedov's note. He quotes stanza 11 of *Olga*. C.R.]

3. "We have all changed, we cure now according to a completely new method" (from Molière's comedy, *A Doctor in Spite of Himself*). [Note of editors of Russian text.]

4. Readers should not be misled by these sharp remarks: They are done only in imitation of the review of *Olga*. [Griboedov's note.]

5. Griboedov parodies Gnedich here. The word in question (*oblechenny*) is a past passive participle which Zhukovsky uses as a predicate adjective. Normally in that usage the participle should have a short adjectival form. Zhukovsky does use a short form, but not one that is totally correct. Instead of spelling the word with one "n," he spells it with two.

6. Rephrasing of those very same two lines from "Apparitions of Lethe's Shores," by Batyushkov, which Gnedich quoted in his article. [Note of editors of Russian text.]

E. A. BARATYNSKY

About Delusions and Truth

What do we call delusion? What do we call truth? I do not speak about historical, mathematical or moral truths; no, I speak about fleeting observations of reason based on opinions which we honor as true and which lead us, one way or another, to accept impressions of objects surrounding us. I ask: why do we call certain impressions, or thoughts born of them, true, but others false?

If on a beautiful evening, watching the setting sun with its last rays gilding the green hills, full of the quiet peace of drowsy nature, I exclaim in a moment of ecstasy: how majestic, how beautiful is creation!—no one would think of calling the feeling which compelled me to express myself in such a way a delusion.—A child chases a butterfly, and after he catches it, cries out: how beautiful is the butterfly! how happy I am that I caught it!—We speak with a feeling of personal superiority: a charming age! A butterfly makes up your happiness; but a time will come when this delusion will disappear!

Why delusion? perhaps because it is a passing thing? But what in the world is not a passing thing? Nature in its entirety does not exist for a child; for him, only a butterfly exists in it; nature delights us, but for us, the butterfly no longer exists. Have we gained a lot in deception? and who guarantees that we see more clearly now than we did before?

They call youth a time of blindess and delusion; autocratic old age is good at defining it in such a way: "Youths," the grumblers say to us, "passions blind you; your daydreams beautify all subjects; imagination uses flowers to cover up the abyss which is ready to open up under your footsteps; but live as long as I have and you will see truth without its cover."

"Granny," I would answer her: "your lessons would have vexed me at another time, but today I'm not in the mood to get angry and I advise you to get out of the habit of your grumpy grumbling. But listen: your eyes are growing weak, but you want to see better than I do! because the years, which have deprived you of sight, have thrown a gloomy pall on all things that surround you, why should I believe that they, as a matter of fact, are covered in fog! Because your imagination has died, why should I call the flowers I see by the light of my imagination daydreams! I cannot doubt their existence because I do see them, but I see them because I have good vision. You are deprived of eyes and of the senses; take mine, my dear, and you will sense the frivolity of your conclusions."

"When I was your age, I thought as you do," the old lady answered me: "experience destroyed my castles in the air; the years may take away my eyes, but they make reason sharp-sighted."

I don't know what you understand by the word, reason. I think that it is nothing other than that sense which, because of notions I acquire through various impressions, forces me to see objects in the very order in which I see them at that minute. And could I see them any other way? Could I separate myself from the dreams and passions which make up an essential part of my very being? You speak to me about experience; but I still don't know what experience is. It will either add something to my being or will destroy some part of it: in both cases I will cease to be myself—only I shall change, the objects will not change. And why should I exchange my dreams for your reason?—You said in some book: judge a man by his actions—shouldn't you then also say: judge the rules of their consequences? Judge then, my dear: you are sad, but I am gay; you are suspicious, but I am trusting; you grow angry and cough, but I laugh and sing a humorous song; I am more intelligent because I am happier.

But there was a time when you built castles out of cards, when you amused yourself with a wax doll, when you fitted out paper boats: toys have already turned simply into toys for you; and soon your daydreams will be only daydreams for you.

I don't argue! But in time I will die too—there is a limit to everything; but castles of marble didn't turn into ones made of cards, nor did boats made of wood turn into ones made of paper: I alone lost a feeling which either deceived me or made me see better; at least the pleasures were true.

You inadvertently agreed that there are objects which exist only for the imagination; consequently they are made of dreams.

Made of dreams because they exist only for the imagination! A playful conclusion! Why trust one feeling more than another? Sounds exist only for hearing; consequently, sounds don't exist! Does nature really do anything without a goal? Imagination is a property itself, just like all other properties. You will say that experience destroys its phantoms. I agree, but a little later we lose sight, hearing, and sometimes, the mind. But isn't losing the physical ability to see really all the same as losing the metaphysical ability to imagine? You say that my dreams deceive me; I have the right, then, to say that your speculations deceive you. Listen: childhood amuses itself with toys, youth amuses itself with dreams, old age amusingly prides itself on its imaginary wisdom, but each plays with a toy peculiar to itself.

I have moved a little away from my subject; at least we saw that it is impossible to force a person to change his thoughts, after not having forced him to change himself, i.e., to lose something or gain something. It remains to define the following: exactly in which cases do we gain and in which do we lose. I do not assert anything and so will only ask a few questions.

What do you consider the truest path to the searching out of truth to be?—Reason and experience.—Agreed.—But let's suppose that you had only sorrowful experiences, that in childhood you depended on a willful tutor; that in youth your lover betrayed you, your friend betrayed you, hope betrayed you; that in old age you remained old and sad.—How would you describe life? For you childhood would be a time of slavery and impotence; youth—a time of rebellious dreams and senseless desires; old age—a triumphant time when truth appears and with a sneer puts out the light in the Chinese lantern of imagination.—In regard to yourself, you are completely right; on the other hand, in childhood, I knew nothing but joys: my kind mother was an indulgent tutor. Now I have merry, dear friends, devoted to me with their whole soul; perhaps I shall also have a dear and true female friend; I hope that my old age will be warmed with reminiscences about my former, diverse, full life; that in my declining years, love for the beautiful will still be preserved, although I will not feel it so vividly; that through my glasses I will still look with pleasure at rosy youth and that at times I will still amuse them with stories about old times. Let's suppose that's what my life will be like; isn't it true that, like you, using reason and experience, I shall make a conclusion completely opposite to yours? and won't we judge each in its turn sensibly?

If fickle youth destroys everything, charms everything with its brilliant imagination—does not grumbling old age darken everything too much with its cold distrustfulness? and is there a minute in life when we are completely immune from this or another bias?

In what instance do we gain and in which do we lose? If in any case there is such an abstract blessing which we call truth, then shouldn't truth be some superficial pleasure which can substitute for all of our former dreamlike, or better to say, inadequate pleasures? But we see the complete opposite. We lose when we become convinced of the authenticity of that which we have become accustomed to calling truth; we respect the axioms of experience and meanwhile often regret the charming delusions which made up our happiness.

Old age has only one advantage over youth: it occurs later; it is indifferent to everything because it has no passions; it sees all objects in the rough because it is incapable of seeing them in another way; it draws sad conclusions from everything because it is sad itself, and still not stripped of its ability to reflect, should form some kind of opinions for itself. But who will guarantee their impartiality?

We call old age a time of prudence and wisdom. But let's suppose then, that with all of its experience, it were the first period of our life and that manhood, youth, and finally, childhood would follow along after it. Feeling the new life pouring into his heart and the new, clear thoughts which little by little refresh his brain and smooth out the wrinkles on his brow, would the old man quite likely conclude that his being is starting to perfect itself? He hears the voice of glory and ambition, he flies to the field of battle, he hurries in counsel to his fellow citizens; he again becomes acquainted with his former dreams and thinks: I used reason to refute that which now I clearly understand with passions and imagination; I erred, but time reveals the truth.— And when the time of love arrives he sees a beautiful woman and is surprised that until now he hasn't noticed that women exist; he perceives in many objects that which he never perceived even a moment ago. He recalls his former prejudices and thinks: Madman! I wanted to understand with cold reason that which one can only understand with heart and with feeling: I clearly see my delusion. Finally, in childhood, setting free soap bubbles, he will say as he catches sight of an old man reading a book—a new inhabitant of the world: look, this is much more useful than your book.

You will find almost more logic in the conclusions of this eccentric going from old age to childhood than in the conclusions of an adolescent going from childhood to old age.

Therefore is there no truth? Who is telling you anything at all like that? But isn't truth something relative to the extreme? Doesn't each age, each minute of our life have its own truths peculiar to it alone? Don't the objects surrounding us also have the same thing to do with our reason that sun rays have to do with the inner layout of our eyes? Isn't it mad then to renounce a pleasant feeling only because others call it a delusion? Isn't it mad to call a person rash only because his acts seem rash to us? Isn't it strange to write a discourse about truth while you are proving that each of us has his own truths?

1820

W. K. KÜCHELBECKER

On the Trend of Our Poetry, Especially the Lyric, in the Past Decade

Deciding to talk about the trend of our poetry during the last decade, I foresee that there are not many whom I will greatly please, and that I will arm many against me. And I, just as much as many people, could go into raptures over the incredible successes of our literature. But a flatterer is always contemptible. As a son of the Fatherland, I set it as my duty to tell the truth boldly.

From Lomonosov to the last transformation of our poetry by Zhukovsky and his followers, there has been in our country, almost without interruption, a generation of lyric poets whose names have remained the heritage of posterity, whose works Russia should be proud of.[1] Lomonosov, Petrov, Derzhavin, Dmitriev, Derzhavin's companion and friend Kapnist, to a certain extent Bobrov, Vostokov, and at the end of the penultimate decade, a poet who deserves to occupy one of the first places of the Russian Parnassus, Prince Shikhmatov, are the leaders of this mighty family; in our time they have almost no successors. Among us the elegy and epistle have supplanted the ode. Let us examine the qualities of these three genres and try to define the degree of their poetic merit.

Power, freedom, inspiration are the three essential conditions for any poetry. In general, lyric poetry is nothing other than the extraordinary, i.e., the powerful, free, and inspired expression of the emotions of the writer himself. From this it follows that the more it is elevated above mundane events, above the base language of the rabble who do not know inspiration, the more excellent it is. All of the requirements which this definition presupposes are fully satisfied only by the *ode*—and therefore without doubt the ode occupies the first place in lyric poetry or, better said, it alone totally deserves the name lyric poetry. But the other genres of versified expression of one's own emotions either subordinate these emotions to narration—as does the hymn and even more so the ballad—and therefore they are a transition to epic poetry, or the insignificance of the subject itself lays chains on genius, smothers the fire of its inspiration. In the latter case these works are distinguished from prose only by the verse form, because just as much charm and euphony (the merits to which they are by necessity limited) can be found in rhetoric as in these genres. The ode soars, thunders, glitters; it enslaves the hearing and soul of the reader as it is carried away by elevated subjects, transmitting to the ages the great deeds of heroes and the Fatherland, soaring to an all-high throne, and making prophecies to a reverential people. In addition, the poet is unselfish in the ode. He is not made joyful by the insignificant events of his own life, he does not lament them; he prophesies the truth and judgment of Providence, he rejoices in the greatness of his native land, he casts lightning bolts at foes, he blesses the pious man of truth, curses the miscreant.

In the elegy—the modern and the ancient—the poet speaks about himself, about *his own* griefs and pleasures. The elegy almost never grows wings, it doesn't rejoice, it *has* to be quiet, smooth, considered; it *has* to, I say, because anyone who is made too ecstatically joyful by his own good fortune is ridiculous; and unrestrained sadness is frenzy, not poetry. The lot of the elegy is moderation, mediocrity (Horace's *aurea mediocritas*):[2]

> Son enthousiasme paisable
> N'a point ces tragiques fureurs;
> De sa veine féconde et pure

Coulent avec nombre et mesure
Des ruisseaux de lait et de miel,
Et ce pusillanime Icare
Trahi par l'aile de Pindare
Ne retombe jamais du ciel![3]

It is only interesting when, like a beggar, it manages to gain sympathy by tears or entreaties, or when the freshness, the playful variety of colors which it scatters on its subject makes one forget its insignificance for an instant. The last requirement is more or less satisfied by the elegies of the ancients and Goethe's elegies, which he called Roman; but our Grays[4] have almost never been tempted by this radiant southern genre of poetry.[5]

Our epistle is the same elegy, only in the most disadvantageous garb possible; or else it is a satirical flourish such as the satires of the wits of prosaic memory, Horace, Boileau, and Pope, or it is simply a letter in verse. It's difficult not to be bored when Ivan and Sidor croon to us about their misfortunes; it's even more difficult not to fall asleep rereading, as they occasionally tell each other in three hundred trimeters, that—glory to God!—they are in good health and that they are dreadfully sorry they haven't seen each other in such a long time! It's easier if at least the ardent writer instead of beginning:

Dear sir NN,

exclaims:

... sensitive singer,
You (and I) are destined for the crown
of immortality!

and then limits himself to the announcement that he is reading du Marsay,[6] studying the alphabet and logic, that he never writes either *semo* or *ovamo*[7] and he desires to be clear! It's easier on the spirit—I say—if he doesn't top that off by supplying us with a detailed description of his pantry or library or Schwabian geese or his friend's Russian ducks.

Now I ask: have we gained by replacing the ode with the elegy and epistle?

Zhukovsky was the first of us to start imitating the *modern* Germans, primarily Schiller. Contemporaneously with him, Batyushkov took two pygmies of French literature—Parny and Millevoye—as models. For a while Zhukovsky and Batyushkov became the leading figures among our poets, especially the school which nowadays is passed off as romantic.

But what is romantic poetry?

It was born in Provence and it educated Dante, who gave it life, power, and boldness; he bravely threw off the yoke of slavish imitation of the Romans, who themselves were only imitators of the Greeks, and he decided to do battle with them. Subsequently in Europe they began to call any free and national poetry "romantic." Does romantic poetry, in this sense, exist among the Germans?

Excepting Goethe, and he only in very few of his works, they were always, in every case, students of the French, Romans, Greeks, English, and finally the Italians and Spanish. What is the echo of their works? What is our romanticism?

Let us not, however, be unjust. Given the total ignorance of ancient languages which, to our shame, is a distinguishing feature of almost all Russian writers who have talent, a knowledge of German literature is indubitably not without use for us. Thus, for example, we are obliged to its influence that now we don't write just in Alexandrines and iambic and trochaic tetrameter.

By their study of nature, their power, their abundance and variety of emotions, tableaux, language, and ideas, by the nationalism of their works, the great poets of Greece, the East, Britain, have ineffaceably chiseled their names into the rolls of immortality. Can it be we dare hope that on the road which we are now traveling we compare with them? No one (except our common translators) translates translators. An imitator does not know inspiration: he does not speak from the depth of his soul, he forces himself to retell other people's ideas and feelings. Power?—Where will we find it in our turbid, vague, effeminate, colorless works? Among us everything is *dream* and *vision,* everything is *imagined* and *seems* or *appears to be,* everything is *just as if, somehow, something or other, something.* Richness and variety?—Having read any elegy of Zhukovsky, Pushkin, or Baratynsky you know everything. We haven't had any feelings for a long time; the feeling of dejection has swallowed up all the others. We all lament to each other about our lost youth; we chew and re-chew this melancholy to infinity and we incessantly flaunt our faintheartedness in periodical publications. If this grief were not simply a rhetorical figure, someone—judging from our Childe Harolds—might think that in our Russia poets are born already old men. The tableaux are the same everywhere: The *moon* which, of course, is *dejected* and *pale,* cliffs and oak groves where they never existed, a forest beyond which the setting sun and dusk has been described a hundred times; sometimes long shadows and ghosts, something or other invisible, something or other unknown, banal allegories, colorless, tasteless personifications of *Labor, Sweet Bliss, Tranquillity, Gaiety, Sadness,* the *Laziness* of the writer and the *Boredom* of the reader, but especially, *fog:* fogs over the waters, fogs over the pine grove, fogs over the fields, fog in the writer's head.

From the rich, powerful, Russian vocabulary they are trying to extract a small, fastidious, cloying, artificially meagre language adapted *for a few, un petit jargon de coterie.* They mercilessly purge it of all Slavic expressions and turns of speech, and they enrich it with *architraves, columns, barons, mournings,* Germanisms, Gallicisms, and barbarisms. Even in prose they try to replace participles and verbal adverbs with an infinity of pronouns and conjunctions. About ideas there's nothing to be said. The stamp of nationality distinguishes about 80 lines of Zhukovsky's *Svetlana* and *Epistle to Voeykov,* a few minor poems by Katenin, and two or three passages in Pushkin's *Ruslan and Lyudmila.*

Freedom, invention, and novelty are the three main advantages of romantic poetry over the so-called classical poetry of the most recent Europeans. The fathers of this seeminly classical poetry were the Romans more than the Greeks. It abounds in versifiers—not *poets,* who are as rare as albinos in the physical world. In France this flaccid tribe dominated for a long time; the best, the true poets of that land, for example Racine, Corneille, Molière, in spite of their inner loathing, had to oblige them, subordinate themselves to their arbitrary rules, to dress in their ponderous *kaftans,* wear their huge powdered wigs, and not infrequently make sacrifices to the ugly idols which they called taste, Aristotle, and nature, bowing down, under these names, to nothing but finicality, decorum, and mediocrity. Then the worthless robbers of ancient treasures were able to vulgarize the best depictions, phrases, and ornaments of those treasures by means of frequent, cold repetition: the helmet and armor of Hercules crushed dwarfs who were not only able to rush into battle and strike hearts and souls, but were deprived of life, movement, and breath beneath their weight. Aren't our repetitions the same thing: *youth* and *joy, dejection* and *voluptuousness,* and those nameless, anonymous, obsolete gripes which even in Byron himself (*Childe Harold*), I hope, are far from worthy of Homer's Achilles, or Ariosto's

Orlando, or Tasso's Tancred, or the glorious Cervantes's knight of sad countenance, which are weak and underdrawn in Pushkin's "Prisoner" and elegies, which are unbearable, ridiculous under the pen of his *copyists*. —Let's be thankful to Zhukovsky for freeing us from the yoke of French literature and from the dominion of the laws of La Harpe's *Lycée* and Batteux's *Course*;[8] but let us not allow him or anyone else, even if he possessed ten times his talent, to place the chains of German or English sovereignty on us!

It is best to have a national literature. But isn't France obliged partly to Euripides and Sophocles for Racine? Working on the path of his great predecessors, a man with talent sometimes discovers spheres of new beauties and inspirations which had hidden from the eyes of these giants, his mentors. So if one is going to imitate, it isn't a bad idea to know which of these foreign writers is worth direct imitation. However, our live catalogers whose "looks," "critiques," and "discussions" one meets in *The Son of the Fatherland, The Emulator of Enlightenment and Philanthropy, The Well-Intentioned,* and *The Messenger of Europe* usually place on the same level: Greek literature—and Latin; English—and German; the great Goethe—and Schiller (who did not mature); the giant among giants Homer—and his pupil Virgil; the luxuriant, thunderous Pindar—and the prosaic versifier Horace; Racine, a worthy heir of the ancient tragedians—and Voltaire, who was alien to true peotry; the vast Shakespeare—and the monotonous Byron! There was a time when we blindly fell down before every Frenchman, Roman, or Greek sanctified by the pronouncement of La Harpe's *Lycée*. Nowadays we venerate any German or Englishman as soon as he is translated into French, for to this time the French have not stopped being our legislators; we have dared to peek at the works of their neighbors solely because *they* started to read them.

With more thoroughgoing basic knowledge and greater love of work on the part of our writers, Russia could, with its geographical position, assimilate all the treasures of the mind of Europe and Asia. Firdausi, Hafiz, Saadi, and Jami await Russian readers.[9]

But, I repeat, it is not enough to assimilate the treasures of other nations: may a truly Russian poetry be created for the glory of Russia, may Holy Russia be the foremost power of the universe in the moral world as well as the political one! The faith of our forefathers, national mores, chronicles, folk songs and legends are the best, the purest, the surest sources for our literature.

Let us hope that finally our writers, of whom a few young ones are especially endowed with real talent, will cast from themselves the shameful German chains and wish to be Russian. Here I have in mind particularly A. Pushkin, whose three poems, particularly the first, offer great hopes. I haven't hesititated to voice my opinion boldly about his shortcomings either, in spite of the fact that I am sure he will prefer this to the loud praises of the publisher of *The Northern Archive.* The public has little need of knowing that I am Pushkin's friend, but this friendship gives me the right to think that he, like his worthy comrade Baratynsky, will not doubt that no one in Russia is gladdened by their successes more than I!

I will answer the Sayids, who certainly will pronounce me a Zoilus and envious man everywhere they can, only when I find their attacks harmful for our country's literature, which is precious to my heart. I will gratefully receive the refutations of conscientious and enlightened opponents; I ask them to send these for publication in *Mnemosyne* and I announce in advance to each and all that I will gladly change my favorite opinion for a better one. Truth is dearer to me than anything in the world!

Mnemosyne, 1824

Translator's Notes

1. V. P. Petrov, S. Bobrov, A. K. Vostokov, V. Kapnist, and S. A. Shirinsky-Shikhmatov—ponderous, old-fashioned, neoclassical poets of the latter part of the eighteenth century and the beginning of the nineteenth century.

2. [Küchelbecker's note]: Voltaire said that all genres are good except the boring; he didn't say that all are equally good. But Boileau, the supreme, indisputable lawgiver in the eyes of the crowd of Russian and French Saint-Maurs and Aujers, declared: "Un sonnet sans défaut vaut seul un long poème!" However, there are barbarians in whose eyes just the boldness of undertaking the creation of an epos outweighs all possible sonnets, triolets, charades, and perhaps, ballads.

Saint Maur (Congrégation Benédictine de)—produced an *Histoire littéraire de la France* (1773-63). Probably Louis S.Auger (1772-1829)—a literary scholar and critic.

3. From Lamartine's ode *L'Enthousiasme (Méditations,* No. XII).

4. Thomas Gray's "Elegy Written in a Country Churchyard" was one of Zhukovsky's first translations.

5. [Küchelbecker's note]: Baron Delvig wrote several poems from which, *as far as I remember,* one could get a fairly accurate idea of the spirit of the ancient elegy. However, I don't know if they have been printed or not.

6. César du Marsay (1676-1756)—grammarian and rhetorician, author of *Traité des tropes.*

7. *Semo, ovamo*—Church Slavonic words meaning hither and thither.

8. Charles Batteux (1713-80)—French pedagogue and aesthetician, translator of Horace.

9. Firdausi, Hafiz, Saadi and Jami—classics of Tadzhik and Persian literature (10th, 14th, and 15th centuries).

P. A. VYAZEMSKY

In Place of a Foreword to The Fountain of Bakhchisarai

A Conversation between the Publisher and a Classicist from the Vyborg Side of Vasilev Island

Classicist: Is it true that young Pushkin is printing a third new poem, a poem, that is, in the romantic sense of the word—I don't know what to call it in our terms.

Publisher: Yes, he has sent *The Fountain of Bakhchisarai,* which is being printed here now.

Classicist: One cannot help regretting that he writes so much; he'll soon write himself out.

Publisher: Prophecies are confirmed by events; one needs time to check them; and meanwhile I will note that if he writes a lot in comparison to our poets, who write almost nothing, he writes little in comparison with his other European colleagues. Byron, Walter Scott, and a number of others write tirelessly and are read tirelessly.

Classicist: You expect to shut the mouths of the critics and their objections by exhibiting these two Britons! In vain! We are not of timid nature. It is impossible to judge a writer's talent by the predilection for him of the superstitious mass of readers. They are capricious, they often pay no attention to the most worthy writers.

Publisher: Isn't it with a most worthy writer that I have the honor to be speaking?

Classicist: An epigram is not an evaluation. The point is that the time of true classical literature has passed in our country . . .

Publisher: And I thought that it hadn't started . . .

Classicist: That nowadays some kind of new school has started up, unacknowledged by anyone except its own, which, not obeying any laws except its own whims, distorts the language of Lomonosov and writes randomly, showing off new expressions, new words . . .

Publisher: Taken from the *Dictionary of the Russian Academy* and to which the new poets have returned the right of citizenship in our language, a right stolen without trial for I don't know what crime; because up until now we have guided ourselves mainly by usage, which can be replaced by new usage. The laws of our language still haven't been codified, and how can one complain about the novelty of expressions? Will you order language and our poets to submit to Chinese immobility? Look at nature! Human faces, which are all made up of the same parts, are not all molded into one physiognomy, and the expression is the physiognomy of words.

Classicist: Well, at least let's not give Russian words a Geman physiognomy then. What do these forms, this spirit mean for us? Who introduced them?

Publisher: Lomonosov!

Classicist: Now that's amusing!

Publisher: What do you mean? Didn't he take a survey of German forms in the prosody which he introduced? Didn't he imitate contemporary Germans? I'll say more. Take the three celebrated poets in the history of our literature—you will find a German imprint on each of them. The epoch of reform made in Russian versification by Lomonosov, the epoch of reform in prose by Karamzin, the present movement, the romantic movement (against laws if you want to call it that)—don't these three clearly show the dominant propensity of our literature? Thus our poet-contemporaries follow the direction given by Lomonosov; the only difference is that he followed Guenther[1] and a few other of his contemporaries rather than Goethe and Schiller. And is it just among us that the German muses are spreading their dominion? Look in France too—a country which, at least in a literary regard, has hardly justified its vainglorious dreams of "universal hegemony"; even in France these kidnappers still receive some sovereignty and replace the local hereditary powers. The poets who are our contemporaries are no more sinful than their poet-predecessors.

We still don't have a Russian cult in literature. Perhaps because there isn't one now, there won't ever be one; but at least modern, so-called romantic poetry is no less native to us than the poetry of Lomonosov or Kheraskov, whom you strive to exhibit as classical. What is national in the *Petriada* and *Rossiada* except the names?

Classicist: What is nationalism[2] in literature? There is no such figure in the poetics of Aristotle or the poetics of Horace.

Publisher: There isn't in Horace's poetics, but there is in his works. It is in feelings, not rules. The imprint of nationalism, of the locale—perhaps it is that which is the most essential merit of the ancients and maintains their right to the attention of posterity. It was not in vain that among his sources in his universal history the profound Müller[3] noted Catullus and referred to him in characterizing that time.

Classicist: It seems you already want to recruit the ancient classics into the band of romantics. I suppose that both Homer and Virgil were romantics.

Publisher: Call them what you wish, but there is no doubt that Homer, Horace, and Aeschylus have much in common, more correlations with the leaders of the romantic school, than with their cold slavish followers who strive to be Greeks and Romans at a later date. Can it be that Homer created the *Iliad* foreseeing Aristotle and Longinus[4] and to please some kind of "classical conscience" which had not been invented yet? And allow me to ask both you and your elders whether it has been defined with exactitude what the "romantic type" is, what relation it has to the "classical," and how it contrasts with it. I confess, for myself at least, that no matter how much I have read about it, how much I have thought about it, neither in books nor in my mind have I yet happened to discover a complete, mathematically satisfactory solution of this problem. Many believe in the classical type because they have been ordered to, many do not acknowledge the romantic type because it doesn't have any legislators who bind one to unconditional and unquestioning faithfulness. They look at romanticism as capricious anarchism, a destroyer of decrees hallowed by antiquity and superstition. Schlegel[5] and Mme de Staël are not clothed in the armor of leaden pedantry, they don't exude the air of scholastic pomposity, and for some people their rules have no weight because they aren't embellished by pomposity; not all of us surrender to allurement and enthusiasm, many are enslaved only by authority. The "herd of imitators" of which Horace speaks[6] is not transferred from type to type. What acts on the minds of many pupils? A good pointer with which teachers pound intelligence into their listeners through the fingers. With what does a shepherd drive his herd along the travelling road? A firm staff. Our brothers love servility....

Classicist: You've calumniated me so much here that I haven't been able to give an appropriate rebuff to you with the following objection: the fact that its very name has no defined sense maintained by a general condition can serve as proof that there is no sense in the romantic school. You yourself acknowledge what classicism is, what it demands....

Publisher: Because its definition has been agreed upon, and there still hasn't been time to agree about romanticism. Its source is in nature; it *is*, it's in circulation; it still hasn't entered the hands of anatomists. Give it time! The hour will come when pedantry will put its leaden brand on romanticism's ethereal clothes, too. In some century, Byron, Thomas Moore will fall beneath the scalpels of experimenters, as Anacreon or Ovid have today, and the blooms of their bright and fresh poetry will grow lusterless from the office dust, from the fumes of the lamps of commentators, antiquarians, scholiasts—only if, let us add, in future centuries there are people who live on other people's intellects and who, like vampires, dig in coffins, gobble and chew dead people, not forgetting to bite living ones too . . . .

Classicist: Permit me, however, to remark to you in passing that your digressions are quite romantic. We had begun to talk about Pushkin; from him we were thrown into antiquity and now we've run ahead into future centuries.

Publisher: Sorry! I forgot that such campaigns are beyond the strength of your classicist brothers. You hold to the unities of time and place. For you the intellect is a stay-at-home. Excuse me, I'll settle down; what do you wish of me?

Classicist: I would like to know about the content of Pushkin's so-called poem. I confess that from the title I don't understand what can be suitable for a poem here. I understand that one can write stanzas, even an ode, *to a fountain.*

Publisher: Yes, all the more that Horace already has *The Fountain of Bandusia.*[7]

Classicist: However, the romantics have accustomed us to accidents. Their titles have an elastic quality. All you have to do is wish and it will embrace everything visible and invisible, or else it promises one thing and does something entirely different. But tell me . . . .

Publisher: A legend well-known in the Crimea even today serves as the basis for the poem. It is told that Khan Kerim-Girey abducted the beautiful Pototskaya and kept her in the Bakhchisarai harem; it is even supposed that he was married to her. This legend is dubious, and in his recently published *Journey in Tavrida,* Muravyov-Apostol attacks the probability of this story, rather soundly, it seems.[8] However that may be, the legend is in the province of poetry.

Classicist: So! In our time the muses have been turned into narrators of all kinds of cock-and-bull stories. Where is the merit of poetry if you feed it nothing but fairy-tales?

Publisher: History should not be credulous; poetry is the opposite. It often values that which the former rejects with scorn, and our poet did very well in assimilating the Bakhchisarai legend to poetry and enriching it with realistic fictions, and even better that he used both elements with perfect artistry. The local color is preserved in the narration with all possible vividness and freshness. There is an eastern stamp on the tableaux, in the emotions themselves, and in the style. In the opinion of judges whose verdict can be considred final in our literature, in the new work the poet showed signs of a talent which is maturing more and more.

Classicist: Who are these judges? We don't acknowledge any except *The Messenger of Europe* and *The Well-Intentioned,*[9] and that because we write in concert with them. Let's wait for what they say!

Publisher: Wait with God! And meantime I will say that Pushkin's story is lively and interesting. There is a lot of movement in the poem. Into a rather tight frame he has put action full not of a multitude of characters and a chain of different adventures, but of artistry—with which the poet was able to depict and add nuances to the main characters of his narration. *Action* depends, so to speak, on the *activity* of talent: style lends its wings or slows its motion with weights. The interest of the reader is maintained from beginning to end in Pushkin's work.—One cannot achieve this secret except with the allurement of style.

Classicist: Nevertheless I am certain that, according to the romantics' custom, all this action is only lightly marked out. In such cases the reader must be the author's apprentice, and finish saying things for him. Slight hints, hazy riddles—those are the materials prepared by the romantic poet, and then let the reader do what he wants with it. The romantic architect leaves the arrangement and structure of the building to the whimsy of each—a veritable castle in the air which has neither plan nor foundation.

Publisher: You aren't satisfied that you see a beautiful building before you; you demand that its frame be visible too. In works of art just the general action is enough; why the desire to see the private production too? A work of art is a deception. The less the prosaic connection between parts is manifested, the more profit in relation to the whole. Personal pronouns in speech retard its flow, make the story cold. Imagination and invention also have their "pronouns," from which talent tries to free itself by means of successful ellipses. Why say everything and press everything when we are dealing with people whose minds are sharp and active? And there's no reason to think about people whose minds are lazy and dull. This reminds me of one classical reader who simply didn't understand what had happened to the Circassian in *A Prisoner of the Caucasus* in the lines:

> And in the moonlit waters which had splashed
> A running circle disappears.

He rebuked the poet for not having made it easier for him by saying straightout and literally that the Circassian had thrown herself into the water and drowned. Let's leave prose to prose! The way it is, there's enough of it in everyday life and in the poems printed in *The Messenger of Europe*.

P.S. Here the classicist left me hurriedly and in anger, and I got the idea of putting the conversation we had had on paper. As I reread it, it occurred to me that I may be suspected of cunning—it will be said: "The publisher purposely concealed everything sensible that he could utter in defense of his opinion!" It's useless to justify oneself to mistrust; but let my accusers take on themselves the labor of rereading everything that has been said over and over in some of our journals about romantic works and about the latest generation of our poetry in general: if one excludes the crude personalities and vulgar jokes, everyone will doubtlessly and easily be convinced that my conversant is on a par with his journalistic minions.

1824

Translator's Notes

1. Johann Guenther (1695-1723)—German poet.
2. *Narodnost'*—Vyazemsky is usually given credit for introducing the concept of *narodnost'* (nationalism, nationality) into Russian literary criticism. In a letter to Alexander Turgenev (November 22, 1819), he discusses the matter, saying "Why not translate *nationalité* as *narodnost'*," adding that "the ending *ost'* is a fine pimp."
3. Johann Müller (1752-1809)—German historian.
4. Cassius Longinus (ca. A.D. 213-73)—rhetorician and philosopher. Best known for his commentaries on Homer.
5. August Schlegel (1767-1845)—both of the Schlegels and Madame de Staël influenced Russian romantic aestheticians.
6. In his *Epistula ad Pisones* (or, *Ars Poetica*).
7. *The Fountain of Bandusia*—Odes, Book IV.
8. Ivan M. Muravyov-Apostol—Pushkin appended part of his travel notes to *The Fountain of Bakhchisarai*.
9. A journal published in 1818-26 by A. E. Izmailov. In their private correspondence Pushkin and Vyazemsky made the title a phallic allusion.

K. F. RYLEEV

A Few Thoughts about Poetry

The argument about romantic and classical poetry has already occupied enlightened Europe for a long time, and not long ago it began among us too. Not only doesn't the heat with which this argument continues, grow cool with time—it keeps increasing. In spite of that, however, neither the romantics nor the classicists can boast of victory. It seems to me that the reason for this is that both sides (as it usually happens) argue more about words than about the substance of the matter, that they give too much importance to forms, and that in fact there is not classical or romantic poetry, but there was, is, and will be only one true self-sufficient poetry, the rules of which always were and will be the same.

Let's get down to business.

In the Middle Ages when the dawn of enlightenment was already beginning in Europe, a few learned men termed "classical," i.e., exemplary, the authors they chose for reading in classes and as models for their students. In this manner Homer, Sophocles, Virgil, Horace and other ancient poets were named classical poets. Teachers and students sincerely believed that only by blindly imitating the ancients both in form and in the spirit of their poetry could they achieve the height which they had achieved; and this unfortunate prejudice, which became general, was the reason for the insignificance of the works of the majority of the modern poets. The exemplary creations of the ancients, which should have served only as encouragement for the poets of our time, took the place of the very ideals of poetry for them. The imitators could never compare with the models, and besides that, they deprived themselves of their strength and originality; and if they did produce anything excellent, it was, so to speak, by chance; and in almost every case it happened when the subjects of their creations were taken from ancient history, primarily Greek, for here imitation of the ancient was replaced by a study of the spirit of the time, the enlightenment of the age, the human and geographical characteristics of the country where the event which the poet wished to present in his work took place. That is why *Mérope, Esther, Mithridate,* and a few other creations of Racine, Corneille, and Voltaire are excellent.[1] That is why all the creations of these or other poets, creations the subjects of which were borrowed from modern history and molded into the forms of the ancient drama, are almost always far from perfection.

Terming many ancient poets of unequal merit "classics," without differentiation, caused perceptible harm to modern poetry; and to this day it serves as one of the most important reasons for the confusion of our ideas about poetry in general and about poets in particular. We often put a poet of originality on the same level with an imitator: Homer with Virgil, Aeschylus with Voltaire. Having enmeshed ourselves in the chains of foreign opinions and used imitation to clip the wings of poetry's geniuses, we were drawn toward the goal which the ferule of Aristotle and his untalented followers had pointed out to us. Only the extraordinary power of genius occasionally forged a new path for itself, and flying around the goal which had been pointed out by the pedants, soared toward its own ideal. But when a few poets appeared who followed the inspiration of their own genius without imitating either the spirit or the forms of ancient poetry, and gave Europe their original works, it was necessary to distinguish classical poetry from modern—and the Germans called this latter poetry "romantic," instead of simply calling it "new." Dante, Tasso, Shakespeare, Ariosto, Calderón, Schiller, Goethe were termed romantics. To this we must add that the very name "romantic" is taken from the dialect in which the first original works of the troubadours appeared. These singers did not imitate the ancients, because then Greek had already been distorted by mixing with various barbaric languages; Latin had branched out, and the literatures of both had become dead for the peoples of Europe.

Thus original, distinctive poetry was called romantic poetry; and in this sense Homer, Aeschylus, Pindar—in a word all the best Greek poets—are romantics, just as the finest works of modern poets written by the rules of the ancients, but the subjects of which were not taken from ancient history, are basically romantic works, although neither the former nor the latter are acknowledged as such. Doesn't it follow from all that has been said above that neither romantic nor classical poetry exists? In its essence true poetry has always been the same, just as its rules have. It differs only in the essence and forms which are lent to it in different ages by the spirit of the time, the degree of enlightenment, and the location of the country where it appears.

In general, poetry may be divided into the ancient and the modern. This would be better grounded. Our poetry has more intellectual than material content; that's why we have more thoughts, the ancients have more tableaux; we have more of the general, they have more particulars. Modern poetry also has its subdivisions, depending on the ideas and spirit of the ages in which its geniuses appear. Such are Dante's *Divina commedia,* the wizardry in Tasso's poem, Milton, Klopstock with his elevated religious ideas, and finally in our time, the poems and tragedies of Schiller, Goethe, and especially Byron, in which the passions of men are depicted, their innermost motives, the eternal battle of the passions with a secret aspiration to something elevated, something infinite.

I said above that in general too much importance is ascribed to the forms of poetry. This is also an important reason for the confusion of the ideas of our time about poetry in general. Those who consider themselves classicists demand blind imitation of the ancients and assert that any deviation from their forms is an inexcusable error. For example, in a dramatic work the three unities are, for them, an indispensable law, the breaking of which cannot be justified by anything. Romantics, on the contrary, reject these conditions as restricting the freedom of genius, and consider unity of goal sufficient for drama. In this case there is basis for the romantics' view. The forms of the ancient drama are unsuitable for us, exactly as the forms of the ancient republics are. Pure democracy was convenient for Athens and Sparta and the other republics of the ancient world because all the citizens without exception could participate in it. And the form of their government was not purposely invented, not forcibly introduced; it stemmed from the nature of things; given the position in which civil societies were at that time it was essential. In exactly the same manner the three unities of Greek drama, in the works where they are encountered, were not purposely invented by the ancient poets; they were a natural result of the essence of the subjects of their works. Almost all the activities took place in one city and in one place then; this itself determined both the rapidity and the unity of action.

The populousness and vastness of modern nations, the degree to which their peoples are enlightened, the spirit of the time—in a word, all the physical and moral conditions of the modern world—determine a larger field both in politics and in poetry. For us the three unities no longer should or can be an indispensable law in the drama, because not one city, but an entire nation serves as the theater of our activities—and usually the beginning of the activity is in one place, its continuation in another, and a third sees its end. I don't at all want to say by this that we should banish the three unities from our drama. When the event which the poet wishes to present in his work flows effortlessly into the forms of the ancient drama, then of course the three unities are not only not superfluous, but occasionally even an essential condition.

Only it isn't necessary to distort an historical event purposely in order to observe the three unities, because in this case all probability is destroyed. Given the state of our civil societies, we retain complete freedom, depending on the nature of the subject, to observe the three unities or to content ourselves with one, i.e., the unity of the event or the goal. This frees us from the chains placed on poetry by Aristotle. Let us note, however, that this freedom, just like our civil freedom, places upon us duties more difficult than those which the three unities demanded from the ancients. It is more difficult to unite various events in one whole, so that they form a perfect drama and harmonize in their movement toward a goal, than to write a drama observing the three unities—given, of course, equally fruitful subjects.

Poetry is also harmed a great deal by the vain desire to set up a definition for it, and it seems to me that those who maintain that one should not define poetry in general are right. At least to this time no one has yet defined it in a satisfactory manner: all the definitions have either been specific ones—concerning the poetry of a certain age, a certain people, or a poet—or ones common to all verbal disciplines, like Ancillon's.[2]

The ideal of poetry, like the ideals of all other subjects which the human spirit strives to comprehend, is infinite and inaccessible; and therefore a definition of poetry is impossible and, it seems to me, useless. If it were possible to define what poetry is, then it would be possible to reach its highest summit; and if it were reached in any age, what would be left to future generations? Where would the *perpetuum mobile* be put?

The great labors and superb creations of some of the ancient and modern poets should inspire us with esteem for them, but not at all with piety, because this is contrary to the laws of the purest morality; it lowers the worth of man, and at the same time implants a kind of fear in him which prevents him from getting close to the exalted poet and even from seeing faults in that poet. Therefore, let us respect poetry and not its priests; and leaving the useless argument over romanticism and classicism, let us try to destroy the spirit of slavish imitation and, turning to the source of true poetry, let us employ all efforts to embody in our writings the ideals of elevated emotions, ideas, and eternal truths which are always close to man and always insufficiently well-known to him.

1825, *Son of the Fatherland*

Translator's Notes

1. Racine wrote *Mithridate* and *Esther*, Voltaire *Mérope*.
2. Johann P. Ancillon (1767-1837)—German writer, historian, and political figure. Ryleev had read a volume translated as *The Esthetic Opinions of Mr. Ancillon* (St. Petersburg, 1813). Ryleev included the following note in his article:

> In Ancillon's opinion "poetry is the power of expressing ideas by means of words; or the free power of representing, with the help of language, the infinite in finite and defined forms which in their harmonic activity will speak to the emotions, the imagination, and the judgment." But this definition also fits philosophy; it fits all areas of human knowledge which are expressed in words. Also, many (taking the teaching of modern German philosophy into account) say that the essence of "romantic" (in our terms, "old") poetry consists of the aspiration of the soul to perfection, which is unknown to it itself, but which is an essential aspiration for it—one which possesses every emotion of true poets of this kind. But isn't this the essence and philosophy of all the arts?

D. V. VENEVITINOV

A Critique of an Essay on *Eugene Onegin* Published in *The Telegraph*

If talent always finds the measure of its perceptions and its impressions in its own self, if its lot is to scorn the usual prejudices of the crowd (which is one-sided in its opinions) and to feel more vividly than others the creative power of those rare sons of nature on whom genius has put its mark, then what thought struck Pushkin when he read the essay about his new poem in *The Telegraph,* where he is presented not in comparison to himself, not in relation to his goal, but as a faithful comrade of Byron in the field of world literature, standing on the same spot with him?

The Moscow Telegraph has such a number of readers and such curious essays are found in it that any unjust opinion promulgated in it will certainly have an influence on the evaluations made by, if not all, at least many people. In such a case it is the obligation of every conscientious person to correct the errors of the editor and resist, as far as possible, the deluge of delusions. I am sure that Mr. Polevoi will not be offended by criticism written with this aim: in his soul he will admit that in the critique of *Onegin* his pen was perhaps guided partly by a desire to enrich his journal with the works of Pushkin (a desire which, incidentally, is praiseworthy and doubtless shared by all the readers of *The Telegraph*).

And can one fight the spirit of the times? It always remains unconquered, triumphing over all efforts, enclosing in its chains even the thoughts of those who not long before had sworn to be faithful fighters for objectivity!

Mr. Polevoi's first error, it seems to me, is that he intends to raise Pushkin's worth by excessively lowering the critics of our literature. This is an error against the most ordinary prudence, against the politics of getting along with people—which requires always assuming as much intellect as possible in others. It is difficult to fight with opponents whom you make talk without sense. I confess it is an unenviable victory. Let's listen to the critics invented in *The Telegraph:*

"What is Onegin," they ask, "what kind of poem is it that has chapters like books," etc.?

I don't think anyone has asked, nor probably will ask such a question; and so far no literary person except the editor of *The Telegraph* has tried to note the difference between *a poem and a book.*

The answer is worth the question.

"*Onegin,*" answers Pushkin's defender, "is a novel in verse, therefore it is permissible to use a division into chapters," etc.

If Mr. Polevoi permits himself this kind of conclusion, won't I be right in concluding, in the same way, the opposite and saying:

"*Onegin* is a novel in verse, *therefore* in verse it is not permissible to use a division into chapters." But our bold syllogisms prove nothing either in favor of *Onegin* or against it, and it's better to leave it to Mr. Pushkin to justify his work by the division which he has used.

Let us leave off the picayune criticism of each sentence. How can one avoid mistakes of this kind in an essay in which the author did not posit a *single* goal for himself, in which he discussed things without resting on *a single fundamental idea?* We are going to speak only of those errors which can spread false conceptions about Pushkin and about poetry in general.

Who denies Pushkin has *true talent?* Who has not been enraptured by his verses? Who will not admit that he has gifted our literature with fine works? But why always compare him to

Byron, to a poet who in spirit belongs not just to England, but to our time, who concentrated the aspiration of a whole era in his fiery soul, and who would forever remain in the chronicles of the human mind even if he could be effaced from the history of the special sphere of poetry?

All of Byron's works bear the imprint of one profound idea—an idea about man in his relation to the nature which surrounds him, in a struggle with himself, with the prejudices which have engraved themselves in his heart in contradiction to his feelings. It is said: there is little action in his poems. True—his aim is not the *narrative tale;* it is *the character of his heroes,* the *connection* between descriptions. He does not describe objects for the sake of the objects themselves, not to present a *series of tableaux,* but with the intention of expressing the impressions these have on the character whom he has put on stage. A truly poetic, creative idea.

Now, Mr. Editor of *The Telegraph,* I repeat your question, "What is *Onegin?*" You *know* him; you *love* him. So! But in your own words the hero of Pushkin's poem is a "prankster with wit, a flibbertigibbet with heart" and nothing more. Like you, I am judging just by one chapter, the first; perhaps we will both be mistaken and justify the caution of the experienced critic who, fearing his ideas would be cockeyed, did not wish to utter his judgment prematurely.

Now dear sir, allow me to ask: what is it you call the "new inventions of the Byrons and the Pushkins?" Modern poetry is proud of Byron, and in a few lines I have already tried to point out to you that the character of his works is truly new. We are not going to question his fame as an inventive person. The singer of *Ruslan and Lyudmila, A Prisoner of the Caucasus,* and so forth has the unquestionable endorsement of his fellow countrymen for having enriched Russian literature with beauties hitherto unknown to it; but I confess to you, and to our poet himself, that I do not see inventions in his works which, like Byron's ,"do honor to the century." The lyre of Albion has acquainted us with sounds entirely new to us. Of course no one could have written Pushkin's poems in the age of Louis XIV, but this does not prove that he is better. Many critics, says Mr. Polevoi, assert that *A Prisoner of the Caucasus* and *The Fountain of Bakhchisarai* are in general taken from Byron. We do not assert so definitely that our poet borrowed the structure of his poems, the character of the protagonists, the descriptions from Byron; but we will say only that Byron leaves deep impressions in his heart, ones which are expressed in all his works. I am speaking boldly about Pushkin, because among our poets he stands on a level where truth is not hard to swallow.

And Mr. Polevoi pays his due to current fashion. How can one not make a dig at Batteux in an article on literature?[1] But is it magnanimous to use the superiority of one's age to abase old Aristarchs? Isn't it better not to disturb the peace of the deceased? We all know that their worth is only relative; but if one is going to attack prejudices, isn't it more useful to harass them in the living? And who is free of them? In our time one does not judge poetry according to a book on poetics; one doesn't have an arbitrary number of rules according to which the levels of works of art are defined. True. But isn't an absence of rules for judgment a prejudice too? Aren't we forgetting that there should be a positive foundation in poetics, that every positive science borrows its strength from philosophy, that poetry too is inseparable from philosophy?

If from this point of view we cast a dispassionate look at the development of enlightenment among all nations (evaluating the literature of each as a whole by the level of philosophy of that age, as separate parts according to the relation of the ideas of each writer to contemporary concepts of philosophy), everything, it seems to me, will be cleared up. Aristotle will not lose his claims to profundity of thought, and we will not be surprised if the French, subordinating themselves to his rules, have no independent literature. Then we will judge the literature of modern times according to the right rules too: then the reason for romantic poetry will not consist of "an indefinite state of the heart."

We have seen how the editor of *The Telegraph* judges poetry; let's listen to him when he talks about art and music, comparing the artist to the poet.

"The sketches of Raphael show an artist capable of the great: it is his will to take up the brush, and the great will amaze your eyes; unless he himself wants to, no threats of a critic make him paint what others want." Further:

"In music there is a special type of work called the *capriccio*—and they exist in poetry. *Onegin* is one."

What! In Raphael's sketches you see only the capability of the great? Must he *take up* the brush and complete the painting to amaze you? Now I'm not surprised that Onegin pleases you as a *series of tableaux;* but it seems to me that the first merit of any artist is strength of thought, strength of feelings; and this strength is revealed in all the sketches of Raphael in which one can already see the size of the subject. The artist's ideal and of course, the coloring, which is essential for detailed expression of feeling, also function toward the beauty and harmony of the whole; but these only spread the main idea—which is always reflected in the character of the subjects and in their arrangement. And what kind of comparison is this of an epic poem to a painting and *Onegin* to a sketch?

"He doesn't wish to write what others wish and no threats of the critics will make him."

Do Raphael and Mr. Pushkin enjoy the exclusive right of not submitting to the will and threats of their critics? You yourself, Mr. Polevoi, will not renounce this right; and, for example, if you do not wish to agree with me about the mistakes I have noticed, surely threats will not force you to.

There is also a constant rule in the special genre of musical composition called the *capriccio*. The *capriccio,* like every musical work, must contain a complete idea, without which art cannot exist. "Such is Onegin?" I don't know and I repeat to you: we have no right to judge it until we have read the whole novel.

After all the noisy praise which the publisher of *the Telegraph* heaps on Pushkin, and which, incidentally, is perhaps more dangerous than "silent thundering," who would expect this in the same essay: "Pushkin stands in the same relation to the earlier writers of comic Russian poems as Byron stands to Pope."[2]

One musn't forget that on the preceding page Mr. Polevoi says that in our country "nothing at all bearable has been written in this genre."[3] We remind him of I. I. Dmitriev's "Fashionable Wife" and Bogdanovich's *Dushenka*.

A few words about the nationalism which the publisher of *The Telegraph* finds in the first chapter of *Onegin:* "We see what is our own," he says, "we hear our native sayings, we look at our own oddities—to which we were not always alien."[4] I don't know what there is that is national here except the names of Petersburg streets and restaurants. In France and in England, too, corks pop to the ceiling, devotees go to theaters and to balls. No, Mr. Publisher of *The Telegraph!* Attributing the superfluous to Pushkin means taking away that which truly belongs to him. In *Ruslan and Lyudmila* he proved to us that he can be a national poet.

To this point Mr. Polevoi has spoken decisively; he has defined the merit of the *future Onegin* without any difficulty. His review poured out of his pen by itself and, it seems, without the author's knowledge—but here is the keystone. His effusion stops: "Where is a reviewer of Pushkin's poems to find mistakes?" Dear sir! Sometimes a whole work can be one mistake; I am not saying this about *Onegin,* but only to assure you that mistakes too are defined only in relation to the whole. However, let us be just, even in the chapter of *Onegin* which has been printed, strict taste will perhaps note a few lines and digressions which are not completely consonant with the elegance of poetry—which is always noble, even in a joke. Concerning the expression you have called "imprecise," I am not agreed with everything. In poetry "the lyre sighs" is fine; "to waken a smile" is good and correct; one can hardly express one's idea more clearly.

It remains for me to point out to Mr. Polevoi that instead of making such decisive conclusions about the novel from the first chapter, which has something whole and complete only in one respect, i.e., as a picture of Petersburg life, it would have been better to dilate on the poet's conversation with the bookseller. In the poet's words one can see a soul which is free, ardent, capable of powerful efforts. I confess, I find more true poetry in this conversation than in *Onegin* itself.

I have tried to point out that poets do not fly without a goal and solely to spite the poetics, that poetry is not an indefinite fever of the mind but (like its subjects, humor, nature, and the human heart) has in itself its own permanent rules. Our attention has been turned now on the critique of the publishers of *The Telegraph,* now on *Onegin* itself. Now, what will I say in conclusion?

Of Mr. Polevoi's essay—that I would like to find in it criticism based more on positive rules, without which all judgments are shaky and inconsistent.

Of Mr. Pushkin's new novel—that it is a beautiful new flower in the field of our literature, that in it there is not a description in which one cannot see an artful brush guided by a lively, sportive imagination; there is hardly a line which does not bear the stamp of either playful wit or enchanting talent in the beauty of expression.

Son of the Fatherland, 1825

Translator's Notes

1. Polevoi makes fun of Batteux's formalistic listing of rules for the epic.

2. Polevoi complains that Russian comic poems are filled with dirty taverns, card players, and cachinnating drunkards. Pushkin is above this, and: "In general recent poets have discovered new aspects of work in this genre, aspects unknown to the old writers."

"*The Rape of the Lock* is monotonous, the poet just makes you laugh. But Byron doesn't just make you laugh, he goes much further. In the middle of a stanza he displays the heart of a man, his gaiety blends with dejection, his smile with a sneer; and Pushkin stands in the same relation to the earlier writers of comic Russian poems as Byron stands to Pope."—N. Polevoi, *The Moscow Telegraph,* No. 5, 1825.

3. Venevitinov's note: "Mr. Publisher of *The Telegraph!* Allow me, for the sake of clarity, to give the equation for the two aspects you have chosen in the accepted form. We will call the letter "X" the sum of all the unknown (in your opinion) Russian writers of comic poems, and we will say: Byron:Pope = Pushkin: X.

4. Polevoi writes: "The same philosopher says that national (*nationale*) literature takes from the imagination that which speaks most strongly to the mind and character of a nation [*narod,* people or nation], and Pushkin has expressed this nationalism, this harmony in the description of contemporary manners, in a masterful fashion. *Onegin* is not copied from the French or English; we see what is our own . . . ."

A. S. PUSHKIN

On Classical and Romantic Poetry

Our critics still have not agreed on a clear difference between the classical and the romantic. For the inconsistent conception of this subject we are obliged to the French journalists, who usually regard as romanticism everything which seems to them marked with the stamp of dreaminess and German idealism or based on the superstitions and legends of the simple folk: a most imprecise definition. A poem may manifest all these features and still belong to classicism.

If instead of the *form* of a poem we take as a basis only the *spirit* in which it is written we will never disentangle ourselves from definitions.[1] Of course, in its spirit J. B. Rousseau's hymn differs from Pindar's ode, Juvenal's satire from Horace's satire, *Jerusalem Delivered* from the *Aeneid;* however, they all belong to classicism.

We should regard as this type those poems the forms of which were known to the Greeks and Romans and models of which they left us; therefore, here belong: the epic, didactic poem, tragedy, comedy, ode, satire, epistle, heroic poem, eclogue, elegy, epigram, and fable.

But what kinds of poem should be regarded as romantic poetry?

Those which were not known to the ancients and those whose previous forms have changed or have been replaced by others. I do not consider it necessary to talk about the poetry of the Greeks and Romans: every educated European should have a sufficient understanding of the immortal works of majestic antiquity. Let us glance at the origin and gradual development of the poetry of the more modern peoples.

The western empire rapidly headed toward its collapse, and with it the sciences, literature, and the arts. Finally it fell; enlightenment was extinguished. Ignorance darkened a blood-imbrued Europe. Latin literature barely survived; in the dust of monastery archives monks scraped the verses of Lucretius and Virgil from the parchment and in their place wrote their chronicles and legends on it.

Poetry awakened under the sky of southern France—rhyme echoes in the romance language; this new decoration of verse, at first glance of so little significance, had important influence on the literature of modern peoples. The ear was delighted by the doubled accents of sounds; a difficulty overcome always brings us pleasure—that of loving the proportionality and harmony characteristic of human intellect. The troubadours played with rhyme, invented all possible alterations of verse for it, contrived the most difficult forms; the virelay, ballade, rondeau, sonnet, etc., came into being.

From this came an unavoidable strain in the manner of expression, a kind of affectation completely unknown to the ancients; a trifling wittiness replaced feeling, which cannot express itself in triolets. We find these unfortunate traces in the greatest geniuses of more modern times.

But the intellect is not satisfied with just toys of harmony; the imagination demands scenes and stories. The troubadours turned to new sources of inspiration; they glorified love and war, enlivened the folk legends—the lay, romance, and fabliau were born.

Church festivals and murky conceptions of the ancient tragedy gave rise to the composition of mystery plays (*mystères*). They were almost all written on one model and came under one code of rules, but unfortunately at that time there was no Aristotle to establish unalterable laws of mystery dramaturgy.

Two circumstances had a decisive influence on the spirit of European poetry: the attacks of the Moors and the crusades.

The Moors inspired it with the frenzy and tenderness of love, an attachment to the miraculous, and the luxurious eloquence of the East; knights imparted to it their piety and openheartedness, their concepts of heroism, and the freedom of morals in the field camps of Gottfried and Richard.

Such was the humble beginning of romantic poetry. If it had stopped with these experiments, the stern judgments of the French critics would be just; but its offshoots blossomed rapidly and sumptuously, and it manifests itself to us as a rival of the ancient muse.

Italy appropriated the epic for herself; half-African Spain took possession of the tragedy and novel; opposite the names of Dante, Ariosto, and Calderón, England proudly displayed the names of Spenser, Milton, and Shakespeare. In Germany (which is rather strange) a new, caustic, witty satire stood out, whose monument was left as Reineke Fuchs.

In France then poetry was still in its infancy: the best versifier of the time of Francis I

rima des triolets, fit fleurir la ballade.

Prose already had a strong preponderance: Montaigne and Rabelais were contemporaries of Marot.

In Italy and Spain folk poetry already existed prior to the appearance of her geniuses. They traveled along a road already paved: there were long poems before Ariosto's *Orlando;* there were tragedies before the creations of de Vega and Calderón.

In France enlightenment caught poetry in its childhood without any direction, without any strength. Educated minds of the age of Louis XIV rightly despised its insignificance and turned to ancient models. Boileau promulgated his Koran, and French literature bowed down to him. This pseudoclassical poetry, which was born in the anteroom and never got further than the drawing-room, could not disaccustom itself from a number of congenital habits; and in it we see all the romantic affectation enveloped in strict classical forms.

P.S. However, one should not think that no monuments of purely romantic poetry were left in France. The tales of La Fontaine and Voltaire and the latter's *Pucelle* carry its stamp on themselves. I am not talking about the multitudinous imitations of either of them (imitations which are for the most part mediocre: it is easier to surpass the geniuses in forgetting all decorum than in poetic merit).

1825, unpublished

On the Poem "The Demon"

I think the critic has erred.[2] Many are of the same opinion; some have even pointed out the person whom Pushkin supposedly wanted to depict in his strange poem. It would seem they are wrong; at least I see another, more moral, aim in "The Demon."

At the best time of life, the heart, which has not yet been made apathetic by experience, is susceptible to the beautiful. It is credulous and tender. Little by little the eternal contradictions of reality engender doubt in it—a tormenting feeling, but one of short duration. After destroying forever the best hopes and poetic dispositions of the soul, it disappears. The great Goethe has reason to call the eternal enemy of humanity *the negating spirit*. And didn't Pushkin want to personify this spirit *of negation or doubt* in his demon, and in a compact tableau he traced its distinguishing features and lamentable influence on the morality of our age.

1825, unpublished

An Objection to Küchelbecker's Essay in *Mnemosyne*

The essays "On the Tendency of Our Literature" and "A Conversation with Bulgarin" printed in *Mnemosyne* served as the basis for everything that has been said against romantic literature in the last two years.[3]

These essays were written by a learned and intelligent man. Right or wrong, he always requires and gives reasons for his way of thinking and evidence for his judgments—a rather rare thing in our literature.

No one has tried to refute him—either because everyone agreed with him, or because they didn't want to take on an apparently strong and experienced athlete.

In spite of this, many of his judgments are mistaken in all respects. He divides Russian poetry into the lyric and the epic. In the former he includes the works of our old poets, in the latter Zhukovsky and his followers.

Now let us suppose that this division is accurate and see how the critic defines the relative merit of the two types.

* * *

"For example, we . . . ."[4] We quote this opinion because it agrees entirely with our own.

What is power in poetry? Power of invention, structural plan, or style?

Freedom? In style, in structure? But what freedom is there in Lomonosov's style, and what plan can one demand in a triumphal ode?

Inspiration? This is the disposition of the soul to the most vivid perception of impressions, therefore to the rapid assimilation of ideas, which facilitates their explanation.

Inspiration is necessary in geometry just as it is in poetry. The critic confuses inspiration with rapture.

* * *

No, absolutely not: *rapture* precludes *tranquillity,* an essential condition of the beautiful. *Rapture* does not presuppose power of intellect arranging the parts in their relation to the whole. Rapture is discontinuous, inconstant; consequently it hasn't the power to produce truly great perfection (without which there is no lyric poetry).

Rapture is a tense state of nothing but the imagination. There can be inspiration without rapture, but rapture without inspiration does not exist.

Homer is immeasurably higher than Pindar; the ode, not to mention the elegy, stands among the lower levels of poems. Tragedy, comedy, and satire all require more creativity (*fantaisie*), imagination—masterful knowledge of nature—than does the ode.

But there is and can be no *plan* in an ode; the plan alone of the *Inferno* is the fruit of high genius. What plan is there in Pindar's Olympian odes, what plan is there in "The Waterfall,"

Derzhavin's best work?[5]

The *ode* precludes the constant work without which there is nothing truly great.

1825-26, unpublished

Evgeny Baratynsky's Poems, 1827

At last the collected poems of Baratynsky have been published; they were awaited so long and with such impatience. We hasten to use the opportunity to express our opinion about one of the first-rate poets and (perhaps) one who is still unwillingly given his due by his countrymen.

Baratynsky's first works attracted attention to him. With amazement connoisseurs saw extraordinary grace and maturity in his first efforts.

This precocious development of all poetic abilities perhaps depended on the circumstances, but it already predicted for us that which has now been executed by the poet in such a brilliant manner.

Baratynsky's first works were elegies and in this genre he is pre-eminent. Nowadays it has become fashionable to denigrate elegies, as people used to ridicule odes, but if the flaccid imitators of Lomonosov and Baratynsky are equally unbearable, it does not follow from this that the lyrical[6] and elegiac genres should be excluded from the ranked books of the poetic oligarchy.

And besides, the pure elegy barely exists in Russia. Among the ancients it was distinguished by a special prosody, but sometimes it got off into the idyll, sometimes it entered the tragedy, sometimes it took on a lyrical course (of which in modern times we see examples in Goethe).

1827, unpublished

On Byron's Dramas

English critics have disputed Lord Byron's dramatic talent. I think they are right. Byron, so original in *Childe Harold,* in *The Giaour,* and in *Don Juan,* becomes an imitator as soon as he enters the dramatic field: in *Manfred* he imitated *Faust,* replacing the commonfolk scenes and sabbaths with others which in his opinion were more noble; but *Faust* is the greatest creation of poetic spirit, it serves as the representative of modern poetry, exactly as the *Iliad* serves as a monument of classical antiquity.

In other tragedies Byron's model was, it would seem, Alfieri. *Cain* had only the form of a drama; actually its disconnected scenes and abstract discourses are related to the genre of sceptical poetry of *Childe Harold.* Byron threw a one-sided glance at the world and the nature of humanity, then turned away from them and plunged into himself. He presented us with a phantom of himself. He created himself a second time, now under the turban of a renegade, now in the cloak of a corsair, now as a giaour breathing his last under the schema, now, finally, wandering amid . . . . In the final analysis he comprehended, created, and depicted a single character (namely, his own); he connected everything except a few satirical sallies scattered through his works to this dark, powerful character who is so mysteriously captivating. But when he began to compose his tragedy, he doled out one of the component parts of this dark and strong figure to each character, and in this way he splintered his majestic creation into several petty and insignificant characters. Byron felt his error and subsequently took up *Faust* anew, imitating it in his *Deformed Transformed* (intending by this means to improve *le chef-d'oeuvre*).

1827, unpublished

On Poetic Style

In a mature literature there comes a time when, bored with monotonous works of art, with the limited sphere of an arbitrarily selective language, intelligent men turn to the fresh imagination of the common folk and to the strange colloquialism which had at first been scorned. Thus at one time in France, *blasé* society people, were enraptured by the muse of Vadé,[7] thus nowadays Wordsworth and Coleridge have enthralled the minds of many. But Vadé had neither imagination nor poetic feeling; his witty works contain nothing but gaiety expressed in the street language of peddlers and porters. The works of the English poets, in contrast, are filled with profound feelings and poetic thoughts expressed in the language of the honorable common man.[8] For us, praise God, this time has not yet arrived; the so-called language of the gods is still so new to us that we call anyone who can write ten iambic verses with rhymes a poet. Not only have we not yet thought of making poetic style approach noble simplicity—we try to make prose pompous too; we still do not understand poetry freed from the conventional embellishments of versifying. The experiments of Zhukovsky and Katenin[9] were unsuccessful, not in themselves, but in the reaction they produced. Few, extremely few, people understood the merit of the translations from Hebel,[10] and even fewer the force and originality of *The Murderer,* a ballad which can stand beside the best works of Bürger and Southey. What the murderer says when he turns to the moon, the sole witness of his malefaction:

> Look, look, you bald-headed . . .

a line filled with truly tragic force, just seemed ridiculous to hasty people who failed to consider that sometimes terror is expressed in laughter. The ghost scene in *Hamlet* is written entirely in a joking, even a low style; but one's hair stands on end from Hamlet's jokes.

1828, unpublished

A Conversation about Criticism

A. Have you read NN's criticism in the last number of *Galatea?*

B. No, I don't read Russian criticism.

A. In vain. Nothing else will give you a better idea of the state of our literature.

B. What! Do you really suppose journal criticism is the final judge of the works of our literature?

A. Not at all. But it gives an idea about the relations of our writers among themselves, about their greater or lesser degree of fame, and finally, about the opinions which dominate the public.

B. I don't need to read *The Telegraph* to know that Pushkin's poems are in fashion and that no one in our country understands romantic poetry. As for the relations of Mr. Raich and Mr. Polevoi, Mr. Kachenovsky and Mr. Bulgarin, that does not interest me in the least ....[11]

A. However, it is amusing.

B. You like fist fights?

A. Why not? Our boyars were amused by them. Derzhavin also sang of them![12] I like Prince Vyazemsky in a scrap with some literary carouser as much as Count Orlov in battle with a coachman. These are features of nationality.

B. You mentioned Prince Vyazemsky. Admit that he is the only one from higher literature who stoops to polemics.

A. If you please .... First say what it is you are calling higher literature ....

* * *

B. The public is rather indifferent to the successes of literature—true criticism does not interest it. Occasionally it looks at a fight between two journalists, listens in passing to the monologue of an irritated author—or shrugs its shoulders.

A. Have it your way; but I stop, look, and listen until the end, and applaud the one who has beaten his opponent. If I were the author myself, I would consider it meanness not to answer an attack—no matter what kind it might be. What is this aristocratic pride that allows every rogue from the street to fling dirt at you! Look at the English lord. He is ready to answer the polite challenge of a *gentleman* and shoot with Kuchenreiter pistols, or take off his coat and box at the crossroads with a coachman. That is real bravery. But both in literature and in society life we are too fastidious, too ladylike.

B. Our criticism has no wide circulation; probably the writers of the highest circle don't read Russian journals and don't know whether they are being praised or abused.

A. Excuse me. Pushkin reads every number of *The Messenger of Europe,* where he is abused, which means, in his energetic expression, "to overhear at the doors what is being said about him in the anteroom."

B. That's really curious!

A. At least it is very understandable curiosity!

B. Pushkin answers with epigrams, what more do you need?

A. But satire is not criticism—an epigram is not a refutation. I am worrying about the good of literature, not just my own pleasure. If all the writers who deserve the respect and confidence of the public took it upon themselves to direct public opinion, criticism would soon become what it is not. Wouldn't it be interesting, for example, to read Gnedich's opinion of romanticism or Krylov's about present-day elegiac poetry? Wouldn't it be pleasant to see Pushkin analyzing Khomyakov's tragedy?[13] These men are in close contact with each other and probably exchange comments with each other about new works. Why not make us, too, participants in their critical discussions?

1830, unpublished

Yury Miloslavsky, or, the Russians in 1612

In our time, by the term *novel* we mean an historical epoch developed in a fictional narrative. Walter Scott attracted a whole crowd of imitators. But how far they all are from the Scottish wonder-worker![14] Like Agrippa's[15] pupil, having summoned the demon of the past, they didn't know how to control it, and became victims of their own audacity. With a heavy supply of domestic habits, prejudices, and daily impressions, they themselves clamber over into the age into which they want to transport the reader. Under a *beret* topped with feathers you recognize a head combed by your barber; the starched tie of a present-day *dandy* shows through lace collars *à la* Henry IV. Gothic heroines brought up at Madame Campan's[16] and statesmen of the XVIth century read the *Times* and *Journal des débats*. How many incongruities, unnecessary trifles, important omissions! How much refinement! And, above all, how little life![17] However, these bland works are read in Europe. Is it, as Madame de Staël maintained, because people know only the history of their own time,[18] and therefore are incapable of noticing the absurdity of anachronisms in novels? Or because even a weak and inaccurate depiction of the past possesses inexplicable charm for an imagination which has been dulled by the monotonous mottle of the present, the quotidian?

Let us make haste to note that these reproaches are not made apropos of *Yury Miloslavsky*. Mr. Zagoskin really does transport us to 1612. Our good common folk, boyars, Cossacks, monks, brawling rascals—all of them are divined, all of them act and feel as they must have acted and felt during the troubled times of Minin[19] and Avraam Palitsyn.[20] How vivid, how interesting the scenes from ancient Russian life are! How much truth and good-hearted gaiety in the depiction of the characters Kirsha, Alexei Burnash, Fedka Khomyak, Pan Kopychinsky, papa Eremei! The events of the novel fit effortlessly into the very broad framework of historical events. The author does not hurry with his story, he pauses over details, and he looks to the side—but he never tires the reader's attention. The dialogue (lively and dramatic wherever it deals with the common folk) reveals a master of his craft. But the unquestionable talent of Mr. Zagoskin noticeably betrays him when he approaches historical characters. Minin's speech on the Nizhny-Novgorod square is weak; there are no bursts of the common folks' eloquence in it. The boyars' council is depicted coldly. Two or three small anachronisms and several oversights in the language and *costume* can also be noticed. [Here Pushkin gives several examples of linguistic errors and anachronisms. *Trans.*] But these minor oversights and others noted in No. 1 of this year's *Moscow Messenger* cannot hurt the brilliant and entirely deserved success of *Yury Miloslavsky*.

The Literary Gazette, 1830

Baratynsky

Baratynsky is among our finest poets. He is original in Russia because he thinks. He would be original anywhere else, because he thinks in his own way, correctly and independently, while at the same time he feels strongly and profoundly. The harmony of his verse, freshness of style, liveliness and precision of expression have to strike anyone who is even a little endowed with taste and feeling. Besides the charming elegies and small poems which everyone knows by heart and which are constantly being imitated so unsuccessfully, Baratynsky has written two tales which would win him fame in Europe, but in Russia were noticed only by connoisseurs.[21] The first, youthful works of Baratynsky were at one time received with rapture. The latest ones, which are more mature and closer to perfection, have had less success with the public. Let us try to explain the reasons.

This very maturity and process of perfecting his works must be considered the first reason. The ideas, feelings of an eighteen-year-old poet are still close and akin to everyone; young readers accept him, and with ecstasy they recognize in his works their own feelings and thoughts, expressed clearly, vividly, and harmoniously. But the years pass, the young poet matures, his talent grows, his ideas get more elevated, his feelings change. His songs are no longer the same. But the readers are the same and perhaps have just gotten colder in heart and more indifferent to the poetry of life. The poet is separated from them and little by little is completely isolated. He creates for himself, and if he occasionally publishes his works he meets coldness, inattention, and he finds a response to his sounds only in the hearts of a few admirers of poetry who are isolated, forgotten in society, like him.

The second reason is the absence of criticism and public opinion. In Russia literature is not a national demand. Writers become well known due to extraneous circumstances. The public is little interested in them. The class of readers is limited, and they are governed by journals which judge literature as they do political economy, and political economy as they do music, i.e., randomly, by hearsay, without any basic rules and information, but for the most part by personal considerations. While he was the object of their ill-will, Baratynsky never defended himself, never answered a single journal article. It's true that it is rather difficult to justify oneself where there has been no accusation, and that, on the other hand, it is rather easy to scorn childish malice and street-corner sneers; nevertheless their judgments have definite effect.

The third reason: Baratynsky's epigrams—masterful, model epigrams—have not spared the rulers of the Russian Parnassus. Not only did our poet never descend to journal polemic and not once did he compete with our Aristarchs, in spite of the extraordinary force of his dialectic, but he could not keep himself from strongly expressing his opinion in these small satires which are so amusing and stinging. We dare not reproach him for them. It would be too great a pity if they did not exist.[22]

This unconcern about the fate of his works, this unchanging indifference to success and praise, not only with regard to journalists, but also with regard to the public, is quite remarkable. Never did he try meanly to gratify the ruling taste and demands of momentary fashion; never did he resort to charlatanism, exaggeration to produce a big effect; never did he ignore thankless labor, which is rarely noticed, the labor of fine finishing and etching; never did he trail on the heels of the genius who captivated his age, picking up whatever he had dropped; he went his own way, alone and independent. It is time for him to occupy a rank which belongs to him and stand beside Zhukovsky and above the singer of Penates and Tavrida.[23]

1830, unpublished

On Journal Criticism

In one of our journals it is noted that a *Literary Gazette* cannot exist in our country for an extremely simple reason: *we have no literature.*[24] If this were correct, we would not be in need of criticism; but the works of our literature, however rarely they appear, live, and die, and are not evaluated according to their merit. In our journals criticism is either limited to dry bibliographical information, satirical remarks (more or less witty), general praises between friends, or simply turns into a domestic correspondence between the philosopher and his co-workers, the proofreader, etc. "Clear a place for my new essay," says the co-worker. "With pleasure," answers the publisher. And all this is printed.[25] Not long ago there was a reference to *powder* in our journal. "There, now you'll really have powder!" it says in the typesetter's comment, and the publisher himself objects to this:

> Abuse for the mighty prophet,
> Scorn for the weak one.[26]

These family jokes must have their key, and, probably, are very amusing—but for us they make no sense as yet.

It will be said that criticism should concern itself solely with works of obvious merit. I don't think so. A certain work is insignificant in itself, but remarkable for its success or influence; and in this respect moral observations are more important than literary observations. Last year several books were printed (*Ivan Vyzhigin* among others) about which criticism could have said much that is instructive and interesting. But where were they analyzed, explicated? Not to mention living writers, Lomonosov, Derzhavin, and Fonvizin, who still await final and dispassionate evaluation. Grandiloquent nicknames, unconditional praises, banal exclamations can no longer satisfy sensible people. However, *The Literary Gazette* was essential for us not so much for the public as for a certain number of writers who, for different reasons, could not appear under their own name in any of the Petersburg or Moscow journals.

The Literary Gazette, 1830

On Victor Hugo

Everyone knows that the French are the most antipoetic people. Their best writers, the most famous representatives of this witty and practical people—Montaigne, Voltaire, Montesquieu, La Harpe, and Rousseau himself—have demonstrated how alien and incomprehensible esthetic feeling is to them.

If we turn our attention to the findings of their critics which circulate among the people and are accepted as literary axioms, we will be amazed at their insignificance and inaccuracy. In France Corneille and Voltaire are considered equals of Racine as writers of tragedy; to this day J. J. Rousseau has kept the title "great." The insufferable Béranger[27] is now considered their foremost lyric poet—a scribbler of strained and affected little songs which contain nothing passionate or inspired and which are far behind the charming light works of Colnet in gaiety and wit. I don't know whether they have finally admitted the lean and flaccid monotony of their Lamartine, but about ten years ago they were unceremoniously setting him on a level with Byron and Shakespeare. They equate Count de Vigny's mediocre *Cinq Mars* with the great creations of Walter Scott. It goes without saying that their attacks are as unjustified as their love. Among the young talents of the present time, Sainte-Beuve is least well-known, but he is very probably the most remarkable.

Of course his poems are very original, and what is more important, filled with true inspiration. In the *Literary Gazette* they were mentioned with praise which seemed exaggerated. Nowadays V. Hugo, a poet and a man with true talent, has undertaken to justify the opinion of the Petersburg journal: under the title *Les Feuilles d'automne* he has published a volume of poems apparently written in imitation of Sainte-Beuve's book *Les Consolations.*

1832, unpublished

The Poetic Works and Translations of Pavel Katenin

The other day *The Poetic Works and Translations of Pavel Katenin* were published.

In the beginning of an extremely remarkable preface, the publisher (Mr. Baktin) mentioned that almost from the time he entered his literary career P. A. Katenin has been met by the most inaccurate and the most immoderate criticism.

It seems to us that Mr. Katenin (just as all of our writers in general) could complain about the silence of criticism rather than its severity or prejudiced captiousness. Real criticism does not exist in our country: it would be unjust to demand it from us. Our literature barely exists; and "you can't judge nothing," says the irrefutable proverb. If the public can be satisfied with what we call criticism, it proves only that we still have no need of Schlegels or even La Harpes.

As for the unjust coldness the public has shown for Mr. Katenin's works, it does him honor in all respects: first, it proves the poet's abhorrence of the trivial devices for gaining success; and second, his originality. He has never tried to please the public's reigning taste; on the contrary, he has always gone his own way, creating for himself what and how he pleased. He extended his proud independence even to abandoning one offshoot of poetry as soon as it becomes fashionable; and he moved away to where he was accompanied neither by the prejudice of the crowd nor the models of some writer who drew others along after him. Thus having been one of the first apostles of romanticism and the first to introduce language and subjects from the common folk into the sphere of elevated poetry, he was the first to renounce romanticism and turn to classical idols when the reading public began to like the novelty of the literary reform.

The first noteworthy work of Mr. Katenin was a translation of Bürger's famous *Lenore.* It was already well known here from the inaccurate and charming imitation of Zhukovsky, who made of it the same thing Byron made of *Faust* in his Manfred: he weakened the spirit and form of his model. Katenin perceived this and got the idea of showing us *Lenore* in the energetic beauty of its original creation; he wrote *Olga.* But this simplicity and even crudity of expression, this "scum" which replaced the "ethereal chain of shadows," this gallows in place of rural scenes illumined by the summer moon, struck the unaccustomed readers unpleasantly, and Gnedich undertook to state their opinions in an essay the unjustness of which was exposed by Griboedov. After *Olga,* appeared *The Murderer,* perhaps the best of Katenin's ballads. The impression it produced was even worse—in a fit of madness a murderer abusively called the moon (the witness of his malefaction) "bald-headed"! Readers brought up on Florian[28] and Parny burst out laughing and considered the ballad beneath any criticism.

Such were Katenin's first reverses; they had influence on his subsequent works. In the theater he had decisive successes. From time to time his poems appeared in journals and almanacs, and they finally started to be given justice—although stingily and reluctantly. Standing out among these are *Mstislav Mstislavich,* a poem full of fire and movement, and *An Old Tale,* in which there is so much ingenuousness and true poetry.

In the book which has now been published enlightened readers will notice an *idyll*—where he perceives bucolic nature with such charming faithfulness, not Gessner's[29] prim and affected nature, but the ancient, broad, free nature—a melancholy *elegy,* a masterful translation of three cantos from the *Inferno,* and a collection of romances about El Cid, that folk chronicle which is so interesting and poetic. Connoisseurs will render justice to the erudite refinement and sonority of the hexameter and in general to the mechanism of Mr. Katenin's verse, something too much ignored by our best poets.

Literary Supplement to The Russian Invalid, 1833

On the Insignificance of Russian Literature

If[30] Russian literature offers few works which merit the observation of literary criticism, just by itself (like every other phenomenon in the history of humanity) it should attract the attention of conscientious studiers of truth.

Russia long remained alien to Europe. Accepting the light of Christianity from Byzantium, she participated in neither the political upheavals nor the intellectual activity of the Roman Catholic world. The great epoch of the Renaissance had no influence on her; chivalry did not animate her ancestors with pure raptures, and the beneficial shock produced by the crusades was not felt in the regions of the frozen north .... A high destiny had been preordained for Russia .... Her boundless plains swallowed up the power of the Mongols; the barbarians did not dare to leave enslaved Rus at their rear, and they returned to the steppes of their East. Developing enlightenment was saved by a mutilated and expiring Russia ....[31]

For two dark centuries only the clergy, spared because of the amazing perspicacity of the Tartars, preserved the pale sparks of Byzantine learning. In the silence of monasteries, monks kept their uninterrupted chronicles. In their epistles the bishops spoke with princes and boyars, comforting their hearts in onerous times of temptation and hopelessness. But the inner life of the enslaved people did not develop. The Tartars did not resemble the Moors. Having conquered Russia, they did not give it algebra or Aristotle. The throwing off of the yoke, the quarrels of the great principalities with their appanages, absolutism along with the freedoms of the cities, autocracy along with the boyars, and conquests along with the independence of nationalities were not favorable to the free development of enlightenment. Europe was flooded with an incredible multitude of poems, legends, satires, romances, *mystères,* etc., but our ancient archives and libraries offer almost no food for the curiosity of researchers except chronicles. The half-expunged characteristics of our nationality were preserved by a few tales and songs which were constantly revised by oral tradition, and *The Song of Igor's Campaign* rises up as a solitary monument in the desert of our ancient literature.

But in the epoch of storms and upheavals, the Tsars and boyars were agreed on one thing: the necessity of moving Russia toward Europe. Thus the relations of Ivan Vasilevich with England, Godunov's correspondence with Denmark, the conditions presented to the Polish Grand Duke by the XVIIth-century aristocracy, the embassies of Alexei Mikhailovich .... Finally Peter appeared ....

Russia entered Europe like a ship launched with the pounding of an ax and the thunder of cannons. But the wars undertaken by Peter the Great were beneficial and fruitful. The success of the national reform was the result of the Battle of Poltava, and European enlightenment moored at the shores of the conquered Neva.

Much that Peter began, he didn't manage to complete. He died during maturity, in the midst of all his creative activity. He cast a preoccupied but penetrating glance at literature. He promoted Feofan, approved of Kopievich, didn't like Tatishchev because of his frivolity and free-thinking, foresaw an "eternal toiler" in the poor schoolboy Tredyakovsky. Seeds were sown. The son of the Moldavian *hospodar*[32] was educated on his campaigns; and the son of a fisherman from Kholmogorsk,[33] having run away from the White Sea, knocked at the gates of the Zaikonospassk school: a new literature, the fruit of a newly educated society, was soon to be born.

French literature dominated Europe at the beginning of the eighteenth century. It was to have a long and decisive influence on Russia. First of all we must study this.

Examining the innumerable multitude of shallow lyrics, ballades, rondos, virelays, and sonnets, allegorical and satirical poems, chivalric novels, folk tales, fabliaux, *mystères,* etc., with which France was flooded in the beginning of the seventeenth century, it is impossible not to admit the fruitless insignificance of this sham superabundance. The tired researcher is rarely rewarded by a difficulty artfully overcome, a felicitously chosen repetition, lightness of phrase, an ingenuous joke, a sincere maxim.

Romantic poetry had flourished luxuriantly and magnificently all over Europe: Germany had long had its *Niebelungen*; Italy its tripartite poem; Portugal—*The Lusiad*;[34] Spain—Lope de Vega, Calderón, and Cervantes; England—Shakespeare; and among the French—Villon sang of taverns and gallows in his coarse couplets and was considered the foremost national poet! His heir, Marot, lived at the same time as Ariosto and Camoëns,

Rima des triolets, fit fleurir la ballade.[35]

Prose already had a decisive dominance. The sceptic Montaigne and the cynic Rabelais were contemporaries of Tasso.

Men gifted with talent, struck by the insignificance and—one must say—the *baseness* of French versification, decided that the barrenness of the language was to blame for this and started trying to recreate it on the model of ancient Greek. A new school was formed of our Slavist-Russians, among whom there were also men with talent. But the labors of Ronsard, Jodelle,[36] and Du Bellay[37] remained futile. Language rejected a direction alien to it, and again went along its own road.

Finally there came Malherbe—who was evaluated by a great critic with such brilliant precision and such severe justness:

Enfin Malherbe[38] vint et le premier en France
Fit sentir dans les vers une juste cadence,
D'un mot mis en sa place enseigna le pouvoir
Et réduisit la Muse aux règles du devoir.
Par ce sage écrivain la langue réparée
N'offrit plus rien de rude à l'oreille épurée.
Les stances avec grâce apprirent à tomber
Et le vers sur le vers n'osa plus enjamber.[39]

But nowadays Malherbe is forgotten like Ronsard, these two talents who exhausted their powers in a struggle with the mechanism and improvement of the line of verse. Such is the fate which awaits writers who worry more about the external forms of a word than about the thought, its true life which does not depend on usage!

* * *

By what miracle did the group of truly great writers who covered the end of the XVIIth century with such glitter appear amid this pitiful insignificance, lack of true criticism, and shakiness of opinion, amid the general fall of taste? Was it the political generosity of Cardinal Richelieu or the vainglorious patronage of Louis XIV that were the reasons for this? Or does fate predestine for each nation an epoch when a constellation of geniuses suddenly appears, glitters and disappears? . . . Whatever the case, after a crowd of untalented, mediocre, or unfortunate versifiers who close the period of old French poetry, immediately Corneille, Boileau, Racine, Molière and La Fontaine, Pascal, Bossuet, and Fénelon step forward. And their rule over the intellectual life of the enlightened world is much more easily explainable than their unexpected advent.

Among other European peoples poetry existed before the appearance of the immortal geniuses who gifted humanity with their great creations. These geniuses went along a road which had already been broken. But among the French the elevated minds of the seventeenth century found national poetry in shrouds, scorned its weakness, and turned to the models of classical antiquity. Boileau, a poet gifted with mighty talent and an acute mind, promulgated his codex, and literature submitted to it. Old Corneille alone remained a representative of the romantic tragedy which he had so gloriously introduced on the French stage.

In spite of its manifest triviality, Richelieu felt the importance of literature. The great man who had humbled feudalism in France wanted to tie up literature as well. The writers (in France a poor, insolent, and scornful class) were invited to the court and given pensions like the gentry. Louis XIV followed the cardinal's system. Soon literature was concentrated around his throne. All the writers had their duties. Corneille and Racine entertained the king with tragedies made to order, the historiographer Boileau sang his victories and designated to him the writers worthy of his attention, at court the valet Molière laughed at the courtiers. The Academy set as the first rule of its code: praise of the great king. There were exceptions: a poor noble (in spite of the dominating devoutness) printed his jolly tales about nuns in Holland, and a dulcet-tongued bishop[40] placed a caustic satire on the glorified reign in a book filled with bold philosophy . . . . For that La Fontaine died without a pension, and Fénelon in his diocese, removed from the court for mystical heresy.

Hence the courteous, delicate literature, glittering, aristocratic, somewhat finical—but because of this very thing comprehensible to all the courts of Europe, for the higher society, as a modern writer has accurately remarked, forms one family all over Europe.

Meanwhile the great age was passing. Louis XIV died, having outlived his glory and the generation of his contemporaries. New ideas, a new direction were echoed in minds craving novelty. The spirit of examination and repudiation was beginning to appear in France. Ignoring the blossoms of literature and noble games of the imagination, minds were preparing for the fateful predestiny of the XVIIIth century . . . .

Nothing could be more contrary to poetry than the philosophy to which the XVIIIth century gave its name. It was directed against the dominating religion—the eternal source of poetry for all peoples—and its favorite weapon was cold and sharp irony, rabid and vulgar mockery. Voltaire, the giant of the epoch, had mastered poetry too—as an important branch of the intellectual activity of man. He wrote an epic with the intention of blackening Catholicism. For 60 years he filled the theaters with tragedies in which (without worrying about either the verisimilitude of his characters or the naturalness of his devices) he made his personages, apropos and inapropos, express the rules of his philosophy. He flooded Paris with charming trifles in which philosophy spoke in a joking and easily understandable language which differed from prose only in rhyme and meter; and this lightness seemed the summit of poetry; finally he too, for once in his life, becomes a poet—when with all lack of restraint, all his destructive genius poured out into a cynical poem where all the elevated feelings precious to humanity were brought as sacrifice to the demon of laughter and irony, Greek antiquity was ridiculed, and the sacredness of both testaments blasphemed.

Voltaire's influence was incredible. The traces of the great age (as the French called the age of Louis XIV) disappear. Enervated poetry turns into trivial toys of wit; the novel becomes a boring sermon or a gallery of seductive pictures.

All elevated minds follow Voltaire. The pensive Rousseau proclaims himself his pupil; the ardent Diderot is the most zealous of his apostles. In the persons of Hume, Gibbon, and Walpole, England greets the Encyclopedia. Europe makes pilgrimages to Ferney. Catherine enters into a friendly correspondence with him. Frederick quarrels and makes peace with him. Society is submissive to him. Finally Voltaire dies in Paris giving his blessing to Franklin's son and greeting the New World with words theretofore unheard of!

The death of Voltaire does not stop the deluge. The ministers of Louis XVI step down into the arena with the writers. Beaumarchais drags onto the stage, strips bare, and flails everything that is still considered sacrosanct. The old queen laughs and applauds.

Old society was ripe for a great destruction. Everything is still calm, but already the voice of young Mirabeau, like a distant storm, rumbles remotely from the depths of the dungeons in which he knocks about . . . .

Stunned, enchanted by the glory of French writers, Europe worships them with servile attention. From the height of their chairs, German professors proclaim the rules of French criticism. England follows France in the field of philosophy; Richardson, Fielding, and Sterne maintain the glory of the prose novel. In the fatherland of Shakespeare and Milton, poetry becomes dry and insignificant, as in France; Italy renounces Dante's genius, Metastasio[41] imitates Racine.

Let's turn to Russia . . . .

1834, unpublished

Translator's Notes

1. Here as elsewhere in his literary essays, Pushkin takes what it is now fashionable to call the formalistic approach. For other comments on romanticism see below, "On the Insignificance of Russian Literature." See also John Mersereau, Jr., "Pushkin's Concept of Romanticism," *Studies in Romanticism,* III, 1 (1963), 24-41.

2. The anonymous critic who wrote in *The Son of the Fatherland* (No. 3, 1825): "Pushkin's demon is not an imaginary creation. The author wanted to present a debaucher who tempts inexperienced youth with sensuality and sophistry."

3. Küchelbecker's first essay is translated above. Pushkin refers to the statement, "Power, freedom, and inspiration are the three essential conditions for all poetry" and (from "A Conversation with Bulgarin") " . . . he [Horace] was almost never a truly ecstatic poet. And what can you call a poet if he is alien to true inspiration?"

4. The passage Pushkin probably had in mind is the one beginning, "We all lament . . . ."

5. Gavril Romanovich Derzhavin (1743-1816)—a more or less neoclassical poet in whose thundering verse Pushkin found more brass than gold. Among the scattered lines which make him Russia's best eighteenth-century poet are those of the ode, *The Waterfall* (1793-94), written under the influence of Ossian.

6. Here "lyrical" applies to odes. Lomonosov decreed that odes should have "lyrical disorder." The poet was supposed to let his imagination "soar."

7. Jean Joseph Vadé (1720-57)—author of light verse and comedies in which he used the coarse jargon of the fishmarket.

8. As Wordsworth wrote in the Preface to the *Lyrical Ballads:*

> Low and rustic life was generally chosen because in that situation the essential passions of the heart find a better soil in which they can attain their maturity, are less under restraint, and speak a plainer and more emphatic language; because in that situation our momentary feelings exist in a state of greater simplicity, and consequently may be more accurately contemplated . . . . The language too of these men is adopted (purified indeed from what appear to be its real defects, from all lasting and rational causes of dislike and disgust) because such men hourly communicate with the best objects from which the best part of language is originally derived."

Pushkin would never have said it in such a diffuse manner, but simplicity was one of his most important criteria for poetic diction too. The English Romantics' dissatisfaction with eighteenth-century conventions is paralleled by the Russian Romantics' break with the Slavonic pomposities of Russian pseudoclassicism.

9. Pushkin considered "The Murderer" Katenin's best ballad. See above, "The Poetic Works and Translations of Pavel Katenin."

10. Johann Hebel (1760-1826)—Zhukovsky translated his *Sonntagsfrühe* and several other ballads.

11. There had been unseemly polemics between S. Raich (publisher of *Galatea*) and Polevoi (*The Moscow Telegraph*), also between Bulgarin's *Northern Bee* and Kachenovsky's *Messenger of Europe.*

12. In his ode *Felitsa.* Count Orlov was known to enjoy this pastime.

13. *Ermak* by Alexei Stepanovich Khomyakov (1804-60)—poet, publicist, Slavophil theoretician.

14. Originally Pushkin wrote: "But except for Cooper and Manzoni, how far they all are from the Scottish wonder-worker!"

15. Henry Cornelius Agrippa von Nettesheim (1486-1535)—writer, soldier, physician, and occultist on whose legend Southey wrote his "Cornelius Agrippa, a Ballad of a Young Man who Would Read Unlawful Books, and How He Was Punished" (1798) and Goethe his *Der Zauberlehrling.*

16. Jeanne Campan (1752-1822)—confidante of Marie Antoinette, later an educator, author of *De l'éducation des femmes.*

17. In a draft Pushkin says: "One witty lady compared Alfred de Vigny's novel [*Cinq Mars*] to a bad, pale lithograph."

18. Chapter Two (Part One) of her *Considérations sur les principaux événements de la révolution française* opens with the statement:

> Les hommes ne savent guère que l'histoire de leur temps; et l'on diroit, en lisant les déclamations de nos jours, que les huit siècles de la monarchie qui ont précédé la révolution française n'ont été que des temps tranquilles, et que la nation étoit alors sur des roses. [*Oeuvres Complètes de Mme la Baronne de Staël* (Paris, 1820), XII, 24.]

19. Kozma Minin (d. 1616)—a butcher—and national hero during the Polish invasion of 1612.

20. Avraamy Palitsyn—monk at the Trinity Monastery during the Time of Troubles, one of the leaders of the resistance to the Poles, author of a well-known *Legend* which gives a "history" of the period.

21. The two tales were *Eda* and *The Ball.*

22. Pushkin's note: The epigram defined by the legislator of French poetics:

> Un bon mot de deux rimes orné,

soon grows old, and while it has a more vivid effect the first time—like every *bon mot,* it loses all its force with repetition. Contrariwise, in Baratynsky's less restricted epigram, satirical thought takes now a fairy-tale turn, now a dramatic one, and develops more freely, forcefully. Having smiled at it as a *bon mot,* we re-read it with pleasure as a work of art.

23. The singer of Penates and Tavrida was Konstantin Batyushkov.

24. In "An Epistle from *The Northern Bee* to *The Northern Ant*" (published in No. 3 of *The Northern Bee* for 1830) an anonymous person wrote: "Our literature is an invisible literature. Everyone talks about it, but no one sees it."

25. The examples Pushkin gives are from Nadezhdin's editorial remarks in *The Messenger of Europe.*

26. From Zhukovsky's "A Bard in the Camp of Russian Warriors."

27. Pierre-Jean de Béranger (1780-1857)—in his day an extremely popular poet.

28. Jean-Pierre Florian (1755-94). His poetry is flowery and polite.

29. Salomon Gessner (1730-88)—poet and painter, contemporary of Kleist and Wieland.

30. This is Pushkin's outline of "On the Insignificance of Russian Literature":

    1. A quick outline of French literature in the 17th century.

    2. 18th century.

    3. The beginning of Russian literature. In Paris Kantemir ponders his satires, translates Horace. Dies at 28. Captivated by the harmony of rhyme, Lomonosov writes an ode filled with life in his earliest youth etc., and turns to the exact sciences, *dégoûté* by Sumarokov's fame. Sumarokov. At this time Tredyakovsky is the only one who understands his business. Meanwhile the 18th century *allait son train.*

    4. Catherine—pupil of the 18th century. She alone gives a push to her age. She pleases the philosophers. The *nakaz.* Literature refuses to follow her exactly as the people had (the members of the commission, the deputies). Derzhavin, Bogdanovich, Dmitriev, Karamzin, Cath., Fonvizin, and Radishchev.

    The age of Alexander. Karamzin secludes himself to write his *History.* Dmitriev—a minister. General insignificance. Meanwhile *French literature gone shallow envahit tout.*

    Voltaire and the giants do not have a single follower in Russia; but untalented pygmies, mushrooms grown up at the roots of oaks—Dorat, Florian, Marmontel, Guichard, Mme. Genlis—take over Russian literature. Sterne is alien to us, with the exception of Karamzin. Parny and the influence of sensual poetry on Batyushkov, Vyazemsky, Davydov, Pushkin, and Baratynsky. Zhukovsky and *1812* overcome the German influence.

    The present influence of French criticism and young literature. *Exceptions.*

31. Pushkin's note: And not Poland, as was asserted by the European journals not long ago; but in its relation to Russia, Europe has always been as ignorant as it is ungrateful.

32. Antioch Kantemir (1708-44)—one of Russia's first professional writers, author of ponderous neoclassical satires in syllabic verse.

33. Lomonosov was the son of a fisherman. He studied at the Slavo-Greco-Latin Academy of the Zaikonospassk Monastery in Moscow.

34. *Os Lusíadas*—the Portuguese national epic, written by Luis de Camoëns (1524-80), published in 1572. It deals with heroic Portuguese (Lusians) of all ages, but especially with the adventures of Vasco de Gama.

35. From Boileau's *Art Poétique.*

36. Etienne Jodelle (1532-73)—lyric and dramatic poet.

37. Joachim Du Bellay (1522-60)—member of the Pléiade, pioneer classicist and sonneteer.

38. François de Malherbe (1555-1628)—poet of propriety and prudence—defined in the narrowest sense.

39. From *Art Poétique.*

40. François de Salignac de la Mothe-Fénelon (1651-1715) in *Les Adventures de Télémaque* (1699).

41. Pietro Antonio Domenico Bonaventura Trapassi Metastasio (1698-1782)—Italian poet and dramatist.

N. V. GOGOL

Petersburg Notes of 1836*

I

... Indeed, where was the Russian capital cast—to the edge of the world! The Russian people are strange: the capital was in Kiev—too warm; not cold enough; the Russian capital moved to Moscow, but no, it isn't cold enough there either; by God, let's have Petersburg! The Russian capital will do a keen trick if it snuggles up to the icy pole. I am saying this since its mouth waters just to get a closer look at the polar bears. "Seven hundred versts just to run away from Mother Moscow! What restless feet!"—say the people of Moscow, screwing up their eyes at the Finnish land. But then, what weird wilderness lies between the mother and the son. What sights! What nature! The air is thick with fog; the pale gray-green earth is covered with charred stumps, pines, fir-groves, hummocks ... It's a good thing that the highroad, like an arrow, and the Russians singing and troikas pass by like flashes. But what a difference, what a difference there is between the two! She is still a Russian beard, but he is already a punctilious German. How old Moscow has spread out and broadened! How disheveled she is! How the dandy Petersburg has drawn himself together, standing at attention! There are mirrors on every side of him; the Neva here, the Gulf of Finland there. He always has something in which to see himself. As soon as he notices a feather or a piece of lint on himself, he flicks it off that very same minute. Moscow, the old stay-at-home, bakes *bliny,* looks on from afar and without getting out of her armchair listens to the accounts of what's happening in the world; Petersburg, the sprightly lad, never sits at home, he is always dressed up, and beautifying himself before Europe, exchanging bows with folks from abroad.

From the cellars to the garrets all of Petersburg stirs: at midnight he begins to bake French bread, all of which the Germans will eat the next day, and during the entire night and the next morning, having crossed himself and bowed to all four sides, goes to the market with baked kalaches. Moscow is feminine in gender, Petersburg is male. In Moscow everyone is a bride, in Petersburg everyone is a groom. Petersburg observes more decorum in his dress; he does not like bright colors or any sharp or bold deviation from fashions; Moscow, however, demands something already in fashion to be fashionable in its fullest sense: if waists are long, she makes hers longer still; if coat lapels are large, hers are like barn doors. Petersburg is a punctilious person, a perfect German, who looks calculatingly at everything and who looks in his pocket before planning to give a party; Moscow is a Russian nobleman, who if enjoying himself would enjoy himself until he dropped, not worrying about having already spent more than is in his pocket—Moscow does not like half measures. In Moscow all the journals, no matter how learned they might be, always end with a fashion plate; Petersburg journals rarely include fashion plates—and if they were to, then for want of habit somone glancing at it might take fright. Moscow journals talk about Kant, Schelling, etc., etc; in the Petersburg journals they talk only about the public and loyalty ... In Moscow the journals keep up with the times, but

---

*First published in *The Contemporary* in mid-1837, Gogol's commentary on the theater was originally divided into two separate pieces—"Petersburg and Moscow" and "The Petersburg Stage 1835/36." Most of the plays which he mentions were put on in January of 1836. The surviving drafts of this essay differ radically from this final text.

the issues are late in coming out; in Petersburg the journals do not keep up with the times, but they appear punctually at the prescribed time. In Moscow men of letters spend all their money; in Petersburg they make a fortune. Moscow, wrapped in a fur coat, is always riding somewhere, and mostly to dinner; Petersburg, wearing a flannel frock coat, hands in pockets, dashes at full speed to the exchange or "to the office." Moscow makes merry until four o'clock in the morning and the following day does not get up until after one; Petersburg also makes merry until four o'clock but the following day at nine o'clock, as if nothing had happened, rushes to the bureau office in his flannel frock coat. Rus with money in its pockets drags itself to Moscow and returns empty-handed; penniless people travel to Petersburg and disperse to all corners of the world with a fair amount of capital. Rus drags itself in winter sledges over winter's pits and bumps to Moscow in order to sell and to buy; the Russian people travel on foot to Petersburg in the summertime in order to build and to work. Moscow is a storeroom, she is loaded with bales and bundles and she does not even care to look at a petty salesman; Petersburg has squandered itself by bits and pieces, divided itself, expanded itself into shops and stores catching the petty shoppers. Moscow says: "If the customer needs something, he will find it": Petersburg shoves a sign under you very nose, digs a Rhein wine cellar under your floor, and places a carriage stand at the very doors of your house. Moscow does not look to her residents, but rather sends her wares to all of Russia; Petersburg sells ties and gloves to his own officials. Moscow is a large open marketplace; Petersburg—a well-lighted store. Moscow is necessary to Russia; Russia is necessary to Petersburg. In Moscow you seldom see an official button on a coat; in Petersburg there is not a coat without official buttons. Petersburg loves to make fun of Moscow for her coarseness, her awkwardness, and her lack of taste; Moscow will bite back by saying that Petersburg is a corrupt man and that he cannot even speak Russian. In Petersburg, as if they had stepped out of a newspaper fashion plate displayed in the windows, the people stroll along Nevsky Prospect at two o'clock, even the old women having such narrow waists that it is becoming ridiculous; while strolling in Moscow, in the very middle of a fashionable crowd, one always comes across some kind of matron with a kerchief on her head and already completely without any waist. There is more which could be said, but—

The distance is much too vast!..

II

It is difficult to grasp the general feeling of Petersburg. It is something like a European-American colony: just as few natives and just as many of a mixed ethnic background not yet blended into a solid mass. There are as many layers of Petersburg society as there are nations. These societies are completely separate from one another: aristocrats, civil-service officials, craftsmen, Englishmen, Germans, merchants—all make up completely separate circles, seldom intermingling, mostly living and amusing themselves independently of each other.

And if we were to take a closer look, we would see that each of these classes is made up of a great number of other smaller circles, which also do not intermingle. For example, take the officials: the young assistants to the department chiefs comprise their circle, to which a department chief would not sink for anything. The department chief for his part holds his coiffure a little higher in the presence of a chancery official. German craftsmen and German office workers also comprise two separate circles. Teachers make up their circle, actors theirs; even the man of letters, up until now an ambiguous and dubious character, stands quite apart nowadays. In short, it is as if a huge stagecoach, in which each passenger was sitting the whole way in isolation from the others, arrived at an inn and each passenger went into a common hall, only because there was no other place to go. The attempt at establishing public societies has not met with success so far. The Petersburg resident goes to a club to dine, not to spend time. The only reason Petersburg has not been transformed into a hotel is because of some kind of inner Russian force, one which still stands out as a peculiarity even after endless polish and contact with foreigners. In order to speak about each of these circles and to notice the life current among them with its gaiety, delights, hopes and sorrows—it would be necessary to be one of those who write nothing at all, for they as a reward for their activity would have absolutely no time. And so, bypassing the balls and parties, I will direct my attention to those amusements which maintain the longest memories and which admit all classes. The theater and the concert—here are the spots where the classes of Petersburg societies collide and have the time to look at each other to their hearts' content. The ballet and the opera are the Tsar and the Tsaritsa of the Petersburg theater. They have been more brilliant, tumultuous and rapturous than in previous years; and the intoxicated audiences forgot that there exists majestic tragedy involuntarily instilling lofty sensations into the concordant hearts of this speechless, listening crowd, and that there exists comedy—a true record of the society which is moving in front of us, comedy strictly deliberate and, by the depth of its irony, producing laughter, not that laughter which moves the vulgar crowd for which convulsions and grotesque grimaces are needed, but that electrifying, animating laughter which is involuntarily, freely and unexpectedly expelled straight from the soul when it is struck by a blinding flash of wit, laughter which is born of quiet delight and is produced only by the elevated mind. The audience was correct to be enchanted with the ballet and opera . . . On the dramatic stage appeared the melodrama and the vaudeville, drop-in guests who were masters in the French theater, but who played an extremely strange role in the Russian theater. It has already been known for a long time that Russian actors look rather strange when they play marquises, viscounts and barons, just as the French would probably look ridiculous if they got the idea of imitating Russian peasants; and the scenes of balls, parties and fashionable receptions appearing in Russian plays—what are they like? And the vaudevilles? . . Some time ago vaudevilles wormed their way onto the Russian stage, entertaining folks of the middling sort, since they are glad to have a laugh. Who would think that vaudevilles would not only appear in translation on the Russian stage, but that even original vaudevilles would appear? A Russian vaudeville! It is, indeed, rather strange, strange because this light colorless toy could only have been born among the French, a nation not possessing in its character a profound, impassive physiognomy; but when the Russian character, still rather stern and ponderous as it is, is forced to trip along in pentameters . . . I can just imagine our stout and keen-witted merchant with a broad beard, whose feet have never known anything but his heavy boots, putting on instead one slim little shoe and stockings *à jour,* while his other foot remains snugly in a boot, and dressed like this taking his place in the first pair of a French quadrille.

It has been five years now since melodrama and vaudeville took possession of the theaters of the entire world. What monkey business! Even the Germans—well, who would have thought that now the Germans, a sound people inclined to profound aesthetic pleasure, would be acting in and writing vaudevilles, and adapting and putting together bombastic and cold melodramas! And if only this craze had been brought about by the power of a nod from a genius! When the whole world lived in harmony with Byron's lyre, it was not ridiculous; for there was something comforting in this yearning. But Dumas, Ducange and others have become the universal law-givers! . . I swear, the nineteenth century will be ashamed of these five years. O, Molière, great Molière! You who developed your characters so broadly and completely, who so profoundly traced every nuance in them; you, strict, circumspect Lessing, and you, noble, fiery Schiller, who displayed the dignity of man in such a poetic light!—look, what is happening on our stage after you; look, what a strange monster, in the guise of melodrama, has perched itself among us! Where is our own life? Where are we with all our contemporary passions and peculiarities? If only we could see some sort of reflection of our own life in our melodramas! But our melodrama tells lies in the most shameless way . . .

An unfathomable phenomenon: that which daily surrounds us, that which is inseparably with us, that which is ordinary, can only be observed by a profound, great and extraordinary talent. But that which occurs rarely, that which constitutes exceptions, that which strikes us by its ugliness and disharmony, mediocrity seizes with both hands. And here the life of a profound talent flows in all its flood with all just proportions, clear as a mirror, reflecting with identical clarity both the dark and the light clouds; but mediocrity is attracted to the turbid, dirty waves, reflecting neither the clear nor the dark.

The strange has become the plot of today's drama. The whole point is to tell about some kind of incident, sure to be new, sure to be strange, hitherto unheard of and unseen—murders, fires, the wildest passions, of which there is no trace in present-day society! It is as if the children of burning Africa had changed into our European dress-coats. Executioners, poisons—effect, eternal effect, and there is not a single character who stirs any kind of empathy! Never yet has an audience walked out of the theater deeply moved, in tears; on the contrary, in a somewhat perturbed state they hurriedly get in a coach and for a long time are unable to collect and consider their thoughts. Even within our refined well-educated society this is the sort of spectacle we have. Involuntarily, before our eyes move those bloody contests which all Rome gathered to watch in the epoch of its greatest sovereignty and jaded surfeit. But, thank God, we are not Romans yet and not yet in the twilight of our existence, but only in the dawn! If one were to gather together all of the melodramas presented in our time, one would then think that it was the *Kunstkamera* where deformities and freaks of nature were purposely collected, or better yet, an almanac in which all the strange events are written down with protocol coldness, and where opposite each date is written: today in such and such a place such and such a swindle took place; today the heads of such and such brigands and arsonists were chopped off; such and such an artisan at that time knifed his wife . . . and so on. I can just imagine what sort of strange bewilderment our descendants will experience when they attempt to look for our society in our melodrama.

It is not surprising that ballet and opera are more comforting and provide respite: their delight is serene. We Russians are very hungry for opera. The enthusiasm with which all Petersburg rushed to the lively, colorful music of *Fenella,* and the wild, hellishly delightful music of *Robert le diable* has still not passed. *Semiramide,* to which the public was indifferent for the last five years, now, when the music of Rossini is virtually an anachronism, absolutely enraptures the same public. There is nothing that can be said about the enthusiasm produced by the opera *Life for the Tsar*: it is already understood and well known by all Russia. About this opera it is necessary to say a great deal or else to say nothing at all.

But I do not like to talk about music or singing. It seems to me that all musical treatises and reviews must be tiresome for the musicians themselves: for the vast part of music is inexpressible and unconscious. Musical passions are not everyday passions; music sometimes only expresses or, better yet, imitates the voice of our passions so that by supporting itself on them it can rush with the gushing and singing fountain of other passions into another sphere. I will note only that the love of music is becoming more and more widespread. There are people whom no one would suspect of having a musical way of thinking who sit without moving through *Life for the Tsar, Robert le diable, Norma, Fenella* and *Semiramide*. The operas are presented nearly twice weekly, a countless number of performances are given, but nevertheless it is sometimes difficult to obtain a ticket. Is this not a function of our singing Slavic character? And is not a return to our antiquity after our journey through the alien land of European enlightenment where people always spoke in an unintelligible language around us and where strangers flashed by only for a moment, a return in a Russian troika with ringing bells and us standing up on the run, waving our hats and saying, "There's no place like home!"

What opera could be composed from our own national motifs! Show me a people which has more songs. Our Ukraine rings out with song. Along the Volga from its upper reaches to the sea in every row of hauling barges, barge haulers merrily sing songs. To song, cottages of pine logs are built throughout Russia. To song, bricks are passed from hand to hand, and like mushrooms cities spring up. To the songs of peasant women the Russian is swaddled, married, and buried. Everyone on the road—the nobility and the non-nobility—flies along to the songs of the coachmen. By the Black Sea the beardless, swarthy Cossack with a resinous moustache, while loading his harquebus, sings an ancient song; and there at the other boundary, astride a floating block of ice, the Russian whaler harpoons a whale, striking up a song. As if we did not have anything from which to compose our operas. Glinka's opera is only a beautiful beginning. In his work he was fortunately able to fuse the music of two Slavic peoples; you can hear where the Russian speaks and where the Pole speaks: one breathes of the free and easy motif of the Russian song, the other of the hasty motif of the Polish mazurka.

Petersburg ballets are dazzling. Apropos of ballets in general: the staging of ballets in Paris, Petersburg and Berlin has advanced very far; but one must note that it has been perfected only in the richness of the costumes and decorations; the very essence of the ballet, its invention, does not come up to par with its staging; composers of ballet show very little which is new in the way of dances. Up to now there has been little in the way of characterization. Just look at the folk dances that exist in various corners of the world: the Spaniard does not dance like the Swiss, nor the Scot like the German, nor the Russian like the Frenchman, the Asian. Even in different provincial areas of the same country the dances vary. The northern Russian does not dance like the Little Russian, the southern Slav, the Pole or the Finn: one's dance is communicative—another's is unfeeling; one is furious, rakish, the other is calm; one is strained, serious—another is light, airy. What is the source of such a variety of dances? It arose from the character of the people, their life and the shape of their pursuits. People leading a proud martial life express that same pride in their dance; light-hearted and free people reflect that limitless freedom and poetic nonchalance in their dances; people of a fiery climate retain that sweet bliss, passion and zeal in their national dance. Guiding himself by subtle selectivity, the creator of ballet can take as much as he wants from each of these for use in defining the characters of his dancing heroes. It goes without saying that having caught hold of the primary force in them, he can develop it and surpass by far the original, just as a musical genius creates a whole poem from a simple song which he has just heard in the street. At least dances would have more meaning then, and thus they would better form models of this light, airy, ardent language, which so far has remained somewhat strained and constricted.

Petersburg is a great lover of the theater. If you take a walk along Nevsky Prospect in the fresh, frosty morning when the sky is gold and pink and with intermittent thin clouds from the smoke rising out of the chimneys, take some time to walk into the passage of the Alexandrinksy Theater—you will be struck by the stubborn patience with which the people who have gathered together there frontally besiege the cashier, who thrusts nothing but a hand outside the window. How many lackeys crowd there—of every sort, beginning with the one who comes wearing a gray overcoat and a silk, colored tie but without a hat—to the one who has a three-storied collar on his livery overcoat, similar to the multi-colored woolen butterfly used for wiping off the feathers of a pen. Hanging about here also are those civil servants whose boots are polished by cooks and who have no one to send for their tickets. Here you will see how the purely Russian hero, having finally lost his patience, to the singular amazement of all, goes over the shoulders of the entire crowd to the window and obtains a ticket. Only then will you realize the extent to which our love of the theater is obvious. And what is presented in our theaters?—Melodramas and vaudeville! . . . I am angry at melodramas and vaudevilles.

The position of Russian actors is pitiful. An unspoiled populace flutters and boils in front of them, but they are given characters to play which they have never seen. What are they to do with these strange heroes, who are neither French nor German, but some sort of unbalanced people having absolutely no definite passion or clear-cut physiognomy? Where are they to show themselves off? How are they to develop their talent? For God's sake, give us Russian characters, give us *our own selves,* our swindlers, our cranks! Onto the stage with them, for the people to laugh at! Laughter is a great thing: it takes away neither life nor estate, yet before it a guilty person is like a trapped hare . . . We have become so accustomed to colorless French plays that we are already afraid to see our own. If we were to be presented with some life-like character, we would wonder if this were not some specific real personality—since the character being represented is not quite like the peasant, theatrical tyrant, rhymester, judge or other similar stereotyped characters whom toothless authors drag into their plays, as they drag eternal figurants on stage zestfully dancing the *pas* which they have cleverly memorized in forty years before the audience with the same smile. If, for example, we were to say that in a certain city a certain high-ranking official had unsober conduct, then all high-ranking officials would take offense, and another completely different official would say: "How could this be? I have a relative who is of the same rank, a fine fellow! How can you possibly say that officials of this rank have unsober conduct!" As if one could defame a whole class! And this kind of irritability is really spread among all of our classes! Are examples necessary? Recall *The Inspector General* . . .

It is annoying. Really, it is time to realize that the only true representation of a character is not in general stereotyped features, but in a form that they have assumed as a whole nation; they strike us with their vivacity, so that we say, "But I think that this is someone I know,"—only this kind of representation is useful in essence. We have made a toy of the theater, like those trinkets with which people amuse children, having forgotten that the theater is a rostrum from which a lively lesson is read to an entire crowd at once, where to the solemn magnificence of the lighting, to the thunder of the music, to the unanimous laughter, a familiar but concealed vice is revealed and to the secret voice of general participation a familiar, timidly hiding, lofty emotion is exhibited . . .

But enough about the theater. I was carried away by it. A noisy week in Petersburg closes its winter carnival, when half of the population is swinging on swings or rushing like a whirlwind down icy mountains, and the other half is transformed into a long chain of carriages and hardly moves as these are evened up in a line by the gendarmes; and when performances are given day and night, the entire Admiralty Square is sown with nutshells . . .

Lent is quiet and stern. It seems a voice is heard: "Stop, Christian, look back on your life." The streets are empty. There are no coaches. Reflection is visible on the faces of passers-by. I love you, time of thought and prayer! My thoughts flow more freely, better considered. All the hollow, worthless people will probably be sleepy and tired and forget to come harass me with commonplace conversation about whist, literature, awards or the theater.

Lent in Petersburg is a musician's holiday. At that time they assemble from diverse corners of Europe. The huge concert for the benefit of war wounded is always grand: four hundred musicians! There is something overpowering about it. When the harmonious murmur of four hundred sounds re-echoes under the trembling arches, it seems to me that the shallowest listener's soul must quiver with an uncommon trepidation.

During Lent the sun peeps into the Petersburg atmosphere. The west side by the sea becomes clearer. The north looks on with less severity from its Vyborg side. Carriages stop in the streets more frequently letting out strollers onto the sidewalk. In 1836 Nevsky Prospect, the noisy, perpetually stirring, hustling and bustling Nevsky Prospect, has completely fallen: strolling has shifted over to the English Embankment. The late Emperor loved the English Embankment. It is, indeed, beautiful. But only when the strolling began did I notice that it is rather short. But the strollers all have something to gain since half of Nevsky Prospect is almost always taken up by craftsmen and civil servants, which is why on Nevsky Prospect one was able to suffer half again as many jolts as in any other place . . .

—Why does our irreplaceable time fly by so quickly? Who summons it away from us? Lent, how tranquil, how solitary is its interval! What is there that cannot be done during these seven weeks? Now, finally, I will thoroughly devote myself to my work. Now I will accomplish, finally, what the noise and general agitation kept me from accomplishing; but the first week is already coming to an end; I had not time to begin and already the second week rushes by; now it is the middle of the third week, now the fourth; by now the fair is in Gostiny Dvor and the whole gallery of pussy willows with waxen fruits and flowers is in bloom under its dark arches. When I walked by this motley avenue, under the shadow of which were piled wooden children's toys, I became annoyed. I was angry at the red-cheeked nannies stepping along in a crowd, at the children joyfully stopping in front of heaps of litter which was great fun for them; and at the swarthy, thickset, moustached Greek who had styled himself a Moldavian pastry-cook with his dubious, nondescript jams. The shoe-brushes, little tin monkeys, knives, forks, cakes, and small mirrors lying on the little tables seemed offensive to me. The people all were motley, clustering; the same emotions were expressed on every face; they stare with the same curiosity with which they stared a year ago, two, three, several years ago;—but they and I are no longer the same: their emotions are already different than they were a year ago; their thoughts are already more severe; their souls smile more rarely, and something of their former animation is lost each day.

The Neva broke up early. The ice, undisturbed by the winds, since it had time to melt almost before the break-up of the ice, had already drifted loose and fallen to pieces by itself. The ice on Lake Ladoga broke up almost at the same time. The capital suddenly changed. The spire of the Peter-Paul Bell Tower, the fortress, Vasilevsky Island, the Vyborg side, and the English Embankment—all assumed a picturesque mien. The first steamer rushed by, disgorging smoke. The first boats carrying civil servants, soldiers, old nannies, and English clerks made their way to and from Vasilevsky. It has been a long time since I could remember such calm, bright weather. When I turned on Admiralty Boulevard, it was the eve of Easter Sunday,—when by way of Admiralty Boulevard I reached the pier, before which two jasper vases sparkle, when the Neva opened up before me, when the pink color of the sky steamed from the Vyborg side with a light-blue mist, the buildings of the Petersburg side were dressed in almost a violet color, concealing their plain appearance, and when the churches, the protuberances of which were concealed by a mist like a single colored cover, seemed to be painted on or pasted onto a rose-colored cloth, and in this violet-blue haze only the lone spire of the Peter-Paul Bell Tower shone, also reflected in the infinite mirror of the Neva—it seemed as if I were not in Petersburg. It seemed as if I had moved to another city where I already had been before, where I knew everything and where there was something which was missing in Petersburg . . . Over there is a familiar oarsman whom I have not seen for more than six months, his skiff rocking on the waves near the shore; familiar speeches are heard, and the water, and the summer, things which Petersburg did not have.

I love spring intensely. Even here in this barbarous north, it is mine. It seems to me that no one in the world loves it as I do. With it returns my youth; with it my past is more than memory: it is before my eyes and ready to bring forth tears from my eyes. I had been so intoxicated by the clear bright days of Easter that I had taken no notice of the enormous fair in Admiralty Square. I saw only from afar how the swings would carry off into the air some youth sitting hand in hand with some lady in a dandified hat; my eye caught a sign on the corner booth, on which a very big red devil with an axe in his hand was painted. I did not see anything else.

On Easter it seems as if the capital terminates. It seems that anything not seen on the street is being packed for a trip. After Easter the shows and balls are nothing but the tail-ends of those from before Lent, or better yet, they are like guests who leave later than everyone else, standing by the fireplace uttering a few more words, with one hand covering their yawning mouths. The whole town has dried up, the sidewalks are dry. Petersburg gentlemen wear a certain type of light coat with various walking sticks; instead of cumbersome coaches, light carriages and phaetons rush along the parquet roadway. Books are read more indolently. Summer peak caps and whips are shown in the store windows now, instead of silk stockings. In short, all through April Petersburg seems ready to take off. It is cheering to disdain the sedentary life and continually dream about distant roads under different skies, leading to southern green groves, to countries where the air is new and fresh. It is cheering to the one who sees at the end of a Petersburg street the mountains of the Caucasus reaching to the clouds, or one of Switzerland's lakes, or Italy crowned with anemones and laurels, or Greece, beautiful in its desertion . . . But wait, thought of mine: Petersburg's buildings still loom on either side, all around me . . . .

A Few Words about Pushkin

The name Pushkin immediately calls to mind Russia's national poet. Indeed, none of our poets is superior to him and none is more deserving of being called "national." This right belongs undeniably to him. In him, as in a lexicon, one finds all the richness, power and suppleness of our language. He, more than anyone else, has extended its boundaries outwards and has done more to illustrate its range. Pushkin is an exceptional phenomenon and, perhaps, the only phenomenon of the Russian spirit: he is a Russian developed to a point which perhaps all Russians will achieve in two hundred years. Russian nature, the Russian soul, the Russian language and the Russian character are reflected in him with such unadulterated, pure beauty as one sees in a landscape reflected in the convex surface of an optic lens.

His very lifestyle is nothing if not Russian. During the initial years of his introduction to Russian society he was affected by that same debauchery and liberty for which Russians sometimes strive when they forget themselves and which affords such pleasure to a Russian in the freshness of youth. It was as if fate had deliberately thrown him into that part of Russia where her borders are distinguished by a sharp, majestic strength of character; where the smooth intensity of Russia is interrupted by cloud-covered mountains and is fanned by the south. The gigantic Caucasus, shrouded in eternal snow and surrounded by sweltering valleys, struck him. One may say that he summoned all the strength of his soul and broke free from the last remaining chains which weighed down his free thoughts. The free, poetic life of the daring mountain dwellers captivated him, as did their skirmishes and raids which could not be beaten back; and from that time on his brush acquired that broad sweep, that speed and daring which so amazed and startled a Russia which had only recently begun to read. When depicting a battle skirmish between the Chechens and Cossacks, his style is like lightning: it gleams like a flashing saber and flies swifter than the battle itself. He alone is the singer of the Caucasus: he consciously adores them with his whole soul; he is impregnated and intoxicated by its wonderful scenery, its southern sky, the valleys of beautiful Georgia and the magnificent Crimean nights and gardens. Perhaps this is the reason why, in his works, he is more fiery and passionate wherever his soul is in contact with the south. He involuntarily left the stamp of his strength on them and thus his works, infused with the Caucasus, the freedom of Circassian life and Crimean nights, have a wonderful, magical power; and even those who lacked the discernment and development of their spiritual faculties to be able to appreciate the man were amazed by his works. Bold deeds are easier to understand and they animate the soul more forcibly and expansively, particularly in youth, which always craves the unusual. No other poet in Russia had such an enviable fate as did Pushkin. No one's fame spread so quickly. Everyone considered it a duty to utter, and occasionally to distort, some gleaming extracts from his poems, irrespective of the suitablility to the occasion. There was already something electrifying about his name, and any one of those leisure-time daubers had only to inscribe it on his work, and the work would be a sellout everywhere.[1] From the very beginning he was nationalistic, because true nationalism lies in being able to describe the soul of the nation, not a sarafan. A poet can even be nationalistic when he is describing a completely strange country, although observing it with the eyes of his own national element, the eyes of the whole nation, when he feels in such a way that his fellow countrymen think that they are feeling and saying these things themselves. If one must talk about those achievements which comprise Pushkin's attributes and which distinguish him from other poets, they will be found in the extreme rapidity of his descriptions and in his unusual ability to describe his whole subject in a few lines. He is so daring and apposite with his epithets that on occasion a single one suffices to replace a complete description; his brush flies. His short play always stands like a complete poem. He is a rare poet indeed who can include in a short play so much grandeur, simplicity and power as one finds in Pushkin's.

But Pushkin's last poems, written by him at a time when the Caucasus was hidden, hidden from him, together with all its daunting grandeur and peaks towering imperiously from behind the clouds, when he had been plunged into the heart of Russia, into her ordinary plains and when he had thrown himself into research on the life and customs of his fellow countrymen, in an attempt to become a completely national poet, his poems no longer struck anyone with the brilliance and blinding courage he was able to infuse into anything he wrote about Mount Elbrus, the mountain tribesmen, the Crimea and Georgia.

This characteristic is not so difficult to fathom: being struck by the daring of his brush and the magic of his pictures, each of his readers, educated and uneducated alike, tried to outdo each other in their demands that patriotic and historical events should become the central theme of his poetry, forgetting that it is impossible to depict a more peaceful and far less passion-ridden Russian way of life with the same paints one uses to depict the mountains of the Caucasus and its freedom-loving inhabitants. The mass of the public, representing a nation in their visage, is very strange in its wishes; it shouts out: "Show us as we are, with complete truthfulness, portray the deeds of our forebears just as they were." But if the poet, faithful to their command, attempts to portray everything in a completely truthful way, as it really was, they immediately say: "It's flaccid, weak, and poor. Things weren't at all like that." At such a moment the mass of the people resemble a woman who commissions an artist to paint her portrait as a true likeness, but woe betide him if he proves incapable of covering up her defects. Russian history has acquired a lifelike brilliance only during its latest direction under the Emperors; previously the national character for the most part was colorless; it had but little acquaintance with the variegated nature of passions. The poet is not to blame; even among the people also there is a perfectly excusable taste for exaggerating the magnitude of the deeds of one's forebears. The poet has a choice of two courses of action: he can either make his style as high-sounding as possible, giving strength to what is weak and speaking passionately about things devoid of passion, in which case admirers and the nation will flock to his side and he will never be short of money. Or he can remain true to truth alone, being lofty when his theme is lofty; cutting and audacious where truth is cutting and audacious; being calm and serene when an event calls for calm and serene description. But this method means goodbye to the crowd! It will abandon him even when that very theme which his mind has conceived is so grand and cutting that it cannot but evoke universal enthusiasm. The poet did not elect to take the first course because he wished to remain a poet and because anybody who feels within him the spark of that sacred calling also possesses a keen sense of discrimination which does not allow him to express his talent in such a way. Nobody will dispute that a wild mountain tribesman in his battle-dress, free as the wind, his own judge and master, is far more colorful than any chairman, and despite the fact that the former made a habit of slaughtering his enemies, hidden in some gully, or burned whole villages, he is nevertheless, more appealing, and rouses within us stronger feelings of sympathy than our judge in his tattered, tobacco-stained coat, who has naively ruined a great many serfs and freemen with his documents and corrective measures. But they are both phenomena of our world: they must both have the right to our attention, although, naturally, what we seldom see has a greater effect on our imagination, and to prefer the usual to the unusual is nothing less multitudinous than the waste of a poet—waste from the public's point of view, not the poet's. He in no way lessens his achievement; and even, perhaps, enhances it, but only in the eyes of a few genuine connoisseurs. I recall a certain event from my childhood. I always felt a certain passion for art. I was much preoccupied with a landscape painting I had done, with a dry tree spreading across the foreground. At that time I was living in the country; my experts and judges were my immediate neighbors. One of them, when he had glanced at my picture, shook his head and said, "A good painter chooses a fine, sturdy tree, with fresh leaves, . . . a healthy one, not a dry one." It grieved me, at such a young age, to hear this judgment, but afterwards I was able to detect the wisdom behind it, and to learn what the masses like and do not like. Pushkin's works, from which exudes the breath of Russian nature, are as calm and inexcitable as Russian nature. This can be completely understood only by him whose soul carries within it purely Russian elements and to whom Russia is home, and whose soul is so delicately adjusted and developed in sensitivity that it is capable of understanding the apparently dismal Russian songs and Russian spirit. For this reason, the more unusual the theme, the more talented the poet must be if he is to extract the unusual from it and if the unusual is to be the complete truth. Have Pushkin's last works been justly appraised? Has anyone defined or understood *Boris Godunov,* the lofty, profound work which is contained in an inner, inaccessible poetry which rejects any of the vulgar, garish adornment on which the masses usually gaze?—at least no true assessment of them has appeared in print and to this day they remain neglected.

In that delightful anthology of his shorter works, Pushkin is uncommonly versatile and is even more expansive and more conspicuous than in his poems. Some of these lesser works are so dazzling that anyone is capable of understanding them. But on the other hand the greater part of them (and, moreover, the better part) appear quite ordinary for the vast mass of the people. To be capable of understanding them one must have a keen sense of smell. One's sense of taste must be keener than that of a man who can understand only a few sharp, outstanding lines. In order to do this one needs to be somewhat of a sybarite who has long since satiated himself on coarse, stodgy victuals and who eats, with great relish, a fowl no bigger than a thimble which is of indistinct flavor and which gives no pleasure to one accustomed to swallowing the culinary preparations of some peasant cook. This collection of his lesser verse is a gallery of the most dazzling pictures. It is that bright world which contains so many of those features which were known only to the ancients, where nature is expressed as vividly as in the waters of some silvery river which reflects a pair of dazzling shoulders, white arms or an alabaster neck, over which nightly cascade dark curls, or transparent bunches of grapes, or myrtle and a wooden canopy, created for life. Everything is here: enjoyment, simplicity, the momentary peak of meditation, suddenly shrouded in the saintly chill of the reader's inspiration. There is none of that cascade of eloquence which attracts only by its verbiage, in which each sentence is powerful only because it is combined with others and deafens when it descends in chorus with them but which, once it is separated from the rest, becomes weak and impotent. There is no eloquence here, only poetry; no outward glitter. Everything is simple, decent, and filled with an internal brilliance which is not immediately revealed; there is nothing but laconic brevity, such as one always finds in pure poetry. Words are used sparingly, but they are used with such precision that they convey the poet's meaning exactly. Each word contains an abyss of space; each word is immense, like the poet. Consequently, the lesser works possess the quality of readability which allows them to be read through several times, but one cannot say this of a work containing a single, excessively conspicuous, central idea.

I was always surprised to hear the judgments on these works passed by those who were reputed to be experts and literati, and in whom I had more faith before I heard their discussions on this subject. One may call these smaller works a touchstone on which to try the taste and aesthetic feeling of their discerning critic. It is totally incomprehensible to think that they should not be understood by everyone! They are so uncomplicatedly lofty, so clear, so passionate and sensuous, yet so childishly innocent. How could one not understand them? But, alas, it is an indisputable truth that the more a poet becomes a poet, the more he expresses feelings known only to poets, the more noticeably his entourage diminishes, till it finally becomes so small that he can count on his fingers the number of people who appreciate the true value of his works.

---

1. [Gogol's note:] Many of the most absurd poems were circulated under the name Pushkin. This was the usual fate of a talented person enjoying great renown. At first it entertains, but then it becomes annoying when finally one outgrows one's youth and sees them as unending follies. In this way Pushkin had attributed to him: "A Cure for Cholera," "The First Night," etc., etc.

V. G. BELINKSY

Literary Reveries
(An Elegy in Prose)[1]

> *I'll let you have home truths without all ceremonial,*
> *Truth's worse than any lie. Friend, here's his testimonial:*
> *To speak with due respect and gentleness, I'm staggered with*
> *men like these . . . .*
>
> "Wit Works Woe," Griboedov

> *Have you good books?—No, but we have great writers.—*
> *Then, at least you have literature?—On the contrary, we have*
> *only a book trade.*
>
> Baron Brambeus

Do you remember that blissful time when a breath of life seemed to have stirred in our literature, when talent appeared after talent, poem after poem, novel after novel, periodical after periodical, almanac after almanac; that splendid time when we were so proud of the present, so hopeful of the future and, proud of our reality and still more of our sweet hopes, we were firmly convinced that we had our own Byrons, Shakespeares, Schillers and Walter Scotts? Alas! Where art thou, *O bon vieux temps,* where art thou, fond dreams, seductive hopes! How everything has changed in so short a time! What a terrible, what a heartbreaking disappointment after such a strong, such a sweet enchantment! The stilts of our literary athletes have snapped, the straw stage has collapsed on which golden mediocrity was wont to climb, and silenced, mute and vanished are those few and slight talents we had so fondly believed in. We have slept and dreamt of ourselves as Croesuses, to awaken as Iras. Alas! How aptly do the touching words of the poet fit every one of our geniuses and semi-geniuses:

> Not to blossom but fade away
> In the morn of cloudy days!

Yes—*before and today, then and now!* Good heavens! Pushkin, preeminently a Russian poet, Pushkin, whose powerful and stirring songs first wafted to us the breath of Russian life, whose vivacious and versatile talent Russia so greatly loved and cherished, to whose melodious notes she listened so eagerly and responded so lovingly, Pushkin, the author of *Poltava* and *Godunov*—and Pushkin, too, the author of *Angelo* and other dead and lifeless tales.[2] Kozlov, the wistful bard of the suffering monk, who drew so many tears from the eyes of fair readers, that blind man[3] who gave us such harmonious glimpses of his beautiful visions, and Kozlov, the author of ballads and other poems, long and short, published in the *Readers' Library,* of which all that can be said is that *all's well* with them, as has already been noted on the pages of the *Rumor!* What a difference! We could cite many, too many, such sad comparisons, such deplorable contrasts, but . . . in short, as Lamartine says:

> Les dieux étaient tombés, les trônes étaient vides.

What new gods have filled the thrones vacated by the old ones? Alas, they are substitutes for them but not replacements! Previously our Aristarchuses,[4] carried away by youthful hopes, under whose spell everybody lived at one time, used to exclaim in an intoxication of puerile ingenuous rapture: "Pushkin is the Byron of the North, the representative of present-day humanity!" Today our indefatigable town criers are clamoring loudly on the literary marts:[5] "Kukolnik, the great Kukolnik, Kulkolnik is a Byron, Kukolnik is the valorous rival of Shakespeare! Obeisance to Kukolnik!" Now all the Baratynskys, the Podolinskys, the Yazykovs, the Tumanskys and Oznobishins have been replaced by Messieurs Timofeevs and Ershovs; on the field of their eclipsed glory now ring the names of Messieurs the Brambeuses, Bulgarins, Greches and Kalashnikovs according to the proverb: in a waste everyone can be king. The former either regale us once in a while with old tunes to old measures, or maintain a modest silence; the latter exchange compliments, call each other geniuses and cry from the housetops so that people should hurry to buy their books. We have always been too immoderate in awarding the laurels of genius, in eulogizing the coryphaeuses of our poetry: that is an inveterate vice; at least the cause of it before was an innocent illusion springing from a noble source—love of kin; whereas now absolutely everything is based on self-interest; moreover, we really had something to boast of before, whereas now . . . Far from wishing to cast aspersion on the excellent talent of Mr. Kukolnik we can yet assert without hesitation that between Pushkin and Mr. Kukolnik there lies an immeasurable gulf, that Pushkin is to Mr. Kukolnik:

> As far as the heavenly star!

Yes—Krylov and Mr. Zilov, Zagoskin's *Yury Miloslavsky* and Mr. Grech's *The Black Woman*, Lazhechnikov's *The Last Page* and Mr. Masalsky's *Streltsy* and Mr. Bulgarin's *Mazepa*, the stories of Odoevsky, Marlinsky and Gogol—and the stories, if stories they can be called, of Mr. Brambeus!!! What does this all mean? What are the reasons for this void in our literature? Or can it really be that *we have no literature?* . . .

[. . .]

> *Pas de grâce!*
> Hugo, "Marion de Lorme"

Yes—we have no literature!

"What astonishing news!"—I hear thousands of voices in response to my impertinent sally. "And what about our magazines, unremittingly pursuing for us the quest of European enlightenment, and our almanacs, filled with brilliant fragments of unfinished poems, dramas and fastasies, and our libraries chock-full of thousands of volumes of Russian authorship, and our Homers, Shakespeares, Goethes, Walter Scotts, Byrons, Schillers, Balzacs, Corneilles, Molières and Aristophaneses? Have we not Lomonosov, Kheraskov, Derzhavin, Bogdanovich, Petrov, Dmitriev, Karamzin, Krylov, Batyushkov, Zhukovsky, Pushkin, Baratynsky, etc., etc.? What have you to say to that?"

This, dear sirs: though I have not the honor of being a baron, I am free to have my whims and consequently I stubbornly hold the fateful belief that despite the fact that our Sumarokov has greatly outstripped M. Corneille and M. Racine in tragedy, and M. La Fontaine in fable; that our Kheraskov, in glorifying the fame of the Rosses on the lyre, has become the peer of Homer and Virgil, and under the shield of Vladimir and Ivan[6] has wormed his way unscathed into the temple of immortality;[7] that our *Pushkin* has managed in a very brief space of time to take his place with Byron and become the representative of humanity; that although our prolific Faddei Venediktovich Bulgarin, the veritable scourge and persecutor of evil vices, has been arguing for ten years in his works that a man *comme il faut* should not cheat and swindle, that drunkenness and thievery are unpardonable sins, and whose moral-satirical (would it not be more correct to say *police*) novels and humoristic popular pieces have advanced our *hospitable* country a whole century in the matter of moral reformation;[8] that although the young lion of our poetry, our mighty Kukolnik, has at his first bound overtaken the universal genius of the giant Goethe,[9] and only at his second has fallen somewhat short of Kryukovsky; that though our venerable Nikolai Ivanovich Grech (in concert with Bulgarin) has anatomized and dissected piecemeal our native language and presented its laws in his triple-seried grammar—that authentic tabernacle of the Lord which, except for him, Nikolai Ivanovich Grech, and his friend, Faddei Venediktovich Bulgarin, no profane foot has yet defiled;[10] the Nikolai Ivanovich Grech who has never committed grammatical errors in all his life, and only in his marvellous creation—*The Black Woman*—on the evidence of sensitive Prince Shalikov, did he first fall out with his grammar, apparently having been carried away on the wings of fancy; that although our Mr. Kalashnikov has thrown Cooper into the shade with his magnificent descriptions of the trackless deserts of Russian America—Siberia, and the portrayal of her rugged beauties; that although our genius, Baron Brambeus, with his fat *fantastic* book[11] has dealt a deathblow to Champollion and Cuvier, two of the greatest charlatans and cheats whom ignorant Europe has hitherto been credulous enough to have regarded as great scientists, and in caustic wit has trampled underfoot Voltaire, the world's supreme wit and wag; despite, I say, this convincing and eloquent refutation of the absurd idea that we have no literature, a refutation so cleverly and forcefully proclaimed in the *Readers' Library* by the profound Asiatic critic Tutunji-Oglu[12]; despite all this, I repeat: *we have no literature!* . . . Whew! I'm tired! Let me recover my breath! Such a long period would make even Baron Brambeus gasp for breath, and he is a master of great periods.

What is literatue?

Some say that the literature of a nation comprises the entire scope of all its intellectual activities expressed in letters. Consequently, our literature, for example, would comprise Karamzin's *History* and the *History* of Messieurs Emin and S. N. Glinka, the historical researches of Schlözer, Everts and Kachenovsky, and Mr. Senkovsky's article on "Iceland Sagas," the physics of Vellansky and Pavlov, and *The Destruction of Copernicus' System* with a pamphlet on *bugs* and *beetles;* Pushkin's *Boris Godunov* and some scenes from historical dramas complete with *cabbage soup* and *vodka,* Derzhavin's odes and Mr. Svechin's *Alexandroida,* etc. If so, then we do have a literature, and a literature rich in great names and no less great works.

Others under the word literature understand a collection of a number of elegant productions, or, as the French say, *chefs-d'oeuvre de littérature.* In this sense, too, we have a literature, for we can boast a certain number of works by Lomonosov, Derzhavin, Khemnitser, Krylov, Griboedov, Batyushkov, Zhukovsky, Pushkin, Ozerov, Zagoskin, Lazhechnikov, Marlinsky, Prince Odoevsky and some others. But is there a language in the world which does not possess a modicum of exemplary works of art, though they be only folk songs? Is it surprising that Russia, which exceeds in territory the whole of Europe and in population any single European state, is it surprising that this new Roman empire should have yielded a greater number of talents than, say, a country like Serbia, or Sweden, or Denmark, or other diminutive lands? This is as it should be, and it by no means implies that we have a literature.

But there is a third opinion, resembling neither of the two preceding ones, an opinion which claims that literature is the collective body of such artistic literary productions as are the fruit of the free inspiration and concerted (though uncoordinated) efforts of men, born for art, living for art alone, and ceasing to exist outside of it, fully expressing and reproducing in their elegant creations the spirit of the people in whose midst they have been born and educated, whose life they live and spirit they breathe, expressing in their creative productions its intimate life to its innermost depths and pulsation. In the history of such a literature there are not, nor can there be, any leaps: on the contrary, everything in it is consistent and natural, there are no violent or forced breaks effected by extraneous influences. Such a literature cannot be at one and the same time both French and German, English and Italian. This idea is not novel: it was expounded long ago a thousand times. There would seem to be then no reason in repeating it. But alas! How many common truths there are in our society that have to be repeated every day for everyone to hear! In our society, whose literary opinions are so fickle and precarious, whose literary problems so dark and puzzling; in our society, where one man is displeased with the second part of *Faust,* and another is delighted with *The Black Woman,* one rails at the bloody horrors of *Lucrezia Borgia* and thousands enjoy the novels of Messieurs Bulgarin and Orlov; in our society, where the public represents a veritable Babel, where

> One cries for watermelons,
> Another for pickled cucumbers;

where, lastly, the laurel wreaths of genius are so cheaply sold and bought, where every manifestation of shrewdness, abetted by arrogance and brazenness, wins for itself loud repute, insolently reviling under a baronial mask all that is great and sacred to humanity, in our society; where the purchase-deed on a whole literature and all its geniuses brings thousands of subscribers to a commercial periodical; where preposterous ravings resurrecting the forgotten learned opinions of men like Tredyakovsky and Emin are loudly proclaimed as *universal* articles destined to effect a sweeping change in Russian history! . . . No: you must write, talk, shout—anyone who has the slightest feeling of disinterested love of his country, of truth and goodness; I do not say *knowledge,* for many deplorable experiences have shown us that in the matter of truth, knowledge and profound erudition are by no means identical with impartiality and fairness . . . .

And so, does our literature justify the latter definition which I have cited? To settle this point let us cast a cursory glance at the progress of our literature from Lomonosov, its first genius, to Mr. Kukolnik, its latest genius.

[. . .]

The age of Alexander the Beneficent, like the age of Catherine the Great, belongs to the happiest moments in the life of the Russian nation and, to some extent, was its continuation. It was a carefree and merry life, proud of the present and filled with sanguine hopes for the future. Catherine's wise legislation and innovations had taken root, became naturalized, so to speak; the new beneficial institutions of the young and gentle tsar consolidated the welfare of Russia and accelerated the country's further progress. Indeed, what a lot was done for education! How many universities, lyceums, gymnasiums, county and parish schools were founded! Education began to spread among all classes of the nation, for it became more or less accessible to all classes. The patronage of an enlightened and educated monarch, the worthy grandson of

Catherine, everywhere discovered gifted men and gave them full scope and the wherewithal to pursue their chosen calling. At that time the idea of the country needing a literature of its own first cropped up. In the reign of Catherine literature had existed only at the court; people engaged in it because the empress engaged in it [. . .] Under Alexander everyone began to engage in literature, and title began to be separated from talent. A new and hitherto unheard-of phenomenon made its appearance: writers became the movers, the leaders and educators of society; attempts were made to establish a language and literature. But alas! these attempts were neither durable nor substantial; for attempt presupposes calculation, and calculation presupposes volition, and volition frequently runs counter to circumstances and clashes with the laws of common sense. There were many talents but not a single genius, and all literary phenomena did not arise as the result of necessity, spontaneously and unconsciously, they were not engendered by events and the national spirit. Men did not ask: what must we do and how? They were told: do what the foreigners are doing, and you will be doing the right thing. Is it surprising that, despite all efforts to create a language and literature, we then had neither the one nor the other, nor do we have them now! Is it surprising that at the very commencement of the literary movement we had so many literary schools, but not one that was genuine and fundamental; that they sprang up like mushrooms after a rain and vanished like soap bubbles; and that we, as yet possessing no literature in the full sense of the word, had contrived to become classicists and romanticists, Greeks and Romans, French and Italians, Germans and English? . . .

Two writers met the age of Alexander and were justly considred to be the adornment of that age's dawn: Karamzin and Dmitriev. Karamzin—there was the actor of our literature who, at his very first debut, his first appearance on the stage, was greeted with loud applause and loud hisses! There is a name for which so many sanguinary battles were given, so many fierce skirmishes fought, so many lances broken! And is it long since the turmoil of battle and clash of arms have subsided, since the warring factions have sheathed the sword and now rack their brains to understand what they were fighting about? Which of my readers has not been a witness to those fierce literary battles, has not heard the deafening noise of extravagant and senseless praise and criticism, some just, some ridiculous? And now, on the grave of the never-to-be forgotten-hero—has victory been decided, has one or the other side triumphed? Alas, not yet! On the one hand we are called upon as *loyal sons of the motherland* to *pray on the grave of Karamzin* and *utter his sacred name in a whisper*; and on the other, men listen to this appeal with an incredulous and amused smile. It is a curious spectacle! The conflict of two generations who do not understand each other! [. . .] Karamzin . . . *mais je reviens toujours à mes moutons* . . . . Do you know what has been, still is and, I believe, for a long time will continue to be the greatest hindrance to the spread of serious concepts of literature and the cultivation of taste in Russia? *Literary idolatry!* Children, we all still pray to and worship the numerous gods of our populous Olympus without a thought of more frequently consulting birth certificates to make sure that the objects of our worship are really of celestial origin. It cannot be helped! Blind fanaticism has always been the lot of infant societies. [. . .]

Karamzin's name marked an epoch in our literature; his influence on contemporaries was so great and strong that a whole period of our literature from the nineties to the twenties is, in good reason, called the Karamzin period. This in itself suffciently proves that Karmazin was head and shoulders above his contemporaries in education. Besides his name as an historian he still holds, though not very firmly and definitely, the repute of a writer, poet and artist. Let us examine his claims to these titles. Posterity has not yet come for Karamzin. Who of us in childhood was not solaced with his stories, did not dream and cry over his works? The memories of childhood are so sweet, so alluring—can one be impartial here? However, let us attempt it.

Imagine for yourself a society diverse in character, multifarious, one might say, heterogeneous: one part of it read, spoke, thought and prayed to God in French; the other knew Derzhavin by heart and ranked him not only with Lomonosov, but with Petrov, Sumarokov and Kheraskov; the one part knew Russian very badly; the other had been brought up on the grandiloquent and scholastic language of the author of *Rossiada* and *Cadmus and Harmony*; the common trait of both was a semi-savage, semi-educated condition; in a word, a society disposed to reading, but devoid of any luminous ideas on literature. And there appears a youth with a soul open to all that is good and beautiful, but who, though endowed with happy talents and a great intellect, had not received his fair share of education and scholarship, as we shall see below. Not having raised himself to the level of his age, he was incomparably superior to his society. This youth looked upon life as an exploit, and, full of youthful virility, he craved the fame of authorship, craved the honor of being a promoter of his country's progress along the path of enlightenment, and all his life he was a votary of this sacred and sublime cause. Is not Karamzin a remarkable man, worthy of the highest respect, if not veneration? But do not forget that the *man* must not be confused with the *writer and artist.* [. . .] Now let us see how Karamzin performed his high mission.

He saw how little had been done with us, how little his fellow-writers understood what was to be done, saw that high society had reason to spurn their native language, because the written language was at loggerheads with the spoken. That was an age of *phraseology,* pursuit of words, when ideas were matched to figures of speech merely to make sense. Karamzin was endowed by nature with a musical ear for language and a faculty for facile and eloquent expression; consequently, it was not difficult for him to remodel the language. It is said that he patterned our language after the French, as Lomonosov had patterned it after the Greek. That is true only in part. Probably Karamzin strove to write the language the way it was spoken. In this respect he was to blame for having neglected the idiom of the Russian language, for not having lent an ear to the vernacular of the common people and generally for not having made a study of native sources. But he rectified this mistake in his *History.* Karamzin set before himself the aim of *developing in the Russian public a reading habit.* I ask you: can the vocation of an artist lend itself to a premeditated aim, no matter how splendid that aim may be? More: should an artist debase himself, bend, so to speak, to the public which does not reach above his knees and is therefore incapable of understanding him! Let us presume that it is permissible; then another question crops up: can he in such a case remain an artist in his creations? Undoubtedly not. The person who converses with a child becomes a child himself for the moment. Karamzin wrote for children, and wrote childish-fashion; is it surprising that these children forgot him when they grew up, and in their turn passed his works over to their children? It is in the nature of things: the child listened with rapt credulity to the tales of his old nurse, who held him by leading strings, about ghosts and dead men, and laughed at her stories when he grew up. You have the custody of a child: now mind, that child will become an adolescent, then a youth and eventually a man, therefore watch the development of his gifts and, in conforming with it, change the method of teaching, be always above him; otherwise you will have a bad time: that child will begin to laugh at you to your face. While teaching him, learn still more yourself, or he will outstrip you: children grow quickly. Now tell me frankly, *sine ira et studio,* as our true-bred scholars say, who is to blame that *Poor Liza* is now being laughed at as much as it was once cried over? You can say what you like, messieurs Karamzin admirers, but I would rather read the stories of Baron Brambeus than *Poor Liza* or *Natalia the Boyar's Daughter*! New times, new customs! Karamzin's stories inculcated a desire for reading, and many people learned to read from them;

then let us be grateful to their author; but let us leave them in peace, even tear them out of the hands of our children, for they will cause considerable mischief: they will corrupt their feeling with false sentimentality.

Apart from this Karamzin's works lose much of their value in our day because he was rarely *sincere* and *natural* in them. The epoch of *phraseology* is passing for us; in our conception a phrase should be chosen for the purpose of expressing thought or feeling; formerly thought and feeling were sought for the sake of phrasemongery. I know that we are not entirely blameless even today in this respect; at least, today, if tinsel can easily be foisted off as gold, stilted mind and affected feeling as the play of intellect and the flame of emotion, it is not for long, and the stronger the delusion all the harsher the disillusionment; the greater the veneration of false deities, the more cruelly does disgrace punish the impostor. People have become generally more candid nowadays: any man of true education will sooner admit that he does not understand the beauties of this or that work than adopt an insincere attitude of admiration. Hence you will scarcely find a well-meaning simpleton these days who believes that Karamzin's copious torrents of tears flowed from his heart and soul and were not the favorite coquetry of his talent, the habitual stilts of his authorship. Such falsity and affectation are all the more deplorable when the author is a man of talent. [. . .]

Now another question: did he accomplish as much as he could, or less? I reply emphatically: *less*. He undertook a journey: what a splendid opportunity he had of unfolding before the eyes of his compatriots the great and alluring picture of the fruits of centuries of education, the progress of civilization and social organization of the noble members of the human race!... That was so easy for him to do! His pen was so eloquent! His credit with contemporaries so high! And what did he do instead? What are his *Letters of a Russian Traveller* filled with? We learn from them, for the most part, where he dined, where he supped, what dishes were served him and how much the tavern keeper charged him; we learn how Mr. B—paid court to Madame N—and how a squirrel scratched its nose; how the sun rose above a Swiss village through which a shepherd girl with a bouquet of roses pinned to her breast was driving a cow . . . . Did he have to travel so far to see this? Compare *The Letters of a Russian Traveller* in this respect to Fonvizin's *Letters to a Grandee* of an earlier date: what a difference! Karamzin met many German celebrities—and what did he learn from his conversations with them? That they were all kindhearted people, enjoying peace of mind and sereneness of spirit. And how modest, how commonplace were his talks with them! In France he was more fortunate in this connection, for a well-known reason: remember the meeting of the *Russian Scythian* with the *French Plato*.[13] How did it happen? Because he had not prepared himself properly for the journey he was not sufficiently learned. But, despite this, the triviality of his *Letters of a Russian Traveller* was due more to his personal character than to insufficient information. He was not quite conversant with Russia's requirements in the intellectual field. Of his verses little need be said: they are the same phrases but in rhyme. There, as everywhere else, Karamzin is a reformer of the language, but certainly not a poet.

These are the shortcomings of Karamzin's works, this is the reason why he was so soon forgotten, why he almost outlived his fame. In justice to him it should be said that his works, where he has not been carried away by sentimentality and is sincere, are pervaded by a warm candor; that is especially evident in the passages where he speaks of Russia. Yes, he loved the good, he loved his country and served it to the best of his ability; his name is immortal, but his works, with the exception of his *History,* have died and will never be resurrected despite all the declamations of men like Messrs. Ivanchin-Pisarev and Orest Somov! [. . .]

In brief, according to the expression of one of our critics, *The History of the Russian State* is a monument to our language against which Time will break its scythe. I repeat: the name of Karamzin is immortal, but his works, with the exception of his *History,* are already dead and will never be resurrected!

[. . .] Zhukovsky's appearance amazed Russia, and not without reason. He was our country's Columbus, who discovered for it German and English literatures, the existence of which it had never suspected. Moreover, he completely transformed the language of poetry, and excelled Karamzin in prose: these are his chief merits. He has few original works of his own; his productions are either translations, or adaptations, or imitations of foreign works. A style that was bold, vigorous, though not always concordant with feeling, and a one-sided romantic tendency said to be the outcome of personal experience—such are the characteristics of Zhukovsky's works. It is a mistaken notion that he was an imitator of the Germans and the English: he would not have written otherwise had he not been familiar with them, if he only wished to be true to himself. He was not a son of the nineteenth century, but was, so to speak, a *proselyte;* add to this that his works were perhaps really the outcome of his personal experiences, and you will understand why they do not contain world ideas, ideas of humanity, why *Karamzinian* ideas frequently seem to lurk under the most gorgeous forms (for example *My friend, protector, angel mine!* etc.), why his finest works (as, for example, *The Poet in the Camp of the Russian Warriors*) contain a number of purely rhetorical passages. He was self-contained, and that is the reason for his one-sidedness, which in his case was supreme originality. In the profusion of his translations Zhukovsky is related to Russian literature as Voss or August Schlegel were related to German literature. Authorities assert that he did not translate but assimilated to Russian literature the works of Schillers, Byrons, etc.; that, I believe, is beyond a shadow of doubt. In short, Zhukovsky is a poet with a remarkably vigorous talent, a poet who has rendered Russian literature an inestimable service, a poet who will never be forgotten, who will never cease to be read; but nonetheless, not the kind of poet one would call a genuine Russian poet whose name could be proclaimed at a European tournament where *national* fames contend for supremacy.

Much of what has been said of Zhukovsky applies to Batyushkov. The latter stood definitely on the borderline of two ages; he was alternately captivated and repelled by the past, refused to recognize and was himself denied recognition by the present. He was a man of great talent, though not a genius. What a pity he did not know German literature: he needed little to achieve perfect literary treatment. Read his article on morals, based on religion, and you will understand the yearning of the soul and its craving for the infinite after voluptuous delights which permeate his harmonious creations. He wrote of life and the impressions of a poet where, amid childish thoughts, one catches a gleam of modern ideas, and also wrote of what he called light poetry, as though there were a heavy poetry. Do you not agree that he did not belong entirely to either age? Batyushkov, with Zhukovsky, was the reformer of our poetical language, that is, he wrote in a pure, melodious language; his prose, too, is better than that of Karamzin's minor pieces. In point of talent Batyushkov ranks with our second-rate writers and is, in my opinion, inferior to Zhukovsky; the idea of comparing him to Pushkin is ridiculous. Only in the twenties could people believe in a triumvirate in which our men of letters included Zhukovsky, Batyushkov and Pushkin. [. . .]

Prince Vyazemsky, the Russian Charles Nodier, wrote in verse and prose about all and everything. His critical articles (i.e., prefaces to sundry publications) were quite unusual in their time. Many of his innumerable poems are noteworthy for sparkling wit, both genuine and original, and sometimes feeling; many of them are farfetched, as for instance *No Thank You!* and others. But, generally speaking, Prince Vyazemsky ranks among our distinguished poets and men of letters . [. . .]

The Karamzin period of our literature was followed by the *Pushkin* period which lasted almost exactly ten years. I say the *Pushkin* period, for who will not agree that Pushkin was the head of that decade, that everything then centered around him? I do not, however, mean to say that Pushkin quite signified for his day what Karamzin had been for his. The very fact that his was the unconscious activity of the artist and not the practical and deliberate activity of a writer, implies that there was a great difference between him and Karamzin. Pushkin held sway solely by the power of his talent and the fact that he was the son of his age; Karamzin's sway has latterly been founded on blind homage to his authority. Pushkin did not say that poetry was this and this, and science that and that; no: he provided in his works a standard for the former and to a certain extent showed the *contemporary* value of the latter. At that time, namely, in the twenties (1817-24) the echo of the intellectual revolution that was taking place in Europe had a faint reverberation in our country; men at that time began to say, albeit timidly and uncertainly, that the drunken savage Shakespeare was immeasurably superior to starched Racine, that Schlegel was alleged to know more about art than La Harpe, that German literature, far from being inferior, was incomparably higher than the French; that the honorable Messieurs Boileau, Batteux, La Harpe and Marmontel had unconsciously traduced art, since they had but a faint notion of it themselves. Of course, now no one doubts this, and an attempt to prove such truisms at this time of the day would draw down derision on one's head; but it was really no laughing matter then; for even in Europe in those days such impious ideas were fraught with risk of the inquisitorial *auto-da-fé*; can you imagine the danger people ran in Russia who had the temerity to assert that Sumarokov was not a poet, that Kheraskov was heavy, and so on? It is obvious then that Pushkin's excessive influence was due to the fact that, in relation to Russia, he was the son of his time in the full sense of the word, that he kept abreast of his country, was the representative of its intellectual progress; consequently his sway was legitimate. Karamzin, on the contrary, as we have seen above, was in the nineteenth century the son of the eighteenth, and even that he did not in a certain sense fully express, for he had not even raised himself to its level in his ideas, and consequently his influence might be considered legitimate only until the appearance of Zhukovsky and Batyushkov, when his powerful influence began to act only as a drag on the progress of our literature. Pushkin's appearance on the scene was a touching spectacle; the poet-youth, receiving the benediction of the anointed seer Derzhavin standing on the edge of the grave into which he was making ready to lay his laurelled head; the poet-man stretching forth his hand to him across the vast gulf of a century which morally separated two generations; and, finally, standing beside him and together with him forming a radiant twin constellation in the desolate firmament of our literature.

Classicism and *romanticism*—these were two words that dominated the *Pushkin* period of our literature; these were the two words on which books, dissertations, magazine articles and even verse were written, with which we went to sleep and woke up, for which we fought to the death, over which we argued ourselves to tears in classrooms and drawing rooms, in the streets and on the squares. Now these two words have become somehow vulgar and ridiculous; it is somehow strange and bizarre to come across them in print or hear them in conversation. But is it so long since that *then* ended and that *now* began? How can one help saying after this that everything is rushing onward on the wings of the wind? Unless it be some place like Daghestan where one can still gravely discuss those departed martyrs—*classicism* and *romanticism*—and impart to us as news that Racine is somewhat mawkish, that the Encyclopaedists occasionally blundered, that Shakespeare, Goethe and Schiller are great and Schlegel spoke the truth, and so on. But that is not at all surprising: for is not Daghestan in Asia?

In Europe *classicism* was literary *Catholicism*. The late Aristotle, without his knowledge and consent, was elected its *pontiff* by an unauthorized *conclave; its inquisition* was French *critique;* its grand *inquisitors*: Boileau, Batteux, La Harpe and company; objects of worship: Corneille, Racine, Voltaire and others. Willy-nilly, messieurs the inquisitors enlisted the ancients too, among them the eternal old Homer (together with Virgil), Tasso, Ariosto and Milton who (perhaps with the exception of the bracketed) were innocent of *classicism* both in body and soul, for they were natural in their creations. Such was the state of affairs until the eighteenth century. Then everything turned topsy-turvy: white became black, and black white. The hypocritical, depraved, mawkish eighteenth century breathed its last, and with the advent of the nineteenth century, intellect and taste were reborn to a new and better life. Its dawn was heralded by the appearance of a terrible meteor, the son of Fate, vested with all her appalling might, or, better to say, Fate herself appeared in the form of Napoleon, the Napoleon who became the *master of our thoughts,* in speaking of whom mediocrity itself was exalted to poesy.[14] The age assumed gigantic proportions and prodigious grandeur; France became ashamed of herself and began to point her finger with reviling laughter at the wretched ruins of bygone days which, seemingly oblivious of the great upheavals taking place before their eyes, even at the fateful passage of the Berezina, sat perched on the bough of a tree curling their ringlets with stark hand and sprinkling them with traditional powder, while around them raged the winter blizzard of the implacable North and men dropped by the thousands stricken with terror and cold... And so, the French, stunned by these great events, grew more staid and serious, stopped skipping about on one leg; this was the first step in their conversion. Then they learned that their neighbors, the clumsy Germans, whom they had always held up as an example of aesthetic bad taste, possessed a literature, a literature deserving deep and serious study, and they also realized that their own illustrious poets and philosophers had not by any means set the Pillars of Hercules to the genius of man. Everyone knows how that happened, and therefore I will not expatiate on how Châteaubriand became the godfather and Madame de Staël the midwife of young romanticism in France. I will merely say that *romanticism* was just a return to naturalness and, consequently, to originality and nationality in art, a preference for idea over form and the overthrow of alien and restringent forms of antiquity which suited the works of modern art as much as the Greek tunic or Roman toga would suit a powdered wig, an embroidered vest and a shaved chin. It ensues from what has been said that so-called *romanticism* was a very old novelty and by no means the offspring of the nineteenth century; it was, so to say, the *nationality* of the new Christian world of Europe. Germany since time immemorial was preeminently a romantic country due both to its feudal forms of government and the idealistic trend of its intellectual activity. The Reformation killed capitalism in Germany and, together with it, classicism. The same Reformation, though in a somewhat different shape, enabled England to cast off the trammels: Shakespeare was a romanticist.[15] Romanticism apparently was something new only to France and perhaps to states which had no literature of their own, such as Sweden, Denmark, etc. France pounced upon this novelty with her characteristic vivacity and drew the unliteratured states after her. Youthful literature[16] is merely a reaction to the old; and since public life and literature in France go hand in hand it is no matter for surpise that their present literature is distinguished for its excesses: reactions are never moderate. Today everyone in France, for the sake of mere fashion, wants to be profound and energetic after the style of a Ferragus,[17] as previously everyone for the sake of fashion wanted to be frivolous, nonchalant, gullible and insignificant.

And yet, how strange! never had there appeared in Europe such a unanimous and powerful impulse to throw off the trammels of *classicism, scholasticism, pedantism,* or *stupidism* (they all amount to the same thing). Byron, another *master of our thoughts,*[18] and Walter Scott crushed with the weight of their creations the school of Pope and Hugh Blair and restored romanticism to England. In France there appeared Victor Hugo with a crowd of other potent talents, in Poland Mickiewicz, in Italy Manzoni, in Denmark Oehlenschläger, in Sweden Tegnér. Was Russia alone fated to remain without her literary Luther?

Classicism in Europe was neither more nor less than literary *Catholicism*; then what was it in Russia? That question is not difficult to answer: in Russia *classicism* was merely the faint reverberation of the European echo, for an explanation of which one had no need to travel to India by the *John Bull.*[19] Pushkin was not stilted, he was always truthful and sincere in his feelings, and created his own forms for his ideas: that was his romanticism. In this respect Derzhavin, too, was a romanticist very much after Pushkin's pattern; the reason for this, I repeat, was his *ignorance.* Had that man had learning, we would have possessed two Kheraskovs between whom it would have been difficult to draw the line.

Thus, the third decade of the nineteenth century was notable for the dominant influence of Pushkin. What can I say of this man that the reader has not already heard? I confess that this is the first time I find myself nonplussed in undertaking to pass an opinion on Russian literature; it is the first time I regret that nature has not endowed me with poetical talent, for there are things in nature of which it is a sin to speak in humble prose!

In contrast to the slow and irresolute, or rather limping, pace of the *Karamzin* period, the *Pushkin* period moved along swiftly. It may be affirmed that life came into our literature only in the last decade—and what a life—disturbing, seething, active! Life is action, action is struggle, and at that time people fought a mortal fight.

[. . .]

Like Karamzin, Pushkin was greeted with loud applause and hisses, which have only recently ceased to pursue him. Not a single poet in Russia enjoyed such popularity and fame during his lifetime, and not one was so cruelly insulted. And by whom would you think? By men who first cringed before him in the dust and then cried: *chute complète.* By men who blazed abroad that they had more sense in their little fingers than there was in the heads of all our men of letters: precious little fingers—it would be interesting to take a look at them. But that is not the point. Remember the state of our literature prior to the twenties. Zhukovsky had then run the greater length of his career; Batyushkov was silent for ever. Derzhavin was admired with Sumarokov and Kheraskov in accordance with the lectures of Merzlyakov. There was no life, there was nothing new; everything dragged along in the old rut; then suddenly there appeared *Ruslan and Lyudmila,* a creation that was emphatically peerless both in harmony of verse, form and content. Men without pretension to scholarship, men who believed in their feeling and not in textbooks on poetics, or were at all acquainted with contemporary Europe, were enchanted by this poem. The literary judges, holding in their hand the mace of criticism, gravely opened La Harpe's *Lycée (Lukei* in Mr. Martynov's translation) and Mr. Ostolopov's *Dictionary of Ancient and Modern Poetry,* and finding that the new composition did not tally with any of the known categories and that it had no model in Greek and Latin, solemnly declared it to be a bastard of poetry, an unpardonable aberration of talent. Not everyone believed that, of course. That was when the fun began. Classicism and romanticism fell upon each other tooth and nail. But let us leave them in peace and speak about Pushkin.

Pushkin was the perfect expression of his time. Endowed with sublime poetic feeling and an amazing faculty for receiving and reflecting all possible sensations, he assayed all the timbres, all the tones and chords of his age; he paid his due to all great contemporary events, phenomena and thoughts, to everything that then moved Russia, which had ceased to believe in the infallibility of *age-old rules derived by wisdom itself from the writings of great geniuses,*[20] and learned with surprise of the existence of other rules, of other worlds of thoughts and concepts, and of new, unsuspected views on long-familiar things and events. It is unfair to aver that he imitated Chénier, Byron and others; Byron possessed him not as a standard, but as a fact, as the master of thoughts of the age, and I said that Pushkin had paid his due to every great occurrence. Yes—Pushkin was the expression of his contemporary world, the representative of contemporary men, but of the Russian world, Russian man. It cannot be helped! [. . .]

It is impossible to review all his creations and define the character of each of them, for it would mean enumerating and describing all the trees and flowers in Armida's garden.[21] Pushkin has few, very few, short verses; they are mostly poems: his poetical obits over the urns of the great, namely, his *André de Chénier,* his *mighty discourse* with the sea, his *prophetic meditations* on Napoleon, are poems. But the most precious jewels in his poetical crown are indubitably *Eugene Onegin* and *Boris Godunov.* I would never end did I begin to speak of these works.

Pushkin reigned ten years: *Boris Godunov* was the last of his great deeds; in the third part of his collected poetry the melodious sounds of his lyre are no longer heard. Now we do not recognize Pushkin; he is dead, or, perhaps, only mute for a time. Perhaps he has ceased to be, or maybe he will rise from the dead; the answer to that question, that Hamlet's *to be or not to be,* is wrapped in the mist of the future. At any rate, judging by his poem *Angelo* and other works published in *Novoselye* and *The Readers' Library* we should be lamenting a grievous, irrevocable loss. Where are now those sounds rich with the flavor of rollicking festivities and wistful yearnings, where are those flashes of deep and passionate feeling that thrilled the heart, smote and stirred the soul, those flashes of subtle and caustic wit, that irony at once trenchant and sad whose sparkling play so amazed the mind; where are those scenes of life and nature before which life and nature paled? [. . .] However, let us not be too hasty and precipitate in our conclusions; let us leave this tangled problem to time. It is no easy matter to pronounce an opinion on Pushkin . [. . .]

With Pushkin there arose a host of talents, now mostly forgotten, or being forgotten, who possessed in their time altars and worshippers; now we can say of them:

> . . . Alas, some now are distant,
> Some are no more, as Saadi said.[22]

Mr. Baratynsky has been ranked with Pushkin; their names have always been inseparable, and once even two compositions by these poets were published in one book, under a single cover. Speaking of Pushkin, I forgot to mention that he is only now receiving his due meed, for the reaction has passed, the factions have cooled. And today no one even in jest would place Mr. Baratynsky's name alongside that of Pushkin. That would be a cruel joke on the former and a misjudgment of the latter. Mr. Baratynsky's poetical talent does not raise the slightest doubt. True, he wrote a bad poem *Feasts,* a bad poem *Eda* (a *Poor Liza* in verse), a bad poem *The Concubine,* but he also wrote some excellent elegies pervaded with genuine feeling, of which *On the Death of Goethe* could be called exemplary, and several epistles distinguished for their keen wit. He was formerly exalted beyond his merits; now, it appears, he is being unreasonably humbled. It should be mentioned, too, that Mr. Baratynsky once laid claim to possessing a critical talent; now, I think, he no longer believes in it himself.

Kozlov was one of the remarkable talents of the *Pushkin* period. His compositions in form were always imitative of Pushkin, but in the feeling that dominated them they were, I believe, influenced by Zhukovsky. It is common knowledge that misfortune awakened Kozlov's poetical talent: hence the wistful feeling, the meek resignation to the will of Providence and the hopes of reward beyond the grave that constitute the characteristic feature of his creations. His *Monk,* over which fair readers have shed so many tears and which is a replica of Byron's *Giaour,* is particularly conspicuous for this one-sidedness of character; the poems that followed it were consecutively weaker. Kozlov's minor pieces are remarkable for their genuine feeling, gorgeous picturesqueness, rich and harmonious language. What a pity he wrote ballads. A ballad without nationality is a spurious genus and cannot evoke sympathy. Moreover, he took great pains to create something in the nature of a *Slav* ballad. The Slavs lived a long time ago and we know very little about them; then why go to the trouble of dragging Germanized Vsemilas and Ostans onto the stage? Kozlov further derogated from his artistic fame by giving an impression that he sometimes wrote out of sheer boredom: that particularly applies to his present works.

Yazykov and Davydov (D.V.) have much in common. They are both noteworthy appearances in our literature. One, a student-poet, carefree and bubbling over with youthful ardor, sings the sports of youth feasting at the carnival of life, the rosy lips, black eyes, lily breasts and delicate brows of lovely girlhood, nights of flaming passion and unforgettable scenes,

> Where rollicking youth
> Ran its noisy race.

The other, a warrior-poet, with utter military candor and an ardor uncooled by time and labor, narrates to us in spirited verse the vagaries of youth, wild frolics, dashing sorties, Hussar revels, his passion for some proud beauty. One and the other often pluck loud, strong and triumphal notes from their lyre; often stir us with an expression of vivid and ardent feeling. Their onesidedness constitutes their originality, without which there can be no real talent. Podolinsky held out the most flattering hopes, but, unfortunately, he did not fulfill them. He commanded poetical language and was not devoid of poetic feeling. It seems to me that the reason for his failure to achieve success was that he was unaware of his natural bent and trod the wrong path. [. . .]

Delvig . . . but Yazykov wrote Delvig a beautiful poetical Mass, and Pushkin considers Delvig to be a man of unusual talent; dare I dispute with such authorities as these? Delvig was once considered a Grecized German: is that true? *De mortuis aut bene, aut nihil,* and therefore I will not reveal my own opinion of this poet. This is what the *Moscow Herald* once wrote about his poems: *"They may be read with light pleasure, but not more."* There were many such poets in the past decade.

[. . .]

Land! Land!
A threadbare expression

The *Pushkin* period is remarkable for its unusual number of versifiers: it is emphatically a period of versification that became a perfect mania, to say nothing of poetasters, of authors of

Kirghiz, Moscow and other prisoners, of authors of Belsky and other Eugenes[23] under diverse names, a period teeming with men of surprising *ability,* if not *talent,* for versification, if not poetry. The innumerable magazines and almanacs were flooded with verses and fragments of poems, the bookshops with essays in verse, collections of verse and poems. And Pushkin alone was to blame for it all: that was probably his sole, albeit unintentional, sin against Russian literature. And so the literary hacks can claim neither our attention nor our censure: Lethe dealt out retributive justice to them a long time ago. Better speak of men who were conspicuous for some measure of *talent* or, at least, *ability.* Why were they so soon thrown into the shade? Perhaps they have written themselves dry? Nothing of the sort! Many of them are still writing, or at any rate can still write as well as before; but alas! they can no longer excite the reader's enthusiasm. Why is that? Because, I repeat, they *might have been* or *not have been,* because they mistook youthful ardor for the fervor of inspiration, the faculty of absorbing impressions of the beautiful for an ability of striking others with impressions of the beautiful, the ability of *describing any given matter with some measure of imitative fiction*[24] in melodious verse for an ability to reproduce in words the phenomena of the universal life of nature. They borrowed from Pushkin the musical and sonorous verse and to some extent the poetical beauty of expression that constitute but the outward aspect of his creations; they did not, however, borrow from him the deep and poignant emotion which he breathes and which alone is the source of life of all artistic production. [. . .]

Venevitinov alone was able to combine thought with feeling, idea with form, for of all the young poets of the *Pushkin* period he was the only one who was able to embrace nature with fervid sympathy and not a cold mind, to penetrate her holy places by the power of love, and

> Not merely with a cold and wandering glance
> Thou dost permit me in her depths profound,
> As in the bosom of a friend, to gaze[25]

and then to describe in his works the exalted secrets which he had descried on that inaccessible altar. Venevitinov is the only one of our poets who was understood and duly appreciated even by his contemporaries. That was a fair dawn, the precursor of a fair day; all parties agreed with this. Justice demands mention of Polezhaev, who, though a one-sided talent, was nevertheless remarkable. Who does not know that this man was the sad victim of the aberrations of his youth, the unhappy sacrifice to the spirit of the times, when talented youth rode post haste along the road of life, strove to slake its thirst for the pleasures of life instead of studying it, looked upon life as a boisterous orgy instead of painful achievement? Do not read his translations (except Lamartine's *l'Homme, à Lord Byron*), which somehow do not go to one's heart; do not read his facetious verses, which savor too much of tavern carousal; do not read his bespoken verses; but read those of his works which have some sort of bearing on his own life; read *Thoughts by the Sea,* his *Evening Twilight,* his *Providence*— and you will feel Polezhaev's talent, see feeling! . . .

I must now mention a poet unlike any of those cited above, an original, unique poet who did not come under the influence of Pushkin and was practically his equal: I have in mind Griboedov. That man carried too many hopes away with him to the grave. He was preordained to be the creator of Russian comedy, the creator of the Russian theater. [. . .]

Comedy, in my opinion, is as much drama as what is usually called tragedy; its subject is the presentation of life in opposition to the idea of life; its element is not innocent wit, which makes good-natured fun of everything out of a mere desire to sneer; no, its element is splenetic *humor,* stern indignation, which does not smile jocularly but laughs fiercely, which pursues triviality and egoism not with epigrams but with sarcasm. Griboedov's comedy is truly a *divina commedia!* It is by no means a droll little anecdote in dialogue, not the kind of comedy where the characters are named Goodmans, Sharpsters, Knavesons, etc.; its characters have long been familiar to you in life, you have seen and known them before reading *Wit Works Woe,* yet they strike you as phenomena entirely new to you: there lies the supreme truth of poetical fiction! The personages created by Griboedov are not figments, but life-size copies from nature, drawn from the wells of reality; their virtues and vices are not written on their foreheads; but they are branded with the seal of their own insignificance, branded by the vindictive hand of the artist-executioner. Every line of Griboedov's is sarcasm wrung from the breast in the heat of indignation; his style is colloquial *par excellence.* Recently one of our noted writers, only too familiar with society, remarked that Griboedov alone succeeded in versifying the conversation of our society: without doubt that did not cost him the slightest effort; but nevertheless it is a great merit of his, for the colloquial language of our comic writers .... But I have already promised not to speak of our comedians .... Of course, this work has its faults as an integral piece, but it was the first essay of Griboedov's talent, the first Russian comedy; besides, whatever its faults, it is still an exemplary, brilliant production not only of Russian literature, which, in the person of Griboedov, has lost a Shakespeare of comedy....

Enough of verse poets, let us speak of prose poets. Do you know whose name stands first amongst them in the *Pushkin period* of our literature? The name of Mr. Bulgarin, gentlemen. It is not surprising either. Mr. Bulgarin was a pioneer, and pioneers, as I have already had the honor to inform you, are always immortal, and therefore I dare assure you that Mr. Bulgarin's name is as deathless in the realm of the Russian novel as was that of the Muscovite Matvei Komarov.[26] [. . .]

Mr. Marlinsky entered the literary field almost at the same time as Pushkin. He is one of our most notable writers, and today undoubtedly enjoys immense prestige: everybody now is on his knees before him; if not all unanimously hail him as the *Russian Balzac* it is merely because they are afraid it will debase him, and they expect the French to hail Balzac as the *French Marlinsky.* While waiting for this miracle to happen let us cool-headedly examine his claim to such immense prestige. It, of course, requires great temerity to run a tilt at public opinion and make a set against its idols; but I venture to do so, prompted not so much by contempt of danger as by a disinterested love of truth. Moreover, I am emboldened by the fact that this formidable public opinion is gradually rallying after the tremendous shock inflicted upon it by the publication of Mr. Marlinsky's complete edition of *Russian Stories*; dark rumors are beginning to spread about some kind of affectation, weary monotony and such like. And so, I venture to make myself the mouthpiece of the new public opinion. I know that this new opinion will still find many adversaries, but be that as it may, truth is dearer than all the authorities in the world.

In the dearth of true talents in our literature the talent of Mr. Marlinsky is assuredly a notable phenomenon. He is endowed with genuine wit, is a master of narrative, often vivid and thrilling, and has shown himself able sometimes to hold the mirror up to nature. At the same time it cannot but be admitted that his talent is exceedingly one-sided, that his pretensions to the flame of emotion are extremely dubious, that his creations lack depth, are devoid of philosophy, of dramatism; that, as a result, all the heroes of his stories are cast in the same mould and differ from each other merely in their names; that he repeats himself in each new work; that he has more phrases than thoughts, more rhetoric than expression of feeling. We have few writers who have written so much as Mr. Marlinsky: but this fertility is not due to great giftedness, or a surfeit of creative activity, but is the result of habit and a knack for writing. If you only possess a few gifts, have educated yourself by reading, have laid in some stock of ideas and communicated to them some mark of your own character and personality, you may pick up a pen and boldly write from morning till night. You will eventually achieve the art of being able at any time and in any mood to write on whatever subject you please; if you have prepared some pompous monologues you will not find it difficult to hitch a novel onto them, or a drama, or a story; merely look after form and style: they must be original. [. . .]

And then how much affectation! It could be said that *affectation* is a hobby horse of Mr. Marlinsky's from which he rarely dismounts. Not a single one of his personages says thing simply, they always pose, always speak in epigrams or puns or similes; in short, every word of Mr. Marlinsky's aims at stage effect. It must be admitted in all justice that nature has lavishly endowed him with a sense of humor, gay and good-natured, which pricks but does not wound, titillates but does not bite; but even here he often overdoes it. He has entire voluminous stories, as, for instance, *Incursions,* which are nothing but voluminous affectation. He has a talent, not a great one, but a talent rendered impotent by constant duress, misspent and battered against the molehills of labored wit. I think the novel is not his sphere, for he has no knowledge of the human heart, no dramatic tact. [. . .] In short, Mr. Marlinksy is a writer not devoid of talent, and he would be greater if he were more natural and less given to affectation.

[. . .]

One more, the final record,
And my annals are ended and complete.

Pushkin

The *cholera* year of 1830 was veritably the *black* year of our literature, a truly fateful epoch which inaugurated an entirely new period of its existence, sharply contrasting at its very outset with the preceding period. But there was no transition between these two periods; there was instead a sort of unnatural break. Such abnormal leaps are, in my opinion, the best proof that we have no literature and, consequently, no history of literature; for not one of its phenomena was the outcome of another, not one of its events originated from another. The history of our literature is neither more nor less than a history of abortive effort, by means of servile imitation of foreign standards, to create a literature of our own; literature, however, is not created; it creates itself like language and customs, independently of the will and knowledge of the people. And so, the year '30 terminated, or rather put a sudden end to, the *Pushkin* period, for Pushkin himself had ended and, with him, the influence he had wielded; since then practically not a single familiar note has been plucked from his lyre. His associates, the companions in his artistic activity, sang out their old songs, their usual dreams, but no one listened to them any longer. Old tunes had palled, and they had nothing new to say, for they remained standing on the same spot on which they had first appeared and refused to budge.

And so, a new period in literature set in. Who was the head of this new, the *fourth* period of our callow literature? Who, like Lomonosov, Karamzin and Pushkin, took hold of the public interest, ruled it unchallenged, placed the seal of his genius on the works of his time, imparted life to it and set a trend for contemporary talents? Who, I ask, was the sun of this new world system? Alas! no one, though many claimed that exalted title. Literature found itself for the first time without a sovereign ruler, and its vast monarchy split up into a multitude of petty, hostile and envious independencies; there were many heads, but they fell as quickly as they rose; in a word, this period of our literary history is the dismal period of interregnum and pretenders.

The present period contrasts with the *Pushkin* period in the same way as the latter contrasted with the *Karamzin* period. Life and activity have ended; the clash of arms has died down, and the wearied combatants have sheathed their swords and rested on their laurels, each ascribing victory to himself and none of them having won it in the full sense of the word. [...]

Romanticism was the first word that marked the *Pushkin* period; *nationality* is the alpha and omega of the new period. As every scribbler then stopped at nothing to pass for a *romanticist,* so now every literary buffoon lays claim to the title of *national* writer. *Nationality* is a wonderful tag! Your *romanticism* is not worth a fig in comparison! Indeed this striving after nationality is a striking thing. [...]

Indeed, what is our common conception of *nationality?* Everybody, absolutely everybody, confuses it with *commonalty* and partly with triviality. But this delusion has its reason, its foundation, and should not be attacked with violence. I will say more: as far as Russian literature is concerned *nationality* cannot be interpreted otherwise. What is nationality in literature? The impress of the national character, the type of the national spirit and national life; but do we possess a national character? That is a difficult problem to solve. Our national character is for the most part preserved among the lower orders of the people; that is why our writers, those, of course, who possess talent, are national when they depict in the novel or the drama the morals, customs, notions and sentiments of the rabble. But is the nation made up of the rabble alone? Of course not. As the head is the most important part of the human body, so do the middle and upper estates pre-eminently make up the nation. I know that a man is a man in any condition, that the common man has the same passions, mind and feeling as the grandee and is therefore no less worthy an object of poetical analysis; but the supreme life of a nation is pre-eminently expressed in its upper strata, or, to be more exact, in the integral idea of the people. Hence, if you choose one part of it as the object of your inspiration, you will inevitably be guilty of one-sidedness. Nor will you avoid this extreme by allotting to your creative activity the history of our country up to the time of Peter the Great. The upper strata of our people have not yet acquired a definite form and character; their lives offer little to poetry. Do you not agree that Bezglasny's beautiful story *Princess Mimi* is somewhat shallow and sluggish? Do you remember its epigraph?—*"My colors are pale," said the painter; "but what can I do? There are no better in our town!"* There you have the poet's best vindication, and also the best proof that he is eminently national in this story. Does it mean, then, that nationality in our literature is a dream? Almost so, but not quite. What is the chief element of our productions which are distinguished for their nationality? [...]

Our society is still too young, still in the process of formation, not yet freed from European tutelage; its features have not yet taken form. Any European poet might have written *The Prisoner of the Caucasus,* the *Fountain of Bakhchisaray* or *The Gypsies,* but only a Russian poet could have written *Eugene Onegin* and *Boris Godunov. Absolute* nationality is only within the reach of men who are free from extraneous foreign influences, and that is why Derzhavin is national. Thus, *our nationality consists in a faithful portrayal of scenes of Russian life.* Let us see what progress the poets of our new literary period have made in this respect.

The beginning of this *national* trend in literature had been made during the *Pushkin* period; only then it was not so sharply defined. Its pioneer was Mr. Bulgarin. But as he is not an artist, a fact which no one now doubts except his friends, his novels rendered a service not to literature but to society, i.e., each of them bore out a practical truth of life, namely:

1. *Ivan Vyzhigin:* the harm done to Russia by foreign emigrants and artful dodgers offering their mercenary services in the capacity of tutors, stewards and sometimes writers;

2. *Dmitry the Impostor:* he who is a master-hand at describing petty knaves and rascals should not attempt to describe great scoundrels;[27]

3. *Peter Vyzhigin: it is no use holding a farthing candle to the sun;* in other words: *make hay while the sun shines.*[28] [...]

Yury Miloslavsky was the first good Russian novel. Though lacking artistic completeness and integrity, it displays a remarkable skill in portraying the life of our ancestors, when that life is similar to the present, and it is permeated with unusually warm feeling. Add to this a quality of interesting narrative and the novelty of the chosen field wherein the author had had neither model nor precedent, and you will understand the reason for its extraordinary success. *Roslavlev* is distinguished by the same qualities of excellence and imperfections: incompleteness and lack of unity combined with vivid pictures of the popular life. [...]

The latest period has been marked by the appearance of two new remarkable talents: Mr. Veltman and Mr. Lazhechnikov. Mr. Veltman writes in verse and prose and in both cases reveals genuine talent. His poems: *The Fugitive* and *Murom Woods,* were an anachronism, and consequently met with no success. The latter, by the way, despite its faults, is remarkable for its vivid beauties; who does not know by heart the song of the highwayman: *Why Art Thou Dimmed, Bright Dawn?* The *Pilgrim,* save its excessive pretensions, is notable for its wittiness, which constitutes the predominant element of Mr. Veltman's talent. In this respect, indeed, he rises to lofty heights: *Iskander* is one of the most precious jewels of our literature. Mr. Veltman's best work is *Kashchei the Deathless:* it reveals a deep study of ancient Rus from the chronicles and folklore which the author has comprehended with the feeling of a poet. This is a series of delightful pictures which one cannot admire enough. It should generally be said of Mr. Veltman that he has been making sport too much and too long of his talent, the existence of which no one, except *The Readers' Library,* doubts. It is time he stopped amusing himself, time he presented the public with a work it rightfully expects of him; Mr. Veltman possesses so much talent, so much wit and feeling, so much originality and independence!

Mr. Lazhechnikov is not a new writer; he has long been known for his *Campaign Diary of an Officer.* That work brought him literary fame; but as it was written under the influence of Karamzin, it is now, despite its merits, forgotten and the author himself calls it an aberration of his youth.[29] However that may be, Mr. Lazhechnikov made his reputation as an author by it, and therefore everybody looked forward eagerly to his *Page.* Mr. Lazhechnikov did not deceive these hopes, he even surpassed the general expectation and is rightly acknowledged to be the first Russian novelist. Indeed, the *Page* is an uncommon work, marked with the stamp of consummate talent. Mr. Lazhechnikov possesses all the attributes of the novelist: talent, education, ardent feeling and life's experience. The chief fault of his *Page* is that it was his first work of that kind: hence the duality of interest, here and there an excessive loquacity and a too obvious dependence on the influence of foreign standards. But then what a daring and rich imagination, what perfect portraiture of men and characters, what diversity of scenes, what life and movement in the narrative! The epoch chosen by the author is the most romantic and dramatic episode of our history and offers the richest hunting ground to the poet. Though giving full due to Mr. Lazhechnikov's poetical talent it should be said that he did not quite cope with the epoch of his choice, due, it would seem, to a certain misjudgment of it. This is especially borne out by the chief character of his novel, who, in my opinion, is the worst character in the whole story. Can you tell me what there is in him that is specifically Russian, or at least individual? He is simply a featureless character, and a man of our day rather than of the seventeenth century. Generally the *Page* had many heroes but not a single principal actor. The most noteworthy and interesting is Patkul: he is given a full-length portrait, and is painted with a masterly brush. But the most interesting, the most beloved child of his fantasy, I believe, is the Swiss maid Rosa; this is a character Balzac himself might have envied. I have neither space nor time to give a full analysis of *Page*, though I could say a good deal about it! I conclude: it reveals the author's considerable talent and establishes his claim to the honorable place of first Russian novelist; his faults, it seems to me, are due partly to the fact that the author did not take an altogether direct view of the epoch of Peter the Great, and primarily to the fact that *Page* was his first opus. Judging by fragments of his new novel, there are hopes that it will turn out to be much better than the first and will fully justify the hopes the public places in his talent.

It remains for me now to mention one more highly noteworthy figure of our literature: that is the author who writes under the pseudonym of *Bezglasny.*[30] They say that this is . . . but what has the name of the author to do with us, the more so that he is himself loath to have it published? Since he recently announced that he was neither A, nor B, nor C, I will choose to call him O. This O. has been writing a long time, but his artistic talent has lately revealed itself with great force. This writer has not yet been appreciated by us at his true worth, and requires special attention which I have neither the time nor space now to give him. All his works reveal a powerful and vigorous talent, a deep and sincere feeling, a perfect originality, a knowledge of the human heart, a knowledge of society, a high education and an observant mind. I said: a knowledge of *society,* and will add: especially of *high society,* of which, I have a suspicion, he is a traitor . . . . O, he is a terrible and retributive artist! How deeply and truly has he fathomed the unfathomable nothingness and insignificance of the class of people whom he pursues with such vehemence and unflagging perseverance! He inveighs at their insignificance, he brands them with the stigma of shame; he castigates them like Nemesis, he condemns them for having lost the image and likeness of God, for having bartered the sacred treasures of the soul for the gilded dross, for having renounced the living God and worshipped the idol of worldliness, for having substituted conventions for mind, feeling, conscience and rectitude! He . . . why tell you so much about him? If you understand my enthusiastic wonder before him, you will the better understand and appreciate the artist; there is no use otherwise in wasting words . . . I take it that you have read his *The Ball,* his *Brigadier,* his *Mockery of the Dead,* his *How Dangerous It Is for Girls to Walk on Nevsky Prospect?* . . .

Mr. Gogol, who has been masquerading so amiably under the name of *Beekeeper,* is an outstanding talent. Who does not know his *Evenings on a Farm near Dikanka*? How full it is of wit and lightness, poesy and nationality! Please God that he justify the promise he holds out! . . .

[. . .] We need, then, not a literature, which will come in due season without any effort on our part, but education! And that education, through the vigilant guardianship of a wise government, will not be allowed to run to seed. The Russian people are intelligent and shrewd, zealous and ardent to all that is good and beautiful, when the hand of the father-tsar points out the goal, when his august voice calls to it! Can we fail to achieve that end when the government represents such a unique, such an unprecedented model of solicitude for the dissemination of education, when it expends such vast sums on the maintenance of schools, encourages teachers and students with magnificent awards, and has thrown open the door to distinction and benefit for the educated mind and talent! Does a year ever pass but an indefatigable government accomplishes new deeds for the benefit of education, or bestows new favors and new bounties upon men of science? The very fact that an institution of *domestic tutors and teachers* has been inaugurated is fraught with incalculable blessings for Russia, whom it will rid of the pernicious effects of foreign education. Yes! we shall soon have *our own,* our Russian, public education; we shall soon show that we have no use for alien intellectual tutelage. And that will not be difficult for us to do, when eminent statesmen, the tsar's associates at the arduous helm of governance, appear amid knowledge-loving youth in the central temple of Russian learning to announce to them the sacred will of the monarch, to point the way to education in the spirit of *Orthodoxy, Autocracy and Nationality* . . .[31]

Our society, too, is nearing its complete enlightenment. The gentle nobility have finally become convinced of the necessity of giving their children a lasting, fundamental education in the spirit of faith, loyalty and nationality. Our young bloods, our *dandies,* possessing no learning other than the facile accomplishment of talking nonsense in French, are becoming ridiculous and pitiful anachronisms. On the other hand can one fail to see how rapidly our merchant class is becoming educated and in this respect approaches high society? Ah, believe me, it was not in vain that they clung so firmly to their venerable flowing beards, to their long-skirted caftans and the customs of their ancestors! The Russian character is more intact in them than in anyone else and they will not lose it in embracing education, but will become the national type. See also what an active part our clergy are beginning to take in the sacred cause of national education . . . . Yes! the seed of the future is ripening today! And it will sprout and blossom, blossom forth in full splendor at the behest of affectionate monarchs! Then shall we have *our own* literature, then shall we be the rivals and not imitators of the Europeans . . . .

And so, I have not only come within sight of land, I am actually ashore, and standing there I gaze back with pride and pleasure upon the way I have travelled. It was certainly a long journey! And I am really tired and worn out! It was an unaccustomed and difficult road. However, before taking leave of you, dear reader, I should like to say another brief word to you. He who ventures to pass judgment on others incurs the risk of still harsher judgment on himself. Moreover, an author's vanity is more susceptible and resentful than any other kind of vanity. When beginning to write this article I merely had a mind to twit our modern literature, and did not imagine I would drift so far. I started out with a toast to the living and ended up with a prayer for the dead. That often happens in the affairs of life. I admit, then, candidly: do not seek strict logical sequence in my *Elegy in Prose.* Elegists were never distinguished for punctilious reasoning. My object was to vent several truths, some of them known before, some of them the result of my own observations; but I had no time to ponder over and polish up my article; I have a love for truth and a desire for the common welfare, though, perhaps, not substantial knowledge. What is to be done? These two qualitites are rarely combined in a single person. However, I never spoke a word about what was beyond my understanding, and have therefore not touched on our *scientific* literature. I think and believe that any man may boldly and candidly express his views in the interests of promoting science and literature, the more so if these views, whether right or wrong, are the outcome of his convictions and do not pursue an ulterior motive. If therefore you find that I have erred, express your opinion in print and charge me with a false view on things: I ask that as proof of your love of truth and as a token of respect for me as a man; but do not be angry with me if you think otherwise. And so, dear readers, let me wish you a happy new year. Farewell!

Chembar, 1834
December 12

Notes*

1. First published in 1834 in the weekly newspaper *Rumor* [*Molva*], under the signature—*on-insky.*

2. A reference to the contradictory criticisms on Pushkin's *Angelo* published in *Rumor.*

3. "That blind man" was I. I. Kozlov, the poet and translator who went blind at the age of 43. The year in which he lost his sight saw the commencement of his literary career.

4. The chief of Russian Aristarchuses, severe critics, was N. Polevoi.

5. The chief of the "indefatigable town criers" who raised a clamor over Nestor Kukolnik was O. I. Senkovsky, better known under the pseudonym of Baron Brambeus.

6. A reference to the better known poems of Kheraskov—*Rossiada,* eulogizing the taking of Kazan by Ivan the Terrible, and *Vladimir Regenerated.*

7. i.e., into Mr. Kaidonov's *Universal History* [Belinsky's note].

8. The words "our hospitable country" contain a hint of F. Bulgarin's Polish origin, his traitorous participation in Napoleon's campaign against Russia, followed by his re-adoption of Russian citizenship.

9. An allusion to Senkovsky, who called Kukolnik "our young Goethe."

10. Reference is made here to N. Grech's three-volume *Grammar.*

11. The "fat fantastic book" was *The Fantastic Travels of Baron Brambeus,* which ridiculed many world-famous scientists and philosophers, among them the French Egyptologist Champollion and the French naturalist Cuvier. V. Odoevsky criticized this gross sally in an article entitled "Hostility to Education."

12. "Tutunji-Oglu"—another of Senkovsky's pseudonyms.

13. "The meeting of the Russian Scythian with the French Plato" applies to Karamzin's meeting with the French archeologist Jean Jacques Barthélemy, author of the novel *Voyage du jeune Anacharsis en Grèce.*

14. "The master of our thoughts" was applied by Pushkin to Napoleon in his poem *To the Sea.*

15. By the end of 1839 Belinsky had rejected his view of Shakespeare and several other writers as romanticists.

16. Belinsky applies the term "youthful literature" to French romanticism.

17. Ferragus is the hero of Balzac's novel *Histoire des treize.*

18. "Another master of our thoughts"—from Pushkin's poem *To the Sea.*

19. An allusion to A. A. Marlinsky, who, in an article on N. Polevoi's novel, wrote with reference to Hindu literature: "Let us take a trip to India, the steamer *John Bull* has long been smoking by the quay."

20. The words given in italics are a paraphrase from Nadezhdin's article *Literary Apprehensions for Next Year.*

21. Armida—the beautiful sorceress, mistress of an enchanted garden, heroine of Tasso's poem *Gerusalemme Liberata.*

22. From *Eugene Onegin,* chapter 8.

23. As early as the twenties, Pushkin's *Prisoner of the Caucasus* and *Eugene Onegin* evoked cheap imitations such as *The Kirghiz Prisoner,* a story in verse by N. Muravyov, *The Prisoner of Moscow,* a story in verse by F. S—v and *Eugene Velsky* (not Belsky, as quoted by Belinsky), a novel in verse.

24. *Vide: Rules of Poetics* by Apollos [Belinsky's note].

25. From Faust's monologue (Goethe).

26. The author of *Policion, My English Lord* and similar famous works [Belinsky's note].

27. The words "foreign emigrant and artful dodger" and "petty knave and rascal" apply to F. Bulgarin.

28. An allusion to the fact that there was very little to distinguish between the merits of the novel *Peter Vyzhigin* and its predecessor *Ivan Vyzhigin.*

29. I beg the pardon of the honorable author of *Page* for an unintentional offence. I knew very well that the beautiful song *Sweetly Sang the Nightingale!* belonged to him, for I had the honor of learning that from himself; my guilt was that I was not sufficiently explicit [Belinsky's note].

30. *Bezglasnyi* was the pseudonym used by V. F. Odoevsky.

31. "Eminent statesman" refers to the Minister of Public Education, S. Uvarov, who in 1832 paid a visit to Moscow University. S. A. Vengerov (1855-1920), the historian of Russian literature and editor and publisher of Belinsky's *Collected Works,* expressed the belief that the lines in praise of the government and the "eminent statesman," which form such an obvious discrepancy with Belinsky's entire outlook, were introduced into his article by the editor and publisher of *Rumor,* N. I. Nadezhdin.

*These notes, unless otherwise marked, were compiled by the editor of V. G. Belinsky *Selected Philosophical Works.* Moscow: Foreign Language Publishing House, 1956, pp. 546-51. The translation in this anthology also comes from this source.

RUSSIAN ARCHIVE

Literary Sources: Circles, Salons and Letters

An important aspect of the literature that developed in early nineteenth-century Russia is its social nature. The trend in literature to become less formal, to find expression in shorter, more intimate genres, parallels the growth of circles, societies and salons.[1] These gatherings played a major role in the formation of Russia's cultural life. At that time writers had no large reading public, and circles, salons and societies gave them an audience for their works. Other reasons led to the formation of these groups.

Intellectuals felt isolated and the circles were a place they could discuss new ideas. Also because they were interested in foreign literature and philosophy, the intellectuals were targets of suspicion. Feeling isolated, they "drew closer to one another. The circle became a close-knit, exclusive group providing for its members the intellectual stimulation that could not be found elsewhere. It also provided comradeship, community of interest, and collective support in all one's affairs."[2]

Meetings of circles and societies were usually friendly gatherings at someone's house and normally had some rules and minutes. Gradually this died out and they became more informal.[3] There were political and philosophical circles as well as literary ones, but they all shared one concern: Russia's backwardness in contrast to Western Europe. And so the writers met, discussed language and literature, but mostly worked to develop a literary language, one suitable for prose as well as poetry.

One of the first major societies was Admiral Shishkov's "*Beseda* (Colloquium) of Lovers of the Russian Word" (1811-16). A formal group with minutes and even an assigned seating arrangement,[4] the *Beseda* tried to uphold Lomonosov's theories of language and genre. One of its members, Prince A. A. Shakhovskoi wrote a play, *A Lesson for Coquettes,* or *Lipetsk Waters,* in which he lampooned Zhukovsky, his style and language. Friends rallied around the poet and formed a group called Arzamas. Basically disciples of Karamzin and his language reforms, some members even wrote parodies of Shakhovskoi in retaliation for his attack on Zhukovsky. Their meetings were parodies of the *Beseda*'s, but their collective interests were sincere. Members of Arzamas were interested in "familiar correspondence, stylistic controversy, the cult of friendship, the appeal to polite society for literary instruction, and the fashionable obsession for literature."[5] They may have been a frivolous group, but their concerns were serious.

Another frivolous group which met informally was the Green Lamp.[6] The most famous member of this society was Pushkin, also a member of Arzamas. Approximately twenty-one members participated in the meetings that took place once every two weeks on Saturdays. They had extraordinarily complex minutes which they had to keep secret in parodic imitation of Masonic rituals. Although they occasionally did stage literary readings, their group was probably only a drinking club where they could get together for fun.

A totally different atmosphere reigned in the *Lyubomudry* (Lovers of Wisdom) circle, a group of serious young men who met in Moscow to read and discuss German philosophy and romantic literature. Idealists, they studied the works of Goethe and Schelling. The forum in which they were able to express their views was the almanac *Mnemosyne*. The group disbanded after the Decembrist uprising, but a number of its members became the leading Slavophiles of their day.

Like the *Lyubomudry* group, the circle formed around Stankevich in the thirties had its beginnings at Moscow University.[7] With the earlier group, the Stankevich circle also shared an interest in German philosophy and literature. Disciples of Schelling, Kant, Fichte and Hegel, "they looked upon a mastery of German philosophy as a necessary attainment of the free mind."[8] What distinguished the Stankevich circle from earlier societies is the social make-up of the members. Earlier the circles were aristocratic, and although the Moscow circles still "retained a semi-aristocratic character,"[9] the membership of the *raznochinets*[10] Vissarion Belinksy in the Stankevich circle set it apart. In the late thirties and forties we begin to see the emergence of a "plebeian" class whose ideas would dominate the Russian cultural scene for many years.

Salons retained their aristocratic nature much longer. The salons were another phenomenon that contributed to Russian culture in the early nineteenth century: "It was in these *salons* that a new Russian culture was forged."[11] More lively than the circles, the salons were freer and their character depended on the personalities running them.[12] Debates on philosophical, historical and literary topics went on in the salons, but their main focus was "culture." Emphasis on music and the arts, as well as literature, took first place. One of the most famous salons was run by Zinaida Alexandrovna Volkonskaya (1792-1862) in Moscow.[13] Educated in the French language and literature, Volkonskaya also had a fair command of Russian and even published poems and excerpts from her travel notes. Lasting for about five years, from 1824 to the beginning of 1829, her salon was devoted entirely to art, poetry and music. Her home was a meeting place for the most famous writers of the day.

In the twenties the salons and circles were closely connected with each other and each visited the other.[14] Another literary outlet in which writers, intellectuals and *littérateurs* debated various topics and exchanged literary news and gossip was the genre of the familiar letter. Letter writing became another means of developing a literary prose language. Although familiar letter writing has a long tradition in the West, in Russia it begins only with Lomonosov in the mid-eighteenth century.[15] But letter writing became a truly popular literary genre only in the "Golden Age" and became a real art in the hands of the members of Arzamas.[16] The best letter writer of the group was Pushkin, whose letters exhibit those same characteristics which make his prose so remarkable at the time. But a fascinating, informative and delightful group of letters forms the extensive correspondence between Prince Pyotr Andreevich Vyazemsky and Alexander Ivanovich Turgenev (1784-1845), "a friend of all the Arzamasians and one of the most intelligent men of the period."[17]

Alexander Turgenev went to the school for nobles connected with Moscow University where his father had been the rector whose educational ideas and Masonic ideals also influenced Karamzin and Zhukovsky. Later Turgenev studied at Göttingen University. Turgenev later worked as the director of the Department of Spiritual Affairs for foreign religions (1810-24); his government career was ruined by his brother's participation in the Decembrist uprising.

A member of Arzamas and a close friend of Vyazemsky, Turgenev also had long-standing close ties with Pushkin, whom he helped get into the lyceum at Tsarskoe Selo. Between 1817 and 1820 Pushkin was a frequent visitor to his home and wrote his famous ode "Freedom" there.[18] Turgenev also contributed letters about European life and letters to Pushkin's journal, as well as to those of his other friends.

The letters quoted below, from the Turgenev-Vyazemsky correspondence,[19] are excellent examples of Arzamas epistolary writing. They are full of information, allusions, wit and feeling. Really "written conversations,"[20] the basic characteristics of the Arzamas letters were "capacity for love and friendship, love of literature, good taste, delight in the pleasure of the mind and flesh, frankness, self-irony, a variety of interests, civility, and a sense of humor."[21] These qualities also describe the talented men who helped to develop Russian language and literature by creating a cultural milieu in which it could thrive.

Notes

1. Approximately twenty-five circles and salons existed in the eighteenth century; fifteen from 1800 to 1810; twenty-six in 1810-20; fifty-four in 1820-30; forty-four in 1830-40; twenty-nine in 1840-50; and sixteen in 1850-60. M. Aronson and S. Reyser, *Literaturnye kruzhki i salony* (Leningrad: Priboi, 1929), pp. 301-6.

2. Edward J. Brown, *Stankevich and His Moscow Circle* (Stanford, California: Stanford University Press, 1966), pp. 12-13.

3. Aronson, p. 32.

4. William Mills Todd, III, *The Familiar Letter as a Literary Genre in the Age of Pushkin* (Princeton, New Jersey: Princeton University Press, 1976), p. 48.

5. Todd, p. 49.

6. Aronson, pp. 260-62.

7. D. S. Mirsky, *A History of Russian Literature* (New York: Alfred A. Knopf, 1966), p. 159.

8. Brown, p. 4.

9. Mirsky, p. 160.

10. Members of non-aristocratic classes, usually members of the intelligentsia.

11. Mirsky, p. 161.

12. Aronson, p. 37.

13. Aronson, pp. 375-77.

14. Aronson, p. 63.

15. Todd, p. 26.

16. Another writer who wrote interesting and witty letters is the playwright Griboedov.

17. Mirsky, pp. 113-14.

18. L. A. Chereiskii, *Pushkin i ego okruzhenie* (Leningrad: Nauka, 1975), p. 424.

19. *Perepiska Aleksandra Ivanovicha Turgeneva s Kn. Petrom Andreevichem Viazemskim,* vol. I: 1814-33. *Arkhiv Brat'ev Turgenevykh, vypusk 6,* ed. M. K. Kulman (Petrograd: Rossiiskaia gosudarstvennaia akademicheskaia tipografiia, 1921).

20. Todd, p. 70.

21. Todd, p. 103.

Circles and Salons[1]

Arzamas

At that time the literary world was divided into two sharply delineated parties—Shishkov's and Karamzin's. To the first group belonged all of the Kutuzovs, Kikin, I. S. Zakharov, Khvostov (Alexander Semyonovich), Prince Shakhovskoi and in general, a large number of the members of the *Beseda*[2] of the Lovers of the Russian Word. To the latter group [Karamzin's] belonged Dmitriev, Bludov, Dashkov, Turgenev, Zhukovsky, Batyushkov, V. L. Pushkin, Vyazemsky, etc. Derzhavin, Krylov and Gnedich stayed in the middle, but leaned more to the latter group.

"Karamzinolatry" reached the highest stage with his readers: whoever dared to doubt the infallibility of their idol was cursed and pursued, not only literarily. It was much easier to get on with Karamzin himself, a man both gentle and placid, than with his frenzied *sayyids*.[3] The spirit of their party was so strong that they not only ostracized the worthiest of people who dared not adore Karamzin, but even drew close vile freaks who imitated their tone . . .[4] Vigel, and the greatest scoundrel of them all, Voyeykov. The second *treasure* of this circle was Zhukovsky. They loved, honored and worshipped him. They considered the smallest doubt in the perfection of his verses to be a crime. Zhukovsky benefited more than anyone. P. A. Nikolsky, publishing *The Pantheon of Russian Poetry,* didn't think that he could harm Zhukovsky by including his verses in *The Pantheon.* A. Turgenev saw this as a financial loss for Zhukovsky . . . and once, after starting to talk about them with Gnedich at a dinner at Countess Stroganov's, he called Nikolsky a thief. Gnedich stood up for Nikolsky. A quarrel ensued, almost ending in a duel. Nikolsky, after he found out about this, stopped printing Zhukovsky's works in *The Pantheon.* These frenzied fanatics demanded not only acknowledgment of Karamzin's talent, respect for him, but blind pagan adoration itself. Whoever dared to judge Karamzin, to find the tiniest blemish in his works, became in their eyes a villain, cruel monster, some type of atheist. V. L. Pushkin said this about Shishkov's followers:

> And if someone dares to praise Karamzin,
> Our obligation, O people, is to destroy the villain.

The same could have been said about the other party, only substituting the first line with

> And if someone dares to judge Karamzin.

Karamzin's followers founded a private, closed literary society under the name of Arzamas, into which they admitted people who swore a vow of adoration of Karamzin and hatred for Shishkov. At the initiation, each one had to give a speech of praise, a satire or something like that, glorifying their idol and humiliating their enemy. I was always an ardent admirer of Karamzin, not because of any connections or party spirit, but because of sincere conviction; I hated Shishkov and his absurd worshippers and imitators, but I did not inflict upon myself the obligation to flatter Karamzin absolutely and continually, and not only because I wasn't accepted into Arzamas, but was made an object of indignation and sneers of its members. The followers of Shishkov also got angry at me for my real opposition. Later on the roles changed. For example, Bludov, the most frenzied of the Karamzinians, became a comrade of Shishkov's through the Ministry of Education. Only Dashkov remained true to his mission. After about fifteen years as the assistant minister of Internal Affairs he asked me when we met:

"And have you turned to Shishkov?"
"No," I answered, "I've kept my former opinion. And you, Dmitri Vasilievich?"
"And I t-t-too. I have two en-en-enemies. Sh-sh-shiskov and the T-t-turks," he said, stuttering.

I. I. Grech, *Notes from my Life*
St. Pete: 1886, pp. 408-10

***

The Arzamas society got its start in the following way: Prince Shakhovskoi wrote the comedy, *Lipetsk Waters* (still earlier he had written a comedy about Karamzin called *The New Sterne*). In *Lipetsk Waters* he exposed the balladeer, i.e., Zhukovsky. To be sure, all of our young tribe were seething and arming themselves. Dmitri Nikolaevich (Bludov) wrote *An Apparition in Arzamas,* similar to the one Abbé Morlet wrote under the title *La Vision,* which owed a debt to the comedy *Les Philosophes* in which Palissot presented many of the encyclopedists of that time. In *Son of the Fatherland* Dashkov wrote and published a letter to the newest Aristophanes and also couplets with the refrain "Praise to you, o Shutovskoi."[5] I brimmed over with a flood of epigrams, and it seems, first gave Shakhovskoi the nickname Shutovskoi ... This *Apparition in Arzamas* really gave our literary society its name. The active founders and later the most zealous members were Dmitri Nikolaevich [Bludov], Zhukovsky and Dashkov. I was then still living in Moscow. Even though I was nominated as a member at its inception, I only began to participate in it later, i.e., in 1816 when I arrived in Petersburg ...

By the way, the following was stated in the society's charter: "According to the example set by all other societies, each new member of Arzamas will have to deliver a speech in praise of his deceased predecessor; but all members of the new Arzamas are immortal," and so, for lack of proper corpses, the new Arzamasians suggested renting corpses from among the Chaldeans of the *Beseda* and Academy. The minutes of the meetings, which always ended with supper where roast goose was an indispensable dish, were put together by Zhukovsky; in them he always gave vent to his love of, outstanding genius for, and ability to sustain, balderdash.

For a long time everything was carried out only as a joke; but later there was expressed a desire to give the society a more serious and exclusively literary direction, and together with this, to publish a journal. It seems that Count Bludov composed a new set of regulations .... But many members drifted away, circumstances changed, and all of these good intentions of reform were left without any results. The society itself died a natural death or came to a halt, and what remained was only a friendly connection among the members and the use of our nicknames in our friendly correspondence.

For details and chronological information about all of this, you could turn to Vigel's notes ...

P. A. Vyazemsky, *Notebooks,*
Collected Works, vol. X (St. P., 1886), pp. 245-47

***

Strictly speaking, Arzamas did not have any form. It was a society of young people, congregating around Karamzin and united only by a lively feeling of love for their native tongue, literature and history . . . The direction of this society, or it would be better to say, of this friendly conversation group, was mainly *critical*. The people who made up the group were concerned with strict analysis of literary works, its application to language and the native lore of all sources of ancient and foreign literature, with the search for their own origins, serving as the foundation of a firm, independent theory of language and so on . . . At that time Zhukovsky, Batyushkov and Pushkin wrote poems under the influence of Arzamas and this influence perhaps even affected some pages of Karamzin's history.

A. V. [S. S. Uvarov], *Literary Reminiscences.*
Collected Works, 1851, vol. XXVII, p. 37

***

The Arzamas society, or simply Arzamas . . . gathered quite faithfully each week on Thursdays at the home of one of the two married members—Bludov and Uvarov. They grew more jolly with every meeting; each joke was followed by new ones, every sharp word was answered with another . . . The evening usually began with the reading of the minutes of the previous meeting, written by the secretary Zhukovsky; these already disposed everyone to hilarity, if it is permissible to say this. It ended with a tasty supper which also was recorded in the minutes. To whom in Russia is not known the glory of the Arzamas geese: Zhukovsky wanted to confer this honor on the society . . . He demanded that at every supper a roast goose be served and wanted to adorn the coat-of-arms of the society with its picture.

F. Vigel, *Notes,* vol. II, part 4, p. 66

***

In this society dedicated to jokes and parodies, each member had his own name. I remember a few: Zhukovsky was called Svetlana; A. I. Turgenev—Aeolian Harp; S. P. Zh[ikharev] *Gromoboi*; D. N. B[ludov]—Cassandra; F. F. Vigel—Crane of Ibycus; D. P. S[everin]—Frisky Tomcat; S. S. Uvarov—Old Lady; V. L. Pushkin—*Vot* [over there]. I don't remember the rest. They read parodies and each meeting began with a speech in honor of one of the literary old-believers, adversaries of Karamzin, or one of the versifiers. These parodies and speeches, read by the members, referred a lot to the famous count D. I. Khvostov . . .[6]

Here's how Vasily Lvovich Pushkin was accepted as a member of the Arzamas society. This happened in the home of S. S. U[varov].

They led Pushkin into one of the front rooms, laid him on a sofa and heaped upon him the fur coats of all of the other members. This . . . meant that the newly accepted member had to endure as his first trial, a *furcoat rotting*, i.e., *to rot* under these *fur coats*.[7]

His second trial consisted of the following: lying under them, he had to listen to the reading of an entire tragedy of some Frenchman, a Petersburg author who read it himself. Then they led him, blindfolded, from one staircase to another and into a room which came before the study. The study in which the meeting was held and where the members were gathered was brightly illuminated, but this room was kept dark and divided from it by an arch with a fiery, orange curtain. Here they took the blindfold from his eyes—and a huge, formless dummy, constructed on a dress hanger which was covered by a sheet, appeared in their midst. They explained that this monster stood for bad *taste,* gave him a bow and arrows and ordered him to use the monster as a target. Pushkin (it is necessary to remember his figure: fat, with a double chin, breathless and gouty) pulled back the bow, released the arrow and fell down because behind the sheet was hidden a little boy who, at that very minute, shot him with a pistol loaded with blanks and brought down the dummy.

Then they led Pushkin behind the curtain and put in his hands the emblem of Arzamas, a frozen Arzamas goose which he had to hold in his hands the whole time that they were reading a long welcoming speech. I think Zhukovsky read the speech. Finally they brought him a silver washtub and washstand to wash his hands and face, explaining that this was patterned on *Lipetsk Waters,* Shakovskoi's comedy. All of this went on either in 1816 or 1817. Of course in this way they took in the good-natured Vasily Lvovich, who believed that everyone else underwent the very same trial. The general title of the members was: *their excellencies, the geniuses of Arzamas.*

> M. A. Dmitriev, *Trifles from the Storehouse of My Memory* (M. 1869), pp. 88ff.

***

29 September 1817, Saturday. Arzamas met at our place the day before yesterday. We accidentally abandoned literature and began to talk about internal politics. Everyone agreed about the necessity of abolishing slavery; but the means suggested were not accepted by everyone. I would also wish that this could be done another way, but since we have no choice, then we must take what they give us.

> N. I. Turgenev, *Diary.*
> *Archive of the Turgenev Brothers,* vol. III, p. 93

***

4 December 1817 . . . The Russian character has a great shortcoming, consisting of the fact that Russians usually cannot devote themselves to any goal, to a simple pursuit; consequently, there is inconstancy. In this we are worse, I think, than the French, who are blamed for flightiness. Arzamas to me is an example and proof of this inconstancy.

> *Ibid.,* p. 108

***

On January 12, 1818 Uvarov was named President of the Academy of Sciences. On January 28, at their suggestion, Karamzin was chosen as an honorary member . . . A. I.

Turgenev also was chosen on February 18. Not long before that, November 5, 1817, D. I. Khvostov was chosen to join the Academy.

V. I. Saitov, *Notes,*
Ostankino Archives, vol. I, p. 467

The Green Lamp

When visiting high society in this capital, even infrequently, one can notice that a large schism exists here in the upper classes of society. The first, whom one may call the True Believers . . . are adherents of ancient customs, despotic rule and fanaticism; the second—the heretics—are defenders of foreign customs and pioneers of liberal ideas. These two parties always find themselves in a kind of war. It seems that you see the spirit of gloom in a skirmish with the genius of light: out of this fight comes an intellectual and moral twilight which still covers our poor motherland.

A. F. Ulybyshev, Letter to a friend in Germany,
Decembrists and Their Time, vol. I (M. no date), p. 44

***

One of the secret circles where discussions about literature and the theater and the reading of literary works accompanied dreams of freedom was the Society of the Green Lamp, which met at its founder's, the gentleman of the chamber, N. V. Vsevolozhsky; its intimate participants were: N. V. Vsevolozhsky, member of the Union of Prosperity;[8] Y. N. Tolstoi, hussar; member of the Union of Prosperity, P. P. Kaverin . . . officer of the household troops . . . D. N. Barkov, often translated for the theater; Uhlan Yuriev and a few others; and the famous member of a secret society, S. P. Trubetskoi also belonged to it, although only for a little while. One of the intimate members of the circle was A. S. Pushkin.

V. Semevsky, *Sketches on the History of the Ideas of the Decembrists,*
Russkoe Bogatsvo, 1908, No. 4, p. 73

***

In 1818 or 1819 a group formed in the house of the Gentleman of the Chamber, Nikita Vsevolozhsky. I was one of the first founders of this group and was chosen as its first chairman. It received the name, Green Lamp, because of a lamp of that color which hung in the room where the members gathered. However, a double implication was concealed under this name, and the words "Counsel and Hope" made up the motto of the group. Rings were also made with lamps engraved on them; each member had to have a ring. Regardless of that, the Society of the Green Lamp had no political goals at all. One circumstance distinguished it from all other learned societies: the statute invited members to speak at the meetings and to write freely, and each member gave his word to keep the secret. For all of this, in the course of a year the society of the Green Lamp did not change; and except for a few republican verses and other fragments read there, no free-thinking plans came up; the number of members reached about twenty or a few more. The meetings took place . . . at Vsevolozhsky's house and, in his absence, at mine.

> Ya. N. Tolstoi, quoted in P. E. Shchegolev, "Green Lamp," in *Pushkin and His Contemporaries,* No. 8, pp. 30-31, 42

***

For their meetings, which usually took place on Saturdays, the Green Lamp adopted a humorous ritual: Amphitryon Nikita fed his friends dinner and gave them champagne to drink during their famous jovial rites. So, for example, his retainer, a Kalmyk servant, was obliged to follow the conversation and if any one of the guests casually uttered an unprintable word, he then had to give him a "penalty" goblet, exclaiming, "I wish you health." Sometimes, of course, actresses took part in the carousals of the Green Lamp and still more often—"Laisas"[9] like Shteingel, Olga Masson, Nadenka and others to whom Pushkin refers in his friendly epistles to members of the circle . . . (in society they told yarns about orgies, Athenian evenings and so on) . . . In reality it's more likely that the "orgies" of the Green Lamp did not go beyond the most ordinary of drinking bouts; more often than not, they were simple suppers, gay, natural, during which they discussed different theatrical news and adventures; the discussions were even noted down in some of the minutes.

> P. Morozov, *From the Lycée until Exile, Works of Pushkin,* ed. S. Vengerov, vol. I, p. 489

***

Once Colonel Zhadovsky, a member of the society, informed us that the police had found out about its existence and that it could be liable to persecution, since no formal permission was given for its establishment: at once they decided not to meet any more and the society was disbanded.[10]

> V. Semevsky, *Sketches on the History of the Ideas of the Decembrists, Russkoe Bogatsvo,* 1908, No. 4, p. 75

***

Thursdays at S. E. Raich's and the Saturdays of the Lyubomudrys[11]

After my translation of Virgil's *Georgics* (1821) I started . . . on a translation of Tasso's *Jerusalem Delivered.* Meanwhile, under my leadership, a small, modest literary group formed at my place; in the last years of its existence it was under the patronage of I. I. Dmitriev and

RUSSIAN ROMANTICISM

Prince Dmitri Vladimirovich Golitsyn. The members of this group were: M. A. Dmitriev, A. I. Pisarev, M. P. Pogodin, V. P. Titov, S. P. Shevyryov, D. P. Oznobishin, A. M. Kubarev, Prince V. F. Odoevsky, A. S. Norov, F. I. Tyutchev, A. N. Muravyov, S. D. Poltoratsky, V. I. Obolensky, M. A. Maximovich, Count [A. A.] Shakhovskoi, N. V. Putyata and a few others: some of them always participated in the society which gathered at my house on Thursdays, others came sometimes. According to the laws of aesthetics which were popular then, we read and discussed works of the members and translations from Greek, Latin, Persian, Arabic, English, Italian, German and, rarely, French ... At the end of April 1825, I went to Little Russia [the Ukraine] with G. N. Rachmanov, whose son and nephew were entrusted to my care ... In August, 1826 I returned to Moscow; my society disintegrated and didn't meet anymore ...

S. E. Raich, *Autobiography.*
Russkii bibliofil, 1913, No. 8, pp. 28-29

***

At that ... time we formed two societies: one was literary and the other was philosophical. The first, under the leadership of the translator of the *Georgics,* S. E. Raich [Amfiteatrov], first met in Muravyov's home ... but then at the apartment of Senator Rachmanov, whose son had Raich for a tutor ... Our meetings were very lively, and a few of them were even brilliant and were honored with the presence of the universally loved and respected Governor-General Prince D. V. Golitsyn, I. I. Dmitriev and other celebrities. Here *belles-lettres* took the forefront; philosophy, history and other sciences only stealthily dared to give voice from time to time. I was fortunate to read a few translations from Thucydides and Plato and fragments from a history of Peter I, with which I was then lovingly occupied.

The other society was especially remarkable. It met *secretly,* and no one spoke of its existence to anyone. Its members were: Prince Odoevsky, Ivan Kireevsky, Dm. Venevitinov, Rozhalin and I. Here ruled German philosophy, i.e., Kant, Fichte, Oken, Görres and others. Here we occasionally read our own philosophical essays; but most often, for the most part we conversed about the works of the German "Lovers of Wisdom" which we had read. The sources on which all types of human knowledge were supposed to be based, made up the primary subject of our conversations; to us, Christian teaching seemed to be fit only for the masses and not for us, the lovers of wisdom. We especially valued Spinoza and considered his works to be on a higher level than the Gospel and other sacred writings. We met at Prince Odoevsky's, in Lanskaya's home ... He presided, but D. Venevitinov spoke more than anyone and led us into ecstasy with his speeches.

A. I. Koshelev, *Notes* (Berlin, 1884), pp. 11-12

***

After he found out that N. A. Polevoi not only had decided to publish a journal, but also had received permission for it, the Prince [V. F. Odoevsky] suggested that my brother get acquainted with his own literary society, which also wanted to publish a journal. Wouldn't it be better to join with him and that way not only avoid rivalry, but also suddenly acquire more active and educated co-workers? Such was the sensible judgment of Prince Odoevsky, with whom N. A.Polevoi enthusiastically agreed. As a matter of fact, it was for the most part made up of excellent young people, former pupils of the prince in the University Boarding School for Nobility. Unfortunately the Chairman of the society was Semyon Egorovich Raich [Amfiteatrov], a mediocre versifier, distinguished by a great originality in conversation and manners . . . It's not surprising that such a man imparted a humorous character to the literary society of young people, who had chosen him as their chairman. The society always met on the designated days and had, besides a chairman, a secretary who kept *minutes* of the meetings, and read members' verses and little prose articles at the meetings—in a word—it childishly imitated the official Society of Russian Literature, which met at Antonsky's.

At first glance the entire comedy did not appeal to my brother; however, he had the patience to show up a few times at the meetings of the Society, where he was accepted as a member . . . Still one more comic scene occurred at the last meeting N. A. attended. I remember that when he returned from there, he laughed and said that he wouldn't be going anymore to the society, to which the witty Sobolensky, who had dealings with all of the educated youth, attached killingly funny epithets, which the members of the Society themselves laughingly repeated.

K. Polevoi, *Notes*, (St. P.,1888), pp. 100-101

***

Tell me, has your correspondence with Venevitinov begun? How I love to recall our winter Saturday evenings! I will tell you frankly that I got a lot out of those conversations—more than from books or personal meditation. Your heated discussions with Venevitinov were the most interesting things for me. Your faces were enlivened with enthusiasm. You argued openly, made heated objections, but agreed with joy.

A. S. Porov, Letter to A. I. Koshelev, in N. Kolyupanov, *Biography of A. I. Koshelev* (M. 1889), vol. I, book II, p. 74

***

I will never forget an evening I spent as an eighteen-year-old youth at the home of my grand-cousin Mikh. Mikh. Naryshkin; this was in February or March of 1825. The following were at the party: Ryleev, Pr. Obolensky, Pushchin and a few others who were subsequently exiled to Siberia. Ryleev read his patriotic ballads; and everyone spoke freely about the necessity—*d'en finir avec ce gouvernement* [of putting an end to the government]. That evening made a very strong impression on me; and the next morning I informed Ivan Kireevsky of all I had heard and then together we went off to D. Venevitinov's, at whose place Rozhalin then lived . . . We talked a lot that day about politics and about how it was imperative to bring to Russia a change in its form of government. For this reason, with special avidity we applied ourselves to Benjamin Constant, Royer-Collard and other French political writers; and for a time German philosophy took second place.

A. I. Koshelev, *Notes* (Berlin, 1884), p. 13

Pogodin, the editor of the *Moscow Herald* came to St. Petersburg from Moscow. Only *in name* is he the editor; his signed letters are proof of this. The main bosses of this editorial board are: Sobolensky, Titov, Maltsov, Poltoratsky, Shevyryov, Ragozin and several other sincerely rabid liberals. A few of them (Maltsov and Sobolensky) have money for the upkeep of the journal and pay Pushkin for poems. Their main goal consists of bringing *politics* into that journal. In 1828 they intended to publish a political newspaper, but since not one of them could present his work as enjoined by censorship regulations, they sent for Pogodin so that he again could use his name to ask permission to bring in politics. Pogodin is an exceptionally ingratiating person. He is under the protection of Uvarov and hopes to receive his desired permission to house in the journal a section of politics, which Titov and Poltoratsky intend to edit. Pogodin doesn't have influence on these people, but depends on them because they are rich and brave and he is poor, has no name and is timid. These youths do not write anything literary, deeming themselves unworthy of it and occupy themselves only with political science. The form of their thoughts, their speeches and judgments resound with blatant *carbonari* spirit. Sobolensky and Titov . . . are the worst of the lot. They meet at Prince Odoevsky's, who has a reputation among them as a philosopher, and at Maltsov's.

> A hand-written note by M. J. von-Foch, 1827,
> *Russian Antiquity,* 1902, book I, p.34

***

These conversations [in the *Lyubomudry* circle] continued until December 14, 1827, when we decided it was imperative to discontinue them, since we did not want to draw the suspicion of the police on ourselves; also because our political activities were taking up all of our attention. I vividly recall how after this unhappy date, Prince Odoevsky summoned us and in a special ceremony gave over the charter and minutes of our Society for the Love of Wisdom to the fire in his fireplace.

> A. I. Koshelev, *Notes,* p. 12

The Circle of N. V. Stankevich and V. G. Belinsky

The very appearance of the circles in question was the natural answer to a deep inner need of Russian life at that time . . . In the university our circle . . . met the already formed circle of Sungurov. Its direction was like ours, more political than scientific. Stankevich's circle, formed at that time, was equally close to and distant from both of them. It went in another direction: its interests were purely theoretical. In the thirties our convictions were much too youthful, much too passionate and ardent not be be exclusive. We could coolly respect Stankevich's circle, but could not draw together. They planned philosophical systems, were occupied with self-analysis and contented themselves with a luxurious pantheism from which Christianity was not excluded. In 1834 Sungurov's whole circle was exiled and disappeared. In 1835 they exiled us; in five years we returned, hardened by our trials. Our youthful dreams were turned into the irrevocable determination of maturity. This was the most brilliant phase of the Stankevich circle. I didn't find him in Russia—he was in Germany, but precisely at that time the articles of

Belinsky all began to draw attention to themselves.

After we returned we began to take each other's measure. The battle was uneven on both sides; the ground, the arms, and the language—everything was different. After fruitless debates we saw that our turn had come to study science and we took up Hegel and German philosophy ourselves. When we mastered it sufficiently, it turned out that there was no disagreement between us and Stankevich's circle.

The Stankevich circle inevitably had to dissolve. It had done its work and done it in a most brilliant manner; its influence on all of literature and on academic teaching was enormous—it is sufficient to name Belinsky and Granovsky; Koltsov was formed in it also. Botkin belonged to it, as well as Katkov and so on. It could not remain a closed circle, not moving to German doctrinairism; living Russian people are not suited to it.

Naturally, the Stankevich society had to divide up between them and us. The Aksakovs, Samarin sided with the Slavophiles, i.e., with Khomyakov and the Kireevskys; Bakunin, Belinsky with us. Stankevich's closest friend, the one most totally like family to him, Granovsky, was ours from the time of his arrival from Germany. If Stankevich had lived, his circle still would not have stood ground; he himself would have come over either to Khomyakov or to us.

> A. Herzen, *Past and Thoughts,* III, 1919, vol. IV, pp. 30, 33

***

While still in the university classroom, he [Stankevich] became the center of a circle of companions, equal to him in intelligence, but eagerly submitting (as only people in their early years are able to submit) to the influence of a bright mind, noble heart and strict moral demands. Stankevich was totally charming with people his own age: he was a living ideal of truth and honor which in the early stages of life passionately and tirelessly is sought after by youth, vividly feeling its vocation.

> P. Annenkov, "N. V. Stankevich. Biographical Sketch," *Reminiscences and Critical Sketches,* 1881, pt. III, pp. 271-72

***

The course of human thought, its stately growth and its increase, eternal truth, clothing itself in various garb in conformity with its age and the people, showing its essence more and more—which other phenomenon could be more diverting? . . I do not consider philosophy my calling: it can be a step I cross over on the way to other fields of study: but first of all I must satisfy a need for it. And the solution of problems does not attract me as much as the method itself, as an expression of the latest successes of the mind. I want to be still more convinced of the worth of man and I confess, I would then want to convince others and awake in them lofty thoughts.

> N. V. Stankevich, Letter to V. M. Neverov, 2 December 1835, *Correspondence* (M, 1914), p. 341

In this circle they had already worked out a general view of Russia, life, literature, the world—a view for the most part negative. The artificiality of Russian jingoism, its claims filling up our literature, the increased fabrication of verses, the insincerity of the lyricism of the press—all of this engendered a justified desire for simplicity and sincerity, engendered a forceful attack on each phrase and effect; this and other things were perhaps first uttered in the Stankevich circle as the opinion of a whole society of people ... Most one-sided of all were their attacks on Russia, excited by false praises of her. As a fifteen-year-old boy ... I was struck by such a trend and it was sometimes painful to me; especially painful to me were the attacks on the Russia I have loved since my earliest days. But observing the constant intellectual interest in this society and hearing the constant speeches about moral questions, once I became acquainted with it, I could not tear myself away from this circle and spent decidedly every evening there.

K. Aksakov, *Day,* 1862, Nos. 39-40

***

Later a group of young people from this circle, Herzen, Ogaryov and others, and those of the Stankevich circle who united with them, sided with Belinsky. A few of them had a large influence on the growth and activities of Belinsky himself. A whole series of figures developed in this way. Their influence appeared in all strata of society, it formed, as it were, one family, the members of which divided among themselves, as they expressed it, "the act of renovation of the obsolescent forms of life." A new spirit began to be embodied everywhere: in literature, in science, in family life, in service; and it put its stamp on everthing.

T. Passek, *From Distant Years,* vol. I (St. P, 1878), p. 465

***

For the most part the friends got together at B[otkin's]. Their conversation was always lively, ardent. Its subject was art from Hegel's point of view: from this point of view they strictly discussed Pushkin and other contemporary poets. They could in no way resign Lermontov, with his demonic and Byronic trend, to this new view. This tortured Belinsky terribly ... He saw that the novice poet displayed enormous poetic force; every one of his new poems in *Notes of the Fatherland* led Belinsky to ecstasy, but at the same time, there was not even a shadow of reconciliation to Hegel's view in these poems. However, they excused Lermontov by the fact that he was young and only just starting out; they calmed themselves a little with the fact that he possessed all the qualities to become, in time ... a great artist and to achieve the crown of creation—artistic composure and objectivity ... Klyushnikov, who had a bit of the demonic about him, was greatly sympathetic to Lermontov's talent ... Katkov and Aksakov read through their translations of Heine, Freiligrath and the other latest German poets ... This circle occupies an important place in the history of Russian growth ... Formed in it, the most ardent and noble figures in the fields of science and literature also emerged from it.

I. I. Panaev, *Reminiscences,* pp. 256-57

The rapture with Hegel's philosophy from 1836 was boundless in the young circle which met in Moscow in the name of the great German teacher . . . The circle considered anyone unfamiliar with Hegel to be almost a non-existent person . . .

P. Annenkov, *Literary Reminiscences,* (St. P., 1909), p. 187

***

In Hoffmann's biography I read that Hoffmann did not read criticism and reviews of his works and was completely indifferent to them. After writing a work, he read it to his friends; if they liked it, then the whole world couldn't make him believe that it was bad. Isn't it the very same in our circle? we have no partiality toward each other—we say about each other what we feel, and therefore we value mutual judgment and care little about what others think of us. When I read my articles to you, I am frightened—I tremble for the fate of what I have written: you praise and I am in ecstasy; you don't like it and I very calmly treat my composition as an unsuccessful attempt. You come to me with the very same attitude.

V. G. Belinsky, Letter to M. Bakunin, June 20, 1839, *Letters,* vol. I (St. P., 1914), p. 196

The Salon of Z. A. Volkonskaya

At that time the splendid home of Princess Zinaida Volkonskaya, born Princess Belozerskaya (-Beloselskaya), served as the common center for the literary set and in general for lovers of all areas of art, music, singing, and painting. This remarkable woman . . . wanted to play the role of Corinne and really was our Russian Corinne.[12] She wrote both prose and poetry . . . Everything in this unusual woman, who totally devoted herself to art, breathed of grace and poetry. Because of her aristocratic connections, the most brilliant society of the first capital [Petersburg] gathered in her home; literary men and artists turned to her as if to some kind of Maecenas, and pleasantly met each other at her splendid evening gatherings, which she knew how to enliven with a special talent. A passionate music-lover, she set up in her home not only concerts, but also Italian opera; and she even appeared on stage herself in the role of Tancredi,[13] striking everyone with her adroit performance and marvelous voice; it was hard to find a contralto equal to her. In the magnificent rooms of the Beloselsky house . . . operas, *tableaux vivants,* and masquerades often took place all of that winter (1826-27), and each presentation was arranged with special taste, because Italians, who even enticed her to Rome, always surrounded her. Here at these very salons one could meet everything distinguished in the Russian Parnassus, for everyone bent down before this woman of genius. Pushkin and Vyazemsky, Baratynsky and Delvig were her constant visitors. Prince Odoevsky, devoted to music as much as he was to poetry, and who at that time published *Mnemosyne,*[14] never missed one of her evening gatherings; the pleasant author of Russian historical novels, M. N. Zagoskin, attended; the sedate Raich, Shevyryov and Pogodin, although not fans of high society, nevertheless were not strangers to her splendid circle: she really knew how to bring everyone together. But there was one youthful, gifted poet similar to André Chénier who was drawn to her not only because of the brilliant society alone; ardent with pure, but passionate love, he dedicated his melodious, melancholy verse to her and went to his grave prematurely, although the princess, friendly with his family, showed him tender goodwill. The young Venevitinov had much promise for the future and his early death was a great loss for poetry. The famous Polish poet, Mickiewicz, visiting Moscow against his will, was also one of the dear guests of the Beloselsky palace; his *Dziady* [Forefathers] and *Crimean Sonnets* enjoyed a very high reputation at that time and he amazed everyone with his unusual improvisation of tragic scenes.

A. N. Muravyov, *Acquaintance with Russian Poets* (Kiev, 1871), pp. 11-13

***

In Moscow the house of Princess Zinaida Volkonskaya was the refined meeting place of all the remarkable and select personalities of contemporary society. Here came together representatives of the high life: dignitaries and beauties, youths and those of mature age, people of intellectual labor, professors, writers, journalists, poets, artists. Everyone in this house carried the mark of service to art and thought. In it took place readings, concerts by dilettantes and performances of Italian opera by amateurs. The hostess herself was counted among the artists and stood at their head. Once having heard her it was impossible to forget the impression she made with her full and melodious contralto voice and with her lively performance in the role of Tancredi in Rossini's opera. I still remember and hear how she, in Pushkin's presence on the first day of their acquaintance, sang his elegy put to music by Genishta:

The daylight sky dimmed,
The evening mist fell over the blue sea.

Pushkin was touched to the quick by this seduction of subtle and artful coquetry. As usual the color flashed in his face . . .

It goes without saying that Mickiewicz, from his very arrival in Moscow, was a zealous visitor and belonged to the ranks of the most beloved and honored guests in the home of Princess Volkonskaya. He dedicated to her a poem known under the name of *Pokój grecki* [Greek room] . . .

P. A. Vyazemsky, "Reminiscences of Mickiewicz," *Russian Archive,* No. 6, pp. 1085ff.

***

She first lived in Moscow, where she met Venevitinov and Mickiewicz. Later she became a Catholic (probably secretly when she was in Moscow). Then she moved to Petersburg. When the news of her conversion reached the Emperor Nikolai Pavlovich, he wanted her to listen to reason and with this goal sent a priest to her. But she had an attack of nerves, convulsions. The tsar let her leave Russia and she chose Italy as her place of residence—probably because of its connection with her change of religion. In Rome they soon nicknamed her Beata . . .

> Report of Princess Repnina in V. Shekrok,
> "N. V. Gogol. Five Years Abroad, 1836-41,"
> *Russian Messenger,* No. 8 (1894), p. 630

Notes

1. The selection of memoirs on the circles and salons comes from M. Aronson and S. Reyser, *Literaturnye kruzhki i salony* (Leningrad: Priboi, 1929). The notes are the translator's unless indicated otherwise.

2. Colloquium of Lovers of the Russian Word. It will appear in the text as *Beseda.*

3. Islamic chief or leader.

4. One line was deleted by the censors. [Note of Aronson and Reyser.]

5. A pun on Shakhovkoi's name based on the Russian word for "joke."

6. History of members (according to Zhukovsky's tally): Bludov, Batyushkov, Vigel, Voyeykov, Vyazemsky, Davydov, Dashkov, Zhikharev, Zhukovsky, Kavelin, N. Muravyov, M. Orlov, Poletika, Pleshcheev, A. S. Pushkin, V. L. Pushkin, Severin, A. Turgenev, N. Turgenev, Uvarov and one other person, "Stately Swan," whose pseudonym has not been revealed. Honorary members (or "honorary geese") were: Karamzin, Dmitriev, Neledinsky-Meletsky, Count Kapodistrias, A. Saltykov, M. Saltykov, G. Gagarin. Also, these are more nicknames: Orlov—Rhine, N. I. Turgenev—Warwick, Kavelin—Hermit, Vyazemsky—Asmodeus. [Aronson and Reyser.]

7. An allusion to Shakhovskoi's comedy, *Abduction of a Furcoat.* [Aronson and Reyser]

8. A circle, the precursors of the *Lyubomudry* group, full of high ideals.

9. Euphemism for women of easy virtue based on the name of an ancient Greek courtesan.

10. Apparently at the end of 1820. [Aronson and Reyser.]

11. Lovers of Wisdom.

12. Heroine of a novel by Mme de Staël, *Corinne, or Italy* (1807). Known for its description of Italian customs and civilization, the novel is a love story which revolves around the heroine, a half-English, half-Italian poetess in self-exile in Rome.

13. Main character in the opera, *Tancredi, melodramma eroico,* by Rossini, based on Tasso's *Jerusalem Delivered.*

14. Chronological error. Odoevsky published *Mnemosyne,* a *Lyubomudry* journal in 1824-25, but doubtlessly at that time, he certainly often frequented this salon. [Aronson and Reyser.]

The Vyazemsky-Turgenev Correspondence*

Prince Vyazemsky to A. I. Turgenev and V. A. Zhukovsky
29 September, 1826. Moscow

Greetings, my dear and beloved friends! I've been here ten days, but left the Karamzins' the night between the third and fourth of September. Their stay in Revel [Tallinn] has been good for them and so they'll stay there for the winter. And that's very well thought out! What awaits them in Petersburg? You, their closest friends, are not there. For the sake of two or three friends they would have to pay the high price of [seeing] a hundred boring, empty acquaintances, [of bearing] the burden of social obligations and so on and so on: at least boredom won't be forced upon them there.

How I envy you, my friends! Send for me: I can't breathe here! Formerly we all somehow were expecting something; now we're like Jean-Paul's *orphans*.[1] Eternity arrived and this eternity is a trifle. I don't hope for anything good. What a new censorship board! Everyone has an obligation to judge: until I see that the Government isn't afraid of enlightenment, but summons it as a helpmate, I shall have no hope for Russia's welfare. Personal measures in the government are not enough. In the regulations it says that History should not include the musings of the historian, but should be a bare story of the events. They say that when he was reading the regulations in manuscript form, the Tsar put a question by this article: "on the strength of this, shouldn't Karamzin's history be passed? Answer simply *yes* or *no.*" They answered: *no!* Here the Tsar added: *nonsense*; but meanwhile this nonsense stays and that's the way it is. We even hear that a storm is brewing against Karamzin's history. Tsesarevich considers it to be a harmful book and Karamzin to be a cunning stepchild of the Martinists.[2] He read it the first time in Ems and there made up his mind about it and about him [Karamzin]. The author does not avoid responsibility because of the Censor's approval or his own remoteness, for the Censor looks the book over superficially, but the Author had time to think over his subject and so on and so forth. And what can one say about the absurdity of the Editorial board? In the first place it's been said that the Censor has a goal, if not to give good direction to Literature and to minds, at least then, to put a stop to a fallacious one; and in the second place: *from this it follows* that all books, journals, pictures and *musical notes* should be censored. Zhukovsky! you should write for the regulations from Perovsky, who, they say, participated [in drawing them up] with his brother Alexei, under the guidance of Shishkov. But better still: make up your mind to write your observations on it and take them to the Tsar. This is your duty! Since Karamzin's death you have been called on to be the representative of Russian Literacy, prostrate at the throne of illiteracy. I'm not joking. Your indifference to such matters would only be cowardice.

They say that the Tsar is intelligent and vainglorious: here are two springs on which loyal and honorable people can act with success. And what can you demand of him when loyal and honorable people leave him in the power of stupid people and idlers, but themselves stand in corners with their fingers in their noses and say: it's not our affair!—I've seen very few people from the world of prominence here, because I finagled to return to Moscow when the show was over and not for the fitting of the cap of Monomakh;[3] but according to all of the opinions and

---

*The selections are taken from *Perepiska Aleksandra Ivanovich Turgeneva s Kn. Petrom Andreevichem Viazemskim,* vol. I: 1814-33. *Arkhiv Brat'ev Turgenevykh,* vypusk 6, ed. M. K. Kulman. Petrograd: Rossiiskaia gosudarstvennaia akademicheskaia tipografiia, 1921.

echoes reaching me, I conclude that there are very few who are pleased and many who are not. The favors themselves, falling like rain, have only aggravated the thirst for ranks and crosses, but have not slaked it: everyone gets insulted when he compares himself with his neighbor, who received more, or even the very same amount. In a word, nothing in the political atmosphere heralds a beneficent regeneration, although they do talk about the many changes in people and departments. For example, generally speaking, they are nominating Kochubey to be Councillor of the Department of Internal Affairs; it's probable that something may very well come of it, since all of the important menials are really paying court to them. They say that Stroganov interceded to Nesselrod so that Kushnikov and Speransky would occupy the ministries of justice and internal affairs. A new Arakcheev is ripening in Dibich, who with his short little hands grabs everything and overshadows the Tsar, so that you have access to him [the Tsar] only though him [Dibich].

Only one rumor made me happy—that Poletika will take Shishkov's place; but somehow this is not to be believed. Prince A(lexander) N(ikolaevich) Golitsyn, they say, is also in power: they say about him that he will be some kind of chief, *maître des requêtes,*[4] as head of State Secretaries, and so on. It seems that Bludov is semi-active: here with Golitsyn, or under A. N. Golitsyn, and with Longinov, he took part in a petition committee, and added to that he orchestrated other *rescripta,* e.g., a *rescriptum*[5] to Nesselrod at the granting to him of lands (which, by the way, scandalized many with its excessive outlay of praise), Russian translations of the declaration of war with Persia and other official papers. But according to all signs, it seems to me that he won't eat his way into power and into public affairs. The new organization of the gendarmerie under the leadership of Benckendorf frightens many: Alexander Volkov is already there, as well as Bibikov, formerly with Tormasov, and their appearance at balls in their light blue uniforms made a wonderful impression. They all didn't know whether they should make up their minds to bow to them or not. But in order not to grieve kind Zhukovsky completely with a stringent review of his friends, I left a joyous piece of news for him, *pour la bonne bouche.* Pushkin is here and is free.[6] In consequence of his letter to the Tsar, or information about him [Pushkin] or in consequence of one and the other, the Tsar sent a courier to the country after him, received him in his study, spoke with him intelligently and affectionately and congratulated him on getting his freedom. Fragments from his elegy *Chénier,* not passed by the censor, were "heated up" by someone and released under the name of the 14th of December. A few young officers were made victims of the forgery, imprisoned and were dispersed among various regiments.[7]

Pushkin read me his *Boris Godunov.*[8] A mature and lofty work. Whether it is a Tragedy or more of a historical picture, I won't say a word: one must listen to it, try to understand it in order to give it a satisfactory definition; but the fact is that the historical veracity of customs, language and poetic colors are completely preserved, that Pushkin's mind didn't turn to joking, that his thoughts matured, his soul brightened up, and in this creation has reached heights he never reached before. Today he's reading it at my place to Bludov and Dmitriev; it will be amusing to see his classical primness under a Romantic line of fire. Pushkin jumps from year to year, from Russia to Poland, from poetry to prose: the monks speak in [. . .], Marzheret speaks in French *et lache de gros mots* [and lets abuse fly]. However, Pushkin is only amusing himself here and, all in all, there is about a page of these fun and games: it's easy to delete. But Dmitriev will be very curious. The next group of songs from *Onegin* has also come a long way from the first. The Tsar himself promised to be his censor. And isn't that great! What a contradiction. The Tsar, or the Government, can give privileges to the detriment of punishment, but how can it give privileges to the detriment of public morality? One or two things: either Censorship is oppressive, then abolish it; or it is a sincere guardian keeping infections out, and then how can you give anyone the right to change it?

After all of these rumors what can I tell you about myself? My arrival in Moscow wasn't happy: on the second day my wife became incapacitated and to this day has not recovered. In the winter we are going to Ostafievo because we have nothing to live on. On top of all that my Kostroma village burned to the ground. I really don't know what I'll be able to do. I have no desire to serve [in the government] and don't foresee any good coming from it. One cannot serve here out of conscience, out of love for goodness, at least to my way of thinking: it's not worth it [to serve] for money, since they don't give you much of it. One would have to work as a cook *out of honor alone.*[9] Meanwhile the children are growing up: our means for education here are difficult. You need luck to hit upon a good choice and money to pay for this luck. And we have neither the one nor the other. Until now we have had surprisingly bad luck with *mesdames* and *mesdemoiselles.* There is one hope in sight: somehow to clamber out of this slough of disordered affairs and Russia and get along in some corner, but somewhere sunny. But when will this hope be realized? If only the Censorship were more reasonable, then I would enthusiastically get started on a journal. We could make ten thousand, but how could we manage with Fedora,[10] who is both great and a fool? Zhukovsky! take our part, [we] the landlords of intelligence, take your own part, you who are our Sheremetev. Get us the right, however small it might be, to be able to use our patrimony. You know I don't have the strength to endure.

I saw Ekat[erina] Fyodor[ovna] Muravyova in Petersburg. That's real hell. Her sons are still in the fortress, just like many other unfortunates. A small number were already sent to Siberia, among them: Volkonsky, Trubetsky[sic], Yakubovich, Davydov. The Muravyovs, mother and wife, are going to follow their family, when they send them off. They still don't know exacly whether they will be working or whether they will be simply kept in a fortress, which (according to local gossip) they are building to this end in Siberia. Trubetskaya also went after her husband, and on the whole it seems that all of the wives will follow this example. God grant at least that they will make up for the infamy of our age. Just imagine that already there is not even a trace of the 13th[11] or the 14th. There is no nation more thoughtless and inhuman than ours. Do you know Ryleev's letter?[12]

Farewell, my dears. I embrace you and Sergei Ivanovich [Turgenev] from the bottom of my heart. How is his health? Write to me and if you have a chance, send a European present— book, e.g., everything you find about Byron in French, English and German; the history of Napoleon by Walter Scott.[13] For God's sake, give me something to chew on. Why am I not with you? Take me as your dependent. Bow to the Pushkins[14] from us.

Zhukovsky, we wrote you from Revel, in answer to your letter. Did you get it?

And Turgenev, you have completely forgotten the Karamzins. While I was there, they had only one letter from you when you first arrived in Dresden.

If you have unpublished poems of mine or Pushkin's, give them to Prince Vasily Golitsyn in gratitude for the tobacco his wife will bring for you.

* * *

Prince Vyazemsky to A. I. Turgenev and V. A. Zhukovsky
November 20, 1826. Moscow.

Un écu, Sire, et votre nom, wrote d'Alembert to Frederick the Great, inviting him to subscribe to the construction of a statue to Voltaire. Your Parnassian Majesty, Vasily Andreevich, a little line and your name! Out of having nothing to do and [because of] my impecunious state, I was obliged to take part in the *Telegraph* and for my participation to take one half of the publisher's profits. Pushkin was obliged to go over to another journal for ten thousand rubles: Pogodin and all of the University youth, brought up on Schelling's German beer, will publish the *Moscow Messenger* next year; they wanted to name it the *Moscow Hermes;* but the Censorship wouldn't allow it because there is a Senator Hermes.[15] And this is the situation: It's equally bad to be like a literate Senator or like an illiterate Journal; consequently the name was improper. But that's not the point; I didn't go to participate in their Journal for many reasons: first, I instigated Pogodin from the beginning to publish a Journal, and it would be shameful to abandon him when another Journal is undermining him. Second, it seems to me that financial speculation is safer with the *Telegraph,* for without a doubt, the lion's share of that Journal belongs by all rights to Pushkin, but an ordinary part would be sent to me; but now, when peasants don't pay their quitrent, one must try to see whether the fools, i.e., readers, will give the quitrent. Third, it goes without saying that I would be happy with Pushkin anywhere; but he won't be here, the running of a journal can bore him; and he would have to be in contact with young people, not without talent, but surprisingly haughty; for haughtiness is a distinguishing trait of the new generation of writers, especially the Moscow writers. Also, as you know, I am not distinguished by humble wisdom and feel that it would turn out badly for me with them. That's an account of the situation for you. I don't ask poems of you because you probably don't have any; but by the way, I ask that you not give anything to anyone but me, if you finally give birth to anything; but give me prose in the form of letters about new books coming out in Germany, or in the form of accounts of your reading, and so on. That's easy for you: it's not easy to play the author here, very likely I won't print your name, but simply call them communications from our Dresden Correspondent. Two or three little pages a month will not burden you, but will enrich me. You can talk about the theater, the city, the weather, the young girls, etc. For this I rely on Turgenev, i.e., I'm not talking about girls but about communiqués to me about the European news. Your Grimmean Majesty, Alexander Ivanovich! help. All joking aside, Turgenev, you love to write, you write letters masterfully, and know how to be a journalist: all of your letters from foreign lands are suitable for publication. Not in vain did Dmitriev call you little Grimm.[16] Be for me the large Grimm; however small your communiqués, for me they will be great as good deeds. I am still waiting for help from you: get me any kind of literary novelties. I'm not asking for completely forbidden political fruits, more so since they would not be appropriate for my Journal; and I do value your loyal conscience, but you know how slowly and stupidly our French booksellers order books. Can't you subscribe to some French literary journal for me and send it, to me, to Zhukovsky through Perovsky or some other good soul? There is some *Revue britannique*[17] published in French in Paris, some sort of *Catholic,*[18] in which, it seems to me, good literary articles are appearing, *Revue encyclopédique.*[19] If you would send me about six hundred rubles worth a year, I would give it to Zhikharev here for you. All of the new *pirogi*[20] of Walter Scott, especially his history of Napoleon; whatever Guizot, Chateaubriand and Casimir Delavigne write; let's have the Germans too; all that is written in any language at all about Byron. In a word, the plums of European Enlightenment. Look, my sweet cows, don't turn me into Perrette[21] with an overturned earthenware pot of hope. No, take my verses as a motto for yourselves:

> A peasant had a cow
> As healthy as a bull.

It will be unconscionable of you not to humor me. Would that each of you could give me, for Christ's sake, two thousand rubles for nuts, plays, trousers and—you're waiting for this— for young girls! No, may the power of the Cross be with us! But I don't want to take a single kopeck from the profits for myself, but to subsist on, clothe myself and amuse myself with my own sweaty, or inky, farthings. Instead of money give me *des billets au porteur* [bill to bearer] for the public. Our journals don't have anything of a European scent about them: A Journal fumigated with fresh European fumes will appeal to our public, however stuffed up its nose is [. . .]me with Europe, my dears! In anticipation I'll say:

> Oh, wind, wind, whatever you may blow,
> Whatever—from Aeolian Harp to me,
> Whatever you may carry to me,
> Sweet-smelling from Svetlana—Martha.

After such verses I can inform you that Shishkov married Lebarzhevskaya. This doesn't amuse me anymore, but infuriates me. When I was younger, I rejoiced at the buffooneries of the Ministers, but now I begin to feel that a Minister who enters his second childhood insults the honor of his fellow citizens. It would be good, if having married him off to Lebarzhevskaya, they could divorce him from the Censorship. However, they are talking about his replacement and are naming candidates: Uvarov, Olenin, Karneev:

> *Dauchet, Hadel et St. Didier*
> *Sont écrivains de même force.*[22]

I am writing to you with the sound of bells in the background. How many hearts in Petersburg are out of sorts now, at least according to local rumors. For a long time they've been predicting great changes of faces in the Ministry by now.

You ask for verses from *Boris Godunov.* Pushkin isn't here; he went to the country to finish writing and took the tragedy with him; moreover his tragedy isn't suitable for a piecemeal [reading]. It is an important juicy *piece of meat,* as the Poles say, in the English taste: you must put it on the table whole. In it there aren't any French verses, upstarts that crawl out of the crowd, breast forward. It is a picture in which everything is in place, where the colors blend into harmonious shades, and nothing can be taken out. But I'll quote to you a speech from the role of Marzheret, who talks *que ces bougres ont du poil au cul* [like fellows with fur on their bottoms]. He says: *quoi?* [what?] but the Russians answer him: *kwa, kwa* [quack, quack], *it's all right for you heathens to quack at our lawful tsar.* Imagine Dmitriev at the reading of this Tragedy, the Actual Privy Councillor and General-Procurator of Classicism. However, we must be fair to him: he displayed great patience and flexibility. Also young Khomyakov has a manuscript of a tragedy, full of, as they say, much poetic beauty, if not a historical one, for Ermak, its hero, is a being rather ideal in his portrayal. A few days ago I also heard extracts from a manuscript-tragedy, *Vladimir,* by young Muravyov,[23] the younger son of Nikolai Nikolaevich, written in French form, but in German spirit. It's young, green, but has vivacity, fire and signs of real talent.

I received a letter from the Karamzins in Revel, dated November 9. They are surviving well and peacefully. Write to them often: in their loneliness letters are a substitute for friends. I haven't heard anything about Bludov and Dashkov since they got to Petersburg. Poletika has been named to inspect the Petersburg *gubernaia*.[24] The Krivtsovs are here. In a few days he is going to his Nizhny *pashalik*,[25] but she'll probably spend the winter here. Bezobrazova is coming later. Agripina Trubetskaya, whom Dashkov courted, got married to a cousin of Mansurov's, an aide-de-camp to the Emperor, with the highest permission, if not the Very Highest, i.e., of his Ministers, because Filaret did not approve the marriage. All of Peter[sburg] and Moscow are full of the break up of the Samoylovs. He found her correspondence with the young La-Ferronays: he sent his wife to the Littes, but they would not receive her; now he is taking her to see her father, Palen, and they are living in Moscow in the very same inn, see each other, and play the roles of *Adolphe and Clara;*[26] they say there won't be a divorce, but the husband has decided firmly to divorce her. Have you had enough of these literary, political and impudent rumors? I really have a great need of letters from you. Don't ignore my requests and I will pray to God for you. I am sincerely happy that our beloved Sergei Ivanovich is better. May you all be healthy and peaceful . . .

* * *

Prince Vyazemsky to A. I. Turgenev and V. A. Zhukovsky
January 6, 1827, Moscow

I thank you, my beloved friends, you, Zhukovsky, for permission to ride on your fields and to take what falls on them, and for your promise to inform me about what's new; you, Turgenev, my priceless Grimm, for your letter, which already is going to be used with your permission, or without your permission; it will be printed, of course, with deletions and without your name, in the first number of *The Telegraph*. Your letter will so inundate our Russian hut with Europe. Do me a favor and write more letters like that. Couldn't Zhukovsky, even through Berlin, send me literary loot and goods. I forewarned Matushevich about this, asking him to open (a channel) of information through him between me and Zhukovsky. Today I am writing about the same thing to Vasily Perovsky and, on trial, I am sending you, through him, some of my articles, published in last year's *Telegraph* and the first issue of *The Moscow Messenger* where you will find a scene from Pushkin's tragedy. Isn't it true that there is an amazing maturity and sobriety in his style, imbued and filled with the spirit of the past? The entire play is so controlled and there are places much more magnificent. But it seems the journal won't be a journal if you judge according to the introduction. It has no character at all. Send my letter to Jullien in Paris. Let them see how we judge them. Couldn't you subscribe to the *Globe*[27] for me, or at least, send me last year's. Karamzin told me a story that somewhere in a home for the insane he found a madman reading a paper more than forty years old, and to his remark about this, he heard from him the answer: "don't forget that we here live in another world. What is old for you is new for us." We also live, in this aspect and in many aspects, in some kind of Bedlam. The new edition of Chateaubriand is not for sale here. There isn't anything here. Each offering of yours will be a blessing, and each gift perfect. Only give and get it done.

Write something about Karamzin, if not a full, systematic biography, then just a remembrance of your friendship with him, of your conversation, etc. You don't need to play author here, but just give freedom to your pen, heart and memory. With this you will fulfill your debt of good will. Ivanchin-Pisarev is getting ready to publish the spirit of Karamzin,[28] about which I already told you, and requested permission for this from Ekaterina Andreevna. Here's what Katinka[29] wrote to me about that: "Nous n'avons pu nous empecher[sic] de sentir une épingle dans le coeur, en pensant que de tant de plumes amies et éloquentes celle de M-r Pissareff est la seule qui entreprenne de rompre le silence" (We weren't able to keep from feeling a prick in the heart, thinking that, of so many friendly and eloquent pens, that of M. Pissareff is the only one to undertake to break the silence). And that's the truth. It seemed to me that it wouldn't be to the point for me, as someone close to him, to be the first to speak out in the matter of national gratitude in the heat of the moment. In time I'm thinking about writing notes about Karamzin and the Karamzin age, as Garat wrote about Suard. Karamzin definitely can be the focus around which we should wind the circle of our enlightenment. Now it is still too early to take up this task, but I must gather my strength and think about it maturely. But you, Zhukovsky, Bludov and Dashkov, should without fail put a few flowers on his grave. You, more than anyone, knew him more than I; for from the time when I began to think, we lived apart from him. You are the living, complete archives, whither his ardent soul and bright mind unloaded their most secret thoughts. Indeed, Turgenev, turn your memory, your loving memory out on paper without any effort of authorship at all, and a living and warm portrayal will pour forth. You know it is shameful that from the circle of Karamzin's enlightened friends, from the legion of honor of the Russian people, not one voice rings out, breaking the silence of the grave. If you will—this is indifference, criminal negligence. Karamzin does not need our praises, we don't need to raise him on our shoulders; he is already so high, without a doubt he is higher than our whole generation. All of this is fine, but all of this resembles a "God will provide" with which an unfeeling miser greets the entreating hand of an unfortunate creature. *God will provide* is, certainly, a Christian message and spiritual alms are loftier than a ruble, and because of that, also cheaper.

Pushkin got his tragedy back from the hands of the highest censor. God grant everyone such a censor. Very little mutilation. The new Censorship board here in Moscow is still not at its full complement. I have hopes that Bludov will completely weaken it. I told him to say that I hope Cassandra soon will be here like the Clytemnestra of his Agamemnon. Pushkin finished the sixth chapter of Onegin. There are perfect gems in it. The provincial country ball is good in an extremely funny way. The duel of two friends, Onegin and Lensky, and the death of the latter are magnificent descriptions.

Poetic liveliness and prosaic truth unite in one bright world, in striking truth. He compares the murdered Lensky to a deserted house: the windows are whitened, the shutters are closed, the mistress is gone and no one knows where she is. How this is all said, how simply and powerfully, with what feeling. I don't know when he'll make up his mind to publish it, but in the meanwhile, everything that will be printed in *The Moscow Messenger* I will send when I can, if only I discover a moneyless way of information between us. He himself is sending you the journal.

... Tomorrow we are seeing off Zhikharev to that very same Turk to which we saw you off. It was sad then, too, but then there were very few bright stars in our sight, and still how many horrors occurred since that time, still how many eclipses and sad appearances. We will drink a toast to you there, absent friends. We dare not lift a cup [to honor] our reunion. God knows, what is there to desire? How will we meet? Perhaps it is better never to meet again. A few days ago we saw those going further, Muravyova-Chernysh[eva] and Volkonskaya-Raevs-[kaya]. What a touching and elevated doom. A thank you to the women: they will give a few beautiful lines to our history. In them really was visible not the exaltation of fanaticism, but some kind of pure, unrebellious obedience of martyrdom, which does not think of Glory, but gets carried away with, gets absorbed in, only a quiet feeling, all-embracing, all-conquering. There is nothing here for the *Gallery:* and where do we have a Gallery? Where is there public appraisal of our deeds?

Farewell, dear, beloved friends—I embrace you from the bottom of my heart—Our children are better, completely better. You've had enough, Turgenev, of quarreling with my wife. She loves you and loves both of you sincerely. She's not at home now, but nevertheless she wanted to write to you.

The Krivtsov sisters and Bezobrazova are here. We often talk with them about you Turgenevs. It seems Bezobrazova was getting ready to write to you. They also mourn for your brother. My heartfelt handshake to those near and far.—See here, Grimm, don't forget me. [. . .]

***

A. I. Turgenev to Prince Vyazemsky
Venice, September 21, 1832

I wrote to you through Moscow from Milan on Sept. 9; but from you—not a word since my departure. I do not lose hope of conquering your laziness with my importuning. Prince Gag[arin] will give you this letter and will tell you about our life of the past 12 days here. We met in Padua and on the next day, here; since then we have not separated, for we live in the very same inn where he once lived with Seryozha. I got ready to write you a long letter from here, but he moved up his date of departure and I am already tired, having written an 8-page letter to Moscow to my sister, which you can copy through the Princess when she sends the enclosed packets to my sister and sends to the Princess the little boxes with Venetian trifles for your three little princesses. I give you Gray in various poses in memory of my Veronese sadness, when I often thought of you as I strolled along near the ruins of the amphitheatre in Rome. The multicolored postcards distribute according to the addresses.

My letter to my dear sister Nefedyeva you can read and relate what I write about Lamennais to whomever you deem necessary. I wanted to describe my meeting with him in Munich and everything that I heard about him here from Schelling, but I won't get it done.

Venice is still so beautiful, still so rich with sights even in its ruins that, according to Gagarin, one must see her only after Rome, after all of Italy. And in 8 days I have hardly succeeded in hastily looking over the main points; much that is curious remains, and there is no time to write down and describe everything the way I would like. I am learning to look at pictures here; the treasures of the Venetian school are almost completely intact, in the churches, in private palaces and in the Academy of Arts. Taken to Paris a long time ago, they were returned together with four gilded horses which gallop on the facade of St. Mark's Cathedral.

What a cathedral! and what a square! It is evident that the *Palais Royal* is built along the lines of this Venetian square; but in an architectural relationship, and especially in approximation of the Greco-Gothic gilded masses and cupolas of the cathedral, the *Palais Royal* yields to the buildings here, surrounding the square on three sides; even on St. Mark's square Napoleon left a reminder of himself, having constructed one side with marble buildings; they are lower than the older ones, but almost in the same style. Toward evening we gather there to drink coffee and eat sorbets; the square is wide and the light which comes from two sides, on which there are shops and coffee houses, is insufficient. The living rooms are not illuminated now, for all are at their summer houses and only the pigeons have not left their roofs for the summer. According to ancient custom they receive food; for by Senate order the Venetian Republic is authorized to preserve them: they think that the Venetians saw in them a living emblem of the origin of their republic—the saving of their ancestors from Atilla; these pigeons, or their ancestors, also once were saved from the barbaric habit of throwing them to the people at certain holidays; since then the pigeons congregate and live without danger all over the square. One pigeon-loving lady, exactly at two o'clock, gives them food daily; yesterday on the tower in front of me, dressed in a suit of armor, a knight struck two times with his hammer: suddenly there appeared clouds of pigeons and they flew together under the windows of the woman who feeds them: they opened and the feed was scattered: but the pigeons arrived at the bell before the food did.

I ride in the gondolas every day, ride around churches, palaces, arsenals and gardens; gondoliers point out to me the home where Byron lived and where, on a wooden pillar to which they hook the gondolas, his half-effaced coat-of-arms still is; but not one *barcarolle* has yet sung to me stanzas from Tasso; and Goethe's epigrams about Venice, written before her total collapse, must now not be applied to her at all: since then much has disappeared; much has grown silent! But for history, for memories—all is still alive here; and the ruins are expressive. The walls still shine with marble, the floors with mosaics, the churches with emeralds; Titian is everywhere—*Emulator de Zeus de degl' Apelli*[30]—Leonardo and Giordano are everywhere— and finally, Canova, who received his first training here, who himself realized here his own Genius! The ride along the canals from church to church, from palace to palace, is also as entertaining as the palace and churches themselves—everywhere and in everything appears "a great shadow of the past"—*Stat magni nominis umbra* . . . But the evening sun! I will never forget how it lay beyond the distant hills of Padua, gilding with its last rays the quiet surface of the waters washing Venice; how the tops of the churches and the cupolas are drawn on the bluish-pink, gilded sky: Giorge maggiore, della Salute, Redentore[31]—memorials of pestilence and Palladio!

All day Venetian harmonies ring out and this disturbed my writing to Moscow; now it's night and under my windows uninvited troubadors are playing Tyrolean and Rossini melodies and are disturbing my writing to you—and even are keeping Turgenev from sleeping: if the music continues I'll go to the theater to watch a play *tutta da riddere!*[sic—all to laugh]. There are always good actors for farces in Italy. The music under my windows has grown silent. It's time [to crawl up] on my high bed. Farewell, Vyazemsky [. . .].

September 22. I forgot the main thing: while still in Moscow before your departure, I received from S[ophia] P[etrovna] Svechina the assignment of collecting manuscripts of famous Russian writers or others, and in this group, she especially demanded yours, Pushkin's, Zhukovsky's, Dmitriev's, Karamzin's and others'. She wanted this for Princess Gagarina. I recently received here a letter from Sophia P[etrovna] about that very thing. The princess confirmed her request and I promised her for you, that you would not only send her your scrawl, but also would write in it a few lines for the album of this sweet Angel. She is passionately devoted to this hobby and is collecting tribute from all over the world. In her album is all of living Rome. Please ask Pushkin for me to give 4 lines, even old ones, if he grudges new ones, but [ask him] to write them in his own hand and give all of this on thin paper to Prince Gagarin, and say that this is for his wife and that he must quickly send it to her. My manuscripts are in Paris and in Munich, but you probably have some notes of Dmitriev's nearby. Request some also from Gnedich and Krylov: they both knew her. And if you have a few lines of Baratynsky's—that wouldn't be bad: in a word, everything that falls into your hands; but you, you and Pushkin, as quickly as possible.

Today I am treating Schelling and his wife to a Venetian meal, but with French wines, under a tent of grapes at Santa Margarita. We are going there on a gondola and will try to see some of Venice.

Evening: I just this hour returned from the grape pavilion where the three of us: Schelling, his wife (she is an intelligent and sweet woman and understands her husband), and I conversed. It can be said that I listened to all of his lecture, at the end of which I left Munich: what simplicity with his profundity! And how clear everything is in the head of the German philosopher, who has not written or printed anything for 15 years, but who has thought everything out! Perhaps it will clear up in my mind. I probably will stop by Munich on my way back from Italy, if Schelling will be teaching there at that time. I feel that I am closer to the sciences than I am to the arts.

September 24, evening. I returned from the island *Lido.* One must be a poet in his heart and soul in order to describe everything that I felt as I was on the boat to the Lido, surrounded by a crowd of other gondolas and wooden barges, at various distances from each other: the gay conversation of the boaters, the cry of children over the boundless water reached me on the even, mirrorlike flatness. To the left is Napoleon's garden, turning green in the water, the Castello of Saint Andrew with its fortifications defending the Lido; to the right the little island of St. Lazare with its Armenian monastery, Hospital and beyond that the *Murazzi;*[32] behind me is a floating city, and in the distance mountains turning blue. Barcarolles in white shirts, with their stately movements over the gondolas, seemed from afar to be like white flying lapwings over the water. They chased each other and flew from various directions to the shores of the Lido. Barges, weighted down with people, with music, with singing islanders, mottled with the multi-colored outfits of dark Venetian women, were also sailing to the Lido; and the closer [we got] to the island, the louder was the noise and conversation of the merrymakers on the island and on the barges: the noise even reached me, lying in a black gondola in luxurious solitude! It wasn't even 4 o'clock in the afternoon yet, but it was already difficult to reach the shore because of the great number of moored gondolas and boats; we had to jump from one to the other in order to get more quickly to the landing stage, i.e., to the two planks thrown across by half-naked boys from the shore to the slimy soil in which we could get stuck while crowding all around. I walked behind the crowds and caught sight of an open cemetery; on the graves [I saw] provisions, wine, oysters, vegetables and, among the monuments to death and human vanity, I saw dancing sailors, *barcarolles,* people of every shape and size in white and multi-colored shirts, in Venetian caps: one should depict all of this with a brush and not with a pen. Troupes of musicians with guitars and contrabasses, girls playing on the French horn! Horns, violins, bassoons and each with its own harmony. To the music, scattered in various places, there were folk dances: wherever the musicians [went], there [went] whole crowds of dancers! and in one spot a single couple dances alone and rejoices to the general noise. Neither in the Tyrol nor in Paris have I seen such a lively picture of native gaiety, such a vivid Bacchanalian joy on faces, such abandon, such lightheartedness!—Everywhere groups were sprawled along with their victuals: greens, cheese, oysters, peaches, figs! Red wine flowed from huge bottles. little boys ran around with pastry, yellow pumpkins, walnuts: they had their own tune (*les cris de Venise* distinguished from all of the others: on the *ponte-Rialto* they drown out the passersby). The native dance resembles the French quadrille, but here there are more airs or turnings on their feet; but this turning is somehow more graceful than the French. The men dance apart from the women: you will not see many elderly women in a separate group with their men. Only Austrian soldiers in their loose overalls wandered like orphans around the subjugated merrymakers: I felt sorry for the victors! . . .

I went to find a Princess . . . whom I met twice on St. Mark's square with her father, and I found myself unobtrusively before cannons, bombs, in front of ramparts: the guard shouted to me to turn back, but I ran up onto the rampart and saw the boundless rosy-blue sea which was merging with the very same-colored sky; involuntarily I glanced at the comely P . . . and I cried out: a gem! She looked back. Here and there little boats and barges were darkening on this blending of sea and sky:

> There, there beyond the blue ocean,
> Far away in the crimson glow.

I sighed for my brother, for myself; but there was no one to whom I could give that with which my heart was filled—with this feeling I wandered over to the merrymakers; everyone was still jumping, laughing, the children were romping, taking the cemetery monuments by storm; regimental songsters, hiding behind their bottles of sour wine, sang out haphazardly their Hungarian-Slavic songs, in view of the fallen Tsaritsa of the Adriatic Sea.

I leaned against a gravestone: under me lay an ambassador of the Court of Great Britian. The setting sun burned in the Italian sky and a fiery pillar was reflected in the Lagoon. I again sat in my black coffin, but the barcarolle Guiseppe repeated some mournful songs with the quiet stroke of the oar along the water. Nearing Venice, again among the islands, the garden: here is another race, other crowds on green paths and along the embankment. The lagoon darkened, the sun hid and on St. Mark's square fires burned under tents; they strummed guitars, and coffee awaited me. I got mixed up in another crowd, didn't find my fellow citizens at Florian's and wandered home. Now I hear under the windows of my room, on the grand canal, a Venetian serenade and the cries of the gondoliers; I am going to spend a last evening with Gagarin. Farewell.

Sept. 25. Here's what I wrote yesterday at my return from the Lido. I give you my impressions just as I got them.

I am sending this to you so that, in similar moments, I will usually think of you, for, with you, my sorrow would be different, weaker. I am going again to say goodbye to Gagarin. Farewell. Embrace Pushkin, Veleursky, and tenderly press the hands of our sweet beauties. Bow to the Kozlovs and read them my letter if they wish you to. You can read the letter I sent to Nefedyeva, but then send it to her quickly.

***

A. I. Turgenev to Prince Vyazemsky
July 9, 1833, *à la balance*

On June 12 I wrote to you from Turin and suggested that it would be the last letter to you if I didn't find a packet of letters from you here; I didn't find anything and have not received anything since then, but I am writing so that I can send a lot with Zhukov[sky] for you and through you, with a list of people [to whom they go]. Here's an account of it and our local life.

From Turin, through Arona, and consequently, lac Majeuire[33] past the Borromeo islands, and after I clambered up in worship of Charles Borromeo, whose colossal statue blesses from the mountains of the islands (created by him), I went on to the Simplon Pass and crossed it, surrounded still by snow, lying in the ravines of the mountains and near the road. In the *Domo d'Ossola*[34] I came to my senses from the wonders of nature and Napoleon. There, dug across arches over the rapids—an indestructible monument to him! Here he destroyed in order to create.

On June 14 I entered the land of Tell and Lavater: I looked back to Italy, where I baked for ten months and descended into Brig. Simplon did not astound me as much as the Tyrolean road into Bad-Gastein; there everything is more majestic and more horrible; and burrowed into cliffs, roads shuffle over precipices in which waterfalls make noise, the mountains there are more picturesque and the bridges are thrown from one cliff to another, so that not even taking their firmness into consideration, it's terrifying to see oneself over the abyss so far away the eye can't see it, under the rocks, from which entire ruins rush into the chasm. Along the local road is a noteworthy waterfall: Pisse-Vache. Others, like silver threads, descend from their heights. Only Terni and Tivoli can compare with the Bad-Gastein waterfalls. In Brig I spent two hours with sheltered Jesuits, inspected their schools and church with the wonders of St. Ignatius and Laynez; I argued with the Rector and Inspector of Instruction about their method of teaching, frankly, not hiding my opinion about the shortcomings of their system of education, out of step with our age. They liked my frankness and they pleaded guilty to many things, after having explained, however, the principle of their being *behind the times.* They have no time to finish their studies: there is such a demand for Jesuits in Europe, that they are forced to send to various places teachers who have not finished their courses; and however much their colleges enrich novices, their number is insufficient for all the sciences and all the classes. But all that aside, they finally decided to look over their old plan of teaching and institute a new one; in conformity with the successes of enlightenment and pedagogy. To do this, deputies from all of the Jesuit *provinces* are assembled, and, the results of these meetings should institute a new plan, or at least, improve and perfect the old system of knowledge, teaching and education in the Jesuit society. We argued about a lot, but sometimes even agreed; I attacked some of their classic books, e.g., the history of France by *Loriquet,* derided, and even slandered in France; they showed me the edition used in their classes and I didn't find that of which the author is blamed. In Brig they have about 200 pupils of all nations; they wander with them along the mountains and place crosses where a raven wouldn't even carry bones.[35] My enemies grew fond of me for my sincerity, took me to a Jesuit whom I used to know in Petersburg, and saw me to my coach. From here I sent them an English book *Hershchel, About the Successes of European Society,*—and found here an intelligent and learned ex-Jesuit with whom I readily chat about the order which he left.

Through St. Maurice, about whose antiquity I recently read in Johann Müller, I arrived in Vernex, stopped by at Zhukovsky's little house, but a family named Reitern met me there. I stopped in Vevey, and towards evening, I set off again on foot, along the shores of Lake Geneva for Vernex and found out that Zhukovsky arrived in Geneva on that very day. The next day, after I looked over the house in Vevey, in which the renowned English fugitives Ludlow and Broughton lived out their days, I got on a steamboat and arrived here. Reitern was sailing from Geneva on another boat; I caught sight of him but I didn't see Zhukovsky: he was riding along the banks in a carriage. He discouraged me from coming to Vernex, the reason for which he hid: on that day he was having an operation. He endured it heroically, and on the third day[after it] I saw him already on his feet. I spent an evening and a day with him and yesterday returned here via Lausanne, where I did not find LaHarpe: he is riding around Switzerland; but I did see Mlle Calame and other governesses of Russia's fair sex, of whom Switzerland is full. The rain disturbed my seeing the charming environs of Lausanne again, but twice I cast a glance at the little house in the vineyard where for six weeks lived my Seryozha in the last year of his life. I was *not alone* on Mont Benon, from whose terraces I looked at the little house, but didn't dare point it out to my other brother, knowing that he's never yet been at his grave . . . in Paris.

Yesterday we came down from Lausanne into *Ouchy,* got on a boat and arrived here by dinnertime. In Lausanne (this was on Sunday) we heard a rather good sermon, looked over the memorials in the cathedral: buried there is Princess Orlova, born Zinovyeva, who died in 1781, and the wife of the English envoy Stratford-Canning, for whom Canova made a beautiful urn with bas-relief. Bookshops in Lausanne are scarcely richer with new books than the local ones; I bought for you: *Scènes du beau monde,* received the day before from Paris, by various authors: Janine, Sue, et al. But it seems that the articles are not provocative. [An article] about the Arts and Literature in Fr[ance] since the times of the *three days* is interesting, but as a match for our *reviews:* one of its just reproaches to the new Literature, especially the dramatic—is that Authors have disfigured, spoiled the richest and greatest subject for Drama and Art: Napoleon! "Ils ont déchiqueté de leurs ongles ce vaste cadavre, dont la tête touchait aux pyramides et les pieds au Kremlin!" (They have torn to shreds with their fingernails this huge corpse, whose head reached to the pyramids and whose feet stretched to the Kremlin). They only knew how to use his grey frockcoat and hat; but not one of the episodes of his dramatic life was appropriately presented, neither on the stage nor in the Poem. "Il y avoit dans cette vie de quoi épouvanter Bossuet, de quoi intimider Corneille!" (There was in this life enough to astonish Bossuet and to frighten Corneille). Delavigne's stanzas and Chateaubriand's sentences do not replace either the tragedy or the orator. Dramatic writers threw themselves on the bloody side of the revolution, resurrected the Jesuits and beat those lying down: "On a gaspillée la révolution en moins de quinze jours," meanwhile as "la seule famille d'Agamemnon a suffi à tous les théâtres du monde, depuis Sophocle jusqu'à Racine" (They squandered the revolution in less than a fortnight . . . by itself, the family of Agamemnon was enough for all the theaters of the world from Sophocles to Racine). Read the rest yourself.

From here I am sending you *Il Pianto,* a poème of your protégé—Aug[uste] Barbier, and also his *iambs,* which you already know. In *Pianto* he wanted to describe Italy in verses as Goethe did in his immortal epigrams; but what's far for a woodcock[36] . . . . He tries hard, though unsuccessfully, like Hugo, but lower than his subject or his subjects, and only in the Pisan *Campo Santo,*[37] described by him do I find a few decent lines characterizing this magnificent temple of death, resembling more a museum because of its memorials, and a picture gallery because of its paintings (of the first and most ancient masters of Italy) than the Père-La-Chaise of Pisa. His description of great artists is arrogant with its pretensions, but he characterizes no one, and who will recognize Raphael—in *jeune homme plein de grâce et de sérénité* (a young man full of grace and serenity)? I thought not of him but of Sasha Karamzin. And Titian is *"un grand Venitien, à l'énorme cerveau!* (a grand Venetian with an enormous brain). But the divine Domenichino got it worst of all in his description:

> Boeuf sublime, à pas lourds il creusa son ornière
> Aux cris des envieux hurlant à son côté.
> (Splendid ox, with heavy tread he digs his rut
> to the shouts of the envious ones beside him.)

It seems that now in Italy calamities are starting to bring Poetry to life. Five issues of a new literary journal *l'Exilé*[38] have already come out in Italian and in French. I subscribed for you for a whole year, but I probably won't send it, although only Literature takes up a large part of it. I am sending two volumes of the prose and poems of Count Pepoli, who lives here. Three more are coming out, which you will receive later. In them there is a lot of poetry, so they assure me. A sonnet about Mary Magdalene appealed to me very much. Your sweet Maria, who will never have to repent of anything, will translate it for you. If she does not read Italian, then give the books to Dubenskaya. Apropos of your Masha: I am sending her my portrait by Bryullov, lithographed in Paris, by means of Zhukovsky, who is setting off for Petersburg in about six days, hoping not to need the waters and to be with you for half of your August. There is also a portrait for you, for Kozlov, Serbinovich, Fyodorov, Bravursha, three for the Putyatins, for Bulgakov, for my family in Moscow and in Simbirsk; Zhukovsky persuaded me to inscribe one for the Karamzins too: I wanted to send it without an inscription and let you do it if the Karamzins would like to have it. Act as you see fit. I would not like to butt my ugly mug in. To Dmitriev I am sending a portrait in exchange for my former, *two-faced* one. Genoan earrings and other jewelry distribute to the Princesses. Send the other packages around more precisely, but if Tatar[inov] is already in P-burg, then the next one is for Arzhevitinov and give it to him (in person). In the little box there are Genoese cufflinks for Arzhevitinov.

This week there was an exhibit here of articles of local industry in the museum of the Russian general *Rat,* founded by his sister in Geneva in his memory. The exhibit is not very rich, although there are new inventions. The main artists, the watchmakers, didn't want to display their machines, fearing imitation and not having time for the preparation of samples; they have never been so busy before; people are demanding watches from all parts of the world; time flies for everyone, and there are few tardy people, even beyond the ocean. Inquiries from America are significant. I am sending you the catalogue of the exhibit.

I met here d'Ivernois, noted for his financial brochures, who came to us in 1812 with a plan of finances for Russia, but having presented them, by command of the Tsar, to a special Committee, in which was Baron Stein, he returned without success to England, where he hid after his banishment from Geneva, and where Pitt rewarded him with a pension in honor of his financial system. He still writes about Political Economics, but has already run to death the subject for which Malthus is famous. His new booklet about the death-rate in Normandy is interesting in his general remarks about the proportions of the death-rates in various countries. In a book written by him about this very same subject, there is a big article about Russia. D'Ivernois asked me about Yakov Alexandrovich Druzhinin, who was with him in his dealings with the finance committee. Give him my greetings.

On the second day after my arrival here I was in the Church of St. Peter during the distribution of prizes to the students of the local Academy, in the presence of all of the public and all of the city officials. The professor's speech about the main methods of writing history, beginning with the ancients to the most recent, was wonderful. Unfortunately it is not yet published; the account of the Rector of the Academy about all branches of Learning and about local Authors in the field of Literature presents a comforting picture of local intellectual activity, although this year little that is especially remarkable came out. The plan of teaching and education will soon go through a reform and because of this the Rector did less this year; among the scholars here there are first-class [people], e.g., the botanist de Candolle, whose Herbarium is the richest in the whole world! Linnaeus praised, by the way, his collection of dry plants which extends to six thousand species: de Candolle *daily* enriches his herbarium with an order of up to six thousand plants from all parts of the world (by the way, even from Russia)! [..] His son is also a botanist and keeper of the garden, in which you see busts of the good Bonnet, the poet Haller, Swiss Naturalists. Another celebrity of the local Academy is the Italian *Refugié,* but already [turned into] a local citizen, *Rossi,* whose book about criminal legislation is a classic; it also summarizes all the improvements in criminal law, which is indebted for its successes to his co-citizens—the Italians. He is now an envoy to Paris, where the Minister of

Foreign Affairs, his friend Broglie, once acquainted the French public with his book in the *Revue française;* he [Broglie], through his superior examination of Rossi's book, joined the ranks of the very best Jurists. Because of his advice I read this book in Paris. The Rector in his account also referred to the local literature which came out during the past year: the best in poetry was the coronation exercise "Les voyages" by M. Manget, a conversation between Horace and Ch-[ristopher] Columbus. It still is not published, but out of other approved literature we know only four lines from the conversation of a hermit-sparrow and a swallow:

> D'accord, repond [sic] la voyageuse
> Cependant je suis plus heureuse;
> Vous apprenez peniblement [sic],
> Moi, je m'instruis en m'amusant.
> (Agreed, answered the traveler.
> However I am the more fortunate;
> You learn with difficulty,
> Myself, I learn while amusing myself.)

Sismondi, at whose summer home in Chêne I spend every Wednesday evening, published the sixteenth part of his *History of the French*; in it is the Reformation. One of the best books around is Mme Necker De Saussure's *l'Education progressive*. Talent here seems to be hereditary, especially in the Necker family. Two parts of her book recently came out. Behind it is the book of Pastor Naville, approved by the Paris "society of Christian morality": *l'Education publique*.[39] They are all in front of me, but are too voluminous for Zhukovsky's knapsacks and too serious for your study. There is still one more important book: *Hist. abrégée de l'église de J. Christ, principalement pendant les siècles du moyen âge, rattachée aux grands traits de la Prophétie,* 1832, 2 parts. I ordered it from Paris; I wanted to send it to Prince A[lexander] N[ikolaevich] Gol[itsyn], but couldn't make up my mind, not knowing whether he would like it.

De Candolle acquainted me with Madame *Marcet,* an Englishwoman known for her works about Political Economy and Chemistry. She lives with her children near Gentu, in a charming cottage on the shore of Lake Geneva: in front of her terrace are Mont Blanc and Salève with their little brothers! Here one must fall in love with the setting of the sun and watch as its last rosy rays fall *auf die vergoldeten Alpenspitzen!* (upon the gilded Alpine peaks). Bonnet used to live in the neighborhood and our Karamzin used to paise his kindness and his Genius. Dining at Mme Marcet's, I renewed my acquaintance with the traveler Basile Hall, who recently, according to the English Tories, described and slandered the United States of America intelligently and ingeniously. He showed us a manuscript of W[alter] Scott's *The Antiquarian* which he bought at an auction for 40 Swiss francs. Meeting with W. Scott in Portsmouth before his departure for Italy, he [Hall] showed him the manuscript. The author wanted to write him a few lines on the manuscript, and after having witnessed its *l'authenticité,* to tell him his own, the author's, opinion of this novel: he considers it his best novel and wrote it with the greatest pleasure, for in it are described scenes of his youth; he wrote in his own hand more than two pages about this. Basile Hall published his testimony in the third part of excerpts of his travels. And W. Scott's second daughter died—from grief: she lived for her father and grieved for him to her last minute. I saw her in Abbotsford, blooming like a rose, and listened as she played Scottish airs on the harp, and her Father echoed her, limping with his diseased leg. Another daughter, wife of the Tory journalist Lockhard, lives in London with her children, whom their grandfather loved so! English families are scattered all over the shores of Leman and they enliven cottages, terraces and Genevan industry. I ride with my brother and with little Carl, vividly and truly reminding us of his father, in a London cabriolet and on a beautiful English horse; I am starting to manage it myself, although recently it carried us off into a ditch, but without misfortune. I get up early, go to the *Terreaux* of St. Anthony or to the *Rampe de la Treille* to read Johann Müller or Goethe, then to the *Cabinet de lecture,* where from 8 o'clock in the morning are all the new French and English journals; from there I drop in at the post office, in order to curse your laziness daily, and then I go home to have breakfast with my brother and Carl; then I finish reading the journals, rest or nap with a book in my hands and until 2 o'clock gad about fashionable candy shops where intelligent and educated pretty little people talk about everything and even about Literature; at noon I refresh myself with ice cream and sit behind books and brochures in another reading room, where there is a large library of old books along with all the new ones coming out here, in Paris and in Italy (but there are very few German ones!). Arnault's (the father) notes, Merimée's memoirs of Spain, the sometimes intelligent ravings of Lerminier and a lot more I would like to send to you, but I have no one to send them with. We dine at the *table d'hôte* with travelers; after dinner we roam about in a cabriolet in the environs or appear at parties at de Candolle's, Constant's (the cousin of Ben[jamin] Constant), Sismondi, Mme Pictet, a madame whose name I've forgotten, a friend of 40 years and cousin of Mme Stahl[sic]. With her for 40 years, in Geneva, lives the German Ress, the translator of Johann Müller's world history. There I also met Eynard, but he is at a distant cottage. They remember and love Kapodistrias here: his portraits are everywhere. In a few days, around July 22, I am setting out for Lugano through Lausanne, Berne, where I will see Severine, Lucerne; in Lugano Naturalists from all of Switzerland and from farther away will meet; this society was founded a *l'instar* of (in imitation of) a German one which he saw in Dresden. From Lugano through Bellinzona, St. Gothard, and so on, again to Vevey, where on August 4 there will be *la fête des Vignerons,* [40] which has not been celebrated since 1819; this society, whose origins are lost in the gloom of Swiss Antiquity, is also called *l'Abbaye des Vignerons.* Eight hundred people will be in the procession and I already saw in Vevey some of the pictures lithographed for this celebration. They're already publishing songs, couplets and a description of the festival—also many poems in the local dialect: *le Vaudois.* Gathering there from all of Switzerland are gardeners, shepherds and farmers. All of the accommodations have been taken for a long time. I'll probably get a room for myself at Zhukovsky's, for Vernex is an hour's walk away from Vevey.—Three days ago I rode around all of the environs of Vernex: the castle *Hauteville* with its charming park on the mountain, from there Lake Geneva with its small coastal towns is visible; the castle *Blonay,* the oldest in Switzerland from the time of Charlemagne; here the family Blonay still lives, as before, with all its neighboring estates, but still respected by the peasants; the castle *Châtelard,* from the fifteenth century at the very entrance to the valley which terminates *par le Col de Jaman.* I descended to the little village, where even the little boys talk on and on about Rousseau and his Héloise;[41] I went past the little village of *Montreux,* about ten minutes away from Zhukovsky, where bloom little oranges under the protection of green mountains and the cliffs of Melier—the only place with a warm climate in Switzerland; from his windows Zhuk[ovsky] showed me the house in which Byron lived, with a view of the lake. Toward evening I went to Chillon, went down into its damp dungeon, again knocked with the ring [knocker] to which Bonnivard[42] was chained. Byron didn't know his story and imitated the episode of Ugolino,[43] imprisoned in the Pisa jail. The dungeon has columns; between two pillars a cross-beam is visible: this was the gallows; now on the facade of this underwater dungeon, toward the river, is the motto of the canton: *liberté, patrie*... On one of the columns in the jail Byron carved out his name, under it Russians read the name of his translator—*Zhukovsky*; farther on [is written] some Tolstoi and a legion of unknowns. In some historical information about the Chillon castle I noticed the following lines:

Qui peut sans être ému voir Chillon,
Qu'ont illustré Rousseau, le malheur et Byron.
(Who, without emotion, can see Chillon, which
Rousseau, misfortune and Byron have rendered famous)

In Clarens they showed us a little corner of former times, called *le bosquet* [the grove], grown over with bushes; in *Chatelard* the study of Julie and the rooms of Baroness d'Etange.[44] But the sneers of the travellers disenchanted this field of ancient industry, and finally they remembered that Rousseau himself admitted that the topography of *The New Héloise* was rarely true. Vevey is the true fatherland of Julie and Mme de Warens. I forgot, while in Vevey, to find out about *La Clef,* the inn where Jean-Jacques lived. But now, to my disappointment, even he himself does not allow us to look for the characters of his novel there: "dites si la nature n'a pas fait ce beau pays pour une Julie, pour une Claire et pour un Saint-Preux; *mais ne les y cherchez pas*" (say whether nature has not made this beautiful countryside for Julie, for Claire and for Saint-Preux; *but don't look for them there).*

Since that time the customs and even the faces of the local female inhabitants could not change: how many well-formed, pretty near-beauties I met along the way, in the vineyard and in the terraces! But for me it is more proper to look for historical recollections *of another kind* in Vevey. I went to the house in which *Ludlow* lived and where still recently could be seen the inscription: "Omne solum forti patria, quia patris."[45] I do not share this feeling. In the cathedral at Vevey are his grave and that of the other fugitive, *Broughton,* but they took the inscription back to England.

I've already gone around Leman three times and each time [went] with new pleasure. What shores! and how fiercely gleam the snows of Mont Blanc and Salève in their inaccessible grandeur! I understood how Gibbon could write about the fall of Rome in sight of unflinching nature! He calls the fall of Rome "the greatest and most awful scene in the history of mankind" [quoted in English in the original], these masses are "the most awful scene" [quoted in English in the original] in our part of the world. The Empire, like its Coliseum is in ruins; on the contrary: *ces masses indestructibles ont fatigué le tems!* [sic] (these indestructible masses have worn out time!)

Again I am setting out to work on the Italian poets and now I am beginning my first Italian lesson with a learned, normal type of professor. In Vernex I read your letters (not to me) and not without annoyance at you for me and for Zhuk[ovsky]: how could one advise him, in his official position, to write *memoirs!* This is the task of Sophia Nikolaevna, who could, no worse than a cousin of Schiller's, write down all that her intelligent, unforgettable father said at the tea table, in the circle of his worshipping friends. The biography of Schiller by Mme Wollzogen and the ideas which she heard at Schiller's, her cousin, would serve as an example to her, since in general this biography of Schiller's is the best work of this kind; but think about the hermit of Vernex and about his obligation! You order him to dig up from his loving memory all that poured out of the soul of the Historiographer and wonderful person; of course, all should be holy for us, but not everything that he thought about out loud and felt is suited for Zhukovsky's supply of pedagogical and political wisdom: we are not allowed, especially after Karamzin, to be mistaken, as sometimes his Russian heart was mistaken; even the *History of the Russian State* will sicken us *jurare in verba*[46] of our kind, sweet Master. We should pour his soul into ours, and try to be the way he would have been in our time and with the revelations of contemporary history. Another friend of Zhukovsky's, Reitern, constantly shoves a pencil into his hands! No! He should remember his orders and devote all of his life to it, to live awhile all alone, only with his books and with that which reflects the spirit of our age, but not the obsolete and already dead one. I never will allow myself to tell him everything about what is in my heart; on the contrary, on the journey I always wanted only to comfort and pamper him, although he complains that I prevented him from stopping at every step to enrich his sketching *album* with Italian views; without my reminders he would not have succeeded in snatching three days for Florence and five for Rome. Come to Italy, but don't delay: we have even seen it too late. For this journey eyes alone are not enough: a soul is still necessary, open with live impressions and great memories. "Der reizendste Anblick einer herrlichen Natur ist nichts für einen traurigen Sinn, und eine Wüste schafft sich ein heiteres leibendes Herz zum Himmel!" (The most charming sight of glorious nature is nothing for a sad spirit, and a joyful, loving heart creates a heaven for itself from a wasteland). Thus spoke Schiller, thus think *le plus gras des hommes sensibles* who spent time in Italy. I became overjoyed looking at Zhukovsky's enthusiasm and disturbed him from sketching, not from being delighted. "O! man soll nicht säumen dem Genius die schnell welkenden Blüthen des Genusses Lebendiger Theilnahm darzubringen!" (Oh, one should not neglect to offer the genius the quickly wilting blossoms of the enjoyment of living participation)—the very same Schiller [. . .]

In front of my windows is the rushing green Rhône, which beyond the mountains unites with the Arva. Their waters flow together for a long time, not merging, and the yellow color of the Arva for a long time is distinguished from the green Rhône. The Arva is colder, although the Rhône flows from the mountains and is formed for the most part from glaciers and melting snow. But it arrives here from the mountains in a few hours, near 8 o'clock in the morning, rather than in the evening, so in the morning it is warmer here than in the evening. The environs of Geneva with their diversity and their beauties cannot bore me; but Geneva is the fatherland of rheumatism. My brother cannot bear the climate. His leg hurts all of the time: what will it be like in autumn and winter! [This] may separate us. The climate of France, especially in the country, is very good for him. He didn't suffer there, but here he hardly walks, and only rides on horseback and in a cabriolet.

Zhuk[ovksy]'s operation lasted 4 minutes; but perhaps he will have another in Petersburg. Zhuk. writes that he is leaving Vernex the 13th. His wound is still not completely healed.

July 10. I am planning to go with the botanist de Candolle and Constant, the cousin of Benj[amin] Cons[tant], to Lugano for the festival of Naturalists and to Vevey, for the Bacchus festival, through St. Gothard. Constant is making the 116th trip of his life: he was in China twice. My brother isn't going; but the mountains still haven't tired me out . . ."[47]

Notes

1. This allusion could refer to several characters in the works of Jean Paul (Jean Paul Friedrich Richter), but Vyazemsky probably has Walt and Vult of *Flegeljahre* in mind. In this comic novel the two brothers are reunited after a long separation.

2. Martinism is a mystical doctrine of the theosophist St. Martin (1743-1803) which was popular with Russian Masons at the end of the eighteenth and the beginning of the nineteenth centuries. At one time Karamzin had been a Mason.

3. The "hat of Monomakh" is a headdress Prince Vladimir Monomakh (1053-1125) received from his grandfather, the Byzantine emperor Constantine Monomakh. Here Vyazemsky may be referring to the coronation of the new emperor.

4. This is a special position instituted by Peter the Great and abolished in the nineteenth century. It began in pre-Revolutionary France as an office that took care of complaints. The office holder was a liaison between other ministers and the tsar.

5. An edict or official document. A *rescriptum* was a reply from the Roman emperor to a question on a point of law.

6. Because of poems the Emperor considered to be politically hostile, he sent Pushkin to the South in 1820. He spent about four years there and then two years at his estate in Mikhailovskoye in exile. Pushkin returned to St. Peterburg in 1826.

7. Pushkin's elegy "André Chénier" was written over six months before the Decembrist uprising and was printed in a collecion of his poems which left the censor's October 8, 1825. It is true that more than 40 lines (21-64 and 150) were not passed, but they were disseminated in manuscript form. Writing down these lines, a candidate of Moscow University, Andrei Leopoldov, gave them the heading "On December 14." An incident ensued, in which Leopoldov, as well as two officers, junior-captain Alexeev and ensign Molchalov suffered; Vyazemsky has them in mind.[Note of N. K. Kulman.]

8. Pushkin's historical play about the Time of Troubles.

9. These words are taken from "The Dangerous Neighbor" of V. L. Pushkin, where the cook says: "From honor alone do I work in this house." [Note of N. K. Kulman.]

10. Here Vyazemsky refers to the Censorship board alluding to a Russian proverb, "Velika Fedora, da dura" (Fedora is great, but a fool).

11. On July 13, 1826, the death penalty was carried out on the Decembrists. [Note of N. K. Kulman.]

12. Before he left, Ryleev sent a touching letter to his wife. Copies went around and everyone read it.[Note of N. K. Kulman.]

13. Here he is talking about Scott's *The Life of Napoleon Buonaparte, Emperor of the French. With a Preliminary View of the French Revolution,* 1827.

14. Elena Grigorievna and her daughters, the wife and children of Alexei Mikhailovich Pushkin, a distant relative of the poet. [N. K. Kulman.]

15. Senator Bogdan Andreevich Hermes (1758-1839). "According to a comment by F. F. Vigel, in Siberia they loved and respected Hermes for his unselfishness, kindness and strictness only in the case of need." *Russian Biographical Dictionary,* Moscow, 1916.

16. Little Grimm was Turgenev's nickname in Arzamas. I. I. Dmitriev gave him this name, because in Vyazemsky's words "he was an active literary correspondent and distributor of all new works of Zhukovsky, Pushkin and others in society." (*Complete Works* of P. A. Vyazemsky, vol. VIII, p. 273.) Dmitriev had in mind the well-known Friedrich Grimm who carried on a wide correspondence even with the Empress Catherine II. It was published in Paris under the title of *Correspondance littéraire, philosophique et critique.* [N. K. Kulman.]

17. *Revue britannique* began to be published in July 1825 under editorship of Amédée Pichot. [N. K. Kulman.]

18. *Le Catholique, ouvrage périodique dans lequel on traite de l'universalité des connaissances humaines sous le point de vue de l'unité de doctrine.* Published from January 1826 to October 1829 under the editorship of publisher and philosopher, Baron Ferdinand Eckstein. In all, 16 volumes came out. Taking in all fields of knowledge, the journal tried to promulgate the ideas of pure Catholicism. It denied the possibility of knowning *man* by way of individual consciousness, which gives meaning exclusively to the individual "I," and preached attention to history and the church, through which alone one could attain the meaning to the essence of humanity in general. [N. K. Kulman.]

19. *Revue encyclopédique—ou analyse raisonée des productions les plus remarquables dans la littérature, les sciences et les arts, par une réunion des membres de l'Institut et d'autres hommes de lettres.* It was published in Paris from 1814 to December 1833 and was the continuation of *Magasin encyclopédique.* Its editor from the beginning to September 1831 was Marc-Antoine Jullien de Paris, but from September 1831 to the end, Hippolyte Carnot and P. Leroux. A. I. Turgenev was personally acquainted with Jullien. [N. K. Kulman.]

20. *Pirogi* are Russian dumplings. Here Vyazemsky refers to Scott's prolific literary output in a jocular fashion, implying that he can write books as quickly as some bakers can make *pirogi.*

21. Perrette is the heroine of LaFontaine's fable "La Laitière et le Pot au lait" (The Milkmaid and the Milkpot)[N. K. Kulman.] In the fable the girl dreams of how she can trade her milk for many things and thus make a considerable profit. While she daydreams she drops the pot of milk and thus, as Vyazemsky says, shatters her hopes.

22. I have been unable to find the source of this quotation.

23. Probably the lyric tragedy *Rogned* of Andrei Nikolaevich Muravyov (1806-1874). [N. K. Kulman]

24. A *gubernaia* is a political division, equivalent to a province.

25. Paşalik—In Turkey during the time of Sultans, this was a region under the rule of a pasha.

26. Heroes of a one-act comedy *Adolphe and Clara, or Two Prisoners,* which appeared in translation in Moscow in 1801. [N. K. Kulman.]

27. *Globe* began to appear September 15, 1824, first twice a week and then daily. Pierre Leroux and Dubois founded it. It had an interesting history and ended up in the hands of St. Simonists. [N. K. Kulman.]

28. The book of Nikolai Dmitrievich Ivanchin-Pisarev, *The Spirit of Karamzin, or selected thoughts and feelings of the writer. With the addition of a few reviews and historical characters;* 2 parts, Moscow, 1827. [N. K. Kulman]

29. Ekaterina Nikolaevna Karamzin, Princess Meshcherskaya by marriage. [N. K. Kulman.]

30. The imitators of Zeus and Apelles—Apelles was a Greek painter from the fourth century B.C.

31. Churches built or begun by Palladio in the sixteenth century.

32. *Murazzi* are seawalls built by the Republic on the edge of the Lido in 1716 to defend the entrance to the city.

33. Lake Maggiore. The text reflects Turgenev's bizarre spelling.

34. Supposedly a small and unimportant town.

35. From a proverb which means "very far away."

36. From a proverb "Daleko kuliku do svoego bolota" (The snipe has a long way to go to his own swamp). Here Turgenev implies that Barbier is not talented enough for his task.

37. According to legend the soil in this cemetery came from Calvary. Located at the north end of the piazza, it was built in 1278 with four corridors around a large central quad (*campo*).

38. *L'Exilé. Journal de la littérature italienne ancienne et moderne.* This was a monthly journal coming out in Paris in Italian with a translation in French on the opposite page. It began in 1832 and evidently lasted only a few months. [N. K. Kulman.]

39. The title of Naville's essay is "De l'éducation publique considerée dans ses rapports avec le développement des facultés, la marche progressive de la civilisation et les besoins actuels de la France." This work, which came out in 1832, won a gold medal at a competition on education. [N. K. Kulman.]

40. Festival of Vintners.

41. The heroine of Rousseau's novel, *Julie, or the New Héloise.*

42. François de Bonnivard, 1495-1570, Genevan prelate and politician. Byron idealized him in *The Prisoner of Chillon.*

43. Ugolino, Count of Pisa (ca. 1220-89). A Guelph leader, one of the most famous characters in Dante's *Inferno.* He is doomed to the ninth circle—for traitors—and is frozen in ice and must gnaw on the head of the Ghibelline Archbishop Ruggiero.

44. Julie's mother in Rousseau's novel.

45. The grammar here is incorrect. It means, "the brave can make every clime their country because of the country." This is a corruption of the motto of Lord Balfour of Burleigh: *Omne solum forti patria est ut piscibus aequor,* i.e., "The brave can make every clime their country, as fish are at home in every sea." *Classical and Foreign Quotations,* by Wm. Francis Henry King (London: Whitaker and Sons, 1889), p. 391.

46. To swear by the words.

47. Here Turgenev is making a pun on the proverb "Ukatali sivku krutye gorki" (Steep hills drive away the gray mare).

AFTERWORD

"Yes, Virginia, There Was a Russian Romantic Movement"

John Mersereau, Jr.

This essay is concerned exclusively with Romanticism in literature, that is, with a historic phenomenon, not with that innate and timeless romanticism of the human psyche which has found expression in riding barrels over Niagara Falls, attempting to better the world's record for teetertottering, or climbing the Matterhorn with one hand tied behind the back. Nor does this essay concern, other than in passing, the so-called philosophy of Romanticism, a perilous topic whose name is Confusion.

Romanticism in literature, wherever it occurred, had denominators in common with its manifestations elsewhere, such as its qualities of dynamism, individualism, freedom, radicalism, idealism—and egotism. But despite some shared characteristics (and one might expand the list), each country, in its own good time, developed its peculiar or national romantic profile. My purpose here is not to present a comparison or contrastive analysis of Russian Romanticism with the various European embodiments of the movement. Rather, I hope to sketch its background in Russia, to show when and how it acquired dominance on the literary scene, and to indicate, at least superficially, how it evolved into Realism.

The study of Romanticism in Russia has been considerably confused by constant acts of what might be called "biased hindsight": that is, by attempts to read into Russian literary history ideas, trends, and developments which will support contemporary ideological postures. This process of *selective* illumination of Russia's literary past has been a continuing one since the days of Belinsky, with the result that much of what has been said about Romanticism is incomplete, based on half-truths, or deliberately false. A few of the terms which have appeared will give an idea of what I mean. In post-revolutionary critical literature we encounter such formulations as "democratic Romanticism," "reactionary Romanticism," "progressive Romanticism," "idealistic Romanticism," "revolutionary Romanticism," "passive Romanticism," "Decembrist Romanticism," and so forth. Strangely, and unhappily, the term "literary Romanticism" is not much heard. The term "esthetic Romanticism" is used, but in a pejorative sense to suggest an art-for-art's-sake motivation.

Among older, pre-revolutionary critics we have some similarly confusing formulations. According to one of these (Sipovsky), Pushkin was responsible for the creation of something called "true Romanticism," which this critic equated with Realism, an equation very congenial to critics who wish to make a realist out of the poet. Some say that Russia had no Romantic movement, that, as it were, there was only a short circuit from Neoclassicism to Realism, the spark consisting of only a handful of *bona fide* romantics, of whom Lermontov was the most flashy. All of these opinions and formulations have been carefully established and proved, notwithstanding their mutual incompatibility (demonstrating the maxim that in research, unless one is careful, one will always find what one is seeking).

But it isn't only Russian critics, tendentious or otherwise, who are responsible for the confusion existing about Romanticism. Among West-European or American students of Russian literature there has been a strong inclination to consider the Russian Romantic movement not on its own terms and in its own context, but to see it as an extension of German, French, or English Romanticisms. There is no question that Russian Romanticism owes a debt to all three, but still it must be accorded the courtesy, and prestige, of being considered an individual movement.

Russian Romanticism may have been less formalized in a philosophical sense than German Romanticism, but then it was more dynamic and did not become anchored in the shallows of mediocrity by its romantic philosophy. Russian Romanticism may have waxed and waned more quickly than its French counterpart, but in its short period it accomplished more. Russian Romanticism may have produced prose inferior to that of the English, but its poets surpassed those of France and Germany. And finally, it can be established that the Russian Romantic movement taken as a whole displays as much unity and cohesiveness as any of the others, assuming that it is proper to speak of cohesiveness in reference to movements whose main features seem to be diversity and individuality.

I would affirm, therefore, that we have the right to speak of a Russian Romantic movement in its own terms. I do not mean that the influences of England, Germany, and France upon this movement should be dismissed or underplayed—objectivity demands otherwise. But it must be remembered that influences occur only if conditions are right. Western Europe did not force Romanticism upon Russia, and in fact did not even offer it—it was Russian literature itself which absorbed some aspects of Western romantic theory and practice, because it was ready for them and found them congenial. The breath of life for Russian Romanticism may have come from the West, but it drew its sustenance from the Russian soil.

Russian Romanticism was an esthetic revolution in reaction to conservative literary norms which were no longer productive. It was a positive movement which sought to free itself from the bonds of Neoclassicism. It was national, or self-centered, in that it concerned itself with Russian history, folklore, traditions, national types, and it derived its settings from its native landscape. It was experimental in that it utilized a new literary language, mixed established genres to form new ones, and engaged in a wide variety of metrical innovations. Russian Romanticism was self-conscious, at least to the extent that critics and writers were aware that they were engaged in a common struggle against the literary conservatives, and to the extent that they called themselves "romantics." Russian Romanticism's greatest achievement was in poetry, but its prose provided the foundaton for the great novels of the second half of the nineteenth century.

For this brief survey it would be a mistake to attempt to trace the domestic roots of Russian Romanticism which, if one looks carefully, may be seen to extend down through the previous centuries even to the Slavic national epic, *The Lay of the Host of Igor.* (Parenthetically, when Andre Mazon challenged the authenticity of this work, one of his arguments was that it seemed too modern, too *romantic,* to have been a product of the twelfth century.) Let us, therefore, start with Nikolai Karamzin, whose tales in the sentimentalist tradition legitimitized prose fiction and laid the groundwork for much that was to follow. Karamzin's *Letters of a Russian Traveller,* published in 1792 and manifestly influenced by Sterne's *Sentimental Journey,* was a deeply subjective and sentimental work incorporating a prose style unlike the heavy Slavono-Russian which had dominated the eighteenth century. Patterning his syntax on French and English, and enriching his language with a host of words and expressions appropriated from French, he achieved a prose which he felt would neither offend polite society nor tax the society matrons' knowledge of Russian or Church Slavonic. (Remember that French was then widely spoken by the gentry, whose understanding of Russian was often imperfect.) Karamzin followed his *Letters* with numerous pieces of short fiction, the most famous of which was "Poor Liza," a lachrymose tale devoted to the theme that even a peasant girl could love. Despite its macaronic quality and its essential artificiality, Karamzin's language took hold and was soon improved upon by the expansion of its lexical content. Meanwhile, his sentimental tales were widely imitated, and "Poor Liza" became godmother to a brood of Unhappy Lizas, Poor Mashas, Comely Tatyanas, and others. Concurrently, sentimental tragedies and tearful comedies usurped the stage, while poets raised their tear-stained handkerchiefs as banners of the new conceit.

In the first two decades of the nineteenth century, Russian readers and writers also became better acquainted with West European pre-romantic or romantic literary works, primarily through the efforts of Vasily Zhukovsky. His translation of Gray's "Elegy" appeared in 1802 and was followed in 1808 by an adaptation of Bürger's ballad "Lenore," which he called "Lyudmila." Ballads immediately became very much in vogue. Zhukovsky continued popularizing Western authors, in particular Schiller, Scott, Thomas Moore, and later Byron. Zhukovsky was the first top-flight poet to demonstrate that a poetic diction based on Karamzin's language reform was especially suitable for the new verse themes and forms, imported or domestic. His efforts were seconded by Konstantin Batyushkov, whose Muse favored Italian poets and the so-called "light poetry" of the late eighteenth-century French transitional poets (Millevoye and Parny). Both Zhukovsky and Batyushkov, especially the latter, became masters of the young Alexander Pushkin, who was destined to become the most famous poet of the Romantic period—or any period, for that matter.

But I am anticipating. The existence of the new poetic language, demonstrated so effectively by Zhukovsky, Batyushkov, and others, opened the way for the renovation of traditional genres, their recombination, and even the creation of new poetic forms. The violent polemics which accompanied these developments during the second and third decades of the nineteenth century testified to the extent of the literary ferment. The literary conservatives, united in their defense of Neoclassical doctrines and the traditional Slavono-Russian literary language, were unable to counter these new developments effectively, for the desire for something new was too intense and the possibilities for change were unlimited. In many instances these conservatives, who mustered around Admiral Alexander Shishkov, were quite right in deploring and mocking some manifestations of this new poetry, such as its imported conceits, its fatuous periphrasis, or its thematic triviality. Indeed, Admiral Shishkov did have some justification for asking why the new poets did not simply say "the moon is shining" rather than "pale Hecate mirrors the wan reflections." Still, the conservatives' attacks were essentially negative, because they offered nothing in exchange but a return to shopworn norms and forms which had lost their magic. Despite its weaknesses, the poetry of Karamzin's disciples was fresh and different, while Shishkov and his camp continued to produce musty works with titles such as: "Ode on the Return of My Beloved Brother from a Sea Voyage of Seventeen Months' Duration."

One must also mention the existence of a small third party which developed along with the Karamzin-Zhukovsky school and which was to exert an influence far out of proportion to its size. Its most important members were Pavel

Katenin and Alexander Griboedov. In 1816 Katenin published his own version of Bürger's "Lenore," which he called "Olga" and intended as a lesson to Zhukovsky and his followers on the proper method of adapting foreign models to domestic literature. Katenin's adaptation featured vernacular Russian and some earthy imagery which sounded uncouth to the tender ears of those accustomed to the sweet sounds of Zhukovsky's lyre. In the polemics following the publication of "Olga," Griboedov sided with Katenin against Zhukovsky. This opposition suggested that Katenin and Griboedov had at least a spiritual alliance with Shishkov and his conservatives. And, in fact, Katenin and Griboedov did share common ground with Shishkov in something which might be called their literary nationalism, but where Shishkov's nationalism was connected with the retention of eighteenth-century norms and the preservation of Slavonic elements in the literary language, Griboedov and Katenin were primarily concerned that Russian literature protect its Russianness and not become the lackey of foreign masters. They deplored the misty Germanic fogs which wafted from Zhukovksy's verse, its ceaseless elegiac tone, its sweet melancholy, and the effete style which eschewed not only Slavonicism but even many perfectly good and unoffensive lexical elements from everyday Russian.

These polemics continued right on into the twenties, and in 1824 we find Wilhelm Küchelbecker echoing the complaints of Griboedov and Katenin—and with good reason. By that time the ballad and the elegy had become so popular that they were cliché-ridden, and their conventionalized poetic language had spread into other kinds of verse as well. It was a language typical of the period, the Romantic period. Küchelbecker, in his essay "On the Direction of Our Poetry," inveighed against this situation, criticizing the imitativeness, vapidity, and repetitiousness of contemporary verse. Though he was a good friend of Pushkin, Zhukovsky, and Baratynsky, he did not hesitate to include them in his critical remarks:

> An imitator knows no inspiration: he speaks not from the depths of his own soul, but forces himself to repeat another's concepts and feelings. Power? Where will we find it in the majority of our turbid, effeminate, colorless works, which define nothing. Everything is *a dream or a vision,* everything *appears to be* or *seems to be* or *gives an impression,* everything is only *as if, as it were, something or other.* Richness and variety? Having read any elegy of Zhukovsky, Pushkin or Baratynsky, you know it all . . . And the imagery is always the same: *a moon,* which it goes without saying is *melancholy* and *pale;* there are cliffs and groves where they never existed, a forest behind which a setting sun appears for the hundredth time, evening glow. Now and then there are long shadows, visions, something unseeen, something unknown, banal allegory, pale, tasteless personifications of *Labor, Bliss, Peace, Joy, Sadness, Laziness* of the author and *Boredom* of the reader. And in particular there is *fog;* fog over the pine woods, fog over the fields, and fog in the writer's head.

The word *romanticism* was first used in Russian criticism by Prince Vyazemsky in 1819, which was considerably later than the initial manifestations of the movement in Russian literature. But it often happens that an affliction (and Romantcism was regarded as such by many) precedes its denotation. The term caught on quickly, and by the early twenties banners were raised in the name of Romanticism and a great deal of attention was focused on the question of its proper meaning, but without much success. A good example is provided by one reception of Pushkin's *Ruslan and Lyudmila,* a mock epic published in 1820. Zhukovksy received it enthusiastically, and the conservatives were perplexed and indignant (for some reason they believed that Pushkin was obligated to create a proper Russian epic, although they had proved incapable of doing so themselves). The writer and critic Alexander Voeikov, who was sympathetic to modernist trends, was entirely at a loss to identify the genre of *Ruslan and Lyudmila,* apparently a matter of importance for him. In grappling with this problem, he provided his own unique definition of Romanticism: the distinguishing elements of Pushkin's poem, in Voeikov's assessment, were its qualities of folklore heroic, folklore fairy tale, and humor. Said he, "Nowadays, this type of poetry is called *romantic.*" A rival commentator advised Voeikov to read Byron and see if he could confirm his definition.

Prince Vyazemsky's introductions to Pushkin's "A Prisoner of the Caucasus" and "The Fountain of Bakhchisaray," published in 1822 and 1824 respectively, were attempts to defend Romanticism and to define it. Although Pushkin was initially grateful for his friend's efforts, in 1825 he wrote to him as follows: "By the way, I have noticed that everyone (and you, too) has the haziest notion of romanticism." Vyazemsky conceded the point in a letter to Zhukovsky, likening Romanticism to *domovoi,* an invisible being which Russians believed inhabited every household. Vyazemsky wrote: "Romanticism is like *domovoi:* many believe in it, there is a conviction regarding its existence, but what are its characteristics, how is one to define it, how is one to put his finger on it?"

Pushkin attempted on several occasions to grapple with the definition of Romanticism, his most extensive effort being an essay entitled "On Classical and Romantic Poetry." His conclusion was that the essential feature distinguishing Romantic poetry from Classical poetry was *not* its spirit but its form: poems with forms not known to the Greeks and Romans, or which represented changes of their forms were, in Pushkin's formulation, to be considered romantic. A simple solution, but its limitations are apparent.

The real theoretician of Romanticism was the critic, journalist and author Orest Somov. In 1823 he published in the *Emulator,* the journal of the Free Society of Lovers of Russian Literature, a three-part essay entitled "On Romantic Poetry." Essential to the whole development of the essay is the idea, expressed early in the first part, that true poetry can be achieved only if no arbitrary rules restrict its creation. The second part of Somov's work is largely a paraphrase, with credit, of Mme de Staël's ideas about national literatures. In the conclusion of his essay, Somov emphasized that Russia possessed in great abundance history, heroes, diversity of ethnic types, variety of landscape, and richness of language; hence it could and should create its own individual and unique Romanticism. Somov exhorted writers to abandon imitation of foreign models and produce works embodying qualities of *narodnost',* or national identity, and *mestnost',* or national locality. Somov, incidentally, paid attention to his own exhortation, and many of his own prose stories present national types, such as provincial gentry, peasants, mendicant religious halfwits, bailiffs, coachmen, all depicted against a rich background of Russian and Ukrainian local color.

Somov's stories appeared in the latter part of the twenties and in the early thirties (he died in 1833), just at that time when prose was asserting its popularity at the expense of poetic genres. Poetry's heyday occurred in the twenties, and I am speaking now of the new poetry, the romantic poetry produced by that galaxy of unusual talents whose principal luminary was Alexander Pushkin. It is not my purpose to provide details about the poetic achievements of this group— these are well known. What I would like to emphasize, however, is that irrespective of their differences, which were considerable, Russian romantic poets were united by their common, conscious debt to Karamzin and their shared views that the aim of poetry was poetry itself. Now, I am aware that claims can and have been made that Pushkin and the best of the Pleiad, including Baratynsky, Delvig, Vyazemsky and Yazykov, display some prominent qualities which are more traditionally associated with Classicism than with Romanticism. The same may be said for Tyutchev. Thus, for example, Baratynsky and Vyazemsky seem almost classical in the restrained exposition of their ideational poems, Delvig's attraction to the idyll and to antique themes suggests a classical orientation, and the cold, controlled brilliance of Yazykov's poetry seems strangely unromantic. Tyutchev's predilection for odes to nature links him with the poets of an earlier tradition. But the presence of non-romantic qualities in the verses of these poets does not make the poets themselves Classicists or Neoclassicists. Prince Vyazemsky, as we have seen, was an ardent champion of Romanticism: it was in the name of Romanticism that he defended Pushkin's Southern Cycle against the attacks of the literary conservatives. Further, Prince Vyazemsky gave financial support to Polevoi to assist in establishing *The Moscow Telegraph,* a bi-monthly founded in 1825 with the deliberate program of supporting the romantic cause. Baratynsky's views on nature and the isolation of the poet define his lyrics as romantic, irrespective of their apparent "Classical" style; Baratynsky's narrative poems, *The Ball* and *The Concubine,* have nothing in common with the literary product of the Shishkov group. Delvig, for all his interest in the idyll, created an exceptional cycle of Russian popular songs. He was also editor of *Northern Flowers,* the literary almanac which annually from 1825 to 1832 presented not only the best offerings of Pushkin and the Pleiad but other poets whose choice and treatment of themes leave no doubt about their romantic orientation, poets such as Zhukovsky, Ivan Kozlov, Vasily and Fyodor Tumansky, and Andrei Podolinsky. And, finally, Tyutchev's worldview and attitudes toward man and nature are romantic; it is not accidental that he, along with the romantic's romantic, Lermontov, became a favorite of the Symbolists at the end of the century.

No, cavils aside, these greater and lesser poets belong to Russian Romanticism. Their works show a definite break with the traditions and restrictions of Neoclassicism, especially with respect to poetic language, the hybridization of genres, the development of new metrical features, the choice and treatment of themes. If these romantic poets respected, and sometimes even imitated, antique and Renaissance poets, it was because they regarded them as poets whose verse reflected—as romantic poetry properly should—their own homeland and their own age. The Russian romantics' quarrel was not with the Classicists but with the neo- or pseudo-classicists, who imposed arbitrary rules on theme and genres and language, and who stifled the freedom and individualism necessary for the creation of new and significant poetry.

The great number of talented poets and their production of excellent works has led the twenties to be classified as the Golden Age of Russian poetry. But gold, as we know, gives way to baser metals, and the generation of poets that followed (Podolinsky, Delaryu, Struisky) showed themselves incapable of the originality, technical perfection, and scope of their masters. The exception was Lermontov, who extended the Golden Age, or at least its sunset, until his death in 1841—an age of Bronze then ensued.

While poetry had been sailing before the winds of popularity through the twenties, prose was beginning to move from the doldrums in which it had languished since the days of Karamzin. Of course, people had been writing prose throughout the first three decades of the century—we have met the names of some of these authors before. Zhukovsky, for example, in 1809 published his "Mary's Grove," a highly sentimentalized tale of unhappy love set in pre-Muscovite times. Batyushkov composed his "Predslava and Dobrynya," a short historical romance set against the background of Kiev court life. Both works betray their debt to Karamzin and to Sentimentalism. Vasily Narezhny, the only notable fiction writer of the period between Karamzin and the mid-twenties, combined elements of picaresque satire with sentimentalism to produce a few works of modest worth, such as *A Russian Gil Blas* and *The Two Ivans*. Notwithstanding Narezhny's concern with national types and local color, his style and attitudes derive from the eighteenth century. Thus, although he was active until his death in 1825, he contributed little to the romantic prose tradition.

In the early twenties prose was largely non-fiction, such as travel notes, military memoirs, sketches. Although the short story and novella were extant to a limited degree, the historical tale seemed to dominate fiction. Most works of this genre show little intrinsic superiority to the sentimental distortions of history made earlier in the century by Zhukovsky and Batyushkov. Plots are improbable, characters one-dimensional, their psychology is arbitrary; and authors (or narrators) and characters are wont to indulge in mawkish rhetoric. Although today the style strikes us as ludicrous, most readers of the twenties and thirties would have been disappointed had they not been permitted to share the emotional seizures of hero and heroine, and an exposition devoid of striking metaphor would have seemed flat and unrealistic. Perhaps the most popular writer of fiction in the early twenties was Alexander Bestuzhev-Marlinsky. Here is a brief sample from his historical tale of fourteenth-century Novgorod, "Roman and Olga," which appeared in the 1823 edition of the famous literary almanac *Polar Star:*

> In the heat of his anger Roman did not notice the supplicating voice of Olga, but having drained his heart of words, he saw her tears. His fury disappeared, like melting snow on red-hot iron.
> "Ungrateful friend," said the beauty. "You could think you could say that I had ceased to love you . . ."
> "Forgive me, forgive me, my priceless one," repeated the touched Roman, kissing her frigid hand.
> Involuntarily the maid inclined against the boiling breast of the youth, the cheeks of both turned red, and their first sweet kiss of love sealed their truce.
> "To live and die with you," Olga pronouced softly, and all of Roman's veins shuddered with an inexpressible feeling.

Marlinsky, in keeping with the norms of the period, then shares a thought with his readers.

> "Ardent souls! You understand, you have experienced these magic moments, when each thought is joy, each sensation is delight, and each feeling is ecstasy!"

So much for life in old Novgorod. In this story Marlinksy did try to fulfill the criteria of *narodnost'* and *mestnost':* he chose his subject from Russian history, he tried to reproduce the image of life in Novgorod during the last days of its independence, he introduced all sorts of antiquarian bric-a-brac to provide an antique flavor.

The biggest problem facing Russian fiction was that whereas poetry had long since developed a real literary language, replete even with its own clichés, prose had not. One of Pushkin's constant complaints throughout the twenties was that Russian prose was at best an awkward and inflexible tool. Orest Somov, in the annual surveys of literature which appeared in the almanac *Northern Flowers,* continually stressed the necessity for the creation of a suitable prose language, noting that the majority of Russian prose writers "either become lost in the rough plowland of antiquated Slavono-Russian or slip and fall over the heaps of foreign languages accumulated in the past (Gallicisms, Teutonisms, and the like), or sink in the low and marshy soil of a rude, uncultivated vernacular."

Throughout the later twenties prose writers persevered, with varying degrees of success, and by the end of the decade we encounter some adequate short stories—often with supernatural content—and the first of a flood of historical novels. It is clear that Russian authors were looking to Western European literatures for their models in prose, just as the poets, but with better results, had once done. E. T. A. Hoffmann, Ludwig Tieck, and Charles Maturin and his disciples of *l'école frénétique* were pilfered for themes and motifs for tales of the supernatual; Walter Scott provided the formula for the historical novel; and Washington Irving contributed the form for the framed tale with its interpolated adventures, not to mention some plots. A very positive influence, at least in the long run, was that of Balzac. His novels and stories of contemporary French life created a thirst among Russian readers for similar exposés of their own high society, a thirst soon slacked by a flood of so-called society tales. A pattern or formula soon dominated the genre. An unhappily married countess or princess, whose husband is always old, fat and stupid (but rich), finds true love with a poet, musician, artist, or sea captain. Usually the hero is socially a few notches beneath his partner in adultery, and therefore is scorned by her circle, a circumstance which enabled authors to inject a note of social protest. Although the adulterous, or would-be adulterous, couple was presented sympathetically, morality demanded that sins be paid for, so the heroes were usually eliminated by duels and the fallen countesses were banished to remote estates where they languished in perpetual contemplation of their transgressions. A special variant of the society tale was the *Künstlernovelle,* which had its origins in German literature. Although the background or setting was often society, the focus was on the sufferings and frustrations of a painter, sculptor, composer, or bard who ineffectually struggled for recognition, or love, or bread, ignored by an insensate society.

Both types of tale, although categorically romantic, bore within them seeds of Realism. This was particularly true of the satirical society tales, the ones which had as their particular aim the exposure of the triviality, corruption, cupidity, and banality of high society. Satire begins with reality, because it is the exaggeration and overstatement of reality that generates the satirical effect. In seeking the essence of the reality they wished to satirize, Russian authors were moving towards Realism—irrespective of the clumsiness of their methods.

Other qualities within Russian romantic prose also caused a natural development towards Realism—that is, the qualities of *narodnost'* and *mestnost';* an author had to study the behavior and habits of his countrymen, to inform himself of the features which distinguished Russian life from that elsewhere, and to incorporate these distinguishing or dominant features into his art. The requirement of *mestnost'* demanded attention to the domestic setting, its peculiarities, its atmosphere. There were, of course, many examples of pseudo-*narodnost'* and distorted *mestnost',* the result of superficial observation and incorrect generalization. But still the trend continued towards the felicitous embodiment of these two qualities in fiction, with the inevitable result of greater realism.

Throughout the thirties Russian authors continued their efforts to master their language. Marlinsky, Polevoi, Titov, and Bulgarin, along with many lesser lights, pretty much stayed on dead center; but others—Perovsky, Pogodin, Odoevsky, Somov, Pavlov, and most notably Pushkin—made real progress. Of course, since artistic virtue is usually recognized and rewarded belatedly, Pushkin's prose (unornamental, matter-of-fact, succinct) passed largely unnoticed, while Marlinsky and Bulgarin shared honors for public popularity. Still, the unrecognized developements taking place in the prose literary language made it possible to expand the range of devices for character delineation, and in this decade we note the first steps toward interior monologue, the differentiation of characters' speech in conformity with class background, profession and personality, the depiction of inner conflict, the correlation of behavior with motivation, the expansion of metonymic means of characterization. The cardboard protagonists of the twenties whose psychology was alien to human understanding and whose emotions were typically expressed by breast beating and teeth gnashing, now give way to characters who are less colorful, less erratic, less rhetorical, and less demonic—but eminently more human.

Simultaneously, new types of prose fiction were evolving. Genres which had dominated fiction in the twenties and early thirties were becoming shopworn through use and abuse. Tales of the supernatural, though still produced, were given ironic treatment. Typical of this trend was Pushkin's "The Queen of Spades," a work which Eikhenbaum has interpreted as an anti-romantic manifesto. Without destroying the credulous faith of his more simple-minded readers, who took the tale as a story of the supernatural (and some still do), Pushkin cleverly satirized the popular romantic themes of ghosts, the superman, madness and genius, unrequited love, demonic interference, the triumph of virtue, the midnight tryst, and so forth. Of course, Pushkin's story was more or less his own private joke, and I mention it here simply as one of the harbingers of that change of taste, and of genres, which was to follow shortly.

But let us turn to Lermontov, the poet who established his reputation with his elegy protesting Pushkin's slaying in 1837. Lermontov's evolution as a prose writer is interesting because in the course of one decade it presents in capsule form many of the evolutionary qualities of Russian romantic prose. Around 1832, when he was an eighteen-year-old cadet in the Guards' School in Petersburg, he began writing a historical novel set against the Pugachev Rebellion of 1774. His hero ws a demonic hunchback named Vadim, who unsuccessfully sought to combine incestuous love for his sister with revenge against the man who ruined his father. Vadim's diabolical genius, his passion, his grotesque appearance, his magnetic eyes, and his grandiloquent rhetoric show that his creator was well acquainted with Byron's *Lara* and *The Deformed Transformed,* Scott's *The Black Monk,* Maturin's *Melmoth the Wanderer,* the young Hugo's *Bug-Jargal,* and Balzac's *Les Chouans,* to mention just some of the authors and works reflected in this juvenile pastiche. Lermontov never finished the novel, which speaks well for his judgment.

In 1836 Lermontov began a society tale entitled "Princess Ligovskaya," a bitter satire on the beau monde. The story centers around the triumphs and tribulations of a young officer, named Pechorin, as he seeks to acquire notoriety in Petersburg high society. Significantly, although Lermontov here followed the formula for the society tale, his work surpassed the usual examples of the genre because of its unusual concern with depiction of the psychological states of the main figures. Despite some flaws, had he finished the work it probably would have been better than any others of its genre, including those of Vladimir Odoevsky.

Lermontov's next prose venture resulted in the famous *A Hero of Our Time* (1840), Russian literature's first modern novel of psychological realism. To create his novel the author imaginatively combined available romantic genres (travel notes, military memoir, physiological sketch, society tale), structuring them in such a way that the reader is provided an increasingly intimate acquaintance with the protagonist, a dynamic but completely alienated officer. Not less important to the illusion of reality which the novel generates is the rich but unobtrusive prose style, which became a model for other writers throughout the century.

Finally, in 1841, in the last year of his life, Lermontov began a *Künstlernovelle.* This tale concerns an artist,

Minsky, who is being driven insane by his inability to realize on canvas his ideal of a woman. Minsky thinks that people have lemons instead of heads. Meanwhile, he is visited by a déclassé spook to whom he loses all of his money gambling. The story does not proceed to the point where Minsky's problems are resolved. Some critics have seen this tale as an unsuccessful attempt on Lermontov's part to compose a story of the supernatural, a preposterous idea. Like Pushkin's "The Queen of Spades," this story parodies the traditional supernatural tale. Common sense tells us that Lermontov, whose fiction had progressed from the egregious romanticism of l'école frénétique to the realism of A Hero of Our Time would not and could not regress to the hackneyed romantic themes of Hoffmann's multitudinous followers. No, the story is a joke, and a parody, and interestingly enough, one of its parodistic barbs was directed at Lermontov's fellow romantic, Nikolai Gogol.

I would like to leave Gogol aside, and I am sure he would prefer that I do so, too. But he must be accounted for— and he was a romantic, irrespective of the unceasing efforts of various critics to prove otherwise. Without going into details, we see in Gogol's development a pattern similar to that of Lermontov—up to a point. Gogol's first published prose was a fragment from a historical novel dealing with the ancient Polish-Ukrainian conflict. The novel was unfinished, a not too unhappy circumstance judging by the published excerpt, which is undistinguished except for a pine tree which drips blood. We know that Orest Somov encouraged the young Gogol to write about the customs and legends of their native Ukraine (Somov mistakenly assumed that Gogol was informed about these matters). So Gogol produced his Ukrainian cycle, with all its comic and not so comic devils, its exuberance, its farce, its romanticized vision of reality—the stories of Evenings on a Farm Near Dikanka and Mirgorod. Then came the Petersburg cycle, including stories of the supernatural, such as "The Portrait," a mishmash of second-hand romantic motifs and tedious philosophizing. The cycle also had a Künstlernovelle, entitled "Nevsky Prospect," an unusual variant of that genre. One might have expected that Gogol would then have developed, as Lermontov did, in the direction of Realism. Some profess that he did with Dead Souls, but that is nonsense. True, that novel, or epic as Gogol called it, is filled with realistic details, but there is only a symbolic "reality" in the culminating image of a world given over to madness, monsters, and mercenary mendacity. As in Sterne's Tristram Shandy, verbal and stylistic conceits further forestall any illusion of reality—and the results are marvelous, one might add.

Russian Romanticism was a broad, dynamic movement. Besides the Literary Mandarins of Petersburg, on whom I have focused my discussion, there were other active and important groups. Of particular importance were the Lovers of Wisdom Society, a Moscow circle united by their mutual interest in German idealistic philosophy and German Romanticism. In 1824-25 they published their own almanac, Mnemosyne. The major figures of this group were Dmitri Venevitinov, philosopher, critic, and talented poet, whose death in 1827 was a severe blow to Russian literature; Vladimir Odoevsky, a neo-Hoffmannist who produced unique variants of the Künsternovelle and several interesting society tales; Wilhelm Küchelbecker, a literary Don Quixote whose conservative critical views were in sharp contrast to his radical political activities.

Another group controlled by romantics or pro-romantics was the Free Society of Lovers of Russian Literature, whose president was the poet and allegorist Fyodor Glinka. The monthly published by this group, The Emulator, was in the service of Romanticism. There were also many informal literary circles, such as those of Zhukovsky, Delvig, Princess Volkonskaya, Sofia Ponomareva, Nikolai Grech, etc. The cause of Romanticism was seriously assisted by the many literary almanacs on the market following the success of Kondraty Ryleev's and Marlinsky's Polar Star, which appeared annually from 1823 to 1825. The 1826 issue, to be called Little Star, was suppressed owing to the editors' involvement in the Decembrist Uprising. Aladin's Nevsky Almanac and Delvig's Northern Flowers were Polar Star's most successful competitors and successors, lasting for eight or more annual issues; both works were organs of Romanticism. There was a host of others, most of which appeared only once or twice: Sirius, Russian Thalia, Urania, Northern Lyre, Snowdrop, Album of Northern Muses, Tsarskoe Selo, Dawn—these were only the most important popularizers of romantic authors and ideology. Polevoi's Moscow Telegraph furthered the movement; the bi-monthly Slav, edited by Alexander Voeikov, also played a role, as did Mikhail Pogodin's Moscow Herald, another bi-monthly initiated in 1827. Also deserving particular mention as an organ of Romanticism was Delvig's Literary Gazette, a periodical devoted to criticism, poetry, and (especially) fiction, which appeared every five days from January 1830 to July 1831.

When did Romanticism end? If we wish to satisfy our tendency to periodize literature, we can say that it came to a conclusion with the death of Lermontov (1841), whose demise marked the end of the twilight of the Golden Age of Russian poetry and whose novel A Hero of Our Time represented the sunrise of the realist tradition. But dates can only be approximate, and I would insist that although one may quite legitimately contrast the canonical features of Romanticism and Realism, the latter evolved from the former's most viable features. In differing degrees and in differing respects one sees the legacy of Pushkin, Gogol, and Lermontov—to mention just the foremost romantics—in the prose of Turgenev, Dostoevsky, and Tolstoy—to mention only the foremost psychological realists.

GLOSSARY

Aeschylus (ca. 525-456 B.C.). Greek tragic poet and dramatist. His plays include *Suppliant Women, Seven against Thebes* and *The Oresteia.*

Aksakov, Konstantin Sergeevich (1817-60). Critic and thinker, leader of the Slavophiles. He also wrote literary criticism.

Alembert, Jean Le Rond D' (1717-83). French mathematician, philosopher, member of the Paris Academy of Sciences, and one of the Encyclopedists.

Alfieri, Vittorio (1749-1803). Italian poet and dramatist, and probably his country's leading pre-Romantic writer. In his works he lashed out against the French and against tyranny.

Annenkov, Pavel V. (1812-87). Literary critic and memoirist, a westernizer and friend of Belinsky and Stankevich.

Antonsky (Antonsky-Prokopovich), Anton Antonovich (1763-1848). Famous professor of natural history at Moscow University.

Arakcheev, Aleksey Andreevich (1769-1834). Count, Minister of War and an extremely influential man during Alexander I's reign. He was hated because of his cruelty.

Ariosto, Ludovico (1471-1533). Italian poet, author of *Orlando Furioso* (1505-15), a long narrative about Orlando and other knights of Charlemagne in wars against the Saracens.

Aristophanes (B.C. about 450-385). Greek dramatist, author of political comedies such as *The Birds.*

Arnault, Antoine Vincent (1766-1834). Dramatic writer and fabulist, author of *Souvenirs d'un sexagénaire,* 4 volumes, 1833.

Arzhevitinov, Ivan Semyonovich (died 1848). A cousin of A. I. Turgenev.

Avdeev, Mikhail Vasilyevich (1821-76). A member of the editorial board of *The Contemporary,* this writer imitated Lermontov and Turgenev with his novels *Tamarin* (1852) and *Underwater Stone* (1860), with their "superfluous men" as heroes.

Bakunin, Mikhail Alexandrovich (1814-76). Radical thinker and one of the founders of political anarchism, he was a member of the Stankevich Circle.

Balzac, Honoré de (1799-1850). French novelist who wrote in the realistic mode. *Le Père Goriot* and *La Cousine Bette* are two of his many famous novels.

Barbier, Henri Auguste (1805-82). French minor poet who wrote satires, especially about profiteers in the July Revolution. *Il Pianto* (1833) is a series of poems about Italy's former glories. He outlived his success.

Barkov, Dmitry Nikolaevich (1796-after 1855). Military man, bureaucrat in the Petersburg customs agency, theater critic and member of the Green Lamp.

Batteux, Charles, abbot (1713-80). French philosopher and aesthetician.

Benckendorf, Alexander Khristoforovich (1783-1844). Chief of the gendarmerie and the Third Section. He was close to the tsar and an adversary of Pushkin.

Bezobrazova, Sofya Fyodorovna (1799-1875). Sister of Decembrist F. F. Vadkovsky.

Bibikov, Dmitry Gavrilovich (1791-1870). Director of External Trade, in which ministry Vyazemsky worked as vice director from 1832.

Blair, Hugh (1718-1800). Scottish theoretician of aesthetics and professor of rhetoric at Edinburgh University.

Blok, Alexander Alexandrovich (1880-1921). One of Russia's greatest Symbolist poets.

Bludov, Dmitry Nikolaevich (1785-1864). Served in Ministries of Foreign Affairs, Popular Education, the Interior, and Justice. He wrote epigrams, historical studies and a satire "Vision in Arzamas." Bludov's nickname was Cassandra in the Arzamas Society.

Bogdanovich, Ippolit Fyodorovich (1743-1803). Russian poet, author of *Dushenka,* a version of LaFontaine's *Les amours de Psyché et de Cupidon.*

Boileau, Nicolas (1636-1711). French poet and critic, he set down the rules of classical poetry.

Bonnet, Charles (1720-1793). Swiss naturalist and philosophical writer who discovered parthenogenesis and developed catastrophe theory of evolution.

Borromeo, St. Charles (1538-84). Cardinal, aristocrat who in 1583 went to Switzerland as an apostolic visitor and worked to combat Protestantism there. A member of the counter-reformation in Italy, he died in Milan.

Bossuet, Jacques Bénigne (1627-1704). French preacher, bishop, theologian, historian and an influential and eloquent spokesman for the rights of the French church against papal authority. He is remembered for his literary works, which include panegyrics for great personages.

Botkin, Vasily Petrovich (1811-69). Writer, critic and translator. He wrote articles on philosophy, literature, art, music and the theater.

Brambeus, Baron. See Senkovsky.

Brantome, Pierre de Bourdeilles de (1504)-1614). French memoirist who paints a lively picture of life at court in the late sixteenth century.

Bravurina-Bravursha. Affectionate terms A. I. Turgenev uses for his close friend Madame Maria Ivanovna Bravoura. She was a celebrated beauty who frequented the salons and hence came to know the leading intellectuals of her day, including Chaadayev.

Brentano, Clemens (1778-1842). German poet, novelist and dramatist. He was mainly interested in a study of Germany's folklore and cultural past. He was also a proponent of strict Catholic asceticism.

Broglie, Victor de (1785-1870). Famous political figure in France.

Broughton. See Ludlow.

Bryullov, Karl Pavlovich (1799-1852). Famous Russian painter.

Bulgakov, Konstantin Yakovlevich (1782-1835). Director of the Petersburg Post Office and friend of Pushkin, Vyazemsky and Turgenev.

Bürger, Gottfried August (1747-94). German poet. Known mostly for his ballad *Lenore* (1774), he greatly influenced several Russian Romantic poets.

Calame, Mlle. A former teacher in the home of princess Sofya Grigoryevna Volkonskaya (1786-1869), a friend of Pushkin, Vyazemsky and Turgenev.

Calderón de la Barca, Pedro (1600-1681). Spanish dramatist who reflects the mood of a nation in decline, upholds a rigorous code of honor and writes plays of thought rather than action.

Camöens, Luis Vaz de (1524?-1580). Portuguese poet, author of epic *Os Lusiadas (The Lusiad),* which chronicles Vasco de Gama's discovery of a sea-route to India. He includes in the epic an entire history of Portugal.

Canova, Antonio (1757-1822). An Italian sculptor.

Candolle, Augustin Pyrame de (1778-1841). Swiss botanist who established scientific structural criteria for determining natural relations among plant genera.

Catullus, Gaius Valerius (87?-54 B.C.). Roman lyric poet famous for his poems which chronicle his infatuation with Lesbia, a character most likely based on a real life woman named Clodia.

Chaadayev, Pyotr Yakovlevich (1793-1856). Philosopher who espoused mystical Christianity. He was very influential, although his *Philosophical Letters* (1836) caused him to be officially declared insane and put under house arrest.

Champollion, Jean François (1791-1832). French Egyptologist and first decoder of hieroglyphics.

Chauteaubriand, François René, Viscount de (1768-1848). French Romantic novelist (*Atala* and *René*), apologist for the Catholic Church.

Chaulieu, Guillaume Amfrye (1639-1729). French poet.

Chénier, André-Marie (1762-94). A French poet, political journalist, liberal monarchist, he was arrested and guillotined during the last days of the Terror. His work is the high point of French poetry of the 18th century. He greatly influenced Romantic poets.

Chesterfield, Philop Dormer Stanhope, fourth earl of (1694-1773). A friend of Alexander Pope and a patron of the arts, his *Letters to His Son* (1774) are a classic portrait of an 18th-century gentleman.

Constant, Benjamin or Henri-Benjamin Constant de Rebecque (1767-1830). A French novelist, exiled because of his politics, his most famous work is the novel *Adolphe* (1816), a psychological analysis of passion.

Corneille, Pierre (1606-84). French dramatist who wrote both tragedies and comedies, with *Le Cid* as his most famous play. He created a new dramatic art.

Cuvier, Georges Léopold (1769-1832). French naturalist and founder of paleontology.

Dante (Alighieri) (1265-1321). Italian poet, most renowned for his masterpiece, *The Divine Comedy*.

Dashkov, Dmitry Vasilievich (1788-1839). A diplomat and literary critic, this member of Arzamas wrote articles opposing Shishkov.

Delaryu, Mikhail (1811-68). A Russian poet who was a follower of Delvig. His poems, which were more classical than romantic, and translations appeared in *Northern Flowers*.

Delavigne, Jean François Casimir (1793-1843). A French poet and dramatist without any marked poetic quality. He celebrated events of national interest. His comedies were better than the tragedies which provided a transition to Romanticism.

Derzhavin, Gavrila Romanovich (1743-1816). Russian poet, known primarily for his odes, especially for his tribute to Catherine the Great, *Felitsa* (1782).

Dibich, Ivan Ivanovich (1785-1831). A general field marshall in the guards during the war of 1812, he informed on Decembrists to Nicholas I.

D'Ivernois, Francis (1757-1842). A Swiss political figure and economist who wrote financial brochures. In 1794 he was sentenced to death by Revolutionary Tribunal, fled to England and returned to Geneva only in 1814. While in England, he went on many diplomatic missions, even to Russia.

Dmitriev, Ivan Ivanovich (1760-1837). Russian writer, author of many satires, epigrams and fables.

Dmitriev, Mikhail Alexandrovich (1796-1866). Nephew of Ivan Ivanovich Dmitriev, poet and literary critic. He was known as a "classicist."

Domenichino—also Domenico Zampieri (1581-1641). Leading painter of the early Baroque eclectic school of Rome and Bologna.

Druzhinin, Yakov Alexandrovich (1771-1849). A member of the Russian Academy and director of the offices of the Ministry of Finance.

Dubenskaya, Varvara Ivanovna. A very close friend of A. I. Turgenev.

Ducange, Victor (1783-1833). French dramatist whose plays look ahead to the prose drama of the Romantic era.

Dumas, Alexandre (Père) (1803-70). French novelist and dramatist, known especially for *The Count of Monte Cristo* and *The Threee Musketeers*.

Emin, Fyodor Alexandrovich (1735-70). Russian writer of tales and adventures, known especially for *The Letters of Ernest and Doravra* (1766), a sentimental novel.

Everts, Johann Gustav (1781-1830). German historian and jurist.

Eynard, Jean Gabriel (1775-1863). A representative of the philhellenic movement, he built a museum in Geneva for the Société des Beaux Arts.

Fichte, Johann Gottlieb (1762-1814). German philosopher, representative of subjective idealism.

Filaret, Metropolitan (Vasily Mikhailovich Drozdov) (1782-1867). A reactionary churchman who complained about a chapter of Pushkin's *Eugene Onegin*.

Fonvizin, Denis Ivanovich (1745-92). Russian playwright whose most famous satires are *The Brigadier-General* (1768-86) and *The Minor* (1782).

Freiligrath, Hermann Ferdinand (1810-76). Translator and German poet of some of the best German revolutionary poetry.

Fyodorov, Boris Mikhailovich (1798-1875). A writer, academician and secret agent of the Third Section. He was a writer of prose, poetry and journalism.

Gagarin, Grigory Ivanovich (1782-1839). Amateur *litterateur* and artist, friend and schoolmate of Alexander Turgenev. He worked as a diplomat in Rome, was an honorary member of Arzamas and wrote erotic verse. His wife was Ekaterina Petrovna Semyonova, sister of Sofia Petrovna Svechina.

Garat, Dominique-Joseph (1749-1833). French writer and politician. His book on Suard is *Mémoires sur la vie de M. Suard, sur ses écrits et sur le dix-huitième siècle*, 1820.

Genishta, Iosif Iosifovich (1795-1853). Moscow composer and pianist who wrote melodies to some of Pushkin's lyrics.

Genlis, Félicité Ducrest de Saint-Aubin Mme de (1746-1830). A writer with a mania for instructing others, she wrote and produced plays. Napoleon paid her to furnish him with letters on literature, politics and various subjects. She wrote popular romances of sentiment, morals and history without simplicity or humor. *Mademoiselle de Clermont* (1802) is her most famous book, along with her memoirs, which give a scandalous account of her era.

Glinka, Fyodor Nikolaevich (1786-1880). Writer of mystical religious poetry who also wrote songs which have survived as folk melodies.

Glinka, Sergei Nikolaevich (1775-1847). Brother of Fyodor Nikolaevich, poet, dramatist, translator, journalist, censor and one of the editors of the *Russian Herald* (1808-24).

Goethe, Johann Wolfgang (1749-1832). Great German poet and prose writer, author of *Faust, The Sorrows of Young Werther* and other works.

Golitsyn, Alexander Nikolaevich (1773-1844). Minister of Religious Affairs and Education under Alexander I. Pushkin in an epigram called him the "destroyer of enlightenment."

Golitsyn, Dmitri Vladimirovich (1771-1844). Prince and military governor general in Moscow, an acquaintance of Pushkin.

Golitsyn, Vasily Sergeevich (d.1836 in Paris) Prince. Son of Sergei Ivanovich and Elizaveta Vasilyevna Priklonskaya, a first cousin of the Bulgakov brothers. This former adjutant of Alexander I, married the former Aglaida Pavlovna Stroganova.

Görres, Joseph J. von (1776-1848). German historian, publicist and Romantic. His book *Christliche Mystik* (1836-42), which blends historical facts and legends of the middle ages, expresses genuine admiration for man's piety in that era. He was an apologist for Catholicism.

Granovsky, Timofei Nikolaevich (1813-55). Historian and professor at Moscow University. A "Westernizer," he was closely associated with Belinsky, Stankevich and Herzen.

Gray, Thomas (1716-71). Poet and letter writer. Most famous for his "Elegy Written in a Country Churchyard" (1751).

Grech, Nikolai Ivanovich (1787-1867). Literary historian, writer and reactionary journalist, he was an associate of Bulgarin and Senkovsky.

Grimm, Friedrich Melchior, Baron von (1723-1807). French critic of German origin and friend of French *philosophes*. He edited *Correspondance littéraire*, a cultural newsletter for foreign sovereigns.

Guizot, François Pierre Guillaume (1787-1874). French historian, political figure and leader of the conservative constitutional monarchy. The "Guizot law" gave all citizens the right to obtain a secular primary education. He was a leader of the French Protestant community.

Hadel. The only source for any information on this author is Fr. J. Querard, a bibliographer who says in *La France littéraire* that Hadel is the author of a five-act comedy in verse, *Contrarion,* published in Paris in 1804.

Hall, Basile (1788-1844). An English traveler and author of *Fragments of Voyages and Travels,* in nine volumes, 1831-33.

Haller, Albrecht von (1708-77). Swiss naturalist and poet, the foremost biologist of the eighteenth century and the father of experimental physiology. An accomplished poet, he wrote a glorification of the Alps called "Die Alpen" in 1732.

Hegel, Georg Wilhelm Friedrich (1770-1830). German philosopher who expounded the dialectic method and developed a phenomenology of culture.

Heine, Heinrich (1797-1856). German poet and prose writer.

Herschel, John Frederick William (1792-1871). English astronomer.

Herzen, Alexander Ivanovich (1812-70). Russian revolutionary thinker and philosopher. *My Past and Thoughts* (1855) is an autobiography and brilliant picture of intellectual life in Russia in the 1840s.

Hoffmann, E. T. A. (Ernst Theodor Amadeus or William) (1776-1822). German prosaist and composer known most for his tales of the grotesque and bizarre.

Horace, Quintus Horatius Flaccus (65-8 B.C.). Roman lyric poet and satirist. Author of *Satires, Epodes, Carmen sacculare, Epistles,* one of which is *Ars Poetica,* a handbook on style. He is most famous for his collections, *Odes I, II, III,* and *IV.*

Irving, Washington (1783-1859). American short story writer and historian. He is probably best known for his "Knickerbocker History" as well as the stories that make up *The Alhambra* (1832) and the *Sketch Book* which contains the tales "Rip van Winkle" and "The Legend of Sleepy Hollow."

Ivanchin-Pisarev, Nikolai Dmitrievich (1790-1849). Poet and prose writer, ardent admirer of Karamzin and author of *The Spirit of Karamzin,* 1827.

Ivanov, Vyacheslav Ivanovich (1866-1949). A Russian symbolist poet, dramatist and historian who eventually emigrated to Italy where he died.

Janin, Jules Gabriel (1804-74). French critic, feuilletonist, dramatist, journalist and literary critic. His judgments lack intellectual consistency and are now generally ignored. He was one of the foremost exponents of the *l'école frénétique.*

Jean-Paul. See Richter.

Jomini, Baron Antoine. Foremost analyst of Napoleonic warfare. His masterpiece is *Précis de l'art de la guerre* (1836).

Jullien, Marc-Antoine (1775-1848). The editor of the monthly radical journal, *Revue Encyclopédique.*

Juvenal (Decimus Junius Juvenalis) (60?-130?). The greatest of Roman satirists.

Kachenovsky, Mikhail Trofimovich (1775-1842). Historian, professor and publisher of the *Herald of Europe.*

Kalashnikov, Ivan Timofeevich (1797-1863). Native Siberian, novelist and ethnographer. His novels include *Daughter of the Merchant Zhelobov, The Kamchadale Girl* and *The Automaton.*

Kant, Immanuel (1724-1804). German philosopher, founder of German classical idealism and author of *The Critique of Pure Reason.*

Kapodistrias, Ioannis Antonios (1776-1831). Governor of Greece 1827, one of Russia's representatives at the Congress of Vienna. He ran the Ministry of Foreign Affairs with Nesselrode. He was assassinated by a rival clan. An honorary member of Arzamas.

Karneev, Yegor Vasilyevich (1773-1849). Civil servant and translator of a mystical composition of a Protestant pastor, Dutoit de Mambrini: *Divine Philosophy in Relation to Immutable Truths, Revealed in a Triple Mirror—The Universe, Man and Holy Scripture.* He also translated Cicero, Montesquieu and Tertullian.

Katkov, Mikhail Nikiforovich (1818-87). Philologist and publicist, an early member of the Stankevich Circle, he turned into a reactionary in his later years.

Kaydanov, Ivan Kuzmich (1782-1845). Adjunct professor of history at the lyceum at Tsarskoe Selo and author of history textbooks.

Khemnitser, Ivan Ivanovich (1745-84). Fabulist, a leading predecessor of Krylov.

Kheraskov, Mikhail Matveevich (1733-1807). Poet, dramatist and writer of epics such as *Rossiada* [Russian Epic, 1779].

Khvostov, Alexander Semyonovich (1753-1820). One of the wits of the age of Catherine the Great. He wrote many popular poems, among them the humorous ode "To Immortality" (1783). He was a cousin of the poet D. I. Khvostov.

Khvostov, Dmitry Ivanovich (1756-1835). Versifier, member of Beseda, and of the Russian Academy. He was known in satires and parodies as a "graphomaniac."

Kikin, Pyotr Andreevich (1775-1834). A member of Beseda and adjutant to the tsar. He later was a state secretary under Alexander I. Kikin was first a student of French literature and progress in general, but later became an ardent Shishkovite.

Kireevsky, Ivan Vasilevich (1806-56). Philosopher, critic and journalist, and one of the leaders of the Slavophile Movement.

Klopstock, Friedrich Gottlieb (1724-1803). German poet, epic writer, author of *Messias,* the life of Christ, and bibilcal dramas.

Klyushnikov, Ivan Petrovich (1811-95). Russian poet and member of the Stankevich Circle.

Kochubey, Viktor Pavlovich (1768-1834). Minister of Internal Affairs, one of the officials who questioned Pushkin during the controversy over Pushkin's *Gavriliada.*

Koshelev, Alexander Ivanovich (1806-83). Worker in the Moscow Archives of the Foreign Ministry, a member of the literary circles around Pushkin, Zhukovsky and the Karamzins.

Krivtsov, Nikolai Ivanovich (1791-1843). A diplomat and brother of a Decembrist. His wife was Ekaterina Fyodorovna (d. 1861), herself a sister of another Decembrist, F. F. Vadkovsky.

Krylov, Ivan Andreevich (1768-1844). Famous Russian fabulist.

Kryukovsky, M. V. (1781-1811). Russian dramatist.

Kubarev, Aleksei Mikhailovich (1796-1881). Historian and adjunct professor of Latin literature at Moscow University.

Kukolnik, Nestor Vasilevich (1809-68). Russian poet, dramatist and novelist, author of overblown, patriotic plays such as *The Hand of the Almighty Has Saved Our Motherland.*

Kushnikov, Sergei Sergeevich (1765-1839). Karamzin's nephew, Suvorov's adjutant and a member of the Supreme Criminal court which judged the Decembrists.

Kutuzov, Mikhail Ilarionovich (1745-1813). General and statesman.

La-Ferronays, Pierre-Louis-Auguste-Ferron,Comte de. The son of the French envoy to Petersburg.

La Harpe, Jean (1739-1803). The tutor of tsar Alexander I, he was a dramatist, journalist and typical critic of the late-eighteenth-century dogmatic school. He was a disciple, friend and critic of Voltaire. His lectures on literature were influential in Russia.

Lamartine, Alfonse Marie Louis Prat de (1790-1869). French poet and statesman. He wrote of spiritual affinities of man and God with a suggestion of emotion rather than with typical Romantic exuberance.

Lamennais (Hughes), Felicité (Robert de) (1782-1854). French publicist and philosopher, priest and political writer, Lamennais tried to combine political liberalism with Roman Catholicism after the French Revolution. In his defense of ultramontanism he saw Catholicism as a key to social regeneration.

Lanskaya, Nadezhda Nikolaevna, née Maslova, Poletika in her first marriage. She was married to Pavel Petrovich Landkoi (1787-1862), mason and member of the Union of Prosperity, senator. He was the brother of V. F. Odoevsky's wife. These people were all in Pushkin's social set.

Lavater, Johann Kaspar (1741-1801). Swiss writer and Protestant pastor. He wrote deeply mystical religious poems in German. He believed piety and religion were products of irrational emotions and supported the *Sturm und Drang* [Storm and Stress] movement in literature.

Laynez, Diego (1512-65). Papal Theologian at the Council of Trent. The second person to join the Jesuits in 1534. He was later General of the Order and was responsible for the direction the Jesuits took in education.

Lazhechnikov, Ivan Ivanovich (1792-1869). A historical novelist in the manner of Sir Walter Scott. His most famous novel is *The House of Ice* (1835).

Lebarzhevskaya, Yuliya Osipovna. Widow of major-general Lebarzhevsky. Her maiden name was Narbut.

Lebrun, Elisabeth Vigée, Mme (1775-1842). A French painter, known especially for her portriats, notably of Marie-Antoinette.

Lerminier, Jean-Louis-Eugène (1803-57). French liberal publicist and jurist.

Lessing, Gotthold Ephraim (1729-81). German writer of criticism in which he espoused naturalness and sincerity in drama. He also wrote some minor plays. His most important work is the *Laokoon* (1766) which limits spheres of art and literature.

Litte, Yuly Pompeevich (1763-1839). Palace official, superior of Pushkin in his court duties. He was an Italian by birth.

Lockhard, John Gibson (1794-1854). English critic, novelist, and biographer, especially of his father-in-law, Walter Scott. He often contributed to the Tory-oriented *Blackwood's Magazine*.

Lomonosov, Mikhail Vasilevich (ca. 1711-65). Classical poet and legislator of Neoclassicism in Russia. He was very important not only for his literary accomplishments but for his activities in the fields of physics, chemistry, mathematics, geography, and mineralogy.

Longinov, Nikanor Mikhailovich (died no earlier than 1839). Brother of the secretary to the Empress Elizaveta Alekseevna. He was a government official and one of Pushkin's Odessa acquaintances.

Lope de Vega (1562-1635). Spain's first great dramatist and poet.

Loriquet, Jean Nicolas (1767-1845). One of the most noted Jesuits. He studied pedagogy and wrote many articles for youths, which were published in 1814. He is known most for his *Histoire de France A.M.D.G.* [*Ad Majorem Dei Gloriam*, to the Greater Glory of God, the motto of the Jesuits].

Loyola, Saint Ignatius (1491-1556). A Spanish soldier and ecclesiastic who founded the Society of Jesus (Jesuits) in 1534.

Ludlow, Edmund (1617-92). English political figure and republican who took part in the reign of Charles I. When the Stuarts were restored, he went to France and then Vevey, where he died. He is mentioned with Broughton, one of the judges who sentenced Charles I to death.

Lyapunov, Procopius. One of Russia's national heroes who fought the Poles during the Time of Troubles.

Macpherson, James (1736-96). Scottish poet, writer, literary forger. Author of *Fragments of Ancient Poetry Collected in the Highlands of Scotland, and Translated from the Gaelic or Erse Language.* Then he published *Fingal, An Ancient Epic,* and *Temora, An Epic Poem,* both supposedly the work of the third-century Gaelic bardic hero Ossian, but in reality a literary hoax.

Malthus, Thomas Robert (1766-1834). English economist.

Maltsov, Ivan Sergeevich (1807-80). Worker in the Moscow Archives of the Ministry of Foreign Affairs and secretary of the Russian Embassy in Persia during the time of Griboedov. An acquaintance of Pushkin.

Mansurov, Alexander Pavlovich (1788-1880). He was a captain of the Izmailovsky regiment and later an adjutant general. He studied literature at Moscow University and published poems in the leading journals.

Manzoni, Alessandro (1785-1873). Italian novelist, known especially for his novel *The Betrothed* (1821-27).

Marcet, Madame, born Haldimand (1785-1850). English writer of popular scholarly books about chemistry and political economics.

Marmontel, Jean-François (1723-99). Frenchman of letters and protégé of Voltaire. He wrote memoirs, and a philosophical tale, *Bélisaire* (1766) in which he advocated religious tolerance, and pleasant little moral tales.

Marot, Clément (1496-1544). Poet who introduced into French poetry new forms such as the elegy, epigram and eclogue. He also may have written the first French sonnet.

Masalsky, Konstantin Petrovich (1802-61). Writer of historical novels, translator, journalist and editor-publisher of *Son of the Fatherland* (1842-49). He was a reactionary and second-rate writer at best.

Maturin, Charles Robert (1782-1824). Irish novelist of Huguenot stock, who is known most for his gothic novel *Melmoth the Wanderer* (1820), a reworking of the wandering Jew motif.

Matushevich, Adam Fadeevich, Count (1791-1842). Russian diplomat.

Maximovich, Mikhail Alexandrovich (1804-73). Professor at Moscow University and later rector of Kiev University where he studied history, philology and folklore. He was also a poet.

Mérimée, Prosper (1803-70). French novelist and short-story writer. He is most known for his story *Mateo Falcone* and his work *Carmen.*

Mesmer, Franz Anton (1734-1815). Austrian physician who practiced hypnotism and was the "founder" of *mesmerism.*

Mickiewicz, Adam (1798-1855). Polish national poet, known especially for his epic poem *Pan Tadeusz.* He was exiled to Russia where he was accepted in the highest literary circles.

Millevoye, Charles-Hubert (1782-1816). French poet who anticipated Romanticism in his elegies.

Mirabeau, Honoré G. V. Riqueti, Comte de (1749-91). A French revolutionary who tried to work out a compromise solution between the liberals and the king. He was a noble who had been elected to the Assembly of the Third Estate; therefore he had the qualities to negotiate between the bourgeoisie and the king.

Mochalov, Pavel Stepanovich (1800-1848). Dramatic and tragic actor in the Moscow Theater.

Molière (pseud. Jean-Baptiste Poquelin, 1622-73). The great French writer of comedies, such as *Tartuffe* (1664) and *The Misanthrope* (1666).

Montaigne, Michel [Eyquem] de (1533-92). French moralist and creator of the personal essay.

Montgolfier, Joesph Michel (1740-1810). A French inventor who, with his brother Jacques Etienne (1745-99), built one of the first hot air baloons.

Moore, Thomas (1779-1852). Songwriter and poet. His best verse is *Irish Melodies* (1808-34) and his most famous is *Lalla Rookh; an Oriental Romance* (1817).

Morlet (Morellet), André, Abbé (1727-1819). Member of Madame de Staël's circle, a contributor to the *Encyclopedia* with articles on theology and metaphysics.

Müller, Johann (1752-1809). The most important Swiss historian of the eighteenth century, he was known as the "Swiss Tacitus." He drew an idealistic picture of the ancient Swiss constitution and influenced the nineteenth-century European view of Switzerland. His works were a source for *Wilhelm Tell* by Schiller, who with Herder and Goethe claimed him as "their" historian.

Muravyov, Andrei Nikolaevich (1806-74). Brother of Nikolai Nikolaevich, government offical, poet, writer, author of books on spiritual topics and member of the Russian Academy.

Muravyov, Nikita Mikhailovich (1796-1843). Army officer, cousin of Batyushkov, a member of Arzamas and a Decembrist exiled to Siberia.

Muravyova, Ekaterina Fyodorovna née Baroness Kolokoltsova (1771-1848). The wife of Mikhail Nikitich, aunt of Batyushkov.

Musset, Alfred Louis Charles de (1810-57). French playwright, poet and novelist. He was a better dramatist than poet, and one of the best of the Romantic dramatists. Author of the influential confessional prose work,*Le Confession d'un enfant du siècle* (1836).

Nadezhdin, Nikolai Ivanovich (1804-56). Journalist, critic, professor of literature at Moscow University. He was an advocate of nationalism and the editor of *The Telescope.*

Naryshkin, Mikhail Mikhailovich (1798-1863). Decembrist colonel of the Farutino Regiment and a member of the Union of Welfare and the Northern Society. He was sentenced to eight years in Siberia and was accompanied there by his wife Elizaveta Petrovna.

Naville, François, Pastor (1784-1846). Swiss philosopher and pedagogue. His book *De l'éducation publique considérée dans ses rapports avec le développement des facultés, la marche progressive de la civilisation et les besoins actuels de la France,* won a gold medal at a concourse on problems of pedagogy.

Necker, Mme Albertine de Saussure (1766-1841). A cousin of Mme de Staël, she received a prize from the French Academy for the book mentioned in the text.

Nefedyeva, Alexandra Ilyinichna (1782-1857). A. I. Turgenev's cousin.

Nesselrode, Count Karl Vasilevich (1780-1862). Russian government official, Minister of Foreign Affairs (1816-56).

Neverov, Yanuary Mikhailovich (1810-93). *Littérateur,* journalist and pedagogue. He belonged to the literary social set.

Nikolsky, Pavel Alexandrovich (1794-1816). Literary man and editor of the *Pantheon of Russian Poetry* (1814-15).

Nodier, Charles (1780-1844). French writer and Romantic novelist. He also wrote a melodrama, lexicography, bibliography, entomology and criticism.

Norov, Avraam Sergeevich (1795-1869). Writer, translator and member of the Russian Academy and the Academy of Sciences. He frequented the salon of Volkonskaya and the Lyubomudry meetings.

Obolensky, Vasily Ivanovich (1790-1847). Adjunct of the Moscow University, a member of Raich's literary circle, expert in ancient languages, *littérateur* and translator.

Oehlenschläger, Adam (1779-1850). Danish poet, dramatist, a disciple of Romanticism. His poem *The Golden Horns* is important for introducing a new style in Danish literature.

Ogaryov, Nikolai Platonovich (1813-77). Poet and publicist, close friend of Herzen. He wrote melancholy as well as revolutionary and civic poetry.

Oken, Lorenz (1779-1851). His original name is Ockenfuss. He was a German naturalist, biologist and natural philosopher.

Olenin, Alexei Nikolaevich (1763-1843). Russian archeologist, historian, artist and President of the Petersburg Academy of Arts.

Orlov, Alexander Anfimovich (1791-1840). Minor poet and prose writer of the thirties.

Ossian. Legendary Gaelic warrior who became a bard in old age, supposedly at the end of the third century. See Macpherson, James.

Ostolopov, Nikolai (1782-1833). Critic, poet, fiction writer and director of the St. Petersburg theaters. He was also a theoretician of Russian Classicism.

Ostrovsky, Alexander Nikolaevich (1823-86). Playwright who wrote works exposing the life of merchants. His most famous plays are *The Bankrupt* or *It's All in the Family* (1850), *Poverty is No Crime* (1854) and *The Thunderstorm* (1859).

Ovid, Publius Ovidius Naso (43? B.C.-A.D. 17). Roman poet, known primarily for his *Metamorphoses.*

Ozerov, Vladislav Alexandrovich (1769-1816). Russian dramatist who wrote sentimental tragedies based on French classical models.

Oznobishin, Dmitry Petrovich (1804-77). Poet and translator from Eastern languages, publisher (with Raich) of the almanac *Northern Lyre* in 1827 and participant in the 1826 edition of *Northern Flowers.*

Palissot De Montney, Charles (1730-1814). French dramatist who wrote light comedies, some ridiculing the *philosophes* and other Enlightenment figures.

Palladio, Andrea (1508-1580). Greatest architect of the 16th century in Northern Italy and one of the most influential figures in Western architecture. He designed churches in Venice, such as the facade for S. Francesco della Vigna, S. Giorgio Maggiore 1566-1610, and Il Redentore 1576-1592.

Panaev, Ivan Ivanovich (1812-62). Writer and journalist, he worked on *The Contemporary* of Nekrasov and *Notes of the Fatherland* with Kraevsky.

Parny, Evariste-Désiré de Forges, Vicomte de (1753-1814). French poet who combines Epicureanism and Voltairean thought in erotic verse.

Passek, Tatyana Petrovna, née Kuchin (1810-89). Cousin of Herzen and memoirist of her period. See Alexander Herzen, *My Past and Thoughts,* trans. Constance Garnett (New York, 1973), pp. 48-52 for Herzen's account of her visit to his home.

Pavlov, Nikolai Filippovich (1803-64). Russian writer who was known mainly for his translation of Balzac. However, he did publish his own verses in journals such as *Mnemosyne* and *The Moscow Telegraph.*

Pepoli, Count Carlo. Italian writer and political figure. After the events of 1831 he had to emigrate from Italy and until 1848 he lived in Paris, Geneva, London. In 1833 he published a two-volume book, *Mélanges,* in prose and poetry.

Perovsky, Alexei Alexeevich (Antony Pogorelsky, 1787-1836). The writer and his brother [Vasily Alexeevich, 1795-1857], who served in the military and civil service, were members of the literary set around Vyazemsky and Pushkin.

Petrarch, Francesco Petrarca (1304-74). Italian poet and scholar. Called the founder of Renaissance humanism, he is best known as the author of love poems to Laura.

Petrov, Vasily Petrovich (1736-99). An eighteenth-century poet who wrote odes and translated Virgil and Pope.

Pictet, Mme. Turgenev has in mind the Pictet family, especially the brothers Mark, August and Carl. They founded the *Bibliothèque britannique* to acquaint the public with scientific discoveries in England.

Pindar (518-438 B.C.). Greek choral lyric poet who wrote of the aristocratic code of values.

Pisarev, Alexander Ivanovich (1803-28). Writer of stage vaudevilles.

Pitt, William (the "Younger," 1759-1806). British statesman and prime minister (1783-1801 and 1804-6).

Podolinsky, Andrei Ivanovich (1806-86). Poet, author of novellas in verse and narrative poems. He also worked for *Northern Flowers* (1828-30).

Pogodin, Mikhail Petrovich (1800-75). Historian, writer, journalist, publisher of *The Moscow Herald* (1827-30) and *The Muscovite* (1841-56) and professor at Moscow University. His journal *The Muscovite* upheld the principles of Autocracy, Orthodoxy and Nationalism as well as Slavophilism.

Poletika, Pyotr Ivanovich (1778-1849). Russian diplomat and a member of Arzamas, he was close to Karamzin.

Polevoi, Xenofont Alexeevich (1801-67). Brother of Nikolai Alexeevich, critic, journalist, translator.

Polevoi, Nikolai Alexeevich (1796-1846). Writer, journalist, critic, playwright, and publisher of the *The Moscow Telegraph* until it was closed in 1834 for publishing a critical article on Kukolnik's patriotic play. Son of a merchant, his liberal views led him to write a history of Russia opposed to Karamzin's monarchist views.

Poltoratsky, Sergei Dmitrievich (1803-84). Russian bibliographer and member of the editorial board of the *Moscow Herald.* He was a rather close friend of Pushkin.

Propertius, Sextus (49-15 B.C.). Roman poet and master of elegiac verse. Approximately two-thirds of his poems deal with his love affair with Cynthia, traditionally identified as Hostia.

Pushchin, Ivan Ivanovich (1798-1859). Pushkin's closest friend from lyceum days, he was a member of the Northern Society of the Decembrists and exiled to Siberia.

Pushkin, Vasily Lvovich (1766-1830). Pushkin's uncle, a poet, author of *The Dangerous Neighbor* (1811) and a member of Arzamas.

Putyata, Nikolai Vasilyevich (1802-77). *Littérateur* and friend of Baratynsky and acquaintance of Pushkin.

Putyatina. A cousin of A. I. Turgenev.

Racine, Jean (1639-99). French tragic poet and playwright who mainly wrote Neoclassical tragedies such as *Andromaque* (1667) and *Phèdre* (1677).

Ragozin, Evgeny Ivanovich (1835-1906). Liberal who took part in the revolutionary movement of the 1860s and became friends with Herzen and Ogaryov while abroad. He worked on the board of the *Moscow Herald* as well as other journals and newspapers.

Raich, Semyon Egorovich (real name Amfiteatrov, 1792-1855). Poet, translator, journalist and tutor to nobles and the poet Tyutchev.

Rat, General. Swiss by birth, he was a general in the Russian service whose sister built a well-known museum in his honor in Geneva.

Reineke Fuchs. *Reynard the Fox,* an animal fable by Goethe based on German folk tales.

Reitern, Gerhardt Wilhelm. Artist, father-in-law of Zhukovsky.

Repnina, Varvara Nikolaevna (1808-91). Close friend and admirer of Nikolai Gogol. She describes him in her memoirs.

Richter, Johann Paul Friedrich (Jean Paul, 1763-1825). German novelist of overly sentimental works.

Rousseau, Jean-Jacques (1712-78). French writer of the eighteenth century known for his *Confessions,* the sentimental novel, *La nouvelle Héloise* and the work of political philosophy, *The Social Contract.*

Rossi, Pellegrino-Luigi (1787-1848). Italian scholar and statesman who was forced to flee Italy in 1815. In Geneva he taught Roman and criminal law and helped draft the 1832 constitution. His book *Traité du droit pénal* is about criminal law.

Rossini, Gioacchino Antonio (1792-1868). Italian composer of operas, much admired by Pushkin.

Royer-Collard, Pierre Paul (1763-1845). French statesman and philosopher, exponent of "spiritualism." A moderate revolutionary who became a liberal legitimist.

Rozhalin, Nikolai Matveevich (1805-34). Literary scholar of Greek, Latin and German literature and translator of Goethe's *Sorrows of Young Werther.*

Saint-Didier, Ignace Francois (1699?-1739). A minor French poet who wrote satire and prose in verse.

Sainte-Beuve, Charles Augustin (1804-69). French critic and novelist who was associated with the Romantics and later with Flaubert.

Saitov, V. I. Editor of the Ostafiev Archives of Vyazemsky.

Samarin, Yury Fyodorovich (1819-76). Russian public figure, thinker, historian and publicist. Member of the Stankevich Circle and theoretician of the Slavophile Movement.

Samoylov, Count Nikolai Alexandrovich (died 1842). He was an uncle of the Raevskys, friends of Pushkin. His wife, Yuliya Pavlovna, was another intimate of the Pushkin social set.

Sand, George (pseudonym of Amandine Aurore Lucie Dupin, Baronne Dudevant, 1804-76). French novelist who was influential in her time. *Indiana* was one of many novels that championed women's right to love.

Sapienza. Another name for the University of Rome.

Schelling, Friedrich Wilhelm Joseph von (1775-1854). German Romantic philosopher—one of the most influential of the period.

Schiller, Friedrich (1759-1805). German dramatist and poet who sang the praises of freedom. He is known especially for *The Robbers, The Maid of Orleans,* and *Wilhelm Tell.*

Schlegel, August Wilhelm von (1767-1845). German poet, critic and scholar and his brother Karl Wilhelm Friedrich von (1772-1829), poet and thinker, were two of the most influential theoreticians of Romanticism.

Schlözer, August Ludwig von (1735-1809). German historian and publicist. In 1761 he went to Russia where Catherine II made him a member of the Academy and professor of Russian history. He was an influential publicist of the German Enlightenment.

Scott, Sir Walter (1771-1832). Scottish novelist, ballad-collector, poet and critic. He is most famous for his historical novels.

Scriabin, Alexander (1872-1915). Russian composer who experimented with musical forms at the turn of the century.

Seneca, Lucius (?) Annaeus, the Elder (55 B.C. - A.D. 40?). Roman rhetorician.

Senkovsky, Osip Ivanovich (1800-58). Journalist, critic, writer and professor of Arabian and Turkish literature at St. Petersburg University. He wrote under the name Baron Brambeus. He was part of the reactionary group which included Bulgarin and Grech.

Serbinovich, Konstantin Stepanovich (1796-1874). Civil servant and journalist.

Severin, Dmitry Petrovich (1792-1865). Chargé d'affaires in the Russian embassy in Switzerland. He was a member of Arzamas.

Sévigné, Marie de Rabutin Chantal, Marquise de (1626-96). Famous European letter writer.

Shakhovskoi, Prince Alexander Alexandrovich (1777-1846). A playwright and literary conservative. His play *A Lesson for Coquettes, or the Lipetsk Waters* (1815) attacked Karamzin and Zhukovsky.

Shalikov, Prince Pyotr Ivanovich (1768?-1852). Poet, imitator of Karamzin, translator, journalist and editor of the *Ladies Journal* (1823-33).

Shevyryov, Stepan Petrovich (1806-64). Literary historian, publicist and professor of literature at Moscow University. He was an ardent Slavophile.

Shishkov, Admiral Alexander Semyonovich (1754-1841). As a writer and literary theoretician he advocated the retention of Church Slavonic forms in Russian.

Sismondi, Jean Charles-Léonard Simonde de (1773-1842). Swiss historian and economist who crusaded against runaway industrialism.

Sobolevsky, Sergei Alexandrovich (1803-70). Booklover, bibliographer and writer of epigrams. He was a close friend of Pushkin.

Sokolovsky, Vladimir Ignatevich (1808-39). Poet and novelist. His works include a dramatic poem *Khever* and a novel *One and Two or The Love of a Poet.* Because of an anti-Nicholas I poem he allegedly wrote and his possession of incriminating letters, he was sent to prison and exile.

Sollogub, Count Vladimir Alexandrovich (1814-82). Playwright and writer of tales, the most famous of which is *Tarantas.*

Somov, Orest Mikhailovich (1793-1833). Writer, journalist, critic and theoretician of Russian Romanticism. He worked with Delvig on *Northern Flowers.*

Southey, Robert (1774-1843). English poet, historian and man of letters. Although he was Coleridge's brother-in-law, he himself was not a Romantic poet. He did experiment with poetic form.

Speransky, Mikhail Mikhailovich (1772-1839). High government official and statesman during the reigns of Alexander I and Nicholas I.

Spinoza, Baruch (1632-77). Dutch philosopher.

Staël, Anne-Louise-Germaine Necker, Mme de (1766-1817). French writer who ran a famous salon. She was influenced by German Romanticism. Her two novels about "modern women" are *Delphine* (1802) and *Corinne* (1807). Two other important works are *De la littérature* (1800) and *De l'Allemagne* (1810).

Stein, Baron (Heinrich Friedrich) Karl, Freiherr vom (und zum). One of the greatest Prussian statesman of the nineteenth century, who carried out reforms after his country's defeat by Napoleon. He was in the Russian service as a personal counselor to Alexander I (1812-15) and influenced the formation of the last European coalition against Napoleon.

Stilling, Heinrich (pseudonym of Johann Heinrich Jung, 1740-1817). A German writer known best for his autobiography. His style is full of piety and simplicity. He was also a physician. He wrote economic textbooks, mystical-pietistic works and novels, the best known of which is the allegorical work *Das Heimweh.*

Stratford-Canning, Stratford de Redcliffe, S. C. 1st Viscount (1786-1880). Diplomatic representative of Great Britain at the Ottoman Court for twenty years. He arranged the Treaty of Bucharest of 1812 between Turkey and Russia.

Stroganov, Grigory Alexandrovich (1770-1857). Count, uncle of Pushkin's wife and ambassador to Turkey.

Struisky, Dmitri (1806-56). A Russian writer whose prolific works include prose, poetry and criticism. His works appeared in the leading journals and almanacs of the day, including *Northern Flowers.*

Suard, J. B. Antoine (1733-1817). French journalist and member of the Paris Academy. During the reign of terror he left Paris, then was exiled from France. When he returned he founded *Le publiciste.* His collected works are *Mélanges de littérature* (1803-5).

Sue, Eugène (1804-57). French novelist who wrote about the sea, Paris life, and social reform. The most famous novels of his large output are *The Mysteries of Paris* (1842-43) and *The Wandering Jew* (1844-45).

Sumarokov, Alexander Petrovich (1717-77). Russian dramatist and poet in the Classical vein. His poems include odes, elegies, eclogues, idylls, songs, fables and satires.

Sungurov, Nikolai Petrovich (1805-?). Leader of a circle at Moscow University. In 1831 he tried to organize a secret "anti-government" society patterned after the Decembrists in order to establish a republican form of government in Russia. He and 25 associates were arrested. At the trial he and one associate were exiled to hard labor in Siberia; others were drafted into the military or put under police surveillance.

Svechin, Pyotr Igorovich (1773-?). Poet, author of *Alexandrida.*

Svechina, Sophia Petrovna (1782-1859). She belonged to the highest circles in the capital. She moved to Paris where she ran a famous Catholic salon frequented by the cream of the Parisian aristocracy. Her memoirs and correspondence were published after her death. She was a close friend of A. I. Turgenev.

Tasso, Torquato (1544-95). Italian poet, author of the epic *Jerusalem Delivered* and *Aminta.* The latter is an idyll about the love of Aminta for Silvia. The epic deals with the recovery of Jerusalem in the First Crusade.

Tatarinov, Alexander Nikolaevich (1810-62). Nephew of A. I. Turgenev.

Tatishchev, Vasily Nikitch (1696-1750). A fmous eighteenth-century Russian historian, who was also one of Peter the Great's administrators and collaborators.

Tegnér, Esaias (1782?-1846). Swedish national poet who combines classical humanism with Norse mythology. He writes in the Romantic mode.

Thomson, James (1700-48). Scottish poet, best known for his *The Seasons* (1730).

Tibullus, Albius (54?-18 B.C.). Roman elegiac poet. He was a friend of Horace and a member of the literary circle of Messalla. In his poems he writes of his love for the woman known as Delia.

Tieck, Ludwig (1773-1853). German Romantic poet, novelist and dramatist.

Timofeev, Alexei Vasilevich (1812-83). Writer of imitative Romantic literature in areas of drama, poetry and prose. He worked with Senkovsky on *The Library for Reading.*

Titov, Vladimir Pavlovich (1807-91). Man of letters and member of the *Lyubomudry* group. He frequented Pushkin's literary circles. He published tales, some under his pseudonym "Tit Kosmokritov."

Tolstoi, Yakov Nikolaevich (1791-1867). Participant in the War of 1812, member of the Green Lamp (1819-20) and from 1837 a secret agent of the Russian government in Paris. He was a theater critic and dilettante poet.

Tormasov, A. P. A general in command of the Third Army in the War of 1812. He defeated the Saxon troops.

Trubetskaya, Agripina Ivanovna. Princess, the wife of Alexander Mansurov.

Trubetskoi, Sergei Petrovich (1790-1860). Member of the Northern Society of the Decembrists and the Green Lamp.

Tsesarevich. The term used for the heir apparent, son of the tsar. In his letter Vyazemsky is probably referring to Konstantin, the brother of Nicholas I.

Tumansky, Vasily Ivanovich (1800-1860). Obscure Russian poet, worked for Delvig's *Northern Flowers* (1825, 1828, 1830-31) and *Literary Gazette* (1830-31).

Turgenev, Nikolai Ivanovich (1789-1871). Brother of A. I. Turgenev and member of the Northern Society of the Decembrists.

Turgenev, Sergei Ivanovich (1792-1827). Brother of A. I. Turgenev. He lived much of his life abroad and died there.

Uhland, Ludwig (1787-1862). A German poet, he is the author of many lyric poems and ballads.

Ulybyshev, Alexander Dmitrevich (1794-1858). Translator for the College of Foreign Affairs, a music critic, journalist and member of the Green Lamp.

Uvarov, Sergei Semyonovich (1786-1855). Tsarist minister of education who originated the slogan "Orthodoxy, Autocracy and Nationality."

Vega, Lope de. See Lope de Vega.

Veleurskaya, Luisa Karlovna. Wife of Mikhail Yuryevich Vielgorsky (1788-1856), amateur musician, connoisseur of the arts and close friend of the Arzamas group.

Vellansky, Danilo Mikhailovich (1774-1847). A Russian philosopher, Schellingian, and professor of the Military Surgical Academy.

Veltman, Alexander Fomich (1800-1870). Russian novelist and poet. He was influenced by Sterne and wrote novels of the fantastic and grotesque.

Verlaine, Paul (1844-96). Important French poet who stood for classical order and clarity. However, most people know him primarily for the musical quality of his work and his lines "De la musique avant toute chose / Et tout le rest est littérature."

Vigel, Filipp Filippovich (1786-1856). Member of Arzamas and author of comprehensive memoirs of the period.

Virgil (Publius Vergilius Maro, 70-19 B.C.). Roman poet, author of *Bucolics, Eclogues, Georgics* and the epic, the *Aeneid.*

Volkonskaya, Zinaida Alexandrovna (1792-1862). She ran one of the most famous salons in Petersburg during the era. Later she moved to Rome.

Volkov, Alexander Alexandrovich (1778-1833). Former officer of the Semenovsky regiment who was wounded severely at Austerlitz, retired and was named Chief of Police in Moscow. In 1826 he entered the gendarmerie under Benckendorf.

Voss, Johann Heinrich (1751-1826). German poet. He is known primarily for his translations from the classics, especially the *Odyssey* and the *Iliad.* He also wrote original lyrics.

Vsevolozhsky, Nikita Vsevolodovich (1799-1862). Government official, lover of theater and literature, translator of French vaudevilles and one of the founders of the Green Lamp.

Wackenroder, Wilhelm Heinrich (1773-98). German Romantic poet who wrote about emotional subjectivity and art as a religion.

Wagner, (Wilhelm) Richard (1813-83). German composer, known for his "Ring Cycle," celebrting Germany's folklore.

Warens, Mme de. Famous protectoress of Rousseau.

Wollzogen, Mme (born Lengefeld, 1763-1847). Biographer of Schiller, who was married to her sister Charlotte.

Weltman. See Veltman.

Werner, Friedrich Ludwig Zacharius (1768-1823). German poet and dramatist.

Yakubovich, Alexander Ivanovich (1792-1845). A Decembrist exiled to Siberia.

Yershov, Pyotr Pavlovich (1815-69). Poet, the author of the fairy tale "Little Humpbacked Pony" (1834).

Young, Edward (1683-1765). English poet, known primarily for his influential work, *The Complaint, or Night Thoughts, or Life, Death and Immortality* (1742-44). This series of poems in blank verse appealed to the moral affinities of the eighteenth-century reader and lasted in appeal to readers and writers of the "Graveyard School" (cf. Gray).

Yuryev, Fyodr Filippovich (1796-1860). Military man and member of the Green Lamp.

Zakharov, Ivan Semyonovich. Well-known writer and member of the Shishkov faction.

Zhadovsky, Ivan Estafevich (died no earlier than 1863). A military man and member of the Green Lamp.

Zhikharev, Stepan Petrovich (1788-1860). Translator, theater administrator, dramatist, memoirist and member of Arzamas.

BIBLIOGRAPHY

This bibliography is by no means complete; its entries concentrate mainly on the authors and works in this anthology. Listed below are the full titles of the abbreviations of the most frequently cited journals in the bibliography.

ASEER	*American Slavic and East European Review*
Cal SS	*California Slavic Studies*
CASS	*Canadian American Slavic Studies*
CL	*Comparative Literature*
CRCL	*Canadian Review of Comparative Literature*
CSP	*Canadian Slavonic Papers*
CSS	*Canadian Slavic Studies*
FMLS	*Forum for Modern Language Studies*
HSS	*Harvard Slavic Studies*
ISS	*Indiana Slavic Studies*
JRS	*Journal of Russian Studies*
MLR	*Modern Language Review*
NZSJ	*New Zealand Slavonic Journal*
OSP	*Oxford Slavonic Papers*
RLT	*Russian Literature Triquarterly*
Rus L	*Russian Literature*
Rus R	*Russian Review*
SEEJ	*Slavic and East European Journal*
SEER	*Slavonic and East European Review*
SIR	*Studies in Romanticism*
Slav R	*Slavic Review*
TSLL	*Texas Studies in Language and Literature*

Please note that in the entries of dissertations I have included their order numbers from University Microfilms wherever available.

General Background: Nineteenth-Century Russia

1. Choldin, Mariana Tax. "A Fence Around the Empire: The Censorship of Foreign Books in Nineteenth-Century Russia." Diss. University of Chicago, 1979.
2. Hingley, Ronald. *Russian Writers and Society in the Nineteenth Century.* 2nd rev. ed. London: Weidenfeld & Nicholson, 1977.
3. Mirsky, D. S. *A History of Russian Literature,* ed. Frances J. Whitfield. New York: Alfred A.Knopf, 1966.
4. Mazour, A. *The First Russian Revolution.* Berkeley: University of California Press, 1937. Paperback ed., Stanford, California: Stanford University Press, 1964.
5. Mazour, A. G. *Women in Exile: Wives of the Decembrists.* Tallahassee, 1975.
6. Riasanovsky, Nicholas V. *A History of Russia.* New York: Oxford University Press, 1977.
7. Riha, Thomas, ed. *Readings in Russian Civilization,* vol. II, *Imperial Russia, 1700-1917.* Chicago: The University of Chicago Press, 1965.

Russian Romantic Age: General Background

8. Busch, Robert. "Russian Freneticism," *CASS,* 14, 269-83.
9. Hollingsworth, Barry. "Arzamas: Portrait of a Literary Society." *SEER,* 44, 306-26.
10. Jacobson, Helen Saltz, ed. and trans. *Diary of a Russian Censor: Aleksandr Nikitenko.* Amherst: The University of Massachusetts Press, 1975.
11. Karkavelas, Sigrid Martha. "The Visual Artist in Russian Literature of the First Half of the Nineteenth Century." Diss. University of California at Berkeley 1980. (8029446).
12. Leighton, Lauren G. *Russian Romanticism: Two Essays.* The Hague: Mouton, 1975.
13. Mersereau, John, Jr. *Russian Romantic Fiction.* Ann Arbor: Ardis, 1983.
14. Monas, Sidney. "Šiškov, Bulgarin, and the Russian Censorship," *HSS,* No. 4 (1957), 127-47.
15. Nilsson, Nils Åke. *Russian Romanticism. Studies in the Poetic Codes.* Stockholm, Sweden: Almqvist & Wiksell International, 1979.
16. Passage, Charles E. "The Influence of Schiller in Russia 1800-1840." *ASEER,* V, 12-13, 111-37.
17. *Russian Literature Triquarterly.* No. 3 (1972). This issue is devoted mainly to Romanticism. See also No. 10 (1974), *The Golden Age.*
18. Struve, Peter. "Walter Scott and Russia." *SEER,* No. 32 (1933), 397-410.
19. Busch, Robert L. "N. A. Polevoy's *Moskovskij Telegraf* and the Critical Debate over *Junaja Francija." CRCL,* 1, 123-27.
20. Leighton, Lauren G. "A Romantic Idealist Nation in Russian Romantic Criticism." *CASS,* 7, 285-95.
21. Nepomnyashchy, Catherine Theimer. "Katkov and the Emergence of the *Russian Messenger." Ulbandus Review* (Columbia University), No. 1 (1977), 59-89.

Drama

22. Pomar, Mark G. "Russian Historical Drama of the Early Nineteenth Century." Diss. Columbia 1978. (78-19413).

Poetry

23. Barratt, Glynn R. "Russian Verse Translations in the Early Romantic Period: A Note on Changing Conventions," in *Canadian Contributions to the 7th International Congress of Slavists, Warsaw, Aug. 21-27, 1973.* The Hague: Mouton, 1973, pp. 41-46.

24. Glassé, Antonia. "The Poet in Search of an Audience: Russian Poetry in the Alexandrine Period." Diss. Columbia 1972. (75-12, 313).

25. Katz, Michael R. *The Literary Ballad in Early Nineteenth Century Russian Literature.* London: Oxford University Press, 1976.

26. Nilsson, Nils Åke. " 'In Vain'—'Perhaps': The Russian Romantic Poets and Fate." *Scando-Slavica,* 25, 71-82.

27. Pigarev, I. "Romantic Poetry in Relation to Painting," in Sötér, I. and I. Neupokoyeva, eds. *European Romanticism.* Budapest: Akad. Kiadó, 1977, pp. 475-501.

28. Pushchin, Helen A. "German and English Influences on the Russian Romantic Literary Ballad." Diss. New York University 1976 (76-19, 535).

29. Stahl, Sandra Gail. "Byron's Influence on the Lives and Works of Representative Russian Poets of the Romantic Period, 1815-1825." Diss. Northwestern 1978. (79-03366).

Prose

30. Fehsenfeld, Nancy Kanach. "Prose in Nicolaevan Russia." Diss. Cornell 1980. (80-20820).

31. Kisseleff, Natalia. "A Study of the Romantic Hero in the Nineteenth Century Novel." Diss. University of Toronto 1976.

32. Mersereau, John Jr. "Normative Distinctions of Russian Romanticism and Realism," in *American Contributions to the Seventh International Congress of Slavists.* Vol 2. The Hague: Mouton, 1973.

33. _____. "The Chorus and Spear Carriers of Russian Romantic Fiction" in Freeborn, Richard, R. R. Milner-Gulland and Charles A. Ward, eds. *Russian and Slavic Literature.* Cambridge, Mass.: Slavica, 1976, pp. 38-62.

34. Phillips, Delbert Darwal. "The Supernatural Tale: An Analysis of Supernatural Elements in Russian Short Fiction of the First Three Decades of the Nineteenth Century." Diss. New York University 1977. (77-21, 311).

35. Proffer, Carl R. ed. *Russian Romantic Prose: An Anthology.* Ann Arbor: Ardis, 1977.

36. Todd, William Mills. *The Familiar Letter as a Literary Genre in the Age of Pushkin.* Princeton: Princeton University Press, 1976.

37. West, James. "Walter Scott and the Style of Russian Historical Novels of the 1830s and 1840s" in Birnbaum, Henrik, ed. *American Contributions to the Eighth International Congress of Slavists,* Zagreb and Lyubljana, Sept. 3-9, 1978. Vol. I, Linguistics and Poetics. Columbus: Slavica, pp. 757-72.

Baratynsky, E. A.

38. Barratt, G. R. ed. *Selected Letters of Evgenij Baratynskij.* The Hague: Mouton, 1973.

39. _____. "Borghese, Baratynsky and the Ideal Italy." *Forum Italicum,* No. 3 (1968), 270-76.

40. _____ "Eighteenth Century Neo-Classical Influences on E. A. Baratynsky and on Pushkin." *CL,* No. 6 (1969), pp. 435-61.

41. Burton, Dora. "Boratynskij: The Evolution of His Style and Poetic Themes." Diss. University of Washington 1975. (76-17, 417).

42. Dees, Joseph B. "Content and Expression in the Poetry of Baratynsky." Diss. Princeton 1967. (68-8917).

43. _____. *Evgeny Baratynsky.* New York: Twayne, 1972.

44. Harvie, J. A. "The Eclipse of the Golden Age," *FMLS,* 9, 170-81.

45. _____. "Russia's Doomsday Poet." *FMLS,* 12, 170-81.

46. _____. "Poet of Nirvana." *Journal of the New Zealand Slavists' Association* (1967). [Now superseded by *NZSJ.*] [Unpaged.]

47. Kovalenko, Tatyana. "The Rhythmic and Syntactic Structure of the *Sumerki* Cycle of E. A. Baratynsky." Diss. New York University 1973. (73-21, 128).

48. Liapunov, Vadim. "Poet in the Middest: Studies in the Poetry of E. A. Baratynsky." Diss. Yale 1969. (70-19, 519). [Portions in French, German and Russian.]

49. Shaw, Joseph Thomas. *Baratynskii: A Dictionary of Rhymes and a Concordance to the Poetry.* Madison: University of Wisconsin Press, 1975.

50. Woodward, James B. "The Enigmatic Development of Boratynsky's Art." *OSP,* No. 3 (1970), 32-44.

> **See also:**
>
> Pratt, Sarah Claflin. "The Metaphysical Poetry of F. I. Tjutčev and E. A. Boratynsky: Alternatives in Russian Romanticism." Diss. Columbia 1978. (78-11149).
>
> Rolich, Andrea M. Sepich. "The Stanzaic Forms of K. N. Batjuškov and E. A. Baratynskij." Diss. University of Wisconsin 1981. (81-16016).

Batyushkov, K. N.

51. Johnson, Doris. "The Comparison in the Poetry of Batiushkov and Zhukovsky." Diss. University of Michigan 1973. (74-15, 765).

52. _____. "The Simile in Batyushkov and Zhukovsky." *RLT,* No. 7 (1973), 407-22.

53. Rolich, Andrea M. Sepich. "The Stanzaic Forms of K. N. Batjuškov and E. A. Baratynskij." Diss. University of Wisconsin 1981 (81-16016).

54. Serman, Ilya Z. *Konstantin Batyushkov.* New York: Twayne, 1974.

55. Shaw, Joseph Thomas. *Batiushkov: A Dictionary of the Rhymes and a Concordance to the Poetry.* Madison: University of Wisconsin Press, 1975.

Belinsky, V. G.

Translations

56. Belinsky, V. G. *Selected Philosophical Works,* Moscow: Foreign Language Publishing House, 1956.

57. Belinksy, V. G., N. G. Chernyshevsky, N. A. Dobrolyubov. *Selected Criticism,* ed. with intro. Ralph E. Matlaw. New York: E. P. Dutton and Co., Inc., 1962.

Criticism

58. Ponomareff, C. V. "Configurations of Poetic Vision: Belinsky as an Idealist Critic." *SEEJ*, No. 14 (1970), 145-59.
59. ___. "V. G. Belinskii's Romantic Imagination." *CASS*, 7, 314-26.
60. Schillinger, Jack A. "The Evolution of Artistic Criteria in the Criticism of Vissarion Belinsky." Diss. University of Wisconsin 1973 (74-500).
61. Terras, Victor. *Belinskij and Russian Literary Criticism: The Heritage of Organic Aesthetics.* Madison: University of Wisconsin Press, 1974.

Bestuzhev-Marlinsky, A. A.

Translations

62. Bestuzhev-Marlinksy, Alexander. "The Test," trans. Lewis Bagby. *RLT*, No. 10 (1975), pp. 95-145.

Criticism

63. Bagby, Lewis. "Prose Fiction of Aleksandr Aleksandrovich Bestužev-Marlinskij." Diss. University of Michigan 1972. (73-6780).
64. Leighton, Lauren. *Alexander Bestuzhev-Marlinsky.* Boston: Twayne, 1975.
65. ___. "Aleksandr Bestuzhev-Marlinskij: The Romantic Prose Tale in Russia." Diss. University of Wisconsin 1968. (68-9096).
66. ___. "Bestuzhev-Marlinskii as a Lyric Poet." *SEER*, No. 47 (1969), 308-22.
67. ___. "Marlinsky." *RLT*, No. 3 (1972), pp. 249-68.
68. ___. "Marlinsky's 'Ispytanie': A Romantic Rejoinder to *Evgenij Onegin*." *SEEJ*, No. 13 (1969), 200-16.

Bulgarin, F.

Translations

69. Bulgarin, Thaddeus. *Ivan Vejeeghen; or, Life in Russia.* 2 vols. London: Whittaker, Treacher, and Co.; Edinburgh: H. Constable, 1831.
70. Bulgarin, Faddei. "Plausible Fantasies or a Journey in the 29th Century." *Pre-revolutionary Russian Science Fiction: An Anthology,* ed. and trans. Leland Fetzer. Ann Arbor: Ardis, 1982, pp. 5-34.

Criticism

71. Alkire, Gilman. "The Historical Novels of Faddej Bulgarin." Diss. University of California at Berkeley 1966. (66-15, 322).
72. Mocha, Frank. "Tadeusz Bulharyn (Faddej V. Bulgarin) 1789-1859: A Study in Literary Maneuver." Diss. Columbia 1970. (73-26, 438).
73. Vaslef, Nicholas P. "Bulgarin and the Development of the Russian Utopian Genre." *SEEJ*, No. 12 (1968), 35-43.

> **See also:**
> Alkire, Gilman H. "Gogol and Bulgarin's Ivan Vyzhigin." *Slav R,* 28, 289-96.

Chaadaev, P. Ya.

74. Chaadayev, Peter Yakovlevich. *Philosophical Letters and Apology of a Madman,* tr. and intro. Mary-Barbara Zeldin. Knoxville: University of Tennessee Press, 1969.
75. McNally, Raymond T. *The Major Works of Peter Chaadaev,* intro. by Richard Pipes. Notre Dame: University of Notre Dame Press, 1969.

Davydov, D.

76. Leighton, Lauren. "Denis Davydov's Hussar Style." *SEEJ*, No. 7 (1963), 349-60.

> **See also:**
> ___. "The Anecdote in Russia: Puškin, Vjazemskij, and Davydov." *SEEJ*, No, 10 (1966), 155-66.

Delvig, A. A.

77. Koehler, Ludmilla. *Anton Antonovič Del'vig: A Classicist in the Time of Romanticism.* The Hague: Mouton, 1970.
78. ___. "Delvig—A Classicist in the Time of Romanticism." Diss. University of Washington 1963. (64-4511).
79. Mersereau, John Jr. *Baron Delvig's "Northern Flowers."* Carbondale: Southern Illinois University Press, 1967.

Gnedich

80. Barratt, Glynn, R. "A View of Petersburg: New Correspondence of M. E. Lobanov and Gnedič 1827-1828." *Rus L,* No. 9 (1975), 25-36.

Gogol, N. V.

Translations

81. Ehre, Milton, ed. and tr. *The Theater of Nikolay Gogol: Plays and Selected Writings.* Chicago: University of Chicago Press.
82. Gogol, Nikolai. *Arabesques,* tr. Alexander Tulloch. Ann Arbor: Ardis, 1982.
83. ___. *Dead Souls,* tr. George Reavey, intro. George Gibian. New York: W. W. Norton and Company, 1971.

84. ___. *Dead Souls,* tr. Andrew R. MacAndrew. New York: Signet, 1961.

85. ___. *Dead Souls,* tr. with foreword Bernard Gilbert Guerney. New York: Modern Library, 1965.

86. ___. *Dead Souls,* tr. Constance Garnett. New York: Modern Library, 1936.

87. ___. *Selected Passages from Correspondence with Friends,* tr. Jesse Zeldin. Nashville: Vanderbilt University Press, 1969.

88. Kent, Leonard J., ed. *The Collected Tales and Plays of Nikolai Gogol.* New York: Pantheon Books, Random House, 1964.

89. Proffer, Carl R., ed. *Letters of Nikolai Gogol.* Ann Arbor: University of Michigan Press, 1967.

Criticism

90. Alkire, Gilman H. "Gogol and Bulgarin's *Ivan Vyzhigin.*" *Slav R,* 28, 289-96.

91. Barratt, Andrew. "Plot as Paradox: The Case of Gogol's *Shinel'* [Overcoat]." *NZSJ* (1979), ii, 1-24.

92. Baumgarten, Murray. "Gogol's *The Overcoat* as a Picaresque Epic." *Dalhousie Review,* XLVI, 186-99.

93. Blankoff-Scarr, Goldie. "The Use of Person in Gogol's *Revizor* [Inspector General]." *Equivalences* 10, i-ii (1979), 71-88.

94. Busch, Robert L. "Gogol' and the Russian Freneticist Cycle of the Early 1830s." *CSP,* 22, 28-42.

95. Cox, Gary. "Geographic, Sociological and Sexual Tensions in Gogol's Dikan'ka Stories." *SEEJ,* No. 24 (1980), 219-32.

96. Debreczeny, Paul. "Gogol's Mockery of Romantic Taste: Varieties of Language in the Tale of the Two Ivans." *CASS,* No. 7, 327-41.

97. DeJonge, A. "Gogol'." *Nineteenth-Century Russian Literature,* ed. John Fennell. Berkeley and Los Angeles: University of California Press, 1973, pp. 69-129.

98. Ehre, Milton. "Laughing through the Apocalypse: The Comic Structure of Gogol's *Government Inspector.*" *Rus R,* 39, 137-49.

99. Eichenbaum, Boris. "The Structure of Gogol's *The Overcoat.*" *Rus R,* 22, 377-99.

100. Fanger, Donald. "*Dead Souls:* The Mirror and the Road." *Nineteenth-Century Fiction,* 33, 24-47.

101. ___. *The Creation of Nikolai Gogol.* Cambridge: Harvard University Press (Belknap), 1979.

102. Friedeberg Seeley, Frank. "Notes on Gogol's Short Stories." *Annali Instituto Universitario Orientale, Napoli, Sezione Slava.* 19 (1976), 3-44.

103. Gippius, V. V. *Gogol,* ed. and trans. Robert A. Maguire. Ann Arbor: Ardis, 1981.

104. Gustafson, Richard F. "The Suffering Usurper: Gogol's *Diary of a Madman.*" *SEEJ,* No. 9 (1965), 268-280.

105. Harvie, J. A. "The Demonic Element in Gogol and Baratynsky." *NZSJ* (Summer 1970), 77-85.

106. Hughes, Olga Raevsky. "The Apparent and the Real in Gogol's 'Nevskij Prospekt'." *Cal SS,* 8, 77-91.

107. Jennings, Lee B. "Gogol's Dead Soul Grotesqueries," in Jennings, Lee B. and George Schulz-Behrend. *Vistas and Vectors: Essays Honoring the Memory of Helmut Rehder.* Austin: Department of Germanic Languages, University of Texas at Austin, 1979.

108. Karlinsky, Simon. *The Sexual Labyrinth of Nikolai Gogol.* Cambridge: Harvard University Press, 1976.

109. Maguire, Robert A. ed. and tr. *Gogol from the Twentieth Century: Eleven Essays.* Princeton, New Jersey: Princeton University Press, 1974.

110. McLean, Hugh. "Gogol's Retreat from Love: Towards an Interpretation of 'Mirgorod'," *American Contributions to the Fourth International Congress of Slavists: Moscow, Sept. 1958.* The Hague: Mouton, pp. 225-43.

111. Nabokov, Vladimir. *Nikolai Gogol.* New York: New Directions, 1944.

112. Oulianoff, Nicholas I. "Arabesque or Apocalypse? On the Fundamental Idea of Gogol's Story *The Nose.*" *CSS,* 1, 158-71.

113. Peace, R. A. "The Logic of Madness: Gogol's *Zapiski sumasšedšego* [Notes of a Madman]." *OSP,* No. 9 (1976), 28-45.

114. Poggioli, Renato. "Gogol's 'Old-fashioned Landowners': An Inverted Eclogue." *ISS,* III (1963), pp. 54-72.

115. Pomorska, Krystyna. "On the Problem of Parallelisms in Gogol's Prose: *A Tale of the Two Ivans*" in Kodjak, Andrej, Michael J. Connolly and Krystyna Pomorska, eds. *The Structural Analysis of Narrative Texts: Conference Papers.* (New York University Slavic Papers 2.) Columbus: Slavica, 1980.

116. Proffer, Carl R. "Gogol's Definition of Romanticism." *SIR,* 6, 120-27.

117. ___. *The Simile and Gogol's Dead Souls.* The Hague: Mouton, 1967.

118. ___. "Gogol's *Taras Bulba* and the *Iliad.*" *CL,* 17, 1424-50.

119. Proffitt, Edward. "Gogol's 'Perfectly True' Tale: 'The Overcoat' and Its Mode of Closure." *Studies in Short Fiction,* 14, 35-40.

120. Rowe, William Woodin. *Through Gogol's Looking Glass: Reverse Vision, False Focus, and Precarious Logic.* New York: New York UP, 1976.

121. Setchkarev, Vsevolod. *Gogol: His Life and Works,* tr. Robert Kramer. New York: New York University Press, 1965.

122. Sobel, Ruth. "Gogol's Views on Art and Literature in *Selected Passages from a Correspondence with Friends.*" *Journal of Russian Studies,* 31, 29-37.

123. Spycher, Peter C. "N. V. Gogol's *The Nose:* A Satirical Comic Fantasy Born of an Impotence Complex." *SEEJ,* No. 7 (1963), 361-74.

124. Trahan, Elizabeth, ed. *Gogol's "Overcoat": An Anthology of Critical Essays.* Ann Arbor: Ardis, 1982.

125. Troyat, Henri. *Divided Soul. The Life of Gogol,* tr. Nancy Amphoux. New York: Minerva Press, 1975.

126. Waszink, Paul M. "Mythical Traits in Gogol's *The Overcoat.*" *SEEJ,* No. 22 (1978), 287-300.

127. Woodward, James B. *Gogol's Dead Souls.* Princeton, New Jersey: Princeton University Press, 1978.

128. ___. "The Threadbare Fabric of Gogol's *Overcoat.*" *CSS,* 1, 95-104.

129. Zeldin, Jesse. *Nikolai Gogol's Quest for Beauty: An Exploration into His Works.* Lawrence: Regents' Press of Kansas, 1978.

See also:
Cosman, Tatiana M. "The Letter as a Literary Device in the Fiction of Puškin, Lermontov and Gogol'." Diss. New York University 1973. (74-1867).

Griboedov, A. S.

Translations

130. Griboyedov, Aleksandr Sergeyevich. *The Trouble with Reason,* tr. F. D. Reeve, in *An Anthology of Russian Plays,* vol. I, ed. F. D. Reeve. New York: Vintage, 1961, pp. 85-163.

131. Griboyedov, Alexander Sergeyevich. *Wit Works Woe,* tr. Sir Bernard Pares in *Masterpieces of the Russian Drama,* vol. I, ed. George Rapall Noyes. New York: Dover Publications, Inc., 1961.

Criticism

132. Janacek, Gerald. "A Defense of Sof'ja in *Woe from Wit.*" *SEEJ,* No. 21 (1977), 318-31.
133. Harden, Evelyn Jasiulko. "Griboedov in Persia: December 1828." *SEER,* No. 57 (1979), 255-67.
134. Richards, D. J. "Two Malicious Tongues—the Wit of Chatsky and Pechorin." *NZSJ,* No. 11 (Winter), 11-28.

Grigoriev, A.

Translations

135. Grigoryev, Apollon. *My Literary and Moral Wanderings,* tr. Ralph E. Matlaw. New York: E. P. Dutton and Co., Inc., 1962.

Criticism

136. Jerkovich, George C. "Apollon Grigor'ev as a Literary Critic." Diss. University of Kansas 1970. (70-25, 354).
137. Talbot, Elizabeth M. "Apollon Grigoriev as a Literary Critic." Diss. Brown 1973. (74-3080).
138. Terras, Victor. "Apollon Grigoriev's Organic Criticism and Its Western Sources," in Mlikotin, M., ed. *Western Philosophical Systems in Russian Literature: A Collection of Critical Studies* (Series in Slavic Humanities 3). Los Angeles: University of Southern California Press, pp. 71-88.

Herzen, A.

139. Herzen, Alexander. *My Past and Thoughts,* ed. and abridged by Dwight Macdonald. New York: Alfred A. Knopf, 1973.

Karamzin, N. M.

Translations

140. Karamzin, N. M. *Letters of a Russian Traveler,* tr. and abridged by Florence Jonas. New York: Columbia University Press, 1957.
141. Nebel, Henry M. tr. *Selected Prose of N. M. Karamzin.* Evanston: Northwestern University Press, 1969.

Criticism

142. Anderson, Roger B. *N. M. Karamzin's Prose, The Teller in the Tale.* Houston: Cordovan Press, 1974.
143. Black, J. L., ed. *Essays on Karamzin: Russian Man-of-Letters, Political Thinker, Historian, 1766-1826.* The Hague: Mouton, 1975.
144. Cross, A. G. *N. M. Karamzin.* Carbondale: Southern Illinois University Press, 1971.
145. Kochetkova, Natalya. *Nikolay Karamzin.* Boston: Twayne Publishers, 1975.
146. Nebel, Henry M. Jr. *N. M. Karamzin. A Russian Sentimentalist.* The Hague: Mouton and Co., 1967.

Katenin, P.

147. Sussex, Roland. "Poetic Translation and Literary Polemics in Katenin's 'Olga'." *Melbourne Slavic Studies,* 9-10 (1975), 39-53.

Kozlov, I.

148. Barratt, G. R. V. *Ivan Kozlov: A Study and a Setting.* Toronto: Hakkert, 1972.
149. ___. *I. I. Kozlov: The Translations from Byron.* Berne and Frankfurt/M: Herbert Lang and Co. Ltd., 1972.
150. ___. "Somov, Kozlov and Byron's Russian Triumph." *CRCL,* 1, 104-22.

Küchelbecker, W.

151. Baxter, Norman Allen. "The Early (1817-25) Literary Criticism of Wilhelm Küchelbecker." Diss. University of California at Berkeley 1977. (78-12, 484).

Lazhechnikov, I. I.

Translations

152. Lazhechnikov, Ivan Ivanovich. *The Heretic,* tr. Thomas B. Shaw. Edinburgh and London: W. Blackwood and Sons, 1844.

Criticism

153. Twarog, Leon I. "The Soviet Revival of a Nineteenth-Century Historical Novelist: I. I. Lažečnikov." *HSS,* IV, 107-26.
154. Wowk, Vitaly. "The Historical Novels of I. I. Lažečnikov." Diss. Ohio State University 1972 (73-11, 606).

Lermontov, M. Yu.

Translations

155. Daniels, Guy, ed. and tr. *A Lermontov Reader.* New York: The Universal Library, 1967.
156. Lermontov, Michail. *The Demon and Other Poems,* tr. Eugene M. Kayden. Intro. by Sir C. Maurice Bowra. Yellow Springs, Ohio: Antioch Press, 1965.
157. ___. *A Hero of Our Time,* tr. Paul Foote. New York: Penguin Books, 1979.

158. ——. *A Hero of Our Time,* tr. Philip Longworth. New York: A Signet Classic, 1962.
159. ——. *A Hero of Our Time,* tr. Vladimir Nabokov. Garden City, New York: Doubleday Anchor Books, 1958.
160. ——. *Masquerade,* tr. Roger W. Phillips. *RLT,* No. 7 (1974), pp. 67-116.
161. ——. *Selected Works.* Moscow: Progress Publishers, 1976.

Criticism

162. Bagby, Lewis. "Narrative Double-Voicing in Lermontov's *A Hero of Our Time.*" *SEEJ,* No. 22 (1978), 265-86.
163. Binyon, T. J. "Lermontov, Tyutchev and Fet." *Nineteenth-Century Russian Literature,* ed. John Fennell. Berkeley and Los Angeles: University of California Press, 1973, pp. 168-224.
164. Cameron, Alan H. "Byronism in Lermontov's *A Hero of Our Time.*" Diss. University of British Columbia 1974.
165. Debreczeny, P. "Elements of the Lyrical Verse Tale in *A Hero of Our Time* by M. I. Lermontov," in VII *Międzynarodowy Kongress Slawistów w Warszawie.* Warsaw: PAN, 1973.
166. Eagle, Herbert. "Lermontov's 'Play' with Romantic Genre Expectations in *A Hero of Our Time.*" *RLT,* No. 10 (1974), pp. 299-315.
167. Eikhenbaum, B. M. *Lermontov,* tr. by Ray Parrott and Harry Weber. Ann Arbor: Ardis, 1981.
168. Faletti, Heidi E. "Elements of the Demonic in the Character of Pechorin in Lermontov's *A Hero of Our Time.*" *FMLS,* 14, 365-77.
169. Goscilo, Helena. "Lermontov's Sketches: From Poetic City to Prosaic Man." *CASS,* No. 14 (1980), 21-35.
170. Harvie, J. "Lermontov's 'Demon'." *Journal of the Australasian Universities Language and Literature Association,* 29, 25-32.
171. Hecht, Leo. "Lermontov and the German Poets." *CASS,* No. 10 (1976), 400-409.
172. Hopkins, William H. "Lermontov's Hussar Poems." *RLT,* No. 14 (1976), 36-47.
173. Kelly, Laurence. *Lermontov: Tragedy in the Caucasus.* New York: Braziller.
174. Lavrin, Janko. *Lermontov.* London: Bowes and Bowes; New York: Hillary House, 1959.
175. Lavrin, Yanko. "Some Notes on Lermontov's Romanticism." *SEER,* 36, 58-68.
176. Michailoff, Helen. "The Death of Lermontov (The Poet and the Tsar)." *RLT,* No. 10 (1974), 279-98.
177. Mersereau, John, Jr. "Lermontov and Balzac" in *American Contributions to the Fifth International Congress of Slavists:* Sofia, Sept. 1963. Vol. II. The Hague: Mouton, 1963, pp. 233-58.
178. ——. "Lermontov's *Shtoss:* A Hoax or a Literary Credo?" *Slav R,* No. 21 (1962), 280-95.
179. ——. *Mikhail Lermontov.* Carbondale: Southern Illinois University Press, 1962.
180. ——. "M. Yu. Lermontov's *The Song of the Merchant Kalashnikov:* An Allegorical Interpretation." *CAL SS,* No. 1 (1960), 110-33.
181. ——. " 'The Fatalist' as a Keystone of *A Hero of Our Time.*" *SEEJ,* No. 4 (1960), 137-46.
182. Peace, R. A. "The Role of 'Taman' in Lermontov's *Geroy nashego vremeni* [A Hero of Our Time]." *SEER,* 45, 12-29.
183. Pervushin, N. V. "Lermontov's Poetic Apprenticeship." *Etudes Slaves et Est-Européennes,* 12, 25-43.
184. Reed, Walter L. *Meditations on the Hero: A Study of the Romantic Hero in Nineteenth-Century Fiction.* New Haven: Yale Univesity Press.
185. Reid, Robert. "Eavesdropping in *A Hero of Our Time.*" *NZSJ,* 1, 13-22.
186. Ripp, Victor. "*A Hero of Our Time* and the Historicism of the 1830's." *Modern Language Notes,* 92, 969-86.
187. Shaw, J. T. "Byron and Lermontov: The Romantic Verse Tale." Diss. Harvard University, 1950.
188. ——. "Byron, the Byronic Tradition of the Romantic Verse Tale in Russian and Lermontov's *Mtsyri.*" *ISS,* I, 165-90.
189. ——. "Lermontov's *Demon* and the Byronic Oriental Verse Tale." ISS, II, 163-80.
190. Sommer, Tamara. "The Image of Loneliness in Lermontov's Lyrics." *NZSJ,* 1, 1-11.
191. Turner, C. J. G. *Pechorin: An Essay on Lermontov's A Hero of Our Time.* Birmingham: University of Birmingham, 1978.
192. Ulph, Owen. "Unmasking the Masked Guardsman." *RLT,* No. 3 (1972), 269-81.
193. Wilkinson, Joel Lynn. "The Development of the Ballad in Russian Literature by Mixail Jur'evič Lermontov (1814-41)." Diss. University of Kansas 1977. (77-28, 924).

      See also:
      Briggs, A. D. P. "*Pikovaya Dama* ["The Queen of Spades"] and *Taman':* Questions of Kinship." *JRS,* 37, 13-20.
      Cosman, Tatiana M. "The Letter as a Literary Device in the Fiction of Pushkin, Lermontov and Gogol'." Diss. New York University 1973. (74-1867).
      Proffer, Carl R. "The Similes of Pushkin and Lermontov." *RLT,* No. 3 (1972), pp. 148-91.
      Rowe, Eleanor. "Pushkin, Lermontov, and *Hamlet.*" *TSLL,* 17, 337-47.

Odoevsky, V. F.

Translations

194. Odoevsky, V. F. "Princess Mimi," tr. David Lowe, *RLT,* No. 9 (1974), 53-86.
195. ——*Russian Nights,* tr. Olga Olienikov and Ralph E. Matlaw. New York: E. P. Dutton and Co., Inc., 1967.
196. ——"The Sylph," tr. Joel Stern. *RLT,* No. 8 (1974), 241-58.
197. ——"The Year 4338. Letters from Petersburg." *Pre-Revolutionary Russian Science Fiction: An Anthology,* ed. and trans. Leland Fetzer. Ann Arbor: Ardis, 1982, 38-54.

Criticism.

198. Karlinsky, Simon. "A Hollow Shape: The Philosophical Tales of Prince Vladimir Odoevsky." *SIR,* 5, 169-82.
199. Linburn, JoAnn H. "A Would-Be Faust: V. F. Odoevsky and His Prose Fiction, 1830-45." Diss. Columbia University 1970. (73-8968).

(Pogorelsky)—Perovsky, A. A.

200. Frantz, Philip Edward. "A. A. Perovskij (Pogorel'skij): Gentleman and *Littérateur.*" Diss. University of Michigan 1981. (81-25113).
201. Passage, Charles E. "Pogorelskij, the First Russian Hoffmannist." *ASEER,* 15, 247-64.

Pushkin, A. S.

Translations.

202. Arndt, Walter, ed. and trans. *Alexander Pushkin: Collected Narrative and Lyrical Poetry.* Ann Arbor: Ardis, 1984.
203. Harkins, William E., tr. and ed. *Pushkin, Three Comic Poems.* Ann Arbor: Ardis, 1977. This book includes *Gavriliada, Count Nulin* and *Little House in Kolomna.*
204. Proffer, Carl R., ed. and tr. *The Critical Prose of Alexander Pushkin.* Bloomington: Indiana University Press, 1969.
205. Pushkin, Alexander. *Eugene Onegin,* tr.Walter Arndt. New York: E. P. Dutton and Co., 1963.
206. ___. *Eugene Onegin,* tr. V. Nabokov. New York: Bollingen, 1964.
207. ___. *The History of Pugachev.* Trans. E. Sampson. Ann Arbor: Ardis, 1983.
208. ___. *A Journey to Arzrum,* tr. Birgitta Ingemanson. Ann Arbor: Ardis, 1974.
209. ___. *Ruslan and Liudmila,* tr. Walter Arndt. Ann Arbor: Ardis, 1974.
210. ___. *Selected Verse,* intro. and tr. John Fennell. Baltimore, Maryland: Penguin, 1964.
211. Shaw, J. T., tr. and ed. *The Letters of Alexander Pushkin.* Madison: University of Wisconsin Press, 1963.
212. Wolff, Tatiana, tr. and ed. *Pushkin in Literature.* London: Methuen; New York: Barnes and Noble, 1971.
213. Yarmolinsky, Avrahm, ed. *The Poems, Prose and Plays of Alexander Pushkin.* New York: The Modern Library, 1936 (1964).

Criticism

214. Akhmatova, Anna. "Benjamin Constant's *Adolphe* in the Work of Pushkin," tr. Sharon Leiter. *RLT,* No. 10 (1974), pp. 157-79.
215. Banerjie, Maria. "Pushkin's *The Bronze Horseman:* An Agonistic Vision." *Modern Language Studies,* 8, ii, 47-64.
216. Bayley, John. *Pushkin: A Comparative Commentary.* Cambridge: Cambridge University Press, 1971.
217. Briggs, A. D. P. "Hidden Qualities of Pushkin's *Mednyi vsadnik* [Bronze Horseman]" *CASS,* No. 10 (1976),.228-41
218. ___. "*Pikovaya Dama* [The Queen of Spades] and *Taman'*: Questions of Kinship." *JRS,* 37 13-20.
219. Brody, Ervin C. "Pushkin's *Boris Godunov:* The First Modern Russian Historical Drama." *MLR,* 72, 857-75.
220. Call, Paul. "Puškin's *Bronze Horseman:* A Poem of Motion." *SEEJ,* No. 11 (1967), 137-44.
221. Cosman, Tatiana M. "The Letter as a Literary Device in the Fiction of Puškin, Lermontov and Gogol'." Diss. New York University 1973. (74-1867).
222. Cross, Anthony. "Pushkin's Bawdy; or, Notes from the Literary Underground." *RLT,* No. 10 (1974), pp. 203-36.
223. Debreczeny, Paul. "Poetry and Prose in *The Queen of Spades.*" *CASS,* No. 11 (1977), 91-113.
224. ___. "Puškin's Use of His Narrator in 'The Stationmaster'." *Rus L,* NS 4, ii (1976), 149-66.
225. Emerson, Caryl Geppert. "Boris Godunov and a Poetics of Transposition: Karamzin, Pushkin, Mussorgsky." Diss. University of Texas at Austin 1980. (81-09159).
226. Faletti, Heidi E. "Remarks on Style as Manifestation of Narrative Techniques in *The Queen of Spades.*" *CASS,* No. 11 (1977), 114-33.
227. Fehsenfeld, Nancy K. "Pushkin's Prose in Nicolaevan Russia." Diss. Cornell University 1980. (80-20820).
228. Fennell, J. "Pushkin." *Nineteenth-Century Russian Literature,* ed. John Fennell. Berkeley and Los Angeles: University of California Press, 1973, pp. 13-68.
229. Gibian, George. "Narrative Technique and Realism: *Evgeny Onegin* and *Madame Bovary* in *Actes du VIIIe Congrès de la Fédération Internationale des Langues et Littératures Modernes.* (Bibliothèque de la Faculté de Philosophie et Lettres de l'Université de Liege, facs. CLXI.) Paris: Société d'Edition "Les Belles Lettres," 1961, p. 339.
230. Greene, Militsa. "Pushkin and Sir Walter Scott." *FMLS,* 1, 207-15.
231. Gregg, Richard A. "Balzac and the Women in *The Queen of Spades.*" *SEEJ,* No. 10 (1966), 179-82.
232. ___. "The Nature of Nature and the Nature of Eugene in *The Bronze Horseman.*" *SEEJ,* No. 21 (1977), 167-79.
233. Grossman, Leonid. "The Art of the Anecdote in Pushkin," tr. Sam Cioran. *RLT,* No. 10 (1974), pp. 129-48.
234. Gustafson, Richard F. "The Metaphor of the Seasons in *Evgenij Onegin.*" *SEEJ,* No. 6 (1962), 6-20.
235. ___. "The Upas Tree: Pushkin and Erasmus Darwin." *The Publication of the Modern Language Association,* 75 (1960), 101-9.
236. Hoisington, Sona Stephen. "*Eugene Onegin:* An Inverted Bryonic Poem." *CL,* 27, 136-52.
237. Ingemanson, Birgitta Maria. "On Pushkin and Travel Literature: *Puteshestvie v Arzrum.*" Diss. Princeton 1974. (75-23, 212).
238. Jocelyn, Michael. "Pushkin and Barclay de Tolly." *RLT,* No. 10 (1974), pp. 237-44.
239. Kappler, Richard G. "Pushkin and Benjamin Constant" in Baldner, R. W. *Proceedings, Pacific Northwest Conference on Foreign Languages.* 17-18 March 1967. Victoria, B.C., Canada: University of Victoria, 1967.
240. Karpiak, Robert. "Pushkin's *Little Tragedies:* The Controversies in Criticism." *CSP,* 22, 80-91.
241. Katz, Michael R. "Dreams in Pushkin." *Cal SS,* 11, 71-103.
242. Kodjak, Andrej. "Puškin's Utopian Myth." Kodjak, Andrej, Krystyna Pomorska, and Kiril Taranovsky, eds. *Alexander Puškin: Symposium II.* Columbus: Slavica, 1980, pp. 117-30.
243. Kirtley, Basil F. "National Character and Folklore in Pushkin's *Skazki.*" *West Virginia University Philosophical Papers,* No. 11 (1958), 22-32.
244. Konick, Willis. "Categorical Dreams and Compliant Reality: The Role of the Narrator in *The Tales of Belkin.*" *CASS,* No. 11 (1977), 75-90.
245. Kopelev, Lev. "Pushkin," tr. David Lapeza. *RLT,* No. 10 (1974), 185-97.
246. Leighton, Lauren G. "Gematria in 'The Queen of Spades': A Decembrist Puzzle." *SEEJ,* No. 21 (1977), 455-69.
247. ___. "Numbers and Numerology in 'The Queen of Spades'." *CSP,* 19, 417-43.
248. ___. "The Anecdote in Russia: Puškin, Vjazemskij, and Davydov." *SEEJ,* No. 10 (1966), 155-66.
249. Lezhnev, Abram. *Pushkin's Prose.* Trans. R. Reeder. Ann Arbor: Ardis, 1983.
250. Magarshack, David. *Pushkin.* New York: Grove Press, Inc., 1969.
251. Matlaw, Ralph E. "The Dream in *Yevgeniy Onegin,* with a Note on *Gore ot uma* [Woe from Wit]." *SEER,* No. 89 (1959), 487-504.
252. ___. "Poetry and the Poet in Romantic Society as Reflected in Pushkin's *Egyptian Nights.*" *SEER,* 33, 102-19.
253. Mersereau, John, Jr. "Pushkin's Concept of Romanticism," *SIR,* No. 3 (1963), 24-41.
254. Mirsky, D. S. *Pushkin.* New York: E. P. Dutton and Co., Inc., 1963.
255. Monter, Barbara Heldt. "Love and Death in Pushkin's *Little Tragedies.*" *RLT,* No. 3 (1972), 206-14.
256. Newman, John Kevin. "Pushkin and Horace: Remarks on 'Exegi Monumentum' and 'Pamyatnik'." *Neohelicon* 3, i-ii, 331-42.
257. ___. "Pushkin's *Bronze Horseman* and the Epic Tradition." *CLS,* 9, 173-95.

258. Olcott, Anthony. "Parody as Realism: *The Journey to Arzrum.*" *RLT,* No. 10 (1974), 245-59.
259. Pachmuss, Temira and Victor Terras. "The Shift of the Image of Napoleon in the Poetry of Aleksandr Puškin." *SEEJ,* No. 5 (1961), 311-30.
260. Pomorska, Krystyna. "Structural Peculiarities in 'Putešestvie v Arzrum'" in *Alexander Puškin: A Symposium on the 175th Anniversary of His Birth.* Vol. I. New York: New York University Press, 1976.
261. Proffer, Carl R. "The Similes of Pushkin and Lermontov." *RLT,* No. 3 (1972), 148-94.
262. Reeder, Roberta. "*The Greek Anthology* and Its Influence on Pushkin's Poetic Style." *CASS,* No. 10 (1976), 205-27.
263. Richards, D. J. and C. R. S. Cockrell, ed. and tr. *Russian Views of Pushkin.* Oxford: Willem A. Meeuws-Publisher, 1976.
264. Rosen, Nathan. "The Magic Cards in *The Queen of Spades.*" *SEEJ,* No. 19 (1975), 255-75.
265. Rowe, Eleanor. "Pushkin, Lermontov, and *Hamlet.*" *TSLL,* 17, 337-47.
266. Sandler, Stephanie. "The Problem of History in Pushkin: Poet, Pretender, Tsar." Diss. Yale 1981 (82-10705).
267. Schwartz, Murry M., and Albert Schwartz. "*The Queen of Spades:* A Psychoanalytic Interpretation." *TSLL.* 17, 275-88.
268. Shaw, J. Thomas. "Pushkin's 'The Stationmaster' and the New Testament Parable." *SEEJ,* No. 21 (1977), 3-29.
269. ___. "The 'Conclusion' of Pushkin's *The Queen of Spades*" in Folejewski, Zbigniew et al., eds. *Studies in Russian and Polish Literature in Honor of Waclaw Lednicki.* The Hague: Mouton, pp. 114-26.
270. ___. "Theme and Imagery in Puškin's 'Ja pomnju čudnoe mgnoven'e' [I remember a marvelous moment]" *SEEJ,* No. 14 (1970), 135-44.
271. ___. "The Problem of the *persona* in Journalsim: Puškin's Feofilakt Kosičkin" in *American Contributions to the Fifth International Congress of Slavists: Sofia, Sept. 1963.* Vol. II. The Hague: Mouton, 1963, pp. 301-26.
272. Simmons, Ernest J. *Pushkin.* New York: Vintage Books, 1964.
273. Terras, Victor. "Puškin and Romanticism." Kodjak, Andrej, Krystyna Pomorska, and Kiril Taranovsky, eds. *Alexander Puškin:* Symposium II. Columbus: Slavica, 1980, pp. 49-59.
274. Vickery, Walter. "Anchar': Beyond Good and Evil." *CASS,* No. 10 (1976), 175-88.
275. ___. "*Mednyj vsadnik* [The Bronze Horseman] and the 18th Century Heroic Ode." *ISS,* No. 3 (1963), 140-62.
276. ___. *Pushkin: Death of a Poet.* Bloomington: Indiana University Press, 1968.
277. ___. " 'The Water-Nymph' and 'Again I Visited . . .': Notes on an Old Controversy." *RLT,* No. 3 (1972), pp. 195-205.
278. Walter, Starling. "The Conversation of a Poet and a Miserly Knight." *RLT,* No. 3 (1972), pp. 215-28.
279. Weil, Irwin. "Onegin's Echo." *RLT,* No. 10 (1974), pp. 260-73.
280. Wreath, Patrick J. and April I. Wreath, comps. "Alexander Pushkin: A Bibliography of Criticism in English, 1920-75." *CASS,* No. 10 (1976), 279-304.

Pushkin, V. L.

281. Pushkin, Vasily Lvovich. "A Dangerous Neighbor," tr. Thomas Barran. *RLT,* No. 14 (1976), pp. 314-20.

Ryleev, K.

282. Rickwood, T. M. " 'Poet v dushe': A Re-Appraisal of Ryleev's Verse" in Baldner, Ralph W., ed. *Proceedings: Pacific Northwest Conference on Foreign Languages, Twenty-First Annual Meeting, 3-4 April 1970.* Vol. 21. Victoria, B. C.: University of Victoria.
283. Walker, Franklin. "K. F. Ryleev: A Self-Sacrifice for Revolution." *SEER,* No. 47 (1969), 436-46.

Senkovsky, I.

284. Pedrotti, Louis. *Józef-Julian Sękowski—The Genesis of a Literary Alien.* University of California Publications in Modern Philology. Vol. 3. Berkeley and Los Angeles: University of California Press, 1965.

Shakhovskoi, A. A.

285. Malnick, Bertha. "A. A. Shakhovskoy." *SEER,* No. 78 (1953), 29-51.

Somov, O.:

Translation

286. Somov, Orest. "Mommy and Sonny," tr. John Mersereau Jr. *RLT,* No. 8 (1974), pp. 259-77.

Criticism

287. Mersereau, John Jr. "Orest Somov: An Introduction." *SEER,* No. 101 (1965), 354-70.
288. ___. "Orest Somov and the Illusion of Reality." *American Contributions to the Sixth International Congress of Slavists.* The Hague: Mouton, 1968, Vol. II, pp. 307-31.

Stankevich, N. V.

289. Brown, E. J. "The Circle of Stankevich." *ASEER,* 16, 349-68.
290. ___. *Stankevich and His Moscow Circle 1830-1840.* Stanford, California: Stanford University Press, 1966.
291. Kostka, Edmund. "At the Roots of Russian Westernism: N. V. Stankevich and His Circle." *Etudes Slaves et Est-Européenes.* 6, 158-76.

Tyutchev, F. I.:

Translation

292. Zeldin, Jesse, tr. *Poems and Political Letters of F. I. Tyutchev.* Knoxville: University of Tennessee Press, 1973.

Criticism

293. Bilokur, Borys. *A Concordance to the Russian Poetry of Fedor I. Tiutchev.* Providence: Brown University Press, 1975.
294. ____. "Lexical Elements of Tjutčev's Poetry." Diss. University of Illinois 1968. (69-1298).
295. ____. "On Tjutčev's Archaisms." *SEEJ,* No. 18 (1974), 373-76.
296. ____. "Statistical Observations on Tjutčev's Lexicon." *SEEJ,* No. 14 (1970), 302-16.
297. Coates, W. A. "Tiutchev and Germany: The Relationship of His Poetry to German Literature and Culture." Diss. Harvard University 1950.
298. Chopyk, D. B. "Schelling's Philosophy in F. I. Tyutchev's Poetry." *Russian Language Journal,* 96, 17-23.
299. Florovsky, G. "Historical Premonitions of Tyutchev," *Slavonic Review,* No. 3 (December 1924), 337-49.
300. Gifford, H. "The Evolution of Tyutchev's Art." *SEER,* No. 37 (December 1958-June 1959), 378-86.
301. Gregg, Richard. "Dream at Sea: Tiutchev and Pascal." *Slav R,* 23, 526-30.
302. ____. *Fedor Tiutchev. The Evolution of a Poet.* New York: Columbia University Press, 1965.
303. ____. "The Evolution of Tiutchev." Diss. Columbia 1962. (65-7491).
304. Lane, Ronald C. "Bibliography: Tiutchev in English Translation: 1873-1974." *Journal of European Studies,* 5, 153-75.
305. ____. "Russia and the West in Tyutchev's Poetry: On the Origins of Some Poems of 1830." VII *Międzynarodowy Kongres Slawistów w Warszawie.* Warsaw, PAN, 1973.
306. ____. "Tyutchev in Russian Fiction." *NZSJ,* 2, 17-32.
307. ____. "Tyutchev's Place in the History of Russian Literature." *MLR,* 71, 344-56.
308. Matlaw, R. E. "The Polyphony of Tyutchev's 'Son na more'." *SEER,* 36 (December 1957-June 1958), 198-204.
309. Pratt, Sarah Claflin. "The Metaphysical Poetry of F. I. Tjutčev and E. A. Boratynsky: Alternatives in Russian Romanticism." Diss. Columbia 1978. (78-11149).
310. Rydel, Christine A. "A Formal Analysis of the Poems of Fedor Ivanovič Tjutčev." Diss. Indiana University 1976. (76-21, 546).
311. Safonov, Sidonie H. "The Metaphors in Tiutchev's Philosophical Poems." *Bulletin of the Rocky Mountain Modern Language Association,* 26, 55-64.
312. Wehrle, Albert James. "Tensions in the Poetry of F. I. Tjutčev." Diss. Ohio State University 1974. (74-24, 425).

Turgenev, A. I.

313. Hollingsworth, Barry. "Aleksandr Turgenev and the Composition of *Khronika russkogo:* A Note and A Query." *SEER,* 45, 531-36.
314. ____. "The Friendly Literary Society." *NZSJ,* 1, 23-41.
315. Struve, Gleb. "Alexander Turgenev, Ambassador of Russian Culture in *Partibus Infidelium.*" *Slav R,* 29, 444-59.
316. Waddington, Patrick H. "Document: Some Letters from A. I., I. S. and N. I. Turgenev to Richard Monckton Milnes (Lord Haughton)." *NZSJ,* 2, 61-83.

Venevitinov, D. V.

Translations

317. Andrews, Larry R. "The Complete Poetry of D. V. Venevitinov; Translation with Critical Introduction." Diss. Rutgers 1971. (72-805).
318. Venevitinov, D. V. "Sculpture, Painting, and Music," "Morning, Midday, Evening and Night," and "Anaxagoras: A Platonic Dialogue," tr. Larry Andrews. *RLT,* No. 11 (1975), pp. 179-85.
319. ____. "Complete Poetry," tr. Donald R. Boucher and Larry Andrews. *RLT,* No. 8 (1974), pp. 84-130.

Criticism

320. Andrews, Larry R. "D. V. Venevitinov." *RLT,* No. 8 (1974), pp. 373-84.

Vyazemsky, P. A.

321. Little, T. E. "P. A. Vyazemsky as a Critic of Pushkin" in Freeborn, Richard, R. R. Milner-Gulland and Charles A. Ward, eds. *Russian and Slavic Literature.* Cambridge, Massachusetts: Slavica, 1976, pp. 1-16.
322. Meijer, Jan M. "Vjazemskij and Romanticism," in Holk, André van, ed. *Dutch Contributions to the Seventh International Congress of Slavists.* The Hague: Mouton, 1973, pp. 271-304.

> **See also:**
> Leighton, Lauren G. "The Anecdote in Russia: Puškin, Vjazemskij, and Davydov."*SEEJ,* No. 10 (1966), 155-66.

Yazykov, N. M.:

Translation

323. Yazykov, Nikolai. "Selected Poems," tr. Benjamin Dees. *RLT,* No. 8 (1974), 69-71.

Criticism

324. Dees, Benjamin. "Yazykov's Lyrical Poetry." *RLT,* No. 10 (1974), 316-30.
325. Lilly, Ian Kenneth. "The Lyric Poetry of N. M. Jazykov: A Periodization Using Objective Criteria." Diss. University of Washington 1977. (77-18, 378)

Zagoskin, M. N.

Translation

326. Zagoskin, Michael. *Tales of Three Centuries,* tr. Jeremiah Curtin. Boston: Little, Brown and Company, 1891.

Criticism

327. Schwartz, Miriam Golin. "M. N. Zagoskin as a Historical Novelist." Diss. Ohio State University 1979. (79-16, 024)

Zhukovsky, V. A.

328. Brown, William Edward. "Vasily Andreevich Zhukovsky." *RLT,* No. 8 (1974), pp. 295-328.
329. Galer, Dorothea D. "Vasilii Andreevich Zhukovskii: His Theory of Translation." Diss. Northwestern 1975. (75-29, 636)
330. Hewton, Ainslie. "A Comparison of Sir Walter Scott's *The Eve of St. John* and Zhukovsky's Translation of the Ballad." *NZSJ,* 11, 145-50.
331. Ober, Kenneth H. and Warren U. Ober. "Zukovskij's Early Translations of the Ballads of Robert Southey." *SEEJ,* No. 9 (1965), 181-90.
332. ___. "Zukovskij's Translation of Oliver Goldsmith's 'The Deserted Village'." *Germano-Slavica,* 1, 19-28.
333. Semenko, Irina Mikhailovna. *Vasily Zhukovsky.* Boston: Twayne, 1976.

      See also:
      Johnson, Doris. "The Comparison in the Poetry of Batiushkov and Zhukovsky." Diss. University of Michigan 1973. (74-15, 765)
      ___. "The Simile in Batyushkov and Zhukovsky." *RLT,* No. 7 (1973), pp. 407-22.

Addendum: William Edward Brown, *A History of Russian Literature of the Romantic Period,* 4 volumes. Ardis, forthcoming (1985). This is the most comprehensive work on the Romantic period in English.